# Hunting and Animal Exploitation in the Later Palaeolithic and Mesolithic of Eurasia

Gail Larsen Peterkin,
Harvey M. Bricker,
and Paul Mellars, Editors

Contributions by

Christopher A. Bergman
Katherine V. Boyle
Harvey M. Bricker
Ariane Burke
Steven E. Churchill
Geoffrey A. Clark
Francis B. Harrold
Heidi Knecht
Steven L. Kuhn
Daniel E. Lieberman
Paul Mellars
Steven Mithen
Michael P. Neeley
Deborah I. Olszewski
Marcel Otte
Gail Larsen Peterkin
Anne Pike-Tay
T. Douglas Price
Peter Rowley-Conwy
John J. Shea
Mary C. Stiner
Lawrence Guy Straus

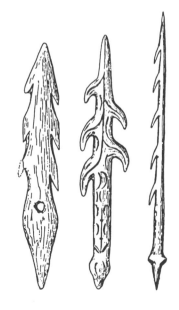

1993
Archeological Papers of the
American Anthropological Association Number 4

*About the Editors . . .*

Gail Larsen Peterkin was born in Waukegan, Illinois. She received a
B.A. from the University of Kansas and an M.A. from Tulane
University. She has done fieldwork in southwestern France and in
the midwestern and southeastern United States. She is currently a
Ph.D. candidate in Anthropology at Tulane University.

Harvey M. Bricker was born in Johnstown, Pennsylvania. He
received an A.B. degree from Hamilton College and M.A. and
Ph.D. degrees from Harvard University. His fieldwork experience is
with Upper Palaeolithic sites in southwestern France. He is
Professor of Anthropology at Tulane University in New Orleans.

Paul Mellars was born in Sheffield, England, and carried out his
undergraduate and doctoral studies in archaeology at Cambridge
University. His research has been concerned with the Middle and
Upper Palaeolithic periods in France and with the British
Mesolithic. He has carried out fieldwork on Mesolithic sites in the
Hebrides and Yorkshire. He is currently Reader in Archaeology at
Cambridge University and President of Corpus Christi College.

The logo for AP3A No. 4 is a trio of harpoons from the very end of
the Upper Palaeolithic sequence (late Magdalenian and Azilian) in
southwestern France. Such antler weapon armatures were probably
propelled by atlatls in the hunting of large terrestrial mammals.
These three classic artifacts were among those used by Henri Breuil
in 1912 as evidence for the first definitive periodization of the
Upper Palaeolithic *(Les subdivisions du Paléolithique supérieur et leur
signification).*

**Library of Congress Cataloging-in-Publication Data**

Hunting and animal exploitation in the later Palaeolithic and
    Mesolithic of Eurasia / Gail Larsen Peterkin, Harvey M. Bricker
    and Paul Mellars, editors ; contributions by Christopher A.
    Bergman . . . [et al.].
        p.   cm.   (Archeological papers of the American
    Anthropological Association ; no. 4)
    Includes bibliographical references.
    ISBN 0-913167-61-4
    1. Paleolithic period  Eurasia. 2. Mesolithic period–Eurasia.
    3. Hunting, Prehistoric  Eurasia. 4. Tools, Prehistoric  Eurasia.
    5. Animal remains (Archaeology) Eurasia. 6. Eurasia
    Antiquities.  I. Peterkin, Gail Larsen.  II. Bricker, Harvey M.
    III. Mellars, Paul.  IV. Series.
    GN772.2.A1H85  1993
    950  dc20                                        93-40095
                                                        CIP

# Contents

# List of Contributors

Christopher A. Bergman
3D/Environmental Services, Inc.
781 Neeb Road, Suite 5
Cincinnati OH 45233

Katherine V. Boyle
10 Conington Road
Fenstanton
Huntingdon
Cambs. PE18 9LB
U. K.

Harvey M. Bricker
Department of Anthropology
Tulane University
New Orleans LA 70118

Ariane Burke
Canadian Museum of Civilization
100 Laurier Street
P. O. Box 3100, Station B
Hull, Quebec J8X 4H2
Canada

Steven E. Churchill
Department of Anthropology
University of New Mexico
Albuquerque NM 87131

Geoffrey A. Clark
Department of Anthropology
Arizona State University
Tempe AZ 85287

Francis B. Harrold
Department of Sociology and Anthropology
University of Texas at Arlington
Box 19599
Arlington TX 76019

Heidi Knecht
Department of Anthropology
University of Miami
Coral Gables FL 33124

Steven L. Kuhn
Department of Sociology and Anthropology
Loyola University of Chicago
Lake Shore Campus
6525 North Sheridan Road
Chicago IL 60626

Daniel E. Lieberman
Department of Anthropology
Harvard University
Cambridge MA 02138

Paul Mellars
Department of Archaeology
Downing Street
Cambridge University
Cambridge CB2 3DX
U. K.

Steven Mithen
Department of Archaeology
University of Reading
Whiteknights
P. O. Box 218
Reading RG6 2AA
U. K.

Michael P. Neeley
Department of Anthropology
Arizona State University
Tempe AZ 85287

Deborah I. Olszewski
Department of Anthropology
University of Arizona
Tucson AZ 85721

Marcel Otte
Préhistoire
Université de Liège
7, place du 20 Août
Liège B-4000
Belgium

Gail Larsen Peterkin
Department of Anthropology
Tulane University
New Orleans LA 70118

Anne Pike-Tay
Department of Anthropology
Vassar College
Poughkeepsie NY 12601

T. Douglas Price
Department of Anthropology
University of Wisconsin--Madison
Madison WI 53706

Peter Rowley-Conwy
Department of Archaeology
University of Durham
46 Saddler Street
Durham DH1 3NU
U. K.

John J. Shea
Department of Anthropology
State University of New York at Stony Brook
Stony Brook NY 11794

Mary C. Stiner
Department of Sociology and Anthropology
Loyola University of Chicago
Lake Shore Campus
6525 North Sheridan Road
Chicago IL 60626

Lawrence Guy Straus
Department of Anthropology
University of New Mexico
Albuquerque NM 87131

# Acknowledgements

The editors wish to thank the contributors to the volume for their unfailing cooperation during the preparation process. We also wish to acknowledge the invaluable assistance of Geoffrey A. Clark, General Series Editor of the AP3A, who guided this volume to fruition. We also thank the Archeology Division's Editorial Board, who accepted the manuscript for publication, and the reviewers, who provided many helpful suggestions for revisions to the original manuscript. Finally, Gail Larsen Peterkin wishes to thank John, Lewis, and Gavin for their patience and forbearance during the course of the entire project.

# Introduction:
# The Study of Palaeolithic
# and Mesolithic Hunting

**Harvey M. Bricker**
**Tulane University**

**Paul Mellars**
**University of Cambridge**

**Gail Larsen Peterkin**
**Tulane University**

From the very beginnings of systematic research in Palaeolithic archaeology, hunting was, along with tool-making, one of the two cultural behaviors attributed with great certainty to our earliest human or hominid ancestors. With few exceptions, the tight geological associations of chipped stone artifacts with the smashed bones of nonhuman animals were interpreted not only as proof of contemporaneity, but also, in a usually unquestioned fashion, as the discarded skeletal remains of the prey animals killed by the prehistoric hunters who were the makers of the stone artifacts. This view of hunting in the Old Stone Age appears explicitly in some of the early-twentieth-century didactic works written for nonspecialists. For example, Déchelette's *Manuel d'archéologie* (1908: 62) speaks of the earliest then-known Palaeolithic inhabitants of Europe (those making Lower Palaeolithic "Chellean" artifacts) as small groups of people, "devoted to the hunt," roaming fertile plains and tree-lined river valleys during a time of mild climate, who were able to obtain the means of subsistence without too much difficulty.[1] An influential work in English during this period was William Sollas's *Ancient Hunters and Their Modern Representatives*, which appeared in several editions beginning in 1911. As the title of his book implies, Sollas believed that hunting was of central importance throughout the Palaeolithic. Referring to the same "Chellean" groups discussed by Déchelette, Sollas (1924:135) wrote: "Man as we first meet with him is a hunter, not by choice but from necessity, winning a precarious existence from the chase of wild beasts and the collection of grubs, eggs, and other edible products, especially those afforded by wild plants." Similar views on hunting continued to appear in textbooks well into the post-World-War-II era--for example, in a chapter entitled "Lower and Middle Palaeolithic Hunters" in the revised edition of Grahame Clark's standard work on world prehistory (Clark 1969:32-33).

Now, however, at the end of the twentieth century, our understanding of the place of hunting in the Palaeolithic is very different. An abundant literature, richest and deepest for the Early Stone Age of Africa (e.g., Brain 1981; Shipman 1983, 1986; Potts 1988), shows that hunting cannot simply be assumed to have been present at the beginning of the archaeological record. Indeed, the complex behavior that we recognize as "hunting" may have appeared quite late in the Pleistocene (the "later Palaeolithic" of this volume's title) and in the course of human evolution. The study of the development of hunting behavior in relation to human biological evolution has been one of the more interesting research directions of recent paleoanthropology. For example, Lewis Binford has suggested that the emergence of highly structured and focused **hunting** (as opposed to more opportunistic **scavenging**) may have been a central aspect of the transition from anatomically and behaviorally "archaic" to fully "modern" populations. Summarizing a variety of data, Binford (1985:321) concluded:

> At present the inevitable conclusion seems to be that regular, moderate- to large-mammal hunting appears simultaneously with the foreshadowing changes occurring just prior to the appearance of fully modern man. ... Systematic hunting of moderate to large animals appears to be a part of our modern condition, not its cause.

Whatever may be the analytic utility of any specific model (Binford's or anyone else's) for the early development of hunting behavior, the broader question of the relationship between **behavioral** modernity and **anatomical** modernity at the end of the Pleistocene is a matter of widespread concern within anthropology (e.g., Trinkaus 1989; Mellars and Stringer 1989; Mellars 1990; Aiello 1993; Frayer et al. 1993). Regardless of when technologically assisted hunting may have started, it is clear that hunting was practiced during the later Palaeolithic and Mesolithic. Whether or not it is uniquely "modern," hunting is undeniably an important part of "modern" human behavior. Because the technology associated with hunting activities became more complex and more elaborated during the course of the Upper Pleistocene, and because the hunting weaponry and the osteological results of hunting form such major parts of the relevant archaeological record, the study of animal exploitation strategies and associated technology provides some of the most direct insights into the development of human societies existing at and immediately following the end of the Pleistocene.

This present volume, which brings together recent work by North American and British scholars on the general topic of hunting and other techniques for exploiting animal populations during the later Palaeolithic and Mesolithic of Europe and southwest Asia, grew out of two closely integrated symposia organized by the three co-editors and held in New Orleans in April 1991 as part of the 56th Annual Meeting of the Society for American Archaeology. The contributors to the volume use a wide variety of techniques to investigate the relationships between animal prey species and prehistoric human groups. Some concentrate on the evidence from prehistoric artifacts, some derive their information from the archaeologically recovered faunal samples, some deal with present-day information provided by ethnography and ethnoarchaeology, and some are using computer simulation data in their attempts to understand the more restricted data from the past. Attempts to expand the ways in which information about seasonality of occupation may be obtained are central to some research reported here, and the more appropriate use of such information is of general concern. Several of the studies focusing on artifacts show again the great importance of use-wear analysis, particularly as combined with experimental replication. In short, the studies chosen for this volume provide an excellent sample of the latest work being done in the field of human/animal relations during the late Pleistocene and earliest Holocene, and the contributors to the volume comprise a broad sample of the leading contributors to that field now writing in English. As such, the volume takes its place alongside other works published on both sides of the Atlantic during the past decade--for example, Clutton-Brock and Grigson (1983), Martin and Klein (1984), Price and Brown (1985), Nitecki and Nitecki (1987), and Stiner (1991). Although the volume finds its home among such literature, its particular strength is the extent to which it, and the symposia from which it springs, has brought together the "bones" people and the "weapons" people in a very useful encounter.

An obvious place to begin the study is the consideration by STEVEN E. CHURCHILL (Chapter 1) of what can be learned from the ethnographic record that is of relevance to hunting in the Palaeolithic and Mesolithic. His sample includes 96 ethnographically known groups ranging from the Arctic to equatorial forests in Oceania and from all continents except Europe. His examination of the contemporary record focuses on the relationships among weapon systems (thrusting spears, hand-thrown spears, spears or darts propelled from an atlatl, and nonpoisoned arrows propelled from a bow), hunting strategy (ambush, pursuit, etc.), and prey choice (emphasizing particularly prey size). From the point of view of the prehistoric archaeologist, both the positive and negative findings of Churchill's ethnographic survey are very useful. There is not, for example, much of an operational distinction between thrusting spears and hand-thrown spears. In the ethnographic present, the thrusting spear is used mainly to finish off an animal that has been disadvantaged or wounded, and spears thrown by hand are used only in specific circumstances when the prey has been disadvantaged by features of the terrain. The lack of importance of spears as hunting weapons in the groups surveyed by Churchill reflects, certainly, their replacement by more effective delivery systems, specifically atlatls and bows. An obvious suggestion for the Palaeolithic is that, before the invention of the atlatl, hunters may have been restricted to terrain-dependent techniques, perhaps involving cooperative group efforts, for really effective hunting. However, the limitation of using ethnographically derived data is exemplified by the fact that ethnographic cases of using atlatls to hunt terrestrial mammals are limited to Australia, where only small game exists. In other world areas, the atlatl was, probably rather quickly, replaced by the bow and arrow for hunting large mammals. Therefore, the ethnographic record is not very helpful concerning a weapon system that was of great importance during the later Upper Palaeolithic. It is not clear, for example, that the atlatl dart was an effective "shock" weapon against large mammals, and Churchill suggests that the Magdalenian and Azilian harpoons of Europe may represent an attempt to use the atlatl to propel a large projectile with effective killing power against large mammals. In any event, Churchill's results add clear support to the idea that some of the documented changes through time in

Palaeolithic and Mesolithic weapon armatures do indeed reflect the development of technologies for more effective "killing at a distance."

Most of the chapters in the volume are concerned largely with the analysis of data from the past, not the ethnographic present. The European archaeological coverage begins with the study by STEVEN L. KUHN (Chapter 2) of lithic technology at several Mousterian sites in Italy. If one considers only the variation in form of what may be weapon armatures, mainly Mousterian points and Levallois points, the lack of formal variability would suggest very little variation in the hunting techniques employed during the Middle Palaeolithic or Middle Stone Age throughout western Eurasia and Africa. Kuhn's conclusion from this formal monotony is that the study of weapons alone can tell us little about resource procurement during the Middle Palaeolithic. He looks, instead, at items other than weapons and at the relationships between making and using tools, on the one hand, and foraging for food, on the other. The case study reported here concerns four caves on the coast of Italy, southeast of Rome, where lithic raw materials are extremely scarce. In the two caves occupied before ca. 55,000 BP, Grotta Guattari and Grotta dei Moscerini, the faunal remains (almost entirely cervid cranial parts) have been diagnosed by Mary Stiner (1990 and this volume) as resulting from scavenging. Occupations dating from ca. 55,000 BP or later in the other two caves, Grotta di Sant'Agostino and Grotta Breuil, have more varied faunal remains of the sort that suggest the practice of ambush hunting. The lithic industries varied between the two types of sites, not in the forms of the probable weapon tips, but rather in what kinds of flakes were produced from what kinds of raw materials. In the scavenging sites, which were probably occupied during only brief intervals, the emphasis was on producing and reusing large flakes from nonlocal raw material that was probably being carried around with the toolmakers. Occupations at the hunting sites were probably somewhat more lengthy, and the emphasis here was on the most efficient production of numerous small flakes from the locally available small pebbles. Although the patterns associated with the specialized case of scavenging on the Italian coast cannot be extended uncritically to other regions, Kuhn's research shows very clearly how the relationship between a lithic technology and the broader aspects of resource procurement can, in itself, be extremely informative.

The more explicit and more diverse weaponry of the European Upper Palaeolithic is the subject of the next five chapters, beginning with the examination by HEIDI KNECHT (Chapter 3) of bone and antler projectiles in western Europe. Hypotheses about how organic weapon armatures were manufactured and used were tested by the study of prehistoric artifacts from Aurignacian and Gravettian sites in France, Belgium, and Germany and by a program of experimentation. Replicas of bone and antler projectile points were made and hafted onto wooden spear shafts. The spears were shot into suspended goat carcasses using a cross-bow calibrated to apply just enough force to penetrate the carcass. In this way, Knecht was able to assess patterns of weapon efficacy, damage, and breakage under known conditions. The results of Knecht's research support some long-held opinions about organic weapons of the earlier Upper Palaeolithic, but others are challenged. For example, the so-called split-based bone points of the early Aurignacian are made almost exclusively of reindeer antler, and Knecht's experiments show the efficacy of a hafting technique not previously suggested--a technique that provides a more satisfactory explanation for the function of the distinctive objects called "tongued pieces" that are often found in association with split-based points. At a more general level, Knecht's work with the Aurignacian of western Europe has shown the presence of a very sophisticated organic technology that contrasts strongly with that of the western European Mousterian. In the Gravettian samples studied by Knecht, organic weapon armatures feature textured surfaces, flattened surfaces, or notched/incised lateral edges, all of which probably have to do with how the different elements that combined to make one functional weapon were fastened together. Her ballistic experiments invite us to consider the weapon as a whole (armature[s] plus haft) when attempting to understand the changes through time in Upper Palaeolithic weapons systems.

Although the real (as opposed to replicated) hafts of almost all Upper Palaeolithic weapon armatures are unknown to us, very large and very varied samples of the armatures themselves are available for study. The work of GAIL LARSEN PETERKIN (Chapter 4) is based on the subtypological analysis of more than 3,200 armatures, both lithic and organic, from 19 Upper Palaeolithic sites in southwestern France. Discriminant analysis and other multivariate statistical techniques permit her to recognize four general "morpho-functional" classes of lithic weapons armatures--backed points, backed side-elements, foliate points, and points with specialized hafting modifications (tangs, shoulders, etc.). The kinds of variation that are most important in discriminating among these classes include dimensions of the hafted end of the armature, the sharpness of its edges, and the acuity of its tip. Peterkin's work documents in detail the general reduction in armature size during the later Upper Palaeolithic--a change that almost certainly reflects the adoption of the atlatl as the preferred weapon (as discussed by Straus, this volume). On the other hand, some variables (tip thickness, penetrating angle, etc.) are shown to be very nearly constant throughout the Upper Palaeolithic. This chapter also deals with two classes of organic armatures, the spear or dart points called *sagaies* and the barbed points or harpoons of the very late Upper Palaeolithic. There is, Peterkin shows, a fundamental difference between the split-based points of the early Aurignacian and all other later sagaies (it seems possible, in light of Knecht's experimental work reported in this volume, that this finding reflects a difference in "whole-weapon" profile between earliest Upper Palaeolithic spears/darts and later ones). The same sort of analyses applied to Magdalenian and Azilian harpoons focuses attention on hafting technique, particularly the more efficaceous retrieval technology represented by harpoons with basal perforations. In addition, the overall salience of harpoon width and its interaction with both hafting details and barb morphology point to an emphasis on robusticity, which may provide supporting data for Churchill's suggestion (this volume) about the development of harpoons as heavy shock weapons. Finally, some preliminary results of ongoing work suggest that it will be possible to document regularities, across time and tool-making traditions, between variability in the weapon armatures and variability in the prey profiles for different occupations--for example, the tendency for haft length of lithic armatures (of whatever kind) to be greater in assemblages with bovine-rich faunal samples.

In the third chapter dealing with European Upper Palaeolithic weapons, FRANCIS B. HARROLD (Chapter 5) concentrates on Gravette points from southwestern France. Because organic weapons are very rare in many of the assemblage samples studied, the traditional assumption has been that lithic armatures were of primary importance to Gravettian hunters. Harrold's work, a subtypological examination of nearly 1,500 Gravette points from 10 sites in France, provides useful new information bearing on the old question of the function of these artifacts. The results of his research offer good reason for accepting the traditional identification of Gravette points as projectile points in many cases, but he provides good metric documentation for the belief that some Gravette points functioned, instead, as knives.

In his chapter on hunting tactics and weapons, LAWRENCE GUY STRAUS (Chapter 6) uses his wide experience with and eclectic knowledge of Upper Palaeolithic sites in western Europe to provide a critical overview of some old concerns centering on the relationship of a given prehistoric site to its immediate geographic locus. Using prehistoric data that resonate in a very clear fashion with the ethnographic data of Churchill (this volume) about terrain-dependent hunting, Straus emphasizes how Upper

Palaeolithic hunters learned to fit weapons systems to landscape features in order to increase their ability to procure large ungulate prey animals. He shows, in a region by region review, the importance of relief (hills, valleys, canyons) to Upper Palaeolithic site location; in a chronological review, he specifies the improvements that were made in the weapons systems themselves. In the latter, he touches upon themes dealt with in greater detail by the authors of other chapters of this volume--for example, the development of more gracile armatures, both organic and lithic, in the Gravettian as compared to the organic armatures of the Aurignacian; the probable invention of the atlatl during the Solutrean and its ascendancy to predominance during the Magdalenian; and the shift in emphasis toward the later part of the Upper Palaeolithic from "single-element weapon tips" to "multi-element weapon tips." In terms of the themes pursued by Straus, weaponry in the Upper Palaeolithic reached its peak in the Magdalenian, with an emphasis on delivery systems--atlatls and harpoons.

The chronologically latest improvement in weapons delivery that is considered in this book, the early record of the bow and arrow in European prehistory, is the subject of the chapter by CHRISTOPHER A. BERGMAN (Chapter 7). Although some later Upper Palaeolithic stone armatures (for example, tanged points from the Spanish Solutrean site of Parpalló) may be arrowheads, neither arrows nor bows have been documented before the very end of the Pleistocene. The earliest European evidence--nocked arrowshafts made of pine, which were apparently tipped with Ahrensburg points fitted onto separate foreshafts--comes from Stellmoor, Germany, in occupations dated to ca. 11,000-10,300 BP. The Stellmoor bow is not known. Much richer data are available from Mesolithic sites of the early Holocene. Replicative experiments reviewed by Bergman suggest that European Mesolithic bows were able to propel an arrow for 150 to 200 m; they would have delivered arrows with a sufficiently high impact velocity to have killed by trauma and blood loss without the use of poisons. The replacement of the atlatl by the bow at or near the end of the Pleistocene is one of the principal processes in the history of weaponry in Europe (and, as Churchill's data in this volume show, in most other regions of the world as well). Bergman concludes that, although the bow came into use in northern Europe before the Holocene reforestation, it was indeed this reforestation that emphasized the advantages of the bow and arrow and resulted in its complete replacement of the atlatl.

The next four chapters report research based primarily on the study of faunal material from European Palaeolithic sites. The first of these zooarchaeological studies is that of MARY C. STINER (Chapter 8) on the exploitation of small animals at one of the

Mousterian sites of coastal Italy (Grotta dei Moscerini) whose lithic technology was discussed in an earlier chapter by Kuhn. Work reported previously by Stiner has suggested that the faunal remains attributable to the Mousterian occupations, dating to between ca. 115,000 and 65,000 BP, represent the scavenged remains of large ungulates, primarily the crania of red deer. Even though the Mousterian occupations were small and apparently short-lived, these scavenged resources are not considered by Stiner to represent the principal element of the human diet. Additional contributions were made by small animals--both aquatic and terrestrial species of tortoises and several kinds of marine invertebrates, predominately clams and mussels--but the quantities of these resources brought to the cave were not great. A comparison among Grotta dei Moscerini and three other Mousterian cave sites in the immediate vicinity indicates that Mousterian people brought shellfish only to Moscerini, which is the closest of the four sites to the beach or rocky shore. No small terrestrial mammals were brought to any of the caves during the Middle Palaeolithic (rabbit and hare bones in several of the sites were probably introduced by canids, not hominids). Upper Palaeolithic and Mesolithic foragers collected and brought to coastal caves larger quantities of shellfish, as well as the carcasses of both large and small terrestrial mammals and of birds. The Mousterian pattern of relationships between "collected" food resources and the locus of shelter that Stiner has demonstrated is, therefore, quite clearly different from later patterns.

The chapter by ANNE PIKE-TAY and HARVEY M. BRICKER (Chapter 9) uses zooarchaeological, artifactual, and paleoenvironmental data for an integrated examination of hunting strategies employed in the Gravettian of southwest France during the latest part of the Early Upper Palaeolithic, between ca. 28,000 and 23,000 BP. New dental cementum annuli data produced by Pike-Tay (1991) on red deer, taken in combination with data on reindeer obtained previously by other workers, allows the probable identification of three different patterns of seasonally limited hunting in different occupations of several sites: cold-season hunting of both red deer and reindeer, warm-season hunting of red deer, and perhaps "migration hunting" (spring and fall only) of reindeer. The age-at-death data for the two species studied produce profiles that indicate a foraging strategy characterized by taking very limited numbers of animals during each hunting episode, but doing so with enough skill to obtain prime-age individuals as successfully as very old and very young animals. Some special attention to the prime-age animals may be suggested by the profiles for the latest Gravettian occupations. Gravettian weaponry, which is characterized in terms of

Bleed's (1986) distinction between "maintainable" and "reliable" design alternatives, consists, for the most part, of highly maintainable lithic weapon armatures (Gravette points, etc.), consistent with a foraging strategy rather than specialized collecting. In the several occupations that may result from migration hunting of reindeer, it is the large, heavy, and arguably "reliably" designed organic armatures that dominate the weaponry. The latest occupations, in which there may have been some selection for prime-age individuals of the prey species, are the ones in which there is the first evidence for microlith-armed composite weapons of the sort that became so crucial to hunting strategies later in the Upper Palaeolithic.

A second study using analyses of cementum annuli is reported in the chapter by ARIANE BURKE (Chapter 10), but, in this case, the animal in question is the horse. Her research is based on a modern control sample of 36 horses and an Upper Palaeolithic sample from three Magdalenian sites (Laugerie-Haute Est, Le Rond du Barry, and Le Roc de Marcamps) in southwestern France. This work is designed specifically to supplement that of Gordon (1988) on reindeer in the French Magdalenian, and the combination of her results and his leads to some extremely provocative conclusions. For example, the seasonality data on horse (Burke) and reindeer (Gordon) from Locus 1 at the Roc de Marcamps are cited in table form below:

| | **Horse** | **Reindeer** |
|---|---|---|
| Spring | -none- | MOST |
| Summer | MOST | -none- |
| Fall | some | -none- |
| Winter | some | some |

The same kind of seasonal "complementarity" between horse hunting and reindeer hunting may exist in some Magdalenian levels at Laugerie-Haute Est. If the kinds of results reported here by Burke are borne out by further research, and if they really apply to minimal stratigraphic units (the nearest we can come to individual occupations), then their importance can hardly be overstated. Burke's study demonstrates the absolute necessity of using more than one species in determining seasonality of occupation. Traditional understandings of Upper Palaeolithic occupations in the rockshelters of southwestern France may be seriously in error with respect to occupational duration and both the nature and scheduling of faunal resource procurement.

The following study also deals with Magdalenian faunal samples from rockshelters of southwestern France. In her work with materials excavated some time ago from Reignac, Limeuil, and St.-Germain-la-Rivière, KATHERINE V. BOYLE (Chapter 11) uses her own anatomical element counts to arrive at new understandings of these sites. All sites provide quantitatively adequate samples of taxa other than reindeer, bones from all the sites bear cut-marks that can be attributed to hominid action, and evidence of carnivore activity (gnaw marks) is virtually absent at Limeuil and completely so at the other two sites. Boyle uses the measures and interpretative techniques developed by Binford (1978, 1981) in his research among the Nunamiut of Alaska. This is the first major attempt to apply the ethnoarchaeologically derived techniques of Binford, developed in contexts where caribou is of major importance, to the classic Upper Palaeolithic sites of southwestern France, where reindeer dominates the faunal assemblages. In Magdalenian France, as in modern Alaska, the greater the availability of a species, the greater the selectivity in using carcass parts. For example, at Reignac the anatomical element counts of the most common species, reindeer and red deer, define a so-called "gourmet curve" (only body parts of the very highest value were chosen), whereas the much less common horse, boar, and saiga have "bulk curves" (all body parts were chosen for use, except those of the very lowest utility). In this and several other important ways, the points of comparison and contrast are very clearly documented by Boyle's research, and the ethnoarchaeological data are shown to be directly relevant to the interpretation of the Magdalenian sites.

In the last chapter to deal with Upper Palaeolithic fauna of Europe, STEVEN MITHEN (Chapter 12) uses computer simulation techniques, which he has used previously to investigate reindeer and red deer populations, to model mammoth hunting and extinction. Using as a base the life-history characteristics of the elephant, Mithen investigates the impact of a variety of different hunting strategies and environmental events on a simulated mammoth population. His simulations indicate that mammoths were very sensitive to predation, suggesting that human hunters could have played a role in mammoth extinction in both the Old and New Worlds. In this chapter, Mithen applies his simulation results to the archaeological record of the Central Russian Plain. The Late Pleistocene hunter-gatherers of this region are well known for their extensive exploitation of mammoth bone and ivory (e.g., mammoth-bone structures), for over 7,000 years, but it has been uncertain whether these animals were actively hunted in large numbers or were merely collected. Mithen's simulations suggest that the sensitivity of mammoth to even low rates of predation make it unlikely that large-scale hunting was involved. Instead, the simulations support Soffer's (1985) assertion that carcass scavenging was responsible for this accumulation of material.

In the final chapter that discusses European faunas, the focus shifts to the Danish Mesolithic and the work of PETER ROWLEY-CONWY (Chapter 13). Seasonality information derived from patterns of tooth eruption and bone growth of boar indicates that lakeside sites of the Danish interior were used at different seasons and for different purposes during different stages of the Mesolithic. The earlier Mesolithic or Maglemosian sites were all occupied during the summer, whereas the later Mesolithic or Ertebølle site in the sample was occupied during the winter and spring. Rowley-Conwy uses these data to point out the limitations of attempting to interpret a site based primarily on the chacteristics of the individual site location ("site catchment analysis" techniques). Although all the sites in his sample have very similar locations, they represent two very different settlement systems and, apparently, different hunting strategies. These differences in site function could not be understood without a determination of site seasonality based on the detailed examination of faunal remains.

The second part of the book deals with the late Pleistocene and early Holocene prehistory of southwest Asia. The first such chapter is the presentation by JOHN J. SHEA (Chapter 14) of the results of his use-wear analysis of Levantine Mousterian assemblages from Kebara, Tabun, Hayonim, and Qafzeh caves and Tor Faraj rockshelter. The Levantine sites are important because they are associated with both anatomically modern humans (Skhul and Qafzeh) and Neanderthals (Tabun, Amud, and Kebara). All of the sites, however, have a similar Levantine Mousterian lithic complex. Shea is particularly interested in the use-wear traces present on pointed forms, such as Levallois points, triangular flakes, and pointed blades. The distribution of such use-wear traces is consistent with experimental wear produced by use as a combination hafted spear point and butchery knife. Sociobiological and behavioral aspects of hunting suggest that both types of hominid were competing for the same niche in the Levantine ecosystem, and the results of the lithic microwear analysis suggest that **both** used hafted stone spear points in hunting.

The chapter by DEBORAH I. OLSZEWSKI (Chapter 15) examines three common microlithic forms from the Zarzian Epipalaeolithic occupation of Warwasi Rockshelter in Iran--scalene triangles, elongated scalene triangles, and truncated bladelets. Her analysis of metric and non-metric attributes indicates that truncated bladelets represent unfinished or rejected attempts to manufacture the two scalene forms, thus representing a stage in the reduction process associated with the manufacture of the two types of scalene triangles. A macroscopic examination of wear patterns implies that scalenes were most likely used as arrow tips or barbs rather than as components of composite plant-harvesting tools. The location of the site, environmental reconstruction, and faunal evidence suggest that the site would have been an effective hunting and butchering station. Olszewski compares metric attributes of the scalenes from Warwasi with those of lunates from Abu Hureyra 1, which, according to microwear analysis, were hafted as transverse arrowheads or barbs. The scalenes from Warwasi were most likely arrow barbs, with one of the triangle tips of an elongated scalene triangle serving as an arrowtip.

The chapter by DANIEL E. LIEBERMAN (Chapter 16) represents another shift from the consideration of artifacts to a primary concern with faunal assemblages. His research is another example of the utility of cementum increment analysis in the determination of the seasonal use of resources; in this case, gazelle is the species studied. Lieberman investigates the relationship of the season of death of gazelles to the economies and behavioral variables of hunter-gatherer populations in the southern Levant from the Middle Palaeolithic through the Natufian. Data from five deeply stratified caves from Israel were studied-- Qafzeh, el-Wad, Tabun, Kebara, and Hayonim. Late Palaeolithic and Epipalaeolithic hunter-gatherer mobility patterns were complex, and several models of mobility strategy are proposed. Although there is evidence for increasingly complex mobility strategies in the southern Levant at the end of the Epipalaeolithic, with multiseasonal and perhaps permanent use of some Natufian sites, multiseasonal site use was present as early as the Middle Palaeolithic (Kebara XII-VII and Tabun B). Lieberman suggests that Neanderthals moved across the landscape in a different, less mobile manner than anatomically modern humans, an essential element of contrast between the two kinds of humans.

The last chapter of the book to present a full research report is by MICHAEL P. NEELEY and GEOFFREY A. CLARK (Chapter 17); they re-examine Flannery's (1969) idea that a "broad-spectrum revolution" preceded domestication and Edwards's (1989) recent claim that this "broad-spectrum revolution" is not present in Levantine archaeofaunas. Edwards's formulations are compared with the expectations of long-term, diachronic niche-width models developed by Clark and other workers. Neeley and Clark test implications of the "broad-spectrum revolution" and other general models of subsistence change, with a summary of Edwards's results. The Levantine archaeofaunal data analyzed by Edwards are re-analyzed using a superior measure of diversity (richness vs. evenness) and Kintigh's (1984, 1989) simulation approach. These simulations tentatively support the existence of an Epipalaeolithic/Neolithic "broad-spectrum revolution" in the Levant and tend to confirm that, although they leave a lot of variation unexplained, models based on the concept of a "broad spectrum revolution" retain significant explanatory potential.

The final two chapters of the book are reflective comments by the two scholars who were discussants for the 1991 symposia in New Orleans that served as the impetus for this book. T. DOUGLAS PRICE (Chapter 18), an American trained specialist on archaeological chemistry, prehistoric diet, and the Mesolithic cultures of northwestern Europe, comments generally on the recurring themes of the volume and on the implications of the research reported here for some broader issues in the archaeology of hunter-gatherers. In commenting on the work of Stiner (this volume) in coastal Italy, Price reminds us how much of the archaeological record has been "drowned" by the Holocene marine transgression. The data he cites on stable isotope analysis from the Danish Mesolithic and Neolithic show just how skewed our notions of prehistoric subsistence strategies might be as a result of looking only at large-game hunting at interior sites.

In recognition of the fact that the data in the volume were collected from areas on the Eurasian continent where languages other than English are spoken, whereas the contributors are all anglophone scholars from the United Kingdom, Canada, and the United States, the symposia organizers (the volume editors) invited MARCEL OTTE (Chapter 19), a European trained specialist on the Palaeolithic cultures of western and central Europe, to comment on the relationship between the work done by the contributors to this volume and work done by nonanglophone specialists in continental Europe. This choice was particularly fruitful because Otte was co-organizer of a European conference on early prehistoric hunting held at Treignes (Belgium) just a few months before the New Orleans symposia. Otte's comments, delivered with directness and vigor, show clearly that there is more than just a language difference at work here. His forthright criticism of the anthropological approach to archaeology ("...an excess that merits reconsideration...") may well serve as a useful antidote to complacency about what we are doing and why we are doing it. In any case, that these views appear here, in a publication of the American Anthropological Association, seems particularly appropriate.

In conclusion, we should perhaps underscore two of the more general and more central themes that recur repeatedly throughout this volume. The first theme--the crucial importance of seasonality data--is an obvious one, but it deserves to be noted explicitly, if only for the benefit of nonspecialists. The ability of zooarchaeologists and others who work with archaeofaunas to specify when during the year prey animals were killed and when sites were occupied leads to information about hunting strategies and site functions that would otherwise remain unknown. Such information is used by Stiner, and indirectly by Kuhn, for elucidating the coastal Mousterian sites in Italy.

Seasonality data are essential to the efforts of Pike-Tay and Bricker to understand Gravettian hunting in southwestern France, to Burke's attempt to specify Magdalenian site function in the same region, to Rowley-Conwy's explanation of functional differences among Mesolithic sites in Denmark, and to Lieberman's efforts to understand changes in prehistoric human behavior during the Palaeolithic and Epipalaeolithic of Israel. The techniques whereby seasonality can be determined are varied, and they are, happily, increasing in both number and effectiveness.

The second defining theme that recurs in the volume is the critical importance of not merely hunting **technology**, but rather the underlying **strategies** of hunting activities. This implies, of course, much more than the simple killing of game. It involves the systematic and predictive planning of individual hunting episodes, the coordination of the social units needed both to pursue (or intercept) and process animal prey, the capacity to obtain and disseminate information on the distribution and movement of the animal herds, and, indeed, the closely associated patterns of settlement and mobility of the human groups themselves. There is, in other words, a whole network of social, cognitive, and communicative patterns involved in the successful exploitation and harvesting of animal populations that goes far beyond the mere technology used to kill and process the game. As the papers by Churchill, Stiner, Straus, and several other contributors make clear, it is almost certainly in these closely interrelated social and cognitive domains that many of the most significant developments in the strategies and efficiency of hunting activities throughout the course of later human evolution were achieved.

Now that we are well into our second century of systematic research on Palaeolithic and Mesolithic hunting, it is clear that both the bones and teeth of the prey animals and the weapons and other artifacts of the hunters are being interrogated more closely and more effectively than was possible until quite recently. The papers in the present volume, which are very representative of the kinds of questions that are being asked and the kinds of answers that are being obtained, will serve to emphasize just how many different dimensions there are to the basic notion of "hunting" in prehistory and how rapidly our ideas on this have developed over the past few years.

## NOTES

[1] "Disséminées par petits groupes, les tribus de cette période erraient dans la prairie fertile, où la douceur d'un climat très humide, mais tempéré et assez uniforme, entretenait, en dehors des zones glaciaires, une abondante végétation. Sur un sol où croissaient naturellement, aux bords d'immenses fleuves semblables à ceux du Nouveau Monde, le laurier, le figuier, et l'arbre de Judée, nos premiers ancêtres, adonnés à la chasse, pouvaient, sans de trop grands efforts, assurer leur subsistance" (Déchelette 1908:62).

## REFERENCES

Aiello, L. C.
1993    The fossil evidence for modern human origins in Africa: A revised view. *American Anthropologist* 95:73-96.
Binford, L. R.
1978    *Nunamiut Ethnoarchaeology*. New York: Academic Press.
1981    *Bones: Ancient Men and Modern Myth*. New York: Academic Press.
1985    Human ancestors: Changing views of their behavior. *Journal of Anthropological Archaeology* 4:292-327.
Bleed, P.
1986    The optimal design of hunting weapons: Maintainability or reliability. *American Antiquity* 51:737-747.
Brain, C. K.
1981    *The Hunters or the Hunted? An Introduction to African Cave Taphonomy*. Chicago: University of Chicago Press.
Clark, J. G. D.
1969    *World Prehistory: A New Outline*. Cambridge: Cambridge University Press.
Clutton-Brock, J., and C. Grigson, eds.
1983    *Animals and Archaeology. Volume 1. Hunters and their Prey*. BAR International Series 163. Oxford: British Archaeological Reports.
Déchelette, J.
1908    *Manuel d'archéologie préhistorique celtique et gallo-romaine. I.--Archéologie préhistorique*. Paris: Librarie Alphonse Picard et Fils.
Edwards, P. C.
1989    Revising the broad spectrum revolution: Its role in the origins of southwest Asian food production. *Antiquity* 63:225-246.
Flannery, K. V.
1969    Origins and ecological effects of early domestication in Iran and the Near East. In *The Domestication and Exploitation of Plants and Animals*. P. J. Ucko and G. W. Dimbleby, eds. Pp. 73-100. Chicago: Aldine.
Frayer, D. W., M. H. Wolpoff, A. G. Thorne, F. H. Smith, and G. G. Pope
1993    Theories of modern human origins: The paleontological test. *American Anthropologist* 95:14-50.
Gordon, B.
1988    *Of Men and Reindeer Herds in French Magdalenian Prehistory*. BAR International Series 390. Oxford: British Archaeological Reports.
Kintigh, K.
1984    Measuring archaeological diversity by comparison with simulated assemblages. *American Antiquity* 49:44-54.
1989    Sample size, significance, and measures of diversity. In *Quantifying Diversity in Archaeology*. R. D. Leonard and G. T. Jones, eds. Pp. 25-36. Cambridge: Cambridge University Press.
Martin, P. S., and R. G. Klein, eds.
1984    *Quaternary Extinctions: A Prehistoric Revolution*. Tucson: University of Arizona Press.
Mellars, P., ed.
1990    *The Emergence of Modern Humans: An Archaeological Perspective*. Edinburgh: Edinburgh University Press.
Mellars, P., and C. Stringer, eds.
1989    *The Human Revolution: Behavioral and Biological Perspectives on the Origins of Modern Humans*. Edinburgh: Edinburgh University Press.

Nitecki, M. H., and D. V. Nitecki, eds.
  1987   *The Evolution of Human Hunting*. New York: Plenum Press.
Pike-Tay, A.
  1991   *Red Deer Hunting in the Upper Paleolithic of Southwest France: A Study in Seasonality*. BAR International Series 569. Oxford: Tempus Reparatum.
Potts, R.
  1988   *Early Hominid Activities at Olduvai*. New York: de Gruyter.
Price, T. D., and J. A. Brown, eds.
  1985   *Prehistoric Hunter-Gatherers: The Emergence of Cultural Complexity*. Orlando: Academic Press.
Shipman, P.
  1983   Early Hominid lifestyle: Hunting and gathering or foraging and scavenging? In *Animals and Archaeology. Volume 1. Hunters and their Prey*. BAR International Series 163. J. Clutton-Brock and C. Grigson, eds. Pp. 31-49. Oxford: British Archaeological Reports.
  1986   Scavenging or hunting in early hominds: Theoretical framework and tests. *American Anthropologist* 88:27-43.

Soffer, O.
  1985   *The Upper Palaeolithic Settlement of the Russian Plain*. London: Academic Press.
Sollas, W. J.
  1924   *Ancient Hunters and their Modern Representatives*. 3rd revised edition. New York: Macmillan.
Stiner, M. C.
  1990   *The Ecology of Choice: Procurement and Transport of Animal Resources by Upper Pleistocene Hominids in West-Central Italy*. Ph.D. dissertation, Department of Anthropology, University of New Mexico. Ann Arbor: University Microfilms.
Stiner, M. C., ed.
  1991   *Human Predators and Prey Mortality*. Boulder: Westview Press.
Trinkaus, E., ed.
  1989   *The Emergence of Modern Humans: Biocultural Adaptations in the Later Pleistocene*. School of American Research Advanced Seminar Series. Cambridge: Cambridge University Press.

# 1

# Weapon Technology, Prey Size Selection, and Hunting Methods in Modern Hunter-Gatherers: Implications for Hunting in the Palaeolithic and Mesolithic

Steven E. Churchill
University of New Mexico

## ABSTRACT

The ethnographic and ethnohistoric literature on a global sample of 96 recent hunting peoples was surveyed to explore the relationships between weapons, prey body-size, and terrestrial hunting techniques. Findings include: (1) an association between the use of hand-delivered spears, large-bodied prey, and hunting techniques dependent on physiographic features and specific terrain types; (2) less dependence on terrain features in hunting with atlatl-propelled darts, and; (3) use of the bow and arrow without regard to prey size or terrain features. Findings also suggest that technologically aided hunting of medium-to-large game before the development of long-distance projectile weaponry involved a narrow range of strategies and limitations of prey choice. The effective exploitation of a wide range of terrestrial mammals characteristic of modern humans occurred after the advent of efficient projectile weapons.

## INTRODUCTION

Along with faunal remains, archaeologically recovered components of hunting tools provide a valuable source of information about the subsistence practices of past peoples. Weapons affect hunting search and pursuit times and, ultimately, diet breadth (see Winterhalder 1981; Shott 1990). Prey selection is a function of the range of body sizes the predator can kill and the range of prey speeds the predator can effectively overtake (Binford 1984). For hominids biologically ill-adapted to a predatory niche (i.e., lacking claws, large fangs, or great speed), weapons expand the capturable prey size range, and, for projectile weapons capable of "killing at a distance" (see Binford 1984), reduce problems of overtaking swift prey. These factors affect prey selection decisions and weigh heavily in search costs for hunters, while the efficiency of the weapons in wounding and killing prey greatly affects pursuit costs. Weapon technology makes hunting a workable foraging strategy for hominids.

There is a natural congruence between the properties of a particular weapon and the predatory capabilities of its users. Delineating the development of weapons during human evolution is critical to understanding hominid predatory behavior and subsistence and the evolution of technology-as-adaptive strategy.

Unfortunately, interpreting the lithic, wood, and osseous artifact record of hunting tools has not been easy. Two complementary lines of research have greatly added to our understanding. Experimental work with bone and stone weapon tips on spears, darts, and arrows has documented their ability to kill a variety of animals, provided information about their ranges, and shown the limitations inherent to these technologies (e.g., Frison 1986, 1989; Odell and Cowen 1986; Bergman et al. 1988). Use-wear analysis (e.g., Beyries 1984, 1987; Shea 1989a, 1989b, this volume; Anderson-Gerfaud 1990) provides additional information about the actual functions of pointed lithics and the origins of composite weaponry. The ethnographic record of recent hunters provides a third perspective. Recent hunters employ a wide range of weapon systems and hunting techniques, and thus provide the potential for better understanding the interrelationships among weapon system, hunting strategy, and prey choice. Information also can be gained about the practical, as opposed to experimental, limits of various weapons, and, ultimately, what the occurrence of various weapons in the archaeological record indicates about past human behavior.

## WEAPON DEVELOPMENT AND HUNTING

### Middle Pleistocene to Early Holocene

Pointed wood, lithic, and osseous artifacts comprise most of the evidence for weapon technology in Old World archaeological assemblages from the Middle Pleistocene to recent times. To prehistorians working in the "man the hunter" paradigm predominant for most of this century, the meaning of these artifacts was self-evident: they were components of the weapons that early man used in his pursuit of prey (e.g., Bordes 1968). Challenges to this paradigm have questioned the role of hunting in human evolution (e.g., Binford 1981, 1984, 1985; Brain 1981) and, consequently, have raised doubts about the meaning of artifacts once thought to represent hunting technology. What, then, is the evidence for technologically aided hunting in the later Pleistocene and early Holocene, and what does it imply about human predatory capabilities during this time? Addressing these questions is important before exploring the ethnographic and ethnohistorical record of hunter-gatherer behavior.

Sharpened wooden staves, perhaps the earliest spears, have been recovered from several late Middle Pleistocene sites, most notably Clacton-On-Sea (Warren 1911; Oakley et al. 1977) and Lehringen (Movius 1950; Tode 1954). Comparisons with recent hunter-gatherer wooden tools show these staves to be similar in size and design to untipped thrusting spears (Tode 1954; Oakley et al. 1977). The association of these early spears with large animal remains (esp. Lehringen) further suggests that they were hunting weapons (but see Gamble 1987). However, reinterpretations of the faunal remains from key Middle Pleistocene sites (see Binford 1977, 1987; Binford and Stone 1986; Klein 1987; Villa 1990) have cast doubt upon the capabilities of *Homo erectus* and archaic *Homo sapiens* to hunt the large game with which these tools are found. At present these artifacts only tell us that, by the end of the Middle Pleistocene, hominids were capable of making and using durable wooden spears; whether they were regularly used in hunting is open to question.

The issue of hunting medium-to-large mammals is no better resolved for the Middle Palaeolithic/Middle Stone Age than it is for the Lower Palaeolithic (see Binford 1984, 1985, 1989; Chase 1988, 1989; Klein 1986). Pointed lithics are abundant in archaeological deposits from this period (Levallois and Mousterian points from Europe and the Levant; Stillbay and Bambata points and Lupemban foliates from Africa), but their function as armatures is uncertain. Bone points make their earliest, albeit infrequent, appearance in the African Middle Stone Age (Clark et al. 1950; Singer and Wymer 1982), although they do not appear in Europe until the early Upper Palaeolithic.

The addition of a lithic or bone point to a wooden spear increases its penetration and cutting ability, and thus its killing power. Experimental work with stone-tipped spears (Frison 1986) and ethnohistorical references to their use among modern hunters attest to the capabilities of this weapon to inflict mortal wounds in even very large animals. Edge-wear evidence (Beyries 1987; Shea 1989; Anderson-Gerfaud 1990) and the recovery of a resin haft (Mania and Toepfer 1973) show that, by the Middle Palaeolithic, hominids were regularly hafting a variety of lithics, including points, to produce composite tools.

Analyses of Middle Palaeolithic points from Levantine sites report edge-wear and impact damage consistent with their use as projectile armatures (Shea 1988, 1989, 1990, this volume; but see Holdaway 1989, 1990). Similar evidence is lacking in points from European contexts (Beyries 1984, 1987; Anderson-Gerfaud 1990), which is surprising given that hominids living in periglacial conditions, with fewer edible plants, would have required a greater amount of meat in their diets than their temperate- and tropical-adapted contemporaries (see Gamble 1986). If hunting were an important component of subsistence, we would expect artifacts referable to a weapon function to be relatively more abundant in colder environments. While this expectation holds for bone points from Aurignacian levels, it does not for pointed lithics from the Middle Palaeolithic (Kuhn 1989). The lithic and osseous record of the Middle Palaeolithic/Middle Stone Age seems to indicate that, in some places and at some times during this period, hominids were using composite spears as an aid to protein capture. Understanding geographical variation in technologically aided hunting in the Upper Pleistocene presents an interesting challenge to Palaeolithic archaeologists.

Near the end of the Middle Palaeolithic, pointed elements began to display morphological features characteristic of later projectile armatures. These features occur variably at first, but with increasing consistency in the Upper Palaeolithic, and include: relatively small size, greater symmetry about the long axis, basal modification to facilitate hafting, and size standardization of the proximal end. If the properties of lithic armatures reflect properties of the total composite weapon (Christenson 1986), these design features may reflect a concern for projectile aerodynamics and penetration capability (see Guthrie 1983; Christenson 1986; Odell and Cowan 1986). Certain basal modifications, such as the addition of a stem or tang (evident first in Aterian points, later in Solutrean shouldered points, Teyjat points, and Azilian points) may reflect a concern for positioning the haft material (either sinew or resin) away from the cutting edge to reduce drag and increase penetrating ability (see Guthrie 1983). Haft drag is a greater problem in projectiles than in hand-thrust weapons, where muscu-

**Table 1.1.** Hunter-gatherer groups by biogeographical regions.

*Arctic (North America and Asia):*

| | |
|---|---|
| Aleut | Koniag |
| Caribou Eskimo | Netsilik Eskimo |
| Copper Eskimo | Polar Eskimo |
| Gilyak | W. Greenland Eskimo |
| Iglulik Eskimo | Yukaghir |

*North American Northwest Coast:*

| | |
|---|---|
| Alsea | Quileute |
| Bella Coola | Tlingit |
| Hupa | Tolowa |
| Klamath | Twana |
| Modoc | Yurok |
| Nootka | |

*Boreal Forest and Northern Deciduous Forest (North America and Asia):*

Ainu
Chipewyan (Caribou-Eater)
Eastern Ojibwa
Emo Ojibwa (Rainy River)
Kaska (Nahani)
Micmac (Souriquois)
Montagnais
Mistassini Cree
Naskapi
Northern Salteaux and Pekangekum
Slave
Southern Ojibwa (Katikitegon)

*North American Desert/Great Basin:*

| | |
|---|---|
| Cahuilla (Desert) | Ute |
| Seri | Washo |

*North American Great Plains:*

| | |
|---|---|
| Arapaho | Crow |
| Assiniboin | Gros Ventre (Atsina) |
| Blackfoot | Piegan (Pikuni) |
| Blood | Shoshoni |

*North American California Indians:*

| | |
|---|---|
| Achomawi (Pit River) | Pomo |
| Atsugewi | Sinkyone |
| Chumash | Tubatulabal |
| Gabrieleño | Wappo |
| Luiseño | Wintu |
| Maidu | Wiyot |
| Miwok | Yana |
| Mono (Western) | Lake and North Foothill |
| Nisenan | Yokuts |
| Nomlaki | Coast Yuki |
| Patwin | |

*South American Tropical Forest:*

| | |
|---|---|
| Ache | Cuiva |
| Aweikoma (Caingang) | Siriono |
| Bororo | Waorani |
| Botocudo | |

(Table 1.1 continued)

*Southern South America:*

| | |
|---|---|
| Alacaluf | Ona (Selk'nam) |
| Tehuelche | Yahgan (Yamana) |

*Africa:*

| | |
|---|---|
| Dorobo | Hadza |
| Efe (Mbuti) and | !Kung |
| Bambote Pygmy | |
| G/wi | |

*Indonesia:*

| | |
|---|---|
| Agta (Aeta) | Punan |
| Andaman Islanders | Rock Vedda ("Wild") |
| Kubu | Semang |
| Mlabrai | Semaq Beri |

*Australia:*

| | |
|---|---|
| Aranda | Tasmanians |
| Mardudjara | Tiwi |
| Murngin | Yiwara |
| Pintupi | |

lar effort of the hunter insures the continued penetration of the point. Standardization of stem width in Solutrean points also may denote a concern for ease of replacement of stone tips in costly foreshafts after breakage due to projectile use (Straus 1990). The greater investment in stone armatures evident in the Upper Palaeolithic may attest to pressure to produce flight-stable, accurate projectiles.

These changes in lithic points, along with increasing frequencies of small, symmetrical bone points, might have something to do with the advent of long-range weaponry--a concern for "killing at a distance"--at the boundary between the Middle and Upper Palaeolithic. True long-distance projectile weaponry, in the form of spearthrower (atlatl) and dart, is clearly established for the later Upper Palaeolithic, based on Solutrean atlatl hooks from La Placard and Combe-Saunière (Breuil 1912; Cattelain 1989), but may have come into regular use somewhat earlier. While changes in the morphology of armatures at the Middle/Upper Palaeolithic border suggest increased emphasis on projectile technology, they do not preclude an earlier development of long-range weapons. The use of large, imperfectly symmetrical Leilira points as dart tips in parts of Australia (McCarthy 1967; Mulvaney 1969) shows that some dedicated atlatl users are indifferent to the projectile point characteristics discussed above. Given the similarity of elongated Levallois points to Leilira points, it is reasonable to think that they might have tipped atlatl darts during the Middle Palaeolithic. Pinpointing the introduction of this weapon requires recovery of the spearthrower itself, since even sharpened wooden spears serve as adequate darts (see Oakley et al. 1977). The appearance of atlatls in the Solutrean, and their increased frequency in Magdalenian deposits, may represent nothing more than an

**Table 1.2.** Mean animal body weights (kg)[a].

(Table 1.2 continued)

| Species | x̄M | x̄F | x̄M&F |
|---|---|---|---|
| North America | | | |
| Elk (*Cervus elaphus*)[p] | 360 | 258 | 309 |
| Tule Elk (*C.e. nannodes*)[p] | 182 | 153 | 168 |
| Mule Deer (*Odocoileus hemionus*)[c] | 132 | 52 | 92 |
| White-tailed Deer (*O. virginianus*)[p] | 113 | 76 | 95 |
| Moose (*Alces alces*)[c] | 453 | 350 | 402 |
| Caribou (*Rangifer tarandus*)[c] | 110 | 81 | 96 |
| Pronghorn (*Antilocapra americana*)[c] | 51 | 42 | 47 |
| Bison (*Bison bison*)[c] | 570 | 420 | 495 |
| Mt. Goat (*Oreamnos americana*)[c] | 85 | 62 | 74 |
| Muskox (*Ovibos moschatus*)[c] | 340 | 287 | 314 |
| Bighorn Sheep (*Ovis canadensis*)[c] | 143 | 63 | 103 |
| Wild Boar (Feral Hog) (*Sus scrofa*)[i] | - | - | 265 |
| Collarded Peccary (*Tayassu tajacu*)[n,r] | 22 | - | 21 |
| Coyote (*Canis latrans*)[c] | - | - | 13 |
| Wolf (*C. lupus*)[c] | - | - | 53 |
| Arctic Fox (*Alopex lagopus*)[c] | 4 | 3 | 4 |
| Red Fox (*Vulpes vulpes*)[c] | - | - | 5 |
| Grey Fox (*Urocyon cinereoargenteus*)[c] | 4 | 4 | 4 |
| Black Bear (*Ursus americanus*)[c] | 169 | 136 | 153 |
| Grizzly Bear (*U. arctos*)[c] | - | - | 331 |
| Polar Bear (*U. maritimus*)[c] | - | - | 460 |
| Racoon (*Procyon lotor*)[c] | 9 | 8 | 9 |
| River Otter (*Lontra canadensis*)[c] | 8 | 7 | 8 |
| Mt. Lion (*Felis concolor*)[c] | 85 | 48 | 67 |
| Lynx (*Lynx lynx*)[c] | 11 | 9 | 10 |
| Whitetail Jackrabbit (*Lepus townsendii*)[c] | 3 | 3 | 3 |
| Blacktail Jackrabbit (*L. californicus*)[g] | 5 | - | - |
| Snowshoe Hare (*L. americanus*)[c] | 1 | 2 | 2 |
| Arctic Hare (*L. arcticus*)[c] | 5 | 5 | 5 |
| East. Cottontail (*Sylvilagus floridanus*)[c] | 1 | 1 | 1 |
| Armadillo (*Cabassous Sp.*)[m] | - | - | 4 |
| South and Central America | | | |
| White-Lipped Peccary (*Tayassu pecari*)[r] | - | - | 33 |
| Brocket Deer (*Mazama americana*)[r] | - | - | 42 |
| Marsh Deer (*Blastocerus dichotomus*)[n] | - | - | 109 |
| Pampas Deer (*Ozotoceros bezoarticus*)[n] | - | - | 35 |
| Huemul (*Hippocamelus bisulcus*)[n] | - | - | 70 |
| Guanaco (*Lama guanicoe*)[n] | 119 | 121 | 120 |
| Vicuna (*Vicugna vicugna*)[n] | - | - | 50 |
| Tapir (*Tapiros terrestris*)[r] | - | - | 164 |
| Spider Monkey (*Ateles paniscus*)[f] | 9 | 9 | 9 |
| Woolly Monkey (*Lagothrix lagothricha*)[f] | 9 | 6 | 8 |
| Howler Monkey (*Alouatta seniculus*)[f] | 8 | 6 | 7 |
| Capuchin Monkey (*Cebus apella*)[f] | 3 | 2 | 3 |
| Saki Monkey (*Pithecia monachus*)[f] | 3 | 2 | 3 |
| Squirrel Monkey (*Saimiri sciureus*)[f] | 1 | 1 | 1 |
| Crab-Eating Racoon (*Procyon cancrivorus*)[n] | - | - | 9 |
| Coati (*Nasua nasua*)[n] | 5 | 4 | 5 |
| Bush Dog (*Speothos venaticus*)[n] | - | - | 6 |
| Crab-Eating Fox (*Cerdocyon thous*)[n] | - | - | 6 |
| Jaguarundi (*Felis yagouaroundi*)[n] | - | - | 3 |
| Margay (*F. wiedii*)[n] | - | - | 3 |
| Ocelot (*F. pardalis*)[n] | - | - | 8 |
| Puma (*Puma concolor*)[n] | - | 24 | 35 |
| Jaguar (*Panthera onca*)[n] | 100 | 76 | 89 |
| Tayra (*Eira barbara*)[r] | - | - | 4 |
| Giant River Otter (*Pteronura brasiliensis*)[n] | - | - | 27 |
| Giant Anteater (*Myrmecophaga tridactyla*)[n] | 32 | 29 | 31 |
| Tamandua (*Tamandua tetradactyla*)[n] | - | - | 6 |
| Armadillo (*Dasypus Sp.*)[n] | - | - | 2 |
| Giant Armadillo (*Priodontes maximus*)[n] | - | - | 27 |
| Forest Rabbit (*Sylvilagus brasiliensis*)[n] | - | - | 1 |
| Paca (*Agouti paca*)[n] | - | - | 8 |
| Agouti (*Dasyprocta sp.*)[n] | - | - | 3 |
| Capybara (*Hydrochaeris hydrochaeris*)[n] | 43 | 40 | 42 |
| Tucotuco (*Ctenomys sp.*)[n] | - | - | 1 |
| Cayman (*Caiman sclerops*)[r] | - | - | 20 |
| Africa | | | |
| Giraffe (*Giraffa camelopardalis*)[j] | 1100 | 700 | 900 |
| Okapi (*Okapia johnstoni*)[j] | - | - | 230 |
| Dik Dik (*Madoqua sp.*)[j] | - | - | 5 |
| Impala (*Aepyceros melampus*)[h] | 63 | 50 | 57 |
| Eland (*Taurotragus oryx*)[j] | 690 | 450 | 570 |
| Lesser Kudu (*Tragelaphus imberbis*)[j] | 100 | 63 | 82 |
| Greater Kudu (*T. strepsiceros*)[j] | 257 | 170 | 214 |
| Gemsbok (*Oryx gazella*)[h] | - | - | 203 |
| Springbok (*Antidorcas marsupialis*)[h] | 35 | 25 | 30 |
| Steinbok (*Raphicerus campestris*)[h] | - | - | 13 |
| Klipspringer (*Oreotragus oreotragus*)[j] | - | - | 13 |
| Common Reedbuck (*Redunca arundinum*)[j] | 68 | 48 | 58 |
| Waterbuck (*Kobus ellipsiprymnus*)[j] | 240 | 180 | 210 |
| Hartebeeste (*Alcelaphus buselaphus*)[h] | 168 | 150 | 159 |
| Cape Hartebeeste (*A.b. caama*)[h] | 168 | 150 | 159 |
| Wildebeeste (*Connochaetes taurinus*)[h] | 228 | 200 | 214 |
| Sable Antelope (*Hippotragus niger*)[h] | 235 | 210 | 223 |
| Roan Antelope (*H. equinus*)[h] | 280 | 250 | 265 |
| Bongo (*Boocercus eurycerus*)[j] | 300 | 240 | 270 |
| Pygmy Antelope (*Neotragus batesi*)[j] | 2 | 3 | 3 |
| Blue Duiker (*Cephalophus monticola*)[j] | - | - | 6 |
| Bay Duiker (*C. dorsalis*)[j] | - | - | 22 |
| Yellow-Backed Duiker (*C. sylvicultor*)[j] | - | - | 63 |
| Black-Fronted Duiker (*C. nigrifrons*)[h] | - | - | 15 |
| Thompson's Gazelle (*Gazella thomsoni*)[h] | 25 | 19 | 22 |
| Water Chevrotain (*Hyemoschus aquaticus*)[j] | 10 | 12 | 11 |
| Buffalo (*Syncerus caffer*)[j] | 680 | 480 | 580 |
| Forest (Dwarf) Buffalo (*S.c. nanus*)[h] | - | - | 285 |
| Cape Buffalo (*S.c. caffer*)[h] | - | - | 650 |
| Bush Pig (*Potamochoerus porcus*)[j] | - | - | 70 |
| G. For. Hog (*Hylochoerus meinertzhageni*)[j] | 230 | 180 | 205 |
| Wart Hog (*Phacochoerus aethiopicus*)[j] | 85 | 57 | 71 |
| Common Zebra (*Equus quagga*)[j] | 250 | 220 | 235 |
| Hippo (*Hippopotamus amphibius*)[j] | 1475 | 1360 | 1418 |
| Pygmy Hippo (*Choeropsis liberiensis*)[j] | - | - | 237 |
| White Rhino (*Ceratotherium simum*)[j] | - | - | 2950 |
| African Elephant (*Loxodonta africana*)[j] | - | - | 4350 |
| Forest (Pygmy) Elephant (*L.a. cyclotis*)[h] | 1350 | 1000 | 1175 |
| Chimpanzee (*Pan troglodytes*)[f] | 60 | 47 | 54 |
| Olive Baboon (*Papio anubis*)[f] | 25 | 14 | 20 |
| Colobus Monkey (*Colobus sp.*)[f] | 8 | 7 | 8 |
| Common Jackal (*Canis aureus*)[j] | - | - | 11 |
| Bat-Eared Fox (*Otocyon megalotis*)[j] | - | - | 4 |
| Striped Hyena (*Hyaena hyaena*)[j] | - | - | 46 |
| Spotted Hyena (*Crocuta crocuta*)[j] | - | - | 63 |

(Table 1.2 continued)

| Species | x̄M | x̄F | x̄M&F |
|---|---|---|---|
| Lion (*Felis leo*)[j] | 172 | 151 | 162 |
| Leopard (*F. pardus*)[j] | 60 | 50 | 55 |
| Swamp Cat (*F. chaus*)[h] | 9 | 5 | 7 |
| Golden Cat (*F. aurata*)[j] | - | - | 11 |
| Wild Cat (*F. sylvestris*)[j] | 5 | 4 | 5 |
| African Civet (*Civettictis civetta*)[j] | - | - | 12 |
| Common Genet (*Genetta genetta*)[j] | - | - | 2 |
| Mongoose (subfamily *Herpestinae*)[j] | - | - | 2 |
| Porcupine (*Hystrix sp.*)[h] | - | - | 21 |
| Cape Hare (*Lepus capensis*)[h] | - | - | 4 |
| Spring Hare (*Pedetes capensis*)[j] | - | - | 4 |
| Hyrax (*Procavia sp.*)[j] | - | - | 3 |
| Honey Badger (*Mellivora capensis*)[j] | - | - | 8 |
| Tree Pangolin (*Manis tricuspis*)[j] | - | - | 2 |
| Giant Pangolin (*M. gigantea*)[j] | - | - | 33 |
| Cape Pangolin (*M. temmincki*)[h] | - | - | 17 |
| Antbear (*Orycteropus afer*)[j] | - | - | 66 |
| Monitor Lizard (*Varanus albigularis*)[e] | - | - | 3 |
| Ostrich (*Struthio sp.*)[k] | - | - | 95 |
| **Asia and Indonesia** | | | |
| Asian Elephant (*Elephas maximus*)[l] | 2489 | 3022 | 2756 |
| Tapir (*Tapirus indicus*)[l] | - | - | 318 |
| Sambar (*Cervus unicolor*)[l] | 162 | 223 | 193 |
| Japanese Deer (*C. nippon*)[b] | 100 | - | - |
| Barking Deer (*Muntiacus muntjak*)[d] | - | - | 15 |
| Axis Deer (*Cervus axis*)[d] | - | - | 50 |
| Chinese Water Deer (*Hydropotes inermis*)[d] | - | - | 15 |
| Lesser Mouse Deer (*Tragulus javanicus*)[l] | - | - | 1 |
| Lesser Mouse Deer (*T. napu*)[l] | - | - | 5 |
| Manchurian Elk (*Alces alces*)[p] | 360 | 258 | 309 |
| Gaur (Seladang) (*Bos frontalis*)[d] | - | - | 850 |
| Sumatran Rhino (*Didermocerus sumatrensis*)[l] | - | - | 900 |
| Wild Pig (*Sus scrofa*)[d] | - | - | 91 |
| Bearded Pig (*S. barbatus*)[l] | - | - | 80 |
| Flying Fox (*Pteropus vampyrus*)[l] | - | - | 1 |
| Flying Squirrel (*Petinomys Sp.*)[l] | - | - | 1 |
| Bamboo Rat (*Rhizomys sumatrensis*)[l] | - | - | 2 |
| Leaf Monkey (*Presbytis sp.*)[f] | 7 | 6 | 7 |
| Crab-Eating Macaque (*Macaca fascicularis*)[f] | 5 | 3 | 4 |
| Pig-Tailed Macaque (*M. nemestrina*)[f] | 10 | 6 | 8 |
| Otter (*Lutra lutra*)[d] | - | - | 10 |
| Civit (*Viverra sp.*)[l] | - | - | 6 |
| Brown Bear (*Ursus arctos*)[e] | - | - | 331 |
| Asiatic Black Bear (*Ursus thibetanus*)[d] | - | - | 150 |
| Malayan Sun Bear (*Helarctos malayanus*)[l] | - | - | 46 |
| Tiger (*Felis tigris*)[l] | - | - | 178 |
| Malayan Porcupine (*Hystrix brachyura*)[l] | - | - | 8 |
| Lesser Titil Bonor (*Atherurus macrourus*)[l] | - | - | 3 |
| **Australia** | | | |
| Red Kangaroo (*Megaleia rufa*)[o] | 82 | 27 | 55 |
| Wallaroo (*Macropus robustus*)[d] | - | - | 40 |
| Forest Kangaroo (*M. giganteus*)[d] | 91 | - | - |
| Rock Wallaby (*Petrogale penicillata*)[d] | - | - | 7 |
| Red-Bellied Wallaby (*Thylogale billardieri*)[d] | - | - | 6 |
| S. Hairy-Nosed Wombat (*Lasiorhinus latifrons*)[d.] | - | - | 27 |
| Emu (*Dromiceius novaehollandiae*)[q] | 82 | 72 | 77 |

(Table 1.2 continued)

[a]When only body weight ranges were available, the mean weight was taken as the middle of the published range. If mean body weight for the combined sexes of a species was not published, then the average of the means of males and females was used. Prey body weights by biogeographical region were non-normally distributed, and sample variances covaried positively with sample means because of the inclusion of very large animals (elephants, hippos, etc.) in some of the samples. Thus, raw body weight values were log10 transformed before averaging. After the construction of samples by biogeographical region, weighted means for the combined global sample were taken for each combination of weapon system and hunting technique. Pairwise Behrens-Fisher t-tests (Fisher and Yates 1963) were used to evaluate differences in mean animal body weights across hunting techniques and weapon systems. The sequential Bonferroni technique (Holm 1979) was used to control the inflated family-wide Type I error rates that occur with pair-wise testing.
[b]Allen 1940; [c]Banfield 1974; [d]Boitani and Bartoli 1983; [e]Brain 1981; [f]Fleagle 1988; [g]Hall and Kelson 1959; [h]Haltenorth and Diller 1980; [i]Jameson and Peeters 1988; [j]Kingdon 1971; [k]Lee 1979; [l]Medway 1969; [m]Meritt 1985; [n]Redford and Eisenberg 1992; [o]Ride 1970; [p]Schmidt and Gilbert 1978; [q]Serventy and Whittell 1962; [r]Yost and Kelly 1983 (Average body weights from Yost and Kelly [1983] were obtained by dividing the total capture weight of a species [Table 6.1] by the total number of animals captured of that species [Table 6.2].).

increased use of less perishable materials (antler vs. wood) in their manufacture.

Irrefutable evidence of archery in the latest Palaeolithic and Mesolithic of Europe comes from the recovery of partial arrows from Stellmoor at 10,500 years BP (Rust 1943) and wooden self bows from several sites dated to around 8,000 years BP (Rausing 1967). As with other weapons, identifying the origins of the bow and arrow is problematic. Several small Upper Palaeolithic points (Font-Robert, Gravette, and el-Wad) would have served well as arrowheads, and the sophistication of bow design in the European Mesolithic suggests that this weapon system had by then been in use for some time, perhaps since the middle of the Upper Palaeolithic (see Bergman et al. 1988; Bergman and Newcomer 1983; Bergman, this volume).

Regardless of when particular weapons first appear, it is apparent that, between the Middle Pleistocene and the Early Holocene, hominids added new weapons capable of "killing at a distance" (atlatl darts and the bow and arrow) to their existing arsenal of short-range weapons (thrust and thrown hand spears, rocks, sticks, etc.) What does this mean in terms of subsistence strategies overall, about hunting behavior itself, and about the evolving capabilities of hominid hunters? With these questions in mind, we can turn to the ethnographic and ethnohistoric literature on recent hunter-gatherer use of hand-delivered and projectile weapons in terrestrial hunting.

## THE ETHNOGRAPHIC DATA

Two relationships between hunting technology and hunting behavior are explored in this paper: (1) weapon system to hunting technique and (2) weapon system and hunting technique to prey-size selection. **Weapon system** refers to a weapon type plus its method of employment (e.g., thrusting spears and hand-thrown spears are considered two different weapon systems). For each hunter-gatherer group, the weapon system and techniques used in hunting, animals hunted with each system and technique, and the distance between hunter and prey were noted. Weapon systems included thrusting spears, hand-thrown spears, atlatl-delivered spears, and bow with nonpoisoned arrows. Hunting techniques were classified as follows:

**Disadvantage**: includes any technique that limits the escape of an animal or exploits an animal naturally disadvantaged to gain time or access so that a weapon can be employed. Game drives were included if the expressed aim was to force the animal into a handicapped position in which the weapon was applied. Examples include impeding animals by driving them into water, deep snow, or mud; treeing an animal or forcing it into a defensive stance with dogs; or attacking an animal during hibernation in its den.

**Ambush**: involves instances in which hunters wait in hiding, whether behind man-made blinds or natural features, for animals to pass within effective range of their weapons. Drives were considered ambushing if the intent was to force animals past concealed hunters.

**Approach**: includes stalking free-moving animals to within effective weapon range. The object of approach hunting is to avoid evoking the prey's flight response before the hunter is within effective weapon range. Luring of animals was also included in this category.

**Pursuit**: entails chasing an animal to overtake it and place the hunter within effective weapon range or to exhaust and thus disadvantage it. With pursuit hunting the weapon system is used after the animal has taken flight, and, in some cases (running an animal to exhaustion), the flight response is used as an aid to capture. Pursuit may involve domesticated animals such as horses to close the distance between hunter and prey or dogs to keep the animal moving until exhaustion.

**Encounter**: refers to hunting in which animals are taken, either jumped from the bush or spotted in trees, as they are encountered. Hunters are often within effective weapon range when the animal is found and often do not pursue the animals if they move out of range.

Data on hunting behavior was culled from the primary ethnographic and ethnohistoric literature for 96 recent human groups (Table 1.1: bibliographic references available from the author upon request). Although the literature does not provide a fine-grained picture of hunting behavior, it does allow for the establishment of basic patterns regarding who was hunting what, with which weapons, and by which methods. The object of this research was to establish basic associations among weapon systems, hunting methods, and prey sizes, which could then be applied to the archaeological record.

Although the aim of the research was pattern recognition, mean prey body weights for different weapon system/hunting method combinations were compared statistically to evaluate the relationship between prey size, weapons, and techniques. Hunter-gatherers were grouped by biogeographical region (Table 1.1), and mean prey body weights across hunting techniques and weapon systems were calculated for each region (see Table 1.2).

## WEAPONS, TECHNIQUES, AND PREY SIZE

### Hand-Delivered Spears

Although 95% of the surveyed groups used spears, only 50% used them in terrestrial hunting; other uses include hunting marine mammals, fishing, warfare, and defense from predators. Thrusting spears clearly dominate the reported cases of terrestrial spear hunting, while accounts of hand-thrown spears are relatively rare. Two things are readily apparent about modern hunter-gatherer use of thrusting spears: they are predominately directed against larger animals, and they are mostly associated with disadvantaging prey (Table 1.3). The large variances surrounding the mean body weights for the thrusting spear (i.e., the large standard errors in Table 1.3) reflect the versatility of this weapon with respect to prey size. Animals of any size can be dispatched by spear, provided the hunter has the time and close access necessary to repeatedly deliver well-placed stabs. Because the hunting of elephant and hippo with hand spears by a few groups greatly inflates the mean body weights, sample medians have also been included in Table 1.3. These medians underscore the point that, even though there is great variability in the size of animals taken by thrusting spear, modern hunters tend to direct this weapon system at large prey.

The thrusting spear is used primarily as a dispatching tool after prey have been placed in a disadvantaged position. Disadvantaging with thrusting spears is also strongly associated with cooperative drive techniques and use of domesticated animals (mostly dogs) or other technology (such as boats, snowshoes, snares, or other weapons). Only 14 cases (out of 69: a given group may hunt more than one species with the same combination of weapon system and technique, such that the number of "cases" often exceeds the number of groups that use a particular

**Table 1.3.** Mean animal body weights[a] taken by various hunting methods: thrusting spears vs. hand-thrown spears.

| | | | Thrusting | | Thrown | | p |
|---|---|---|---|---|---|---|---|
| Disadvantage | Mean | [Median] | 326.8 | [195.9] | 200.7 | [163.9] | 0.054 |
| | SE | (N) | 139.7 | (33) | 55.0 | (8) | |
| Ambush | Mean | [Median] | 197.8 | [164.3] | 127.3 | [91.0] | 0.843 |
| | SE | (N) | 50.3 | (7) | 36.2 | (5) | |
| Approach | Mean | [Median] | - | - | 42.2 | [42.2] | - |
| | SE | (N) | | | 12.2 | (2) | |
| Pursuit | Mean | [Median] | 378.3 | [460.0] | 341.4 | [277.0] | 0.752 |
| | SE | (N) | 67.1 | (5) | 125.1 | (3) | |
| Encounter | Mean | (N) | 26.5 | (1) | 26.5 | (1) | - |
| TOTAL (all | Mean | [Median] | 283.4 | [163.9] | 146.2 | [74.7] | 0.006* |
| techniques) | SE | (N) | 101.2 | (46) | 42.8 | (15) | |

[a]All weights in kilograms. * = p significant at family-wide $\alpha$ = 0.05. p-values reflect pairwise comparisons of weighted means of logged body weights. **Key:** SE = standard error of the mean; N = number of groups comprising the weighted mean (i.e., number of groups that used each combination of weapon system and technique).

method) lacked cooperative drives, dogs, or accessory technology. In these cases the hunters required only suitable landscape features with which to disadvantage the animals, most commonly snow drifts, but also valleys and swamps--some cases also involved hunters taking advantage of hibernating bears naturally "trapped" in their dens.

The thrusting spear is associated less frequently with ambush and pursuit hunting (Table 1.3). The few reported cases of ambushing with thrusting spears also involved either suitable terrain or cooperative hunting, namely driving animals toward concealed hunters. Most ambushing spear hunters used trees, rocks, and other physiographic features for concealment while waiting for the animal to come within effective weapon range. Ambush hunting with thrusting spears involved smaller prey on average than either disadvantage or pursuit hunting. Cases of pursuit with thrusting spears involved either the use of horses (to close the gap between mounted hunter and fleeing prey), dogs (to catch the animal and then hold it at bay), or a hot and dry environment where endurance pursuit tactics could be employed. Only one case of encounter hunting with thrusting spears (peccaries in the South American tropics) was noted. No reports of approach hunting with thrusting spears were found.

Reports of hand-thrown spears in terrestrial hunting were relatively rare, and most were found in descriptions of thrusting spear use. This suggests that the distinction between these two weapon systems may not be entirely meaningful. Lack of significant differences in mean body weights between thrust and hand-

thrown spears for most hunting techniques further supports this idea (Table 1.3). While there is a non-significant trend for hand-thrown spears to be directed at smaller game, both thrusting and hand-thrown spears are large-animal procurement tools primarily associated with disadvantaging and, to a lesser degree, ambush hunting. Both are also short-range weapon systems (Table 1.4). For these reasons data for thrust and thrown spears were pooled for comparisons with other weapon systems (see Table 1.6). This allowed for incorporation of accounts of hand-spear use that did not specify method of employment (thrust vs. hand-thrown), thus increasing sample sizes for some comparisons.

The notable difference between thrust and hand-thrown spears involves approach hunting. Both the Tiwi (Melville Island, Australia) and Tasmanians were reported to hand throw very thin and light spears during approach hunting of wallabies and kangaroo. These two cases are the only reports of hand spears used with approach hunting techniques.

### Atlatl Darts

The atlatl-propelled dart is markedly different from hand-delivered spears. In this sample atlatl darts were never associated with disadvantage, pursuit, or encounter tactics (Table 1.5). Atlatl spear hunting is associated with a shift in techniques to ambushing and approaching much smaller prey. With an average effective range of 39.6 m (Table 1.4), the atlatl-delivered dart is a true long-range projectile. It is

**Table 1.4.** Effective range in meters of various weapon systems.

| Weapon System | Effective Range | SE | N |
|---|---|---|---|
| Thrusting Spear | Contact | --- | -- |
| Hand-Thrown Spear | 7.8 | 2.2 | 14 |
| Atlatl Spear | 39.6 | 5.5 | 9 |
| Bow and Arrow | 25.8 | 2.4 | 25 |

undoubtedly this feature that makes this weapon system effective with approach and ambush hunting. Although the atlatl is in wide use as a marine and waterfowl hunting tool among Eskimos and as a waterfowl weapon among the agricultural Tarasco of Mexico, all the terrestrial hunting data for this weapon system comes from Australia. The small size of all terrestrial game on the Australian continent makes it impossible to evaluate the relationship between atlatl darts and prey size.

**Bow and Arrow**

The bow and arrow is used with all the hunting techniques examined. Average prey body weights show a trend towards differentiation of prey size with different techniques (Table 1.6). Except for encounter hunting, the differences are not statistically significant --likely due to the large variances surrounding each mean (Tables 1.6 and 1.7). The bow and arrow is a weapon conducive to hunting by any technique, allowing the hunter to tailor the technique to the behavioral characteristics of a given prey species, rather than having the limitations of the weapon system dictate the type and size of prey.

With disadvantage, approach, and pursuit hunting the bow and arrow is used "surgically," directed towards the thoracic cavity with the goal of striking a vital organ and inducing death by hemorrhage. The ability to use it in this way makes the bow and arrow effective against even large game. The need to place an arrow precisely between ribs or behind the shoulder blade, however, makes for a relatively small target area even on large animals (see Guthrie 1983; Frison 1986; Friis-Hansen 1990). This is one reason the bow and arrow have a shorter effective distance than the atlatl spear--25.8 m on average. Disadvantage, ambush, and pursuit tactics may allow the hunter the close shot necessary to bring down large game or may buy time to fire repeated shots. With ambush hunting the arrow is used both as a surgical and a "shock" weapon (causing sufficient tissue damage, regardless of where it hits, to kill or immobilize in a relatively short time). Failing a well-placed, surgical shot, the ambush hunter hopes to place enough arrows into the

animal to cause it to lie down or drop within a reasonable distance. A large number of cervid, bovid, and suid bones with healed arrow wounds from Mesolithic sites (Noe-Nygaard 1974) attest to the limits of the bow and arrow as a shock weapon against medium-to-large game when the thorax is missed. With encounter hunting, which is primarily directed at smaller prey, the bow and arrow is an effective shock weapon capable of bringing down an animal struck anywhere on the body.

**DISCUSSION**

The strong association between hand-delivered spears and disadvantaging suggests limitations on hunting with this weapon system alone. Disadvantaging is highly dependent upon physiographic features for success, requiring natural or man-made traps such as narrow arroyos, box canyons, corrals, swamps, snow drifts, or bodies of water, or the assistance of dogs to surround and impede an animal so that the technology can be employed. Even ambushing, though used much less often, requires physical features suitable for concealing hunters until the animal is within effective range of the weapon--within 5-10 m for hand-delivered spears. These terrain features must not only be suitable for disadvantaging or ambushing, they also must be located in places where desirable game animals occur. It is only with pursuit techniques that the hand-spear hunter is freed somewhat from terrain constraints. Chasing animals to exhaustion is not the most energy efficient means of hunting, however, and may be even less so in colder environments, such as Pleistocene Europe.

The relationship of hand-delivered spears to terrain dependent hunting techniques in northern latitudes suggests that, prior to the development of long-range weapons, hunters may have been restricted to places in the environment where the technology was most effective for the hunting of medium-to-large

**Table 1.5.** Mean prey body weights[a]--atlatl hunting.

| Technique | Mean | [Median] | SE | N |
|---|---|---|---|---|
| Disadvantage | ----- | | --- | - |
| Ambush | 42.2 | [42.2] | 1.4 | 3 |
| Approach | 39.8 | [39.8] | 0.0 | 2 |
| Pursuit | ----- | | --- | - |
| Encounter | ----- | | --- | - |
| TOTAL (all techniques) | 43.1 | [44.7] | 3.8 | 5 |

[a]All weights in kilograms. **Key:** SE = standard error of the mean; N = number of groups comprising the weighted mean.

**Table 1.6.** Mean animal body weights[a] taken by various hunting methods: hand spears vs. bow and arrow.

| | | | Hand Spear | | Bow and Arrow | | p |
|---|---|---|---|---|---|---|---|
| Disadvantage | Mean | [Median] | 504.1 | [202.5] | 230.8 | [141.2] | 0.357 |
| | SE | (N) | 183.9 | (37) | 42.1 | (18) | |
| Ambush | Mean | [Median] | 185.2 | [161.8] | 131.8 | [95.5] | 0.077 |
| | SE | (N) | 53.1 | (7) | 19.9 | (25) | |
| Approach | Mean | [Median] | 42.2 | [42.2] | 170.4 | [101.8] | 0.000* |
| | SE | (N) | 12.2 | (2) | 43.9 | (28) | |
| Pursuit | Mean | [Median] | 349.1 | [368.5] | 200.1 | [129.8] | 0.025 |
| | SE | (N) | 78.0 | (4) | 39.3 | (15) | |
| Encounter | Mean | [Median] | 26.5 | - | 23.2 | [9.9] | 0.999 |
| | SE | (N) | - | (1) | 12.6 | (7) | |
| TOTAL | Mean | [Median] | 324.0 | [160.2] | 151.6 | [118.8] | 0.001* |
| | SE | (N) | 104.3 | (48) | 17.2 | (72) | |

[a]All weights in kilograms. "Hand spears" = pooled data for thrust and hand-thrown spears. * = p significant at family-wide $\alpha$ = 0.05. p-values reflect pairwise comparisons of weighted means of logged body weights. **Key:** SE = standard error of the mean; N = number of groups comprising the weighted mean (i.e., number of groups that used each combination of weapon system and technique).

terrestrial game. Even cooperative hunting techniques aimed at driving animals into a disadvantaged position or past concealed hunters depend upon appropriate terrain features for success (see Straus, this volume). Cooperative techniques are important because they allow large-scale harvesting of gregarious animals, whereas disadvantaging and ambushing by one or two hunters alone, using only hand spears, generally produces individual animal kills. In addition, selective predation of prime-aged animals, which seems to begin in the Middle Palaeolithic, would most likely have required cooperative hunting tactics in the absence of long-range weaponry (Stiner 1990, 1991). Thus, arguments about the origins of social hunting are important to our understanding of the organization of hominid subsistence behavior. Nevertheless, until man-made drive lines or corrals came into use, even cooperative hunters would have been largely dependent upon landscape features where they could disadvantage or ambush animals (see Stiner 1990).

The Tiwi and Tasmanian cases are curious exceptions to an otherwise robust pattern of hand spears used with disadvantage, ambush, and pursuit hunting. These cases show that hand-propelled spears can be used as long-range projectiles with approach hunting--although it was only the Tasmanians who threw the spear long distances (30-40 m) (Roth 1890); the Tiwi approach prey closely before throwing (Goodale 1971). If the Tasmanians are excluded, the average

effective distance of the hand-thrown spear drops to 5.7 ± 0.9 m (N=13). Hand spears among most groups are short-range weapons, whether thrust or thrown, which raises a question about the use of hand spears as long-range projectiles. Perhaps hand spears are inefficient as long-range/approach hunting weapons, and the Australian island cases are related to unique circumstances involving prey and environment characteristics that make this technology/hunting method combination economical. The inefficiency of hand-thrown spears may be due in part to problems of accuracy. There is very little mention of the accuracy of this weapon in the ethnographic literature, although there is ample evidence from experimental research that it is an inaccurate weapon in the hands of anthropologists (see Guthrie 1983; Odell and Cowan 1986). Another possibility is that hand spears are inefficient in this capacity relative to other projectile technologies and that the development of other projectiles superseded the use of hand-thrown spears in most parts of the world, although, for some reason, not on the islands around Australia.

Hand-delivered spears, whether thrust or thrown, are large animal weapons (Tables 1.3 and 1.6). This may be because spears are the best tool for dispatching large animals or because the hunting techniques required to take game with hand spears generally work better with larger prey. Disadvantaging is more successful with larger prey, since smaller, fleeter

**Table 1.7.** Statistical comparisons (p-values) of body weights[a] between bow and arrow hunting techniques.

| | Ambush | Approach | Pursuit | Encounter | Total |
|---|---|---|---|---|---|
| **Disadvantage** | 0.1295 | 0.2016 | 0.4338 | 0.0010* | 0.0006* |
| **Ambush** | - | 0.5944 | 0.0097 | 0.0018* | 0.0000* |
| **Approach** | | - | 0.0171 | 0.0016* | 0.0000* |
| **Pursuit** | | | - | 0.0007* | 0.0000* |
| **Encounter** | | | | - | 0.0064* |

[a]All weights in kilograms. * = p significant at family-wide $\alpha$ = 0.05. p-values reflect pairwise comparisons of weighted means of logged body weights.

animals can more readily escape traps and impediments. Disadvantaging allows a spear to be applied repeatedly against an animal incapable of escaping, so even the largest animals (e.g., elephants) (see Frison 1986) can be dispatched once disadvantaged. Ambushing also may be more effective with larger, slower prey, allowing the hunter more time to place a spear thrust or throw before the animal moves away. Similarly, large game may be the focus of pursuit hunting, as respiratory and heat exchange physiology make larger animals easier to exhaust, at which point spears can be used to kill them.

Reduced effectiveness of hand spears with smaller game may represent another limitation to hunters armed only with this weapon. Modern hunters must often employ additional technology, such as other weapons, boats, or snowshoes, in order to disadvantage an animal or to exploit one already disadvantaged. When cases of disadvantaging involving accessory technology are compared with cases where spears were used alone, a significant difference in body weight is observed (mean kg body weight of disadvantaging with accessory technology = 340.5 $\pm$ 118.0 [median 152.5], N = 55; mean kg body weight of disadvantaging without other technology = 894.6 $\pm$ 438.0 [median 309.0], N = 14; one-tailed p value = 0.0170). Disadvantaging without the aid of other technology, as likely practiced in the Middle and early Upper Pleistocene, is directed at much larger prey. The single-kill focus of this type of spear hunting also places a premium on larger animals, since prey size is the limiting factor for caloric return from a single hunting episode.

The ethnographic evidence suggests that hominids armed only with hand spears may have faced constraints on prey body weight ranges and hunting locales that limited the productivity of hunting. It could be argued that the greater muscularity of *Homo erectus* and archaic *Homo sapiens* (Trinkaus 1987) helped them overcome these limitations by allowing them to hurl spears harder and farther. However, there is limited evidence in the anatomy of Neandertal shoulders that suggests low frequencies of throwing (Churchill and Trinkaus 1990). Whether the same

applies to their contemporaries in other parts of the Old World cannot be determined from the current fossil record. In any case, it does seem that the development of true long-range projectile weaponry would have widened the spectrum of hominid predatory abilities. More research aimed at identifying the origins of long-range weaponry is needed if we want to understand the predatory behavior of archaic members of the genus *Homo*.

The faunal record for the European late Upper Palaeolithic indicates a broadening of the subsistence base (Straus 1985; Straus and Clark 1986), most notably the inclusion of smaller, more agile alpine game (Straus 1987a, 1987b, this volume). It is also with the late Upper Palaeolithic that we find the first unambiguous evidence of long-range weaponry in the form of atlatl components (Breuil 1912; Cattelain 1989). It is certainly reasonable to think that there is a relationship between the two. The greater effective range of an atlatl dart frees the hunter somewhat from terrain constraints, and stalking in a more open environment is possible. Hunting of agile animals like ibex and chamois would have been greatly facilitated by use of such a long-range projectile weapon system.

The atlatl as used by recent hunters in terrestrial hunting is directed at small-to-medium sized animals. This may be because groups using atlatl-delivered spears in terrestrial hunting are restricted to areas without large mammals. It also could be argued that the atlatl was retained in these areas because it is well suited for smaller game. The atlatl is an effective method of delivering a spear at high velocity (Raymond 1986). Against small-bodied animals, the atlatl spear is an effective shock weapon, but with large game its utility may be limited. Although atlatl darts carry a great deal of kinetic energy, and thus penetrating power (Raymond 1986), it may still be necessary to penetrate the thoracic cavity of a large animal to immobilize it and minimize pursuit time. It is possible that the larger antler harpoon heads and barbed points of the European Magdalenian and Azilian represent the efforts of terrestrial hunters to improve the killing power of their atlatl darts. (Although harpoon heads and barbed points are generally thought to represent fishing and marine hunting tools [see Andersen 1971; Julien 1982], the association of two barbed points with an adult male moose skeleton at Poulton-le-Fylde [Barnes et al. 1971] shows that they were at least occasionally used for terrestrial hunting.) Detachable, barbed harpoon heads will work their way deeper into a fleeing animal because of its muscular contractions. The addition of grooves along some of these armatures would have increased hemorrhage (see Rozoy 1978: Fig. 279). These features likely improved weapon effectiveness by increasing success rates with animals struck in the abdomen or hind limbs.

Because of the limited number of contexts in which modern hunters use atlatls, it is difficult to assess its effectiveness with large game. Accounts of atlatl use in the modern record do, however, suggest that it may be a better tool for smaller animals. Several dedicated marine-hunting atlatl users, such as the Aleuts (Veniaminov 1840; Shade 1949; Antropova 1964) and Koniags (Clark 1974) of southwestern Alaska, used other technology, such as bow and arrow, when hunting medium-to-large terrestrial game. In fact, when hunting walrus (mean weight of males = 1,500 kg; females = 900 kg: Ridgway 1972) on shore, which is thus equivalent to terrestrial hunting, the Aleuts abandoned their atlatl darts in favor of thrusting spears (Veniaminov 1840). In marine hunting, atlatl darts represent a highly effective means of delivering a detachable harpoon head that serves the double function of wounding the animal and affixing it to a line, often with floats, that helps to exhaust the animal and prevent it from escaping or sinking to the bottom. In hunting either waterfowl or marine mammals from a boat, the atlatl also has several advantages over the bow and arrow: long range, slight recoil, and the freeing of one hand to control the boat (Nuttall 1891; Jochelson 1933; Kellar 1955; Stirling 1960). In terrestrial hunting its range and velocity may not outweigh problems of accuracy in killing large animals. Again, data on the accuracy of this weapon are lacking in ethnographic accounts. Experimental research with this weapon system, however, demonstrates the difficulty of accurately placing shots by even experienced users (Frison 1989).

I predict that, when hunting large game, atlatl hunters would have either reverted to hand spears or would have adjusted their hunting techniques to compensate for the limitations of the atlatl. For instance, disadvantaging would allow for multiple spear shots to be delivered to a single animal, thus increasing the atlatl's effectiveness against large game. Atlatls may have been used with disadvantaging, using natural "traps," in large animal procurement at North American Paleo- and Archaic Indian bison kill sites (see Frison et al. 1976; Frison 1978; Stanford 1979).

The bow and arrow allows hunters to harvest consistently animals of all sizes with a variety of hunting techniques. The appearance of this weapon system in the late Upper Palaeolithic or Mesolithic (see Bergman et al. 1988; Bergman, this volume) may reflect pressures to improve hunting success rates, perhaps in response to population growth around the Pleistocene-Holocene boundary. It is also possible that subsistence diversification in the later Upper Palaeolithic (Straus 1985; Straus and Clark 1986) created pressures favoring the bow. As diet breadth increases, pursuit time averaged across all prey classes must decline accordingly or the economic benefit of hunting declines (Shott 1990). Increasing projectile accuracy is one way to reduce pursuit time. It is also likely that the reforestation of post-glacial Europe favored a weapon that could be used in dense vegetation (Bergman et al. 1988). Wooden spears were retained by Mesolithic hunters (Becker 1945), but, by this time, they were employing multiple weapon systems with multiple techniques--possibly even involving domestic dogs, as is common among recent hunter-gatherers (see Noe-Nygaard 1974).

Finally, while there is undoubtedly a component of innovation and invention in the development of weapon technology over time, the observed patterning in the ethnographic record suggests that the development of specific weapons in prehistory reflects responses to changing needs or conditions rather than inevitable technological progress. In many respects the bow and arrow is decidedly superior to the atlatl-propelled dart. It can be fired easily and swiftly from a variety of positions. Accuracy is better with the bow, because aim is usually taken from a stationary position (Bergman et al. 1988). Throwing a dart with an atlatl requires a more difficult set of coordinated body movements, and the violent motion of the hunter may frighten the quarry (Raymond 1986). However, the bow fires a projectile with less penetrating power (Odell and Cowan 1986; Raymond 1986) and effective range than an atlatl-propelled dart. The greater kinetic energy of atlatl darts gives this weapon some advantages in warfare, particularly against armor-clad or shield-carrying opponents (see Townsend 1983; Raymond 1986). The atlatl's value in warfare undoubtedly led to its retention by groups that had turned to other subsistence technologies (e.g., the Aztec) (Nuttall 1891). The weapon superiority view, by assuming to know in advance why hunting technology changed over time, precludes a serious evaluation of the causal factors surrounding weapon development. It is encouraging that this view is now being tested more rigorously (e.g., Hames 1979; Townsend 1983; Yost and Kelley 1983), as this will surely lead to a more complete understanding of the relationship between technology and subsistence behavior.

## ACKNOWLEDGEMENTS

I wish to thank Robert Franciscus, Trent Holliday, John Shea, and Erik Trinkaus for their insightful comments on earlier drafts of this paper and for engaging in numerous discussions on this topic. Steve Kuhn and Mary Stiner provided countless suggestions and helped me greatly to clarify my thoughts on the nature of weaponry and hunting in the later Pleistocene. Special thanks go to Bryan Curran for his editorial support and help in refining this study. I am especially grateful to Lewis Binford and Lawrence Straus for encouraging me to pursue these issues.

## REFERENCES

Allen, G. M.
1940    *The Mammals of China and Mongolia.* New York: American Museum of Natural History.

Andersen, S. H.
1971    Ertebölle kulturens harpuner. *Kuml*:73-125.

Anderson-Gerfaud, P.
1990    Aspects of behavior in the Middle Paleolithic: Functional analysis of stone tools from southwest France. In *The Emergence of Modern Humans: An Archaeological Perspective.* P. Mellars, ed. Pp. 389-418. Ithica: Cornell University Press.

Antropova, V. V.
1964    The Aleuts. In *The People of Siberia.* M. G. Levin and L. P. Potapov, eds. Pp. 884-888. Chicago: University of Chicago.

Banfield, A. W. F.
1974    *The Mammals of Canada.* Toronto: University of Toronto Press.

Barnes, B., B. J. N. Edwards, J. S. Hallam, and A. J. Stuart
1971    Skeleton of a late Glacial elk associated with barbed points from Poulton-le-Fylde, Lancashire. *Nature* 232:488-489.

Becker, C. J.
1945    En 8000-Aarig stenalderboplads i Holmegaards Mose. *Fra National-museets Arbejdsmark* 1945:61-72.

Bergman, C. A., and M. H. Newcomer
1983    Flint arrowhead breakage: Examples from Ksar Akil, Lebanon. *Journal of Field Archaeology* 10:238-243.

Bergman, C. A., E. McEwen, and R. Miller
1988    Experimental archery: Projectile velocities and comparison of bow performances. *Antiquity* 62:658-670.

Beyries, S.
1984    *Approche fonctionnelle de la variabilité des différents faciès du Moustérien.* Thèse de 3ème cycle, Université de Paris X, Nanterre.

1987    Quelques examples de stigmates d'emmanchements observés sur des outils du Paléolithique Moyen. In *La main et l'outil: Manches et emmanchements préhistoriques.* D. Stordeur, ed. Pp. 55-64. Lyon: Travaux de la Maison de l'Orient.

Binford, L. R.
1977    Olorgesailie deserves more than the usual book review. *Journal of Anthropological Research* 33:493-502.

1981    *Bones: Ancient Men and Modern Myths.* New York: Academic Press.

1984    *Faunal Remains from Klasies River Mouth.* New York: Academic Press.

1985    Human ancestors: Changing views of their behavior. *Journal of Anthropological Archaeology* 4:292-327.

1987    Were there elephant hunters at Torralba? In *The Evolution of Human Hunting.* M. H. Nitecki and D. V. Nitecki, eds. Pp. 47-105. New York: Plenum Press.

1989    Isolating the transition to cultural adaptation: An organizational approach. In *The Biocultural Emergence of Modern Humans in the Later Pleistocene.* E. Trinkaus, ed. Pp. 18-41. Cambridge: Cambridge University.

Binford, L. R., and N. Stone
1986    Zhoukoudian: A closer look. *Current Anthropology* 27:453-475.

Boitani, L., and S. Bartoli
1983    *Simon and Schuster's Guide to Mammals.* New York: Simon and Schuster.

Bordes, F.
1968    *The Old Stone Age.* New York: McGraw-Hill.

Brain, C. K.
1981    *The Hunters or the Hunted?* Chicago: University of Chicago.

Breuil, H.
1912    Les subdivisions du Paléolithique supérieur et leur signification. *Compte Rendu de la XIVème Session, Congrès International d'Anthropologie et d'Archéologie Préhistorique (Genève)*:5-78.

Cattelain, P.
1989    Un crochet de propulseur solutréen de la grotte de Combe-Saunière 1 (Dordogne). *Bulletin de la Société Préhistorique Française* 86:213-216.

Chase, P. G.
1988    Scavenging and hunting in the Middle Paleolithic: The evidence from Europe. In *The Upper Pleistocene Prehistory of Western Eurasia.* H. Dibble and A. Montet-White, eds. Pp. 225-232. University Museum Monograph 54. Philadelphia: The University Museum, University of Pennsylvania.

1989    How different was Middle Palaeolithic subsistence? A zooarchaeological perspective on the Middle to Upper Palaeolithic transition. In *The Human Revolution: Behavioural and Biological Perspectives on the Origins of Modern Humans.* P. Mellars and C. Stringer, eds. Pp. 321-337. Edinburgh: Edinburgh University Press.

Christenson, A. L.
1986    Projectile point size and projectile aerodynamics: An exploratory study. *Plains Anthropologist* 31:109-128.

Churchill, S. E., and E. Trinkaus
1990    Neandertal scapular glenoid morphology. *American Journal of Physical Anthropology* 83:147-160.

Clark, D. W.
1974    *Koniag Prehistory: Archaeological Investigations at Late Prehistoric Sites on Kodiak Island, Alaska.* Stuttgart: Verlag W. Kohlhammer.

Clark, J. D., K. P. Oakley, L. H. Wells, and J. A. C. McClelland
1950    New studies on Rhodesian Man. *Journal of the Royal Anthropological Institute* 77:7-32.

Fisher, R. A., and F. Yates
1963    Footnote to Table VI. *Statistical Tables for Biological, Agricultural and Medical Research.* 6th edition. Edinburgh: Oliver and Boyd.

Fleagle, J. G.
1988    *Primate Adaptation and Evolution.* New York: Academic Press.

Friis-Hansen, J.
1990    Mesolithic cutting arrows: Functional analysis of arrows used in the hunting of large game. *Antiquity* 64:494-504.

Frison, G. C.
1978    *Prehistoric Hunters of the High Plains.* New York: Academic Press.

1986    Mammoth hunting and butchering from a perspective of African elephant culling. In *The Colby Mammoth Site.* G. C. Frison and L. C. Todd, eds. Pp. 115-134. Albu-

querque: University of New Mexico.
1989 Experimental use of Clovis weaponry and tools on African elephants. *American Antiquity* 54:766-784.
Frison, G. C., M. Wilson, and D. J. Wilson
1976 Fossil bison and artifacts from an early altithermal period arroyo trap in Wyoming. *American Antiquity* 41:28-57.
Gamble, C.
1986 *The Palaeolithic Settlement of Europe.* Cambridge: Cambridge University.
1987 Man the shoveler: Alternative models for Middle Pleistocene colonization and occupation of northern latitudes. In *The Pleistocene Old World: Regional Perspectives.* O. Soffer, ed. Pp. 81-98. New York: Plenum Press.
Goodale, J. C.
1971 *Tiwi Wives: A Study of the Women of Melville Island, North Australia.* Seattle: University of Washington Press.
Guthrie, R. D.
1983 Osseous projectile points: Biological considerations affecting raw material selection and design among Palaeolithic and Palaeoindian peoples. In *Animals and Archaeology. Volume 1. Hunters and their Prey.* J. Clutton-Brock and C. Grigson, eds. Pp. 273-294. BAR International Series 163. Oxford: British Archaeological Reports.
Hall, E. R., and K. R. Kelson
1959 *The Mammals of North America.* New York: The Ronald Press Company.
Haltenorth, T., and H. Diller
1977 *A Field Guide to the Mammals of Africa including Madagascar.* London: Collins.
Hames, R. B.
1979 A comparison of the efficiencies of the shotgun and the bow in neo-tropical forest hunting. *Human Ecology* 7:21-52.
Holdaway, S.
1989 Were there hafted projectile points in the Mousterian? *Journal of Field Archaeology* 16:79-85.
1990 Mousterian projectile points--reply to Shea. *Journal of Field Archaeology* 17:114-115.
Holm, S.
1979 A simple sequentially rejective multiple test procedure. *Scandinavian Journal of Statistics* 6:56-70.
Jameson, E. W., Jr., and H. J. Peeters
1988 *California Mammals.* Berkeley: University of California Press.
Jochelson, V. I.
1933 *History, Ethnology and Anthropology of the Aleut.* Washington: Carnegie Institution.
Julien, M.
1982 *Les harpons magdaléniens.* Supplément à *Gallia Préhistoire* 17. Paris: Editions du Centre National de la Recherche Scientifique.
Kellar, J. H.
1955 The atlatl in North America. *Indiana Historical Society, Prehistory Research Series* 3:281-352.
Kingdon, J.
1971 *East African Mammals. Volumes I-III.* London: Academic Press.
Klein, R. G.
1986 Review of Faunal Remains from Klasies River Mouth by L. R. Binford. *American Anthropologist* 88:494-495.
1987 Reconstructing how early people exploited animals: Problems and prospects. In *The Evolution of Human Hunting.* M. H. Nitecki and D. V. Nitecki, eds. Pp. 11-45. New York: Plenum Press.
Kuhn, S. L.
1989 Projectile weapons and investment in food procurement technology in the Eurasian Middle Paleolithic. *American Journal of Physical Anthropology* 78:257 (abs.).

Lee, R. B.
1979 *The !Kung San.* Cambridge: Cambridge University Press.
Mania, D., and V. Toepfer
1973 *Königsaue: Gliederung, Oekologie und mittelpaläolithische Funde der Letzten Eiszeit.* Berlin: VEB Deutscher Verlag der Wissenschaften.
McCarthy, F. D.
1967 *Australian Aboriginal Stone Implements: Including Bone, Shell and Teeth Implements.* Sydney: Australian Museum.
Medway, Lord
1969 *The Wild Mammals of Malaya and Offshore Islands Including Singapore.* London: Oxford University Press.
Meritt, D. A., Jr.
1985 Naked-tailed armadillos *Cabassous sp.* In *The Evolution and Ecology of Armadillos, Sloths, and Vermilinguas.* G. B. Montgomery, ed. Pp. 25-33. Washington, D.C.: Smithsonian Institution.
Movius, H. L.
1950 A wooden spear of Third Interglacial age from Lower Saxony. *Southwestern Journal of Anthropology* 6:139-142.
Mulvaney, D. J.
1969 *The Prehistory of Australia.* New York: Frederick A. Praeger.
Noe-Nygaard, N.
1974 Mesolithic hunting in Denmark illustrated by bone injuries caused by human weapons. *Journal of Archaeological Science* 1:217-248.
Nuttall, Z.
1891 *The atlatl or spear-thrower of the ancient Mexicans.* Peabody Museum of American Archaeology and Ethnology Papers 1(3).
Oakley, K. P., P. Andrews, L. H. Keeley, and J. D. Clark
1977 A reappraisal of the Clacton spearpoint. *Proceedings of the Prehistoric Society* 43:13-30.
Odell, G. H., and F. Cowan
1986 Experiments with spears and arrows on animal targets. *Journal of Field Archaeology* 13:195-212.
Rausing, G.
1967 *The Bow: Some Notes on its Origin and Development.* Lund: C. W. K. Gleerups.
Raymond, A.
1986 Experiments in the function and performance of the weighted atlatl. *World Archaeology* 18:153-177.
Redford, K. H., and J. F. Eisenberg
1992 *Mammals of the Neotropics: The Southern Cone. Volume 2.* Chicago: University of Chicago Press.
Ride, W. D. L.
1970 *A Guide to the Native Mammals of Australia.* Melbourne: Oxford University Press.
Ridgway, S. H.
1972 *Mammals of the Sea.* Springfield: C. C. Thomas.
Roth, H. L.
1890 *The Aborigines of Tasmania.* London: Kegan Paul, Trench, Trubner and Co.
Rozoy, J.-G.
1978 *Les derniers chasseurs: l'Epipaleolithique en France et en Belgique. Essai de synthèse. Tome 2.* Bulletin Spécial de la Société Archéologique Champenoise. Reims: Imprimerie de Compiègne.
Rust, A.
1943 *Die Alt-und Mittelsteinzeitliche Funde von Stellmoor.* Neumünster: Wachholtz.
Schmidt, J. L., and D. L. Gilbert
1978 *Big Game of North America.* Harrisburg: Stackpole Books.
Serventy, D. L., and H. M. Whittell
1962 *Birds of Western Australia.* Perth: Paterson Brokensha.

Shade, C. I.
1949    *Ethnological Notes on the Aleuts.* Unpublished honors thesis, Harvard University.

Shea, J. J.
1988    Spear points from the Middle Paleolithic of the Levant. *Journal of Field Archaeology* 15:441-450.
1989    A functional study of the lithic industries associated with hominid fossils in the Kebara and Qafzeh Caves, Israel. In *The Human Revolution: Behavioural and Biological Perspectives on the Origins of Modern Humans.* P. Mellars and C. Stringer, eds. Pp. 611-625. Edinburgh: Edinburgh University Press.
1990    A further note on Mousterian spear points. *Journal of Field Archaeology* 17:111-114.

Shott, M. J.
1990    Stone tools and economics: Great Lakes Paleoindian examples. *Research in Economic Anthropology, Supplement* 5:3-43.

Singer, R., and J. Wymer
1982    *The Middle Stone Age at Klasies River Mouth in South Africa.* Chicago: University of Chicago.

Stanford, D.
1979    Bison kill by ice-age hunters. *National Geographic* 155:114-121.

Stiner, M. C.
1990    The use of mortality patterns in archaeological studies of hominid predatory adaptations. *Journal of Anthropological Archaeology* 9:305-351.
1991    An interspecific perspective on the emergence of the modern human predatory niche. In *Human Predators and Prey Mortality.* M. C. Stiner, ed. Pp. 149-185. Boulder: Westview Press.

Stirling, M. W.
1960    The use of the atlatl on Lake Patzcuaro, Michoacan. *Smithsonian Institution, Bureau of American Ethnology Bulletin* 173:265-268.

Straus, L. G.
1985    Stone Age prehistory of northern Spain. *Science* 230:501-507.
1987a   Hunting in late Upper Paleolithic western Europe. In *The Evolution of Human Hunting.* M. H. Nitecki and D. V. Nitecki, eds. Pp. 147-176. New York: Plenum Press.
1987b   Upper Paleolithic ibex hunting in southwest Europe. *Journal of Archaeological Science* 14:163-178.
1990    The original arms race: Iberian perspectives on the Solutrean phenomenon. In *Feuilles de pierre: Les industries à pointes foliacées du Paléolithique supérieur européen.* J. Kozlowski, ed. Pp. 425-447. ERAUL 42. Liège: Université de Liège.

Straus, L. G., and G. Clark
1986    *La Riera Cave: Stone Age Hunter-Gatherer Adaptations in Northern Spain.* Anthropological Research Papers 36. Tempe: Arizona State University.

Tode, A.
1954    *Mammutjäger vor 100,000 Jahren: Natur und Mensch in Nordwestdeutschland zur letzten Eiszeit, auf Grund der Ausgrabungen bei Salzgitter-Lebenstedt.* Brunswick: E. Appelhans.

Townsend, J. B.
1983    Firearms against native arms: A study in comparative efficiencies with an Alaskan example. *Arctic Anthropology* 20:1-33.

Trinkaus, E.
1987    Bodies, brawn, brains and noses: Human ancestors and human predation. In *The Evolution of Human Hunting.* M. H. Nitecki and D. V. Nitecki, eds. Pp. 107-145. New York: Plenum Press.

Veniaminov, I. E. P.
1840    *[Notes on the Islands of the Unalaska District. Volume 3.]* Sanktpeterburg: Metropolitan of Moscow.

Villa, P.
1990    Torralba and Aridos: Elephant exploitation in Middle Pleistocene Spain. *Journal of Human Evolution* 19:229-309.

Warren, S. H.
1911    First published report and exhibition of the specimen, May 10th, 1911. *Quarterly Journal of the Geological Society* 67:xcix.

Winterhalder, B.
1981    Foraging strategies in the boreal forest: An analysis of Cree hunting and gathering. In *Hunter-Gatherer Foraging Strategies: Ethnographic and Archaeological Examples.* B. Winterhalder and E. Smith, eds. Pp. 66-98. Chicago: University of Chicago.

Yost, J. A., and P. M. Kelley
1983    Shotguns, blowguns, and spears: The analysis of technological efficiency. In *Adaptive Responses of Native Amazonians.* R. B. Hames and W. T. Vickers, eds. Pp. 189-224. New York: Academic Press.

# 2

# *Mousterian Technology as Adaptive Response: A Case Study*

**Steven L. Kuhn**
**Loyola University of Chicago**

## ABSTRACT

**Research on Mousterian assemblages from west-central Italy reveals one way that variation in patterns of stone tool manufacture and use may reflect changes in hominid foraging behavior, land use, and mobility. In these cases, frequent movement and wide-ranging foraging, associated with evidence for scavenging of large game, appears to be linked to the production and extensive resharpening of relatively large tool blanks and possibly to greater evidence for artifact transport. More intensive and prolonged occupations, marked by the introduction of entire carcasses of hunted animals into cave sites, are associated with less intensive reduction of tools and greater reliance on immediately available raw materials.**

## INTRODUCTION

Researchers have long been concerned with the ways stone tools might reflect the subsistence behavior of Palaeolithic hominids. Past attempts to link Mousterian technology with foraging have concentrated primarily on hypothetical functional implications of the various artifact forms defined in Bordes's (1961) widely used typology. The scarcity and formal monotony of the most likely "extractive tools" in Eurasian Mousterian assemblages suggest that such design-oriented approaches are of limited utility. Research on Mousterian assemblages from west-central Italy described in this paper illustrates an alternative approach, which relates different tactics of core reduction and stone tool transport and resharpening to changing patterns of foraging and land use.

## LINKING TECHNOLOGY AND SUBSISTENCE

Archaeologically oriented studies investigating the connections between technology and subsistence adaptations can be divided into two major groups (for a more comprehensive review, see Nelson 1991). One type of study focuses on the design of implements, and especially weapons. The variables of interest in discussions of tool design include not only attributes of direct functional relevance, but also more abstract properties like complexity, maintainability, and cost of manufacture (e.g., Bleed 1986; Myers 1989; Shott 1986, 1989; Torrence 1983). Other researchers have chosen to concentrate on how tool manufacture,

maintenance, and discard might have been organized around the energetic and temporal limitations imposed by foraging and mobility. Discussions of what might be termed the technological delivery system (e.g., Binford 1977, 1979; Bamforth 1986, 1990; Goodyear 1989; Kelly 1988; Kuhn 1989; Torrence 1989) are most often framed in terms of the economic aspects of different tactics of implement manufacture and maintenance, transport, and discard.

Tool design and strategies of tool manufacture, maintenance, and discard are linked to the larger subsistence sphere in somewhat different ways. As a general rule, we can expect design (i.e., morphology) to vary as a function of how tools are used and what they are used for, while tactics of manufacture, repair, and abandonment are more directly contingent on the timing and spatial distribution of use events. As a result, the potential utility of the two alternate approaches varies according to the nature of the technological items available for study as well as the research problem at hand.

Most past attempts to understand how Middle Palaeolithic technologies "mapped onto" the ways hominids made a living have taken a design-based line of attack. Using Bordes's (1961) type list as a starting point, a number of somewhat ambiguous statistical associations between tool forms, climate, and faunal remains have been described (e.g., Bordes and de Sonneville-Bordes 1970; Chase 1986a). The "Functional Argument" (Binford and Binford 1966), which was arguably the most comprehensive attempt to interpret Mousterian assemblages in terms relevant to larger issues in human adaptation, postulated that variation in artifact morphology and assemblage content reflected largely utilitarian factors. Lewis Binford did not pursue this line of inquiry, specifically because there were no clear guidelines for interpreting the shapes of retouched tools (Binford 1973), and recent studies of microwear on Mousterian tools have produced mixed results concerning possible formal/functional correlations (cf. Beyries 1988; Shea 1989). Although no longer pursued by its originators, the "Functional Argument" has resurfaced to some extent in the controversy over the existence and nature of hafted weapons tips in the Mousterian (e.g., Holdaway 1989; Shea 1989, this volume). Even though the focus of debate is somewhat more restricted, the primary aim is to demonstrate whether a particular class of artifacts defined by Bordes's typology--in this case Mousterian and Levallois points--did or did not serve a specific range of functions.

Certainly, if one is interested in connections between tool form and function and their possible relevance to understanding prehistoric food-getting, it makes sense to focus on potential components of weapons. Most successful studies of artifact design (e.g. Bleed 1986; Churchill, this volume; Myers 1989; Torrence 1983) deal with extractive technology (sensu Binford and Binford 1966)--the implements used to harvest or capture resources--because extractive tools, weapons in particular, are frequently employed in high-stress applications where the range of design alternatives is tightly constrained and where variation in the morphology of artifacts has direct and perceptible consequences on their functionality.

While studies of weapons design have produced both strongly patterned and intriguing results in the context of ethnographic data, the findings are often of limited applicability in archaeological contexts and may be particularly difficult to apply to the Middle Palaeolithic. The archaeological record generally contains parts of composite implements, such as components of projectile weapons. Fine-grained studies of artifact complexity or design can only be conducted when there is some idea of the association of the different parts. The forms of the implements found in the archaeological record are also the products of a series of manufacture, use, and renewal events, and the morphology of an archaeological specimen may be quite different from that demanded by its original intended use (e.g., Dibble 1987, 1988; Holdaway 1989).

In the specific case of the Middle Palaeolithic, the utility of studying the design of potential extractive tools seems to be further constrained by the lack of variation in the artifacts themselves. A number of researchers (e.g., Straus 1989; Peterkin, this volume; Pike-Tay and Bricker, this volume) have documented the impressive variety of stone and bone "point" forms

in the Upper Palaeolithic and Mesolithic of Eurasia. Whether or not all things called "points" were actually parts of weapons, there are nevertheless a wide array of possibilities to choose from after 35,000 BP. In contrast, the most likely candidates for weapons tips in the Eurasian Middle Palaeolithic are remarkably monotonous. From the Levant to northern France and even eastern Europe, the same two basic forms are found: retouched Mousterian points and unretouched Levallois points. Both types are relatively large, triangular pointed objects, usually with thick bases. Points, retouched or unretouched, vary somewhat in size and degree of elongation across and within geographical regions, but this seems most directly attributable to the use of different raw materials and core reduction techniques rather than to differences in function.

If hunting is, in fact, limited by technology, the uniformity of "point" morphology in the Mousterian suggests that a restricted range of hunting techniques was used over a vast span of time and space. More importantly, however, it appears that the study of weaponry or potential weaponry, as currently defined, provides relatively little information about variation in subsistence during the Middle Palaeolithic. The question is not whether Middle Palaeolithic hominids were capable of procuring large animals. Faunal studies leave little doubt that they could do so, with or without the aid of stone-tipped spears (e.g., Chase 1986b; Stiner 1990a, 1991). However, the most basic ecological principles indicate that, for populations of omnivorous hominids, the importance of and means for obtaining animal protein should have varied considerably across the extensive temporal and geographic span of the Middle Palaeolithic. Yet, looking at the technology from a purely formal, design-oriented perspective, it is difficult to find any evidence of local or regional adaptive variation.

This does not mean that Mousterian tools are devoid of information about prehistoric subsistence behavior. Rather, it suggests that we must look elsewhere for the connections between making tools and making a living. Weaponry or potential weaponry is generally only a small part of Palaeolithic assemblages. The most common artifacts in the Mousterian toolkit (scrapers, denticulates, and the like) were most likely employed to process other materials, either to render them edible or to make tools and implements from them. The manufacture of tools, weapons, and other items and the secondary processing of food resources would not have entailed the kind of intense time stress (sensu Torrence 1983) that can occur in the context of procuring large game. Moreover, most manufacture and/or processing activities are fairly high-tolerance situations, in which the overall form of the tool used has relatively little effect on the successful completion of the task at hand. As such, it is

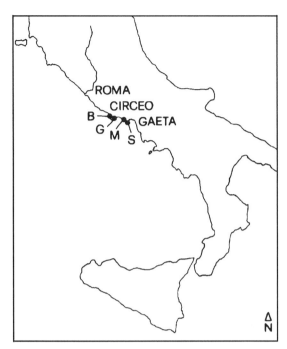

**Figure 2.1.** Geographical distribution of cave sites discussed in the text: B = Grotta Breuil; G = Grotta Guattari; M = Grotta dei Moscerini; S = Grotta di Sant'Agostino (scale 1 cm = 75 km).

unrealistic to expect many strong links between form and function among artifacts used in non-extractive tasks. Instead, it is more profitable to concentrate on the second set of connections between subsistence and technology: how the economics of tool manufacture and use might have been effected by the larger concerns of foraging and moving about the landscape.

Because manufacture and processing are energetically secondary to the procurement of resources, the spatial and temporal scheduling of opportunities for manufacture and processing are determined by patterns of foraging and mobility (Torrence 1983, 1989). The making and mending of things tends to occur whenever or wherever time is not taken up by the concerns of foodgetting (see references in Kuhn 1989:35). Although tools used to work other materials or to process food may not be subject to the intense physical stresses experienced by weapons, they do wear out. At the same time, the practicality and cost of making or replacing such tools is determined in large part by the distribution of appropriate raw materials, which may be quite independent of where people need to go to obtain vital subsistence resources. Inevitably, there will be discontinuities between opportunities to make tools and the need for them; a variety of strategies must be adopted to make sure that people are kept supplied with tools and raw materials. Techniques of artifact production that influence their

immediate utility and long-term durability, as well as decisions about artifact transport and maintenance, are particularly important in bridging the spatial and temporal gaps between generalized needs for tools and opportunities to make them. In the case of Palaeolithic stone tools, evidence for these strategies should be found in patterns of core reduction/blank production, tool resharpening, and the movement or displacement of raw materials across the landscape.

## A CASE STUDY

Results of studies of Middle Palaeolithic lithic assemblages and faunas from central Italy illustrate some intriguing points of correspondence between modes of ungulate procurement and the manufacture and treatment of stone tools. The connection between these two disparate phenomena is argued to relate to patterns of foraging and residential mobility. Only basic findings and their implications are discussed here; methods and results of the respective studies are presented in more comprehensive form elsewhere (Kuhn 1990, 1991; Stiner, 1990a, 1990b, 1991; Stiner and Kuhn 1992).

The data at hand come from studies of 16 Mousterian assemblages from four coastal caves located in the region of Latium, southeast of Rome, Italy (see also Stiner, this volume). Two of the sites, Grotta Guattari and Grotta Breuil, are on Monte Circeo, while the other two caves, Grotta dei Moscerini and Grotta di Sant'Agostino, are situated near Gaeta, some 50 km southeast (Figure 2.1). Topographically, this region is marked by poorly drained coastal plains or basins bounded by mountain ranges with peaks rising to between 1,000 and 1,500 m. It is also a raw material "stressed" zone; the only locally available flint occurs as very small pebbles, rarely over 8-10 cm in length, which are rather irregularly distributed along the beaches and across the coastal plains. The subject assemblages have been classified as representing the Pontinian (Bietti 1980; Taschini 1979), a local facies defined, at least in part, by characteristics linked to the use of these pebble raw materials (i.e., small artifact sizes, large numbers of cortical flakes).

Taphonomic analyses, studies of the age structure of ungulate death assemblages, and studies of patterns of anatomical part representation have revealed the existence of two distinct patterns of ungulate procurement in these Mousterian assemblages. These separate by cave site and quite possibly in time as well, with evidence of a major shift in foraging around 55,000 years ago. Differences and similarities in the treatment of faunas do not seem to be a function of the geographic proximity of the different sites, suggesting that variation in large animal exploitation was not due simply to local topographic factors.

Studies of the faunas from Grotta Guattari and Grotta dei Moscerini indicate that the bulk of ungulate resources used by Mousterian hominids occupying these sites were obtained by scavenging (Stiner 1990a, 1990b, 1991). Scavenging produces relatively low returns (few parts per carcass), and, in fact, these Mousterian faunas consist almost exclusively of cranial parts of various species of cervid. Since MNE (minimum number of skeletal elements) data for different anatomical regions were calculated using only bony elements (mandibles, maxillae, occipitals, etc.) and excluding teeth, this peculiar anatomical pattern should represent the result of procurement and transport by hominids; it should not be an effect of differential preservation. Head parts of scavenged animals may have been preferred because neurocranial tissue maintains a high fat content even in nutritionally stressed animals (Stiner 1991). Two observations also suggest that small-package-sized, gathered resources may have been exploited in conjunction with scavenging: (1) there is no statistical relationship between the abundance of lithics and the abundance of bone in these deposits, suggesting that something other than the success in obtaining ungulate resources determined technological activities in caves (Kuhn 1990); and (2) there is direct evidence for the use of shellfish and marine turtles at Grotta dei Moscerini (Stiner 1990a, this volume).

In the Mousterian faunas from the other two sites, Grotta di Sant'Agostino and Grotta Breuil, all of which date to 55,000 BP or later, age structure and anatomical representation provide strong evidence for a very different form of ungulate procurement--ambush hunting. This mode of procurement yields larger quantities of meat per carcass, as indicated by the relatively complete range of anatomical elements introduced into the cave sites. Stone artifacts and bones are also found in more constant proportions (i.e., are highly correlated among the assemblages), suggesting that the scale of technological activity was roughly correlated with the amount of meat procured (Kuhn 1990).

I emphasize that the contrasts between the two groups of Mousterian faunas represent general tendencies played out over prolonged periods. Like both extant carnivores (e.g., Houston 1979) and modern human foragers (O'Connell et al. 1988), Mousterian populations probably both hunted and scavenged; one tactic or the other simply dominated particular assemblages. Furthermore, because the assemblages are defined in terms of geological strata or groups of adjacent strata, the patterns observed resulted from repeated behavior over long periods of time and thus probably do not represent short-term seasonal or year-to-year variance.

Comparisons of lithic assemblages from strata showing evidence of radically different modes of

ungulate procurement reveal virtually no variation in what might be construed as procurement technology. Pointed elements of all sorts (Mousterian points, Levallois points, and convergent scrapers) are not especially common and are actually slightly less abundant in Mousterian assemblages associated with evidence of hunting. Although possible impact fractures have been recognized, they are very rare--no more than one or two have been noted. On the other hand, major differences in the manufacture and treatment of stone tools associated with the two patterns of ungulate procurement suggest that the ways game was obtained were tied, however indirectly, to the "economics" of lithic technology. These differences can be summarized as follows: (1) There is a marked frequency shift in core-reduction techniques. Evidence of scavenging (at Moscerini and Guattari) is associated with relatively heavy reliance on disc-core or Levallois techniques involving centripetal (radial) preparation of cores. When applied to the small pebbles available in the study area, these techniques enabled the production of a relatively small number of flakes that are fairly large and broad in comparison to the size of the core. Evidence for successful ambush hunting (Breuil and Sant'Agostino) is accompanied by a shift towards very different modes of flake and blank production. In these assemblages, centripetal core preparation is at least partially replaced by techniques of both Levallois and non-Levallois character in which flakes were detached in parallel from one or two platforms located at the ends of a core. Using small pebble raw materials, these modes of core reduction produce relatively large numbers of flakes per core; as expected, however, the resulting flakes and blanks are somewhat smaller and narrower than those produced using radial preparation (Kuhn 1990; Stiner and Kuhn 1992). (2) Lithic assemblages associated with scavenging show evidence of rather intensive exploitation of available tool blanks. The frequency of retouch is quite high, and the retouched pieces have often been extensively reduced or resharpened. Potential tool blanks in assemblages found with evidence of hunting are less frequently modified and were less often or repeatedly resharpened (Kuhn 1990, 1991). (3) In spite of the poor quality of local flint resources, the frequency of exotic artifacts is low throughout the Mousterian in west-central Italy, especially when compared to later Upper Palaeolithic assemblages. However, artifacts likely to have been made on raw materials not immediately available at the four coastal cave sites are most abundant in the assemblages associated with scavenged faunas. Evidence of hunting appears to be associated with more complete reliance on local sources of flint pebbles (Kuhn 1990; Stiner and Kuhn 1992).

While there are clearly parallel shifts in foraging and technology in these central Italian Mousterian sites, there is no obvious functional connection; it is difficult to identify anything about scavenging or hunting per se that would favor producing tools by a particular technique or resharpening them to a greater or lesser extent. Instead, I argue that the technological variation observed represents the influence of foraging and mobility patterns on strategies for making and maintaining general purpose, non-extractive implements--sidescrapers for the most part.

Scavenging, characteristic of the Mousterian faunas from Grotta Guattari and Grotta dei Moscerini, targets relatively dispersed resources with low returns per procurement event. Exploitation of such scattered resources, and evidence for the use of other small-package-sized foods, implies relatively frequent movement and wide-ranging patterns of land use (Stiner and Kuhn 1992). High residential mobility, in turn, often entails greater reliance on transported tool kits (e.g., Goodyear 1989; Kelly 1988; Kuhn 1989), and the characteristics of the lithic assemblages are consistent with such a scenario. The artifacts associated with scavenged faunas show evidence of extensive resharpening and reduction, implying prolonged use, and there is also the suggestion of more frequent long-distance transport. Moreover, the predominant core-reduction techniques, with radial preparation of cores, produced relatively large flakes and tool blanks that would have been especially suitable for being carried around and used over long periods in a raw-material-poor environment.

Compared with scavenging, evidence for hunting in the Mousterian faunas from Grotta Breuil and Grotta di Sant'Agostino implies greater returns per foraging event, as well as targeting of fairly concentrated food patches--red deer congregate, while their carcasses may not. The presence of a wide array of heavily processed anatomical elements further indicates that virtually entire carcasses were carried to caves and consumed. In these Mousterian cases, we are probably dealing with evidence of relatively less wide-ranging land use and more prolonged occupational events, at least as far as these particular cave sites are concerned. More stable residential patterns would entail less reliance on transported toolkits, reducing the need to repeatedly renew a limited toolkit and making it less beneficial to produce the largest possible tool blanks. In the context of more prolonged occupations, it might well have been possible to stockpile scarce pebble raw materials at residential locations and to employ numerically more productive platform core reduction techniques to make smaller blanks destined for light use and little transport. The ability to collect and process local pebbles "at leisure" could relax the need to repeatedly resharpen tools, while the processing of animal carcasses might also have created a special demand for unretouched or lightly resharpened edges.

## DISCUSSION AND CONCLUSION

Human technologies can be shown to vary in response to both the external context and the nature of the larger system of which they are parts. Some of this variation, most notably in the design of extractive tools, may reflect more or less direct interaction with aspects of the environment, such as the nature of prey and consequent limitations on prey-capture techniques. Variation in other dimensions of technology (e.g., raw material economy) is indirectly influenced by the energetically primary concerns of making a living. From the perspective of artifact morphology, there seems to be little functional variation in potential extractive technology within the Middle Palaeolithic. Instead, it has been more profitable to focus on the ways tool manufacture and use were organized to cope with the demands imposed by mobility, the scheduling of foraging activities, the organization of labor, and the duration of occupations--in other words, to think about how Middle Palaeolithic foragers might have used time, energy, and the landscape, rather than just about how they might have used tools.

In the coastal Italian caves, radical shifts in ungulate procurement by Middle Palaeolithic hominids are associated with pronounced changes in the economics of stone tool manufacture and maintenance. It is important to emphasize that these four sites represent only one small part of the Mousterian geographic and temporal range. Although the Mousterian is often treated as a single chrono-stratigraphic unit, albeit a very generalized one, there is no reason to expect a single system of technological behaviors to characterize the length and breadth of the Middle Palaeolithic. Understanding how Mousterian technologies might represent the adaptive responses of archaic and early modern *Homo sapiens* will ultimately require documenting the ranges of technological variation across time and space, along with independent information about the subsistence and environmental factors that may have altered or influenced it.

In the long run, it is unlikely that the specific patterns and associations observed here will be precisely replicated in other contexts (cf. Marks 1988; Rolland 1981; Rolland and Dibble 1990). Unlike the kinds of one-to-one correlations that have been sought between tool form and tool function, the connections between technology, mobility, and foraging organization are highly contingent on external factors such as the nature and distribution of subsistence resources and lithic raw materials. The variability documented among Mousterian assemblages from coastal Latium represents responses to changing patterns of land use in a particular raw material environment: it is not related in a direct mechanical or functional way to what people ate and how they got their food. Although similar kinds of technological behaviors may be observed elsewhere, it is by no means a given that they will have the same subsistence correlates. The limitations imposed and opportunities offered by differing biotic and raw material environments produce different kinds of strategic responses. As long as the goal is to understand the role of Palaeolithic technologies within the larger sphere of human subsistence adaptations, and not simply to identify technological "flags" for non-technological behaviors, documenting and explaining this kind of diversity can only enhance the interest and value of research.

## ACKNOWLEDGEMENTS

The ideas and observations presented in this paper have been formed as a result of innumerable discussions and arguments with teachers and colleagues, particularly Lewis Binford, Steve Churchill, Mary Stiner, and Lawrence Straus. Access to Italian archaeological collections, as well as invaluable information and advice, were generously provided by Prof. A. Bietti, Prof. A. Segre, Dressa. E. Segre-Nardini, and Prof. C. Tozzi. Research in Italy was funded by the L. S. B. Leakey Foundation and the Institute for International Education (Fulbright Program). Finally, Harvey Bricker, Paul Mellars, and Gail Peterkin should be recognized for putting together a stimulating symposium and for seeing this volume to fruition.

## REFERENCES

Bamforth, D.
  1986  Technological efficiency and stone tool curation. *American Antiquity* 51:38-50.
  1990  Settlement, raw material and lithic procurement in the central Mojave desert. *Journal of Anthropological Archaeology* 9:70-104.
Beyries, S.
  1988  Functional variability of lithic sets in the Middle Paleolithic. In *The Upper Pleistocene Prehistory of Eurasia*. H. Dibble and A. Montet-White, eds. Pp. 213-225. University Museum Monograph 54. Philadelphia: The University Museum, University of Pennsylvania.
Bietti, A.
  1980  Un tentativo di classificazione quantitativa del "Pontiniano" laziale nel quadro delle industrie Musteriane in Italia: Problemi di derivazione e di interpretazione culturale. *Rivista di Antropologia* 61:161-202.
Binford, L. R.
  1973  Interassemblage variability: The Mousterian and the "Functional Argument." In *The Explanation of Culture Change: Models in Prehistory*. C. Renfrew, ed. Pp. 227-254. London: Duckworth.
  1977  Forty-seven trips: A case study in the character of archaeological formation processes. In *Stone Tools as Cultural Markers*. R. V. S. Wright, ed. Pp. 24-36. Canberra: Australian Institute of Aboriginal Studies.
  1979  Organization and formation processes: Looking at curated technologies. *Journal of Anthropological Research* 35:255-273.

Binford, L. R., and S. R. Binford
  1966  A preliminary analysis of functional variability in the Mousterian of Levallois facies. *American Anthropologist* 68:238295.
Bleed, P.
  1986  The optimal design of hunting weapons. *American Antiquity* 51:737-747.
Bordes, F.
  1961  *Typologie du Paléolithique ancien et moyen*. MIPUB 1. Bordeaux: Delmas.
Bordes, F., and D. de Sonneville-Bordes
  1970  The significance of variability in Paleolithic assemblages. *World Archaeology* 2:61-73.
Chase, P.
  1986a  Relationships between Mousterian lithic and faunal assemblages at Combe Grenal. *Current Anthropology* 27:69-71.
  1986b  *The Hunters of Combe Grenal: Approaches to Middle Paleolithic Subsistence in Europe*. BAR International Series 286. Oxford: British Archaeological Reports.
Dibble, H.
  1987  The interpretation of Middle Paleolithic scraper morphology. *American Antiquity* 52:109-117.
  1988  Typological aspects of reduction and intensity of utilization of lithic resources in the French Mousterian. In *The Upper Pleistocene Prehistory of Western Eurasia*. H. Dibble and A. Montet-White, eds. Pp. 181-198. University Museum Monograph 54. Philadelphia: The University Museum, University of Pennsylvania.
Goodyear, A.
  1989  A hypothesis for the use of cryptocrystalline raw materials among Paleoindian groups of North America. In *Eastern Paleoindian Lithic Resource Use*. C. Ellis and J. Lothrop, eds. Pp. 1-10. Boulder: Westview Press.
Holdaway, S.
  1989  Were there hafted projectile points in the Mousterian? *Journal of Field Archaeology* 16:79-85.
Houston, D. C.
  1979  The adaptations of scavengers. In *Serengeti: Dynamics of an Ecosystem*. A. R. E. Sinclair and M. Norton-Griffiths, eds., Pp. 263-286. Chicago: University of Chicago Press.
Kelly, R. L.
  1988  The three sides of a biface. *American Antiquity* 53:717-734.
Kuhn, S.
  1989  Hunter-gatherer foraging organization and strategies of artifact replacement and discard. In *Experiments in Lithic Technology*. D. Amick and R. Mauldin, eds. Pp. 33-48. BAR International Series 528. Oxford: British Archaeological Reports.
  1990  *Diversity Within Uniformity: Tool Manufacture and Use in the "Pontinian" Mousterian of Latium (Italy)*. Ph.D. dissertation, Department of Anthropology, University of New Mexico. Ann Arbor: University Microfilms.
  1991  "Unpacking" reduction: Lithic raw material economy in the Mousterian of west-central Italy. *Journal of Anthropological Archaeology* 10:76-106.
Marks, A.
  1988  The Middle to Upper Paleolithic transition in the southern Levant: Technological change as an adaptation to increased mobility. In *L'homme de Neandertal. Tome 8. La mutation*. M. Otte, ed. Pp. 109-123. ERAUL 35. Liège: Université de Liège.
Myers, A.
  1989  Reliable and maintainable technological strategies in the Mesolithic of mainland Britain. In *Time, Energy and Stone Tools*. R. Torrence, ed. Pp. 122-129. Cambridge: Cambridge University Press.

Nelson, M.
1991 Technology as dynamic: Review of studies of technological organization. In *Archaeological Method and Theory. Volume 3*. M. Schiffer, ed. Pp.57-100. Tucson: University of Arizona Press.

O'Connell, J. F., K. Hawkes, and N. G. Blurton-Jones
1988 Hadza scavenging: Implications for Plio/Pleistocene hominid subsistence. *Current Anthropology* 29:356-363.

Rolland, N.
1981 The interpretation of Middle Paleolithic variability. *Man* 16:15-42.

Rolland, N., and H. Dibble
1990 A new synthesis of Middle Paleolithic variability. *American Antiquity* 55:480-499.

Shea, J.
1989 A functional study of the lithic industries associated with hominid fossils in the Kebara and Qafzeh Caves, Israel. In *The Human Revolution: Behavioural and Biological Perspectives in the Origins of Modern Humans*. P. Mellars and C. Stringer, eds. Pp. 611-625. Princeton: Princeton University Press.

Shott, M.
1986 Settlement mobility and technological organization: An ethnographic examination. *Journal of Anthropological Research* 42:15-51.
1989 On tool-class use lives and the formation of archaeological assemblages. *American Antiquity* 54:9-30.

Stiner, M. C.
1990a *The Ecology of Choice: Procurement and Transport of Animal Resources by Upper Pleistocene Hominids in West-Central Italy*. Ph.D. dissertation, Department of Anthropology, University of New Mexico. Ann Arbor: University Microfilms.
1990b The use of mortality patterns in archaeological studies of hominid predatory adaptations. *Journal of Anthropological Archaeology* 9:305-351.
1991 Food procurement and transport by human and nonhuman predators. *Journal of Archaeological Science* 18:455-82.

Stiner, M., and S. Kuhn
1992 Subsistence, technology and adaptive variation in the Middle Paleolithic. *American Anthropologist* 94:306-339.

Straus, L. G.
1990 The original arms race: Iberian perspectives on the Solutrean phenomenon. In *Feuilles du pierre: Les industries à pointes foliacées du Paléolithique supérieur européen*. J. Kozlowski, ed. Pp. 425-447. ERAUL 42. Liège: Université de Liège.

Taschini, M.
1979 L'industrie lithique de Grotta Guattari au Mont Circe (Latium): Definition culturelle, typologique et chronologique du Pontinien. *Quaternaria* 21:179-247.

Torrence, R.
1983 Time budgeting and hunter-gatherer technology. In *Hunter-Gatherer Economy in Prehistory: A European Perspective*. G. Bailey, ed. Pp. 11-22. Cambridge: Cambridge University Press.
1989 Re-tooling: Towards a behavioral theory of stone tools. In *Time, Energy and Stone Tools*. R. Torrence, ed. Pp. 57-66. Cambridge: Cambridge University Press.

# 3

# Early Upper Paleolithic Approaches to Bone and Antler Projectile Technology

## Heidi Knecht
## University of Miami

## ABSTRACT

Results of a study of Early Upper Paleolithic bone and antler projectile points indicate that different strategies of design, manufacture, and performance of projectile technology were emphasized throughout the Early Upper Paleolithic. An integrated analysis of morphology and wear, as well as experimentation in the production and use of various Early Upper Paleolithic projectile technologies has demonstrated that, while there is change through time in Early Upper Paleolithic projectile technology, there are considerable similarities among contemporaneous approaches to organic projectile technology. Moreover, while Aurignacian organic projectile technology was the same throughout western Europe, Gravettian organic projectile point design varied among regions.

## INTRODUCTION

Results of a study of 659 Early Upper Paleolithic bone and antler projectile points from 31 sites in France, Belgium, and Germany indicate that Early Upper Paleolithic projectile technologies differ over time in technique of manufacture, morphology, hafting, and performance. The design of all Early Upper Paleolithic organic projectile points was, of course, concerned with the efficient performance of these objects as the armatures of projectile weapons. There is, however, a great deal of variation among the solutions chosen in the design of different types of organic projectile points. While several strategies of design, manufacture, and performance were emphasized throughout the Early Upper Paleolithic, an effective hunting weapon was always produced. The changes evident in the design of projectile points over time represent different technological approaches to the production and use of the weapons.

## METHODS

Several analytical methods were used in this study to elucidate questions concerning production techniques, morphological standardization and variability, hafting techniques, and characteristics and effectiveness of performance of Early Upper Paleolithic bone and antler projectile points.

### Technique of Manufacture

Raw material selected for production, manufacturing waste, pieces at various stages of completion, and micro- and macroscopic manufacturing stigmata on completed projectile points provided clues to the sequence of production. The procedures adopted for traceological examination followed those developed by the extensive work of several researchers including Olsen (1984), Peltier and Plisson (1986), Peltier (1986), d'Errico (1987), and Campana (1989). The hypothesized manufacturing strategies were tested through experimental replication of the projectile points.

### Morphology

Morphological analyses of the various types of projectile points were designed to elicit formal variations and discontinuities and to assess the range of variability. Patterning was sought through basic statistical manipulations of both metric dimensions and geometric forms. Although space does not permit elaboration of the results, most dimensions are nor-

**Table 3.1.** Sources of Early Upper Paleolithic organic projectile points included in this study.

| Site | Split-Based Points | Lozenge-Shaped Points | Spindle-Shaped Points | Single-Beveled Points | Lateral-Beveled Points | Mammoth-Rib Points |
|---|---|---|---|---|---|---|
| FRANCE: | | | | | | |
| Abri Blanchard | 50 | 3 | | | | |
| Abri Castanet | 55 | 2 | | | | |
| Abri Cellier | 18 | 2 | 1 | | | |
| Aurignac | 2 | | | | | |
| Cro-Magnon | 1 | | | | | |
| Abri Lartet | 4 | | | | | |
| Abri du Poisson | 13 | | | | | |
| Isturitz | 75 | | | | | |
| La Ferrassie | 17 | | | | | |
| La Quina | 22 | | | | | |
| La Rochette | 6 | | | | | |
| La Souquette | 8 | | | | | |
| Laussel | 11 | | | | | |
| Les Vachons | 1 | 4 | | 1 | | |
| St.-Jean-de-Verges | 33 | | | | | |
| Tarté | 25 | | | 2 | | |
| Grotte XVI | | 2 | | | | |
| Le Flageolet I | | | 1 | | | |
| Les Rois | | 2 | | | | |
| Laugerie-Haute | | | | 68 | 19 | |
| | | | | | | |
| BELGIUM: | | | | | | |
| Grottes de Goyet | 1 | 1 | 3 | 1 | | |
| Trou du Surreau | 1 | | | | | |
| Spy | 6 | | | | | |
| Trou al' Wesse | 1 | 1 | | | | |
| Trou Magrite | 6 | | 1 | | | |
| Grotte Walou | 5 | | | | | |
| | | | | | | |
| GERMANY: | | | | | | |
| Brillenhöhle | 2 | | | | | 38 |
| Geissenklösterle | 8 | | | | | |
| Vogelherd | 15 | 1 | 1 | | | |

mally distributed (see Knecht 1991b for details). The forms and sizes of the various types of projectile points studied are highly standardized (Knecht 1991b).

## Hafting

The hypothesized systems of hafting the different projectile points were primarily suggested by (1) the morphology of the proximal ends of the projectile points; (2) additional technological elements associated with the projectile points in archaeological assemblages; and (3) ethnographic and modern hafting technologies. The hypothesized hafting techniques

were tested through replicative construction and experimental use, as described below.

## Performance

The discussion of the use and performance of Early Upper Paleolithic organic projectiles is based upon the results of a series of preliminary experiments conducted in conjunction with the program of TFPPP (*Technologie fonctionelle des pointes de projectiles préhistoriques*; Functional Technology of Prehistoric Projectile Points). Bone and antler projectile points, identical in size and form to particular Paleolithic specimens, were attached to wood spear shafts. The spears were launched with a calibrated crossbow into fresh goat cadavers suspended in anatomical position.

The amount of force necessary for the projectile point to penetrate the hide of the goat was initially determined (cf. Carrère and Lepetz 1988; Cotterell and Kamminga 1990). The force with which the projectiles hit the animal was then kept constant. For each shot, velocity of the projectile, location of contact, depth of penetration, and any damage to the projectile were noted.

Each spear was used repeatedly until it (1) was unusable because of breakage of the projectile point or shaft or separation of the projectile point from the shaft; (2) was damaged in such a manner that it was judged of interest to preserve the fracture for comparative purposes; (3) was embedded in bone and could not be removed without breakage; or (4) was unbroken despite repeated use.

Since the goals of the experiments were both to assess the performance capabilities of the projectile points and to determine any diagnostic patterns of breakage[1], each spear was first shot into soft tissue (usually the abdomen); then into small bones or bony areas (e.g., the vertebrae, ribs, and upper limbs); and finally, if it had not yet broken or become embedded in bone, into larger bones like the cranium, mandible, or pelvis.

## ON THE TYPOLOGY AND CHRONOLOGY OF EARLY UPPER PALEOLITHIC ORGANIC PROJECTILE POINTS

A typology of Paleolithic organic projectile points has evolved during the past century. Points have most often been assigned to typological categories on the basis of the morphology of the proximal ends (cf. D. Peyrony 1933, 1934; D. Peyrony and E. Peyrony 1938; Leroy-Prost 1975; Delporte et al. 1988). For example, split-based points and simple-based points are described as characteristic of the Aurignacian, while points with single-beveled bases are thought to typify the Perigordian in Aquitaine.

Nearly 60 years ago, Denis Peyrony (1933) distinguished five types of Aurignacian organic projectile points among the assemblages from La Ferrassie and Laugerie-Haute, which he viewed as index fossils of successive stages of the Aurignacian:

Aurignacian I:   *pointe à base fendue* (split-based point);

Aurignacian II:  *pointe losangique aplatie* (lozenge-shaped point);

Aurignacian III: *pointe losangique à section ovale* (lozenge-shaped point with oval section);

Aurignacian IV:  *pointe biconique* (biconical point);

Aurignacian V:   *pointe cylindro-conique à biseau simple* (cylindro-conical point with single-beveled base).

It has since been recognized that this sequence of bone and antler point forms does not strictly apply to the sequence of assemblages at several Early Upper Paleolithic sites, including La Ferrassie itself (de Sonneville-Bordes 1960; Leroy-Prost 1974, 1975; Brooks 1979; Knecht 1991b). Moreover, the distinctions between some of Peyrony's "types" of organic projectile points have been shown to be dubious at best (Leroy-Prost 1974, 1975; Knecht 1991b).

The Early Upper Paleolithic organic projectile points studied were all from Aurignacian and Gravettian (including "Upper" Perigordian) levels of sites in France, Belgium, and Germany (Table 3.1). The analysis and results presented below concern six kinds of Early Upper Paleolithic bone and antler projectile points (Figure 3.1): split-based points, lozenge-shaped simple-based points, spindle-shaped simple-based points, single-beveled points, lateral-beveled points, and mammoth-rib points. The delineation of these categories of projectile points was suggested not only by the morphological characteristics of the objects, but also, and perhaps more significantly, by continuities and variability in techniques of manufacture and use (Knecht 1991a, 1991b).

## AURIGNACIAN SPLIT-BASED POINTS

On the basis of their presence in Level F of La Ferrassie, Denis Peyrony (1934) designated split-based points (Figure 3.1a) as the index fossil of his Aurignacian I. All recent research indicates that split-based points are limited to the earlier portions of the Aurignacian (cf. Albrecht et al. 1972; Leroy-Prost 1975, 1979; Hahn 1988; Knecht 1991b).

### Technique of Manufacture

Contrary to their designation as split-based **bone** points in much of the archaeological literature, split-based points were virtually always manufactured of antler. Of 381 split-based points studied, the raw material of 371 was definitively identified as antler, while that of only one was definitively identified as bone.

Denis Peyrony (1928) reconstructed the process of manufacture of split bases as involving the removal of a tongued piece from between the two wings of the split (Figure 3.2). Beginning with Henri-Martin in 1930, the notion that the bases of the points were split by true cleavage has been suggested sporadically by several researchers (cf. J. Vézian and Jos. Vézian 1966; Leroy-Prost 1975; Hahn 1988). Nevertheless, it

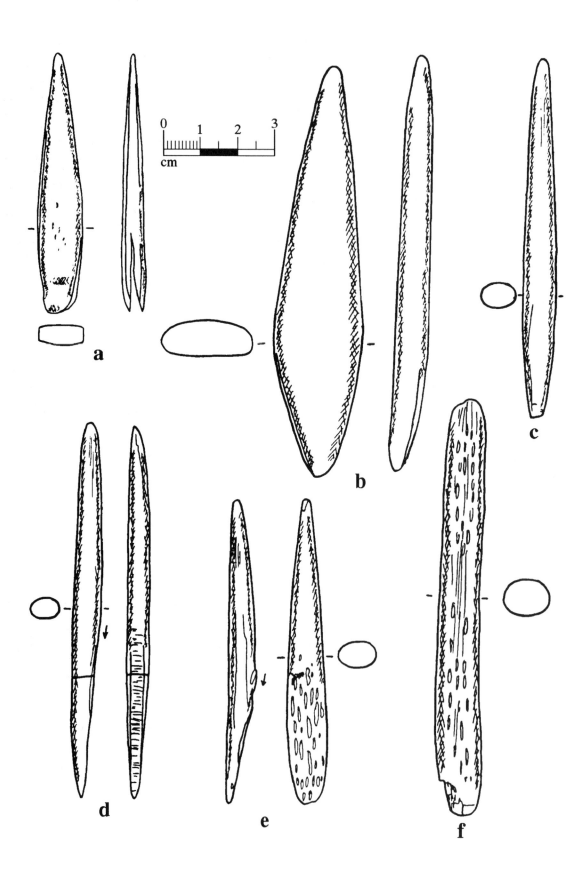

a

b

c

d

e

f

is Peyrony's method for the production of split bases which has been perpetuated in the Paleolithic literature.

My own observations of Aurignacian split-based points and experimental production of split bases demonstrate that the splits were indeed manufactured by simple cleavage of the antler (Knecht 1993). All of the split bases of which the interior surfaces of the two wings can be observed show the surfaces to be negative imprints of one another. In some cases, there is material removed from a portion of the interior of the split. In each instance, this can be demonstrated to have been caused by either (1) correction of an imperfect split by manufacture of a second split or (2) reparation of the split subsequent to breakage.

Split-based points were manufactured from semicylindrical segments of antler (Figure 3.3). The projectile point blank was shaped primarily by removal of material from the lateral edges and the inferior (cancellous) surface. Observation of unfinished split-based points indicates that the split was produced after only preliminary shaping of the piece. Once a successful split was obtained, the final shaping of the piece, including shaping of the distal point, was achieved by additional removal of material from the surfaces and lateral edges.

### Hafting

An association between tongued pieces (*pièces à languette*) (Figure 3.4) and split-based points has long been recognized. Since Denis Peyrony's (1928) suggestion that tongued pieces are by-products generated during the fabrication of split-based points, this explanation of their association has been accepted.

The organic assemblage from Abri Castanet at the Musée National de Préhistoire at Les Eyzies includes 27 pieces which appear to be the negative removals from tongued pieces (Figure 3.5). Observation of these small rectangular pieces and numerous tongued pieces from several sites, in conjunction with experimental replication of the objects, has allowed for the delineation of the sequence of manufacture of tongued pieces (Figure 3.6) (Knecht 1993). Examples of each stage of this sequence of production have been observed among archaeological assemblages.

Experimentation supports the probability that the small wedges removed from tongued pieces were used in hafting split-based points (Figure 3.7). It is likely that split-based points were attached to shafts by wedging. When antler is split by cleavage, the split remains closed. For the experimental reconstructions, a U-shaped housing was whittled out of the distal end of a wooden spear shaft. The split-based point was inserted into the handle and held in place by a sinew ligature. When the ligature was wrapped around the point, an opening was left so that the split was accessible. Once the point was bound to the shaft, a small wedge, like those removed from tongued pieces, was inserted into the split by gentle tapping. The wedge forced open the split until the wings of the base pressed firmly against the inside of the housing in the wood shaft. Hafting of a split-based point in this manner requires lashing and wedging, but not the use of resin.

### Performance

During experimentation, spears armed with split-based points penetrated the hide and soft tissue of the goat with no damage to the point or haft, regardless of the size or form of the point. When a point was projected into bone, its penetration was halted, but the point and haft usually remained intact. Projectile experimentation has demonstrated that an organic projectile point need not have a sharply pointed distal end to be an effective hunting weapon. It is the direction at which and the force with which the spear hits the animal, as well as the overall morphology of the projectile point and haft, which determine the effectiveness of the weapon.

## AURIGNACIAN SIMPLE-BASED POINTS

Subsequent to the Early Aurignacian, simple-based organic projectile points appear in the archaeological record. On the basis of morphology, two types of simple-based points, lozenge-shaped points (Figure 3.1b) and spindle-shaped points (Figure 3.1c) are usually distinguished. Significantly, results of traceological and experimental analyses indicate that the

**Figure 3.1.** Early Upper Paleolithic bone and antler projectile points: (a) split-based point (Abri Castanet, Musée National de Préhistoire, Les Eyzies); (b) lozenge-shaped point (La Ferrassie, Musée des Antiquités Nationales, Saint-Germain-en-Laye); (c) spindle-shaped point (La Ferrassie, Musée des Antiquités Nationales, Saint-Germain-en-Laye); (d) lateral-beveled point (Laugerie-Haute, Musée National de Préhistoire, Les Eyzies); (e) single-beveled point (Laugerie-Haute, Institut du Quaternaire, Université de Bordeaux I); (f) mammoth-rib point (Brillenhöhle, Württembergisches Landesmuseum, Stuttgart).

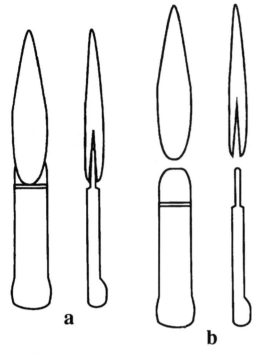

**Figure 3.2.** Manufacture of split-based points according to Denis Peyrony (1928).

techniques of manufacture, hafting, and use of lozenge-shaped points and spindle-shaped points were quite distinct.

## Technique of Manufacture

Both lozenge-shaped and spindle-shaped points were usually manufactured from antler (Table 3.2). Lozenge-shaped points were manufactured from semi-cylindrical segments of antler, i.e., a fragment of antler cut in half along its length (Figure 3.8). As with split-based points, the lateral edges of lozenge-shaped points were worked to form by longitudinal scraping, separate from the smoothing of the superior and inferior surfaces. The curvature of the diameter of the antler dictated to some degree the final cross-section of the lozenge-shaped points; some portion of the exterior surface of the antler remains along extensive portions of the surface of many lozenge-shaped points.

Spindle-shaped points were manufactured from a segment of antler sectioned along its length (Figure 3.9). Analysis of manufacturing stigmata indicates that the blank was shaped by longitudinal scraping, most likely with retouched flint blades. Unlike lozenge-shaped points, material was removed from all surfaces simultaneously. Spindle-shaped points were manufactured "in-the-round;" the flat lateral edges so clearly visible on many lozenge-shaped points are never seen on spindle-shaped points.

## Hafting

The basal thinning of simple-based points clearly allows for their insertion into a shaft. Experimentation demonstrated at least two possible hafting strategies:

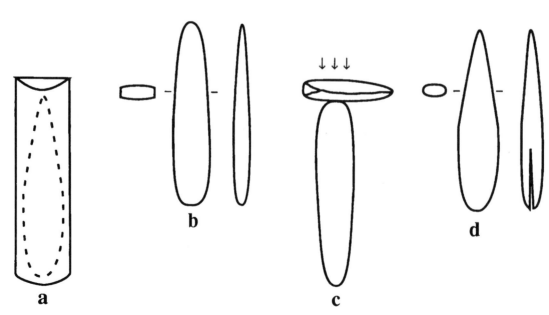

**Figure 3.3.** Manufacture of split-based points.

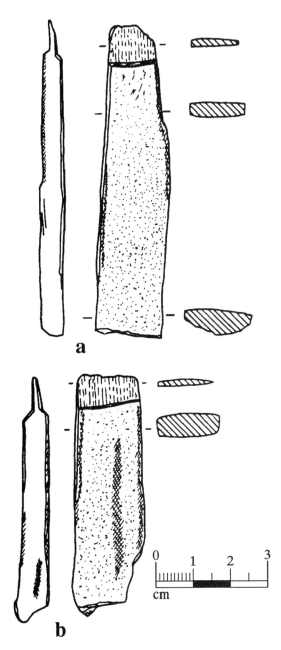

**Figure 3.4.** Tongued pieces (*pièces à languette*) from Abri Cellier (Logan Museum of Anthropology, Beloit, WI).

(1) Like split-based points, the lozenge-shaped points may have been set into a U-shaped housing whittled out of the distal end of a wood shaft (Figure 3.10). During experimentation, the attachment was stabilized by insertion of the nubby proximal end of the point into a socket at the bottom of the housing. Experimentation has shown that use of resin or lashing

alone is insufficient for maintenance of the attachment upon impact with the hunted animal or the ground; it is necessary to fasten the point to the shaft with both ligature and resin.

(2) It is possible that the nearly round spindle-shaped points were inserted into a socket at the distal end of a spear shaft (Figure 3.11). When inserted into a handle to just short of the maximum width, the spindle-shaped point could not move back-and-forth or side-to-side. During experimentation, when spindle-shaped points were inserted in handles and affixed with both ligature and natural plant resin, the attachment was strong enough to withstand impact with either soft or hard animal tissue or with the ground.

### Performance

Because of the marked expansion of lozenge-shaped points at the point of maximum width, the contours of the completed spear bulge just distal to the haft regardless of the hafting technique used. Provided that the spear hits the animal with a force great enough to penetrate the hide, it continues its trajectory so that the spear enters the animal past the point of maximum width of the projectile point. The hide of the animal then closes around the spear shaft. The weapon effectively becomes lodged inside the animal.

Insertion of the tapered proximal end of a spindle-shaped point into a handle allows for the construction of a streamlined spear with no bulge in width or thickness at the level of the ligature--the wrapping and resin protrude no further than the slight bulge in maximum width of the projectile point itself. Unimpeded by changing contours, the spear enters the animal, stopping only when it hits bone or hard tissue

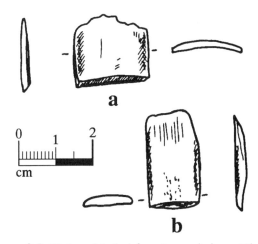

**Figure 3.5.** Wedges detached from tongued pieces (Abri Castanet, Musée National de Préhistoire, Les Eyzies).

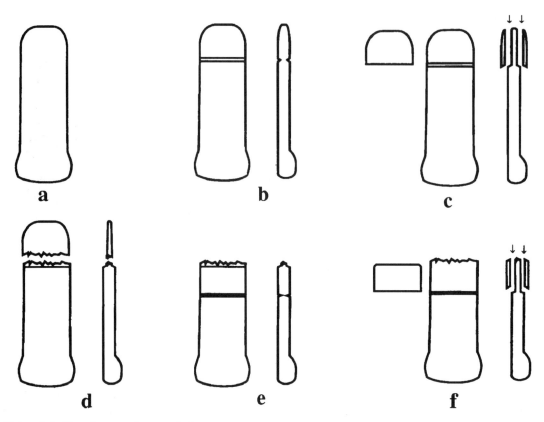

**Figure 3.6.** Manufacture of tongued pieces.

or when its velocity is slowed to a stop by the friction generated through contact with soft tissue.

When all other factors are held constant, the depth of penetration of spears tipped with spindle-shaped points exceeds that of spears equipped with lozenge-shaped points. While the performance qualities selected for in the design of lozenge- and spindle-shaped points appear to have been quite different, both allowed for the construction of effective hunting weapons.

## GRAVETTIAN SINGLE-BEVELED POINTS

Objects classified as single-beveled points from Early Upper Paleolithic assemblages from sites in the Aquitaine Basin are actually of two varieties. Some of these points have a single bevel on their inferior surface, while others are beveled along a lateral edge. The technique of manufacture, as well as the morphology of the two kinds of bevels, are quite distinct. They have therefore been separated into two categories for analysis: (1) single-beveled points with the bevel on the inferior surface (Figure 3.1e) and (2) lateral-beveled points with the bevel along a lateral edge (Figure 3.1d). Notably, single-beveled points and lateral-beveled points are differentiated not only by the location of the beveled surface, but also by raw material of manufacture, technique of manufacture, and differences in the sequence of production.

Single-beveled points are known from levels described as Aurignacian V, Protomagdalenian, and Perigordian VI, whereas lateral-beveled points are known from Protomagdalenian and Perigordian VI levels (Bordes and de Sonneville-Bordes 1966; Bricker and David 1984; D. Peyrony and E. Peyrony 1938; Pike-Tay and Bricker, this volume; de Sonneville-Bordes 1980). In other words, both single-beveled and lateral-beveled points date to the Perigordian, i.e., the period broadly described as the Gravettian throughout most of Europe.

### Technique of Manufacture

Even though antler was available from both red deer and reindeer during the Perigordian in southwest France (Delpech 1983), single-beveled points were manufactured from long bones (Table 3.3). The bone

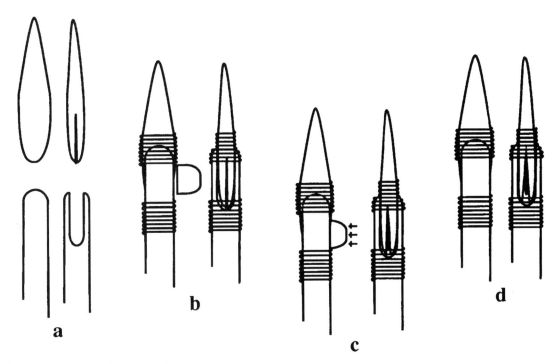

**Figure 3.7.** Hafting of split-based point.

was broken into large splinters (Figure 3.12). Observation of unfinished single-beveled points indicates that the blank was worked to a gentle taper by removal of material along the longitudinal axis of the splinter. Cancellous material was usually left along the proximal end of the blank. The bevel was manufactured by whittling or scraping the cancellous surface at the proximal end.

The thickest part of single-beveled points, the portion just distal to the bevel, often displays some cancellous bone. Cancellous material often remains on the beveled bases of these points. On single-beveled points with the bevel on smooth compact bone, the surface of the bevel was scored with oblique incisions or textured with irregular grooves.

### Hafting

Experimental manufacture and use of single-beveled bone points has demonstrated the efficacy of the hafting mechanism proposed by the Peyronys (D. Peyrony and E. Peyrony 1938:23, Fig. 12d) (Figure 3.13). The distal end of a wood shaft was whittled down to form a bevel at an angle which matched that of the beveled bases of the points. During experimentation, a step-like structure was manufactured at the end of the bevel on the handle to impede dislocation of the point upon impact.

During experimentation, resin was applied to the beveled surfaces to increase adhesion. The irregular surface of the bevel created by the natural openings of the cancellous bone increased the tenacity between the base and the end of the handle. Smooth surfaces would have allowed for slippage. During the Perigordian, the shafts of single-beveled points were sometimes scored with incisions perpendicular to the axis at the distal end of the bevel. It is likely that these incisions reduced slippage of the ligature that bound the point to the shaft. The superior surface opposite the distal end of the bevel of some Perigordian single-beveled points is flattened and marked with oblique or perpendicular incisions. This combination of features would allow for additional cohesion of lashing and/or adhesive.

**Table 3.2.** Raw material of lozenge-shaped and spindle-shaped points.

|  | Lozenge-Shaped | Spindle-Shaped |
|---|---|---|
| Antler | 101 | 35 |
| Antler? | 2 | 0 |
| Bone or antler | 0 | 2 |
| Ivory | 1 | 0 |
| TOTAL | 104 | 37 |

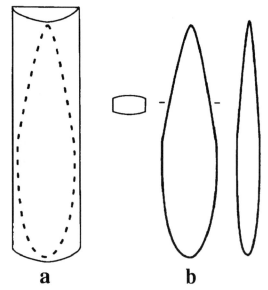

**Figure 3.8.** Manufacture of lozenge-shaped points.

### Performance

Armed with these weapons, Paleolithic hunters would have been capable of maiming or killing both large and small animals. During projectile experimentation, the spears were found to enter easily and even pass through the goat. The projectile trajectory was unimpeded by the streamlined contours of the single-beveled points attached to single-beveled handles.

## GRAVETTIAN LATERAL-BEVELED POINTS

Lateral-beveled points are known from Perigordian VI and Protomagdalenian levels of the sites of Laugerie-Haute and Abri Pataud (Bricker and David 1984; Pike-Tay and Bricker, this volume). In contradistinction to Perigordian single-beveled points, Perigordian lateral-beveled points usually were manufactured from antler, either from longitudinal segments of the antler beam or from tines with appropriately shaped sections. The lateral bevel was manufactured by longitudinal scraping of an edge. The end was shaped subsequent to manufacture of the bevel. Interestingly, this sequence is the inverse of that for single-beveled points, of which the manufacture of the shaft was followed by formation of the bevel. When manufactured from compact tissue, the bevels of lateral-beveled points are marked with either long oblique striae or short perpendicular incisions.

Because of limitations of time and budget, lateral-beveled points were not used experimentally. Several features of the points suggest possibilities for their

**Table 3.3.** Raw material of Aurignacian V, Protomagdalenian, and Perigordian VI single-beveled points from Laugerie-Haute.

|  | Aur.V | PMag. | Per.VI |
|---|---|---|---|
| Antler | 0 | 2 | 0 |
| Antler? | 1 | 1 | 0 |
| Bone | 50 | 6 | 1 |
| Bone? | 4 | 0 | 0 |
| Bone or antler | 1 | 0 | 0 |

manner of use. Some of the lateral-beveled points have pointed distal ends, suggesting that, like single-beveled points, they may have functioned as projectile points. Other lateral-beveled points are beveled at both proximal and distal ends, on opposite edges. These may also be projectile points, or they may represent intermediate elements of a multi-component composite tool technology. The textured beveled surfaces, as well as the regularity of the contours of the bevels on the different pieces, indicate the possibility that these objects were designed for attachment to either similar pieces or to other objects manufactured of wood, bone, antler, or stone.

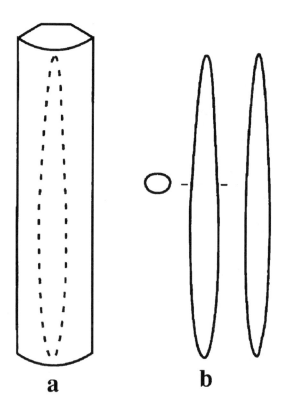

**Figure 3.9.** Manufacture of spindle-shaped points.

## MAMMOTH-RIB POINTS

In southern Germany, mammoth-rib points (Figure 3.1f) are known from Gravettian levels of Geissenklösterle, Brillenhöhle, and Weinberghöhlen. Pieces representative of each stage of the manufacturing process of mammoth-rib points were studied (Plate 3.1). The mammoth rib was first divided into flat segments. The segment was next sectioned longitudinally. The rib fragment was then reduced to form by longitudinal scraping. The resultant piece was a gently tapered point that was most often elliptical, circular, or subrectangular in section. With the exception of small portions of the superior surface, the resultant point was formed entirely of cancellous bone.

Many mammoth-rib points are scored with fine incisions which run either perpendicular or oblique to the longitudinal axis of the piece. Some mammoth-rib points have flattened portions along their otherwise rounded shafts. The flat segment of the shaft is often marked with perpendicular incisions. The system for hafting mammoth-rib points remains to be explored.

## CONCLUSION: EARLY UPPER PALEOLITHIC PROJECTILE TECHNOLOGIES

There are distinct differences among the various Early Upper Paleolithic organic projectile technologies. These technologies are distinguishable from the outset of the manufacturing process on the basis of the selection of bone or antler as the raw material for production. Given the selected raw material, techniques suitable for working of that material were used to produce different types of projectile points designed to be hafted by various techniques. Attached to shafts, the different types of projectile points would have allowed for the construction of several different hunting weapons. While all of these weapons were undoubtedly effective in dispatching the hunted prey animals, different characteristics of performance (see also Knecht 1991a) were sought in the design of the various projectile points.

The techniques of manufacture, hafting, and use of split-based points are reflective of a fully developed organic technology at the beginning of the Aurignacian in western Europe. Antler was worked with techniques completely adapted to its material characteristics. Splitting and wedging permeate the technological system in both manufacture and use (Knecht 1993). The techniques of splitting and wedging of antler were essential not only to the manufacture of split-based points, but also to their hafting. The wedges, which were likely used to wedge open the split base inside a haft, were themselves manufactured by splitting.

The manufacture of lozenge-shaped points involved the reduction of longitudinal segments of antler. The artisan was concerned with working down the antler blank by removing cancellous material. The

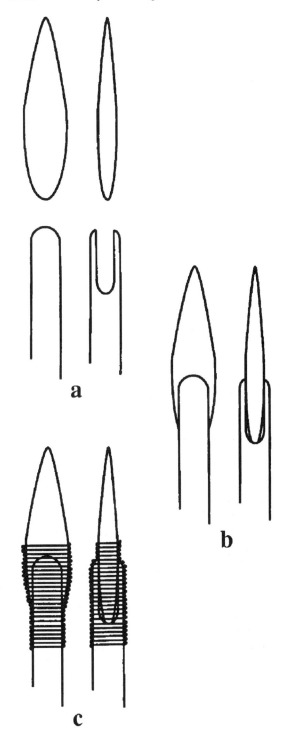

**Figure 3.10.** Hafting of lozenge-shaped points.

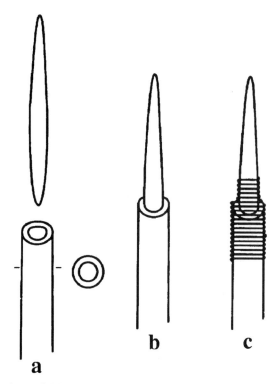

**Figure 3.11.** Hafting of spindle-shaped points.

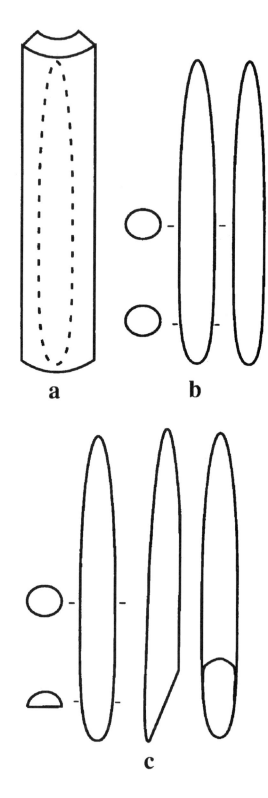

**Figure 3.12.** Manufacture of single-beveled points.

ultimate form of a particular lozenge-shaped point was determined, to a large extent, by the contours of the antler from which it was manufactured.

Unlike split-based points and lozenge-shaped points, spindle-shaped points were manufactured as a whole. During manufacture, once the cancellous tissue had been removed from the piece, no distinction was made between lateral edges and superior and inferior surfaces. If spindle-shaped points were inserted into a hole in the end of a spear shaft as has been postulated, the hafting of spindle-shaped points, like their manufacture, was carried out with no distinction between lateral edges and superior and inferior surfaces. The complete spear, like the projectile point itself, was likely viewed "in the round." This perception of an object as having no sides is inherently different from that of both previous forms of organic projectile points and hafting techniques.

While several kinds of organic points, including single-beveled points, lateral-beveled points, and mammoth-rib points, were in use during the Gravettian, a number of characteristics pervade all Gravettian organic projectile technology: (1) textured surfaces formed either by the natural crevices of cancellous tissue or by intentionally made striae; (2) notched or incised lateral edges; and (3) flattened portions of otherwise rounded surfaces. These features

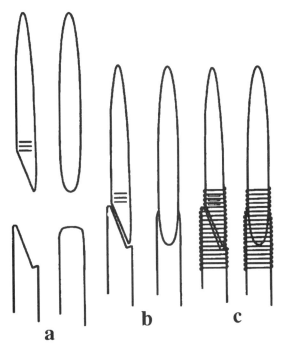

**Figure 3.13.** Hafting of single-beveled points.

are most likely associated with the manner in which objects were fastened together--either the attachment of a point to a shaft or the splicing of components of a multi-element composite tool technology. Moreover, due to their form, all hafted Gravettian projectile points yielded streamlined spears with no bulge in width or thickness along either the projectile point itself or at the level of the haft.

Differences among Aurignacian and Gravettian organic projectile technologies reflect the existence of varied technological systems throughout the Early Upper Paleolithic. Technological systems result from a group's response to a technical problem which is largely a matter of technical choices (Knecht 1991a, 1991b). A technical system may be viewed as a signifying system, which may even be indicative of group identity.

Results of the analyses described above suggest that contemporaneous Aurignacian organic projectile technologies were identical across widely separated geographical regions extending, at the very least, from southwest France to southern Germany. During the Gravettian, certain techniques were used in the design, construction, maintenance (see Knecht 1991a and 1991b for discussion of maintenance and re-use of

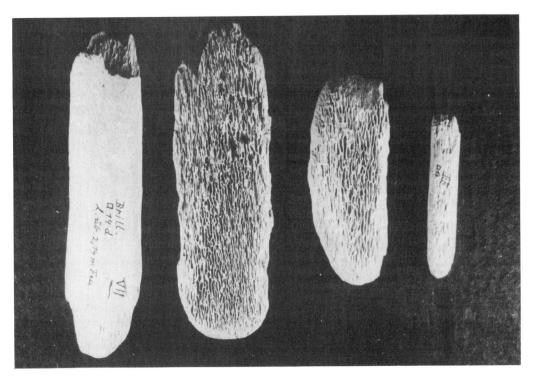

**Plate 3.1.** Manufacture of mammoth-rib points (Brillenhöhle, Württembergisches Landesmuseum, Stuttgart).

Gravettian organic projectile points), and use of organic projectile technologies everywhere, but, at a lower level, the specifics of projectile point design varied among regions. Certain technological approaches are evident in all Gravettian organic projectile technology, but technical choices were made within micro-regions in order to create objects which may be characteristic of different regional groups.

## ACKNOWLEDGEMENTS

I would like to thank Kathy Ehrhardt and Anne Pike-Tay for their comments on earlier drafts of this paper. The research presented in this paper was made possible by the generous support of the National Science Foundation (Grant #BNS-8711320), the L. S. B. Leakey Foundation, the Wenner-Gren Foundation, and New York University.

## NOTES

[1] As has been noted by other researchers (Odell and Cowan 1986), the use of stationary targets may well produce patterns of breakage or wear that differ significantly from those produced when a projectile hits a moving animal.

## REFERENCES

Albrecht, G., J. Hahn, and W. G. Torke
  1972    *Merkmalanalyse von Geschosspitzen des mittleren Jungpleistozäns in Mittel- und Osteuropa.* Archaeologica Venatoria 2. Tübingen: Insitut für Urgeschichte.
Bordes, F.
  1978    Le Protomagdalénien de Laugerie-Haute-Est (fouilles F. Bordes). *Bulletin de la Société Préhistorique Française* 75:501-521.
  1984    *Leçons sur le Paléolithique. Tome II. Le Paléolithique en Europe.* Cahiers du Quaternaire 7. Paris: Editions du Centre National de la Recherche Scientifique.
Bordes, F., and D. de Sonneville-Bordes
  1966    Protomagdalénien, ou Périgordien VII? *L'Anthropologie* 70:113-122.
Bricker, H. M., and N. David
  1984    *Excavation of the Abri Pataud, Les Eyzies (Dordogne). The Périgordian VI (Level 3) Assemblage.* American School of Prehistoric Research Bulletin 34. Cambridge: Peabody Museum, Harvard University.
Brooks, A.
  1979    The Significance of Variability in Palaeolithic Assemblages: An Aurignacian Example from Southwestern France. Ph.D. dissertation, Department of Anthropology, Harvard University.
Campana, D. V.
  1989    *Natufian and Protoneolithic Bone Tools: The Manufacture and Use of Bone Implements in the Zagros and the Levant.* BAR International Series 494. Oxford: British Archaeological Reports.
Carrère, P., and S. Lepetz
  1988    Etude de la dynamique des pointes de projectiles: Elaboration d'une méthode. Mémoire de Maitrise de l'Univer-

sité de Paris I--Panthéon Sorbonne.
Cotterell, B., and J. Kamminga
  1990    *Mechanics of Pre-Industrial Technology.* Cambridge: Cambridge University Press.
Delpech, F.
  1983    *Les faunes du Paléolithique supérieur dans le sud-ouest de la France.* Cahiers du Quaternaire 6. Paris: Editions du Centre National de la Recherche Scientifique.
Delporte, H., J. Hahn, L. Mons, G. Pinçon, and D. de Sonneville-Bordes
  1988    *Fiches typologiques de l'industrie osseuse préhistorique. Cahier I. Sagaies.* Commission de Nomenclature sur l'Industrie de l'Os Préhistorique. Aix-en-Provence: Université de Provence.
d'Errico, F.
  1987    Nouveaux indices et nouvelles techniques microscopiques pour la lecture de l'art gravé mobilier. *Comptes Rendues de l'Academie Science de Paris Série II* 304:761-765.
Hahn, J.
  1988    Fiche sagaie à base fendue. In *Fiches typologiques de l'industrie osseuse préhistorique. Cahier I. Sagaies.* Commission de Nomenclature sur l'Industrie de l'Os Préhistorique. Aix-en-Provence: Université de Provence.
Henri-Martin (see Martin, H.)
Knecht, H.
  1991a   The role of innovation in changing Early Upper Paleolithic organic projectile technologies. *Techniques et Culture* 17-18:115-144.
  1991b   *Technological Innovation and Design during the Early Upper Paleolithic: A Study of Organic Projectile Technologies.* Ph.D. dissertation, Department of Anthropology, New York University.
  1993    Splits and wedges: The techniques and technology of Early Aurignacian antler working. In *Before Lascaux: The Complex Record of the Early Upper Paleolithic.* Heidi Knecht, Anne Pike-Tay, and Randall White, eds. Pp. 137-162. Boca Raton: CRC Press.
Leroy-Prost, C.
  1974    Les pointes en matière osseuse de l'Aurignacien. Caractéristiques morphologiques et essais de définitions. *Bulletin de la Société Préhistorique Française* 71:449-458.
  1975    L'industrie osseuse aurignacienne. Essai régional de classification: Poitou, Charentes, Périgord. *Gallia Préhistoire* 18:65-156.
  1979    L'industrie osseuse aurignacienne. Essai régional de classification: Poitou, Charentes, Périgord (suite). *Gallia Préhistoire* 22:205-370.
Martin, H.
  1930    La station aurignacienne de La Quina (Charente). *Bulletin de la Société Archéologique et Historique de la Charente.*
Odell, G. H., and F. Cowan
  1986    Experiments with spears and arrows on animal targets. *Journal of Field Archaeology* 13:195-212.
Olsen, S. L.
  1984    Analytical approaches to the manufacture and use of bone artifacts in prehistory. Ph.D. dissertation, Insitute of Archaeology, University of London.
Peltier, A.
  1986    Etude expérimentale des surfaces osseuses façonnées et utilisées. *Bulletin de la Société Préhistorique Française* 83:5-7.
Peltier, A., and H. Plisson
  1986    Micro-tracéologie fonctionnelle sur l'os: Quelques résultats expérimentaux. *Artefacts* 3:69-80.

Peyrony, D.
    1928    Pièces à languette de l'Aurignacien moyen. *Association Française pour l'Avancement des Sciences*, 52ᵉᵐᵉ session, La Rochelle:439-441.
    1933    Les industries "aurignaciennes" dans le bassin de la Vézère. *Bulletin de la Société Préhistorique Française* 30:543-558.
    1934    La Ferrassie. *Préhistoire* 3:1-92.
Peyrony, D., and E. Peyrony
    1938    *Laugerie-Haute près des Eyzies (Dordogne)*. Archives de l'Institut de Paléontologie Humaine Mémoire 19.

de Sonneville-Bordes, D.
    1960    *Le Paléolithique supérieur en Périgord*. Bordeaux: Imprimeries Delmas.
    1980    L'évolution des industries aurignaciennes. In *L'Aurignacien et le Gravettien (Périgordien) dans leur cadre écologique*. L. Bánesz and J. Kozlowski, eds. Pp. 255-273. Nitra: Institut Archéologique de l'Académie Slovaque des Sciences à Nitra and Institut Archéologique de l'Université de Cracovie.
Vézian, J., and Jos. Vézian
    1966    Les gisements de la Grotte de Saint-Jean-de-Verges (Ariège). *Gallia Préhistoire* 9:93-129.

*4*

# *Lithic and Organic Hunting Technology in the French Upper Palaeolithic*

**Gail Larsen Peterkin**
**Tulane University**

ABSTRACT

The application of multivariate statistical techniques to the analysis of lithic and organic (bone, antler, and ivory) weapon armatures from the French Upper Palaeolithic has demonstrated that the traditional typological classification systems are underlain by broad, morpho-functional classes of artifacts which transcend cultural and temporal boundaries. These morpho-functional classes enable the examination of isochrestic variability in hunting technology across time and space. Further analysis suggests that morpho-functional classes are related to other aspects of hunting, including the exploitation of preferred prey species and the use of appropriate hunting strategies and techniques.

## INTRODUCTION

French Upper Palaeolithic archaeology has long been dominated by the typological approach to the classification of artifacts. This type-centered approach was epitomized by the publication of the 92-type list for Upper Palaeolithic lithic artifacts by Denise de Sonneville-Bordes and Jean Perrot in 1954-1956 and by the widespread use of an updated, although as yet unpublished, 105-type list for Upper Palaeolithic stone tools (see, for example, Bordes 1978). The presence of certain lithic types, such as the Noailles burin, are considered markers or *fossiles directeurs* for specific cultural traditions, while distinctive typological profiles in the form of cumulative graphs describe broad cultural traditions, depicting, for example, the predominance of leaf-shaped forms in the Solutrean.

Many organic artifacts from the French Upper Palaeolithic are also index fossils for specific cultural traditions (e.g., split-base points in the Early Aurignacian and bilaterally barbed harpoons in the Final Magdalenian). However, no single typological scheme has as yet received universal acceptance, although recent efforts by the *Commission de nomenclature sur l'industrie de l'os préhistorique* under the direction of Henriette Camps-Fabrer have sought to standardize type definitions for bone and antler artifacts and to

establish a formal classification system for organic tools (Cattelain 1988; Delporte et al. 1988; see Camps-Fabrer 1974 and 1977 for preliminary efforts toward this goal). Much of this research has been centered around broad classes of artifacts, such as sagaies[1] (Delporte et al. 1988) or harpoons (Julien 1982), or on the establishment of a working typology for a temporally and/or geographically bounded organic technology (Campana 1989; McComb 1989).

This longstanding interest in and reliance on typological classification, although it has proved useful in the discrimination of the gross temporal phases of the Aurignacian, Perigordian, Solutrean, and Magdalenian, has hindered the meaningful cross-cultural analysis of technological and behavioral variability within functionally equivalent classes of artifacts. Because of the economic primacy of hunting to fulfill subsistence needs during the Upper Palaeolithic, the tool complex associated with hunting is an ideal test case for a multivariate statistical approach to artifactual variability. Recent academic interest in hunting techniques and technology (e.g., Winterhalder and Smith 1981; Bailey 1983; Price and Brown 1985; Nitecki and Nitecki 1987; Soffer 1987; Bettinger 1991) and on animal exploitation (e.g., Spiess 1979; Gordon 1988; Boyle 1990; Mithen 1990; Pike-Tay 1991; Stiner 1991a, 1991b) provides an ample data base for the consideration of such artifactual variability, along with its relationship to the exploitation of

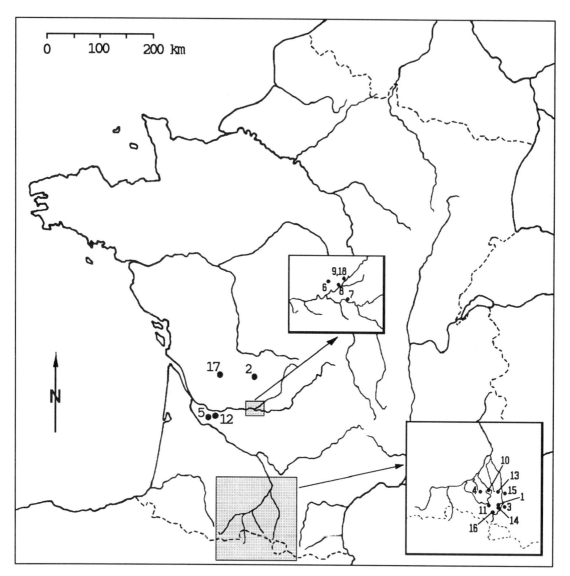

**Figure 4.1.** Location of sites included in the study. Map redrawn from Bordes (1984) with additional material from Bahn (1984), Clottes (1974), and Lenoir (1976). **Key:** 1 = Bédeilhac; 2 = La Chèvre; 3 = Les Eglises; 4 = Enlène; 5 = Abri Faustin; 6 = La Ferrassie; 7 = Flageolet I and II; 8 = Laugerie-Haute; 9 = La Madeleine; 10 = Mas d'Azil; 11 = Massat; 12 = Le Morin; 13 = Le Portel; 14 = Abri Rhodes II; 15 = Tuto de Camalhot; 16 = La Vache; 17 = Les Vachons; 18 = Abri de Villepin.

preferred prey species and to other behavioral correlates of hunting.

## METHODOLOGY

The study included the analysis of over 3,200 lithic and organic weapon armatures from the Upper Palaeolithic levels of 19 archaeological sites in several *départements* of southwest France (Ariège, Charente, Dordogne, and Gironde) (Figure 4.1) and housed in public and private museum collections. Forty-six metric and non-metric variables were recorded for each artifact, including provenience and raw material data; metric dimensions of the tip, shaft, and base; and special features to facilitate hunting, such as the presence of barbs or runnels. As a result of their superior preservation, lithic weapon armatures com-

**Table 4.1.** Lithic and organic weapon armatures from French Upper Palaeolithic sites studied.

| | Lithics | | Organics | |
|---|---|---|---|---|
| | Total | Complete | Total | Complete |
| *Ariège:* | | | | |
| Bédeilhac | 0 | 0 | 2 | 0 |
| Les Eglises* | 14 | 8 | 35 | 6 |
| Enlène* | 29 | 10 | 58 | 7 |
| Mas d'Azil | 2 | 2 | 4 | 2 |
| Massat | 0 | 0 | 40 | 20 |
| Le Portel | 7 | 2 | 4 | 2 |
| Abri Rhodes II | 0 | 0 | 9 | 2 |
| Tuto de Camalhot | 10 | 2 | 44 | 13 |
| La Vache | 47 | 29 | 30 | 8 |
| La Vache/Massat (mixed sample) | 0 | 0 | 23 | 4 |
| *Charente:* | | | | |
| Les Vachons | 202 | 69 | 15 | 5 |
| *Dordogne:* | | | | |
| La Chèvre* | 158 | 59 | 9 | 2 |
| La Ferrassie* | 217 | 52 | 74 | 14 |
| Flageolet I* | 128 | 65 | 10 | 3 |
| Flageolet II* | 0 | 0 | 10 | 2 |
| Laugerie-Haute* | 638 | 178 | 192 | 39 |
| La Madeleine* | 253 | 133 | 316 | 38 |
| Abri de Villepin | 41 | 38 | 2 | 0 |
| *Gironde:* | | | | |
| Abri Faustin* | 36 | 21 | 10 | 1 |
| Le Morin* | 494 | 463 | 44 | 21 |
| TOTAL | 2,276 | 1,131 | 931 | 189 |

*Sites with quantified faunal data that were included in the lithic/faunal analyses described later in this paper.

prised more than two-thirds of the total artifactual sample. In addition, lithic weapon armatures were more often intact, whereas many bone and antler armatures were fragmented as a result of the vagaries of use, preservation, and/or recovery techniques (Table 4.1). This paper presents the analysis of the entire sample of 984 complete lithic weapon armatures and the two largest classes of complete organic weapon armatures, sagaies and harpoons.

Over 30 Upper Palaeolithic lithic tool types were tentatively defined as weapon armatures, based upon traditional typological definitions (de Sonneville-Bordes and Perrot 1954-1956; Brézillon 1968; 105-type list as used in Bordes 1978). Organic weapon armatures were identified by basic techno-functional classes, including *baguettes* (some of which may have been weapon armatures [Bricker and David 1984: 100]), *hameçons* or gorges, harpoons, proto-harpoons, sagaies, tridents, and hunting accoutrements such as spearthrowers.

The preliminary identification was corroborated by "circumstantial" evidence from ethnographic analogy (see Churchill, this volume), ethnoarchaeology, and contextual finds from the archaeological record of other geographic regions (e.g., Noe-Nygaard 1974). More direct evidence of employment as weap-

on armatures came from macroscopic fracture patterns, such as "burination" of the tip (Bergman and Newcomer 1983:239; Christenson 1986b:25; Epstein 1963; Shea 1988, this volume), as well as evidence of hafting damage (Keeley 1982; Odell 1980) and occasionally even the presence of mastic (Allain 1979; Leroi-Gourhan 1983). Several use-wear studies of similar weapon armatures from France and other European settings and of experimentally produced projectile points have confirmed the use of similar weapon armatures as hafted projectile points (Donohue 1988; Fischer et al. 1984; Keeley 1988; Odell 1978; Odell and Cowan 1986).

## LITHIC WEAPON ARMATURES

The statistical examination of 984 complete lithic weapon armatures suggests that classic Upper Palaeolithic weapon armatures can be grouped into several broad morpho-functional classes based on general morphology and on the mechanics of hafting; these classes remained static throughout the French Upper Palaeolithic and transcended both cultural and temporal boundaries (Peterkin n.d.b):

**Class 1:** Backed points, including Gravette points, Azilian points, and pointed backed geometric microliths (Figure 4.2).

**Class 2:** Backed side elements, including *éléments tronqués* and non-pointed backed geometric microliths. These artifacts were most likely used as the side elements of a composite weapon armature, although some may have been used as paired elements of a projectile tip or even as transverse projectile points (Deacon 1984a, 1984b; Olszewski, this volume; Vayson de Pradenne 1936; Vignard 1935).

Despite the wide range of variation in overall size within these two morpho-functional classes, the variability is normally distributed from small backed microliths through large macrolithic backed points. There is thus no statistical basis for the further subdivision of these two classes on the basis of size.

**Class 3:** Foliate or leaf-shaped points, such as *flèchettes*, *dards*, Laugerie-Basse points, and the Solutrean forms (Figure 4.2).

**Class 4:** Points with hafting specializations, such as shoulders or tangs, including Font-Robert points, Magdalenian shouldered points, and Teyjat points (Figure 4.3).

This morpho-functional classification scheme was corroborated by a series of discriminant function analyses run within specific cultural and industrial traditions and for the Upper Palaeolithic as a whole. This statistical technique is ideal for testing typological categories, because it "allows the researcher to study the differences between two or more groups of objects with respect to several variables simultaneously" (Klecka 1980:7). Since the technique requires the use of interval or ratio-scale variables (Klecka 1980:8), 14 continuous variables of the tip, edge, and haft were selected for discriminant function analysis: length, width, thickness, weight, tip length, tip thickness, penetrating angle, left divergence, right divergence, high edge angle, low edge angle, haft length, haft width, and haft thickness.

The artifacts were first analyzed within the context of 15 specific cultural and industrial traditions of the French Upper Palaeolithic: Middle Aurignacian (i.e., Aurignacian II with Font-Yves points), Châtelperronian, Middle Perigordian or Gravettian, Upper Perigordian, Final Perigordian, Noaillian, Protomagdalenian, Proto- and Early Solutrean, Middle Solutrean, Late Solutrean, Early Magdalenian, Middle Magdalenian, Late Magdalenian, Final Magdalenian, and Azilian. The Early Aurignacian, Late Aurignacian, and Aurignacian V industrial traditions were omitted from this analysis because of the absence of distinctive lithic weapon armatures.

A series of 49 discriminant function analyses using BMDP-7M for stepwise discriminant function analysis (Jennrich and Sampson 1983:519-537) were run within these specific cultural and industrial traditions in order to test the applicability of the morpho-functional classification system. Overall correct reclassification ranged from a low of 28.1% for the Final Perigordian to 100% for the Middle Aurignacian, Châtelperronian, Middle Perigordian, and Protomagdalenian (Table 4.2). The low percentage of correct reclassification for the Final Perigordian may reflect the typological distinctiveness of the segmented backed bladelet, which Bricker and David (1984:28) think represents a population quite distinct from Gravette points and other Perigordian backed pieces. On the other hand, the four perfect reclassifications may be the result of small sample sizes--even though discriminant function analysis handles small samples very well, requiring only that each group consist of at least two cases (Klecka 1980:11). In spite of the poor showing of the Final Perigordian, the mean correct reclassification rate for all 15 samples was 85.1%, thus validating the broad utility of the proposed morpho-functional classes.

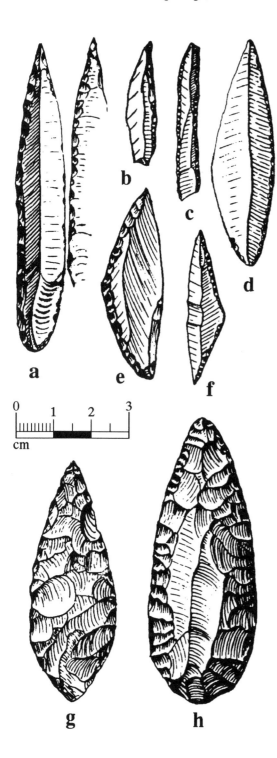

0    1    2    3
cm

**Figure 4.2.** Representative French Upper Palaeolithic lithic weapon armatures. *Backed Points:* (a) Gravette point from Pair-non-Pair (Cheynier 1958:Fig. 3); (b,c) backed bladelets from La Madeleine (de Sonneville-Bordes and Perrot 1956b:Fig. 5); (e) Azilian point from Abri de Villepin (de Sonneville-Bordes and Perrot 1956b:Fig. 5) (f) triangle (de Sonneville-Bordes and Perrot 1956b:Fig. 5). *Foliate Points:* (d) flèchette from La Gravette (Cheynier 1958:Fig. 3); (g) Solutrean bifacial laurel-leaf point from Badegoule (Cheynier 1958:Fig. 5); (h) Solutrean unifacial point from Le Trilobite (Cheynier 1958:Fig. 4). All illustrations are actual size.

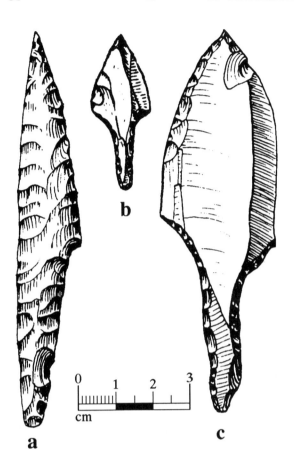

**Table 4.2.** Results of discriminant function analyses of lithic weapon armatures by morpho-functional classes.

| Cultural Affiliation | Mean Correct Reclassification | Variables |
|---|---|---|
| Middle Aurignacian | 100.0% | HiEA, HW |
| Châtelperronian | 100.0% | HW, LoEA |
| Middle Perigordian | 100.0% | HiEA, RD |
| Upper Perigordian | 81.1% | HiEA, HL |
| Final Perigordian | 28.1% | HiEA |
| Noaillian | 95.8% | PA |
| Protomagdalenian | 100.0% | Wt, LD |
| Proto- & Early Solutrean | 94.4% | Wt, HTh |
| Middle Solutrean | 57.1% | PA |
| Late Solutrean | 75.0% | RD |
| Early Magdalenian | 88.9% | PA |
| Middle Magdalenian | 89.1% | W, HL |
| Late Magdalenian | 89.7% | PA, TL |
| Final Magdalenian | 84.3% | HL, L |
| Azilian | 93.2% | W, RD |
| | | |
| Average Correct Reclassification | 85.1% | HiEA, PA, HL |
| | | |
| Upper Palaeolithic Combined Sample | 85.5% | HL, HW, HiEA |

**Key:** L = length; W = width; Wt = weight; TL = tip length; PA = penetrating angle; LD = left divergence; RD = right divergence; HiEA = high edge angle; LoEA = low edge angle; HL = haft length; HW = haft width; HTh = haft thickness.

**Figure 4.3.** Representative French Upper Palaeolithic lithic weapon armatures. *Shouldered/Tanged Points:* (a) Solutrean shouldered point from Le Fourneau du Diable (Cheynier 1958:Fig. 6); (b, c) Font-Robert points from Font-Robert (Cheynier 1958:Fig. 1 and Fig. 3). All illustrations are actual size.

A final confirmatory discriminant function analysis was run on a combined Upper Palaeolithic sample of 829 complete lithic points. The non-pointed backed forms, the so-called side elements, were excluded from this phase of analysis. The overall correct reclassification for the combined sample averaged 85.5%, which is quite consistent with the average computed for the individual runs (see Table 4.2).

Several variables were most valuable in discriminating among the four morpho-functional classes of lithic weapon armatures. They include measurements of the hafting element, primarily haft length and haft width, along with high edge angle, defined as the greatest of the two edge angle measurements, and penetrating angle.

Based on research in North America, I expected variables such as gross weight and haft width to differentiate most clearly among the four morpho-

functional classes of Upper Palaeolithic weapon armatures (Peterkin n.d.a). For example, Fenenga (1953) and Corliss (1972, 1980) attempted to distinguish functional classes of projectile points (i.e., dart points, arrow points, and spear points) by attributes such as gross weight and neck width. Other North American archaeologists (Christenson 1986a; Patterson 1985; Thomas 1978; Tucker 1980) employed multivariate statistical techniques to consider simultaneously a variety of important metric attributes. Their results suggest that, in many cases, functional classes of projectile points can be distinguished on the basis of weight alone.

In spite of its correlation with metric dimensions such as length and width, weight is considerably less important in differentiating among the morpho-functional classes of the French Upper Palaeolithic--even given the presence of geometric microliths in several of the industrial traditions. Consistent with the work in North America, however, measurements of the hafting element are of considerable utility. On the other hand, the importance of variables such as high edge angle and penetrating angle reflect the unique character of the French Upper Palaeolithic traditions. High edge angle, for example, reveals the importance of backed forms to industrial traditions like the Perigordian,

**Table 4.3.** Means and standard deviations (±) for four functional variables of lithic weapon armatures.

| | Tip Thickness | Penetrating Angle | Left Divergence | Right Divergence |
|---|---|---|---|---|
| *Backed Points:* | | | | |
| Aurignacian | 3.00 ± 1.10 | 45.8 ± 13.2 | 5.00 ± 3.46 | 4.33 ± 2.34 |
| Earlier Perigordian | 3.10 ± 1.01 | 60.3 ± 19.5 | 8.10 ± 2.88 | 9.52 ± 3.32 |
| Later Perigordian | 2.41 ± .82 | 38.5 ± 14.8 | 5.05 ± 2.92 | 5.82 ± 2.77 |
| Solutrean (n = 2) | 2.00 ± 0 | 25.0 ± 0 | 6.50 ± .71 | 2.00 ± 0 |
| Earlier Magdalenian | 1.68 ± .68 | 35.9 ± 13.3 | 3.90 ± 1.41 | 3.61 ± 1.39 |
| Later Magdalenian | 2.24 ± .90 | 46.2 ± 14.8 | 4.67 ± 2.16 | 4.87 ± 2.27 |
| *Foliate Points:* | | | | |
| Perigordian | 1.67 ± .52 | 40.8 ± 8.0 | 8.00 ± 3.03 | 7.50 ± 3.67 |
| Solutrean | 3.23 ± 1.17 | 54.8 ± 12.5 | 12.79 ± 4.44 | 12.27 ± 4.77 |
| Magdalenian | 2.16 ± .68 | 47.6 ± 11.8 | 7.58 ± 2.49 | 6.77 ± 2.46 |
| *Shouldered & Tanged Points:* | | | | |
| Upper Perigordian | 3.42 ± 1.75 | 49.2 ± 12.7 | 8.69 ± 3.58 | 9.31 ± 3.51 |
| Solutrean (n = 4) | 2.00 ± 0 | 41.2 ± 8.5 | 5.75 ± .50 | 6.75 ± 1.50 |
| Magdalenian | 1.80 ± .52 | 46.5 ± 10.1 | 6.18 ± 1.77 | 5.85 ± 1.94 |

while penetrating angle distinguishes between pointed forms and the so-called side elements, which may have been components of a composite-weapon delivery system.

The same 14 continuous variables were examined within morpho-functional classes, in order to identify any patterning in metric variability over time and across industrial traditions. Several variables, including mean tip thickness, penetrating angle, and left and right divergence, were remarkably consistent throughout the French Upper Palaeolithic, probably because of their importance to the performance of an effective hunting technology (Table 4.3). Mean tip thickness, for example, is related to the penetrating power required to disable prey, while the acuity of the penetrating point and its resistance to breakage are measured by penetrating angle. The consistent values for left and right divergence are a result of the symmetrical configuration necessary to the delivery of an aerodynamically effective projectile weapon.

Several other variables, however, exhibit some degree of diachronic variability within morpho-functional classes. For example, backed points became somewhat smaller late in the French Upper Palaeolithic, obviously reflecting the increasing importance of geometric microliths in the Magdalenian industrial traditions (Figure 4.4). The largest backed points were present in the Châtelperronian and Late Perigordian samples, although those of the Châtelperronian were more than twice as heavy as their Late Perigordian counterparts. This observation is probably related to the inclusion of the controversial Châtelperron point/knife. Current research indicates that the asymmetrical Châtelperron point/knife was most likely used as a knife, although some of the more symmetrical forms may have been hafted weapon armatures (Bricker 1978:180; Harrold, this volume). The average penetrating angle of 62.5° (s = 18.0) also sug-

gests that the Châtelperron point/knife might not have been an ideal weapon armature.

The same general trend towards a reduction in size is also evident in the backed side-element class, again reflecting the increasing predominance of backed microlithic forms in the Magdalenian (see Figure 4.4). This trend suggests the increasing sophistication of composite weapon armatures in the later Upper Palaeolithic, with several small backed geometric microliths fulfilling the same functional role as the larger backed points of the earlier Upper Palaeolithic (see Deacon 1984a, 1984b; Olszewski, this volume; Vayson de Pradenne 1936; and Vignard 1935 for reconstructions of composite weapon armatures utilizing geometric microliths).

Foliate points were fairly similar in terms of overall metric dimensions during the Perigordian,

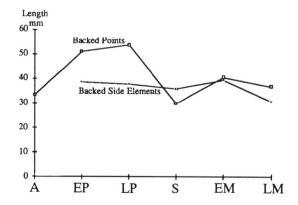

**Figure 4.4.** Size reduction in backed points and backed side elements during the French Upper Palaeolithic. **Key:** A = Aurignacian; EP = Earlier Perigordian; LP = Later Perigordian; S = Solutrean; EM = Earlier Magdalenian; LM = Later Magdalenian.

Solutrean, and Magdalenian. Solutrean bifacial laurel leaves, however, were considerably heavier than the other foliate points included in the study (Figure 4.5). Perhaps the more robust laurel-leaf points were used as armatures for thrusting spears rather than throwing spears. In addition, it is sometimes difficult to distinguish between a laurel-leaf point and a bifacially worked piece abandoned at a penultimate stage in the manufacturing process (Otte and Keeley 1990:579-580). A penetrating angle of approximately 55° is virtually a constant for all Solutrean foliate points ($\bar{X}$ = 54.78, s = 12.47), confirming the great degree of standardization which has long been assumed for the Solutrean. Haft dimensions are always large in the foliate point category, since the points in this morpho-functional class generally lack any obvious specialized hafting mechanism, with the exception of several rare subtypes of Solutrean laurel-leaves (Brézillon 1968; Smith 1966).

Points with hafting specializations are represented by a variety of shouldered and tanged points from the Late Perigordian, Solutrean, and Magdalenian. Because of the presence of a clearly defined penetrating triangle combined with an elongated hafting mechanism, this class tends to be rather long and thin. Nevertheless, shouldered and tanged points became narrower and thinner over time (Figure 4.6), suggesting the more efficient use of raw material in the standardized production of suitable blade blanks. The tip also became smaller over time, although haft length reached its apogee with the distinctive Magdalenian shouldered point.

Thus, the morpho-functional approach has proved useful to the analysis of lithic weapon armatures from the French Upper Palaeolithic. The use of powerful multivariate statistical techniques such as discriminant function analysis has confirmed the reality of the four broad morpho-functional classes, transcending the

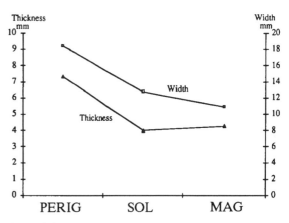

**Figure 4.6.** Change in dimensions of shouldered and tanged points during the French Upper Palaeolithic. **Key:** PERIG = Perigordian; SOL = Solutrean; MAG = Magdalenian.

traditional system of lithic typology and facilitating the examination of variability across cultural and temporal boundaries. Moreover, the morpho-functional classification scheme presented here closely corresponds to the point types recently defined and described by Demars and Laurent (1989), thus providing a bridge between subjective and objective, mathematically derived classification systems.

## ORGANIC WEAPON ARMATURES

### Sagaies

Sagaies were the numerically predominant class of complete organic weapon armatures represented in my sample (n = 141). They were present in almost all of the cultural/industrial traditions included in the study and were recovered from 17 of the 19 sites studied, making them particularly amenable to effective multivariate analysis. The same continuous variables were selected to ensure that results would be comparable to those from the analysis of the lithic weapon armatures: length, width, thickness, weight, tip length, tip thickness, penetrating angle, left divergence, right divergence, haft length, haft width, and haft thickness. The attributes high and low edge angle, which obviously do not pertain to organic weapon armatures, were eliminated from analysis. In addition, because basal treatment is so important in the definition and description of sagaie types (see, for example, Delporte et al. 1988), nominal-scale variables describing the hafting element (e.g., split-base, single vs. multiple bevels) were also included in some of the analyses (Figure 4.7).

The results suggest that the sagaies of the French Upper Palaeolithic were remarkably consistent in size range and in the profile of the longitudinal axis,

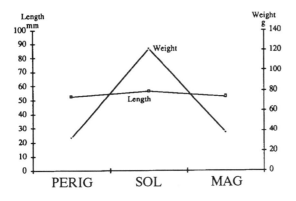

**Figure 4.5.** Weight of foliate points during the French Upper Palaeolithic. **Key:** PERIG = Perigordian; SOL = Solutrean; MAG = Magdalenian.

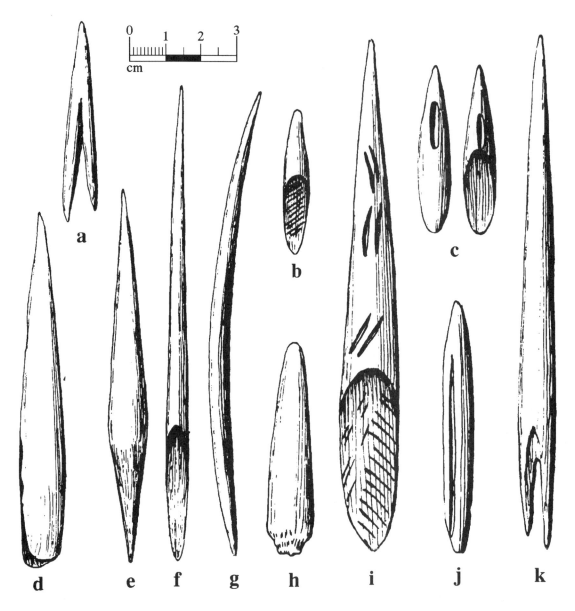

**Figure 4.7.** Representative French Upper Palaeolithic sagaies: (a,d) split-base sagaies from Isturitz (Cheynier 1958:Fig. 2); (b) bevel-base sagaie (Cheynier 1958:Fig. 7); (c) grooved bevel-base sagaie (Lussac-Angles type) from Laugerie-Haute (Cheynier 1958:Fig. 7); (e) lozenge-shaped sagaie from La Ferrassie (Cheynier 1958:Fig. 2); (f) bevel-base sagaie from Laugerie-Haute (Cheynier 1958:Fig. 4); (g) curved, bi-pointed sagaie from Laugerie-Haute (Cheynier 1958:Fig. 4); (h) whittled-base sagaie from Isturitz (Cheynier 1958:Fig. 4); (i) incised bevel-base sagaie from Le Placard (Cheynier 1958:Fig. 7); (j) grooved sagaie from Abri Reverdit (Cheynier 1958:Fig. 7); (k) forked-base sagaie from Isturitz (Cheynier 1958:Fig. 7). All illustrations are actual size.

irrespective of a variety of distinctive basal treatments and hafting techniques (Peterkin n.d.d). The sole exception in my sample is the split-base point of the Early Aurignacian, which differed in overall size as well as in the characteristics of the hafting element.

Histograms and scatter diagrams of the 12 continuous variables revealed a virtually normal distribution for the total sample of Upper Palaeolithic sagaies, with no evidence of multi-modality. An exploratory factor analysis using BMDP-4M (Davis 1986:516; Frane et

**Table 4.4**. Unrotated and rotated factor loadings (pattern) and other results of the factor analysis of French Upper Palaeolithic sagaies.

| | Commu- nalities | Unrotated Factors | | | Rotated Factors | | |
|---|---|---|---|---|---|---|---|
| | | 1 | 2 | 3 | 1 | 2 | 3 |
| Length | .5711 | .681 | .297 | -.140 | .524 | -.028 | .432 |
| Width | .8989 | .928 | -.067 | -.185 | .897 | .034 | .108 |
| Thickness | .7784 | .790 | -.116 | .374 | .407 | .609 | .060 |
| Weight | .8029 | .895 | .001 | -.052 | .748 | .159 | .178 |
| Tip Length | .6635 | .342 | .730 | .114 | -.101 | .105 | .820 |
| Tip Thickness | .8492 | .511 | -.001 | .767 | -.143 | .948 | .142 |
| Penetrating Angle | .4924 | .589 | -.227 | .306 | .340 | .502 | -.097 |
| Left Divergence | .7453 | .831 | -.022 | -.233 | .837 | -.048 | .133 |
| Right Divergence | .8069 | .827 | -.107 | -.334 | .940 | -.145 | .040 |
| Haft Length | .7413 | .585 | .631 | -.029 | .235 | .022 | .760 |
| Haft Width | .6718 | .768 | -.257 | -.130 | .806 | .080 | -.114 |
| Haft Thickness | .5760 | .679 | -.340 | -.012 | .684 | .197 | -.211 |
| | | | | | | | |
| Eigenvalues | | 6.2399 | 1.2827 | 1.0751 | | | |
| Cum. % of Total Variance Explained | | 52.00% | 62.69% | 71.65% | | | |

al. 1983:480-499) with factor extraction by principal components analysis and direct quartimin oblique rotation was employed to pinpoint any significant patterning of attribute variability.[2] Although the first factor identified is typically a factor of gross size (Sneath and Sokal 1974), length itself was not an important consideration in the patterning of variability described by any of these factors. Instead, the factors indicate a strong relationship among width, weight, left and right divergence, and, to a lesser degree, thickness and haft width (Table 4.4).

A series of additional statistical tests incorporated information on important nominal-scale variables such as raw material, cross-section of the shaft, and specialized basal treatments. One-way analyses of variance using these nominal-scale data along with factor scores for each sagaie suggest several relationships between factor scores and specific basal treatments (Table 4.5). For example, sagaies with high loadings for factor one tend to have bases that are split rather than beveled.

Because these results describe the stereotypical Aurignacian lozengic-shaped point, and especially the split-base points of the Early Aurignacian, an additional series of factor analyses were run based on assemblage samples. Site-specific samples of complete Upper Palaeolithic sagaies were characterized as Earlier Aurignacian (Early and Middle Aurignacian), Later Aurignacian (Late Aurignacian and Aurignacian V), Upper Perigordian (Perigordian Va, Perigordian Vb, Final Perigordian, and Protomagdalenian), Earlier Magdalenian (Early and Middle Magdalenian), and Later Magdalenian (Late and Final Magdalenian). Two complete Solutrean sagaies were dropped from this phase of analysis.

Mean metric data for the 12 continuous variables were considered, along with percentage of split, beveled, and stemmed bases and the presence of blood runnels. As expected, the split-base sagaies of the Earlier Aurignacian loaded high on factor one.

The subdivision of Upper Palaeolithic sagaies into two underlying groups, split-base points versus all other sagaies, was confirmed by two discriminant function analyses utilizing BMDP-7M for stepwise discrimination of variables (Jennrich and Sampson 1983:519-537). The first discriminant function analysis considered 37 complete Aurignacian sagaies, classified as split-base or other. Split-base points were correctly reclassified 83.3% of the time. As predicted from the earlier factor analyses and from the graphic representation of mean metric data, the variables haft width, tip length, haft thickness, and length were the most important variables distinguishing between split-base points and other Aurignacian sagaies.

A second discriminant function analysis based on the entire collection of Upper Palaeolithic sagaies substantiated these results with an overall correct reclassification rate of 97.2%. The same discriminating variables were joined by tip thickness and width. The presence of width is related to the difference in geometric configuration between the lozengic-shaped sagaies of the Aurignacian and the slender sagaies typical of the other Upper Palaeolithic traditions. Tip thickness is probably a function of the rather blunt tips characteristic of Earlier Aurignacian sagaies; their mean penetrating angle is 36.25° (s = 19.44), while the other Upper Palaeolithic samples average 30° (s = 11.9) (Figure 4.8).

The use of these multivariate statistical techniques thus confirm the notion that Upper Palaeolithic sagaies can be subdivided into two distinctively different classes, the split-base points of the Early Aurignacian and all other sagaies. Perhaps the Early Aurignacian split-base points represent the beginning of a techno-

**Table 4.5.** Results of one-way analyses of variance between nominal-scale data and factors 1, 2, and 3 for Upper Palaeolithic sagaies.

| Variables | Factor 1 | Factor 2 | Factor 3 |
|---|---|---|---|
| Raw Material | F=9.92, p<.001 | F=11.67, p<.001 | |
| Shaft Cross-Section | F=2.91, p=.011 | F=3.08, p=.007 | |
| Beveled Base | F=2.77, p=.044 non > beveled | F=4.32, p=.006 single > non & double | F=5.30, p=.002 single > non & double |
| Split Base | F=34.54, p<.001 split > non | | |
| Stemmed/Whittled Base | F=7.63, p=.001 non > stemmed | | F=11.31, p<.001 non > stemmed |
| Grooved | | F=8.96, p=.003 grooved > non | |

evolutionary process in the production of organic weapon armatures. By the Later Aurignacian, however, an aerodynamically effective organic weapon armature had been perfected. Although later modifications were made in terms of basal treatment and concomitant hafting technology, as well as in increasing decorative elaboration, the basic dimensions and geometric profile of sagaies varied little throughout the rest of the French Upper Palaeolithic (see Knecht 1993 and this volume for a comprehensive treatment of Early Upper Palaeolithic sagaies, including techniques of manufacture and experimental performance).

It should be noted that two other sagaie types, which were not present in great numbers in my Upper Palaeolithic sample, might represent additional subclasses of Upper Palaeolithic sagaies. The curved, bi-pointed sagaies from the Perigordian VI at Abri Pataud and the Perigordian VI and Aurignacian V at Laugerie-Haute might represent a unique, self-barbed sagaie which was hafted along the incised central portion of the shaft (Bricker and David 1984:95; D. Peyrony and E. Peyrony 1938:23; Pike-Tay and Bricker, this volume). Nevertheless, these sagaies fall within the expected range of variation for the metric variables studied, differing only in hypothetical mode of hafting. The distinctive Isturitz sagaie was not represented in my sample. Only a small number of these large sagaies are complete. The average length for the five complete specimens in *Fiches typologiques I* (de Sonneville-Bordes 1988:8) is 150.8 mm (s = 50.9) as compared to an overall average of 85.86 mm (s = 39.72) for my Upper Palaeolithic sample.

I also tested my data against the eight sagaie subtypes proposed by the authors of *Fiches typologiques I* on sagaies (Delporte et al. 1988): (1) Aurignacian sagaies with simple bases; (2) split-base sagaies; (3) sagaies with single-beveled bases, including Lussac-Angles sagaies; (4) sagaies with double-bev-

eled bases; (5) sagaies with *"raccourcie"* or "whittled" bases (McComb 1989:273, Fig. 4:10);[3] (6) forked-base sagaies; (7) bi-pointed sagaies; and (8) Isturitz sagaies. Because Isturitz sagaies were not present in my sample, they were omitted from this analysis.

A series of four discriminant function analyses, again using BMDP-7M (Jennrich and Sampson 1983: 519-537), were run to determine if this typological classification system for Upper Palaeolithic sagaies was corroborated by my metric data on the same 12 continuous variables considered before. Mean reclassification rates for the seven remaining types, with the distinctive Lussac-Angles sagaies considered as a separate type, yielded an overall correct reclassification rate of only 48.2%. Several additional discriminant analyses, using somewhat different groupings of sagaie types, produced reclassification rates that were little better than 50% and never exceeded 70%. It is apparent that the distinctions made by this new typological classification system for Upper Palaeolithic sagaies do not conform very closely to the results of

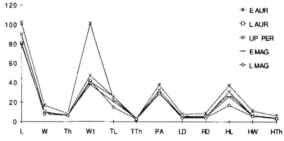

**Figure 4.8.** Means of the major continuous variables used in the analysis of French Upper Palaeolithic sagaies. **Key:** L = length; W = width; Th = thickness; Wt = weight; TL = tip length; TTh = tip thickness; PA = penetrating angle; LD = left divergence; RD = right divergence; HL = haft length; HW = haft width; HTh = haft thickness.

**Table 4.6.** Unrotated and rotated factor loadings (pattern) and other results of an exploratory factor analysis of Magdalenian and Azilian harpoons.

| | Commu-nalities | Unrotated Factors | | | | Rotated Factors | | | |
|---|---|---|---|---|---|---|---|---|---|
| | | 1 | 2 | 3 | 4 | 1 | 2 | 3 | 4 |
| Length | .8994 | .624 | -.647 | .150 | -.263 | -.034 | .911 | .117 | -.035 |
| Width | .9135 | .741 | .564 | -.172 | -.128 | .946 | .006 | -.015 | .096 |
| Thickness | .8286 | .777 | -.427 | .055 | .198 | .111 | .520 | .566 | -.061 |
| Weight | .9220 | .902 | -.289 | .111 | -.110 | .349 | .696 | .281 | .065 |
| Tip Length | .7229 | .155 | .337 | .763 | -.051 | .016 | .075 | .018 | .848 |
| Tip Thickness | .6828 | .644 | -.226 | -.465 | .032 | .431 | .303 | .251 | -.476 |
| Penetrating Angle | .6873 | .586 | -.020 | -.316 | .494 | .334 | -.114 | .659 | -.293 |
| Left Divergence | .6574 | .634 | .448 | .223 | -.071 | .618 | .097 | .076 | .414 |
| Right Divergence | .9082 | .607 | .553 | -.439 | -.202 | .990 | -.067 | -.164 | -.163 |
| Barbed Length | .9018 | .387 | -.642 | .198 | -.549 | -.112 | .993 | -.243 | .012 |
| Haft Length | .6227 | .644 | .453 | .019 | -.051 | .708 | .034 | .074 | .224 |
| Haft Width | .5884 | .294 | .519 | .481 | .038 | .316 | -.108 | .080 | .652 |
| Haft Thickness | .9004 | .434 | -.307 | .352 | .703 | -.295 | .040 | .955 | .209 |
| Eigenvalues | | 4.7465 | 2.6561 | 1.6026 | 1.2302 | | | | |
| Cum. % of Total Variance Explained | | 36.51% | 56.94% | 69.27% | 78.73% | | | | |

a multivariate statistical analysis of the major continuous variables.

## Harpoons

Only 26 complete harpoons were represented in my sample, from the Late Magdalenian, Final Magdalenian, and Azilian levels of eight archaeological sites in Ariège, Dordogne, and Gironde (Figure 4.9). The same 12 continuous variables (length, width, thickness, weight, tip length, tip width, penetrating angle, left and right divergence, haft length, haft width, and haft thickness), along with a measurement recording barbed length, were considered in the application of a variety of multivariate statistical techniques. Preliminary results indicate that harpoons with perforated bases are morpho-functionally distinct from other harpoons; the presence of such a perforation certainly suggests the existence of a sophisticated technology for the retrieval of game and/or expended weapon armatures (Peterkin n.d.d).

An exploratory factor analysis using BMDP-4M (Davis 1986:516; Frane et al. 1983:480-499) with factor extraction by principal components analysis and direct quartimin oblique rotation was employed to pinpoint any significant patterning of harpoon variability. Once again, the first factor identified does not reflect the typical factor of gross size (Sneath and Sokal 1974); instead, this factor represents a more specific index of overall robusticity (thickness and weight) (Table 4.6). Further examination of the factor scores generated by this analysis, however, suggests that factor 1 is clearly associated with flattened Azilian harpoons, which have broad, perforated bases (see Figure 4.9).

Additional statistical tests incorporated important information on nominal-scale variables, including raw material, cross-section(s) of the tip and shaft, uniserial vs. biserial barbs, the presence of grooves and decorative elaboration, as well as specific basal modifications such as perforations and collars. One-way analyses of variance using these nominal-scale data along with factor scores for each harpoon again distinguish harpoons with perforated bases, including both Magdalenian and Azilian forms, from other harpoons (Table 4.7).

A series of discriminant function analyses using BMDP-7M for stepwise discrimination of variables (Jennrich and Sampson 1983:519-537) was employed to highlight other potential models for the subdivision of harpoons, based on morphological features and/or cultural historical context (Table 4.8). All four of the discriminant function analyses yielded good results, with correct reclassification rates ranging from 84.6%, when Late Magdalenian, Final Magdalenian, and Azilian harpoons were considered as discrete analytical units, to 100%, when harpoons were subdivided into only two groups, Magdalenian vs. Azilian. In all cases, attributes of the hafting element, such as haft width and haft thickness, discriminate most clearly among the various classes of harpoons, again suggesting that harpoons with basal perforations form a discrete morpho-functional category.

Width is also important in some of the discriminate function analyses, which suggests that uniserially barbed harpoons can be distinguished from biserially barbed harpoons on the basis of width. Thickness is a consideration only when discriminating between the rounded Magdalenian harpoons and the flattened deer antler harpoons of the Azilian.

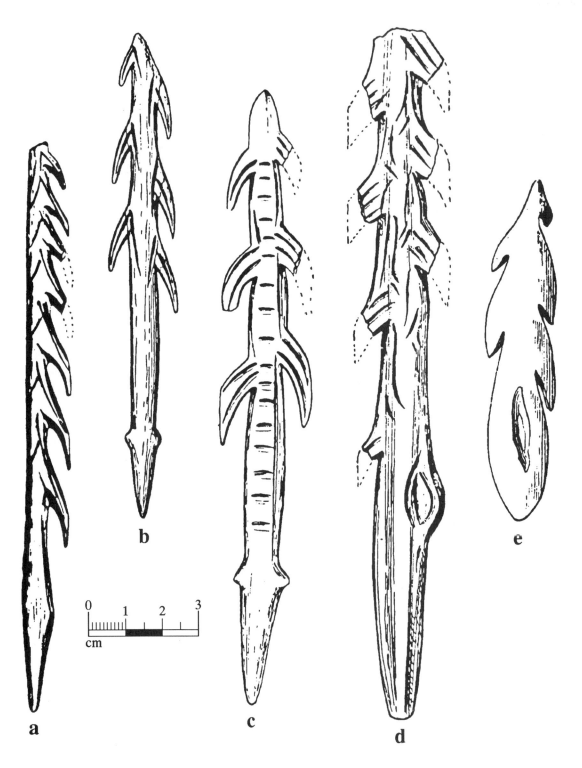

**Figure 4.9.** Representative Magdalenian and Azilian harpoons: (a) uniserial harpoon from Mas d'Azil (Breuil 1912:Fig. 32); (b) biserial harpoon from Massat (Breuil 1912:Fig. 34); (c) biserial harpoon from La Madeleine (Breuil 1912:Fig. 34); (d) biserial harpoon with perforated base from La Madeleine (Breuil 1912:Fig. 35); (e) flattened Azilian harpoon with perforated base from Mas d'Azil (Peyrony 1923:Fig. 56). All illustrations are actual size.

**Table 4.7.** Results of one-way analyses of variance between nominal-scale data and factors 1, 2, 3, and 4 for Magdalenian and Azilian harpoons.

| Variables | Factor 1 | Factor 2 | Factor 3 | Factor 4 |
|---|---|---|---|---|
| Raw Material | | F=6.32, p=.019 bone > antler | | |
| Tip X-Section | F=5.12, p=.033 planoconvex > biconvex | F=12.14, p=.002 planoconvex > biconvex | | |
| Barbs | | | F=5.34, p=.030 uniserial > biserial | |
| Basal Striations | | | F=16.39, p=.000 | |
| Stemmed Base | | | | F=7.99, p=.009 non > stemmed |
| Perforated Base | F=4.45, p=.045 | | | F=6.90, p=.015 |
| Grooved | | F=9.21, p=.006 | | |

This small series of harpoons was also examined using both continuous and nominal-scale variables as input for several additional factor analyses. Nominal-scale variables are obviously crucial to understanding the variation among harpoons, but frequency data from such small assemblage-based samples must be treated with care. Following the suggestion of Binford (1987) in his analysis of the data from Torralba, harpoon attribute frequencies were standardized within each attribute set by converting them to signed Chi-square values. The Chi-square distribution is, of course, particularly appropriate when dealing with small samples. These values and the assemblage means for the continuous variables were transformed to z-scores and entered as input for the factor analyses.

Seven assemblage samples, representing seven archaeological sites from Ariège, Gironde, and Dordogne, were analyzed. The small number of assemblage samples, however, limited the number of variables that could be considered. Several continuous variables that were important in the previous factor analysis and discriminant function analyses of harpoons were selected, including length, barbed length, haft width, and haft thickness. Nominal-scale variables recording barb characteristics (uniserial vs. biserial), perforated basal treatment, and the presence of grooved blood runnels were considered in dichotomous form.

The results from this trial study of Magdalenian and Azilian harpoons complement those obtained from the earlier analyses of the continuous variables alone. Separate factor analyses were run considering uniserial and biserial barbed harpoons. Three factors were identified in the analysis of uniserial harpoons (Table 4.9). Factor 1 indicates a very strong relationship between haft width and the presence of perforated basal

treatment, which is logical because this basal treatment requires the hafting element to be wide enough to accommodate a perforation. The relationship between length and barbed length is described by factor 2, while factor 3 suggests that uniserially barbed harpoons have thick hafting elements.

Biserially barbed harpoons, on the other hand, are described by a pair of significant factors (Table 4.10). Again, the first factor shows a strong relationship between haft width and the existence of perforations. Factor 2 indicates a strong negative relationship between haft thickness and the presence of biserial barbs, suggesting that uniserially barbed harpoons are considerably thicker at the base than biserially barbed harpoons. This observation is no doubt due to the presence of four Azilian harpoons, with their characteristic flattened cross-sections and large basal perforations. Thus, the typological distinctiveness of perforated harpoons has been substantiated by this technique.

The analysis of the factor scores for each assemblage sample presents a slightly different picture of harpoon variability in the very late French Upper Palaeolithic. The graphic plots of the factor scores

**Table 4.8.** Results of discriminant function analyses of Magdalenian and Azilian harpoon types.

| Harpoon Types | Overall Correct Reclassification | Variables |
|---|---|---|
| Uniserial, biserial | 88.5% | HTh, W, L |
| Uniserial, biserial, & Azilian | 88.5% | HW, HTh, W |
| Late & Final Magdalenian, Azilian | 84.6% | HW, HTh, L |
| Magdalenian, Azilian | 100.0% | HW, Th |

**Key:** L = length; W = width; Th = thickness; HW = haft width; HTh = haft thickness.

**Table 4.9.** Unrotated and rotated factor loadings (pattern) and other results of a factor analysis of Magdalenian and Azilian harpoons, using both continuous and standardized nominal-scale data. This factor analysis selected for the presence of uniserial harpoons.

| | Commu-nalities | Unrotated Factors | | | Rotated Factors | | |
|---|---|---|---|---|---|---|---|
| | | 1 | 2 | 3 | 1 | 2 | 3 |
| Length | .9902 | .867 | -.149 | .464 | -.162 | .855 | .196 |
| Barbed Length | .9913 | .647 | -.427 | .625 | .055 | 1.031* | -.111 |
| Haft Width | .9425 | -.775 | .261 | .523 | 1.023* | .080 | .119 |
| Haft Thickness | .9860 | .376 | .885 | .248 | .199 | .030 | 1.018* |
| Uniserial | .9838 | .774 | .612 | -.098 | -.429 | -.028 | .808 |
| Perforated Base | .9430 | -.906 | .288 | .197 | .817 | -.296 | .047 |
| Grooved | .9818 | .956 | .065 | -.251 | -.813 | .121 | .301 |
| | | | | | | | |
| Eigenvalues | | 4.2477 | 1.5177 | 1.0530 | | | |
| Cum. % of Total Variance Explained | | 60.68% | 82.36% | 97.41% | | | |

*Factor loadings slightly greater than unity are likely a result of rounding error.

clearly indicate some temporal patterning, with the Late Magdalenian and Azilian samples distinct from the more numerous Final Magdalenian assemblages. The plots also suggest a degree of geographic variability, with the Pyrenean sites clustered together.

Thus, while the continuous metric variables represent functional attributes shared by all harpoons, the nominal-scale variables add a potential stylistic component to the patterning of variability. These temporal/spatial clusters may, in fact, correspond to what Sackett (1977, 1982, 1985, 1986a, 1986b, 1990) terms isochrestic style--i.e., stylistic variation within functionally equivalent tool forms.

## FAUNAL CORRELATIONS

The ultimate goal of this statistical approach, however, is to examine the complex interrelationships among hunting technology, prey exploitation, and the behavioral correlates of hunting (i.e., hunting strategies and techniques) in the French Upper Palaeolithic, including, for example, the joint analysis of Upper Palaeolithic lithic weapon armatures and associated faunal assemblages (Peterkin n.d.c). A model for such an approach was provided by Clark's (1989) analysis of the material from La Riera, which included the examination of the covariation of lithic and faunal variables. Results of an R-mode factor analysis found the persistent association of some lithic variables (retouched tools, debitage, and cores) to MNI (minimum number of individuals) data on six economic species. For example, ibex was repeatedly associated with Solutrean points, while red deer was associated with chunks, nuclei, and shatter (Clark 1989:41-43).

For the Upper Palaeolithic sites included in my study, faunal information was gathered from published compilations and relevant site reports (Bouchud 1964 for La Chèvre; Delpech 1981 for Enlène; Delpech 1983 for all other sites studied) (see Table 4.1). Percentage of faunal representation was calculated for 13 species of common large terrestrial mammals from the orders Perissodactyla and Artiodactyla: ibex (*Capra ibex*), chamois (*Rupicapra rupicapra*), saiga antelope (*Saiga tatarica*), mammoth (*Mammuthus primigenius*), woolly rhinoceros (*Coelodonta antiquitatis*), reindeer (*Rangifer tarandus*), horse (*Equus caballus*), bovines (*Bos primigenius* and *Bison priscus*), red deer (*Cervus elaphus*), roe deer (*Capreolus capreolus*), moose (*Alces alces*), Irish elk (*Megaloceros*), and boar (*Sus scrofa*). Several species were combined into climatic/environmental complexes for analysis--ibex and chamois were combined into a mountain complex, mammoth and woolly rhino into a steppe complex, and roe deer, moose, and *Megaloceros* into a forest complex (Delpech 1983; Kurtén 1968).

**Table 4.10.** Unrotated and rotated factor loadings (pattern) and other results of a factor analysis of Magdalenian and Azilian harpoons, using both continuous and standardized nominal-scale data. This factor analysis selected for the presence of biserial harpoons.

| | Commu-nalities | Unrotated | | Rotated | |
|---|---|---|---|---|---|
| | | 1 | 2 | 1 | 2 |
| Length | .8580 | .915 | .143 | -.727 | .424 |
| Barbed Length | .5677 | .748 | .087 | -.611 | .317 |
| Haft Width | .8266 | -.736 | .533 | .934 | .297 |
| Haft Thick. | .7410 | .334 | .794 | .134 | .884 |
| Biserial | .8449 | -.640 | -.660 | .207 | -.847 |
| Perf. Base | .9315 | -.897 | .356 | .980 | .073 |
| Grooved | .8390 | .896 | -.191 | -.890 | .089 |
| | | | | | |
| Eigenvalues | | 4.0677 | 1.5411 | | |
| Cum. % of Total Variance Explained | | 58.11% | 80.13% | | |

**Table 4.11.** Assemblage samples with quantifiable faunal information: percentage of representation for eight economic species and/or climatic complexes (without reindeer) and prey profile and index of diversity (with reindeer).

| Assemblages | Ib/Ch | Saiga | Mm/Rh | Horse | Bovs | Red | Roe/M | Boar | PrPr | ID |
|---|---|---|---|---|---|---|---|---|---|---|
| La Chèvre EA | 1.69 | 0.00 | 1.69 | 76.27 | 20.34 | 0.00 | 0.00 | 0.00 | 256.18 | 2 |
| La Chèvre MA | .66 | 0.00 | 0.00 | 17.22 | 71.52 | 8.61 | 0.00 | 1.99 | 495.38 | 4 |
| La Chèvre LP* | 0.00 | 0.00 | 25.00 | 37.50 | 12.50 | 25.00 | 0.00 | 0.00 | 667.94 | 5 |
| La Chèvre MP* | 0.00 | 0.00 | 0.00 | 71.43 | 14.29 | 0.00 | 14.29 | 0.00 | 235.52 | 2 |
| Les Eglises FM* | 99.95 | 0.00 | 0.00 | 0.00 | 0.00 | 0.04 | 0.02 | 0.00 | 53.66 | 1 |
| Enlène MM* | 2.34 | 0.00 | 0.00 | 17.73 | 79.93 | 0.00 | 0.00 | 0.00 | 689.85 | 2 |
| Abri Faustin FM* | 0.00 | 0.00 | 0.00 | 54.76 | 21.43 | 17.86 | 4.76 | 1.19 | 393.76 | 4 |
| La Ferrassie EA | 4.00 | 0.00 | 0.00 | 14.00 | 74.00 | 6.00 | 0.00 | 2.00 | 289.22 | 2 |
| La Ferrassie MA | 1.41 | 0.00 | 0.00 | 3.52 | 56.34 | 20.42 | 3.52 | 14.79 | 481.92 | 4 |
| La Ferrassie LA | 7.21 | 0.00 | 0.00 | 11.86 | 26.51 | 43.72 | 8.60 | 2.09 | 292.40 | 6 |
| La Ferrassie LP* | 0.00 | 0.00 | 0.00 | 9.68 | 87.10 | 0.00 | 0.00 | 3.23 | 410.68 | 2 |
| La Ferrassie UP* | 1.78 | 0.00 | 0.00 | 1.97 | 5.43 | 84.21 | 5.92 | 0.69 | 192.84 | 3 |
| Flageolet I EA | 50.00 | 0.00 | 0.00 | 50.00 | 0.00 | 0.00 | 0.00 | 0.00 | 194.95 | 3 |
| Flageolet I MA* | 5.00 | 0.00 | 0.00 | 25.00 | 10.00 | 50.00 | 5.00 | 5.00 | 247.60 | 4 |
| Flageolet I UP* | 8.19 | 0.00 | 0.00 | 8.95 | 11.24 | 69.33 | 2.29 | 0.00 | 221.85 | 5 |
| Flageolet I PVc* | 14.29 | 0.00 | 0.00 | 42.86 | 10.71 | 28.57 | 0.00 | 3.57 | 192.99 | 1 |
| Flageolet I FP* | 0.00 | 0.00 | 0.00 | 10.00 | 10.00 | 80.00 | 0.00 | 0.00 | 192.14 | 2 |
| Flageolet II FM | 9.76 | 21.95 | 0.00 | 14.63 | 9.76 | 43.90 | 0.00 | 0.00 | 187.91 | 1 |
| Laugerie-Haute FP | 16.67 | 0.00 | 0.00 | 0.00 | 0.00 | 83.33 | 0.00 | 0.00 | 183.81 | 1 |
| Laugerie-Haute PM* | 42.19 | 0.00 | 0.00 | 3.13 | 3.13 | 51.56 | 0.00 | 0.00 | 178.17 | 3 |
| Laugerie-Haute AV | 50.00 | 0.00 | 0.00 | 50.00 | 0.00 | 0.00 | 0.00 | 0.00 | 198.80 | 3 |
| Laugerie-Haute ES* | 9.73 | 0.00 | 21.24 | 63.72 | 2.65 | 2.65 | 0.00 | 0.00 | 229.21 | 1 |
| Laugerie-Haute MS* | 9.30 | 0.00 | 53.49 | 36.05 | 1.16 | 0.00 | 0.00 | 0.00 | 385.95 | 2 |
| Laugerie-Haute LS* | 1.33 | 0.00 | 28.00 | 65.33 | 1.33 | 4.00 | 0.00 | 0.00 | 234.43 | 1 |
| Laugerie-Haute EM* | 15.16 | 11.76 | 0.23 | 59.95 | 7.01 | 5.88 | 0.00 | 0.00 | 199.84 | 2 |
| La Madeleine MM* | 1.25 | 0.00 | 0.00 | 96.25 | 2.50 | 0.00 | 0.00 | 0.00 | 232.24 | 2 |
| La Madeleine LM* | 4.94 | 0.00 | 0.00 | 56.17 | 38.27 | 0.00 | 0.62 | 0.00 | 198.66 | 1 |
| La Madeleine FM* | 9.38 | 0.00 | 0.00 | 15.63 | 75.00 | 0.00 | 0.00 | 0.00 | 199.02 | 1 |
| Le Morin LM* | 0.00 | 0.00 | 0.00 | 0.00 | 10.00 | 0.00 | 0.00 | 0.00 | 297.45 | 2 |
| Le Morin FM* | 0.00 | 0.00 | 0.00 | 28.34 | 45.98 | 17.23 | 0.96 | 7.48 | 363.15 | 4 |
| Abri Rhodes AZ | 14.29 | 0.00 | 0.00 | 0.00 | 0.00 | 21.43 | 16.67 | 47.62 | 106.90 | 4 |

*Assemblage samples included in the lithic/faunal factor analyses. **Key:** *Assemblages:* EA = Early Aurignacian; MA = Middle Aurignacian; LA = Late Aurignacian; AV = Aurignacian V; LP = Châtelperronian; MP = Middle Perigordian; UP = Upper Perigordian; FP = Final Perigordian; PVc = Noaillian; PM = Protomagdalenian; ES = Proto- & Early Solutrean; MS = Middle Solutrean; LS = Late Solutrean; EM = Early Magdalenian; MM = Middle Magdalenian; LM = Late Magdalenian; FM = Final Magdalenian; AZ = Azilian. *Fauna:* Ib/Ch = ibex/chamois; Saiga; Mm/Rh = mammoth/woolly rhino; Horse; Bovs = *Bos* and *Bison*; Red = red deer; Roe/M = roe deer/moose/*Megaloceros*; Boar; PrPr = prey profile; ID = simple index of diversity. Percentages calculated from raw bone counts in Bouchud (1964) and Delpech (1981, 1983).

Reindeer, of course, dominate many Upper Palaeolithic assemblages. In fact, reindeer comprise more than 75% of the large vertebrate fauna in 17 of the 31 assemblages with quantifiable faunal information. Because the presence of reindeer masks other patterning of faunal variability, they were not included in this analysis.

I derived five basic faunal clusters using BMDP clustering algorithms (BMDP-2M for cluster analysis of cases [Engelman 1983:456-463] and BMDP-KM for K-means clustering of cases [Engelman and Hartigan 1983:464-473]): bovines, red deer, ibex, horse, and a mixed group with a diversified faunal profile. Two other measurements of faunal variability were also utilized, the prey profile and a simple index of diversity. The prey profile is the total of the products of the raw percentage of each species present times the mean

body weight for the species. Mean body weights were estimated from information on extant species compiled from standard reference works (Keienburg 1990; Macdonald 1984; Walker 1975). The index of diversity is the simple count of the number of major mammal species present at a pre-determined level of five percent of the total faunal assemblage (see Grayson 1984 and Neeley and Clark, this volume for a more sophisticated approach to the measurement of taxonomic richness and the calculation of diversity indices).

Lithic and faunal data were combined for the next stage of analysis, a series of exploratory R-mode factor analyses with factor extraction by principal components analysis and direct quartimin oblique rotation using BMDP-4M (Davis 1986:516; Frane et al. 1983:480-499; Rummel 1967:446). Based on the earlier discriminant function analyses of complete lithic weapon armatures, the seven continuous variables that were most important in distinguishing among morpho-functional classes were adopted for these factor analyses: length, width, penetrating angle, right divergence, high edge angle, haft length, and haft width. Means were computed for each assemblage sample.

Numerical faunal data for each assemblage sample were provided by percentage of representation, along with canonical variables from a previous discriminant function analysis and the figures for prey profile and index of diversity (Table 4.11). Although faunal information was available for 31 assemblage samples, 10 of the cases were eliminated because they possessed only organic weapon armatures. These assemblages included all Early Aurignacian, Late Aurignacian, and Aurignacian V assemblages, as well as several other assemblage samples which lacked lithic weapon armatures.

Results from these preliminary factor analyses suggest some patterning in faunal variability, with possible relationships between bovines and red deer and between ibex and horse (Table 4.12). In addition, the lithic variable of haft length is positively associated with the proportion of bovines present at a site (e.g., La Ferrassie Lower Perigordian and La Madeleine Final Magdalenian). This relationship, which is being investigated in ongoing research, suggests that the efficient procurement of bovines necessitated a durable hafting technology coupled with specific hunting techniques.

**Table 4.12.** Results from a series of factor analyses including lithic and faunal data for French Upper Palaeolithic assemblage samples. These preliminary results are being investigated in continuing research.

| Factor Analysis | Factor | Rotated Factor Loadings | Correlation |
|---|---|---|---|
| % of Bovines, FnX, FnY, lithic variables | 2 | FnX = .979 Bov = .929 | .890 |
| % of Bovines, lithic variables | 2 | Bov = .778 HL = .861 | .473 |
| % of Horse, FnX, FnY, lithic variables | 2 | FnX = .881 Hrs = -.821 | -.586 |
| % of Ibex, FnX, FnY, lithic variables | 2 | FnX = .889 Ibx = -.716 | -.430 |
| % of Red Deer, FnX, FnY, lithic variables | 2 | FnY = .967 Red = .977 | -.990 |

**Key:** *Lithic variables:* length, width, penetrating angle, right divergence, high edge angle, haft length, and haft width. *Faunal variables:* % of representation, FnX, and FnY. FnX and FnY are canonical variables for each assemblage sample that were derived from a stepwise discriminant function analysis of Upper Palaeolithic faunal assemblages. They are another quantifiable representation of the faunal profile of each assemblage sample.

## CONCLUSION

The application of multivariate statistical techniques to the analysis of lithic and organic weapon armatures from the French Upper Palaeolithic has demonstrated that the traditional typological distinctions are underlain by broad, morpho-functional classes which encourage the examination of isochrestic variability across cultural and temporal boundaries (Chase 1991; Sackett 1977, 1982, 1985, 1986a, 1986b, 1990). Although the organic weapon armatures did not fall into neat morpho-functional classes like those defined for lithic weapon armatures, certain distinctive organic weapon armatures--e.g., the Early Aurignacian split-base point and harpoons with basal perforations--nevertheless form discrete classes which remain separate from the continuum of variation represented by the other types of sagaies and harpoons.

Although a consideration of continuous variables alone was adequate to establish broad morpho-functional classes of lithic weapon armatures, the inclusion of nominal-scale data is crucial to a complete assessment of organic weapon armatures. This difference, which has been intuitively recognized in the construction of formal typological systems for organic weapon armatures, has now been validated by a multivariate statistical approach. In fact, organic weapon armatures may be more sensitive indicators of isochrestic variability, perhaps as a result of the technological constraints of working with organic materials. Because bone and antler are more malleable than lithic raw materials, they are more suited to a variety of hafting techniques and/or to the incorporation of extraneous features, such as the presence of grooved blood runnels, striations, and even non-utilitarian decorative elaboration.

Preliminary results of a broader analysis suggest that morpho-functional classes of lithic weapon armatures are, in turn, related to the exploitation of preferred faunal species and to specialized hunting techniques and other behavioral correlates of hunting. The investigation of such inter-relationships among lithic and organic weapon armatures, faunal exploitation, and hunting methods and techniques represents the final phase of this comprehensive research project.

## ACKNOWLEDGEMENTS

I would like to thank Harvey M. Bricker, my dissertation advisor at Tulane University, for his years of advice and support and Dan M. Healan, also of Tulane University, for his suggestions on statistical methodology. I would also like to acknowledge all the individuals in France who allowed me to study materials then under their curation: Robert Bégouën, Jean-Marc Bouvier, Jean Clottes, Jean Guichard, Henri Laville, Michel Lenoir, André Morala, the Musée de Brantôme, Jean-Philippe Rigaud, Robert Simmonet, Denise de Sonneville-Bordes, and Jean Vézian. This research was partially funded by a generous Selley Dissertation Fellowship.

## NOTES

[1]The French word "sagaie" is widely used by archaeologists working in the European Upper Palaeolithic to refer to the bone and antler points that tipped projectile weapons. The word is probably derived from Arabic and is much more common than the English equivalent "assegai."

[2]Prior to any factor analysis, the computational techniques proposed by Vierra and Carlson (1981) were used to verify that the data were suitable for factor analysis.

[3]The French word "*raccourci*" is literally translated as "shortened" or "abridged," which is not useful in the description of the proximal extremity of sagaies. Although I originally used the English word "stemmed" to describe this type of basal treatment, I have since decided that "whittled," as used by Patricia McComb (1989:273, Fig. 4:10), is a more accurate description.

## REFERENCES

Allain, J.
1979    L'industrie lithique et osseuse de Lascaux. In *Lascaux Inconnu*. A. Leroi-Gourhan and J. Allain, eds. Pp. 87-120. Supplément à *Gallia Préhistoire* 12. Paris: Editions du Centre National de la Recherche Scientifique.

Bahn, P. G.
1984    *Pyrenean Prehistory: A Palaeoeconomic Survey of the French Sites*. Warminster: Aris and Phillips.

Bailey, G. (ed.)
1983    *Hunter-Gatherer Economy in Prehistory*. Cambridge: Cambridge University Press.

Bergman, C. A., and M. H. Newcomer
1983    Flint arrowhead breakage: Examples from Ksar Akil, Lebanon. *Journal of Field Archaeology* 10:238-243.

Bettinger, R. L.
1991    *Hunter-Gatherers: Archaeological and Evolutionary Theory*. New York: Plenum Press.

Binford, L. R.
1987    Were there elephant hunters at Torralba? In *The Evolution of Human Hunting*. M. H. Nitecki and D. V. Nitecki, eds. Pp. 47-105. New York: Plenum Press.

Bordes, F.
1978    Le protomagdalenien de Laugerie-Haute Est. *Bulletin de la Société Préhistorique Française* 75:501-521.
1984    *Leçons sur le Paléolithique. Tome II. Le Paléolithique en Europe*. Cahiers du Quaternaire 7. Paris: Editions du Centre National de la Recherche Scientifique.

Bouchud, J.
1964    Etude sommaire de la faune du gisement de La Chèvre. In *Le Gisement de la Chèvre à Bourdeilles (Dordogne)*. R. Arambourou and P. E. Jude. Pp. 115-120. Périgueux: Imprimerie Magne.

Boyle, K. V.
1990    *Upper Palaeolithic Faunas from South-West France*. BAR International Series 557. Oxford: British Archaeological Reports.

Breuil, H. M.
1912    Les subdivisions du Paléolithique supérieur et leur signifcation. *Compte Rendu de la XIV^ème Session, Congrés International d'Anthropologie et d'Archéologie Préhistoriques (Genève)*:165-238.

Brézillon, M. N.
1968    La dénomination des objets de pierre taillée: Matériaux pour un vocabulaire des préhistoriens de langue française. Supplément à *Gallia Préhistoire* 4. Paris: Editions du Centre National de la Recherche Scientifique.

Bricker, H. M.
1978    Lower to Middle Perigordian continuity. In *Codex Wauchope: A Tribute Roll*. M. Giardino, B. Edmonson, and W. Creamer, eds. Pp. 165-182. New Orleans: *Human Mosaic*, Tulane Univeristy.

Bricker, H. M., and N. C. David
1984    *Excavation of the Abri Pataud, Les Eyzies (Dordogne): The Perigordian VI (Level 3) Assemblage*. American School of Prehistoric Research Bulletin 34. Cambridge: Peabody Muuseum, Harvard University.

Campana, D. V.
1989    *Natufian and Protoneolithic Bone Tools: The Manufacture and Use of Bone Implements in the Zagros and the Levant*. BAR International Series 494. Oxford: British Archaeological Reports.

Camps-Fabrer, H. (ed.)
1974    *Premier colloque international sur l'industrie de l'os dans le préhistoire*. Aix-en-Provence: Université de Provence.
1977    *Méthodologie appliquée à l'industrie de l'os préhistorique*. Paris: Editions du Centre National de la Recherche Scientifique.

Cattelain, P.
1988    *Fiches typologiques de l'industrie osseuse préhistorique. Cahier II. Propulseurs*. Aix-en-Provence: Université de Provence.

Chase, P. G.
1991    Symbols and Paleolithic artifacts: Style, standardization, and the imposition of arbitrary form. *Journal of Anthropological Archaeology* 10:193-214.

Cheynier, A.
1958    Impromptu sur la séquence des pointes du Paléolithique supérieur. *Bulletin de la Société Préhistorique Française* 55:190-205.

Christenson, A. L.
1986a   Projectile point size and projectile aerodynamics: An exploratory study. *Plains Anthropologist* 31:109-128.
1986b   Reconstructing prehistoric projectiles from their stone points. *Journal of the Society of Archer-Antiquaries* 29:21-27.

Clark, G. A.
1989    Romancing the stones: Biases, style, and lithics at La Riera. In *Alternative Approaches to Lithic Analysis*. D.

O. Henry and G. H. Odell, eds. Pp. 27-50. Archeological Papers of the American Anthropological Association 1. Washington, D.C.: American Anthropological Association.

Clottes, J.
1974 Le Paléolithique supérieur dans les Pyrénées françaises. *Cahiers d'Anthropologie et d'Ecologie Humaine* 2:69-88.

Corliss, D. W.
1972 Neck width of projectile points: An index of cultural continuity and change. *Occasional Papers* 29. Pocatello: Idaho State University.
1980 Arrowpoint or dart point: An uninteresting answer to a tiresome question. *American Antiquity* 45:351-352.

Davis, J. C.
1986 *Statistics and Data Analysis in Geology*. 2nd edition. New York: John Wiley and Sons.

Deacon, J.
1984a *The Later Stone Age of Southernmost Africa*. BAR International Series 213. Oxford: British Archaeological Reports.
1984b Later Stone Age people and their descendants in southern Africa. In *Southern African Prehistory and Paleoenvironments*. R. G. Klein, ed. Pp. 221-328. Rotterdam: A. A. Balkema.

Delpech, F.
1981 La faune magdalénienne de la Salle des Morts à Enlène, Montesquieu-Avantès (Ariège). In *Nouvelles fouilles dans la Salle des Morts de la caverne d'Enlène à Montesquieu-Avantès (Ariège)*. R. Bégouen and J. Clottes. Pp. 65-69. Issoudun: Imprimerie Laboureur et Cie.
1983 *Les faunes du Paléolithique supérieur dans le sud-ouest de la France*. Cahiers du Quaternaire 6. Paris: Editions du Centre National de la Recherche Scientifique.

Delporte, H., J. Hahn, L. Mons, G. Pinçon, and D. de Sonneville-Bordes
1988 *Fiches typologiques de l'industrie osseuse préhistorique. Cahier I. Sagaies*. Aix-en-Provence: Université de Provence.

Demars, P.-Y., and P. Laurent
1989 *Types d'outils lithiques du Paléolithique supérieur en Europe*. Cahiers du Quaternaire 14. Paris: Editions du Centre National de la Recherche Scientifique.

Donohue, R.
1988 Microwear analysis and site function of Paglicci Cave, Level 4A. *World Archaeology* 19:357-375.

Engelman, L.
1983 Cluster analysis of cases. In *BMDP Statistical Software*. W. J. Dixon, ed. Pp. 456-463. Berkeley: University of California Press.

Engelman, L., and J. A. Hartigan
1983 K-means clustering. In *BMDP Statistical Software*. W. J. Dixon, ed. Pp. 464-473. Berkeley: University of California Press.

Epstein, J. F.
1963 The burin-faceted projectile point. *American Antiquity* 29:187-201.

Fenenga, F.
1953 The weights of chipped stone points: A clue to their functions. *Southwestern Journal of Anthropology* 9:309-323.

Fischer, A., P. V. Hansen, and P. Rasmussen
1984 Macro and micro wear traces on lithic projectile points. *Journal of Danish Archaeology* 3:19-46.

Frane, J., R. Jennrich, and P. Sampson
1983 Factor analysis. In *BMDP Statistical Software*. W. J. Dixon, ed. Pp. 480-499. Berkeley: University of California Press.

Gordon, B.
1988 *Of Men and Reindeer Herds in French Magdalenian Prehistory*. BAR International Series 390. Oxford: British Archaeological Reports.

Grayson, D. K.
1984 *Quantitative Zooarchaeology: Topics in the Analysis of Archaeological Faunas*. Orlando: Academic Press.

Jennrich, R., and P. Sampson
1983 Stepwise discriminant analysis. In *BMDP Statistical Software*. W. J. Dixon, ed. Pp. 519-537. Berkeley: University of California Press.

Julien, M.
1982 *Les harpons magdaléniens*. Supplément à *Gallia Préhistoire* 17. Paris: Editions du Centre National de la Recherche Scientifique.

Keeley, L. H.
1988 Lithic economy, style, and use: A comparison of three Late Magdalenian sites. *Lithic Technology* 17:19-25.

Keienburg, W. (editor-in-chief)
1990 *Grzimek's Encyclopedia of Mammals*. English edition edited by S. P. Parker. New York: McGraw-Hill.

Klecka, W. R.
1980 *Discriminant Analysis*. Quantitative Applications in the Social Sciences 19. Beverly Hills: Sage Publications.

Knecht, H.
1993 Splits and wedges: The techniques and technology of Early Aurignacian antler working. In *Before Lascaux: The Complex Record of the Early Upper Paleolithic*. H. Knecht, A. Pike-Tay, and R. White, eds. Pp. 137-162. Boca Raton: CRC Press.

Kurtén, B.
1968 *Pleistocene Mammals of Europe*. Chicago: Aldine Publishing Co.

Lenoir, M.
1976 Les civilisations du Paléolithique supérieur dans le sud-ouest (Gironde). In *La préhistoire française. Tome I. Les civilisations paléolithiques et mésolithiques de la France*. Henry de Lumley, ed. Pp. 1252-1256. Paris: Editions du Centre National de la Recherche Scientifique.

Leroi-Gourhan, A.
1983 Une tête de sagaie à armature de lamelles de silex à Pincevent. *Bulletin de la Société Préhistorique Française* 80:154-156.

McComb, P.
1989 *Upper Palaeolithic Osseous Artifacts from Britain and Belgium*. BAR International Series 481. Oxford: British Archaeological Reports.

Macdonald, D. W. (ed.)
1984 *The Encyclopedia of Mammals*. New York: Facts on File Publications.

Mithen, S. J.
1990 *Thoughtful Foragers: A Study of Prehistoric Decision Making*. Cambridge: Cambridge University Press.

Nitecki, M. H., and D. V. Nitecki (eds.)
1987 *The Evolution of Human Hunting*. New York: Plenum Press.

Noe-Nygaard, N.
1974 Mesolithic hunting in Denmark illustrated by bone injuries caused by human weapons. *Journal of Archaeological Science* 1:217-248.

Odell, G. H.
1978 Préliminaires d'une analyse fonctionnelle des pointes microlithiques de Bergumermeer (Pays-Bas). *Bulletin de la Société Préhistorique Française* 75:37-49.

Otte, M., and L. H. Keeley
1990 The impact of regionalism on Palaeolithic studies. *Current Anthropology* 31:577-582.

Patterson, L. W.
1985    Distinguishing between arrow and spear points on the Upper Texas coast. *Lithic Technology* 14:81-89.

Peterkin, G. L.
n.d.a    Small stone points of the French Upper Palaeolithic. Paper presented at the 54th Annual Meeting of the Society for American Archaeology, Atlanta, 1989.
n.d.b    Lithic hunting technology in the French Upper Palaeolithic. Paper presented at the 89th Annual Meeting of the American Anthropological Association, New Orleans, 1990.
n.d.c    Lithic hunting technology and faunal exploitation in the French Upper Palaeolithic. Paper presented at the 56th Annual Meeting of the Society for American Archaeology, New Orleans, 1991.
n.d.d    Organic hunting technology in the French Upper Palaeolithic. Paper presented at the 58th Annual Meeting of the Society for American Archaeology, St. Louis, 1993.

Peyrony, D.
1923    *Eléments de préhistoire*. Ussel: G. Eyboulet et Fils.

Peyrony, D., and E. Peyrony
1938    *Laugerie-Haute*. Archives de l'Institut de Paléontologie Humaine Mémoire 19. Paris: Masson et Cie.

Pike-Tay, A.
1991    *Red Deer Hunting in the Upper Paleolithic of South-West France: A Study in Seasonality*. BAR International Series 569. Oxford: Tempus Reparatum.

Price, T. D., and J. A. Brown (eds.)
1985    *Prehistoric Hunter-Gatherers: The Emergence of Cultural Complexity*. Orlando: Academic Press.

Rummel, R. J.
1967    Understanding factor analysis. *Journal of Conflict Resolution* 11:444-480.

Sackett, J. R.
1977    The meaning of style in archaeology: A general model. *American Antiquity* 42:369-380.
1982    Approaches to style in lithic archaeology. *Journal of Anthropological Archaeology* 1:59-112.
1985    Style and ethnicity in the Kalahari: A reply to Wiessner. *American Antiquity* 50:154-159.
1986a    Isochrestism and style: A clarification. *Journal of Anthropological Archaeology* 5:266-277.
1986b    Style, function, and assemblage variability: A reply to Binford. *American Antiquity* 51:628-634.
1990    Style and ethnicity in archaeology: The case for isochrestism. In *The Uses of Style in Archaeology*. M. W. Conkey and C. A. Hastorf, eds. Pp. 32-43. Cambridge: Cambridge University Press.

Shea, J. J.
1988    Spear points from the Middle Paleolithic of the Levant.

*Journal of Field Archaeology* 15:441-450.

Smith, P. E.
1966    *Le Solutréen en France*. Publications de l'Institut de Préhistoire de l'Université de Bordeaux Mémoire 5. Bordeaux: Imprimeries Delmas.

Sneath, P. H. A., and R. R. Sokal
1973    *Numerical Taxonomy*. San Francisco: W. H. Freeman and Co.

Soffer, O. (ed.)
1987    *The Pleistocene Old World: Regional Perspectives*. New York: Plenum Press.

de Sonneville-Bordes, D.
1988    Fiche sagaie d'Isturitz. In *Fiches typologiques de l'industrie osseuse préhistorique. Cahier I. Sagaies*. H. Delporte, et al. Pp. 1.8:1-9. Aix-en-Provence: Université de Provence.

de Sonneville-Bordes, D., and J. Perrot
1954-    Lexique typologique du Paléolithique supérieur: Outillage
1956    lithique. *Bulletin de la Société Préhistorique Française* 51:327-335; 52:76-79; 53:408-412, 547-559.

Spiess, A. E.
1979    *Reindeer and Caribou Hunting: An Archaeological Study*. New York: Academic Press.

Stiner, M. C. (ed.)
1991a    *Human Predators and Prey Mortality*. Boulder: Westview Press.

Stiner, M. C.
1991b    The use of mortality patterns in archaeological studies of hominid predatory adaptations. *Journal of Anthropological Archaeology* 9:305-351.

Thomas, D. H.
1978    Arrowheads and atlatl darts: How the stones got the shaft. *American Antiquity* 43:461-472.

Tucker, G. C., Jr.
1980    Quantitative affirmation of intuitive typology. *Tebiwa* 22:1-11.

Vayson de Pradenne, A.
1936    L'utilisation de certains microlithes géométriques. *Bulletin de la Société Préhistorique Française* 3:217-232.

Vierra, R. K., and D. L. Carlson
1981    Factor analysis, random data, and patterned results. *American Antiquity* 46:272-283.

Vignard, E.
1935    Armatures de flèches en silex. *L'Anthropologie* 45:85-92.

Walker, E. P., et al.
1975    *Mammals of the World*. 3rd revised edition by J. L. Paradiso. Baltimore: Johns Hopkins University Press.

Winterhalder, B., and E. A. Smith (eds.)
1981    *Hunter-Gatherer Foraging Strategies: Ethnographic and Archaeological Analyses*. Chicago: University of Chicago Press.

# 5

# *Variability and Function among Gravette Points from Southwestern France*

## Francis B. Harrold
## University of Texas at Arlington

## ABSTRACT

A number of morphological and metric variables were recorded for a sample of 1,451 Gravette points deriving from ten sites in southwestern France. Size, macrowear, and base treatment covaried in a manner suggesting that some Gravette "points" in fact functioned as knives. The sample artifacts, however, did not segregate neatly into two distinct morphological-functional types of knives and points, but rather formed a continuum from more knife-like to more point-like pieces. Some probably functioned in both ways during their use lives. Considerable differences in size and other attributes between collections suggest different activity emphases at different sites. Some stylistic variation is apparent, but the bulk of the variation observed seems to be functional.

## INTRODUCTION

Probably the most natural question to arise when one examines an ancient stone tool is, "How was this used?" Such a simple question may be exceedingly difficult to answer. It is generally agreed today that the names traditionally supplied for retouched Paleolithic artifacts, like "point," "scraper," or "knife," are, in effect, hypotheses to be tested.

One Upper Paleolithic artifact type which has received little scrutiny in this regard is the Gravette point (or simply "Gravette") (Figure 5.1). Recognized as a type since early excavations at the eponymous site of La Gravette (Dordogne) in the last century, these artifacts are characterized as elongate, pointed blades with one straight lateral margin backed by abrupt retouch (de Sonneville-Bordes and Perrot 1956).

This report examines a large sample of Gravette points, primarily regarding the functional implications of several morphological and metric attributes. It derives from a comparative study of large samples of Châtelperron knives and Gravette points (Harrold n.d.). Large and significant differences in aspects of shape, symmetry, and butt preparation were found between the two collections. It was concluded that Châtelperron knives, unlike Gravettes, usually functioned as cutting tools.

The Gravette sample, however, was quite variable in many respects. For instance, while mean maximum length in the two groups was nearly identical at just

over 55 mm, the standard deviation of Gravette points exceeded that of Châtelperron knives (20.5 to 15.7). The "average" Gravette point, drawn from the mean values of various shape indicators, was slimmer than the average Châtelperron, but fatter than the examples usually seen in published illustrations (Figure 5.2). During data collection, I noticed many large and wide Gravettes, as well as some with notable traces of macrowear along the unbacked margin. The question of functional differentiation among Gravette points seemed worth pursuing.

## PREVIOUS WORK

The modal shape and size of Gravette points make their traditionally ascribed function seem intuitively likely, but little systematic attention has been given to this issue. No Gravette points have been reported in archeological contexts (e.g., embedded in animal bones) which would demonstrate their use as armatures (Bergman and Newcomer 1983).

Bordes (1952) experimentally mounted a Gravette on a spear, and, with the use of a spear thrower, achieved good range and accuracy and stable trajectory. These results indicated to him that Gravettes were indeed used mainly as armatures, though he allowed for a secondary function as knives. Although spear throwers are not known to date from the Gravettian, Bordes did show the practicability of tipping a spear with a Gravette point.

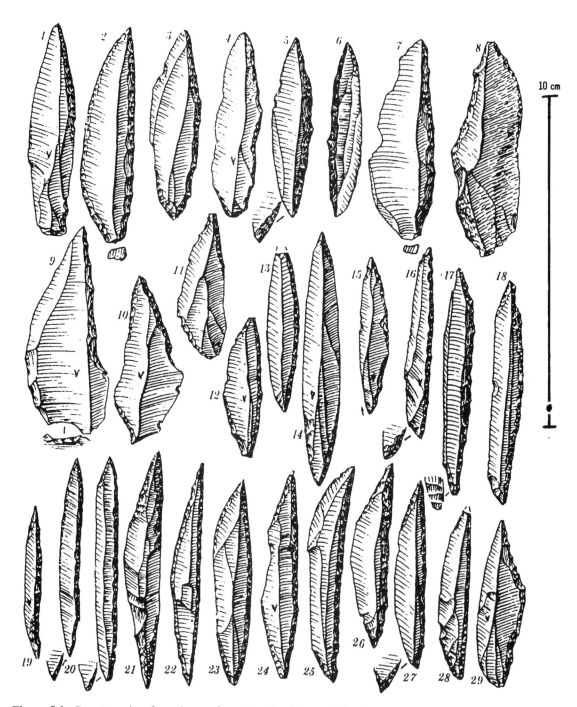

**Figure 5.1.** Gravette points from the *couche noire* at La Gravette (after Lacorre 1960:181, Pl. XXXII).

Some more recent studies are relevant, although none directly treats Gravette points. Bergman and Newcomer (1983) tipped arrows with experimental points of two Upper Paleolithic types from Ksar Akil (Lebanon), *pointes à face plane* and Ksar Akil points. They fired them into a target of meat backed by bone and compared the resulting damage to that on points excavated at the cave. They concluded that several characteristic types of use damage may result from typical head-on armature impact, including burin-like

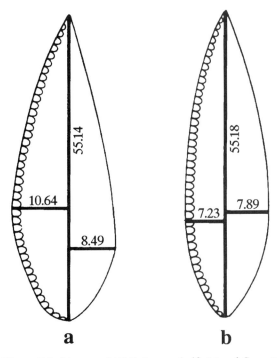

**Figure 5.2.** "Average" Châtelperron knife (a) and Gravette point (b), based on mean values in mm of shape indicators in two large samples (Harrold n.d.).

removals from the point along one margin. They also found that breakage patterns were conditioned by a point's length and cross-section.

Fischer et al. (1984) duplicated several north European final Paleolithic and Mesolithic point types in an experimental program which led to a classification of armature use-damage similar to that described by Bergman and Newcomer, although more complex. However, they did not establish experimentally that such macrowear is caused uniquely by use as a point.

Donohue (1988) made functional attributions for artifacts from an Italian Epigravettian assemblage based on microwear study. He inferred two functions for the assemblage's backed points, which are similar to but generally smaller than Gravettes. Most were projectile tips, but some of the larger ones (some 25-60 mm long, to judge from his illustrations) showed evidence of being used to slice meat.

Finally, in a microwear analysis of 32 Gravettes and microgravettes from Upper Perigordian Level 7 at Le Flageolet I (Dordogne), Kimball (1989) found two main use modes. Some of the points were used first as projectiles and then, usually after breaking, served as butchering knives. Most of them, however, showed only butchering microtraces.

Kimball's microwear study indicates that Gravette points in at least one assemblage were used as both

armatures and knives, sometimes successively; Donohue's (1988) study has a similar import. Other recent studies discussed above imply, although they do not prove, that some types of macro-damage could be unique to projectile tips. Even if this is so for the types tested, Gravettes may be another case altogether; their cross-section, which Bergman and Newcomer (1983) cite as important to use damage, tends to differ from those of the types tested. A Gravette's abrupt backing typically removes the thin margin of one side of the blade, resulting in a narrower, thicker, and perhaps more stress-resistant cross-section than the flattish ones of the types mentioned above. Indeed, Gravettes may have been backed, thus losing one sharp margin, in an attempt to enhance cross-sectional strength.

In any event, all putatively diagnostic macrowear traits would be worth examining. However, the data reported here were collected in 1976 and 1984, before

**Table 5.1.** Gravette points used in the study.

| Collection | Number of Gravette Points |
|---|---|
| Abri Pataud: | |
|     Level 5 Front Lower 2 | 80 |
|     Level 5 Front Lower 1 | 43 |
|     Level 5 Front Middle 2 | 37 |
|     Level 5 Front Middle 1 | 26 |
|     Level 5 Front Upper | 16 |
|     Level 5 Rear Lower | 16 |
|     Level 5 Rear Middle | 1 |
|     Level 5 Rear Upper | 21 |
|     Level 4 | 26 |
| Abri Vignaud | 12 |
| La Ferrassie, Grand Abri: | |
|     Level J | 189 |
|     Indeterminate Perigordian V | |
|       (J, K, or L) | 18 |
| La Ferrassie, Grotte | 64 |
| Laussel, Grand Abri, Couche 3 | 120 |
| Laussel, Petit Abri | 61 |
| Roque-Saint-Christophe, Couche A | 45 |
| La Gravette, Lacorre Collection: | |
|     "Aurignacien et Bayacien" | 3 |
|     Couche Jaune | 11 |
|     Couche Rouge | 78 |
|     Couche Noire | 62 |
|     No provenience | 15 |
| La Gravette, Coste Collection | 270 |
| La Chèvre, Couche 5 | 58 |
| La Faurélie, Hauser Collection | 3 |
| Les Vachons, Abris 1 and 2 (Charente), | |
|     Coiffard Collection: | |
|     Couche 3 | 77 |
|     Couche 4 | 92 |
| Roc de Combe (Lot), Couche 4 | 7 |
| TOTAL | 1,451 |

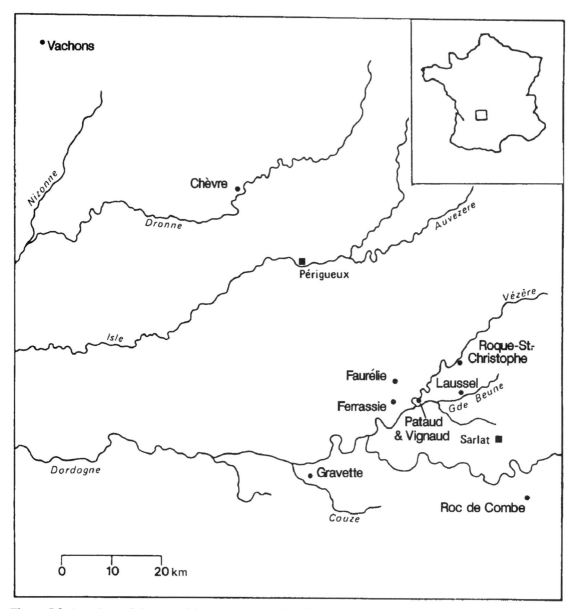

**Figure 5.3.** Locations of sites containing the study sample collections.

the above research came to my attention; only one attribute isolated by them, burin-like removal from the tip, was recorded.

## THE STUDY SAMPLE

The Gravettes in the study number 1,451 complete and fragmentary artifacts and come from 27 collections deriving from ten sites in southwestern France (Tables 5.1 and 5.2; Figure 5.3). Efforts were made to examine as many large collections as possible from the Périgord and its immediate environs in the limited time available, in order to maximize the sample while minimizing possible inter-regional stylistic differences. In the Upper Paleolithic typology of de Sonneville-Bordes and Perrot (1956), these artifacts fall into three types: Type 48, Gravette points (n=990); Type 49, atypical Gravettes with thin marginal backing or other anomalies (n=127); and Type 50, microgravettes less than 50 mm long (n =

**Table 5.2.** Collections used in the study.

| Site | Excavations | Location | Sources |
|------|-------------|----------|---------|
| Abri Pataud | Movius, 1958-1964 | a | 1,2,3 |
| La Ferrassie, Abri, J | Peyrony & Capitan, 1896-1929 | a | 4 |
| La Ferrassie, Grotte | Peyrony & Capitan, 1902 | a | 5 |
| Laussel, Grand & Petit Abris | Lalanne, 1908-1914 | b | 6,7:79-82 |
| Roque-Saint-Christophe | Peyrony, 1912-1913 | a | 8,7:184-189 |
| La Gravette, Coll. Lacorre | Lacorre, 1930-1939, 1945-1949 | c | 9 |
| La Gravette, Coll. Coste | Coste & Tabanou, 1880s | b | 9,7:180-181 |
| La Chèvre | Jude & Arambourou, 1948-1955 | d | 10 |
| La Faurélie | Hauser, before 1914 | a | 7:203 |
| Abri Vignaud | Bourlon, 1920-1921 | e | 7:182-183 |
| Les Vachons, Coll. Coiffard | Coiffard, before 1900 | a | 11,12, 7:191 |
| Roc de Combe | Bordes & Labrot, 1966 | f | 13 |

**Locations:** (a) Musée National de Préhistoire, Les Eyzies; (b) Musée d'Aquitaine, Bordeaux; (c) Musée des Antiquités Nationales, Saint-Germain-en-Laye; (d) Musée de Brantôme; (e) Institut de Paléontologie Humaine, Paris; (f) Institut du Quaternaire, Université de Bordeaux I. **Sources:** (1) Movius, ed., 1975; (2) Bricker 1973; (3) David 1984; (4) Peyrony 1934; (5) Capitan and Peyrony 1912; (6) Lalanne and Bouyssonie 1941-1946; (7) de Sonneville-Bordes 1960; (8) Peyrony 1939; (9) Lacorre 1960; (10) Jude and Arambourou 1964; (11) Bouyssonie 1948; (12) Bouyssonie and de Sonneville-Bordes 1957; (13) Bordes and Labrot 1967.

334). Unless otherwise specified, the term "Gravette point" refers here inclusively to Types 48-50.

Two of the sites in Table 5.1 have been radiocarbon dated (Mellars and Bricker 1986; Mellars et al. 1987). At the Abri Pataud, the levels (5 and 4) yielding the sample Gravettes are in the range of 26,000 to well over 28,000 years old, while recently excavated and dated levels at La Ferrassie, which are probably equivalent to Peyrony's Level J, are about 27,000-28,000 years in age.

These sites and two additional ones, Roc de Combe and La Chèvre, are included in Laville's chronostratigraphy for the Périgord. Their relevant levels are variously assigned to phases V, VI, and VII of the Late Würm (Laville et al. 1980; Laville 1988; Farrand 1988), which probably date from about 24,500 to over 28,000 BP. The remaining artifacts in the study probably fall between the age extremes just cited.

The study collections are conventionally assigned to the Upper Perigordian or Gravettian culture-stratigraphic unit, specifically to the Perigordian IV and V (Rigaud 1988), although David (1985) includes some of them in the Noaillian. Since the dating and cultural taxonomy of the collections in Table 5.1 are of secondary interest here, their complexities will not be further pursued.

Variables recorded for each artifact included metric ones, like maximum length and width, and morphological ones, such as the presence of deliberate retouch on the unbacked margin and the degree of macrowear on the unbacked margin (Table 5.3). Raw material variation was not controlled for, but no place in the study area is far from flint of reasonably good quality and abundance, and such flint types were characteristic of all collections.

This data set has distinct strengths and weaknesses. On the one hand, most of the sample comes from old, poorly controlled excavations, with significant resultant information loss. Only the Pataud, La Chèvre, and Roc de Combe collections (about 23% of the total sample) derive completely from post-1945 excavations. Most others represent rather gross stratigraphic units. Couche 3 at Laussel, for instance, which comes from Lalanne's 1908-1914 campaigns, was about 80 cm thick--comparable to the entire Level 5 Front complex at Pataud, with 19 archeological

**Table 5.3.** Variables considered in the study.

Length
Width
Degree of macrowear on unbacked margin (evidenced by irregular flaking, notching, striations):
    0    absent
    1    light (a few small traces)
    2    moderate
    3    heavy (most of original sharp margin obliterated)
Base modification:
    0    none
    1    some retouch
    2    truncation (or basal point) obliterating striking platform
State of fragmentation:
    0    whole piece
    1    proximal or distal fragment (piece was broken at least once)
    2    mesial fragment (piece was broken at least twice)
Retouch on distal unbacked margin:
    present/absent
Burination from tip:
    present/absent
Side of backing (piece oriented tip up, dorsal face visible):
    left/right

levels grouped into five analytical units. The old collections were subject during excavation to selection in favor of large and unbroken items and *belles pièces*. Afterwards, some were divided and scattered. Paleoenvironmental, faunal, and other contextual data are limited at best.

On the other hand, the sample is large and involves consistent recording of a large number of variables (Harrold n.d.) If it had been restricted to recent excavations, it would have been far smaller. As is, it allows the study of relationships between variables (e.g., size and macrowear) over hundreds of cases and confirmation of patterning at statistically significant levels. It also can be broken down into subsamples representing spatial or temporal segments of the whole. In this way, valuable information can still be extracted from the old lithic collections that make up the bulk of the Paleolithic archeological record in southwestern France.

## HYPOTHESES

If some Gravette points actually functioned as knives, one could expect certain concomitants. For example, knives should be larger than at least the smallest projectile points in the sample, which are often less than 40 mm long, in order to be handled effectively and to slice meat and other materials adequately. They should also receive more macrowear damage along the unbacked margin.[1] Unhafted knives (armatures must be hafted, while knives need not be) and prior work (Harrold n.d.) suggest that Châtelperron knives were usually unhafted. Thus, they should reveal less base preparation for hafting than points, in the form of basal retouch or truncation (Keeley 1982). Another expectation relates to previously established Gravette-Châtelperron differences: deliberate retouch on the distal, unbacked margin was far more common among Gravettes, arguably because their tips needed to be carefully shaped as piercing points. One could thus expect that such retouch would be less common on Gravettes used as knives. Finally, one specific type of use damage suggested experimentally as associated with armature use, burination from the tip, was recorded. If diagnostic, such damage should occur differentially between knives and points.

These expectations are congruent with some findings of Bricker's (1973) analysis of the lithic assemblages from Pataud Level 5. In that level's upper units, he reported a distinct subgroup of large Gravettes. Compared with the others, they had a significantly higher frequency of unmodified bases and a lower frequency of distal retouch, along with the frequent occurrence of an asymmetrical, curved morphology of the backed margin reminiscent of

Châtelperron points. All of these traits would be consistent with the proposition that some Gravettes functioned as knives, to the extent that the variables indicating such use should co-vary in the expected directions. For instance, size should vary positively with edge macrowear, but negatively with tip burination.

## RESULTS

Statistical results are presented below and summarized schematically in Table 5.4; all relationships are significant, unless otherwise noted, at the .001 level or less.

### Macrowear, Size, and Shape

Size was measured by a piece's maximum length and width, and shape (its slenderness or fatness) by width over length. Overall macrowear (that visible to the unaided eye) was measured on an ordinal scale (Table 5.3). Table 5.5 presents means and standard deviations for the sample's measures of form, as well as their correlations with macrowear using the nonparametric Kendall's tau and, for comparative purposes, Pearson's r.

Length and, even more strongly, width correlate positively with wear; the longer and wider a Gravette, the more microwear it tends to exhibit. Somewhat less strongly, slenderness is negatively correlated with wear; i.e., more slender pieces tend to show less wear. Since the relationship with slenderness is the weakest, width and length will be the only form variables discussed in subsequent analyses.

**Table 5.4.** Summary of relationships tested for Gravette points.

| Wear | Wear | L | W | Base | Ret. |
|---|---|---|---|---|---|
| Length | + | | | | |
| Width | + | . | | | |
| Base modification | + | + | + | | |
| Distal retouch | 0 | 0 | 0 | + | |
| Burination | 0 | - | - | 0 | 0 |

Key:  + predicted relationship, statistically significant
0 no significant relationship established
- relationship other than predicted, statistically significant
. not relevant to model.

**Table 5.5.** Size (in mm), shape, and correlation with macrowear. Correlation coefficients shown are Kendall's tau and Pearson's r.

| Variable | N | Mean | S.D. | tau | r |
|---|---|---|---|---|---|
| Length | 416 | 55.175 | 20.492 | .3049 | .3783 |
| Width | 1030 | 10.341 | 4.485 | .3861 | .4493 |
| W/L | 416 | 5.903 | 1.744 | -.2242 | -.2667 |

These correlations using Kendall's tau are fairly strong; Pearson's r for the same data is even higher (strictly speaking, r should not be used when one variable is ordinal-level, but it is a robust statistic and often so used [Labovitz 1970]). Considering the other factors potentially constraining the size of Gravettes (e.g., raw material) and the sources of noise in the archeological record (e.g., artifact loss, breakage and damage before and after deposition, and collection bias), this size-wear relationship is a real and strong one: the widest and longest Gravettes tend to show the most edge damage of the sort likely to be caused by use as knives.

### Base Modification, Macrowear, and Size

Many of the Gravettes in the sample (27.9% of those with bases preserved) had essentially unmodified bases, with striking platform and bulb of percussion still in place. Some 47% had bases bearing some retouch, which often reduced but rarely obliterated, the striking platform and bulb of percussion. Finally, other bases (25.1%) were abruptly truncated or, more rarely, pointed, with the talon and most or all of the bulb removed. Among this latter group, about two-thirds (17.1% of the total) featured a characteristic

**Table 5.6.** Percentages of right-backed Gravettes, for collections exceeding 20 artifacts.

| Collection | | %|
|---|---|---|
| Pataud | 5 Front Lower 2 | 95 |
| | 5 Front Lower 1 | 95 |
| | 5 Front Middle 2 | 97 |
| | 5 Front Middle 1 | 100 |
| | 5 Rear Upper | 81 |
| | 4 | 67 |
| La Ferrassie (Abri) J | | 62 |
| La Ferrassie (Grotte) | | 59 |
| Laussel, Grand Abri | | 74 |
| Laussel, Petit Abri | | 83 |
| Roque Saint-Christophe | | 78 |
| La Gravette c. rouge | | 81 |
| | c. noire | 87 |
| | coll. Coste | 89 |
| La Chèvre | | 86 |
| Les Vachons c. 3 | | 73 |
| | c. 4 | 74 |

oblique truncation (Figure 5.1, no. 16); this subtype was most often encountered in the Pataud collection.

Such base-thinning modification is generally related to hafting (Keeley 1982). If knives were unhafted or hafted less often than points, base thinning should correlate negatively with evidence of knife use such as wear. To test this relationship, base modification was treated as an ordinal variable (Table 5.3). Correlation between macrowear and basal modification was -.2187 (tau); the more wear points showed, the less they tended to have basal modification--again fulfilling expectations.

It was further expected that the degree of base modification should vary inversely with size; smaller pieces, more likely to serve as points, should show more base preparation for hafting. This was the case, as the Kendall correlation of degree of base modification with length was -.2046 and, with width, -.2107.

### Distal Retouch

Regular, deliberate retouch of the unbacked margin along its distal third was found on 52.3% of the 709 pieces which allowed determination of this characteristic. If this retouch was applied to produce a sharp, regular point tip, it should covary with base modification, thus suggesting point hafting. Indeed, artifacts with distal retouch were significantly more likely than those without it to have retouched or truncated bases (Chi-square=27.3532, Cramer's V = .2537).

Contrary to expectations, however, Chi-square tests found no significant relationships between distal retouch and either macrowear or, when microgravettes were compared to other Gravettes, size. A possible explanation is that the same set of flintknapping habits, including distal retouch, sometimes produced knives as well as points, and perhaps even pieces that could serve either function.

### Burination

One final relevant variable is the presence of burin-like removals from the tip, which was expected to covary with other indicators of point use. However, only 27 pieces, barely 1.9% of the total sample, bore such burination. Bergman and Newcomer (1983) reported an even lower frequency of damage putatively diagnostic of point use, only 1% for archeological specimens from Ksar Akil. There may be good reasons for this low frequency, such as the possible rarity of such damage during use or points (and especially tips) lost during hunts and left in animal carcasses. Nonetheless, a trait found so infrequently, even if diagnostic, would be of limited analytical value.

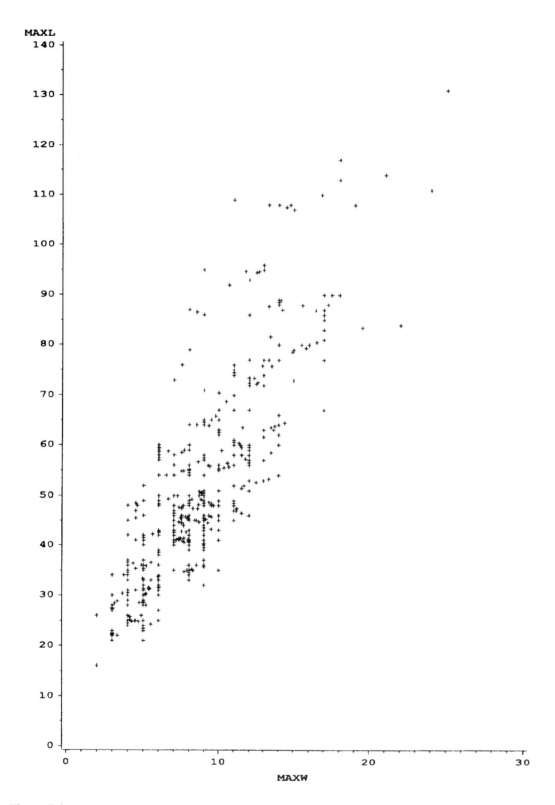

**Figure 5.4.** Scattergram of maximum length (MAXL) and maximum width (MAXW), in mm, for pieces in study sample which allowed determination of both measures.

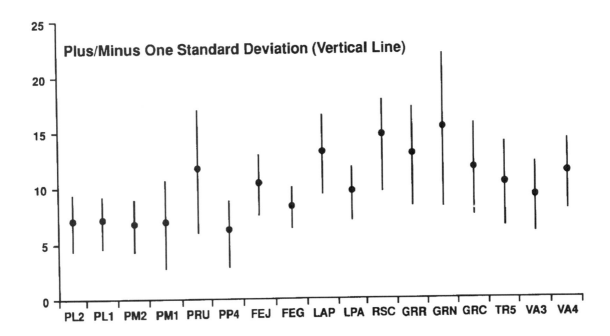

**Figure 5.5.** Mean maximum width for each collection exceeding 20 artifacts.

Key:
| | | | | | |
|---|---|---|---|---|---|
| PL2 | Pataud 5 Front Lower 2 | FEJ | Abri de la Ferrassie J | GRN | La Gravette c. noire |
| PL1 | Pataud 5 Front Lower 1 | FEG | Grotte de la Ferrassie | GRC | La Gravette col. Coste |
| PM2 | Pataud 5 Front Middle 2 | LAP | Laussel Grand Abri 3 | TR5 | La Chèvre 5 |
| PM1 | Pataud 5 Front Middle 1 | LPA | Laussel Petit Abri | VA3 | Les Vachons 3 |
| PRU | Pataud 5 Rear Upper | RSC | Roque-Saint-Christophe | VA4 | Les Vachons 4 |
| PP4 | Pataud 4 | GRR | La Gravette c. rouge | | |

In any case, there was no support for the diagnostic value of tip burination. Chi-square tests found no significant relationships between burination and macrowear, base modification, or distal retouch. And in the study's only case of results contrary to expectations (that smaller Gravettes were more likely to be burinated), the 27 burinated pieces were shown by t-tests to be significantly wider than all others (mean maximum width 14.57 mm vs. 10.58) as well as longer (66.47 mm vs. 54.57, $p < .02$). These results accord with Christenson's (1986) suggestion that burination may result from knife use.

**Summary**

Some Gravette points tend to combine size (especially width), macrowear, and base modification in a way consistent with use as knives. The status of distal retouch is more ambiguous; although it related as expected to base treatment, it is unrelated to size or wear. Burination does not vary with the other variables as expected and does not seem to be particularly diagnostic of point use.

The measures of association expressing the expected relationships are moderate rather than high, in part due to noise in the archeological record--although another factor may be involved as well. If Gravettes had been consistently manufactured as two discontinuous morphological-functional types--Gravette points and Gravette knives--it is likely that the patterning detected would have been more dichotomous, with higher correlations. On the other hand, if Gravettes were made in a range of sizes and morphological configurations (varying with time, space, and site activities), and if they were at least sometimes situationally used as knives, points, or both, we might expect this more continuous patterning. Larger pieces do show more wear, but there are large, unworn pieces and small, worn ones.

Some pieces probably underwent varying uses during their life cycles--for example, beginning as points, then being used as knives after initial breakage (as Kimball's [1989] microwear study indicates). This latter inference is supported by a modest correlation (tau = .1772) between macrowear intensity and degree of fragmentation.[2] Thus, a "Frison effect"

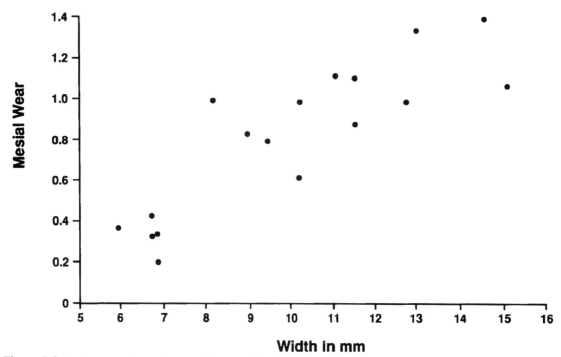

**Figure 5.6.** Scattergram of maximum width on mesial segment of piece vs. mesial segment macrowear for the same collections depicted in Figure 5.5.

seems to exist even among artifacts traditionally thought of as manufactured for a single purpose.[3]

### Discontinuity or Functional Continuum?

In defense of the suggestion that Gravettes were actually two distinct morpho-functional types, one might cite Bordes's (1967:32) argument for the typological distinctiveness of microgravettes. He produced a scattergram of length vs. width for 107 points from the Upper Perigordian site of Corbiac (Dordogne), indicating discontinuity in size between microgravettes and others. Similarly, Bricker (1973:392-465) reported two modes for width (5 mm or less and 6 mm or more) from several Level 5 collections at Pataud.

The large sample studied here, however, does not include Corbiac. In this sample, microgravettes merged into a continuous range of size variability, as a scattergram of length vs. width shows for the cases in which both measurements could be determined (Figure 5.4). Similarly, in some levels at Pataud, the two distinct width modes merged into a continuum or were joined by a third, wider mode (the knife-like pieces mentioned above) (Bricker 1973:392-465). Discontinuity between small and large Gravettes seems to exist in some collections, but not in others and not in general.

### INTERSITE VARIABILITY

We have so far considered a large aggregate sample. The cases of Corbiac and Pataud, however, demonstrate the importance of variability within and between collections. Significant intercollection variability does exist in the study sample. Unfortunately, the weaknesses of the sample become salient at this point. Contextual data and fine stratigraphic distinctions are lacking for most artifacts.

Nonetheless, intercollection variability is easily found. For instance, Figure 5.5 depicts mean width for the 17 collections which contain at least 20 artifacts (mean length showed similar patterning, although it was measurable for fewer pieces). Mean width is as little as 5.92 mm at Pataud 4: Front Lower 2 and as great as 15.06 at La Gravette *couche noire*. Sampling bias, favoring large pieces in old collections, may be a factor here, but intercollection differences are real, as can be seen in different old collections dug by the same excavator (e.g., the Laussel sites).

Suggestive patterns are apparent. The Pataud artifacts tend to be small, as do several other collections from the middle Vézère valley. And there are two cases, Ferrassie Abri and Grotte and Laussel Grand Abri and Petit Abri, where a small site is close to a larger, richer one; in both cases, the smaller site yielded smaller Gravette points. The possibility arises that the smaller and larger sites may have had persistently different functions, perhaps respectively as hunting stations (with more points and fewer knives?) and processing or occupation sites.

Finally, inspection of average macrowear also found notable intercollection differences. As might be expected from the global analysis described above, collections with larger pieces tend to show more wear. At Pataud, for instance, the largest points are from Level 5 Rear Upper. These points also show the most wear, with an average of 0.952, while no other Pataud collection exceeds 0.500. As Figure 5.6 indicates, there is a clear linear relationship between size and wear when collection means are compared. This again suggests that Gravette size differences between collections may be related to differing activity patterns between sites. Future research relating size and wear variations to contextual evidence for site function should be of interest, especially for the numerous and well-documented Pataud artifacts.

## THE QUESTION OF STYLE

There is considerable dispute over just what relationships exist between stylistic variation in artifacts, such as stone tools, and human groupings, such as mating networks, language groups, ethnic entities, and so on (e.g., Sackett 1990; Clark 1989). My concern here is not to attack these complex issues, but to briefly explore potential stylistic variability in the study sample.

Style is understood here as artifact variability that is referable primarily to spatio-temporally bounded craft norms rather than to the constraints of raw material or artifact function. Many attributes which can be vehicles for stylistic expression may also be related to these constraints of function or raw material. Artifact size, for example, could vary with function (as suggested here for Gravettes), raw material quality and nodule size, or stylistic choice (cf. the stylistic variation in spear blade sizes among African pastoralists discussed by Larick [1985]). Given the risk of mistaking one of the other controlling factors for style, it seems preferable to seek style in variation primarily when other factors can be ruled out. The difficulty lies in isolating variability which is **not** related to function or raw material. On the one hand, these artifacts are made in the relatively intractable medium of stone, with its severe constraints on artifact form. On the other hand, ethnographic evidence (e.g., Wiessner 1983; Larick 1985) indicates that projectiles and their points can be important vehicles for stylistic expression.

Two possible cases of stylistic variability will be considered here. One concerns the incidence of the oblique basal truncation mentioned earlier. Since such truncation is but one of various ways to ready a base for hafting, it might have been selected for essentially stylistic reasons. These truncations, interestingly, are frequent in most of the collections from Pataud, while absent or infrequent elsewhere (never exceeding 6%). Even so, they are usually found on fewer than half the bases at Pataud, where their maximum representation in any level is 56%. Thus, while they may represent a highly local, "microstylistic" preference which endured for some time, their expression was far from constant even at one site.

Another potentially stylistic attribute is the side to which backing was applied. Overall, 73% of the sample was backed on the right side (with the piece oriented tip up, butt down, and dorsal face visible), with considerable variation among collections (Table 5.6). Four of the Pataud collections had 95% or more right-backed pieces, while at the Grotte de La Ferrassie artifacts were only 59% right-backed. One might argue that these figures result from small-group, even individual, preferences without functional implications.

Nicholas Toth (personal communication, 1991), however, has suggested a functional implication for the side of backing of backed knives, based on his experimental work. For right-handers, meat-filleting is easier with a right-backed knife because it is the knife's smooth ventral face which contacts bone, rather than the dorsal face, whose ridges are more likely to catch on the bone. One might suggest that, since about 90% of most human populations are right-handed (Toth 1985), a similar proportion of backed knives should be right-backed. Points, meanwhile should be free to vary without functional constraints on the side of backing.

Two findings do not seem consistent with this suggestion. First, the proportion of right-backing does not predict how relatively point-like or knife-like collections are in terms of the criteria discussed earlier. For instance, right-backing is most frequent in the Pataud 5 Front levels, where artifacts are particularly point-like (small, unworn, etc.). Second, a prior study (Harrold, n.d.) found only 50% right-backing among Châtelperron knives, which functioned usually as knives. Thus, a general stylistic preference for right-backed Gravettes, variably expressed from place to place, may account for the distribution of this trait in the study sample, despite the functional drawbacks of right-backed knives.

The overall importance of style among attributes isolated in this study, however, seems relatively small. This should not be surprising, both because of the factors mentioned above and the restricted area occupied by the sites in question (all of the sites are within a few dozen kilometers of each other). Stylistic variation might well loom larger if this sample were compared with some from farther afield (e.g., Spain or central Europe).

## CONCLUSIONS

Old collections can still be of use. Data from mostly old excavations indicate that Gravettes were sometimes used as knives as well as projectile points. There apparently was some selection of points for modification and use based on size. At the same time, sharp metric or morphological discontinuity indicative of separate point and knife types was not established. It is likely that at least some Gravettes were used as both armatures and knives, alternately or successively. The makers of some of these artifacts may have envisioned them as dual-purpose implements, with their use conditioned not only by size, but also by whether they happened to be attached to a shaft at the moment. They were thus probably indispensable components of a hunter's kit.

Intercollection differences in the variables studied suggest different activity suites at different sites and levels. In this regard, the generally small pieces from Abri Pataud contrast intriguingly with most collections.

Various lines of future research can enlarge our knowledge of Gravettes. Microwear analysis and experiment may provide a crucial independent assessment of artifact function. In addition, the comparison of Gravette data with paleoenvironmental, faunal, spatial, and other contextual information, especially at sites such as the well-documented Abri Pataud, promises to help us better understand the functions of these artifacts and the sites where they are found.

## ACKNOWLEDGEMENTS

The following individuals gave permission to study lithic collections or otherwise facilitated their study: the late F. Bordes and H. Movius; A. Roussot (Musée d'Aquitaine, Bordeaux); D. de Sonneville-Bordes (Université de Bordeaux I); H. Bricker (Tulane University); J. Guichard and A. Morala (Musée Nationale de Préhistoire, Les Eyzies); H. Delporte and D. Buisson (Musée des Antiquités Nationales, Saint-Germain); M. de Bayle des Hermens and H. de Lumley (Institut de Paléontologie Humaine); and M. Bonnet (Brantôme). I thank J.-Ph. Rigaud and N. Toth for stimulating discussions regarding the issues treated in this report. This research was supported in part by a grant from the Organized Research Fund at the University of Texas at Arlington, where, additionally, Nancy Rowe and Martin Heltai were very helpful.

## NOTES

[1]Although irregular flaking along an unretouched margin can occur in used experimental projectile points (Fischer et al. 1984), it is not a characteristic form of damage from point use.

[2]This variable may have interpretive potential for Gravette function. For example, distal tips of points might be expected to occur disproportionately rarely, having been broken off and lost away from sites. However, confounding factors intervene. Point fragments may also return to sites in animal carcasses (Bergman and Newcomer 1983). More fundamentally, we lack a developed model of **knife** fragmentation to contrast with that of points. Finally, most old collections in this sample are doubtless biased against inclusion of fragmentary pieces, and their comparison with other assemblages in this respect is thus of limited value.

[3]The term "Frison effect" refers to the successive stages of use, modification, and re-use through which a lithic implement may pass during its use life, falling into different typological categories (like "point," "knife," and "burin") along the way.

## REFERENCES

Bergman, C., and M. Newcomer
1983    Flint arrowhead breakage: Examples from Ksar Akil, Lebanon. *Journal of Field Archaeology* 10:238-243.
Bordes, F.
1952    A propos des outils à bord abattus. *Bulletin de la Société Préhistorique Française* 49:645-647.
1967    Considérations sur la typologie et les techniques dans le Paléolithique. *Quartär* 18:25-55.
Bordes, F., and J. Labrot
1967    La stratigraphie du gisement de Roc de Combe et ses implications. *Bulletin de la Société Préhistorique Française* 64:15-28.
Bouyssonie, J.
1948    Un gisement aurignacien et périgordien. Les Vachons (Charente). *L'Anthropologie* 52:1-42.
Bouyssonie, J., and D. de Sonneville-Bordes
1957    L'abri No. 2 des Vachons. Fouilles J. Coiffard. *Congrès Préhistorique de France, Comptes Rendus de la XVᵐᵉ Session, Poitiers-Angoulême, 1956.* Pp. 271-309. Paris: Société Préhistorique Française.
Bricker, H.
1973    *The Périgordian IV and Related Cultures in France.* Ph.D. dissertation, Department of Anthropology, Harvard University.
Bricker, H., and P. Mellars
1987    Datations $^{14}$C de l'Abri Pataud (Les Eyzies, Dordogne) par le procédé "accélérateur-spectromètre de masse." *L'Anthropologie* 91:227-234.
Capitan, L., and D. Peyrony
1912    Station préhistorique de la Ferrassie. Commune de Savignac-du-Bugue (Dordogne). *Revue Anthropologique* 22:29-50, 84-99.
Christenson, A.
1986    Projectile point size and projectile aerodynamics: An exploratory study. *Plains Anthropologist* 31:109-128.
Clark, G.
1989    Romancing the stones: Biases, style and lithics at La Riera. In *Alternative Approaches to Lithic Analysis.* D. Henry and G. Odell, eds. Pp. 27-50. Archeological Papers of the American Anthropological Association 1. Washington, D.C.: American Anthropological Association.
David, N.
1985    *Excavation of the Abri Pataud, Les Eyzies (Dordogne).*

*The Noaillian (Level 4) Assemblages and the Noaillian Culture in Western Europe.* American School of Prehistoric Research Bulletin 37. Cambridge: Peabody Museum, Harvard University.

Donohue, R.
1988  Microwear analysis and site function of Paglicci Cave, Level 4A. *World Archaeology* 19:357-375.

Farrand, W.
1988  Integration of Late Quaternary climatic records from France and Greece: Cave sediments, pollen, and marine events. In *Upper Pleistocene Prehistory of Western Eurasia.* H. Dibble and A. Montet-White, eds. Pp. 305-320. University Museum Monograph 54. Philadelphia: The University Museum, University of Pennsylvania.

Fischer, A., P. Hanson, and P. Rasmussen
1984  Macro and micro wear traces on lithic projectile points. *Journal of Danish Archaeology* 3:19-46.

Harrold, F.
n.d.  A comparative morphometric analysis of Châtelperron knives and Gravette points. Paper presented at the 86th annual meeting of American Anthropological Association, Chicago, 1987.

Keeley, L.
1982  Hafting and retooling: Effects on the archaeological record. *American Antiquity* 47:798-809.

Kimball, L.
1989  *Planning and Functional Variability in the Upper Palaeolithic: Microwear Analysis of Upper Perigordian Tools from Le Flageolet I.* Ph.D. dissertation, Northwestern University. Ann Arbor: University Microfilms International.

Lacorre, F.
1960  *La Gravette: Le Gravétien et le Bayacien.* Laval: Barnéoud.

Labovitz, S.
1970  The assignment of numbers of rank order categories. *American Sociological Review* 35:515-524.

Lalanne, J., and J. Bouyssonie
1941-  Le gisement paléolithique de Laussel. *L'Anthropologie*
1946  50:1-163.

Larick, R.
1985  Spears, style, and time among Maa-speaking pastoralists. *Journal of Anthropological Archaeology* 4:206-220.

Laville, H.
1988  Recent developments on the chronostratigraphy of the Paleolithic in the Périgord. In *Upper Pleistocene Prehistory of Western Eurasia.* H. Dibble and A. Montet-White, eds. Pp. 147-160. University Museum Monograph 54. Philadelphia: The University Museum, University of Pennsylvania.

Laville, H., J.-Ph. Rigaud, and J. Sackett.
1980  *Rock Shelters of the Perigord.* New York: Academic Press.

Mellars, P., and H. Bricker
1986  Radiocarbon accelerator dating in the earlier Upper Palaeolithic. In *Archaeological Results from Accelerator Dating.* J. Gowlett and R. Hedges, eds. Pp. 73-80. Oxford University Committee for Archaeology Monograph 11. Oxford: Oxford University Press.

Mellars, P., H. Bricker, J. Gowlett, and R. Hedges
1987  Radiocarbon accelerator dating of French Upper Palaeolithic sites. *Current Anthropology* 28:128-133.

Movius, H., ed.
1975  *Excavations of the Abri Pataud, Les Eyzies (Dordogne).* American School of Prehistoric Research Bulletin 30. Cambridge: Peabody Museum, Harvard University Press.

Peyrony, D.
1934  La Ferrassie. *Préhistoire* 3:1-92.
1939  Fouilles de la Roque-Saint-Christophe. *Bulletin de la Société Historique et Archéologique du Périgord* 66:248-269, 360-387.

Rigaud, J.-Ph.
1988  The Gravettian peopling of southwestern France: Taxonomic problems. In *Upper Pleistocene Prehistory of Western Eurasia.* H. Dibble and A. Montet-White, eds. Pp. 387-396. University Museum Monograph 54. Philadelphia: The University Museum, University of Pennsylvania.

Sackett, J.
1990  Style and ethnicity in archaeology: The case for isochrestism. In *The Uses of Style in Archaeology.* M. Conkey and C. Hastorf, eds. Pp. 32-43. Cambridge: Cambridge University Press.

de Sonneville-Bordes, D.
1960  *Le Paléolithique supérieur en Périgord.* Bordeaux: Delmas.

de Sonneville-Bordes, D., and J. Perrot
1956  Lexique typologique du Paléolithique supérieur: Outillage lithique (suite et fin). *Bulletin de la Société Préhistorique Française* 53:547-559.

Toth, N.
1985  Archaeological evidence for preferential right-handedness in the Lower and Middle Pleistocene, and its possible implications. *Journal of Human Evolution* 14:607-614.

Wiessner, P.
1983  Style and social information in Kalahari San projectile points. *American Antiquity* 48:253-276.

*6*

# Upper Paleolithic Hunting Tactics and Weapons in Western Europe

Lawrence Guy Straus
University of New Mexico

## ABSTRACT

There is extensive evidence of subsistence intensification by Upper Paleolithic people in Europe, particularly based on the records from Spain, France, Belgium, and Germany. In addition to diversifying their subsistence base wherever and whenever possible, Upper Paleolithic hunters made efficient use of landforms and developed new types of weapon-delivery systems to procure large numbers of herd game. In so doing, they seem to have preferentially chosen to inhabit regions with significant hills and valleys. This allowed them to channel game movements and to hinder or trap herds, thereby facilitating mass kills. Specific physical features (rivers, cliffs, gorges, box canyons, blind valleys, etc.) were of proven use especially to late Upper Paleolithic hunters in their planned, scheduled mass kills of such species as horse, reindeer, red deer, bison, and ibex. The most dynamic component of Upper Paleolithic technologies was weaponry. New types of weapon tips, shafts, hafts, and propulsion devices were developed at an ever-accelerating rate throughout the Upper Paleolithic and into the Mesolithic, between at least 35,000-40,000 BP and ca. 7000 BP.

## INTRODUCTION

The intensification of subsistence-gathering activities, especially in the late Upper Paleolithic, has been well established on the basis of faunal analyses, particularly in Spain, France, Belgium, and Germany (see Straus 1987a with references). The purpose of this paper is to look at how Upper Paleolithic hunters maximized the use of physical features of the landscape and made rapid readjustments in weapons technology to efficiently, effectively procure large numbers of ungulates.

The general points I wish to make are simple and derived from the research of numerous European and American colleagues and from my own observations: (1) Upper Paleolithic people did not evenly occupy the land surface of Europe; they seem to have preferred regions with moderate relief (e.g., hills, deep valleys). (2) Within these regions, Upper Paleolithic bands located many of their sites near specific landforms that would have been useful in mass kills of herd ungulates. (3) The most dynamic component of the Upper Paleolithic technologies was weaponry, and an "arms race" seems to have accelerated through time.

## UPPER PALEOLITHIC HUMAN GEOGRAPHIC DISTRIBUTIONS

Looking at the overall distribution of Upper Paleolithic sites on the broadest scale, an understanding of how hunters exploited medium and large herd ungulates may help explain why there appear to be distinct clusters of sites (and "empty quarters") in terminal Pleistocene Europe. The known geographic distribution of sites is, of course, subject to the geological and vegetational influences of differential preservation and visibility. It is also subject to the vagaries of archeolgical survey and sampling.

Obviously part of the explanation for the distribution of sites, especially during the Last Glacial maximum centered on 18,000 BP, is the existence of ice and polar desert in northern and northwestern Europe and generally rigorous, resource-poor conditions in many other northerly and highland regions (such as the Mesetas of the Iberian Peninsula) (see papers in Soffer and Gamble 1990). People were attracted to coastal regions because of their relatively temperate climates and their variety and wealth of both terrestrial and aquatic food resources (see Straus 1991).

Otherwise, areas characterized by complex physiographic relief but relatively low absolute elevation seem to have been favored, probably for a number of reasons: shelter (good solar exposures, the presence of horizontal cave mouths and of rockshelters, protection from dominant winds), the presence of vegetation for food and especially fuel, the close proximity of diverse habitats and faunas (ecotonal situations), and the existence of natural features advantageous to mass killing of herd animals (e.g., corridors, funnels and chokepoints, steep-sided valleys and culs-de-sac, canyons and gorges, obligatory water crossings). The latter aspect of site selection by Upper Paleolithic hunters is examined here.

## TACTICAL USE OF TOPOGRAPHIC FEATURES IN HUNTING

An examination of the general distribution of Upper Paleolithic site clusters will reveal that people seem to have been attracted to regions with hills and canyons, although they only conquered the highest elevations at the end of the Ice Age, with the retreat or disappearance of mountain glaciers. Thus, for example, there are dense clusters of sites around the Pavlov Hills in the middle of the Moravian Basin; in the Swabian Alb of southwest Germany; in the hills, valleys, and canyons of southwest and southeast France--notably in the drainages of the Vézère, Lot, Gard, and Ardèche rivers; along the northern flanks of the Pyrénées; in the broken relief of the narrow Cantabrian region between the Cordillera and the shore; and in the hilly coastal zones of eastern and southern Spain and of Portuguese Estremadura. Other things being equal, it would seem that there was a distinct preference for areas with relief, probably because of the combined advantages of shelter, diversity of food and fuel resources, and an abundance of topographic features useful in momentarily "corraling" and then slaughtering herd animals.

These environments could be most useful to people who hunted on foot, with weapons of limited range and without dogs. The idea, of course, is to use natural features to stop, enclose, funnel and/or hinder the flight of massed animals that had been driven into or against them. The importance of such corralling has been emphasized in recent years by Kehoe (1990a, 1990b) in his interpretations of some cave art representations, and, while I do not share the "domestication" hypotheses of certain members of the Cambridge University group of economic prehistorians (e.g., Bahn, Bay-Peterson, Sturdy, Davidson, and other students of the late Eric Higgs), I think they have been correct in emphasizing the role of the landscapes surrounding sites in determining human ability to acquire substantial amounts of meat and other wild animal products during the Upper Paleolithic.

The specifics of how animals, such as reindeer, red deer, horses, bison, aurochs, and even, occasionally, mammoths, may have been trapped with the aid of natural features can be elucidated by a few examples.

At Miloviče, a side valley cul-de-sac in the Pavlov Hills excavated by Martin Oliva, a Gravettian deposit dated to about 22,000 BP contains the massed bones of about 100 young mammoths associated with both large and small Gravette backed points (Oliva 1988, 1989).

At Solutré in east-central France, Olsen (1989) has convincingly demonstrated the use of a small valley at the base of the side (not the end) of "the Rock" to trap small bands of migrating horses that were repeatedly driven up against the cliff from the valley between the parallel Solutré and Pouilly ridges. This tactic was so successful that it was apparently used for over 20 millennia, during most of the Upper Paleolithic--resulting in a massive deposit of bones known as the Horse Magma.

In other regions, striking landmarks, such as the pyramidal Monte Castillo in Santander, Spain, have repeatedly drawn human occupation. The cave sites of Monte Castillo dominate both a narrow gorge that connects a broad intermontane basin with the Cantabrian coastal plain and a cul-de-sac side valley. Migrating herds of red deer, horses, and bovines could have been driven and surrounded at either of these points, as well as at crossings of the Río Pas at the base of the hill. Many of the Upper Paleolithic faunas (especially the Magdalenian) of El Castillo are very rich in red deer remains (Cabrera 1984; R. G. Klein, personal communication, 1988).

A rapid north to south tour of some of the many spots also favored for use by Upper Paleolithic people follows; these locations were selected, in large part, because of their advantageous natural features. Two major open-air Magdalenian sites dating to 12,000-13,000 BP, Andernach and Gönnersdorf, are situated, respectively, near the left and right banks of the Rhine in central Germany, exactly at the mouth of the Rhine Gates gorge at the northern end of the broad Neuwied Basin. These sites saw repeated slaughters of horses and reindeer, perhaps along the narrow benches of the gorge (Bosinski 1988 with references).

Numerous Upper Paleolithic sites are located along the cliff-lined Achtal valley (a paleo-Danube channel) in the Swabian Alb of southwest Germany. They include Geissenklösterle, Brillenhöhle, Sirgensteinhöhle, and Höhlerfels (see Hahn 1977, 1988). Herd hunting would have been facilitated by use of small side valleys and embayments. A similar set of circumstances exists in the nearby Lonetal (the loca-

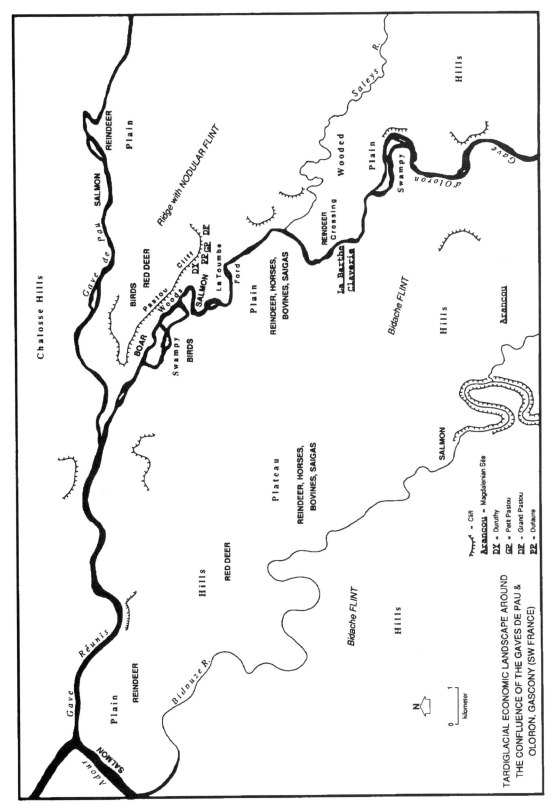

**Figure 6.1.** Economic map of the area around the Pastou sites.

tion of Vogelherd), as well as in other valleys of this hilly region (for example, at Petersfels on the Brüdertal [Albrecht 1979, 1983]).

Deep gorges along the Meuse and its tributaries in southern Belgium, such as the Lesse, likewise created ideal conditions for trapping migrating herds near numerous Upper Paleolithic sites, including the rich Magdalenian site of Chaleux (see Otte 1984) and the multicomponent (Aurignacian-Gravettian-Magdalenian) Trou Magrite (Straus et al. 1992; Straus et al. 1993). The open-air site of Huccorgne-Hermitage, which yielded horse and mammoth remains associated with Gravettian artifacts such as Gravette and Font-Robert points, and several adjacent cave sites are strategically located where the Méhaigne River cuts through the Hesbaye Plateau to the Meuse, where an ancient, steep-ridged oxbow nearly blocks the gorge (Froment 1980; Straus et al. 1992; Straus et al. 1993).

White (1985) has pointed out the importance of fords in the distribution of Upper Paleolithic sites in the Périgord. These would have been especially useful in giving humans access to both sides of the valleys and in fishing at rapids. However, the narrow, steep-sided canyons and culs-de-sac side valleys around Les Eyzies would have also been particularly advantageous in killing large numbers of migratory ungulates. The narrow terrace between the cliffs of Laugerie, adjacent to the blind side canyon of Gorge d'Enfer, and the Vézère River was the location of an early-twentieth-century discovery of 21 pits said to have contained Solutrean artifacts. This site was appropriately named "Les Trappes" (Hauser 1911). The sites of Les Eyzies are famous for their rich, reindeer-dominated faunas, most recently studied by Delpech (1983) and Spiess (1979). Similar deep main and side canyon situations characterize other regions of south-central France, including the Lot, a region rich in both Upper Paleolithic art and habitation sites, such as Pech-Merle.

All along the northern edge of the Pyrénées, there are clusters of sites (mostly Magdalenian) where rivers cut through the mountain chain and flow out onto the plains of the Aquitaine and Toulouse Basins (thoroughly described in Bahn [1984] and Clottes [1976, 1989]). Sometimes these main gorges are associated with steep-sided culs-de-sac and other topographic features useful in the surrounding and slaughter of reindeer and other migratory game. The Basin of Tarascon within the Pyrénées is located at a strategic confluence of two streams, the upper Ariège and the Vicdessos, that are major avenues of communication up to the high Pyrénées below Andorra. This basin is ringed with sites, and the upper valleys are lined with others--including the cave sites of Niaux, Bédeilhac, La Vache, Les Eglises, and Fontanet--most with both cave art and archeological deposits.

At the southern edge of the Aquitaine Basin, near the confluence of three major rivers, there is a striking, isolated landmark, the Pastou Cliff. Along its south-southwest-facing base, there is a cluster of Magdalenian rockshelter and talus sites, including Duruthy, le Petit Pastou, le Grand Pastou, and Dufaure (Arambourou 1978; Straus 1988, n.d.). The clifftop provides a commanding view of the Gave d'Oloron valley as it descends from the Basque Pyrénées. There is a permanent ford in front of the sites, and cliffs abut the river in several places just upstream of the sites. These cliffs may have forced migrating reindeer bands to cross the river at specific spots, making them vulnerable to slaughter in the water or on the banks, at places such as la Barthe Claverie, where there are nineteenth-century reports of discoveries of reindeer bones and Magdalenian artifacts in a bog (Figure 6.1).

The Basque country, with its extremely broken relief albeit low elevations, provided innumerable opportunities to well-organized Upper Paleolithic hunters. For example, a blind valley containing a cluster of Upper Paleolithic sites, Aitzbitarte IV, is located off the south side of the low pass that connects the French and Spanish Basque provinces at the western end of the Pyrénées (Altuna et al. 1982). Similar valleys are abundant along the northern flanks of the Cantabrian Cordillera (see discussions in Straus 1992) (Figure 6.2).

The heavily karstified landscapes of the Cantabrian coastal plain contain many deep, steep-sided *dolinas* ("sinkholes"), which often drain into caves that would have provided excellent shelter. These *dolinas* would have been very useful in the common slaughter of red deer hind herds, as attested by masses of bones in late Upper Paleolithic sites throughout the region, notably at El Juyo cave excavated by Barandiarán, Freeman, González Echegaray, and Klein (1985). Many major interior basins between the coastal hills and the Cordillera have side valleys; at the heads of these valleys, there are sites such as Hornos de la Peña off the Saja basin in Santander. Other main valleys had critical chokepoint gorges and steep, rocky slopes that were the preferred habitats of ibex, which were hunted from specialized sites such as Bolinkoba, El Rascaño, and Collubil (Straus 1987b).

The Río Bedón valley is the main avenue of access between the coast of eastern Asturias and the Picos de Europa; it passes through a narrow gorge in the coastal range. It is probably no accident that the Posada cluster of Upper Paleolithic sites, including La Riera, Cueto de la Mina, and many other caves, is located where it is--along a sheltered south-facing ridge near the spot where this valley breaks out onto the coastal plain (Straus 1986; Straus and Clark 1986).

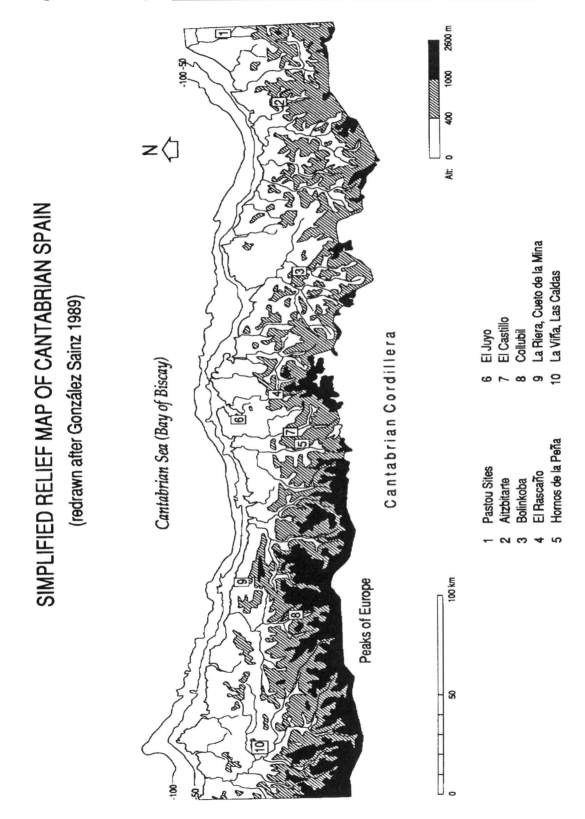

**Figure 6.2.** Relief map of Cantabrian Spain (redrawn after González Sainz 1989).

**Table 6.1.** Lithic weapon elements from modern excavations of Solutrean sites in the Franco-Cantabrian region.

| Site | Level | Age in Millennia BP | % Backed[a] Bladelets | % Solutrean Points |
|------|-------|---------------------|-----------------------|--------------------|
| La Riera | 2/3 | | 2.0 | 5.9 |
| | 4 | 20.9 | 14.2 | 26.4 |
| | 5/6 | | 10.3 | 31.8 |
| | 7 | | 5.4 | 18.8 |
| | 8 | 20.7 | 4.3 | 5.2 |
| | 9 | | 0.0 | 0.9 |
| | 10 | 19.8 | 0.0 | 7.0 |
| | 11 | | 3.1 | 0.0 |
| | 12/13 | 17.2 | 3.1 | 0.0 |
| | 14 | | 2.9 | 1.0 |
| | 15 | 17.2 | 11.8 | 1.3 |
| | 16 | 18.2 | 23.8 | 0.0 |
| | 17 | 17.0 | 70.9 | 0.7 |
| Amalda | V | 19.0 | 28.0 | 3.0 |
| | IV | 16.0-17.5 | 43.0 | 1.5 |
| Las Caldas | Sol. médio | 19.0-19.5 | 1.5 | 12.2 |
| | Sol. super | 19.0-19.5 | 0.5 | 13.9 |
| | Sol. term | 17.0-18.3 | 1.5 | 2.5 |
| Chufín | 1 | 17.4 | 9.9 | 18.8 |
| Cueva Morín | 3 | | 13.8 | 10.9 |
| Aitzbitarte IV | 8 | 17.9 | 13.1 | 9.6 |
| Ambrosio | VI | 16.6 | 0.0 | 22.0 |
| | IV | 16.6 | 1.4 | 22.0 |
| | II | 16.5 | 18.0 | 19.5 |
| Parpalló | 4-4.5m | 17.9 | 17.0 | 0.4 |
| C. Saunière | IVb | 18.9-19.4 | 40.1 | 22.7 |

[a]% Backed Bladelet includes backed micropoints (microgravette and Azilian types). **Sources:** Altuna et al. 1990; Cabrera 1977; Corchón 1981; Fullola Pericot 1979; Geneste and Plisson 1986; González Echegaray and Freeman 1971; Ripoll 1988; Straus 1983; Straus and Clark 1986.

Likewise, the Río Nalón is the major valley connecting the mountains and the coast in central Asturias. It is lined with Upper Paleolithic sites (Fortea et al. 1990), some near the gorge at Puerto, notably La Viña, and others on culs-de-sac, such as Las Caldas, which is located at the head of a narrow, steep-sided valley into which it would have been advantageous to drive game from a broad interior basin of the Nalon.

Many of the important Upper and Epipaleolithic sites of Portuguese Estremadura are also located on gorges, blind valleys, or other places useful in mass hunting. These include Lapa do Suão (Roche 1982), Caldeirão (Zilhão 1987, 1990), and Bocas (Straus et al. 1988). Red deer was the main herd game in this region, as it was in other parts of the Iberian Peninsula, such as Levante and Andalusia, where favorable topographic features were also most probably exploited by humans (see Davidson 1989).

## OF ARMS AND HUMANS

The Upper Paleolithic in general is also characterized by what I have called "the first arms race" (Straus 1990). The most dynamic aspect of the technologies of the last 30,000 years of the Pleistocene was weaponry, both weapon tips and delivery systems. Despite limited data suggesting occasional hafting of Mousterian "points" developed by Shea (1989), most Middle Paleolithic weapons were probably simple affairs: clubs, stones, and sharpened sticks. Then, in the widespread Aurignacian beginning around 40,000 BP, weapons must have been rather large thrusting spears. If the large split-base and lozenge-shaped bone points really were weapon heads, the emphasis seems to have been on bone tips (see Albrecht et al. 1972; Knecht, this volume).

This changed, however, with the beginning of the downturn in global temperatures at the outset of the Upper Pleniglacial around 25,000 years ago, in the Gravettian. Throughout Europe these assemblages are characterized by the presence of narrow, elongated, straight-backed stone Gravette points, along with other types such as the tanged Font-Robert point. These gracile, light-weight points were possibly hafted onto throwing spears. But there are clearly long and short Gravettes; both regular and microgravettes are recognized in the de Sonneville-Bordes/Perrot typology and

**Table 6.2.** Lithic weapon elements from modern excavations of Magdalenian sites in the Franco-Cantabrian region.

| Site | Level | Age in Millennia BP | % Backed[a] Bladelets |
|---|---|---|---|
| La Riera | 18 | | 69.3 |
| | 19 | 16.4-15.2 | 61.9 |
| | 20 | 17.2-12.4 | 63.1 |
| | 21/23 | 12.6-10.3 | 16.4 |
| | 24 | 10.9 | 54.0 |
| Tito Bustillo | 1b/c | 14.9-13.5 | 24.0 |
| | 1a&b | 15.4-14.2 | 30.1 |
| Las Caldas | S.II | 12.9-13.3 | 7.2 |
| Cueva Morín | 2 | | 14.8 |
| El Rascaño | 5 | 16.4 | 3.9 |
| | 4b | | 0.0 |
| | 4 | 16.0 | 6.1 |
| | 3 | 15.2 | 4.9 |
| | 2b | 12.9 | 1.5 |
| El Juyo | 7 | 14.4 | 14.1 |
| | 6 | | 32.9 |
| | 4 | 13.9 | 10.6 |
| Ekain | VII | 16.5-15.4 | 72.1 |
| | VI | 12.1 | 48.7 |
| Erralla | V | 16.2-15.7 | 49.0 |
| | III | 12.3 | 65.6 |
| Abauntz | E | 15.8 | 41.3 |
| Dufaure | 5 | 14.5-15.7 | 44.0 |
| | 4 | 12.2-10.9 | 48.0 |

[a]% Backed Bladelet includes backed micropoints (microgravette and Azilian types). Many Magdalenian assemblages also include small percentages of shouldered and other types of points. **Sources:** Altuna and Merino 1984; Altuna et al. 1985, 1990; Barandiarán et al. 1985; Corchón 1981; González Echegaray and Barandiarán 1981; González Echegaray and Freeman 1971; Moure and Cano 1976; Straus 1988; Straus and Clark 1986; Utrilla 1982.

are described by Bricker and David (1984) at the Abri Pataud, where there is evidence of decreasing size for both types through time (see also Harrold, this volume). There are also some bone, antler, and ivory points in the Gravettian. Bricker and David have suggested that there is an inverse relationship between the organic points and the Gravette points through time, with an increase in bone points toward the end of the Pataud Gravettian sequence.

The Last Glacial maximum (ca. 21,000-17,000 BP) saw the development of new kinds of weapon tips, primarily stone weapon tips such as Solutrean foliate, tanged, and shouldered points (Smith 1966; Straus 1983, 1990, 1991a). Invasive and bifacial flaking techniques were re-invented or elaborated, perhaps at first to produce large, portable knife/cores ("the Protosolutrean"), followed by the development of leaf and shouldered points. A dichotomy appears between large points (for spears) and small points. The latter were probably tips for darts propelled by

atlatl--since the spearthower was invented in Solutrean times, as the recent discovery at Combe Saunière (Dordogne), dated to about 18,000 BP, has proven (Cattelain 1989). There is a decline, although not a total absence, of bone points in most of the Solutrean time range. The Solutrean technology (which is certainly not an ethnic group) first appears ca. 21,000 BP. In some regions it "begins" with leaf points; in others, with both leaf and shouldered points, as shown by finds from La Riera (Straus and Clark 1986) and Vale Almoinha in Portugal (Zilhão 1984; Zilhão et al. 1987). In some places the shouldered points appear early, in others late, and in still others, such as Solutré, they never appear at all. This may have been a matter of site function, hunting type, or local custom. There is a great deal of interregional variability in the timing of the appearance of different basic point types and in point forms (first noted by Smith [1973; see also Straus 1983; Fullola Pericot 1979; Ripoll 1988; Zilhão 1987]) within the primary types of leaf and shouldered points--for example, Asturian concave-base points; Montaut asymmetrical points; Serinya asymmetrical points; Parpalló tanged points; Basque rhomboidal points; le Volgu "monster" laurel leaves; elongated Périgord willow and shouldered points; short, hooked, unifacial Cueto de la Mina shouldered points; backed Mediterranean shouldered points; and so on. Specimens of some of these regional types have sometimes been found hundreds of kilometers from their apparent places of origin, as in the case of tanged points in Portugal, although convergence cannot as yet be totally ruled out.

Although the unilineal cultural evolutionary scheme based on the sequence of point types found in the unique stratigraphy at Laugerie-Haute is not universally valid, as I and others (e.g., Straus 1975; Zilhão 1990) have shown, there is another temporal trend in weapons development that may have some overall validity: namely the isofunctional replacement of Solutrean points (single-element weapon tips) by backed bladelets plus sagaies (multi-element weapon tips). Not widely accepted 15 years ago (but see Straus 1975, 1983; Straus and Clark 1986), it is now clearly a fact that many assemblages with foliate and/or shouldered points in the Solutrean of France, Spain, and Portugal and in the early Epigravettian of Italy (Mussi 1990; Bietti 1990) have moderate or even large quantities of backed bladelets. These are sometimes associated with antler points, including grooved sagaies. Fine screening in modern excavations at such sites as Combe Saunière, Amalda, Chufín, La Riera, and Ambrosio has yielded high percentages of backed bladelets, and, in some stratified sequences, the percentages increase through time as Solutrean points decrease (Table 6.1). This is a trend that was observed by M. de la Rasilla (1989) in his comparison of the sequences of La Riera and the adjacent Cueto de la

Mina, which was recently re-excavated by him. In elegant functional studies of the backed bladelets and shouldered points of Combe Saunière and other Solutrean sites, Geneste and Plisson (1986, 1990; Plisson and Geneste 1989) argue that the two types of tips may have been used for different kinds of game or in different types of hunting. What seems clear is that the Solutrean points were gradually phased out and replaced by the sagaie plus backed bladelet weapon tips. This replacement seems to have been achieved by about 18,000 BP in some regions, such as the Périgord, while in others it came by only about 17,000 or even 16,000 BP, as in some regions of Iberia (Straus 1991). What followed is the suite of technologies collectively known as the Magdalenian or as the Epigravettian in the Mediterranean Basin.

The Magdalenian is characterized by general increases in antler points, backed bladelets, and backed micropoints, although the percentages are variable from level to level and from site to site (Table 6.2). Antler points, and eventually harpoons, are the hallmarks of the Magdalenian, but there are also specialized lithic points, some with regionally specific distributions, such as the Hamburgian and other shouldered and tanged points (see papers in Rigaud 1989 and Rigaud et al. 1992). The Magdalenian is also rich in atlatls, much more so than the Solutrean, as propulsion technology became increasingly important. Some "harpoons" may, in fact, have been elements of tridents or leisters, while true harpoons (whose geographical distribution coincides mainly with that of salmon streams draining into the Atlantic) have basal elements suggesting that they were detachable and equipped with a lanyard (see Julien 1982; Weniger 1987). The stockpile of Magdalenian weapons was, above all, diverse. There were many types of weapon tips and delivery systems. (The bow may have been invented as early as the Solutrean, although the first positive proofs thereof are Mesolithic in date [see Rozoy 1989; Bergman, this volume].) Magdalenian weapons included systems and elements that had been invented thoughout the course of the Upper Paleolithic; they gave hunters specific, specialized capabilities for different game, tactics, milieux, and situations--both on land and in water. Such specialization may have lessened the risk of failure and helped maximize returns per hunting episode.

## MAN-MADE FACILITIES AND THE ROLE OF ART

We have focused on terrain and on active weapons in showing how Upper Paleolithic hunters helped insure success in subsistence acquisition. But there may have been a third aspect to the efficient, effective mass hunting done by these people: the construction, deployment, and use of facilities useful in drives and surround. These may have included nets, portable fences, and drive lines. Of course, nets and weirs may well have been used in birding and fishing, particularly in light of the frequency and sometimes quantity with which remains of these animals appear, especially in Magdalenian sites. I think it is worth considering how effective Upper Paleolithic hunters could have been if they closed off cul-de-sac valleys or gorges after game had been driven into them. Artificial facilities to prevent or hinder escape would have insured massive slaughters. While we obviously have no material proof of such facilities, one could speculate upon the significance of grid-like symbols, so common in cave art, especially in the Cantabrian region. For example, in the small Solutrean cave site of El Buxú, located at the head of a blind valley off the intermontane basin of eastern Asturias, there are numerous such signs engraved on the walls (Obermaier and Vega del Sella 1918; Straus 1983; Menéndez and Soto 1984). They could represent fences or corral sections.

Upper Paleolithic hunters intensified the food quest by diversifying their subsistence base and by developing tactics and weapons that allowed them to maximize their kills of key ungulate species. As Mithen (1990) has cogently argued, they also developed means of extending their cybernetic capacities to deal with uncertainty. It is not a coincidence that cave art flourished in the same regions of southwestern Europe with favorable relief and diverse resources, and at a time when abandonments of the northerly parts of the human range helped cause relatively high population densities in precisely the same favored regions (Straus 1991b). All these phenomena are undoubtedly related to one another. Under these circumstances all means were used to insure human survival.

Without pretending to revive Breuil's (e.g., 1952) pervasive "hunting magic" theory of Franco-Cantabrian art, I believe it is important to keep in mind that this art was created by people who depended fundamentally on hunting for their continued existence. While direct statistical relationships do not exist between the representations of species in archeofaunal assemblages and in works of art in the same sites (e.g., Straus 1976-1977; Altuna 1983; Delporte 1985) and many depicted animals (e.g., large carnivores) were rarely if ever hunted, it is nonetheless true that there are relationships of a less direct sort between actual regional game and artistic images (Rice and Patterson 1985, 1986; González Sainz 1988). Alongside the central place of animals in Upper Paleolithic ideologies, the art of these hunting peoples is both a faithful representation of their world and lives, and a window through which we can glimpse their means of exploiting animal resources. The art goes beyond portraiture to encode seasonal, behavioral, and anatomical data about game, useful in teaching, storing, and organizing survival skills across generations and across fluctuating environmental conditions. Accessing the *etic* meanings of this art should be an important goal of pragmatic, ecologically or economically oriented archeologists, much as deductions about *emic* meanings have tempted so many structuralist or postprocessual prehistorians in recent years. I believe the art cannot be understood without placing it fully within its context: an Ice Age world of hunters living on the edge and by their wits ....

## REFERENCES

Albrecht, G.
1979    *Magdalénien-Inventare vom Petersfels*. Archaeologica Venatoria 6. Tübingen: Institut für Urgeschichte.
Albrecht, G., J. Hahn, and W. Torke
1972    *Merkmalanalyse von Geschossspitzen des mittleren Jungpleistozäns in Mittel- und Osteuropa*. Archaeologica Venatoria 2. Tubingen: Institut für Urgeschicte.
Albrecht, G., H. Berke, and F. Poplin
1983    *Naturwissenschaftliche Untersuchungen an Magdalénien-Inventaren vom Petersfels*. Tübinger Monographien zur Urgeschichte 8. Tübingen: Universität Tübingen.
Altuna, J.
1983    On the relationship between archeofaunas and parietal art in the caves of the Cantabrian region. In *Animals and Archaeology. Volume 1. Hunters and their Prey*. J. Clutton-Brock and C. Grigson, eds. Pp. 227-238. BAR International Series 163. Oxford: British Archaeological Reports.
Altuna, J., A. Baldeón, and K. Mariezkurrena
1985    Cazadores magdalenienses en la Cueva de Ekain. *Munibe* 37:1-206.
1990    *La cueva de Amalda*. San Sebastián: Sociedad de Estudios Vascos.
Altuna, J., K. Mariezkurrena, A. Armendariz, L. del Barrio, T. Ugalde, and J. Peñalver
1982    Carta arqueologica de Guipuzcoa. *Munibe* 34:1-242.
Altuna, J., and J. Merino
1984    *El yacimiento prehistórico de la cueva de Ekain*. San Sebastián: Sociedad de Estudios Vascos.
Arambourou, R.
1978    *Le gisement préhistorique de Duruthy*. Mémoires de la Société Préhistorique Française 13. Paris: Société Préhistorique Française.
Bahn, P.
1984    *Pyrenean Prehistory*. Warminster: Aris and Phillips.
Barandiarán, I., L. Freeman, J. González Echegaray, and R. Klein
1985    *Excavaciones en la cueva del Juyo*. Monografías del Centro de Investigación y Museo de Altamira 14. Madrid: Ministerio de Cultura.
Bietti, A.
1990    The late Upper Paleolithic in Italy. *Journal of World Prehistory* 4:95-155.
Breuil, H.
1952    *Four Hundred Centuries of Cave Art*. Montignac: Centre d'Etudes et de Documentation Préhistoriques.
Bricker, H., and N. David
1984    *Excavation of the Abri Pataud: The Perigordian VI*

*(Level 3) Assemblage*. American School of Prehistoric Research Bulletin 34. Cambridge: Peabody Museum, Harvard University.
Cabrera, V.
1977    El yacimiento solutrense de Cueva Chufín. *Actas del XIV congreso nacional de arqueología*. Pp. 157-164.
1984    *El yacimiento de la cueva de El Castillo*. Bibliotheca Praehistorica Hispana 22. Madrid: Consejo Superior de Investigaciones Cientificas, Instituto Español de Prehistoria, and Departamento de Prehistoria de la Universidad Complutense.
Cattelain, P.
1989    Un crochet de propulseur solutréen de la grotte de Combe Saunière I. *Bulletin de la Société Préhistorique Française* 86:213-216.
Clottes, J.
1976    Les civilisations du Paléolithique supérieur dans les Pyrénées. In *La préhistoire française. Tome I*. H. de Lumley, ed. Pp. 1214-1231. Paris: Editions du Centre National de la Recherche Scientifique.
1989    Le Magdalénien des Pyrénées. In *Le Magdalénien en Europe*. J.-Ph. Rigaud, ed. Pp. 281-357. ERAUL 38. Liège: Université de Liège.
Corchon, M.
1981    *Cueva de Las Caldas, San Juan de Priorio (Oviedo)*. Excavaciones Arqueológicas en España 115. Madrid: Ministerio de Cultura.
Davidson, I.
1989    *La economía del final del Paleolítico en la España oriental*. Trabajos Varios del Servicio de Investigación Prehistórica 85. Valencia: Servicio de Investigación Prehistórica, Diputación Provincial de Valencia.
Delporte, H.
1985    Réflexions sur la chasse à la période paléolithique. *Jahrbuch des Bernischen Historischen Museums* 63-64:69-80.
Fortea, J., M. Corchón, M. González Morales, A. Rodríguez, M. Hoyos, H. Laville, M. Dupré, and J. Fernández Tresguerres
1990    Travaux récents dans les vallées du Nalón et du Sella. In *L'art des objets au Paléolithique. Tome 1*. J. Clottes, ed. Pp. 219-243. Paris: Direction du Patrimoine.
Froment, S.
1980    *Contribution à la géologie du quaternaire de la vallée de la Méhaigne*. Thèse de Licence, Faculté de Sciences, Université Libre de Bruxelles.
Fullola Pericot, J.
1979    *Las industrias líticas del Paleolítico superior ibérico*. Trabajos Varios del Servicio de Investigación Prehistórica 60. Valencia: Servicio de Investigación Prehistórica, Diputación Provincial de Valencia.
Geneste, J.-M., and H. Plisson
1986    Le Solutréen de la grotte de Combe Saunière I. *Gallia Préhistoire* 29:9-27.
1990    Technologie fonctionelle des pointes solutréennes. In *Feuilles de pierre: Les industries à pointes foliacées du Paléolithique supérieur européen*. J. Kozlowski, ed. Pp. 293-320. ERAUL 42. Liège: Université de Liège.
González Echegaray, J., and I. Barandiarán
1981    *El Paleolítico superior de la cueva del Rascaño*. Monografías del Centro de Investigación y Museo de Altamira 3. Santander: Ministerio de Cultura.
González Echegaray, J., and L. Freeman
1971    *Excavaciones en Cueva Morín: 1966-1968*. Santander: Patronato de las Cuevas Prehistóricas.
González Sainz, C.
1988    Le fait artistique. *Bulletin de la Société Préhistorique de l'Ariège-Pyrénées* 43:35-62.
1989    *El Magdaleniense superior-final de la región cantábrica*. Santander: Tantin.

Hahn, J.
1977    Zur Abfolge des Jungpaläolithikums in Sudwestdeutsch-
        land. *Kölner Jahrbuch fur Vor- und Frühgeschichte*
        15:52-67.
1988    *Das Geissenklösterle*. Stuttgart: Konrad Theiss Verlag.
Hauser, O.
1911    *Le Périgord préhistorique*. Le Bugue: Georges Réjou.
Julien, M.
1982    *Les harpons magdaléniens*. Supplément à *Gallia Pré-
        histoire* 17. Paris: Editions du Centre National de la
        Recherche Scientifique.
Kehoe, T.
1990a   Corralling life. In *The Life of Symbols*. M. Foster and L.
        Botscharow, eds. Pp. 175-192. Boulder: Westview Press.
1990b   Corralling: Evidence from Upper Paleolithic cave art. In
        *Hunters of the Recent Past*. D. Reeves, ed. Pp. 34-45.
        London: Allen Unwin.
Menéndez, M., and E. Soto
1984    La cueva del Buxu. *Boletín del Instituto de Estudios
        Asturianos* 38:143-186,755-810.
Mithen, S.
1990    *Thoughtful Foragers*. Cambridge: Cambridge University
        Press.
Moure, J., and M. Cano
1976    *Excavaciones en la cueva de Tito Bustillo*. Oviedo:
        Instituto de Estudios Asturianos.
Mussi, M.
1990    Continuity and change in Italy at the Last Glacial Maxi-
        mum. In *The World at 18,000 B.P.* O. Soffer and C.
        Gamble, eds. Pp. 126-147. London: Unwin Hyman.
Obermaier, H., and R. Conde de la Vega del Sella
1918    *La cueva del Buxú*. Memoria de la Comisiónes de Investi-
        gaciónes Paleontológicas y Prehistóricas 20. Madrid:
        Museo Nacional de Ciencias Naturales.
Oliva, M.
1988    A Gravettian site with mammoth-bone dwelling in
        Milovice. *Anthropologie (Brno)* 26:105-112.
1989    Excavations in the Palaeolithic site of Milovice I (south-
        ern Moravia) in the year 1988. *Anthropologie (Brno)*
        27:265-271.
Olsen, S.
1989    Solutré: A theoretical approach to the reconstruction of
        Upper Paleolithic hunting strategies. *Journal of Human
        Evolution* 18:295-327.
Otte, M.
1984    Paléolithique supérieur en Belgique. In *Peuples chasseurs
        de la Belgique préhistorique dans leur cadre naturel*. D.
        Cahen and P. Haesaerts, eds. Pp. 157-179. Brussels:
        Institut Royal des Sciences Naturelles.
Plisson, H., and J.-M. Geneste
1989    Analyse technologique des pointes à cran solutréennes.
        *Paléo* 1:65-106.
de la Rasilla, M.
1989    Secuencia y crono-estratigrafía del Solutrense cantábrico.
        *Trabajos de Prehistoria* 46:35-46.
Rice, P., and A. Patterson
1985    Cave art and bones. *American Anthropologist* 87:94-100.
1986    Validating the cave art-archeofaunal relationship in
        Cantabrian Spain. *American Anthropologist* 88:658-667.
Rigaud, J.-Ph. (ed.)
1989    *Le Magdalénian en Europe*. ERAUL 38. Liège: Univer-
        sité de Liège.
J.-Ph. Rigaud, H. Laville, and B. Vandermeersch (eds.)
1992    *Le peuplement Magdalénien*. Paris: Editions du Comité
        des Travaux Historiques et Scientifiques.
Ripoll, S.
1988    *La cueva de Ambrosio*. BAR International Series 462.
        Oxford: British Archeaogical Reports.

Roche, J.
1982    A gruta chamada lapa do Suão. *Arqueologia* 5:5-18.
Rozoy, J.-G.
1989    The revolution of the bowmen in Europe. In *The Meso-
        lithic in Europe*. C. Bonsall, ed. Pp. 13-28. Edinburgh:
        John Donald.
Shea, J.
1989    Spear points from the Middle Paleolithic of the Levant.
        *Journal of Field Archaeology* 15:441-450.
Smith, P.
1966    *Le Solutréen en France*. Bordeaux: Delmas.
1973    Some thoughts on variations among certain Solutrean
        artifacts. In *Estudios dedicados al prof. Dr. Luis Pericot.
        Volume 1*. J. Maluquer, ed. Pp. 67-75. Barcelona:
        Instituto de Arqueología y Prehistoria.
Soffer, O., and C. Gamble (eds.)
1990    *The World at 18,000 B.P.: High Latitudes*. London:
        Unwin Hyman.
Straus, L.
1975    *A Study of the Solutrean in Vasco-Cantabrian Spain*.
        Ph.D. dissertation, Department of Anthropology, Univer-
        sity of Chicago.
1976-   The Upper Paleolithic cave site of Altamira. *Quaternaria*
1977    19:135-148.
1983    *El Solutrense vasco-cantábrico*. Monografías del Centro
        de Investigación y Museo de Altamira 10. Madrid:
        Ministerio de Cultura.
1986    Late Würm adaptive systems in Cantabrian Spain.
        *Journal of Anthropological Archaeology* 5:330-368.
1987a   Hunting in late Upper Paleolithic western Europe. In *The
        Evolution of Human Hunting*. M. H. Nitecki and D. V.
        Nitecki, eds. Pp. 147-176. New York: Plenum.
1987b   Upper Paleolithic ibex hunting in southwest Europe.
        *Journal of Archaeological Science* 14:163-178.
1988    The uppermost Pleistocene in Gascony: A view from
        Abri Dufaure. In *Upper Pleistocene Prehistory of
        Western Eurasia*. H. Dibble and A. Montet-White, eds.
        Pp.41-60. University Museum Monograph 54. Philadel-
        phia: The University Museum, University of Pennsylva-
        nia.
1990    The original arms race: Iberian perspectives on the
        Solutrean phenomenon. In *Feuilles de pierre: Les indus-
        tries à pointes foliacées du Paléolithique supérieur
        Européen*. J. Kozlowski, eds. Pp. 425-447. ERAUL 42.
        Liège: Université de Liège.
1991a   Southwest Europe at the Last Glacial Maximum. *Current
        Anthropology* 32:189-199.
1991b   Human geography of the late Upper Paleolithic in
        Western Europe. *Journal of Anthropological Research*
        47:259-278.
1992    *Iberia Before the Iberians*. Albuquerque: University of
        New Mexico Press.
n.d.    *Les derniers chasseurs du renne le long des Pyrénées:
        l'Abri Dufaure, un gisement tardiglaciaire en Gascogne*.
        Mémoires de la Société Préhistorique Française. (in
        press).
Straus, L., and G.Clark
1986    *La Riera Cave*. Anthropological Research Papers 36.
        Tempe: Arizona State University.
Straus, L., J. Altuna, M. Jackes, and M. Kunst
1988    New excavations in Casa da Moura and at the Abrigos de
        Bocas, Portugal. *Arqueologia* 18:65-95.
Straus, L., M. Otte, J.-M. Léotard, A. Gautier, and P. Haesaerts
1992    Middle and Early Upper Paleolithic excavations in
        southern Belgium: A preliminary report. *Old World Ar-
        chaeology Newsletter* 15(2):10-18.
Straus, L., M. Otte, A. Gautier, P. Haesaerts, A. Martinez, M.

Newman, and C. Schutz
    1993    Paleolithic excavations in Belgium by the Universities of New Mexico and Liège. *Old World Archaeology Newsletter* 16(2):1-11.
Utrilla, P.
    1982    El yacimiento de la cueva de Abauntz. *Trabajos de Prehistoria Navarra* 3:203-358.
Weniger, G.-C.
    1987    Der Kantabrische Harpunentyp. *Madrider Mitteilungen* 28:1-43.
White, R.
    1985    *Upper Paleolithic Land Use in the Perigord.* BAR International Series 253. Oxford: British Archaeological

Reports.
Zilhão, J.
    1984    O Solutrense superior de facies cantabrico de Vale Almoinha. *O Arqueologo Português* 4:15-86.
    1987    *O Solutrense da Estremadura portuguesa.* Trabalhos de Arqueologia 4. Lisbon: Instituto Português do Patrimonio Cultural.
    1990    The Portuguese Estremadura at 18,000 B.P.: The Solutrean. In *The World at 18,000 B.P.* O. Soffer and C. Gamble, eds. Pp. 109-125. London: Allen Unwin.
Zilhão, J., F. Real, and E. Carvalho
    1987    Estratigrafia e cronologia da estacão solutrense de Vale Almoinha. *O Arqueologo Português* 5:23-35.

*7*

# The Development of the Bow in Western Europe: A Technological and Functional Perspective

**Christopher A. Bergman**
**3D/Environmental Services, Inc.**
**and Northern Kentucky University**

## ABSTRACT

The development and use of archery equipment in prehistoric Europe has always stimulated archaeological interest. Much of the focus of research has been concerned with the temporal origins of the bow. Surviving examples of prehistoric bows and arrows make it possible to evaluate the functional capabilities of these weapons. Experimental replication of prehistoric European archery equipment shows that early bow and arrow designs were well engineered and adapted to maximize hunting efficiency.

## INTRODUCTION

The development of the bow in western Europe has always stimulated considerable interest on the part of Old World prehistorians. Much of the focus of research has been concerned with the temporal origins of the bow, rather than assessments of the nature of bow design and function. It is not known precisely where and when the bow was first developed, although there has been endless speculation on the subject. It is probably safe to assume that various cultural groups in different locations began experimenting with archery equipment during the Upper Paleolithic. Such assumptions, however, are not the main focus of this paper, which reviews the functional data available on early European bows and arrows.

Functional assessments of archery equipment have been conducted by a number of scholars, including Pope (1923), Klopsteg (1935), Elmer (1946), Hickman et al. (1947), McEwen (1978), Miller et al. (1986), and Bergman et al. (1988). The pioneering work of Dr. Saxton Pope compared the performance of a number of different bow types, including North American ethnographic examples and experimental replicas. To gauge the performance of the various bows he tested, Pope utilized a single criterion: the **cast** or distance a bow can shoot an arrow. In so doing, his work fails to take account of the fact that different bows and their designs are often used for different purposes. For example, a South African Kalahari Bushman bow, which shoots a poison tipped,

unfeathered arrow for no more than 25 m, is just as capable of effectively delivering its projectile as an English yew longbow with a cast of over 200 m.

Hickman et al. (Klopsteg 1935; Hickman et al. 1947) studied the scientific background to archery, especially in relation to the self longbow and the Asian composite bow. Specifically, they conducted experiments aimed at describing the technical and mechanical performance of bows and arrows. An examination of the design of bow limbs by Klopsteg (1935) revealed that flatbows with widened limbs tapering toward the tips have high mechanical efficiency values. This design type was favored by Mesolithic bowyers, as evidenced by extant examples recovered from waterlogged contexts in northwest Europe.

Most recent experimental research on archery tackle has attempted to examine the effect of raw materials, manufacturing techniques, and intended function upon design. McEwen (1978) has examined the role of the composite bow among the nomadic horse cultures of the Asian steppes. He suggests that design modifications in these weapons were closely linked to changes in functional requirements. Specifically, changes in battle armor and tactics necessitated the development of composite bows with greater impact velocity and penetrating power. Miller et al. (1986) have also studied the effects of the use of composite bows in ancient warfare; they discuss changes in battle tactics and siegecraft after the introduction of this weapon during the 3rd millennium B.C. in southwestern Asia.

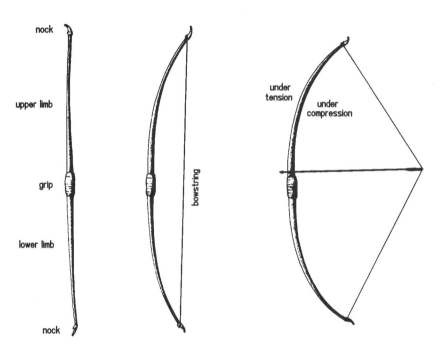

**Figure 7.1.** Longbow labelled according to the terminology used by European bowyers for several centuries.

## TERMINOLOGY

### The Bow

Any discussion of archery tackle must first be prefaced by an understanding of the terms used by bowyers to describe bows and arrows. Figure 7.1 labels the parts of a bow according to the terminology used by European bowyers for at least five centuries (see Ascham 1545).

Two authors, Grahame Clark (1963) and Gad Rausing (1967), have presented data on extant prehistoric archery tackle from western Europe. Clark dealt with northwestern Europe and provided information on Mesolithic and Neolithic bows, as well as arrows. Rausing presented an overview of the development of the bow in both the prehistoric and historic periods. His synthesis of the available data on the subject included a worldwide review of archaeological specimens, historical records and accounts, as well as artistic representations. In addition to these larger works, numerous site reports have described bows and arrows from the European Upper Paleolithic and Mesolithic periods, including Rust (1943), Becker (1945), Behrens et al. (1956), Bröndsted (1957), Troels-Smith (1959), Larsson (1983), Andersen (1985, 1987), and Sheridan (1992).

In mechanical terms, the bow is simply a two-armed spring, spanned and placed under tension by a string. When an arrow is placed on the string and drawn, the bow stores potential energy. Upon release, this energy is transferred to the arrow that is thrown into flight. As a bow is drawn, tensile stress increases along the **back** or outside curve simultaneously with compressive forces developing along the inside curve or **belly**. Any bow must be able to adapt to these forces in order to avoid being broken and successfully to propel the arrow.

Bows are classified into four main groups based on the raw materials and methods of construction, but only one type is relevant to the present discussion: the **self bow**. A self bow, the simplest and oldest form of bow, is any bow made of a single material; in the prehistoric period, self bows are always made from single staves of wood. Self bows often have long limbs up to 6 ft (1.8 m) in length, hence the term longbow, in order to provide an increased draw length and reduce the risk of breakage. The long limbs distribute the tensile stress more evenly over the surface of the back and contribute significantly to the energy transferred to the arrow.

### The Arrow

The **arrow** is the projectile which is shot by a bow, and its design shows considerable morphological variation based on raw materials and function. The basic morphological difference between an arrow and a spear thrower-launched **dart** is the presence of a slot, the **nock**, to fit the bowstring. Darts usually have a small depression or **cup** to fit the **spur** of the spear thrower.

The raw material used for arrows is largely dependent on the local environment. Basically, any straight-growing sapling or reed can be used; in addition, it is also possible to split shafts from larger pieces of wood. To make arrows from saplings, branches or reeds, it is often necessary to heat and straighten them by bending. A variety of tools which act like vises are used for this purpose by modern hunter-gatherers, and one European Upper Paleolithic analogue is the so-called *bâton de commandement*. Arrows made of wooden shafts which have been split or riven from larger branches or trunks are less prone to warping and remain straight for long periods of time. Reeds like *Phragmites*, which are lightweight, rigid, and naturally grow relatively straight, are also suitable for arrowshafts (cf. Elmer 1946:278; McEwen 1978). The manufacture of arrows from reeds necessitates the use of a **foreshaft** because of the lack of solid material into which to cut a notch for mounting a point.

The **fletching** on an arrow, if it is used at all, generally will consist of two to four feathers placed at the nock end. While two to four feathers are most common, some African arrowshafts, for example, are fletched with as many as eight feathers (Dr. C. E. Grayson, personal communication, 1992). The fletching helps to stabilize the arrow during flight and allows it to travel straight; at the same time, it also acts to slow the arrow down. The height and length of the fletching above an arrowshaft must be carefully balanced in order to avoid unnecessary drag. Feathers can be obtained from an almost unlimited variety of birds, and both wing and tail feathers can be used. The way in which the feathers are attached to a shaft involves the use of an adhesive and/or some sort of thread or sinew to bind them down; in some instances feathers are actually sewn onto the shaft. In the most common form of fletching, **radial fletching**, three or four split feathers are fastened separately to the arrowshaft in equidistant units. Another type, **tangential fletching**, uses two whole feathers bound back to back.

**Arrowheads** take a variety of forms and include sharpened wooden points, blunts for bird hunting, antler or bone harpoons primarily for aquatic fauna, and chipped or ground stone points. The **self arrow** has an arrowshaft that tapers into a sharp point or a carved **blunt**. Blunt arrowheads consist of a rounded protuberance at the end of the shaft; they are typically used for hunting small game or birds. Stone points

may be placed on an arrow in a number of ways. The point may be fixed to a foreshaft that is then set into a fletched **mainshaft**. The use of a foreshaft helps to protect the mainshaft, which represents the greatest investment of time during manufacture, from damage due to impact (Hamilton 1982:15; Bergman 1987). Another method is to cut a slot at the end of the arrowshaft and place the point directly into it.

Sinew may be used to bind a projectile point into place, while heat activated resins such as pine pitch can be used as adhesives. In the case of Upper Paleolithic and Mesolithic projectiles with lateral cutting edges, it is highly likely that resins were used to make the backed bladelets or microliths adhere to the shaft (cf. Allain 1979:Fig. 80; Larsson 1983). Bone or antler harpoons are usually attached to an arrowshaft by sinew binding or, in some cases, friction. Historic-period Inuit tie a sinew cord to the arrowshaft and to the base of a small, friction-hafted harpoon used in hunting sea otters (Mason 1893:Pl. LII).

## PREHISTORIC ARCHERY TACKLE FROM THE WESTERN EUROPEAN UPPER PALEOLITHIC AND MESOLITHIC

### Prehistoric Self Bows

All of the surviving examples of prehistoric bows from western Europe are self bows made from single staves of wood. Most of these have been recovered from waterlogged contexts in Scandinavia, particularly Denmark and Sweden. The following section describes some of these finds and provides data on their morphology and construction.

Perhaps the best known Mesolithic bows are those from the site of Holmgaard IV on the Danish island of Zealand (Figure 7.2). This site was occupied beginning in the Late Boreal period or ca. 6000 B.C. The Holmgaard bows are believed to have originally measured 154 cm and 184 cm, respectively. They were made of narrow-grained elm (*Ulmus glabra*) staves, and the maximum width of the limbs on the two bows ranges between 4.5 cm and 6 cm (Rausing 1967:39-40). The limbs are plano-convex and taper evenly toward the pointed nock ends. The handle is constricted and relatively thick on both bows, indicating that this part of the weapon did not bend.

It is not possible to determine the orientation of the growth rings on the Holmgaard bows; thus, it is not easy to identify which of the two surfaces represents the back or belly. Rausing (1967:49), based on the "feel and balance of the staves," suggests that the flattened, split wood surface was the back, while the belly was convex. Such an orientation is similar to the traditional English longbow, which has a D-shaped

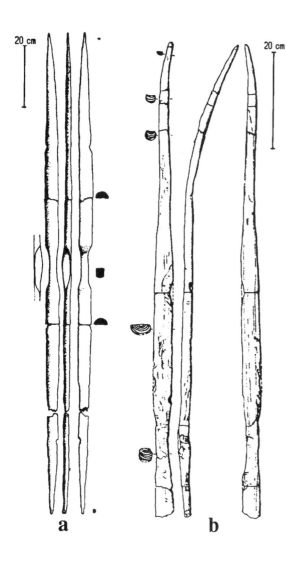

20 cm

20 cm

**a**                    **b**

**Figure 7.2.** (a) Self longbow, made of elm, recovered from Holmgaard IV, Zealand, Denmark (after Clark 1963:Pl. VI); (b) self longbow, made of elm, from Tybrind Vig, Fyn, Denmark (after Andersen 1985:Fig. 161).

suggested here that the Holmgaard bows were shaped in a similar manner.

Ageröd V, an Atlantic period bog site in southern Sweden dated to 6860-6540 radiocarbon years BP, produced two different types of bows. The first is described by Larsson (1983:57) as having a rounded back and a belly which is a flattened, split wood surface. The bow may have originally measured up to 170 cm in length; it was made of a narrow-grained elm (*Ulmus* sp.) stave which was roughly 36 years old when it was cut down. The bow has no apparent incisions for the nocks, but this feature is not essential, and the string can be tied into place without slipping. The surviving fragments of the bow display no pronounced thickening of the grip area, and no obvious constriction is evident. The bow tapers towards narrow, pointed ends from the central section of the grip.

The second bow from Ageröd V (Larsson 1983:59) was made from a European mountain ash or rowan-tree (*Sorbus aucuparia*) branch; it is fragmentary and presently measures 61.7 cm. The bow is generally oval in cross-section and appears to have been minimally shaped, except at the nock ends where two notches were cut for the string. There is no discernable grip area, and the bow undoubtedly was D-shaped, bending through the grip and along its length.

The Ertebølle period (4600-3200 B.C.) bows recovered from Tybrind Vig (Figure 7.2b) probably measured 160 cm in length and were made from knot-free elm (*Ulmus* sp.) staves. They were apparently made from small trunks that were split into two halves (Andersen 1985:61). The orientation of the growth rings of the staves (see Figure 7.2b) suggest the back was rounded in section, while the belly appears to have been the flat, split wood surface. As the bows taper toward their nock ends, the limbs display a pronounced constriction and become more rounded in cross-section. The more complete example has a waisted grip, and this area also appears to be the thickest portion of the bow.

In summary, five of the weapons described above are wide-limbed flatbows, and four of these have narrow, constricted, and rigid grips. Originally, they were between 154 and 184 cm in length and, thus, would be considered longbows. When these prehistoric bows were strung and drawn they would have displayed simple D-shaped profiles (as in Figure 7.1). Finally, it should be noted that the wide-limbed flatbow represents a sophisticated design type undoubtedly requiring significant time and effort to manufacture. It is certain that Mesolithic peoples also made more simple weapons, as evidenced by the round-sectioned bow from Ageröd V, which displays minimal modification. Bows of this type, which may have

cross-section with a flat back and rounded belly. Evidence from other Scandinavian Mesolithic sites, however, indicate this may not be the case. The bows recovered from Ageröd V, central Scania, southern Sweden, and Tybrind Vig, Fyn, Denmark, can be properly oriented by an examination of the position of the tree's growth rings. Bowyers typically orient the back of a bow so that it follows the natural growth rings and curvature of the outside of the tree, closest to the bark. The belly is usually formed of the interior heartwood. The Ageröd V bows and those from Tybrind Vig would thus appear to have convex backs and flattened bellies (cf. Larsson 1983:57-58). It is

been employed briefly for expedient purposes or even by juveniles, would have been less efficient, as well as less powerful.

### Prehistoric Arrows, Arrowshafts, and Projectile Points

A variety of projectile types were utilized by the Late Glacial and Mesolithic peoples of western Europe. During the Upper Paleolithic period, hunters began to experiment with **composite projectile points**. At the 13th millennium BP Magdalenian site of Pincevent in the Paris basin, a reindeer antler point with backed bladelets adhering to its sides was recovered near a hearth (Leroi-Gourhan 1983). This object consisted of a narrow antler point into which two slots had been grooved on opposite surfaces (Figure 7.3a). Backed bladelets were inserted in these grooves and presumably held in place by a heat-activated adhesive such as pine resin; its association with the nearby hearth may be related to replacement of the backed bladelet cutting edges. The design of the point incorporates the impact resisting capabilities of antler (Albrecht 1976; Guthrie 1983; Bergman 1987) with the cutting power of chert. In many respects it anticipates the modern hunting broadhead, which utilizes interchangeable razor inserts for the blades. Points of this type are extremely effective for hunting because they penetrate and open a wide wound channel, maximizing blood loss. It is not known whether such points were ever used in conjunction with a bow (Julien 1982). However, the example from Pincevent is quite thin at its base, ca. 6 mm, and could have easily been slotted into an arrowshaft.

The composite point persisted in use into Mesolithic times, as evidenced by the site of Ageröd V (Larsson 1983:47-50). A broken, grooved bone point measuring 15.6 mm x 9 mm was among the bone and antler tool assemblage. The point had four bladelets attached to its midsection; resin traces on the surface indicated that at least 11 more bladelets were originally positioned there (Figure 7.3b). The bladelets were slotted into narrow grooves at oblique angles along both sides of the point.

The harpoon was another type of bone projectile point utilized for hunting by Late Upper Paleolithic/Mesolithic peoples. At the site of High Furlong, Lancashire, England, [14]C dated to 12,200 ± 160 BP

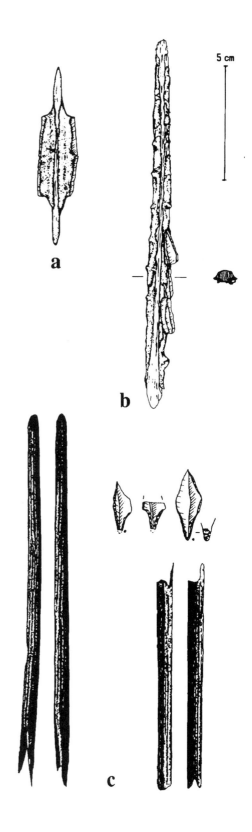

**Figure 7.3.** (a) Experimental reconstruction of the composite point recovered from Pincevent, Seine et Mârne, France (author's reconstruction); (b) Mesolithic composite point recovered from Ageröd V, central Scania, Sweden (after Larsson 1983:Fig. 25); (c) pinewood arrowshaft fragments and Ahrensburg points from Stellmoor, Schleswig-Holstein, Germany (after Rozoy 1989:Fig. 1).

(IGS-C14/134, St-3832; Campbell 1977:Tab. 4), a uniserial barbed harpoon was recovered in association with the left metatarsal and phalanges of a moose (Br. elk) (*Alces alces*). How often harpoons were utilized for hunting terrestrial game or, indeed, whether the shafts they were attached to were propelled by a bow remains uncertain.

Late Glacial arrowshafts were recovered in an Ahrensburgian level at Stellmoor, Schleswig-Holstein, Germany (Figure 7.3c). The site dates to the Younger Dryas phase or approximately 9000-8300 B.C. More than 100 pinewood (*Pinus* sp.) foreshafts and nocked mainshafts were recovered at the site (Rust 1943; Clark 1963:62). Several examples of broken shafts had the tangs of Ahrensburg points still in place. Ahrensburg points are small, tanged projectiles with tips which are typically formed by an oblique truncation (Figure 7.3c). These points were most likely to have been bound with sinew onto the arrowshafts. Experimental studies (Madsen 1983; Fischer et al. 1984; Ataman 1986; Barton and Bergman 1988) show that similar tanged points will break upon impact at the junction of the tang and main body of the point. The tang, held firmly in place by the sinew binding, remains lodged in the arrowshaft. Finally, it should be noted that the two pinewood staves recovered by Rust (1943) at Stellmoor and described by Rausing (1967:33) as bow limbs are not very convincing as such.

At Lilla Løshult, Scania, southern Sweden, a Mesolithic arrow dated to the Early Boreal period or ca. 7000 B.C. was recovered from waterlogged moor deposits (Petersson 1951; Clark 1975). This arrow consists of a pinewood (*Pinus* sp.) shaft tipped by a stone point, probably a triangular microlith, and a microlith side barb (Figure 7.4a). This design relies on the point to penetrate the hide, while the size of the wound channel is increased by the added width of the barb. Another possible example of a Mesolithic arrow with lateral cutting edges was recently recovered from waterlogged peat at Seamer Carr, North Yorkshire, England (Andrew David, personal communication, 1991). Here, a group of 17 microliths appeared to be associated with a fragment of wood (*Populus* or *Salix* sp.), perhaps the remains of a shaft, which has been radiocarbon dated to 8210 ± 150 BP and is therefore Late Mesolithic in age. While the tiny backed bladelets could be interpreted as having been attached to either side of the shaft, it is unclear whether there was a stone tip. Experimental replicas with sharpened wooden points seem to function effectively, however, and the use of backed bladelet cutting edges along the shaft serve to increase the wound diameter.

Transverse arrowheads, still affixed to their shafts, have been recovered from a variety of water-logged contexts in Jutland and Zealand, Denmark, as

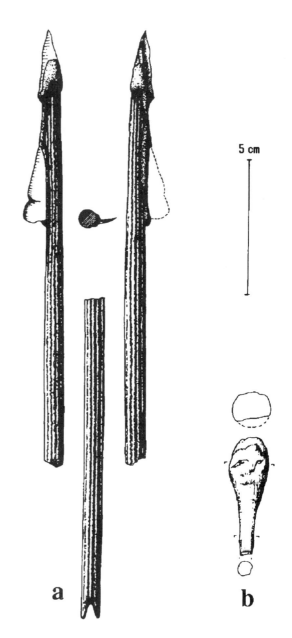

5 cm

a          b

**Figure 7.4.** (a) Arrow recovered from Lilla Løshult, Scania, Sweden (after Rozoy 1989:Fig. 2); (b) blunt arrow-head recovered from Tybrind Vig, Fyn, Denmark (after Andersen 1987:Fig. 161).

well as Petersfehn, Lower Saxony, Germany (Brønd-sted 1957; Troels-Smith 1959; Clark 1963:95-97). Unlike most conventional projectile point types, the transverse examples are trapezoidal in shape and lack an acutely pointed tip. Instead, they utilize an unretouched, straight cutting edge to slice an opening in the hide of an animal. The effectiveness of the transverse arrowhead (see Miller et al. 1980) is evidenced by the recovery of examples of this type embedded in animal bones excavated from Danish Mesolithic settlement sites (Noe-Nygaard 1974). One badly broken specimen was extracted from the proximal epiphysis of the left humerus of a *Cervus elaphus*. The remains of this red deer were excavated from an Atlantic zone VI (6600-4400 B.C.) Kongemosen settlement site in the Aamose, Zealand.

Self arrows have been excavated from several occupations, including the submerged Ertebølle site of Tybrind Vig (Figure 7.4b). Self arrows in the Mesolithic period are represented by examples tipped with wooden blunts; the specimen from Tybrind Vig is made of hazel (*Corylus* sp.). In general, the use of blunt-tipped arrows requires accuracy in aiming and delivering the shot; they function by delivering a crushing blow which breaks bones and injures vital organs without penetration. The advantage of using these types of arrows would be to avoid damage to the hide or feathers. In order to successfully kill an animal, the arrow should contact the cranium or chest, crushing the skull or collapsing the lungs.

## Bow Technology

Several factors must be considered when studying the technology of bow manufacture. Perhaps the most important of these is the wooden stave from which a bow is made. The basic requirement of any wood to be used for a bow is that it be sufficiently elastic to handle the tensile stress along the back, while also being capable of resisting compression of the belly. According to Clark (1963) and Rausing (1967), most of the Mesolithic and Neolithic bows in western Europe were made of two woods: yew (*Taxus baccata*) or elm (*Ulmus glabra* or *Ulmus* sp.). Rausing notes a single example of a Neolithic bow from Branbransø, Denmark, made of European ash, *Fraxinus excelsior*, while Larsson (1983:59) describes a Mesolithic bow made from a European mountain ash or rowan-tree (*Sorbus aucuparia*) branch.

Yew, a narrow-grained hardwood, consists of two visibly distinct layers of wood: the white sapwood and orange-red heartwood. The sapwood layer of yew is strong, fibrous, and elastic. These characteristics make it ideally suited for the back of a bow which must endure tensile stress. Yew heartwood, on the other hand, is more brittle and better suited to handle compression of the belly. The combination of these two layers of wood, each with different properties, made yew one of the better bow woods available to prehistoric Europeans.

The other wood commonly utilized by prehistoric European bowyers, particularly during the Mesolithic period, was elm. Elm, which includes several different species, is also a narrow-grained hardwood, and its sapwood tends to be pink/red in color, while the heartwood is whiter. Elm sapwood is fibrous and has high tensile strength, making it suitable for bow manufacture (Elmer 1946:128). In general, bowyers do not regard elm as highly as yew for the manufacture of bows; Elmer (1946:128), for example, states that elm self bows are "of indifferent merit."

Once a suitably straight, knot-free branch or small trunk has been selected and cut down, the wood can be left to season as is or worked while still green. Stone axes, whether they are ground or flaked, such as the small Mesolithic *tranchet* type, tend to work best at low angles, producing a short, shallow cut. Thus, the number of blows required to cut down a small tree or branch is greater than that needed by metal tools (Coles and Orme 1985:30). Because of the fact that non-metal tools operate at a lower degree of efficiency than metal ones, a wooden stave is more easily shaped with stone tools while it is still fresh or green. Thus, seasoning of the wood, an essential for producing an effective weapon, would take place after the bow had been shaped. While working green wood, rapid drying and checking can be avoided by rubbing animal fat into the stave, a method practiced by historic period Native American bowyers (Mason 1893:10).

In order to prepare a bowstave from a tree trunk or large branch, the wood must first be split with some form of wedge. Seasoned hardwood wedges, as well as those made from large bovid limb bones or deer antlers, are effective for this purpose. Splitting the wood is always preferable to cutting out a stave because it allows the bowyer to examine, as well as to follow, the grain during manufacture. Some woods are more easily riven than others; elm, in particular, is extremely difficult to split successfully. In the case of elm wood, the manufacturing technique may have involved removing the surface forming the belly with an axe, rather than splitting the wood. Finally, another possible method of preparing bow wood, practiced by Paiute Indians in Nevada, is to "block out" the stave on a living tree (Wilke 1988). A pair of parallel, longitudinal grooves is cut by stone tools to define a suitable, branch-free surface area along the trunk. After seasoning for a year or more, the stave is then pried out of the tree with the use of wedges. This method, seemingly used in areas where good timber is scarce, has the advantage of being economical with raw materials, as well as avoiding the time and labor spent in chopping down an entire tree and splitting out bow blanks.

An examination of Mesolithic bows from Europe indicates that some examples have a rounded back which follows the natural curvature and growth rings of the wood. The belly is flattened and coincides with the split or cut surface of the branch or trunk. Shaping of the back consists of little more than removing the bark to the depth of the sapwood layer, a practice both time and energy efficient. In addition, by utilizing a rounded back, the layers of wood beneath the bark are disturbed as little as possible, making it less likely for the bowyer to cut across the grain inadvertently. Most bows break due to tensile stress causing failure on the back or outside curve of the bow. Frequently, the point at which this occurs coincides with an area where the grain has not been followed, causing the wood fibers to separate and crack the bow.

Aside from providing the overall plan shape of the weapon, most woodworking on Mesolithic bows would have occurred on the belly. However, this appears to have not always been the case, and Larsson (1983:57) states that one of the Mesolithic bows from Ageröd V was fashioned mainly by removing wood from the obverse side or back. The belly is scraped and thinned until the bow bends in an even curvature. This process is referred to as **tillering** and involves the gradual reduction of the thickness of both limbs. In general, most prehistoric bows appear to have been well-tillered and taper evenly from the grip area toward the nock ends.

European Mesolithic bows, dated to ca. 6000-3200 B.C., display grips which are often rigid and constricted. The rigid grip area, which is structurally inert and does not bend, prevents the bow from kicking in the hand when the string is released. Wide-limbed flatbows also require a narrowing of their grips in order to compensate for the phenomenon known as the **archer's paradox** (see Miller 1986:Fig. 4). This term refers to the fact that, upon release of the bow-string, an arrow bends, imperceptibly to the eye, around the handle and oscillates before regaining a straight flight pattern. A constricted or waisted grip facilitates the forward movement of the arrow around the handle and helps to increase accuracy. In addition, a narrow grip is obviously easier to handle while shooting a bow.

## Function

During the Late Glacial period in western Europe, the bow seems to have replaced the spear thrower as the primary hunting weapon. There are probably a number of reasons for this, but these are among the advantages of the bow to a hunter: that it can be shot quickly with greater ease from a variety of positions; the bow can be used in a variety of environmental settings, including dense forests; when aiming a bow, an archer is able to sight along the arrow contributing to greater accuracy; finally, the bow utilizes relatively small, lightweight projectiles that can easily be carried in large numbers while hunting.

Experimental replication of European prehistoric flat-limbed bows indicates that they had extended draw lengths, as well as heavy draw weights. Specifically, facsimiles of the Holmgaard bows made by the author show that they probably had draw weights between 70-90 lbs (31.75-40.82 kg) at a 30-in (76.20 cm) draw length. It should be noted that heavy draw weights up to 90 lbs (40.82 kg) do not appear to be unusual among prehistoric bows. McEwen (Bergman et al. 1988) reported that his replica of the Neolithic Meare Heath yew bow from Somerset, England, had a draw weight of 90 lbs (40.82 kg) at 32 in (81.28 cm). The cast of these weapons ranges between 150-200 m, depending on the nature of the wood utilized; yew bows tend to perform better than those of elm, producing a faster and longer cast.

Self longbows are not as mechanically efficient as other bow types, such as the Asian composites (Bergman et al. 1988; McEwen et al. 1991). This inefficiency is directly related to the design and materials used in longbow construction. Depending on the type of wood utilized, the cast and speed of a weapon will vary. Elm, for instance, when compared to yew, is sluggish, and bow limbs made of this wood rebound relatively slowly upon release of the bowstring. The forward movement of the long, heavy limbs uses up some of the bow's stored potential energy, resulting in a diminished transfer of energy to the arrow. In manufacturing weapons with heavy draw weights, prehistoric European bowyers were able to partially counteract this problem. However, this solution would never compensate for the mechanical inefficiency inherent in longbow construction.

Based on ethnographic comparisons (e.g., Weissner 1983 and Deriha 1990), the Mesolithic wide-limbed flatbow would not have required the use of poisoned arrows in order to function effectively. Rather, European prehistoric bows delivered their projectiles with a relatively high impact velocity, and the arrow, upon penetration, damaged tissue and arteries, causing rapid blood loss and inducing cerebral anoxia. Successful hunting with a bow relies upon careful stalking and accurate shooting, specifically the placement of the arrow in an area of the body which induces the maximum amount of bleeding. The chest cavity is an ideal location due to its concentration of major arteries, but lethal shots can also include areas such as the hind quarters surrounding the femoral artery (Dr. Charles E. Grayson, personal communication, 1992). In aiming for the chest, the best shot is behind the scapula, allowing the arrow to pass through to the heart and lungs unhindered by contact with bone. Neck shots can also be fatal, but these are more difficult due to the decreased size of the target area.

The repertoire of projectile types utilized by late and post-glacial hunters performed adequately in the task of bringing down large game such as aurochs, red deer, and moose (Noe-Nygaard 1974; Fischer 1989). Noe-Nygaard (1974) discussed a sample of 26 bones which display hunting injuries, including those from red (*Cervus elaphus*) and roe deer (*Capreolus capreolus*), wild boar (*Sus scrofa*), and aurochs (*Bos primigenius*). They were excavated from Danish waterlogged bog sites including both Mesolithic settlements and isolated finds. Significantly, most of the bones in the sample are associated with the chest area and consist of scapulae, vertebrae, and rib bones. Noe-Nygaard (1974:244) concludes that the damage patterns on the various bones clearly reflects "the knowledge of the prehistoric hunter as to the best region to aim at to wound the animal fatally."

In Noe-Nygaard's (1974) sample there was a marked incidence of healed injuries on the red and roe deer bones. This illustrates the high frequency of the repeated hunting of individual animals by Mesolithic people. An examination of the faunal material, specifically reindeer (*Rangifer tarandus*) bones from the Late Glacial site of Stellmoor, revealed no such pattern of repeated injury. This is because of the different behavioral habits of reindeer when compared to red and roe deer. Reindeer migrate over wide, open tundra landscape in relatively large herds, while red and roe deer are forest animals which live in smaller groups. Both red deer and roe deer are generally territorial, with the bucks remaining sedentary for periods of up to two years (Strangaard 1972; Noe-Nygaard 1974). Thus, the chances of hunters encountering an individual animal over repeated instances were higher than with a migratory reindeer herd with a population of several thousand (Clark 1972:20). The changes in the post-Pleistocene environment, and its accompanying fauna, were undoubtedly reflected in the nature of hunting equipment and strategies. The bow was an ideal weapon for post-glacial hunters needing increased accuracy and easy handling for hunting solitary animals in a forested landscape (cf. Guthrie 1983:293).

## CONCLUDING REMARKS

The limited amount of data on prehistoric archery equipment makes it impossible to determine where and when the bow first came into use in western Europe. Archaeological evidence suggests that the spear thrower and dart have earlier origins in the European Upper Paleolithic than the bow and arrow. Straus (this volume) suggests that the spear thrower was invented no later than the Solutrean period in western Europe. Broken fragments of spear throwers have been recovered from Solutrean and Magdalenian contexts at a number of localities. Solutrean spear throwers have

been identified at both Combe Saunière I and Le Placard in the Dordogne and Charente, France, respectively (Cattelain 1989). Perhaps the best known spear throwers are the carved reindeer antler examples, which come from sites in southwestern France such as Laugerie-Basse, Bruniquel, and Mas d'Azil (Muller-Karpe 1966; Gamble 1986). These objects mostly belong to Magdalenian stages IV-V, which date from approximately 15,500 to 13,000 BP (Brézillon 1969:201; Laville et al. 1980; de Sonneville-Bordes 1988:Tab. 1).

Indirect evidence for the early use of the bow in Europe has often centered around the morphology and technology of projectile point types in the Upper Paleolithic (Clark 1963; Odell 1978). The barbed and tanged points recovered from the upper Solutrean levels of Parpalló, eastern Spain, date to approximately 19,900 B.C. (Davidson 1974). In terms of their overall size and morphology, these pieces would fit comfortably into the ranges displayed by ethnographic examples of arrowheads. Hamilton (1982:27) in discussing North American Indian stone points states, "in the case of the chipped stone projectile point, the critical dimension is the thickness of the stem of the point, which ... is seldom over 3/16 of an inch (5 mm)." The Parpalló points meet this criteria as, indeed, do many other Upper Paleolithic types, such as some of the Perigordian Font-Robert points and Solutrean shouldered points. Patterson (1985) and Christenson (1986:114) caution against using size as a criteria for distinguishing arrowheads from dart points. Using a sample of 142 North American ethnographic dart and arrow points still hafted in their shafts, Thomas (1978) demonstrated that dart points were, on average, larger and heavier (4.40 g) than arrowheads (2.07 g). However, the considerable overlap in the size ranges makes positive identification of the two types difficult, if not impossible, without the corroborating evidence of the shafts. In this context, the recent assertion of Rozoy (1989) that Upper Paleolithic projectile points are, in general, too large to have served as arrowheads should be treated with caution. Fischer (1989), for example, in his extensive study of projectile point function, clearly shows that large, tanged Bromme-type points could easily have served as tips for arrows.

As stated previously, the earliest hard evidence for the use of the bow in Europe appears to be Late Upper Paleolithic, specifically the Younger Dryas phase or 9000-8300 B.C. The recovery of nocked arrowshafts from the site of Stellmoor indicates that the bow was used for hunting reindeer by at least the terminal portion of the glacial period. By later Mesolithic times ca. 6000 B.C., the number of bows and arrows excavated from waterlogged deposits would seem to indicate that archery tackle was distributed throughout northwestern Europe. The fact that evidence exists for the use of the bow in both the glacial and post-glacial periods suggests that the appearance of this hunting technology was not related to environmental changes alone.

The flat-limbed longbows of the Mesolithic period display sophisticated designs with rigid, constricted grips and well-tillered limbs. These bows must have been the end product of repeated experimentation by prehistoric bowyers. Indeed, a similar bow design to that used by Mesolithic peoples was scientifically tested by Klopsteg (1947:100), who stated that it "stresses the limbs equally at all directions" and has "decidedly more cast" than the traditional English longbow of many millennia later.

The data discussed above indicates that the bow was undergoing development during the European Upper Paleolithic. As far as the author is aware, there have been no examples of bows recovered from Upper Paleolithic contexts to date. However, it is easy to imagine that the earliest examples consisted of little more than bending sticks. With the changes in habitat brought about by the end of the Pleistocene period, the functional advantages of bow hunting over the use of spear thrower and dart became more pronounced. Although it seems certain that the changing environment favored the use of the bow, it does not appear to have been the catalyst for its origin. Rather, the new forested habitats emphasized the technological capabilities of archery equipment to better respond to hunting situations less commonly found in the glacial period.

## REFERENCES

Albrecht, G.
1976 Testing of materials as used for bone points in the Upper Palaeolithic. In *Methodologie a l'industrie de l'os préhistorique*. H. Camps-Fabrer, ed. Pp. 119-124. Paris: Editions du Centre National de la Recherche Scientifique.

Allain, J.
1979 L'Industrie lithique et osseux de Lascaux. In *Lascaux inconnu*. A. Leroi-Gourhan and J. Allain, eds. Pp. 87-120. Supplément à *Gallia Préhistoire* 12. Paris: Editions du Centre National de la Recherche Scientifique.

Andersen, S. E.
1985 Tybrind Vig: A preliminary report on a submerged Ertebølle settlement on the west coast of Fyn. *Journal of Danish Archaeology* 4:52-69.

1987 Tybrind Vig: A submerged Ertebølle settlement in Denmark. In *European Wetlands in Prehistory*. J. M. Coles and A. J. Lawson, eds. Pp. 253-280. Oxford: Clarendon Press.

Ascham, R.
1545 *Toxophilus*. 1985 edition. Manchester: Simon Archery Foundation.

Ataman, K.
1986 A group of projectile points from Çan Hasan III. *Arastirma Sonuclari Toplantisi*. Volume IV. Pp. 339-346. Ankara: Kültür ve Türizm Bakanligi Eşki Eserler ve Muzeler Genel Müdurlügü.

Barton, R. N. E., and C. A. Bergman
1988 The Upper Palaeolithic tool assemblage from Hengistbury Head. In *De la Loire a l'Oder: Les civilisations du Paléolithique final dans la nord-ouest Européen*. M. Otte, ed. Pp. 447-464. BAR International Series 444. Oxford: British Archaeological Reports.

Becker, C. J.
1945 En 8000-Aarig stenalderboplads i Holmegaards Mose. *Fra National-Museets Arbejdsmark*:61-72. Copenhagen: National Museet.

Behrens, H., P. Fasshauer, and H. Kirchner
1956 Ein neues Innenverziertes Steinkammergrab der Schnurkeramik aus der Dolauer Heide bei Halle. *Jahresschrift Halle* 40.

Bergman, C. A.
1987 Hafting and use of bone and antler points from Ksar Akil, Lebanon. In *La main et l'outil*. D. Stordeur, ed. Pp. 117-126. Lyon: Travaux de la Maison de l'Orient Mediterranéen.

Bergman, C. A., E. McEwen, and R. Miller
1988 Experimental archery: Determination of projectile velocities and comparison of bow performances. *Antiquity* 62:658-670.

Brézillon, M.
1969 *Dictionnaire de la préhistoire*. Paris: Larousse.

Brøndsted, J.
1957 *Danmarks Oldtid. Volume 1*. Copenhagen: Gyldendal.

Campbell, J. B.
1977 *The Upper Palaeolithic of Britain: A Study of Man in the Late Ice Age*. Oxford: Oxford University Press.

Cattelain, P.
1989 Un crochet de propulseur solutréen de la grotte de Combe Saunière 1 (Dordogne). *Bulletin de la Société Préhistorique Française* 86/87:213-216.

Christenson, A. L.
1986 Projectile point size and projectile aerodynamics: An exploratory study. *Plains Anthropologist* 31:109-128.

Clark, J. G. D.
1963 Neolithic bows from Somerset, England, and the prehistory of archery in north-western Europe. *Proceedings of the Prehistoric Society* 3:50-98.

1974 *The Earlier Stone Age Settlement of Scandinavia*. Cambridge: Cambridge University Press.

Coles, J. M., and J. B. Orme
1985 Prehistoric woodworking from the Somerset Levels: Species selection and prehistoric woodlands. *Somerset Levels Papers* 11:25-51.

Davidson, I.
1974 Radiocarbon dates for the Spanish Solutrean. *Antiquity* 48:63-65.

Deriha, K.
1990 Introduction to the arrow materials of the Ainu stored in the Historical Museum of Hokkaido. *Memoirs of the Historical Museum of Hokkaido* 28:17-29.

Elmer, R. P.
1946 *Target Archery*. New York: Alfred A. Knopf.

Fischer, A.
1989 Hunting with flint-tipped arrows: Results and experiences from practical experiments. In *The Mesolithic in Europe*. C. Bonsall, ed. Pp. 29-39. Edinburgh: John Donald Publishers.

Fischer, A., P. V. Hansen, and P. Rasmussen
1984 Macro and microwear traces on lithic projectile points: Experimental results and prehistoric examples. *Journal of Danish Archaeology* 3:19-46.

Gamble, C.
1986 *The Palaeolithic Settlement of Europe*. Cambridge: Cambridge University Press.

Guthrie, R. D.
1983 Osseous projectile points: Biological considerations affecting raw material selection among Paleolithic and PaleoIndian peoples. In *Animals and Archaeology. Volume 1. Hunters and their Prey.* J. Clutton-Brock and C. Grigson, eds. Pp. 273-294. BAR International Series 163. Oxford: British Archaeological Reports.

Hamilton, T. M.
1982 *Native American Bows.* Missouri Archaeological Society Special Publication 5. Columbia: Missouri Archaeological Society.

Hickman, C. N., F. Nagler, and P. Klopsteg
1947 *Archery: The Technical Side.* National Field Archery Association.

Julien, M.
1982 *Les harpons magdaléniens.* Supplément à *Gallia Préhistoire* 17. Paris: Editions du Centre National de la Recherche Scientifique.

Klopsteg, P.
1935 Science looks at archery. *Archery Review* 1.
1947 *Turkish Archery and the Composite Bow.* Evanston: Klopsteg.

Larsson, L.
1983 *Ageröd V: An Atlantic Bog Site in Central Scania.* Acta Archaeologica Lundensia Number 12. Lund: C. W. K. Gleerups.

Laville, H., J.-Ph. Rigaud, and J. R. Sackett
1980 *Rockshelters of the Perigord.* New York: Academic Press.

Leroi-Gourhan, A.
1983 Une tête de sagaie à armature de lamelles de silex à Pincevent (Seine & Mârne). *Bulletin de la Société Préhistorique Française* 80:154-156.

Madsen, B.
1983 New evidence of Late Palaeolithic settlement in East Jutland. *Journal of Danish Archaeology* 2:12-31.

Mason, O. T.
1893 *North American Bows, Quivers and Arrows.* Smithsonian Annual Report 1891-1892. Washington, D.C.: Smithsonian Institution.

McEwen, E.
1978 Nomadic archery: Some observations on composite bow design and construction. In *Arts of the Eurasian Steppelands.* P. Denwood, ed. Pp. 188-203. London: School of Oriental and African Studies.

McEwen, E., R. L. Miller, and C. A. Bergman
1991 Early bow designs and construction. *Scientific American* 264(6):76-82.

Miller, R. L., C. A. Bergman, and I. Azoury
1980 Additional note on reconstructing aspects of archery equipment at Shams ed-Din Tannira. *Berytus* 30:53-54.

Miller, R. L., E. McEwen, and C. A. Bergman
1986 Experimental approaches to ancient Near Eastern archery. *World Archaeology* 18:178-195.

Müller-Karpe, H.
1966 *Handbüch der Vorgeschichte. Band 1.* Munich: C. H. Beck'sche.

Noe-Nygaard, N.
1974 Mesolithic hunting in Denmark illustrated by bone injuries caused by human weapons. *Journal of Archaeological Science* 1:217-248.

Nuzhnyi, D.
1990 Projectile damage on Upper Paleolithic microliths and the use of the bow and arrow among Pleistocene hunters in the Ukraine. *Aun* 14:113-124.

Odell, G. H.
1978 Préliminaire d'une analyse fonctionelle des pointes microlithiques de Bergumermeer (Pays-Bas). *Bulletin de la Société Préhistorique Française* 75:37-49.

Otte, M.
1988 Le Paléolithique final: Bilan d'une rencontre. In *De la Loire a l'Oder: Les civilisations du Paléolithique final dans la nord-ouest Européen.* M. Otte, ed. Pp. 723-781. BAR International Series 444 (ii). Oxford: British Archaeological Reports.

Patterson, L. W.
1895 Distinguishing between arrow and spear points on the upper Texas coast. *Lithic Technology* 14:81-89.

Petersson, M.
1951 Microlithen als Pfielspitzen; ein fund aus dem Lilla Løshult Moor, Ksp. Løshult, Skäne. *Meddelanden fran Lunds Universitets Historiska Museums* 1950-1951:123-137.

Pope, S.
1923 *A Study in Bows and Arrows.* University of California Publications in American Archaeology and Ethnology 13. Berkeley: University of California.

Rausing, G.
1967 *The Bow: Some Notes on its Origin and Development.* Acta Archaeologica Lundensia Number 6. Lund: C. W. K. Gleerups.

Rozoy, J.-G.
1989 Evolution of the Bowmen of Europe. In *The Mesolithic in Europe.* C. Bonsall, ed. Pp. 29-39. Edinburgh: John Donald Publishers.

Rust, A.
1943 *Die alt- und mittelsteinzeitliche von Stellmoor.* Neumünster: Wachholtz.

Schwartz, C. W., and E. R. Schwartz
1981 *The Wild Mammals of Missouri.* Columbia: University of Missouri Press and Missouri Department of Conservation.

Sheridan, A.
1992 *Treasure Trove 444: Fragmentary Longbow from Rotten Bottom, Dumfriesshire.* Report to the Historic Buildings and Monuments Commission of Great Britain.

de Sonneville-Bordes, D.
1988 Les pointes à affinités nordiques dans le Paléolithique final au sud de la Loire. In *De la Loire à l'Oder: Les civilisations du Paléolithique final dans la nord-ouest Européen.* M. Otte, ed. Pp. 621-653. BAR International Series 444 (ii). Oxford: British Archaeological Reports.

Strangaard, H.
1972 The roe deer (*Capreolus capreolus*) population at Kalo and the factors regulating its size. *Danish Review of Game Biology* 7.

Troels-Smith, J.
1959 En Elmetraes-bue fra Aamosen og andre Traesager fra tidlig-neolitisk-tid. *Aaborger*:122-146.

Weissner, P.
1983 Style and social information in Kalahari San projectile points. *American Antiquity* 48:253-276.

Wilke, P. J.
1988 Bowstaves harvested from juniper trees by Indians from Nevada. *Journal of California and Great Basin Anthropology* 10:3-31.

*8*

# Small Animal Exploitation and its Relation to Hunting, Scavenging, and Gathering in the Italian Mousterian

Mary C. Stiner
Loyola University of Chicago

## ABSTRACT

The remains of small aquatic animals are preserved in many Mousterian caves along the Mediterranean coast. These faunas offer clues about hominids' strategies of searching for and transporting small food packages, an important complement to information on ungulate exploitation in the same region. Marine shellfish and tortoise remains from Grotta dei Moscerini, a shallow cave on the Tyrrhenian (west-central) Italian coast, are examined from taphonomic, zooarchaeologic, and biogeographic perspectives. Mousterian use of large mobile versus small sessile prey are compared to related practices by some "fully modern" human cultures.

## INTRODUCTION

For reasons of preservation, most direct evidence of Palaeolithic subsistence is restricted to faunal remains. Of these materials, however, large mammal bones are the bases for virtually all inferences about hunting and land use practices of Palaeolithic peoples. Whereas ungulate remains are, without question, the most conspicuous and abundant taxa in archaeofaunas across Eurasia, studies of modern hunter-gatherers show plants and other potentially gatherable resources to be essential to most economies. Only a small leap of faith is required to impose the same basic expectation upon hominid lifeways of the past.

Small prey may be considered relatively sessile in habit, either because they are truly immobile (as are plants) or because their territories are so small that the effect is one of immobility from the human point of view. Small prey can also require different, sometimes incompatible, search and collection tactics relative to hunting large game. The ways that and the places where sessile species were exploited, therefore, are important for understanding the nature of Mousterian (and other archaic hominid) foraging systems. The shellfish faunas in Middle Palaeolithic caves lining the Mediterranean coast of southern Europe and North Africa offer unique information about the contingencies of food transport, how search and procurement strategies may have been organized, and the contexts of site use. All such clues in some way reflect the

structures of ancient human societies, a key issue in human evolution research.

Background information on use of large terrestrial game at Moscerini and neighboring caves in the coastal area (Stiner 1990b, 1991a, 1991b, 1991c, 1992), along with a general review of shellfish faunas reported in Mousterian-aged sites elsewhere on the Mediterranean, set the stage for discussion of small game use. The presentation then focuses on shellfish and tortoise exploitation by Mousterian hominids at Grotta dei Moscerini (Vitagliano 1984; Stiner 1990a; Kuhn 1990), a littoral cave in the Italian province of Latium. Analyses begin from a taphonomic perspective: can the shellfish and tortoise assemblages of Moscerini be attributed to hominid economic activities at the site or were they collected by other bone- and shell-gathering agencies? Wave action, for example, represents a potential explanation for the presence of marine shellfish throughout the many strata of this seaside cave, whereas tortoises could have been attracted to the soft sediments inside as places to hibernate, and some subsequently perished there. Damage patterns presented below effectively eliminate these possibilities, instead linking the mollusk shells and tortoise bones to human processing activities in nearly every stratum. Variation in shellfish species representation through the vertical sequence of Moscerini and biogeographic characteristics of these taxa reveal some interesting facts about the circumstances of procurement. The data on small animal use by

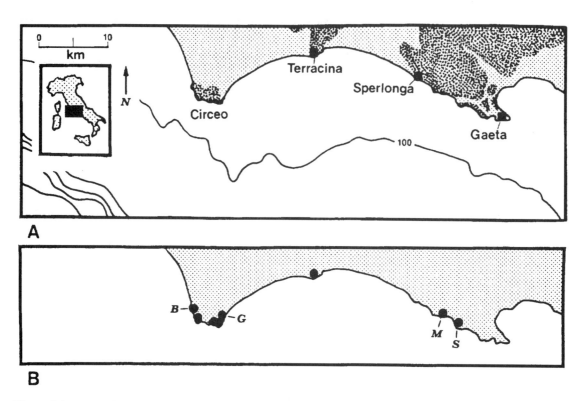

**Figure 8.1.** Terrestrial and subaqueous topography of the Latium coast of Italy and the geographical distribution of the four Mousterian cave sites discussed. **Key:** Heavy stippling = limestone massif; filled circles = caves or shelters containing Upper Pleistocene and/or early Holocene cultural deposits; B = Grotta Breuil; G = Grotta Guattari; M = Grotta dei Moscerini; and S = Grotta di Sant'Agostino.

Mousterian hominids are discussed and compared to patterns of shellfish exploitation documented for certain modern human groups today and in the more recent past.

## THE STUDY AREA AND ARCHAEOLOGICAL SAMPLES

Mousterian faunal assemblages, some of which contain substantial small animal components, occur in a series of cave sites in Latium, on the Tyrrhenian (west-central) coast of Italy (Figure 8.1). North-south trending mountains lie just inland, often separated from the sea by flat, marshy plains and basins. At a few points along the coast, however, uplifted limestone formations rise directly out of the sea (Figure 8.1a), the products of tectonic activity in the region. The caves in these steep, rocky outcrops are relatively shallow solution features, lying between 2 and 50 m above modern sea level (reviewed in Stiner 1990a, 1994).

Today, the caves lie very close to the Mediterranean shore and never were more than 5 to 10 km from the sea during the period under discussion,

usually much closer. Figure 8.1a shows that the subaqueous topography of the coast descends gradually until after the 100 m line, so considerable amounts of land could have been exposed in front of each cave during cooler periods in the past. The chronology of Mousterian site occupations relative to changes in sea level suggest, however, that the sites were used during relatively higher sea stands, in contrast to the situation expected for the Upper Palaeolithic at around 18,000 BP (see Stiner 1990a:24-51).

Most of the faunal collections discussed were excavated by members of the Istituto Italiano di Paleontologia Umana (IIPU) research group, but the sample also includes recently excavated material from Grotta Breuil. The associated lithic assemblages in the four caves belong to a regional facies of the Pontinian Mousterian, pebble-based industries named for the Pontine Plain where they were first identified (Blanc 1937; Taschini 1972). The caves yielding Middle Palaeolithic faunal assemblages are Grotta Breuil (Taschini 1970; Bietti et al. 1988) and Grotta Guattari (Blanc and Segre 1953; Piperno 1976-1977; Taschini 1979) on Monte Circeo, and Grotta dei Moscerini (Vitagliano 1984) and Grotta di Sant'Agostino (Laj-Pannocchia 1950; Tozzi 1970) in the coastal cliffs northeast of Gaeta. Although each of the four sites contains substantial ungulate faunas, only Moscerini also contains significant quantities of shellfish and tortoises.

The faunal assemblages from the four sites collectively span a period beginning just after the last Interglacial, roughly 115,000 years ago, and ending around 35,000 years ago. Chronological assessments are based on electron spin resonance (ESR) dating of ungulate teeth, Uranium-series dating of calcite flowstone layers (Schwarcz et al. 1990-1991, 1991), and geochronological studies (e.g., Blanc and Segre 1953; Segre 1982, 1984). Together, the assemblages probably span Stages 5e/5d through 3 of the classic isotopic chronology based on deep sea cores (Shackleton and Opdyke 1973). This time frame represents a very general trend towards colder, possibly wetter conditions but incorporates several minor warm-cold oscillations. The shellfish faunas of Moscerini formed in the earlier portion of the sequence, roughly between 115,000 and 65,000 BP.

Because the collections of Grotta dei Moscerini were excavated over 40 years ago, they are defined according to vertical geological units only (Segre's unpublished notes, Stiner 1990a). The analyses here consider both fine and grosser vertical level units, the latter following shifts in faunal content and changes in sediment composition (Stiner 1990a). Because of ambiguities in the ESR analyses at Moscerini, radiometric dates are averaged to produce an estimated date for each strata group (Schwarcz et al. 1990-1991).

## TWO MODES OF UNGULATE EXPLOITATION

The large mammal assemblages from the four coastal Mousterian caves in west-central Italy typically contain, in descending order of importance, red deer (*Cervus elaphus*), aurochs (*Bos primigenius*), ibex (*Capra ibex*), fallow deer (*Dama dama*), roe deer (*Capreolus capreolus*), wild boar (*Sus scrofa*), horse (*Equus caballus*), and rarely pachyderms (Stiner 1992). Analyses of age structures and anatomical part representation reveal the existence of at least two distinct ways of exploiting the most common ungulate species--red deer, fallow deer, and aurochs. Independent control research on nonhuman predators, using mortality patterns (Stiner 1990b, 1991b) and the arrays of skeletal parts transported to shelters (Stiner 1991a, 1991b), indicates that the two kinds of assemblages were derived mainly by hunting and **non-confrontational** scavenging, respectively. Non-confrontational scavenging, as envisioned here, contrasts with "aggressive" scavenging by human hunters, who are armed with weapons and may displace another predator at a fresh kill, as documented, for example, for the modern-day Hadza (O'Connell et al. 1988)

The hunted faunas of Grotta Breuil and Grotta di Sant'Agostino associate with relatively prolonged occupations of caves centering on fall-winter, places to which most or all skeletal parts of ungulate prey were transported for processing and consumption. Procurement in these cases was either nonselective with regard to prey age or, more commonly, focused on prime adult individuals. The hunted ungulate faunas of Breuil and Sant'Agostino suggest relatively intensive use of concentrated resource patches. Comparisons of lithic and large mammal abundances indicate that stone tools and associated debris cycled through the system at roughly equal rates to ungulate bones at these sites (documented in Stiner and Kuhn 1992:327-328).

The apparently scavenged ungulate faunas in two other caves, Grotta dei Moscerini and Grotta Guattari, associate with what appear to be more ephemeral occupations. Ungulate procurement may have centered on spring-early summer, but the seasonality results are unclear (Stiner 1990a). Many fewer ungulate parts were moved to these caves for processing per carcass source, mostly heads from old adult animals. Rates of stone artifact and ungulate bone accumulation occurred more or less independently of one another, an observation that cannot be explained by recovery practices of past decades or by differing preservation conditions among the sites or assemblages (Stiner 1990a, 1994). The findings suggest that, while passive scavenging was practiced at the two sites, it did not provide the mainstay of the diet. Evidence of scavenging of ungulates and core reduction strategies facilitating curation and transport of stone tools (Kuhn 1990, 1991, and this volume) together suggest more extensive ranging patterns by hominids while occupying Moscerini and Guattari (Stiner and Kuhn 1992).

Regardless of the exact nature of each foraging pattern outlined above, the Mousterian evidence from west-central Italy indicates that hominids were quite flexible in their responses to foraging opportunities. The two ungulate procurement modes, one apparently emphasizing hunting and the other emphasizing a "low investment" version of scavenging, could correspond to fundamentally different tactics of searching for and procuring food. Ungulate hunting involves capturing large, whole prey that may move about in groups while alive. In contrast, non-confrontational scavenging requires finding and picking up what one can from animals already dead and often dispersed on landscapes (e.g., Houston 1979). Non-confrontational scavenging could occur in the context of hunting, but it could just as easily occur in the context of collecting other kinds of resources. Indeed, picking up things that are scattered and immobile makes passive scavenging much more like gathering than hunting, even

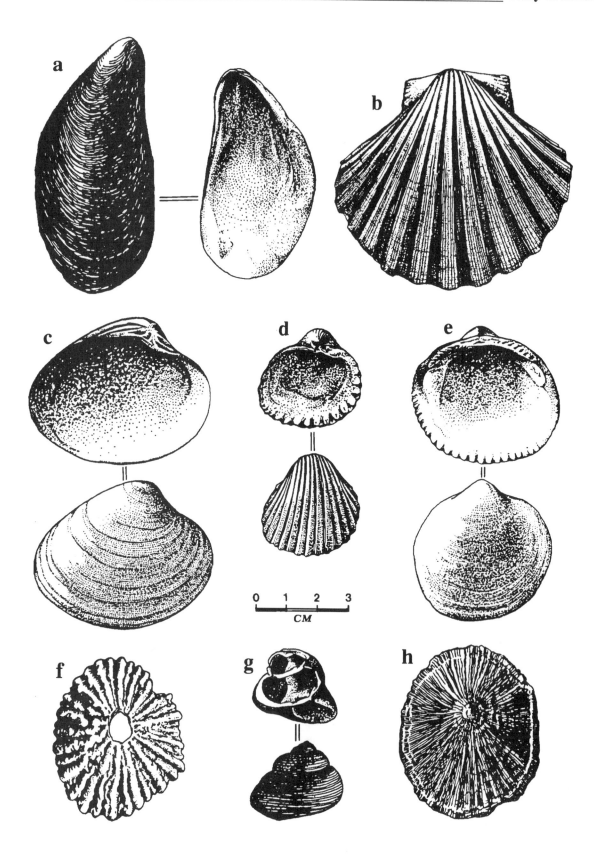

**Table 8.1.** Tortoise counts and damage data for the interior strata series of Grotta dei Moscerini, listed by fine level and level group. Bone specimen counts and frequencies of damage[a] based on NISP.

| Fine level (& level group) | Spur-thigh NISP | Pond NISP | Total NISP | Burned | Impact cones or dents | Crushed | Gnawed |
|---|---|---|---|---|---|---|---|
| 1A-D (M5) | 49 | 14 | 63 | .05 | .05 | .05 | .03 |
| 2 (M5) | 3 | 1 | 4 | - | - | - | - |
| 3 (M6) | 17 | 6 | 23 | .22 | .09 | .09 | - |
| 4 (M6) | 12 | 4 | 16 | .12 | .12 | .06 | - |

[a]Value represents the proportion of total NISP exhibiting the specified type of damage.

though, as in the Italian cases, hunting and scavenging involved exactly the same prey species--principally red deer and aurochs.

The demands of procurement by hunting and by scavenging can differ in terms of the actions required, the spatial distributions of foraging opportunities, and the nutritional yields of the targeted resources. In the Italian study sample, only the scavenged ungulate faunas associate with evidence of small animal use at a shelter by Mousterian hominids. This association provides some unusual clues about the context in which hominid foragers turned to scavenging, as well as some general information about gathering practices, which represents the "other," too often invisible, side of subsistence.

## METHODS FOR ANALYZING SMALL ANIMAL REMAINS

Taxonomic classifications of the reptiles and mollusks of Grotta dei Moscerini are based on comparative skeletal and shell collections of the IIPU. Because species diversity is great in marine communities of the Mediterranean, and taxonomic research on mollusks spans many centuries and many generations of natural historians, two or more Latin synonyms frequently exist for the same animal. My classifications primarily follow Durante (1974-1975; see also Bucquoy et al. 1882; Canavari 1916; Durante and Settepassi 1972; Leonardi 1935) but are keyed to the nomenclature used in Simon and Schuster's *Guide to Shells* whenever possible. Figure 8.2 illustrates the shell forms of most of the marine shellfish taxa found at Grotta dei Moscerini. Terrestrial gastropods also occur in some levels, but, because their presence does not relate to hominid feeding activities there, they will not be discussed (see Stiner 1990a:304-311, 1994).

The taphonomic analyses are based on two types of specimen counts: (1) bone or shell NISP (see below) and (2) mollusk shell hinge counts. NISP is defined as the number of identifiable specimens (Grayson 1984)--in other words, those items in each assemblage assignable to species or a more generic taxonomic level. In the case of mollusks, NISP refers to any sort of shell fragment (shell NISP), whereas "hinge" refers to an anatomically unique hard structure on the shell. In bivalves, the hinge is the location where the two valves articulate in the living animal. The internal coil serves the same purpose in snail-like gastropods, as does the apex of the shell in limpet-like gastropods. Hinge counts provide an independent measure of the degree of shell breakage and, when divided by two for bivalve species (e.g., clams, mussels, scallops), represents the number of individual animals (hinge/2 = MNI) in each vertical provenience. Hinge counts for gastropods correspond

**Table 8.2.** Tortoise counts and damage data for the interior strata series of Grotta dei Moscerini, listed by fine level and level group. Tortoise counts and damage frequencies based on MNI[a].

| Fine level (& level group) | MNI for both species | Number of specimens with impact cones or dents | Number of specimens with Crushing |
|---|---|---|---|
| 1A-D (M5) | 6 | 3 | 3 |
| 2 (M5) | 2 | - | - |
| 3 (M6) | 2 | 2 | 2 |
| 4 (M6) | 3 | 2 | 1 |

[a]Tortoise MNI is determined from the most common portion of the most common right or left limb element for each species in a level. Crushing force always originated from the shell exterior.

**Figure 8.2.** Shell forms of some molluskan taxa from Grotta dei Moscerini: (a) *Mytilus galloprovincialis*; (b) *Pecten jacobaeus*; (c) *Callista* [=*Meretrix*] *chione*; (d) *Cerastoderma edule*; (e) *Glycymeris* [=*Pectunculus*=*Axinea*] spp.; (f) *Patella ferruginea*, broken; (g) *Monodonta turbinata*, opened by humans; (h) *Patella caerulea*.

Strata
group

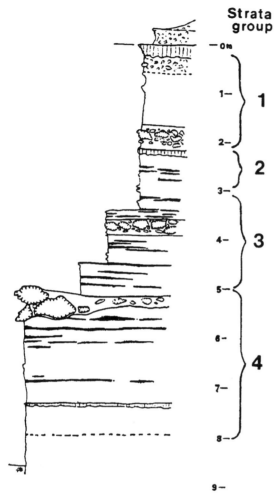

**Figure 8.3.** Schematic of the 9 m exterior strata sequence of Grotta dei Moscerini (adapted from Vitagliano 1984 and based on field drawings by A. G. Segre).

# LINKING TORTOISES AND SHELLFISH TO HOMINID AGENCIES

Grotta dei Moscerini contains a long stratigraphic sequence of 30 fine cultural levels in the exterior series (Figure 8.3) and a more compressed series in the cave interior (Stiner 1990a). The levels contain remains of ungulate head parts and Mousterian stone tools, in addition to the remains of water- and land-dwelling tortoises, marine clams, mussels, certain edible gastropods, and even sponges.

## Tortoises

While uncommon in the deposits overall, most of the aquatic and land tortoises in Moscerini were obtained and processed by hominids. Tortoise remains are confined to the interior level series of the cave: levels 1A-D to 4, or level groups M5 and M6 (Tables 8.1 and 8.2). Level group M5 is primarily a carnivore den (Stiner 1990a, 1994), but it also contains small quantities of flint artifacts. Level group M6 lacks evidence of carnivore activity and is comparatively rich in flint artifacts.

Two types of tortoises occur in the deposits. The land-dwelling variety is a species of *Testudo*, probably the Mediterranean spur-thighed tortoise (*T. graeca*). It is more abundant, comprising 76% of total tortoise NISP, and it occurs in similar proportions throughout the interior levels (Table 8.1). The European pond tortoise (*Emys orbicularis*) is an aquatic species, inhabiting the still or slow-moving waters of ponds, lakes, and rivers (Stuart 1982:71-72). In coastal Latium, this tortoise is also common in brackish water habitats, such as coastal barrier lagoons.

Both tortoise species hibernate in soft or disturbed sediments during the winter, and, because of this behavior, whole specimens are frequently preserved in fine-grained alluvial sediments dating to the Pleistocene. Archaeological sites in west-central Italy often contain soft sediments because of their association with hydrological settings. Tortoises seeking suitable hibernation spots may be attracted to these locations, a possibility that must be addressed in the case of Grotta dei Moscerini.

Tortoise remains in the site include limb bones, carapace, and plastron (belly plate) fragments. The kinds of damage on these remains are very different from naturally fossilized specimens from the Latium region. The latter show much fine abrasion from surrounding sands or silts. To the extent that fragmentation occurs, breaks tend to follow the suture lines joining the bony plates of the shell and to have rectangular contours. All but the smallest tortoise elements in the Moscerini assemblages are broken, and many display green bone fractures (conservatively,

directly to the number of individual animals (hinge = MNI).

The frequencies of damage on shells or bones are expressed as fractions of total NISP. Several classes of damage are considered, depending on the type of material. The bones of tortoises are examined for tool marks, distinctive fracture patterns (e.g., green breaks, impact cones, and impact depressions), burning damage, evidence of gnawing, crushing, abrasion, digestive etching by carnivores, and weathering. Marine shells are examined for beach polish and fractures associated with wave action, based on modern examples. Evidence of shell modification by humans includes burning damage and freshness of break edges. The shell counts also include a small number of specimens retouched into tools (Vitagliano 1984).

**Table 8.3.** Fragment (NISP), hinge, and burning counts for common marine bivalves of Grotta dei Moscerini, listed by fine level.

| Level | *Callista chione* and *Glycymeris* sp. | | | | *Cardium* sp. and *Cerastoderma* sp. | | | | *Mytilus galloprovincialis* | | | |
|---|---|---|---|---|---|---|---|---|---|---|---|---|
| | NISP | NISP Burn | Hinge | Hinge Burn | NISP | NISP Burn | Hinge | Hinge Burn | NISP | NISP Burn | Hinge | Hinge Burn |
| EXT 13 | - | - | - | - | - | - | - | - | 5 | 1 | 1 | 1 |
| EXT 14 | 5 | 1 | - | - | - | - | - | - | 386 | 42 | 88 | 13 |
| EXT 15 | 9 | 2 | 3 | - | 2 | - | 1 | - | 510 | 85 | 126 | 30 |
| EXT 16 | 13 | 10 | - | - | 1 | - | - | - | 63 | 21 | 13 | 5 |
| EXT 17 | 24 | 7 | 2 | 1 | - | - | - | - | 35 | 11 | 9 | 5 |
| EXT 18 | 16 | 7 | 4 | 2 | - | - | - | - | 4 | - | 1 | - |
| EXT 19 | 10 | 6 | 2 | - | - | - | - | - | 2 | 1 | - | - |
| EXT 20 | 12 | 11 | 3 | 2 | 4 | - | - | - | 86 | 33 | 23 | 10 |
| EXT 21 | 259 | 123 | 29 | 16 | 6 | 3 | 1 | - | 45 | 18 | 7 | 4 |
| EXT 22 | 271 | 176 | 37 | 20 | 7 | 4 | 1 | - | 10 | 9 | - | - |
| EXT 23 | 165 | 90 | 22 | 11 | 8 | 2 | 1 | - | 2 | - | 1 | - |
| EXT 24 | 106 | 44 | 23 | 11 | 1 | - | - | - | 3 | - | 1 | - |
| EXT 25 | 96 | 40 | 17 | 9 | 2 | 1 | - | - | 3 | - | - | - |
| EXT 26 | 100 | 23 | 21 | 11 | 2 | 2 | - | 1 | 5 | 2 | - | - |
| EXT 27 | 4 | - | 1 | - | 1 | - | - | - | - | - | - | - |
| EXT 28 | 12 | 4 | 1 | - | - | - | - | - | 6 | 3 | 1 | - |
| EXT 29 | - | - | - | - | - | - | - | - | 4 | 2 | 1 | - |
| EXT 30 | 7 | 2 | - | - | 3 | 2 | - | - | 128 | 61 | 27 | 17 |
| EXT 31 | 6 | 2 | 2 | - | - | - | - | - | 71 | 30 | 9 | 3 |
| EXT 32 | 12 | 4 | 1 | - | 1 | - | - | - | 12 | - | 2 | - |
| EXT 33 | 5 | 3 | - | - | - | - | - | - | 39 | 15 | 7 | 3 |
| EXT 34 | 3 | - | - | - | - | - | - | - | 19 | 9 | 3 | - |
| EXT 35 | 9 | 2 | 2 | 1 | - | - | - | - | 1 | - | - | - |
| EXT 36 | 7 | - | 1 | - | - | - | - | - | - | - | - | - |
| EXT 37 | 32 | 1 | 7 | - | 4 | - | - | - | 26 | 4 | 9 | 2 |
| EXT 38 | 15 | 1 | 3 | - | - | - | - | - | 35 | 11 | 6 | 2 |
| EXT 39 | 30 | 2 | 3 | - | - | - | - | - | 31 | 16 | 5 | 4 |
| EXT 40 | - | - | - | - | - | - | - | - | - | - | - | - |
| EXT 41 | 2 | - | - | - | - | - | - | - | 6 | - | 2 | - |
| EXT 42 | - | - | - | - | - | - | - | - | - | - | - | - |
| EXT 43 | 10 | - | 3 | - | - | - | - | - | - | - | - | - |
| BEACH 44 | 85 | - | 85 | - | 20 | - | 20 | - | - | - | - | - |
| INT 1 | 65 | 1 | 24 | - | - | - | - | - | - | - | - | - |
| INT 1A | 15 | - | 5 | - | - | - | - | - | - | - | - | - |
| INT 1B | 7 | 2 | 1 | - | - | - | - | - | - | - | - | - |
| INT 1C | 22 | 2 | 5 | - | - | - | - | - | - | - | - | - |
| INT 1D | 16 | 1 | 3 | - | - | - | - | - | - | - | - | - |
| INT 2 | 41 | 3 | 10 | - | 1 | - | - | - | - | - | - | - |
| INT 3 | 71 | 1 | 28 | - | 2 | - | - | - | - | - | - | - |
| INT 4 | 21 | 1 | 7 | 1 | 7 | - | - | - | - | - | - | - |

**Key:** NISP = total shell fragment count; NISP Burn = number of shell fragments burned; Hinge = hinge count; Hinge Burn = number of hinges burned.

46% of total tortoise NISP) akin to damage on large mammal bones in the same levels. The shells of the tortoises were opened while fresh, and the break edges seldom are abraded. Impact cones or, more often, impact depressions (Plate 8.1b-d) occur on the exterior surfaces of carapace fragments, on or very near break edges (Table 8.1). The tortoise shells appear to have been struck with a hard, blunt object, such as a rock

**Table 8.4.** Incidence of beach polish relative to shell NISP for common marine bivalves in Grotta dei Moscerini, listed by fine level.

| Level | *Callista chione* and *Glycymeris* sp. | | *Cardium* sp. and *Cerastoderma* sp. | | *Mytilus galloprovincialis* | |
|---|---|---|---|---|---|---|
| | NISP | Number Polished | NISP | Number Polished | NISP | Number Polished |
| EXT 13 | - | - | - | - | 5 | - |
| EXT 14 | 5 | - | - | - | 386 | - |
| EXT 15 | 9 | - | 2 | - | 510 | - |
| EXT 16 | 13 | 1 | 1 | 1 | 63 | - |
| EXT 17 | 24 | 3 | - | - | 35 | - |
| EXT 18 | 16 | - | - | - | 4 | - |
| EXT 19 | 10 | - | - | - | 2 | - |
| EXT 20 | 12 | 2 | 4 | 4 | 86 | - |
| EXT 21 | 259 | - | 6 | - | 45 | - |
| EXT 22 | 271 | - | 7 | - | 10 | - |
| EXT 23 | 165 | - | 8 | - | 2 | - |
| EXT 24 | 106 | - | 1 | - | 3 | - |
| EXT 25 | 96 | - | 2 | - | 3 | - |
| EXT 26 | 100 | - | 2 | - | 5 | - |
| EXT 27 | 4 | - | 1 | - | - | - |
| EXT 28 | 12 | - | - | - | 6 | - |
| EXT 29 | - | - | - | - | 4 | - |
| EXT 30 | 7 | - | 3 | - | 128 | - |
| EXT 31 | 6 | - | - | - | 71 | - |
| EXT 32 | 12 | - | 1 | - | 12 | - |
| EXT 33 | 5 | - | - | - | 39 | - |
| EXT 34 | 3 | 3 | - | - | 19 | - |
| EXT 35 | 9 | - | - | - | 1 | - |
| EXT 36 | 7 | 1 | - | - | - | - |
| EXT 37 | 32 | - | 4 | 4 | 26 | - |
| EXT 38 | 15 | 1 | - | - | 35 | - |
| EXT 39 | 30 | 4 | - | - | 31 | - |
| EXT 40 | - | - | - | - | - | - |
| EXT 41 | 2 | - | - | - | 6 | - |
| EXT 42 | - | - | - | - | - | - |
| EXT 43 | 10 | 7 | - | - | - | - |
| BEACH 44 | 85 | 85 | 20 | 20 | - | - |
| INT 1 | 65 | - | - | - | - | - |
| INT 1A | 15 | - | - | - | - | - |
| INT 1B | 7 | - | - | - | - | - |
| INT 1C | 22 | - | - | - | - | - |
| INT 1D | 16 | - | - | - | - | - |
| INT 2 | 41 | - | 1 | - | - | - |
| INT 3 | 71 | - | 2 | - | - | - |
| INT 4 | 21 | - | 7 | - | - | - |

hammer. As best as can be determined from this small sample, the incidence of cone or impact dents and crushing on carapace fragments in M6 follows tortoise MNI (Table 8.2), as would be expected if only one or two blows were required to open the carapace of each animal. Fewer of these fracture types are represented in relation to MNI in the predominantly hyena components of M5.

A minor fraction of the tortoise bones in 1A-D and 2 (level group M5) are gnawed by a large carnivore (3% of 63 specimens), whereas 5% are burned (Table 8.1). Gnawing and burning damage do not co-occur on the same specimens, however. In levels 3 and 4 (level group M6), tortoise bones are fewer in number (39 specimens) but are more easily tied exclusively to hominid activities. There is no evidence of gnawing by carnivores, and burning is more frequent at 12% and 22% of NISP. Thus, where taphonomic and archaeological evidence on associated large mammal remains and tool frequencies point to hominid activities, evidence of burning on tortoise remains increases markedly.

The data indicate that hominids processed the tortoises found in levels 3 and 4 (M6) and some of those found in levels 1 and 2 (M5). Where the hominids obtained these reptiles is not known, but it is significant that habitats suited to both species would have been present in the immediate vicinity of the

cave. As for the time of year when hominids might have collected them, the tortoises could have been excavated from their winter hiding places inside or near the cave or collected while aboveground and active in the warmer seasons.

## Marine Shellfish

Shells of marine mollusks in association with Mousterian industries are reported for various caves lining the Mediterranean Sea and for roughly contemporaneous Middle Stone Age caves on the shores of South Africa (e.g., Voigt 1973, 1982). Five Mediterranean localities have been noted in particular: the Gibraltar caves (Garrod et al. 1928; Baden-Powell 1964); the Balzi Rossi or Grimaldi caves in Liguria

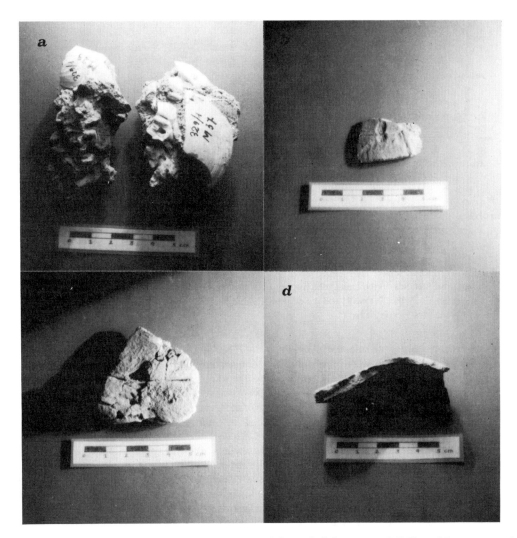

**Plate 8.1.** Aquatic animal remains from Grotta dei Moscerini: (a) shell fragments of *Callista chione* cemented to red deer maxilla and mandible fragments; (b-d) pond tortoise carapace and plastron fragments with green-bone fractures, crushing, and impact depressions.

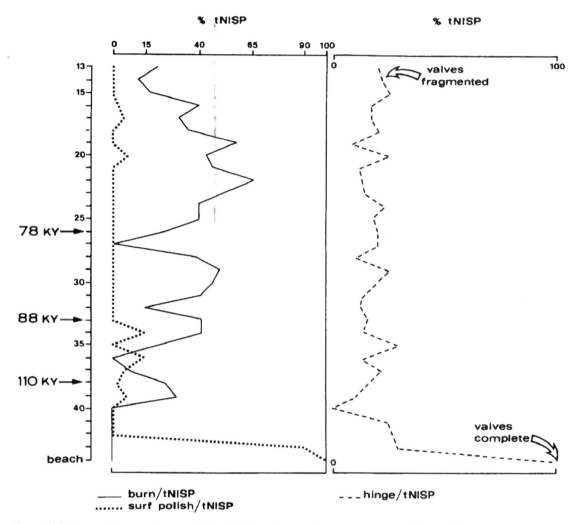

% tNISP

**Figure 8.4.** Damage frequencies on mollusk shells from the exterior strata sequence of Grotta dei Moscerini: surf polish and burning damage on all shells (% tNISP) and the degree of valve fragmentation (hinge/tNISP). Three averaged ESR dates are shown on the stratigraphy axis.

near the Italian-French border (Blanc 1958-1961); Grotta dei Moscerini in Latium, west-central Italy (Vitagliano 1984; Stiner 1990a); coastal caves in Puglia, southern Italy (Palma di Cesnola 1965); and, at Haua Fteah at Cyrenaica in North Africa (McBurney 1967). It is not clear if hominids were the shell collectors at Gibraltar (Freeman 1981), but attributions to hominid activities are more credible in some of the Italian cases. Given the potential implications of shellfish exploitation in the Mousterian--in essence, the earliest evidence of marine resource use by land-bound hominids in Europe--this archaeological phenomenon is underreported. Although several probable cases have been recognized since the late 1920s, no taphonomic inquiry relating these faunas to human diet has been done.

The arrays of molluskan taxa found in coastal Mousterian caves of the Mediterranean vary from east to west, dominated by mussels (*Mytilus gallo-provincialis*, *M. edulis*) and limpets (*Patella caerulea*, *P. ferruginea*) in the Gibraltar and Balzi Rossi cases, and by mussels and two species of marine clam (*Callista* [=*Meretrix*] *chione* and *Glycymeris* [=*Pec-tunculus*=*Axinea*] spp.) in the central and southern Italian cases. The marine gastropod genus *Monodonta* also was eaten by Middle and Upper Palaeolithic peoples in Italy; human-inflicted damage (Figure 8.2g) is characteristic in all sites, usually with a portion of the shell wall sheared away by a sharp, clean blow.

The shellfish species most commonly collected by hominids at Moscerini were bivalves that can be grouped into two categories according to substrate preferences (Table 8.3). Most common are the rock-adhering mussel (*Mytilus galloprovincialis*) and two genera of sand-dwelling clams, *Callista chione* and *Glycymeris* spp. A variety of other marine bivalves and gastropods are also represented in much lower frequencies, including sand clam genera with corrugated shells, such as *Cardium* and *Cerastoderma*, which co-occur with other sand-dwelling taxa in the deposits. Scallops (*Pecten*), oysters (*Ostrea*), Venus shells (*Venus gallina*), and an unidentified conch-form species also occur in very low frequencies. All of these species can be collected from littoral habitats somewhere along the modern sea margin without diving in deep water or using water craft.

The present entrance of Grotta dei Moscerini lies just beyond the reach of the winter sea storm line. Scoured clean by the sea during the last Interglacial, the oldest sediments in the cave postdate this high sea stand. Soon after 120,000 years ago (Blanc and Segre 1953; Schwarcz et al. 1990-1991), waves and littoral drift began depositing sands in the front part of the cave. The stratigraphic sequence thus begins with sandy beach deposits (EXT 44), containing whole or nearly whole sand clam valves (Figure 8.4). Most of these shells display damage characteristic of surf action, including extensive polishing by sand (Figure 8.4 and Table 8.4) and punched-out umbellas caused by collisions with shoreline rocks or other shells. This kind of damage, confined to bivalve umbellas, is not to be confused with randomly placed beveled holes that Natacid predatory snails drill into the shells of their victims (Stiner 1994). All of the kinds of damage on shells from the ancient beach deposit (EXT 44) match examples found on beaches in this locality today.

Sea regression following the last Interglacial left the cave entrance clear of the surf line. The cave was situated only slightly more inland, but enough so that sediment formation involved terrestrial and aeolian phenomena exclusively. Hominids began visiting Grotta dei Moscerini between 115,000 and 110,000 years ago and occupations recurred there until roughly 65,000 years ago. Three ESR averaged dates on red deer tooth enamel (Schwarcz et al. 1991) are shown on the stratigraphy axis of Figure 8.4. Because of ambiguities associated with efforts to date this site (Stiner 1990a:40-51; see also methodological discussion by Grün 1988), the lengths of the time gaps across strata probably are more informative than the absolute values.

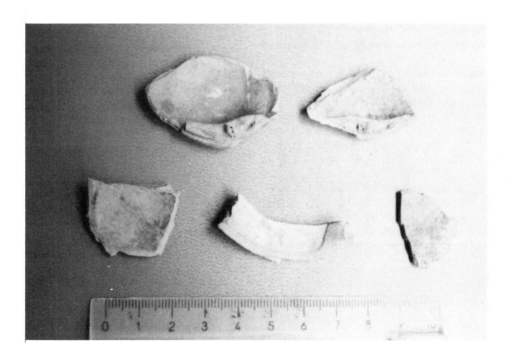

**Plate 8.2.** Marine bivalve shell fragments from Grotta dei Moscerini, modified by hominids and showing burning and/or clean, square-break edges.

Whereas shellfish occur in nearly every cultural (tool-bearing) level of Moscerini, the quantities are low and represent comparatively few individuals, as shown by the hinge counts in Table 8.2. In contrast to the whole valves in the sterile beach level, shells associated with flint tools in EXT 13 through 43 are highly fragmented. The degree of fragmentation (hinge/tNISP) varies, as illustrated in Figure 8.4, but falls within a restricted range throughout this strata series. Nearly all break edges are clean, square, and sharp (Plate 8.2). Surf polish is very rare (Figure 8.4). Sedimentological evidence does not indicate that shells were washed in by waves after the beach (EXT 44) was formed, suggesting that other agencies of collection were responsible for the occasional wave-worn specimens in EXT 13 through 43.

Burning damage is completely absent from shells in the beach level at the base of the sequence, although it is present on shells throughout the levels containing stone tools. The frequencies of burning of shells vary. Where shells are burned, they are also fragmented, but Figure 8.4 shows that the extent of shell fragmentation among levels does not parallel burning frequencies very closely. Burned shells in EXT 13 through 43 signify human activity and suggest that the mollusks were processed and/or discarded in the vicinity of fires. Because the incidence of burning on shell is akin to that on lithic artifacts, however, burning damage is not necessarily the direct result of cooking. Several superficial burn features were noted by the excavators in 1949 (Segre's unpublished field notes), and damage to shells may simply have resulted from, among other things, new fires built atop old debris.

Some valve fragments of *Callista chione* were retouched unifacially to make simple scraper tools (Figure 8.5), a phenomenon also reported for other coastal Mousterian caves in Italy (Palma di Cesnola 1965; Vitagliano 1984). Hominids apparently preferred *Callista* for this purpose; deliberate retouch is not reported for *Glycymeris*, the other common bivalve genus in the deposits with a smooth, porcelain-like shell (compare Figure 8.2c and e). Claims that Mousterian hominids in Italy fashioned highly expedient tools from clam shells appear to be well-founded, although some of the specimens from Moscerini previously identified as "retouched" are ambiguous (see also Kuhn 1990).

Evidence of retouch on *Callista* shells occurs only on the inside lip, and shell tools are rare relative to total *Callista* NISP. Because of the natural curvature of the shell, it is only feasible to produce such retouch by striking or pressing inward from the outside surface of the valve. Force applied from the inside outward, on the other hand, generally results in square-edged breaks. Mousterian hominids undoubted-

ly were aware of this fact, but shell structure, not people, probably limited the orientation of marginal retouch to one direction. Thus, unifacial retouch in itself might not effectively distinguish deliberate tool-making from the accidental trampling of *Callista* shells. More convincing with regard to the authenticity of the retouch is the stark contrast between shell specimens identified as tools and those that are not: tools are completely retouched along the full length of the margin fragment, while other margin fragments are hardly chipped at all. The contrast exists despite uneven cave floors and the pervasive fragmentation of shells throughout the cultural levels. Moreover, if marginal retouch were caused simply by trampling, the same damage should be more evenly distributed on the natural margins of all clams possessing similar valve morphology; as noted above, this phenomenon does not extend to *Glycymeris*.

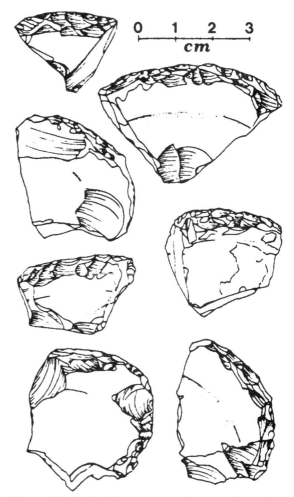

**Figure 8.5.** Unifacial scrapers made on *Callista chione* shells from Grotta dei Moscerini (drawings are adapted from Vitagliano 1984:159).

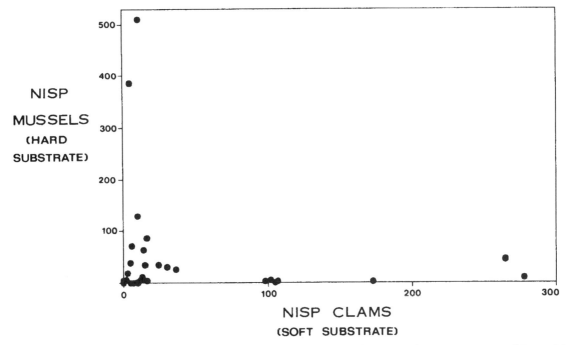

**Figure 8.6.** Scatter plot of sand clam and mussel frequencies (shell NISP) in the exterior strata sequence of Grotta dei Moscerini.

In summary, shellfish and tortoises in Grotta dei Moscerini show every indication of having been brought into the cave and processed there by hominids. Nevertheless, only one of the four seaside caves in the Latium sample contains appreciable evidence of shellfish exploitation. Each of the four caves lies within 1 km of the modern shoreline, and short stretches of sandy beach and rocky shore are, and always were, within a short walk. New excavations at Grotta Breuil (my current research) yield small quantities of shells, but numbers are very low relative to mammal remains, and shellfish exploitation cannot be considered economically significant there.

## AQUATIC RESOURCES AND
## HOMINID FORAGING STRATEGIES

Smooth-shelled clams and mussels are the most common types of shellfish in Grotta dei Moscerini. The relative proportions of these taxa, however, vary greatly among the cultural levels (Table 8.2). This fact could be of tactical significance because the nutritional values of the Mediterranean mussels, clams, and oysters discussed here are roughly equivalent in food mass and nutritional value--at least according to recent summaries and dietary recommendations published in Italy (e.g., Chierchia in *Corriere Salute* 1992). These clam and mussel species clearly differ, however, in

their substrate requirements. Today, the clams inhabit sandy sediments exclusively, while the mussels prefer rocky substrates. Mussel colonies also occur on softer substrates but clearly prefer and thrive on rocky ones, as demonstrated at Porto di Civitavecchia near Rome by Taramelli et al. (1977). Mussels are somewhat more versatile in their preferences for substrate, water salinity, and depth relative to the high tide line than are the clams. And, of the clams, *Callista chione* may be the most sensitive.

Variation in the frequencies of clams and mussels in the exterior strata series of Moscerini is most easily explained by changes in sea level that would have altered shoreline habitats just in front of the cave. The variation probably does not reflect "choosiness" on the part of hominid foragers. Both sand-dwelling clams and rock-dwelling mussels are represented wherever shells are found in the deposits: one class is merely more abundant than the other where samples are large. Figure 8.6 is a scatter plot comparing sand clam and mussel frequencies in the exterior strata, based on total shell NISP for each category. The plot reveals an "either/or" situation wherever shells are abundant. In other words, sand clams dominate or mussels dominate, even though the frequencies are not negatively correlated in a straightforward way. The lack of a simple or direct negative correlation is not surprising. There is no reason to assume that selection criteria or foraging radii of Mousterian hominids should precisely match the spatial distributions of live shellfish patches on rocky outcrops or sandy beds. We only know that, when hominids collected more shellfish at Moscerini, they tended to concentrate on species from one kind of substrate or the other. Indeed, a regression in which samples are weighted by size produces a significant negative correlation (P < .01).

Figure 8.7 illustrates clam and mussel frequencies by fine levels in the exterior Moscerini sequence. Three averaged ESR dates are shown on the stratigraphy axis; as noted above, the beach deposit lying at the base of the sequence formed around the end of the last Interglacial. Alternating series of frequency "pulses" are apparent for mussels and sand clams. The frequency pulses tend to have unidirectional tails, gradually increasing as levels become younger and then ending suddenly. These pulses are evident both from shell NISP (illustrated) and hinge counts (consistently around 10% of NISP, Table 8.3). The unidirectional pulses are not explained by differing degrees of shell fragmentation and/or mechanical sorting by size among the levels, because fragmentation patterns show no such trends (compare Figures 8.4 and 8.7).

Rather than displaying smooth opposing transitions, the mussel pulses closely track declines in sand clam frequencies. The fact that the pulses span thousands of years of sediment formation, evident from the three ESR dates, is also significant. The time frame encompassed by the exterior strata sequence coincides with a general trend towards cooler climatic conditions, but incorporates several minor oscillations in global temperature and sea level. Local topography dictates that, as the level of the sea rose and fell, the proportion of exposed rocky surfaces was altered relative to sandy beach formations in the immediate vicinity of Moscerini. The sequence began with warm temperatures and a sandy beach in front, much like the modern setting of this cave. Sand may have eroded away during certain phases of sea regression, periodically revealing new configurations of limestone bedrock. The relative abundances of rock-dwelling and sand-dwelling mollusks at this locality would have shifted accordingly. The cause of sudden declines in either bivalve category remains a mystery, but, with more extensive intersite comparisons in the future, may also eventually be explained by geological phenomena associated with sea level changes at the small scale.

The comparisons above show that hominids were willing to eat bivalves of either substrate class. Their choices of which shellfish to bring into Grotta dei Moscerini appear to have been guided foremost by locational convenience: one kind of shellfish patch, on rock or in sand, may have been closer to the cave entrance at any given time in the past. Assuming that transport distance was limited by the relatively low caloric yield per bivalve, hominids may have been willing to move them to a shelter only from the closest patches before eating them--otherwise they might eat the shellfish where they found them. The Middle Palaeolithic case from Moscerini, contrasted with the lack of evidence for shellfish exploitation at caves only slightly farther removed from the shore in this area, suggests the influence of this simple energetic principle.

Figure 8.8 shows the relative frequencies of modified ungulate bone, chipped stone artifacts, and shellfish in the exterior strata of Moscerini. These classes of archaeological material do not parallel one another very well at a fine scale, despite being associated in the general sense. Where one class of material is found, one will certainly find the others, but there is no straightforward positive correspondence in abundance. The emphases of hominids on scavenged ungulate parts, small animals, and stone tools were not entirely interdependent. Hominids clearly had a highly varied procurement agenda while occupying this cave (see also Stiner and Kuhn 1992).

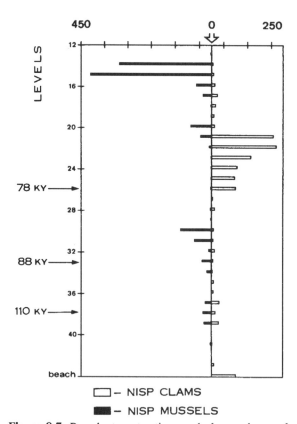

**Figure 8.7.** Bar chart contrasting sand clam and mussel frequencies (shell NISP) in the exterior strata sequence of Grotta dei Moscerini by fine level.

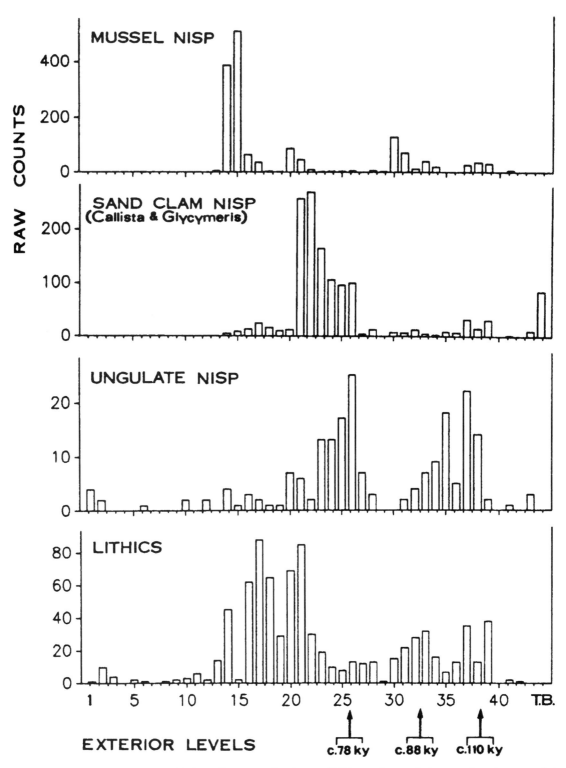

**Figure 8.8.** Relative frequencies of lithic artifacts, ungulate bones (NISP), marine sand clams, and marine mussels in the exterior strata sequence of Grotta dei Moscerini.

Remains of small **terrestrial** mammals are also present in some of the Italian caves, but taphonomic data show that they were the prey of denning carnivores and, in a few instances, owls (Stiner 1990a, 1994). It is significant that Mousterian hominids did not bring small land mammals to any of the four caves and that they brought shellfish only to the one lying closest to the littoral margin. Hominids may well have eaten a variety of small prey while away from caves-- the data show only that hominids did not normally transport these foods to shelter unless they were obtained very close by the shelter. A small difference in distance from shore, on the order of a few hundred meters, apparently determined whether shellfish would be carried to a cave at all. Local distributions of substrate-specific shellfish patches apparently determined which species were deposited inside Moscerini at any given time in the past.

## CONCLUDING DISCUSSION

Some of the findings of this study represent firm conclusions, whereas others serve mainly for refining hypotheses to be tested in a wider array of archaeological circumstances. It is clear from the taphonomic evidence that Middle Palaeolithic foragers made use of littoral marine resources at Grotta dei Moscerini. That people consumed shellfish as early as the Mousterian in the Mediterranean region has been suspected for some time (e.g., Leonardi 1935; Palma di Cesnola 1965), but the Moscerini case represents the first clear demonstration of this important economic phenomenon. With the benefit of taphonomic methods, more Mousterian cases are bound to emerge (e.g., my current research on Riparo Mochi in the Balzi Rossi, Liguria). Shellfish exploitation at Moscerini is generally consistent with cases dating to roughly the same time range in southern Africa (e.g., Voigt 1973, 1982). Whether procuring shellfish, tortoises, or seals, Middle Palaeolithic and Middle Stone Age hominids appear to have been limited to what could be obtained from littoral habitats--and probably not from the deeper waters beyond (on the question of seals in west-central Italy [Stiner 1990a]; aquatic exploitation in southern Africa [Binford 1984; Marean 1986; Voigt 1973, 1982]).

It is interesting that small animal use by Mousterian hominids at caves in west-central Italy is confined to aquatic species and, further, that these resources were transported to shelter only when available in the immediate vicinity. Hominids may have eaten small terrestrial mammals as well, but they evidently did not bring them to the caves before doing so. The principle behind transport of shellfish to shelters may have been the same as that governing the use of terrestrial species; only shellfish patches in the right place at the right times of year permitted hominids to break this rule. Limited willingness to transport small prey to shelters is evident not so much from the fact that hominids consumed clams and mussels at Moscerini as from the patterns of species alternation across 30 cultural layers and several thousand years. Variation in the frequencies of sand-dwelling clams and rock-dwelling mussels can be explained by subtle changes in sea level that altered the extent of rocky versus sand habitats near the cave entrance. Hominids carried to Moscerini only that class of shellfish which was closest at any given time in the past. The few wave-worn specimens that co-occur with shells processed by hominids were probably collected by accident, mixed with other things. Circumstantial as the evidence may be, the rare but persistent presence of wave-worn specimens in non-littoral sediments suggests that the entrance of the cave was never far from the shore.

Foraging tactics involving the selective transport of ungulate head parts, apparently obtained by scavenging, and the gathering of shellfish and tortoises converge at Moscerini. There is little, if any, evidence of ungulate hunting at this site, although faunal records from caves elsewhere on the Latium coast (Grotta di Sant'Agostino and Grotta Breuil) demonstrate that Mousterian hominids were effective hunters in other circumstances. Although the ungulate head-collecting phenomenon appears in two coastal Mousterian sites (Moscerini and Grotta Guattari G4-5), shellfish assemblages occur only in Moscerini. Within the Moscerini sequence, there is no absolute correspondence between evidence of scavenging and the use of small animals at the fine scale. Perhaps the two kinds of foraging tactics (gathering and non-confrontational scavenging) were united foremost by the context of the search process itself.

The search and procurement tactics of gathering and non-confrontational scavenging may have much in common. Both can yield relatively small food packages that must be collected rather than subdued. This basic criterion about food volume per procurement event notwithstanding, the Moscerini case reveals significant differences in hominids' willingness to transport certain kinds of small packages over any distance. Ungulate head parts must have come from multiple terrestrial localities, requiring appreciable movement in order to find and collect, whereas shellfish were concentrated in a more predictable line along the coast. Mousterian lithic technological evidence, associated both with scavenged ungulate remains and shellfish harvesting at Moscerini, also indicates extensive or frequent movement by the hominids relative to other sites in the area, based on comparatively high frequencies of transported tools, core reduction tactics for small flint pebbles that emphasized production of large flakes and tool blanks at the expense of cores, and much resharpening of tools (Kuhn 1990, 1991, this volume; see also Stiner and Kuhn 1992). These secondary sources of evidence suggest that the hominids were distinguishing among small food packages on the basis of their nutritional contents.

The times of year in which modern and archaic humans turned to aquatic resources may have been much the same: limited seasonality data suggest that hominid occupations at Moscerini centered on spring, although the data are unclear (Stiner 1990a, 1994). We know, however, that shellfish were significant additions to the diets of later peoples of the Mediterranean Basin, especially in spring when plant foods and sources of animal fat tend to be scarce (e.g., Deith 1983, 1986, 1989; Deith and Shackleton 1986). I have shown elsewhere that head parts of ungulates are a rich source of fats, even in animals perishing from starvation during late winter through spring (Stiner 1991a, 1993). Because ungulate heads require considerable processing, there is some incentive to move them to foraging hubs (see also technological discussion in Stiner and Kuhn 1992). These qualities of head parts may explain why Mousterian hominids transported scavenged ungulate heads farther and more often than other foods in spite of the small packages they represented. The fats in ungulate head parts may have provided essential temporary supplements to a diet otherwise poor in fat. The Mediterranean bivalves discussed above contain some cholesterol (measures for other kinds of fats are not available), but values are low per 100 g unit if compared to terrestrial and avian prey in well-fed states (Chierchia in *Corriere Salute* 1992). Likewise, plant sources may have been in short supply for at least part of the time that hominids used the cave (see also Stiner and Kuhn 1992), also making animal fat precious for enhancing the nutritional value of other protein-rich foods (see Speth and Spielmann 1983).

Mousterian shellfish exploitation in west-central Italy may have differed from that of later humans in the intensity, or scale, at which it was practiced. It clearly differed from later periods in the kinds of terrestrial resource use with which it alternated or co-occurred at Grotta dei Moscerini. Using lithic artifact frequencies as a point of reference, small quantities of shellfish and ungulate parts were collected at the cave over thousands of years, a relationship that is not explained by in situ decomposition of organic materials (Stiner 1990a, 1994). Low, poorly correlated rates of input of animal remains of all kinds to lithic accumulation may instead suggest periodic emphases on still other resources, namely plants (Stiner and Kuhn 1992). The Mousterian pattern evident at Moscerini also differs from Upper Palaeolithic and Mesolithic cases of the same region, in that the latter peoples brought small terrestrial mammals, birds, and the carcasses of large hunted prey to shelters where they also brought shellfish. Thus, the Mousterian data from west-central Italy suggest some fundamental differences in site use and mobility, as well as in the strategies for offsetting needs for key, seasonally scarce nutrients such as fats. Contrasts in the ways that Mousterian and fully modern humans exploited small game appear to be expressions of how two competent predators used foraging territories differently in order to balance the opportunities to collect various classes of resources with the human need for them.

Gathering practices are among the most poorly understood facets of Middle Palaeolithic adaptations. This is partly because we have few opportunities to investigate gathering directly, but an overly glorified and often vague view of large game hunting in human evolution research is equally to blame. Gathering is about basic economics, logistics, and the necessities that limit human life, and, from a scientific standpoint, evidence relating to gathering warrants more attention than it currently receives. In addition to demonstrating marine exploitation as early as 110,000 BP in Middle Palaeolithic Europe, the perspective gained from the case of Grotta dei Moscerini is important for refining hypotheses about food search tactics, including the economic context of scavenging. Small animal use is less conspicuous in Palaeolithic records than large mammal procurement, and certainly less sensational. However, small animal use implies gathering behavior, the often invisible side of prehistoric foraging systems. If archaeological research questions are about the "structure" of human adaptations and changes therein, gathering practices hold unique keys for understanding how ancient subsistence systems were organized and how they may have differed from those of fully modern peoples.

## ACKNOWLEDGMENTS

I thank Gail Larsen Peterkin, Harvey Bricker, and Paul Mellars for their invitation to participate in the 1991 SAA symposium and for their efforts to see this paper through the publication process. I am grateful to Lew Binford, Steve Kuhn, and Diane Gifford-Gonzalez for their input throughout the course of this study. Thanks are also due to Liz Voigt, whose comments were a great help for developing the shellfish analyses, and to my European colleagues, Prof. A. G. Segre and Drssa. E. Segre-Naldini, for their invitation to work on the Moscerini collection. This research was supported by the American Association of University Women, L. S. B. Leakey Foundation, Institute for

International Education (Fulbright Program), and National Science Foundation.

**REFERENCES**

Baden-Powell, D. F. W.
1964    Gorham's Cave, Gibalter: Report on the climatic equivalent of the marine mollusca. *Bulletin of the Institute of Archaeology* (University of London) 4:216-218.

Bietti, A., G. Manzi, P. Passarello, A. G. Segre, and M. C. Stiner
1988    The 1986 excavation campaign at Grotta Breuil (Monte Circeo LT). *Quaderno Archeologico Laziale* 16:372-388.

Binford, L. R.
1984    *Faunal Remains from Klasies River Mouth.* New York: Academic Press.

Blanc, A. C.
1937    Nuovi giacimenti paleolitici del Lazio e della Toscana. *Studi Etruschi* 11:273-304.
1958-   Industria musteriana su calcare e su valve di *Meretrix*
1961    *chione* associata con fossili di elefante e rinocerante, in nuovi giacimenti costieri del Capo de Leuca. *Quaternaria* 5:308-313.

Blanc, A. C., and A. G. Segre
1953    Excursion au Mont Circe. *Livret/Guidebook, INQUA IV^ème Congrès International*, Roma et Pisa.

Bucquoy, E., P. Dautzenberg, and G. Dollfus
1882    *Les mollusques marins du Roussillon, Volumes I, II & III.* Paris: J.-B. Baillière & Fils.

Canavari, M. (Cerulli-Irelli, S.)
1916    Fauna malacologica mariana. *Paleontolographica Italica, Memorie di Paleontologia.* Pisa: Museo Geologico della Università di Pisa.

Corriere Salute
1992    "Il nuovo colesterolo." L. Bazzoli, G. Cadoria, and R. Renzi, coordinators. Supplemento al *Corriere della Sera*, 21 Settembre 1992.

Deith, M. R.
1983    Seasonality of shell collecting, determined by oxygen isotope analysis of marine shells from Asturian sites in Cantabria. In *Animals and Archaeology. Volume 2. Shells Middens, Fishes and Birds.* J. Clutton-Brock and C. Grigson, eds. Pp. 67-76. BAR International Series 183. Oxford: British Archaeological Reports.
1986    Subsistence strategies at a Mesolithic camp site: Evidence from stable isotope analyses of shells. *Journal of Archaeological Science* 13:61-78.
1989    Clams and salmonberries: Interpreting seasonality data from shells. In *The Mesolithic in Europe.* C. Bonsall, ed. Pp. 73-79. Edinburgh: John Donald.

Deith, M. R., and N. Shackleton
1986    Seasonal exploitation of marine molluscs: Oxygen isotope analysis of shell from La Riera Cave. In *La Riera Cave: Stone Age Hunter-Gatherer Adaptations in Northern Spain.* L. G. Straus and G. A. Clark, eds. Pp. 299-313. Anthropological Research Papers 36. Tempe: Arizona State University.

Durante, S.
1974-   Il Terreniano e la malacofauna della Grotta del Fossel-
1975    lone. (Circeo). *Quaternaria* 18:331-345.

Durante, S., and F. Settepassi
1972    I molluschi del giacimento Quaternario della Grotta della Madonna a Praia a Mare (Calabria). *Quaternaria* 16:255-269.

Freeman, L. G.
1981    The fat of the land: Notes on Paleolithic diet in Iberia. In *Omnivorous Primates, Gathering and Hunting in*

*Human Evolution.* R. S. O. Harding and G. Teleki, eds. Pp. 104-165. New York: Columbia University Press.

Garrod, D. A. E., L. H. Buzton, G. E. Smith, and D. M. A. Bate
1928    Excavation of a Mousterian rock-shelter at Devil's Tower, Gibralter. *Journal of the Royal Anthropological Institute* 58:33-114.

Grayson, D. K.
1984    *Quantitative Zooarchaeology.* New York: Academic Press.

Grün, R.
1988    The potential of ESR dating of tooth enamel. In *L'Homme de Néandertal. Tome 1. La Chronologie.* M. Otte, ed. Pp. 37-46. ERAUL 28. Liège: Université de Liège.

Houston, D. C.
1979    The adaptations of scavengers. In *Serengeti: Dynamics of an Ecosystem.* A. R. E. Sinclair and M. Norton-Griffiths, eds. Pp. 263-286. Chicago: University of Chicago Press.

Kuhn, S. L.
1990    *Diversity within Uniformity: Tool Manufacture and Use in the "Pontinian" Mousterian of Latium (Italy).* Ph.D. dissertation, Department of Anthropology, University of New Mexico. Ann Arbor: University Microfilms.
1991    "Unpacking" reduction: Lithic raw material economy in the Mousterian of west-central Italy. *Journal of Anthropological Archaeology* 10:76-106.

Laj-Pannocchia, F.
1950    L'industria Pontiniana della Grotta di S. Agostino (Gaeta). *Rivista di Scienze Preistoriche* 5:67-86.

Leonardi, P.
1935    *I Balzi Rossi: Parte seconda le faune, 1. I molluschi pleistocenici della Barma Grande.* Istituto Italiano di Paleontologia Umana Anno XIII. Firenze: Istituto Italiano di Paleontologia Umana.

Marean, C. W.
1986    Seasonality and seal exploitation in the southwestern Cape, South Africa. *The African Archaeological Review* 4:135-149.

McBurney, C. B. M.
1967    *The Haua Fteah (Cyrenaica) and the Stone Age of the South-East Mediterranean.* Cambridge: Cambridge University Press.

O'Connell, J. F., K. Hawkes, and N. Blurton Jones
1988    Hadza hunting, butchering, and bone transport and their archaeological implications. *Journal of Anthropological Research* 44:113-161.

Palma di Cesnola, A.
1965    Notizie preliminari sulla terza campagna di scavi nella Grotta del Cavallo (Lecce). *Rivista di Scienze Preistoriche* 25:3-87.

Piperno, M.
1976-   Analyse du sol mousterien de la Grotte Guattari su Mont
1977    Circe. *Quaternaria* 19:71-92.

Schwarcz, H. P., W. Buhay, R. Grün, M. Stiner, S. Kuhn, and G. H. Miller
1990-   Absolute dating of sites in coastal Lazio. *Quaternaria*
1991    *Nova 1 (Nuova Serie)*:51-67.

Schwarcz, H. P., A. Bietti, W. M. Buhay, M. C. Stiner, R. Grün, and A. Segre
1991    On the re-examination of Grotta Guattari: Uranium-Series and Electron-Spin-Resonance dates. *Current Anthropology* 32:313-316.

Segre, A. G.
1982    Considerazioni sulla cronostratigrafia del Pleistocene laziale. *Atti 24ª Riunione Scientifica, Istituto Italiano di Preistoria e Protostoria.* Pp. 23-30. Firenze: Istituto Italiano di Preistoria e Protostoria.
1984    Considerazioni sulla cronostratigrafia del Pleistocene

Laziale. *Estratto dagli Atti della XXIV Riunione Scientifica dell'Istituto Italiano di Preistoria e Protostoria nel Lazio, Ottobre 1982.* Firenze: Istituto Italiano di Preistoria e Protostoria.

Shackleton, N. J., and N. D. Opdyke
1973   Oxygen isotope and palaeomagnetic stratigraphy of equatorial Pacific Core, V28-238. *Quaternary Research* 3:39-55.

Speth, J. D., and K. A. Spielmann
1983   Energy source, protein metabolism, and hunter-gatherer subsistence strategies. *Journal of Anthropological Archaeology* 2:1-31.

Stiner, M. C.
1990a   *The Ecology of Choice: Procurement and Transport of Animal Resources by Upper Pleistocene Hominids in West-Central Italy.* Ph.D. dissertation, Department of Anthropology, University of New Mexico. Ann Arbor: University Microfilms.
1990b   The use of mortality patterns in archaeological studies of hominid predatory adaptations. *Journal of Anthropological Archaeology* 9:305-351.
1991a   Food procurement and transport by human and non-human predators. *Journal of Archaeological Science* 18:455-482.
1991b   An interspecific perspective on the emergence of the modern human predatory niche. In *Human Predators and Prey Mortality.* M. C. Stiner, ed. Pp. 149-185. Boulder: Westview Press.
1991c   A taphonomic perspective on the origins of the faunal remains of Grotta Guattari (Latium, Italy). *Current Anthropology* 32:103-117.
1992   Overlapping species "choice" by Italian Upper Pleistocene predators. *Current Anthropology* 33:433-451.
1993   The place of hominids among predators: Interspecific comparisons of food procurement and transport. In *From Bones to Behavior: Ethnoarchaeological and Experimental Contributions to the Interpretation of Faunal Remains.* J. Hudson, ed. Pp. 38-61. Occasional Paper 21. Carbondale: Southern Illinois University Press.

1994   *Honor Among Thieves: A Zooarchaeological Study of Neandertal Ecology.* Princeton: Princeton University Press. (in press).

Stiner, M. C., and S. L. Kuhn
1992   Subsistence, technology, and adaptive variation in Middle Paleolithic Italy. *American Anthropologist* 94:12-46.

Stuart, A. J.
1982   *Pleistocene Vertebrates in the British Isles.* London: Longman.

Taramelli, E., C. Chimenz, A. Mussino, G. Battaglini, and F. Bianchi
1977   I molluschi del porto di Civitavecchia (Roma). *Atti della Società Italiano di Scienze Naturali e del Museo Civico di Storia Naturale di Milano* 118:299-314.

Taschini, M.
1970   La Grotta Breuil al Monte Circeo, per una impostazione dello studio del Pontiniano. *Origini* 4:45-78.
1972   Sur le Paléolithique de la plaine Pontine (Latium). *Quaternaria* 16:203-223.
1979   L'industrie lithique de Grotta Guattari au Mont Circe (Latium): Definition culturelle, typologique et chronologique du Pontinien. *Quaternaria* 12:179-247.

Tozzi, C.
1970   La Grotta di S. Agostino (Gaeta). *Rivista di Scienze Preistoriche* 25:3-87.

Vitagliano, S.
1984   Nota sul Pontiniano della Grotta dei Moscerini, Gaeta (Latina). *Atti della XXIV Riunione Scientifica dell'Istituto Italiano di Preistoria e Protostoria, Ottobre 1982.* Pp. 155-164. Firenze: Istituto Italiano di Preistoria e Protostoria.

Voigt, E. A.
1973   Stone Age molluscan utilization at Klasies River Mouth Caves. *South African Journal of Science* 69:306-309.
1982   The molluscan fauna. In *The Middle Stone Age of Klasies River Mouth in South Africa.* R. Singer and J. Wymer, eds. Pp. 155-186. Chicago: University of Chicago Press.

# 9

# Hunting in the Gravettian: An Examination of Evidence from Southwestern France

**Anne Pike-Tay**
**Vassar College**

**Harvey M. Bricker**
**Tulane University**

## ABSTRACT

Five southwest French sites containing Gravettian occupations provide zooarchaeological, artifactual, and paleoenvironmental data for an integrated examination of hunting strategies in the region during the latest part of the Early Upper Palaeolithic. New season-of-death and age-at-death data on red deer, based on dental annuli analysis, are combined with previously published data on reindeer to suggest possible hunting patterns. Evidence from these samples is consistent with a foraging strategy where the hunters were skilled enough to obtain prime-age individuals with as much success as they did the very young and very old. A survey of Gravettian weapon armatures notes that (a) lithic armatures are numerically very predominant in most assemblages considered; (b) organic armatures actually outnumber lithic ones in a few assemblages; and (c) microlithic armatures for composite weapons make their first appearance in the region in the latest Gravettian assemblages.

## INTRODUCTION

The recent application of Binford's (1980, 1984) evolutionary forager/collector continuum to materials at the Plio-Pleistocene boundary has focused the attention of scholars on the degree of foresight and cooperation that can be attributed to hominid/human groups of the Middle and Upper Palaeolithic. Some have placed a significant adaptive shift, including a major change from "forager" to "logistical collector" subsistence strategies, at the beginning of the Late Upper Palaeolithic ca. 20,000 BP (e.g., Enloe 1992; Gamble 1986; Lindly and Clark 1990:254), whereas others have cautioned against overstating either the spatial scope or the temporal specificity of such changes (Straus 1990:248). Recent studies, such as that of Enloe and David (1989) for the Magdalenian of Pincevent in the Paris Basin and of Bratlund (n.d.) for the Terminal Palaeolithic of Stellmoor in northwest Germany, strongly support the long-held idea that specialized reindeer hunting was practiced in some areas of Europe by the end of the Upper Palaeolithic.

For the Early Upper Palaeolithic, the subsistence patterns are seen by proponents of a post-20,000 BP adaptive shift as being much the same as the opportunistic forager pattern that has come to characterize the Middle Palaeolithic. (Exactly what Middle Palaeolithic/MSA subsistence strategies were remains unclear, since both Chase [1989] and Klein [1989] have effectively challenged Binford's [1984] interpretation of dichotomy in prey size as a reflection of opportunistic scavenging by arguing that transport decisions were responsible for the differences in skeletal part representation of small and large prey.) With some notable exceptions from Cantabria (e.g., Bernaldo de Quirós 1980a, 1980b; Bernaldo de Quirós and Cabrera Valdés 1992; Cabrera Valdés 1984; Straus and Clark 1986) and southwestern France (e.g., Delpech 1983; Geneste and Plisson 1992), there is the sense that the alleged shift in subsistence adaptations at 20,000 BP has been characterized in terms of extremes, Mousterian and Magdalenian, rather than in terms of archaeological cultures that are closest to the alleged boundary.

| Phase | | FLA-1 | FERR | PAT | R de C | yrs BP |
|---|---|---|---|---|---|---|
| X | | | | 1  Sol | | |
| | | | | | | (21,000) |
| IX | | | | | | |
| VIII | c | | | 2  PM | | (22,000) |
| | b | | | | | |
| | a | 1–3 luPg | | 3  luPg | 1a luPg | (24,500) |
| VII | c | 4  N | B1 ↑ B3 B4  N | 3–4(Red)  N | 1b luPg | (26,000) |
| | b | 5  N | B5 | 3–4(P.R.) ↑ N  3–4(Tan) | 1c luPg | |
| | a | 6  euPg | B6 ↑ C3 C4 D1  euPg | 4:Upper ↑ N  4:Lw(0–3) | 2  N | (27,000) |
| VI | c | 7(Up) euPg | D3–D2 euPg | 4:Lw(0–4) N | | |
| | b | 7(Lw) | E1–D4 euPg | | 3  N | |
| | a | | E4–E2 | | | (28,000) |
| V | | 8(1)  Aur | F1 ↑ G4  Aur | 5:Later ↑ mPg  5:Earlier | 4  ?mPg | |

**Figure 9.1.** Geochronological placement and approximate age BP of archaeological units discussed in the text. **Key:** FLA-1 = Flageolet-1; FERR = La Ferrassie; PAT = Abri Pataud; R de C = Roc de Combe; Sol = Solutrean; PM = Protomagdalenian; luPg = late Upper Perigordian; N = Noaillian; euPg = early Upper Perigordian; mPg = Middle Perigordian; Aur = Aurignacian; P.R. = Pebbly Red.

In this paper, we are concerned with the role and nature of hunting in the latest part of the Early Upper Palaeolithic in one part of Europe, southwestern France, as represented by several variants of one widespread complex, the Gravettian. The assemblages, most of which have been labelled "Perigordian" by regional specialists, date from somewhat before 29,000 to somewhat before 21,000 BP, by which time Solutrean assemblages (of the Later Upper Palaeolithic) are present in the region. We present an overview of the growing body of technological, paleoenvironmental, and zooarchaeological evidence from Gravettian sites, concentrating on the data from Le Flageolet I (Level 7), La Ferrassie (Level D2), Abri Pataud (Levels 5, 4 , and 3), Roc de Combe (Level 1), and Les Battuts (Level 5).

## THE CHRONOLOGY OF THE GRAVETTIAN
## IN SOUTHWESTERN FRANCE

Southwestern France has provided numerous and rich representatives of what is often called the Gravettian, a group of related archaeological cultures of the middle part of the European Upper Palaeolithic, from the Atlantic to the Don (Otte 1985). Gravettian industries are intermediate, both chronologically and in various aspects of technology, between the earlier Upper Palaeolithic European cultures--Aurignacian, Châtelperronian, Szeletian, Bohunician, etc.--and the later Upper Palaeolithic cultures--Solutrean, Magdalenian, etc. The Gravettian, which covers a span of 7,000 to 8,000 years, has recently been divided into three largely successive stages (Otte 1990), which may be recognized across Europe.

The first Gravettian stage, the representatives of which include the eponymous site of La Gravette in France and the earliest of the symbolically complex Pavlovian assemblages of Moravia, began at or shortly after 30,000 BP (Otte 1990). In France, this stage is what has been called Perigordian IV (Peyrony 1933; de Sonneville-Bordes 1960:179-189) or Middle Perigordian (Bordes 1968b; David and Bricker 1987). It is best known from La Gravette (Lacorre 1960) and from Level 5 at Abri Pataud (Movius 1977; Bricker n.d.). This stage at Pataud (Figure 9.1), and probably also at La Gravette, falls entirely within an extended time of mostly warm, humid climate (Farrand n.d.) that can be correlated with Laville's Phase V of the Würm III (Laville 1975:378-379, Tabl. V) or, in the revised terminology, Phase V of the Würm Récent or in the Kesselt interstadial of palynology (Laville and Texier 1986:A13). The Würm Récent corresponds to Oxygen Isotope Stage 2 of the sequence based on deep-sea cores (1986:A20). The beginning of the Middle Perigordian has no acceptable radiocarbon dates, but the end of this stage at Pataud is dated to just before 28,000 BP (Bricker and Mellars 1987; Mellars et al. 1987). In southwestern France, both the Phase V climate and the Middle Perigordian had ended by ca. 28,000 BP.

The second stage of the European Gravettian, dating to between about 28,000 and 25,000 BP (Otte 1990), is particularly well represented in western Europe. Southwest French assemblages containing many tanged Font-Robert points and/or the so-called truncated elements have been called Perigordian Va/Vb (or $V_1/V_2$) (de Sonneville-Bordes 1960:192-195) or early Upper Perigordian (David and Bricker 1987). Assemblages containing high frequencies of several specialized burin forms (Noailles burins, Raysse burins, etc.) have been called Perigordian Vc (or $V_3$) (de Sonneville-Bordes 1960:195) or Noaillian (David 1966, 1985; David and Bricker 1987). Use of the term "Perigordian" is favored by scholars (for

example, Rigaud 1988) who emphasize the undoubted continuities (like the presence of Gravette points) with earlier assemblages of southwestern France, whereas "Noaillian" tends to be used by those working in a broader context of geographic and temporal variation within the European Gravettian (for example, Otte and Keeley 1990).

The early Upper Perigordian stage in southwestern France seems to have begun sometime during the cold and dry phase VI of the Würm Récent (Figure 9.1), the Inter-Kesselt-Tursac cold of the pollen-based terminology (Laville and Texier 1986). We have three samples from this stage. The oldest is Ferrassie:D2, which is placed by both sedimentology (Laville and Tuffreau 1984:49) and palynology (Paquereau 1984:57) at the end of this cold, in Phase VIc, and is radiocarbon dated to shortly after 28,000 BP (Mellars and Bricker 1986). The uppermost part of Level 7 at Flageolet-1 is assigned to Phase VIc as well (Laville 1975:378-379); it is probably somewhat younger than Ferrassie:D2, because some warming was underway by the time of its deposition (Laville 1975:291), whereas Ferrassie:D2 still reflects a very cold, steppic climate (Paquereau 1984: 57). The radiocarbon age of Flageolet-1:7 must be close to 27,000 BP, as indicated by the dates for it and the overlying Flageolet-1:6 (Mellars and Bricker 1986; Rigaud 1988). Battuts:5 is probably a bit younger still. The diagnosis by Delpech (1983:64) that the fauna indicates relatively mild and humid conditions suggests an assignment to the early part of the Tursac oscillation, Phase VIIa of the Würm Récent, but there are no palynological or sedimentological data with which to test this suggestion.

The Noaillian first appears in southwestern France near the end of the pre-Tursac cold climate, in late Phase VI of the Würm Récent (Figure 9.1). The earliest Noaillian occupation at Pataud is in Lens O-4, part of Pataud:4:LOWER. Based on his study of the Pataud sediments, Farrand (n.d.) has determined that only Lens O-4 belongs to phase VIc; contrary to what was originally supposed by Laville (1975:376, 378-379, Tabl. V) on the basis of Farrand's early analyses (and repeated recently by Rigaud [1988:390]), all later sediments at Pataud containing Noaillian archaeological materials must be assigned to Phase VII, the Tursac oscillation. The beginning of the Noaillian at Pataud is well dated by $^{14}$C to about 27,000 BP, and the latest Noaillian occupations, in Pataud:3-4(Red), took place within a few centuries of 26,000 BP (Bricker and Mellars 1987). The Noaillian in southwestern France is not known to postdate Phase VII.

The third and final stage of the European Gravettian, with a general dating of ca. 25,000 to at least 23,000 BP (Otte 1990), is known from only a few French sites. Assemblages from these sites have been referred to as Perigordian VI (Movius 1960: 385; de Sonneville-Bordes 1966:12-13), evolved Upper Peri-

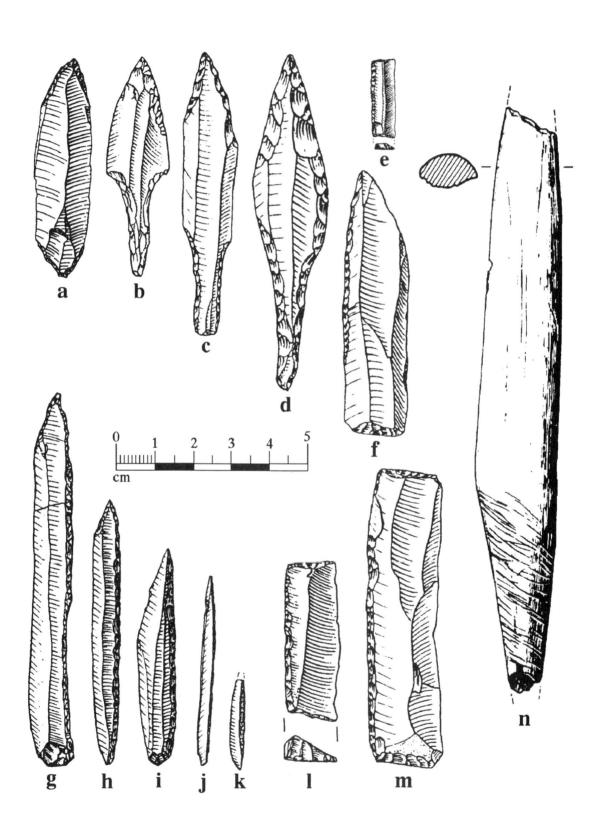

gordian (Bordes 1968a), or late Upper Perigordian (David and Bricker 1987). (The analytic utility of including within the final Gravettian stage younger assemblages [<23,000 BP] known variously as Aurignacian V, Protomagdalenian, Perigordian VII, or Laugerian continues to be debated [de Sonneville-Bordes 1966:13; Rigaud 1988:394; Knecht 1991; Clay n.d.], but we do not consider these assemblages here.) Late Upper Perigordian assemblages appear in southwestern France during Phase VII of the Würm Récent, the Tursac oscillation (Figure 9.1). The base of Roc de Combe:1, which contains most of the archaeological materials, is assigned by Laville to Phase VIIb, whereas the top of the deposit belongs late in Phase VIIc or at the beginning of the Phase VIII cold (Laville 1975:233, 378-379, Tabl. V). Pataud:3 has been shown by Farrand (n.d.) to date to the first episode of post-Tursac cold, Phase VIIIa of the Laville sequence (and not to Phase VIIb, as Laville [1975:378-379, Tabl. V] originally suggested); this series of occupations at Pataud, and therefore Phase VIIIa, began about 24,500 BP according to recently obtained AMS (accelerator mass spectrometer) $^{14}$C dates (Bricker and Mellars 1987:230). Flageolet-1:1-3, with a similar industry and deposited under the same environmental circumstances--first return of frost weathering after a halt in sedimentation during a temperate-climate maximum (Laville 1975:288, 291)--has an essentially identical $^{14}$C date (Mellars and Bricker 1986; Mellars et al. 1987). The Protomagdalenian, which is considered by some to be a very late Gravettian manifestation, is dated to between ca. 22,000 and 21,500 BP at Pataud and two other French sites; the earliest Solutrean, which is certainly post-Gravettian, appears in southwestern France by about 21,000 BP (Bricker and Mellars 1987:230).

## GRAVETTIAN WEAPONRY IN SOUTHWESTERN FRANCE

Archaeologically visible hunting technology from La Gravette and Pataud:5 is limited almost entirely to lithic weapon armatures--the well known Gravette points (Figure 9.2h,i), microgravettes (Figure 9.2k), and *fléchettes*[1] (Figure 9.2a) that serve to define the early Gravettian in much of Europe. Organic weapons are extremely rare at both sites, and, because almost all examples recovered are quite fragmentary, only

two sagaie[2] types can be recognized with certainty. A thin, spiky sagaie, usually bearing a shallow artificial groove or *cannelure* down most of the length of the shaft, is present at both sites (Figure 9.3a,c). (Lacorre [1960:306] regarded the presence of the groove, which he supposed facilitated bleeding from the wound, as a way in which Gravettian weapons technology was superior to that of the Aurignacian.) Both sites also contain broken examples of larger, sturdier sagaies; one example from Pataud (similar to Figure 9.4e) has a base that has been hacked or cut into a crude conical form (sagaie type 5 of Delporte et al. 1988).

Hunting technology of the early Upper Perigordian is, as was the case in the preceding stage, almost entirely limited to lithic weapon armatures. Gravettes and microgravettes continue to be present in large numbers, but *fléchettes* appear only very rarely. The tanged Font-Robert points provide evidence of new hafting techniques for what are otherwise *fléchette*-like armatures (compare Figure 9.2b-d with Figure 9.2a). If they have been interpreted correctly, the so-called truncated elements (Figure 9.2f,l,m) are the first examples in the French Upper Palaeolithic of composite cutting or slashing tools or perhaps weapons armed with multiple lithic components; however, the non-lithic part of these postulated implements has not been identified in the archaeological record, and the large size of the lithic elements makes the composite-tool explanation (Peyrony 1934:86, Fig. 88-10) less than compelling.

Organic weapon armatures in the three early Upper Perigordian assemblages included in our sample (Ferrassie:D2, Flageolet-1:7, and Battuts:5) are almost nonexistent. Although the limited recent excavations at La Ferrassie reported no sagaies in Level D2 or any other "Perigordian V" level (Delporte and Tuffreau 1984:241), Peyrony's previous excavations in the essentially equivalent Level J encountered one complete sagaie (Peyrony 1934:84, Fig. 86-1) that is very similar to a bipointed sagaie from Flageolet-1:7 (Figure 9.5c) and probably to a fragmentary sagaie in Flageolet-1:6, which is also early Upper Perigordian (Rigaud 1982:Fig. 226-3). Such sagaies (sagaie type 7 of Delporte et al. 1988) seem to be very similar to the Aurignacian spindle-shaped points studied experimentally by Knecht (this volume). Organic weapons are not reported as present in Battuts:5 (Alaux 1973), even though bone (i.e., faunal refuse) is well preserved and abundant. The same absence of organic weapons from

**Figure 9.2.** Gravettian weapon armatures: (a) *fléchette*; (b-d) Font-Robert points; (e) segmented backed bladelet; (f,l,m) truncated elements; (g-i) Gravette points; (j-k) microgravette points; (n) Isturitz sagaie. Illustrations adapted from (a) Gravette:Bayacian (Lacorre 1960:63, Pl. VIII); (b,l) Flageolet-1:7 (Rigaud 1982, Fig. 181); (c,d) Ferrassie:J (de Sonneville-Bordes 1960:194, Fig. 117); (e) Pataud:3 (Bricker and David 1984:41, Fig. 9); (f,m) Ferrassie:K (de Sonneville-Bordes 1960:196,Fig.118); (g,j) Pataud:3 (Bricker and David 1984:33, Fig. 8); (h) Gravette:Noire (Lacorre 1960:181, Pl. XXXII); (i) Gravette:Rouge (Lacorre 1960:177, Pl. XXX); (k) Pataud:5 (Bricker n.d., Fig. 6-14); (n) Pataud:4 (David 1985:197, Fig. 46).

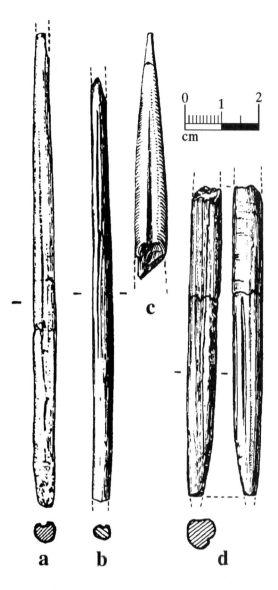

**Figure 9.3.** Gravettian weapon armatures--sagaies: (a) Pataud:5 (Bricker n.d., Fig. 6-17); (b) Pataud:4 (David 1985:193, Fig. 44); (c) Gravette, unspecified Gravettian level (Lacorre 1960:309, Pl. LXXIX); (d) Pataud:3 (Bricker and David 1984:97, Fig. 30).

the early Upper Perigordian occurs in the well-known assemblages of Laraux:5 (Pradel and Chollet 1950: 218; Bricker 1973:1607), Vachons:3 (J. Bouyssonie 1948:22; J. Bouyssonie and de Sonneville-Bordes 1957:289; Bricker 1973:1520), and Roches de Pouligny:3 (Charbonnier 1962:475; Pradel 1965:230; Bricker 1973:1480).

Lithic weapon armatures, predominantly Gravette/microgravette points, are important components of Noaillian (Perigordian Vc) assemblages, but they are much less frequent than in the Middle and early

Upper Perigordian assemblages described above. For example, in the six Noaillian assemblages used by Laville and Rigaud (1973) in their study of typological variation within Perigordian V industries, pooled frequencies of Gravettes and microgravettes range from a low of 0.27% of all retouched lithics in Facteur:10-11 (Delporte 1968:71, Tabl. X) to a high of 6.94% in Jambes:2 (Celerier 1967:66, Tabl. I). Frequencies for the several subdivisions of Pataud:4, all of which are Noaillian, lie between these extremes (David 1985:7-8, Tab. 2). By way of contrast, the corresponding percentages for the Middle Perigordian of Pataud:5(Later Units) is 22.95% (Bricker 1973:188-192, Tab. 4-2); that for Ferrassie:D2, an early Upper Perigordian with Font-Robert points, is 30.24% (Delporte and Tuffreau 1984:246); finally, that for Laraux:5, an early Upper Perigordian with truncated elements, is 21.69% (de Sonneville-Bordes 1960:267-268, Tabl. XXVII). Font-Robert points and truncated elements occur sporadically in Noaillian assemblages, but in frequencies even lower than those of Gravette/microgravettes. The lesser emphasis on lithic armatures is clear from the data available.

Organic weapons, on the other hand, appear to be in substantially higher numbers in the Noaillian than in the Perigordian industries discussed previously. The most characteristic such weapon is the Isturitz sagaie (sagaie type 8 of Delporte et al. 1988), a long, sturdy weapon, usually of antler, with a roughened and sometimes notched conical base (Figures 9.2n and 9.6a,b). A recent inventory lists 247 known Isturitz sagaies, all but three of which are from Noaillian sites in southwestern France (Delporte et al. 1988:I.8.7). The site of Isturitz itself has more than half of the known examples, but 27 Isturitz sagaies come from Pataud:4 (David 1985:195, Fig. 45 and 197, Fig. 46). In fact, Isturitz sagaies outnumber Gravettes/microgravettes in Pataud:4:MIDDLE (6 lithic points to 9 Isturitz sagaies) and Pataud:4:UPPER (6 to 13); when other sagaie types are added, these ratios are 6 : 19 and 6 : 32 (David 1985:7-8, Tab. 2, and 190, Tab. 38)--a decisive preponderance of organic weapons. Other recognizable sagaie types present in Pataud:4 include: (a) long slender sagaies, some with a groove or *cannelure* (Figure 9.3b); (b) sagaies whose base has a single side-bevel (Figure 9.4b; sagaie type 3 of Delporte et al. 1988; the "Gravettian lateral-beveled points" of Knecht, this volume); (c) sagaies with roughly cut or hacked bases (Figure 9.4c); (d) short, bi-pointed or fusiform sagaies with round section (Figure 9.5a; sagaie type 7 of Delporte et al. 1988; similar to the "Aurignacian spindle-shaped points" of Knecht, this volume) or flat section (Figure 9.5b). All these kinds of sagaies appear to be present in the Isturitz:4 assemblages (R. de Saint-Périer and S. de Saint-Périer 1952).

Hunting technology of the late Upper Perigordian is predominantly a question of lithic armatures, including the now familiar Gravette and microgravette points (Figure 9.2g,j), usually, but not always, in high frequencies (20.32% of all retouched lithics in Pataud:3 [Bricker and David 1984:8-9, Tab. 2]; 29.07% in Roc de Combe:1 [Bordes and Labrot 1967:18,20]; ca. 18% and 28% in Laugerie-Haute(Est):B and B', respectively [Bricker and David 1984:105, Fig. 33]; but an anomalously low 2.30% in Flageolet-1:1-3 [Rigaud 1982, Tabl. 6]). There are, in addition, very rare and sporadic occurrences of Font-Robert points and truncated elements. A new and undoubtedly important item of hunting technology in some assemblages is represented by so-called segmented backed bladelets (Clay 1968, n.d.; Movius et al. 1968:49-54). These backed, truncated, and sometimes pointed bladelets (Figure 9.2e) can be seen as the miniaturized versions of the truncated elements, made on full-sized blades, of the early Upper Perigordian. Although they are never numerous in late Upper Perigordian assemblages (the greatest known frequency is in Laugerie-Haute(Est):B', where, according to Clay, segmented backed bladelets account for ca. 3% of the retouched lithics vs. 28% Gravettes/microgravettes), they are important in signalling the first patterned and repeating occurrence in the French Upper Palaeolithic of microlithic armatures for composite weapons, an approach to weaponry that culminates in the atlatl-propelled, microlith-armed, organic projectiles best known from the terminal Palaeolithic.

Organic weapon armatures in the late Upper Perigordian are more numerous and more varied than in the Middle or early Upper Perigordian but less numerous, relative to lithic armatures, than in the Noaillian. With details not available about the several bone sagaies in Roc de Combe:1 (Bordes and Labrot 1967:20), the best information comes from the very similar sagaie samples from Pataud:3 and the Perigordian VI of Laugerie-Haute, which contain, in addition to some hard-to-classify fragments, at least four kinds of sagaies. Long, slender, curved sagaies with a flattened and scored facet along the central portion of the shaft (Figure 9.5d) are the most frequent kind in Pataud:3, and they occur as well at Laugerie-Haute (D. Peyrony and E. Peyrony 1938:15, Fig. 6-9). Both ends are sharply pointed, and the total morphology suggests a self-barbed armature or even, as suggested for some later examples from Laugerie-Haute, a sort of one-barbed harpoon (1938:23-24). The other three sagaie types have all been discussed previously from earlier assemblages--(a) sagaies with roughly cut or hacked conical bases (Figure 9.4d,e); (b) slender sagaies with side-beveled bases (Figure 9.4a) (D. Peyrony and E. Peyrony 1938:15, Fig. 6-6,7); and (c) straight, slender sagaies of unknown base treatment with a groove on one or both sides of the shaft (Fig-

ure 9.3d). The organic portion of the kind of weapon that was armed with segmented backed bladelets has not been recognized in any of the relevant assemblages, but the sagaies with multiple grooves may be appropriate candidates on the basis of size and general configuration.

Taking the descriptive data summarized above as a starting point, one can usefully look at the archaeological remains of Gravettian weapons systems in terms of the optimal-design criteria that Bleed (1986) has shown to be related to overall subsistence strategy. In brief summary, if weapons are to be effective and available--they kill or wound as intended, and they are at hand in good working order when needed--they may

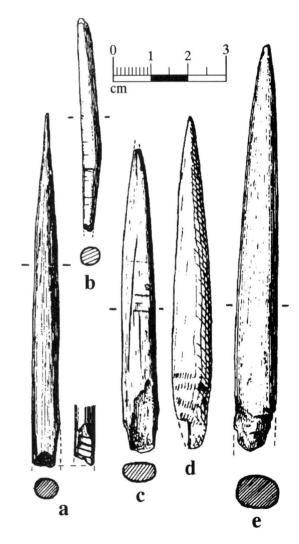

**Figure 9.4.** Gravettian weapon armatures--sagaies: (a, e) Pataud:3 (Bricker and David 1984:98, Fig. 31); (b, c) Pataud:4 (David 1985:193, Fig. 44); (d) Laugerie-Haute, unspecified "Perigordian III" level (D. Peyrony and E. Peyrony 1938:15, Fig. 6).

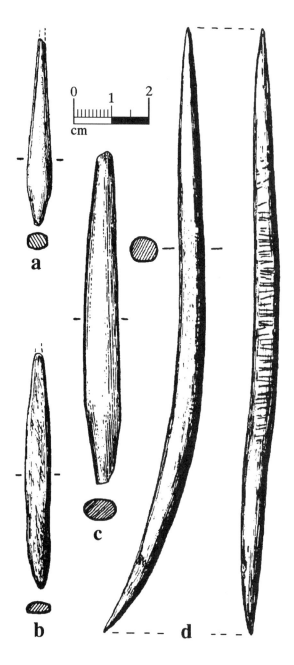

**Figure 9.5.** Gravettian weapon armatures--sagaies: (a) Pataud:4 (David 1985:203, Fig. 49); (b) Pataud:4 (David 1985:193, Fig. 44); (c) Flageolet-1:7 (Rigaud 1982, Fig. 226); (d) Pataud:3 (Bricker and David 1984:98, Fig. 31).

crafted, and likely to be large and sturdy--are produced during the downtime periods when prey is not available; when they break (as they will eventually, of course), they are not easily repaired by the hunter in the field. Maintainably designed weapons would be best in situations where prey animals are constantly available in the region but not predictably so on a day-to-day basis--the situation in which foraging is a likely subsistence strategy. Weapons are in continual demand, at least potentially, for periods of some months, and there is no predictably safe downtime that can be scheduled for the manufacture and repair of weapons. Under these conditions, weapon design tends to be modular, with often small components, and in-field breakage is quickly repaired by replacement of the affected modular unit.

In the context of Bleed's model, the lithic weapon armatures of the southwest French Gravettian can be seen as parts of maintainable weapons. As modular components of total weapons, they are small, portable, quickly made, and disposable. The organic weapon armatures, however, can be alternatively viewed as parts of reliable weapons. Knecht (1991) has pointed out that some aspects of Upper Perigordian single-beveled points, such as standardization of haft angle, are consistent with a portable, replaceable armament, and this is undoubtedly true, particularly in the diachronic perspective of comparisons with earlier Upper Palaeolithic organic weapons. However, within the context of Gravettian weapons systems as a whole, the often larger, sturdier organic armatures--far more time-consuming to manufacture and, as Knecht (1991) notes, sometimes repaired and reworked rather than just discarded--may well provide the reliable counterpart to the maintainable lithics. Future study of technological and functional criteria derived from replication and use experiments such as those of Knecht (1991 and this volume) with Aurignacian samples and Geneste and Plisson (1992) with Solutrean shouldered points would allow for the necessary testing of this hypothesis.

## GRAVETTIAN PREY
## IN SOUTHWESTERN FRANCE

### Species Frequencies and Hunting Strategies

Faunal assemblages from Gravettian and other Early Upper Palaeolithic sites in the Dordogne region of southwestern France are generally dominated by reindeer (Delpech 1983, 1993). Such high frequencies of reindeer remains might be evidence of strategic planning on the part of Early Upper Palaeolithic hunters. White (1985, 1989) has argued, for example, that the apparent relationships among dominant prey

be designed primarily for "reliability" or primarily for "maintainability." Reliably designed weapons would be best when prey would be available during a limited but predictable period; during such a period, the weapons must stand up to repeated use with very low breakage rates. Such weapons--overdesigned, well-

species, site size, topographic location, and site seasonality in the Dordogne result from intentionality and that sites like Abri Pataud provide evidence for seasonal specialization as a hunting strategy--in this case, intensified migration-hunting of reindeer. On the other hand, the high reindeer frequencies may be a function of species availability. Chase (1989) has suggested that Early Upper Palaeolithic subsistence strategy was quite catholic or eclectic and that reindeer-dominated sites like Pataud and Roc de Combe are simply locations where reindeer were always more abundant than other herbivores. Indeed, during the Dryas I (Phase XX of the Würm Récent in the terminology of Laville and Texier 1986), reindeer bone frequencies appear to reflect more- and less-frequented habitats within the animals' range rather than topographic location or site size (Delpech 1983:172).

When trying to deal with what appear to be contradictory interpretations of prey species frequencies, it is important to recognize that two distinct notions of prey movement of different scales are being entertained here. The first concerns the common seasonal movements of a given prey species, and the second concerns long-term shifts in species' range. It is at the short-term/seasonal scale that hypotheses such as migration hunting, with its potential for low-effort/high-benefit returns, must be tested, whereas changes in animal ranges must be investigated in terms of long-term climatic and ecological shifts. One of us has argued elsewhere that, although these two types of movement must not be confused or conflated, information regarding both are essential to the investigation and understanding of Palaeolithic subsistence strategies (Pike-Tay 1993).

In terms of Early Upper Palaeolithic human behavior, a hunting strategy that specializes, even seasonally, on one of several available species implies a different organizational approach from that emphasizing a single species as a by-product of ecological restrictions on availability. The operational question is how to distinguish archaeologically the first approach, which is consistent with a "collector" strategy, from the second, which would seem to reflect "opportunism." Some answers should be obtainable from the study of the archaeofaunas. Information regarding the age at death and season of death of individual prey animals from archaeological assemblages can aid in distinguishing (1) seasonal movements of prey from (2) movements, such as shifts in species range, triggered by long-term climatic change. In addition, it should permit us to distinguish between (3) specialization of hunting strategy on one of several available

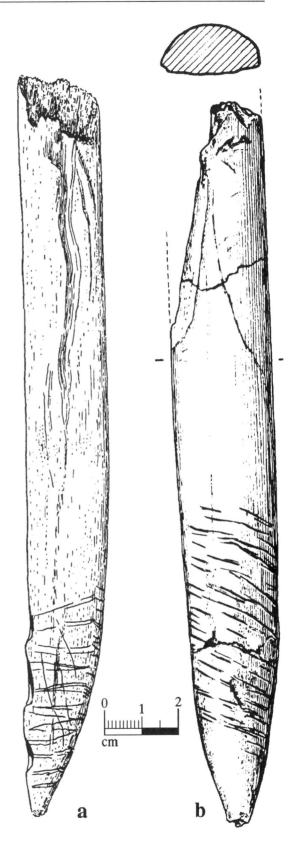

**Figure 9.6.** Gravettian weapon armatures--Isturitz sagaies: (a) Isturitz:Gravettian (R. de Saint-Périer and S. de Saint-Périer 1952:126, Fig. 66); (b) Pataud:4 (David 1985:197, Fig. 46).

species and (4) emphasis on a single species as a by-product of availability. After a brief review of methods and interpretative frameworks, we will discuss how these analytical tools can help read the archaeological traces of "specialization" versus "opportunism" as alternative strategies.

## Seasonality and Prey Mortality

### Dental Annuli Analysis

Skeletochronology is the study of growth marks apparent in mineralized vertebrate tissues, particularly those of bones and teeth. The growth marks normally show a definite periodicity that corresponds to an animal's growth rhythms. For most temperate, sub-arctic, and arctic mammals, a yearly cycle is generally marked by one (growth) zone in addition to one annulus (slow growth) (see Francillon-Vieillot et al. 1991). Recent analyses (e.g., Burke 1992; Lieberman et al. 1990; Pike-Tay 1989, 1991a, 1991b, 1993) of the incremental structure of mammalian teeth demonstrate the potential of even isolated teeth for determining age and season of death of individual animals from archaeological contexts. Modern control samples comprised of sufficient numbers of individual animals are presently under study for a variety of species by the authors cited above, including two important prey species of the southwest French Gravettian--red deer and reindeer (Pike-Tay 1989, 1991b, n.d.). Control samples are studied in order to assess the many variables that affect dental annuli formation and to test assumptions regarding the regularity of annuli formation.

### Prey Mortality Patterns and Their Interpretation

Hunting strategies may sometimes be inferred from the age patterns of prey assemblages. The interpretative framework (based upon the work of Klein 1982, Stiner 1991, and others) is a comparison of characteristic age profiles with catastrophic, attritional, and prime-age dominated patterns. The **attritional pattern** has the highest number of individuals in the youngest age class; frequencies then drop off steeply, with a second rise in the oldest age class. Attritional patterns may reflect the relatively easy catch of youngest and oldest age cohorts or scavenging from natural deaths, since these ages show the highest rate of mortality. The **catastrophic pattern** is characterized by a large number of individuals in the

youngest age class with a gradual decrease in numbers down to the oldest age cohort, reflecting a "natural" population. Catastrophic patterns may result from a drive-style hunt or the natural death assemblage from a catastrophic event. The **prime-age dominated pattern** may reflect selection for prime game after a drive, selection when scavenging from a catastrophic event, or sufficient hunting skill to select prime animals.

The age/mortality profiles of the red deer from the Gravettian assemblages examined here were constructed by Pike-Tay from cementum annuli counts; they concurred with eruption and wear estimates of the partial maxillae and hemi-mandibles whenever these dental series were present.

## Gravettian Red Deer Hunting

Season-of-death determinations and age profiles of the red deer presented below for all sites except Abri Pataud are from Pike-Tay (1989, 1991a). Data on two teeth from Pataud are cited from the analysis of Spiess (1979). In the samples studied by Pike-Tay, all DP4, P4, M1, and M2 red deer teeth recovered were analyzed to insure that every individual red deer in the level was included. Conservative linking of teeth to determine the minimum number of individuals represented by teeth (detailed in Pike-Tay 1991a:Appendix C) precluded problems of over-representation by a single animal. Season-of-death determinations of red deer are as follows:

*Pataud:5:* Spiess (1979:191, 195) diagnosed one incisor from late in the mild and humid Phase V as representing a winter kill. For Pataud:5 as a whole, red deer accounts for less than 1% of the NISP (number of identified specimens) count, which is heavily dominated (98%) by reindeer (Bouchud 1975:120-121, Tabl. XXXII).

*Ferrassie:D2:* In Level D2 at La Ferrassie, red deer dominates the NISP count at 80.1% (Delpech 1983:348). The very high frequency of red deer, a species generally taken to indicate mild and humid climate during the late Pleistocene of southwestern France, has been regarded as anomalous (Delpech 1984:69) in levels that both sedimentology (Laville and Tuffreau 1984) and palynology (Paquereau 1984) show were deposited during a rigorously cold climatic phase. Delpech (1984:69) suggested that the most obvious resolution of the apparent disagreement would regard the faunal samples as representing warm seasons during a time of cold climate; she asked specifically if one should not regard the human occupa-

**Figure 9.7.** Season of death of red deer, as determined by dental annuli analysis, in selected Gravettian faunal samples (all data from Pike-Tay 1989, 1991a): (a) Ferrassie:D2; (b) Flageolet-1:7; (c) Battuts:5; (d) Roc de Combe:1.

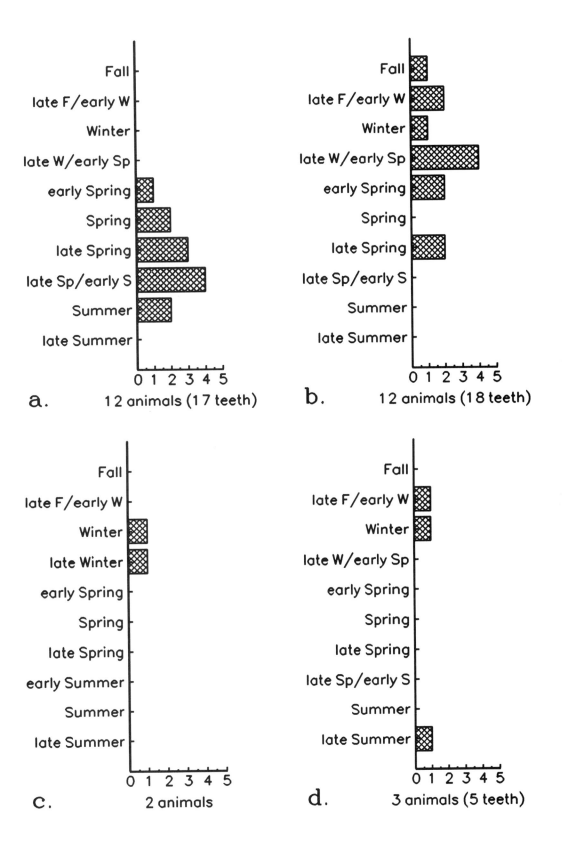

tions represented by Level D2 as "... the remains of summer encampments of Palaeolithic red deer hunters?" The dental annuli analysis (Figure 9.7a) provides the clearest possible confirmation of Delpech's conjecture--red deer hunting at La Ferrassie, Level D2, does indeed occur during the warm season, spring through summer. In addition to answering a very specific question about one site, this combination of data on Ferrassie:D2 shows quite forcefully the value of seasonality information to the proper interpretation of classical paleoclimatic indicators.

*Flageolet-1:7:* Fall through spring (cold season) hunting is indicated at Le Flageolet, Level 7 (Figure 9.7b) during a slightly later and less rigorous part of Phase VIc. NISP counts from this level comprise over 50% red deer, followed by about 36% reindeer, with bovines (*Bos/Bison* sp.), horse (*Equus caballus*), chamois (*Rupicapra*), roe deer (*Capreolus*), and ibex (*Capra ibex* or *Capra pyrenaica*) in decreasing frequencies (Delpech 1983:352). Olivier LeGall's analysis of 20 specimens of fresh water fish vertebrae and otoliths from Level 7 indicate fall, winter, and spring fishing (Pike-Tay 1991:79-80).

*Battuts:5:* Les Battuts, Level 5 shows winter hunting of red deer (Figure 9.7c). In Level 5, red deer comprises nearly 50% of the NISP count, followed by ibex, bovines, horse, and chamois in decreasing frequencies (Delpech 1983:358).

*Pataud:4:* One tooth sectioned by Spiess (1979: 191, 195), coming probably from the mild and humid Phase VIIa, indicates a kill in winter or early spring. The NISP count for Pataud:4 as a whole is dominated by reindeer (90%), with red deer comprising just over 1% (Bouchud 1975:120-121, Tabl. XXXII).

*Roc de Combe:1:* Red deer were taken in the period from late summer through winter at Roc de Combe, Level 1 (Figure 9.7d). Here, reindeer dominate the NISP count at over 80%, with red deer reaching about 5% (Delpech 1983:343).

The age profiles of the red deer from the Upper Perigordian levels sampled at Le Flageolet-1, La Ferrassie, Roc de Combe, and Les Battuts show a broad mix of all age classes--perhaps an overlay of attritional and prime-age patterns (Figure 9.8) resulting from relatively small numbers of individuals in each level. (Age profiles were constructed for each individual site, but, because details are published elsewhere [Pike-Tay 1989, 1991a] and because differences among sites are slight, the data are combined here.)

### Gravettian Reindeer Hunting at Abri Pataud

Based on his study of a sample of faunal material from Pataud:5, Spiess (1979:195, Tab. 6.6) determined that reindeer certainly were killed from October

through February and that the period might extend from September through April. These findings, which are based on data from tooth eruption and wear, fetal long bones, male antlers with skull bones attached, and tooth sectioning, indicate that reindeer hunting in Pataud:5 was primarily a cold-season activity. Two earlier studies by Bouchud (1966, 1975) of the complete Pataud:5 faunal assemblage used techniques for determining seasonality that have been challenged by other workers (as reviewed by Spiess 1979:67-101). For Level 5 and other levels at Pataud, disagreements over details mask the large measure of agreement between the two studies about the seasonality of reindeer hunting by the shelter's inhabitants. For example, Bouchud's (1975:109-110, Tabl. XXV and 113, Pl. XI-2) diagnosis of butchered, as opposed to naturally shed, antler units placed 10 of 13 units in the late fall-winter-spring period (October to June). Bouchud (1966:169, Tabl. XLIV and 175, Fig. 47) concluded, based on dental wear patterns, that a few reindeer were brought back to the shelter in all months of the year, but that the highest kill frequencies occurred in late fall and winter, from early December to mid-April.

For Pataud:4, Spiess (1979:195, Tab. 6.6) based his reindeer seasonality diagnoses on the positive evidence of tooth eruption and the negative evidence (n = 0) of fetal long bones. He concluded that, although the Pataud:4 faunal sample was quite large,

> ... it lacks the definite evidence of January-February occupation provided by fetal long bones. There is evidence of possible occupation anytime in the December through March period, but the only definite evidence in Level 4 is of September-October. Thus we are faced with the possibility of a spring and fall usage of the Abri with winter encamp-

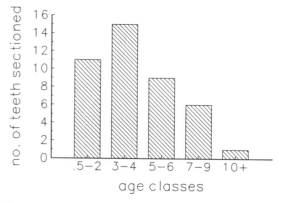

**Figure 9.8.** Composite age profile of red deer in Ferrassie: D2, Flageolet-1:7, Battuts:5, and Roc de Combe:1.

ments elsewhere during the Noaillian (Spiess 1979:194-195).

The seasonality information provided by Bouchud (1975:96, 99, Tabl. XVIII, and 101, Pl. VIII-1) on 22 butchered antlers is quite similar. Most of the kills are diagnosed as occurring in May and/or June, with a secondary frequency peak in October. Although it is calibrated slightly differently, the suggestion of fall and spring reindeer hunting, with little or none during either summer or winter, emerges from both studies.

On the bases of tooth eruption, fetal long bones, and tooth sectioning, Spiess (1979:207) determined that Pataud:3:Lens 2 contained late fall and winter kills, October to March or April. The conclusions reached by Bouchud (1975) are in broad agreement, except that the period is extended from early fall (September) to late spring (June).

Data on the age structure of reindeer in the Pataud faunal samples come from Spiess (1979) for all the Gravettian levels within the shelter and from Bouchud (1966) for the talus deposits in front of the Pataud:5 occupation levels; the resulting age profiles are shown in Figure 9.9. Both samples from the Pataud:5 Middle Perigordian and the Pataud:4 Noaillian closely approximate a classic catastrophic pattern. The late Upper Perigordian sample from Pataud:3, however, has a profile almost identical to that of the composite early-plus-late Upper Perigordian profile for red deer discussed above (Figure 9.8) as a possible overlay of attritional and prime-age patterns. Although sample sizes are too small for confident interpretation, there is a strong suggestion here that the skill and/or technology of Upper Perigordian hunters in southwestern France had become sufficiently developed to allow them to select prime animals of important prey species.

## GRAVETTIAN HUNTING STRATEGIES: PROVISIONAL CONCLUSIONS

We have learned from the archaeofaunal studies that seasonality of hunting of a given species, rather than year-round killing, is a characteristic of all the occupations examined here. Three apparent patterns have emerged: (1) cold-season hunting of red deer in Flageolet-1:7 and reindeer in Pataud:5 and Pataud:3; (2) warm-season hunting of red deer in Ferrassie: D2; and (3) possible migration hunting (spring and fall only) of reindeer in Pataud:4. At sites with long Upper Palaeolithic sequences, one may find either different occupations with different species frequencies during similar climatic phases, as at La Ferrassie, or different seasonality patterns for the same species across climatic phases, as at Pataud. This observation suggests the operation of cultural choice, rather than

an environmental equation involving site location and prey species ranges.

We do not yet have good seasonality information on different species from the same occupation levels at Gravettian sites from southwestern France. Therefore, we must not automatically equate seasonally limited killing with seasonally limited occupation of the rockshelters. The work of Gordon (1988) on reindeer and Burke (1992 and this volume) on horse provides a cautionary tale. In Magdalenian levels at Laugerie-Haute Est, reindeer were killed primarily in winter and spring, whereas horses were killed primarily during the warm season. Information on either species alone would provide an erroneously limited view of occupational seasonality.

The numbers of individual prey animals killed (and/or archaeologically retrieved) are small at all sites considered. For example, Spiess (1979:185) concluded that reindeer hunted during the cold season at Pataud "were killed singly or in small numbers" and that there was no evidence of large-scale drives or mass kills. This pattern is also consistent with Enloe's (1993) conclusions regarding reindeer in the Gravettian occupation of Flageolet-1:5. Mass kills from large-scale drives are highly unlikely, and this kind of specialized collecting can not be attributed to our present sample from the southwest French Gravettian.

Available age-at-death profiles for reindeer in the Middle Perigordian and Noaillian at Pataud are catastrophic in pattern. Because mass kills can be ruled out, this suggests a foraging strategy of taking animals singly or in very limited numbers during each hunting episode--but with enough skill so that prime-age individuals could be obtained with as much success as the very young and the very old. The age profiles examined here for the Upper Perigordian, for both red deer and reindeer, suggest an emphasis on prime-age individuals. This, in turn, suggests more effective selection, but again the overall numbers of kills indicate foraging rather than a fundamental commitment to specialized collection.

The study of Gravettian weaponry both supports and qualifies these interpretations. The very obvious dominance of maintainable (lithic) weapon armatures in most of the assemblages reviewed supports the view that the subsistence system of these occupations was based on foraging rather than specialized collecting. If necessary future experimental research supports the notion of "reliably" designed organic weapon armatures, the fact that such organic armatures dominate at least some Noaillian assemblages will require further consideration. As Bleed (1986: 740) notes, "maintainability and reliability are design alternatives that a tool builder can use to increase the availability of systems in different situations." What may be different about the Pataud:4 occupations in which organic weapons are heavily dominant is the tight seasonal limitation of

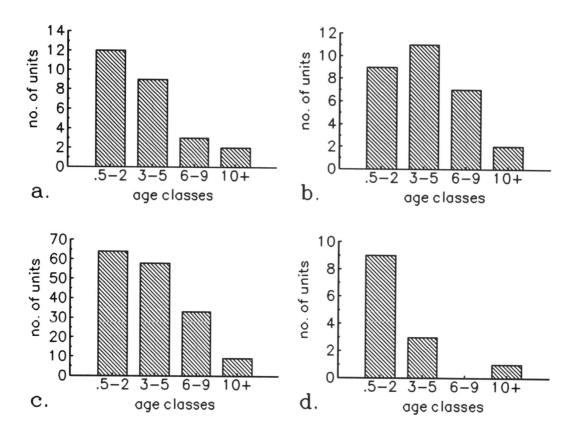

**Figure 9.9.** Age profiles of reindeer in Gravettian levels at Abri Pataud: (a) Pataud:4, n = 26 mandibular units; (b) Pataud:3, n = 29 mandibular units; (c) Pataud:5:Talus, n = 164 mandibular units; (d): Pataud:5, n = 13 mandibular units. Information from Spiess 1979:193, Tab. 6.4 (a, b, d) and Bouchud 1966:169, Tabl. XLIV (c).

reindeer killing--spring and fall only. Even though mass killing eludes us, it may be that short-term seasonal specialization favored the reliable design alternative.

We return, finally, to the question of the dichotomy some have seen between Early and Late Upper Palaeolithic subsistence strategies. Although the picture of Gravettian hunting that emerges from the evidence examined here is not the picture of specialized reindeer hunting we are familiar with from Stellmoor or the Magdalenian levels at Pincevent, it is nevertheless very probable that developmental improvements in both techniques and technology occurred within the Gravettian during the seven or eight millennia of its existence. In the specific cases examined here, this can be inferred from the evidence for age selection in the later assemblages, from the improved hafting techniques for lithic armatures, and from the appearance in the latest Gravettian assemblages of microlith-armed composite weapons. These phenomena suggest that some skills and implements important to later prehistoric cultures were developed

within the Gravettian. The Gravettian itself is most usefully examined as part of a continuum of change, not simply as one pole of a dichotomy.

## ACKNOWLEDGMENTS

Anne Pike-Tay wishes to thank Heidi Knecht, Ariane Burke, and Randy White for valuable comments on an earlier version of this paper. She also thanks Françoise Delpech and Jean-Philippe Rigaud for permission to study faunal materials from southwestern France. The Flageolet I data should be considered preliminary, as the materials await further analysis and publication. Funding for Pike-Tay's archaeofaunal analysis was made possible by the Wenner-Gren Foundation for Anthropological Research and by New York University Dean's Dissertation Fellowship. Current funding for the control sample analysis, with R. White, is from the National Science Foundation (BNS 9023662). Harvey Bricker acknowledges with gratitude numerous discussions with Gail Larsen Peterkin, whose research has significantly shaped his thinking about Upper Palaeolithic weaponry.

## NOTES

[1]The "*fléchette*" is characterized by short, semi-abrupt retouch, sometimes inverse, at one or both extremities of the blade blank, extending sometimes along one or both margins. It is associated with early Gravettian (Middle Perigordian) industries in southwestern France and central Europe.

[2]The French word "sagaie" is widely used by archaeologists working in the Upper Palaeolithic to refer to the organic points that tipped projectile weapons.

## REFERENCES

Alaux, J.-F.
1973 Pointes de la Font-Robert, en place, dans le Périgordien à burins de Noailles de l'abri des Battuts (Commune de Penne, Tarn). *Bulletin de la Société Préhistorique Française* 70:51-55.

Bernaldo de Quirós, F.
1980a *Notas sobre la economia del Paleolítico Superior.* Monografias del Centro de Investigación y Museo de Altamira 1. Madrid: Minsterio de Cultura.
1980b Early Upper Palaeolithic in Cantabrian Spain. In *L'Aurignacien et le Gravettien (Périgordien) dans leur cadre écologique.* L. Bánesz and J. Koslowsky, eds. Pp. 53-64. Nitra: Institut Archéologique de l'Académie Slovaque des Sciences à Nitra and Institut Archéologique de l'Université de Cracovie.

Bernaldo de Quirós, F., and V. Cabrera Valdés
1993 Early Upper Paleolithic industries of Cantabrian Spain. In *Before Lascaux: The Complex Record of the Early Upper Paleolithic.* H. Knecht, A. Pike-Tay, and R. White, eds. Pp. 57-69. Boca Raton: CRC Press.

Binford, L. R.
1980 Willow smoke and dogs' tails: Hunter-gatherer settlement systems and archaeological site formation. *American Antiquity* 44:4-20.
1984 *Faunal Remains from the Klasies River Mouth.* Orlando: Academic Press.

Bleed, P.
1986 The optimal design of hunting weapons: Maintainability or reliability. *American Antiquity* 51:737-747.

Bordes, F.
1968a Emplacements de tentes du Périgordien supérieur évolué à Corbiac (près Bergerac), Dordogne. *Quartär* 19:251-262.
1968b La question périgordienne. In *La préhistoire: Problèmes et tendences.* Pp. 59-70. Paris: Editions du Centre Nationale de la Recherche Scientifique.

Bordes, F., and J. Labrot
1967 La stratigraphie du gisement de Roc de Combe (Lot) et ses implications. *Bulletin de la Société Préhistorique Française* 64:15-28.

Bouchud, J.
1966 *Essai sur la renne et la climatologie du Paléolithique moyen et supérieur.* Périgueux: Imprimerie Magne.
1975 Etude de la faune de l'Abri Pataud. In *Exacavation of the Abri Pataud, Les Eyzies (Dordogne).* H. Movius, ed. Pp. 69-153. American School of Prehistoric Research Bulletin 30. Cambridge: Peabody Museum, Harvard University.

Bouyssonie, J.
1948 Un gisement aurignacien et périgordien, Les Vachons (Charente). *L'Anthropologie* 52:1-42.

Bouyssonie, J., and D. de Sonneville-Bordes
1957 L'abri N° 2 des Vachons, gisement aurignacien et périgordien, commune de Voulgézac (Charente). *Congrès Préhistorique de France, Comptes Rendus de la XV<sup>ème</sup> Session, Poitiers-Angoulême, 1956.* Pp. 271-309. Paris: Société Préhistorique Française.

Bratlund, B.
n.n. The hunting economy of Stellmoor. Paper presented at the international symposium "La chasse dans la préhistoire," October 3-7, 1990, Treignes, Belgium.

Bricker, H. M.
1973 *The Périgordian IV and Related Cultures in France.* Ph.D. dissertation, Department of Anthropology, Harvard University.
n.d. Le Périgordien moyen (niveau 5) de l'abri Pataud. In *Les fouilles Movius à l'abri Pataud, Les Eyzies-de-Tayac (Dordogne).* H. M. Bricker, ed. Paris: Documents d'Archéologie Française. (in press).

Bricker, H. M., and N. David
1984 *Excavation of the Abri Pataud, Les Eyzies (Dordogne): The Périgordian VI (Level 3) Assemblage.* American School of Prehistoric Research Bulletin 32. Cambridge: Peabody Museum, Harvard University.

Bricker, H. M., and P. A. Mellars
1987 Datations [14]C de l'abri Pataud (Les Eyzies, Dordogne) par le procédé « accélérateur - spectromètre de masse ». *L'Anthropologie* 91:227-234.

Burke, A.
1992 *Prey Movements and Settlement Patterns during the Upper Paleolithic in Southwestern France.* Ph.D. dissertation, Department of Anthropology, New York University.

Cabrera Valdés, V.
1984 *El yacimiento de la Cueva del Castillo (Puente Viesgo, Santander).* Bibliotheca Praehistorica Hispana XXII. Madrid: Instituto Español de Prehistoria.

Célèrier, G.
1967 Le gisement périgordien supérieur des "Jambes," commune de Périgueux (Dordogne). *Bulletin de la Société Préhistorique Française* 64:53-68.

Charbonnier, O.
1962 L'abri aurignacien des Roches, commune de Pouligny-Saint-Pierre (Indre). *L'Anthropologie* 66:469-484.

Chase, P. G.
1989 How different was Middle Palaeolithic subsistence? A zooarchaeological perspective on the Middle to Upper Palaeolithic transition. In *The Human Revolution: Behavioural and Biological Perspectives in the Origins of Modern Humans.* P. Mellars and C. Stringer, eds. Pp. 321-337. Princeton: Princeton University Press.

Clay, R. B.
n.d. Le Protomagdalénien (niveau 2) de l'abri Pataud. In *Les fouilles Movius à l'abri Pataud, Les Eyzies-de-Tayac (Dordogne).* H. M. Bricker, ed. Paris: Documents d'Archéologie Française. (in press).
1968 *The Proto-Magdalenian Culture.* Ph.D. dissertation, Department of Anthropology, Southern Illinois University.

David, N.
1966 *The Perigordian Vc: An Upper Palaeolithic Culture in Western Europe.* Ph.D. dissertation, Department of Anthropology, Harvard University.
1985 *Excavation of the Abri Pataud, Les Eyzies (Dordogne): The Noaillian (Level 4) Assemblages and the Noaillian Culture in Western Europe.* American School of Prehistoric Research Bulletin 37. Cambridge: Peabody

Museum, Harvard University.

David, N., and H. M. Bricker
1987 Perigordian and Noaillian in the greater Périgord. In *The Pleistocene Old World: Regional Perspectives*. O. Soffer, ed. Pp. 237-250. New York: Plenum Press.

Delpech, F.
1983 *Les faunes du Paléolithique supérieur dans le sud-ouest de la France*. Cahiers du Quaternaire 6. Paris: Editions du Centre National de Recherche Scientifique.
1984 La Ferrassie: Carnivores, Artiodactyles et Périssodactyles. In *Le grand abri de la Ferrassie. Fouilles 1968-1973*. H. Delporte, ed. Pp. 61-89. Université de Provence Etudes Quaternaires Mémoires 7. Paris: Institute de Paléontologie Humaine.
1993 The fauna of the Early Upper Paleolithic: Biostratigraphy of large mammals and current problems in chronology. In *Before Lascaux: The Complex Record of the Early Upper Paleolithic*. H. Knecht, A. Pike-Tay, and R. White, eds. Pp. 71-84. Boca Raton: CRC Press.

Delporte, H.
1968 L'abri du Facteur à Tursac (Dordogne). Etude générale. *Gallia Préhistoire* 11:1-112.

Delporte, H., J. Hahn, L. Mons, G. Pinçon, and D. de Sonneville-Bordes
1988 *Fiches typologiques de l'industrie osseuse préhistorique. Cahier I. Sagaies*. Aix-en-Provence: Université de Provence.

Delporte, H., and A. Tuffreau
1984 Les industries du Périgordien V de La Ferrassie. In *Le grand abri de la Ferrassie. Fouilles 1968-1973*. H. Delporte, ed. Pp. 235-247. Université de Provence Etudes Quaternaires Mémoires 7. Paris: Institute de Paléontologie Humaine.

Enloe, J. G.
1993 Subsistence organization in the Early Upper Paleolithic: Reindeer hunters of the Abri du Flageolet, couche V. In *Before Lascaux: The Complex Record of the Early Upper Paleolithic*. H. Knecht, A. Pike-Tay, and R. White, eds. Pp. 101-115. Boca Raton: CRC Press.

Enloe, J. G., and F. David
1989 Le remontage des os par individus: Le partage du renne chez les Magdaléniens de Pincevent. *Bulletin de la Société Préhistorique Française* 86:275-281.

Farrand, W. R.
n.d. Etude sédimentologique du remplissage de l'abri Pataud. In *Les fouilles Movius à l'abri Pataud, Les Eyzies-de-Tayac (Dordogne)*. H. M. Bricker, ed. Paris: Documents d'Archéologie Française. (in press).

Francillon-Vieillot, H., V. de Buffrénil, J. Castanet, J. Géraudie, F. J. Meunier, J. Y. Sire, L. Zylberberg, and A. de Ricqlés
1991 Microstructure and mineralization of vertebrate skeletal tissues. In *Skeletal Biomineralization: Patterns, Processes and Evolutionary Trends. Volume 1*. J. Carter, ed. Pp. 471-530. New York: Van Nostrand Reinhold.

Gamble, C.
1986 *The Palaeolithic Settlement of Europe*. Cambridge: Cambridge University Press.

Geneste, J.-M., and H. Plisson
1993 Hunting technologies and human behavior: Lithic analysis of Solutrean shouldered points. In *Before Lascaux: The Complex Record of the Early Upper Paleolithic*. H. Knecht, A. Pike-Tay, and R. White, eds. Pp. 117-135. Boca Raton: CRC Press.

Gordon, B.
1988 *Of Men and Reindeer Herds in French Magdalenian Prehistory*. BAR International Series 390. Oxford: British Archaeological Reports.

Klein, R. G.
1982 Age (mortality) profiles as a means of distinguishing hunted species from scavenged ones in Stone Age archaeological sites. *Paleobiology* 8:151-158.
1989 Why does skeletal part representation differ between smaller and larger bovids at Klasies River Mouth and other archeological sites? *Journal of Archaeological Science* 6:363-381.

Knecht, H.
1991 *Technological Innovation and Design during the Early Upper Paleolithic: A Study of Organic Projectile Technologies*. Ph.D. dissertation, Department of Anthropology, New York University.

Lacorre, F.
1960 *La Gravette. Le Gravétien et le Bayacien*. Laval: Imprimerie Barnéoud.

Laville, H.
1975 *Climatologie et chronologie du Paléolithique en Périgord: Etude sédimentologique de dépôts en grottes et sous abris*. Université de Provence Etudes Quaternaires Mémoires 4. Marseille: Université de Provence.

Laville, H., and J.-Ph. Rigaud
1973 The Périgordian V industries in Périgord: Typological variations, stratigraphy and relative chronology. *World Archaeology* 4:330-338.

Laville, H., and J.-P. Texier
1986 Le Quaternaire en Périgord. In *Quaternaire et préhistoire en Périgord. Excursion de l'A.F.E.Q. 8, 9, 10 mai 1986*. H. Laville, J.-Ph. Rigaud, and J.-P. Texier. Pp. A1-A21. Bordeaux: Institut de Quaternaire de l'Université de Bordeaux I and Direction des Antiquités Préhistoriques d'Aquitaine.

Laville, H., and A. Tuffreau
1984 Les dépôts du grand abri de la Ferrassie: Stratigraphie, signification climatique et chronologie. In *Le grand abri de la Ferrassie. Fouilles 1968-1973*. H. Delporte, ed. Pp. 25-50. Université de Provence Etudes Quaternaires Mémoires 7. Paris: Institute de Paléontologie Humaine.

Lieberman, D. E., T. W. Deacon, and R. H. Meadow
1990 Computer image enhancement and analysis of cementum increments as applied to teeth of *Gazella gazella*. *Journal of Archaeological Science* 17:519-533.

Lindly, J., and G. A. Clark
1990 Symbolism and modern human origins. *Current Anthropology* 31:233-261.

Mellars, P. A., and H. M. Bricker
1986 Radiocarbon accelerator dating in the earlier Upper Palaeolithic. In *Archaeological Results from Accelerator Dating*. J. Gowlett and R. Hedges, ed. Pp. 73-80. Oxford University Committee for Archaeology Monograph 11. Oxford: Oxford University Committee for Archaeology.

Mellars, P. A., H. M. Bricker, J. A. J. Gowlett, and R. E. M. Hedges
1987 Radiocarbon accelerator dating of French Upper Palaeolithic sites. *Current Anthropology* 28:128-133.

Movius, H. L., Jr.
1960 Bas-relief carving of a female figure recently discovered in the Final Périgordian horizon at the Abri Pataud, Les Eyzies (Dordogne). In *Festschrift für Lothar Zotz. Steinzeitfragen der Alten und Neuen Welt*. Gisela Freund, ed. Pp. 377-387. Bonn: L. Rohrscheld.
1977 *Excavation of the Abri Pataud, Les Eyzies (Dordogne). Stratigraphy*. American School of Prehistoric Research Bulletin 31. Cambridge: Peabody Museum, Harvard University.

Movius, H. L., Jr., N. David, H. M. Bricker, and R. B. Clay
1968 *The Analysis of Certain Major Classes of Upper Pa-*

*laeolithic Tools.* American School of Prehistoric Research Bulletin 26. Cambridge: Peabody Museum, Harvard University.

Otte, M.
1985 Le Gravettien en Europe. *L'Anthropologie* 89:479-503.
1990 Révision de la séquence du Paléolithique supérieur de Willendorf (Autriche). *Bulletin de l'Institut Royal des Sciences Naturelles de Belgique, Sciences de la Terre* 60:219-228.

Otte, M., and L. H. Keeley
1990 The impact of regionalism on Palaeolithic studies. *Current Anthropology* 31:577-582.

Paquereau, M.-M.
1984 Etude palynologique du gisement de la Ferrassie (Dordogne). In *Le grand abri de la Ferrassie. Fouilles 1968-1973.* H. Delporte, ed. Pp. 51-59. Université de Provence Etudes Quaternaires Mémoires 7. Paris: Institute de Paléontologie Humaine.

Peyrony, D.
1933 Les industries "aurignaciennes" dans le bassin de la Vézère. *Bulletin de la Société Préhistorique Française* 30:543-559.
1934 La Ferrassie: Moustérien--Périgordien--Aurignacien. *Préhistoire* 3:1-92.

Peyrony, D., and E. Peyrony
1938 *Laugerie-Haute, près des Eyzies (Dordogne).* Archives de l'Institut de Paléontologie Humaine Mémoires 19. Paris: Institut de Paléontologie Humaine.

Pike-Tay, A.
1989 *Red Deer Hunting in the Upper Paleolithic of Southwest France: A Seasonality Study.* Ph.D. dissertation, Department of Anthropology, New York University. Ann Arbor: University Microfilms.
1991a *Red Deer Hunting in the Upper Paleolithic of Southwest France: A Study in Seasonality.* BAR International Series 569. Oxford: Tempus Reparatum.
1991b L'analyse du cement dentaire chez les cerfs: l'Application en préhistoire. *Paléo* 3:149-166.
1993 Hunting in the Perigordian: A matter of strategy or expedience? In *Before Lascaux: The Complex Record of the Early Upper Paleolithic.* H. Knecht, A. Pike-Tay, and R. White, eds. Pp. 85-99. Boca Raton: CRC Press.
n.d. Developing a control sample for archaeology of dental annuli and crown heights in *Rangifer tarandus.* Paper presented at the 57th Annual Meeting of the Society for American Archaeology, Pittsburgh, April 1992.

Pradel, L.
1965 L'abri aurignacien et périgordien des Roches, commune

de Poluigny-Saint-Pierre (Indre). *L'Anthropologie* 69:219-236.

Pradel, L., and A. Chollet
1950 L'abri périgordien de Laraux, commune de Lussac-les-Châteaux (Vienne). *L'Anthropologie* 54:214-227.

Rigaud, J.-Ph.
1982 *Le Paléolithique en Périgord: Les données du sud-ouest sarladais et leurs implications.* Thèse de Doctorat d'État des Sciences, Université de Bordeaux I.
1988 The Gravettian peopling of southwestern France: Taxonomic problems. In *Upper Pleistocene Prehistory of Western Eurasia.* H. Dibble and A. Montet-White, eds. Pp. 387-396. University Museum Monograph 54. Philadelphia: The University Museum, University of Pennsylvania.

de Saint-Périer, R., and S. de Saint-Périer
1952 *La grotte d'Isturitz. III. Les Solutréens, les Aurignaciens et les Moustériens.* Archives de l'Institut de Paléontologie Humaine Mémoires 25. Paris: Institut de Paléontologie Humaine.

de Sonneville-Bordes, D.
1960 *Le Paléolithique supérieur en Périgord.* Bordeaux: Imprimerie Delmas.
1966 L'évolution du Paléolithique supérieur en Europe occidentale et sa signification. *Bulletin de la Société Préhistorique Française* 63:3-34.

Spiess, A. E.
1979 *Reindeer and Caribou Hunters: An Archaeological Study.* New York: Academic Press.

Stiner, M., ed.
1991 *Human Predators and Prey Mortality.* Boulder: Westview Press.

Straus, L. G.
1990 Comment on "Symbolism and modern human origins" by J. Lindly and G. Clark. *Current Anthropology* 31:233-261.

Straus, L. G., and G. A. Clark
1986 *La Riera Cave: Stone Age Hunter-Gatherer Adaptations in Northern Spain.* Anthropological Research Papers 36. Tempe: Arizona State University.

White, R.
1985 *Upper Paleolithic Land-Use in the Périgord: A Topographic Approach to Subsistence and Settlement.* BAR International Series 253. Oxford: British Archaeological Reports.
1989 Husbandry and herd control in the Upper Paleolithic: A critical review of the evidence. *Current Anthropology* 30:609-632.

*10*

# Applied Skeletochronology: The Horse as Human Prey During the Pleniglacial in Southwestern France

**Ariane Burke**
**Canadian Museum of Civilization**

## ABSTRACT

A model for the appositional growth of dental cement in the horse, based on a control sample of recent horse teeth, is applied to the microscopic analysis under transmitted light of petrographic thin-sections of fossil horse specimens from 12 prehistoric sites in southwestern France. This sample is restricted chronologically to the Pleniglacial period (18,000 to 14,000 BP) in order to maintain strict control of environmental variables. The archaeological results of the study include the assessment of the seasonal importance of horse as a human resource during the Pleniglacial, as well as the role of this species in what has been described as a reindeer-based human economy. They also contribute data on season of occupation for the archaeological sites studied, with implications for models of regional seasonal population movements in southwestern France.

## INTRODUCTION

This paper presents the results of a regional analysis of seasonal hunting patterns and site use in the Aquitaine Basin in southwestern France during the Dryas I, the last Pleniglacial, from about 18,000 to 14,000 BP. The principal data are the results of skeletochronological analyses of horse teeth (*Equus caballus*) recovered from controlled archaeological contexts. Comparable data obtained from a study of reindeer (*Rangifer tarandus*) teeth (Gordon 1989) are incorporated as a second index of seasonality. These two species (horse and reindeer) formed the dominant bases for the human hunting economy during the Pleniglacial period in the study region.

The skeletochronological analysis rests on a control sample of 16 modern equids (*Equus caballus*) assembled by the author (Burke 1992) and a sample of 12 feral horses from Sable Island collected by Dr. D. Welsh of the Canadian Conservation Institute (Welsh 1972). The purpose of the control sample is to establish the time of formation of incremental growth structures in the cement of horse teeth and to apply this information to the study of fossil populations of horse.

Research into skeletal growth structures has shown that cement deposition is generally cyclical, with a seasonal periodicity; the usefulness of growth

layers in the dental cement of various marine and terrestrial mammals as an index of absolute age and season of death has been amply discussed in the biological literature (e.g., Klevezal and Kleinenberg 1969; Grue and Jensen 1976; Perrin and Myrrick 1981; Monks 1981; Klevezal 1988).

## METHOD AND MATERIALS

The pattern of cement deposition for a given species must be empirically established through the examination of a control sample of animals of known date of death (e.g., Miller 1974; Pike-Tay 1991). For the present study, a control sample of 16 modern equids was established, with deaths occurring over a period of nine months. Samples of several teeth were taken from each mandible, and undecalcified thin sections were examined under polarized light. Stained, frozen thin-sections were also prepared from demineralized molars from five individuals. Ground, polished, and etched surfaces from molars extracted from two individuals were examined using a scanning electron microscope (SEM). One undecalcified thin-section was also microradiographed. Teeth from 12 feral horses of known date of death, obtained from D. Welsh (Canadian Conservation Institute) and prepared as ground, polished thick-sections, were examined under reflected light.

**Table 10.1.** The provenience of the fossil samples.

| Location, Site, and Collection | Level or Couche | Sample Size |
|---|---|---|
| *Gironde:* | | |
| Moulin Neuf | 2 | 5 |
| Roc de Marcamps, Locus 1 | 2 | 4 |
| | 3 | 2 |
| | 4 | 2 |
| | 5 | 1 |
| Roc de Marcamps, Locus 2 | all | 3 |
| Saint-Germain-la-Rivière | 1 | 3 |
| | 3 | 5 |
| *Dordogne:* | | |
| Badegoule | Mag. | 4 |
| Cap Blanc | Inf. | 3 |
| Esclauzur | Inf. | 4 |
| La Madeleine (Bordes) | 27 | 3 |
| Laugerie-Haute Est (Bordes) | F1-F2 | 3 |
| | F5 | 2 |
| | F1,FM, & FN | 4 |
| Laugerie-Haute Est (Peyrony) | Mag.III | 13 |
| Reignac | all | 5 |
| *Massif Central:* | | |
| Enval | f | 3 |
| Rond du Barry | F2 | 9 |
| | E3 | |
| *Landes:* | | |
| Duruthy | 5 | 5 |
| TOTAL | | 83 |

The archaeological sample originates from 12 sites in southwestern France containing occupation levels firmly attributable to the Dryas I on the basis of chronostratigraphic information (Table 10.1). All sites sampled are cave or rockshelter locations, which imposes recognized limitations on the present research (see Rigaud and Simek 1987; White 1987). This location bias, however, reflects the realities of faunal preservation.

Fossil material was embedded in epoxy resin and thin-sectioned using standard petrographic techniques (Gordon 1989). Longitudinal, labio-lingual sections were made along the columns of the tooth, avoiding infundibulae. In this way, the cementum layers were oriented perpendicular to the surface of the section (Figure 10.1). This orientation was necessary in order to assess the thickness of the growth layers, because layers sectioned diagonally appear thicker under the microscope. Sections were mounted on slides and reduced to a thickness of one or two cells (40 to 60 microns).

Observations of the final incremental layer were made under transmitted ordinary and polarized light.

Two to three slides were prepared per tooth. All of the prepared specimens were photographed, and the photographs were used to compare and verify observations made under the microscope.

Incremental growth was measured on images scanned from photographic negatives of the specimens. The amount of growth of the final increment was expressed as a percentage of the total expected growth, based on the observed width of the previous increment (Gordon 1989; Pike-Tay 1990; Spiess 1990). Measurements of the final and penultimate increments were taken using image processing software (Image 1.23). Increments were counted and measured on histograms (optical density profiles) based on average pixel luminance values for eight-pixel wide cross-sections of the scanned images, normal to the tooth surface (Lieberman et al. 1991).

## RESULTS

### Histological Observations on the Modern Sample

The prismatic, selenodont teeth of equids are distinguished by a prolonged period of growth and continuous eruption. Although in most herbivores

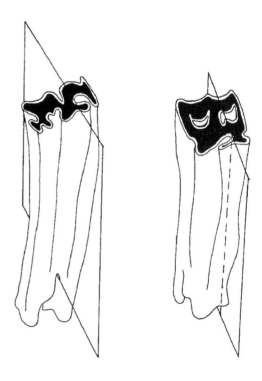

**Figure 10.1.** Orientation of the tooth sections necessary for the production of thin-sections.

**Table 10.2.** Seasonal determinations based on the analysis of the fossil sample.

| Site Name | N | N* | "Summer" May-Oct | Nov | Dec-Jan | Feb-Apr | "Winter" Nov-Apr |
|---|---|---|---|---|---|---|---|
| L.H.E. a | 13 | 5 | N=2 | N=0 | N=2 | N=1 | N=3 |
| L.H.E. b | - | 7 | 6 | 0 | 1 | 0 | 1 |
| L.H.E. t | 22 | 12 | 8 | 0 | 3 | 1 | 4 |
| Badegoule | 4 | 4 | 1 | 0 | 2 | 1 | 3 |
| Duruthy 5 | 5 | 4 | 4 | 0 | 0 | 0 | 0 |
| Madeleine | 9 | 7 | 6 | 0 | 1 | 0 | 1 |
| Rond du Barry | 14 | 14 | 7(8) | 1 | 4 | 1 | 6 |
| Enval | 4 | 3 | 2 | 0 | 1 | 0 | 1 |
| Esclauzur | 4 | 3 | 3 | 0 | 0 | 0 | 0 |
| St.-Germ | 10 | 5 | 3(4) | 1 | 0 | 0 | 1 |
| M. Neuf. | 5 | 5 | 2 | 1 | 1 | 1 | 3 |
| Marcamps 1 | 8 | 6 | 3 | 1 | 2 | 0 | 3 |
| Marcamps 2 | 3 | 2 | 0 | 0 | 1 | 1 | 2 |
| Marcamps t | 11 | 8 | 3 | 1 | 3 | 1 | 5 |
| Reignac | 5 | 1 | 1 | 0 | 0 | 0 | 0 |
| Cap Blanc | 3 | 2 | 1 | 0 | 1 | 0 | 1 |

**Key:** N = number of samples; N* = number of legible samples; L.H.E. a = Laugerie-Haute Est, Bordes sample; L.H.E. b = Laugerie-Haute Est, Peyrony sample; L.H.E. t = Laugerie-Haute Est, both samples; Marcamps 1 and 2 = Roc de Marcamps, Locii 1 and 2; Marcamps t = Roc de Marcamps, both locii.

cement is deposited in relatively thin layers on the dentine surface in the root and cervical regions of the tooth, cementum in equids is deposited on a partially resorbed enamel surface on the crown and root (Jones and Boyde 1974).

As in other ungulates, cementum deposition in equids results from the apposition of thick, successive growth layers deposited parallel to the long axis of the tooth below the gingival cuff. At the gingival cuff, however, growth layers begin tapering towards the root (Figure 10.2). In mature individuals with fully formed roots (7-8 years [Levine 1979]), this asymmetrical pattern of deposition is particularly marked, to the point of presenting apparent discontinuities with preceding growth layers. Readings are considered to be most accurate towards the base of the coronal cement deposit, where layers are almost parallel to each other.

Inter- and intra-individual comparisons of cement formation in the control sample reveal that equid cement possesses an apparently regular, cyclic formation. A primary (first) layer is deposited on a partially resorbed enamel surface (see Jones and Boyde 1974). The distinctly more cellular and chaotic fibrillar organization of this first layer was confirmed by each of the preparation methods (Burke 1992). The exact timing of deposition of this primary growth layer has not yet been determined. Under transmitted light, subsequent growth layers appear as alternating translu-

cent and opaque bands, corresponding roughly to warm and cold season growth.

The wide layer of opaque cementum, (the growth zone, sensu Peabody 1961) is deposited from May to October, inclusively. This period of cementum growth is not easily divisible, as examination of the percentages of expected growth reveals (see also Spiess 1990). Individual variation in rate of growth appears to be high, probably due to a number of factors directly and indirectly affecting physiological growth (e.g., age, hormonal levels, mechanical demands on the tooth, and availability of fodder).

A relatively thin layer of translucent cement, the line of arrested growth or LAG (Baglinière et al. 1992), forms during a rough six-month period corresponding to the temperate zone's "winter" months plus "spring," i.e., November to April. This period can be tentatively divided into two subgroups, with intermittent LAG formation in November and intermittent zonal growth (less than 10% of expected total growth) in February-April. Welsh's sample of 12 animals, dead in March, all showed translucent LAGs with intermittent zonal growth on the tooth margin.

### Archaeological Results

The application of data from a control sample of modern, domestic animals to a fossil population rests on the assumption of uniformity, supported by the

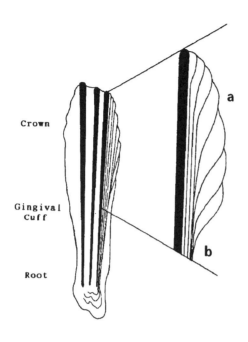

Crown

Gingival
Cuff

Root

**Figure 10.2.** Schematic view of a radial tooth section, showing the asymmetrical pattern of deposition of coronal cement (a) vs. the parallel deposition of cement on the body of the tooth (b).

facts that (1) *Equus caballus* has not diverged genetically since the Pleniglacial, about 14,000 to 18,000 years ago, and (2) there is a high degree of morphological and behavioral similarity among modern equid populations (different species of *Equus*), suggesting a degree of genetic invariance between them (Levine 1982:224).

The application of domestic control data to a wild population can be defended on the grounds that the effects of domestication on the formation of incremental growth lines appears to be minimal (Saxon and Higham 1969; Grue 1976; Grue and Jensen 1979). Differences in the environmental contexts of the modern control populations and Pleniglacial populations in southwestern France undoubtedly exist, but Reimers and Nordby (1968) have shown that intraspecific differences in the pattern of cyclical incremental growth resulting from the exploitation of different ranges within the same climatic zone are not significant. The animals used for the control sample lived in the same broad latitude and climatic conditions and may thus provide a model of incremental growth useful in the investigation of fossil equid teeth.

Globally, histological observations on modern teeth proved valid for the fossil teeth. The rate of attrition resulting from poorly preserved fossil specimens was relatively low; 25% of the teeth did not produce legible slides.

The results of the analysis indicate that all sites in the Dordogne, with the exception of Reignac, where only one tooth was legible, were occupied during both cold and warm seasons (Table 10.2). The same results were obtained for all three sites from the Gironde and both sites in the Massif Central. At Duruthy, on the southernmost fringe of the region, the sample yielded only warm season mortality for horse.

## DISCUSSION

According to the skeletochronological data compiled by Gordon (1988), reindeer were hunted primarily in the winter and spring (December-May) at the sites he surveyed in the Dordogne. At all sites except Reignac, however, horse shows evidence of warm season exploitation (May to October). Two interpretations of the combined seasonal data are possible: (1) the sites surveyed were used year round, or (2) the sites were occupied primarily in the winter and spring (December-May), when reindeer were regionally available. Horse may have been used to extend site occupation into the warm season, after the reindeer had migrated but before a shift to summer residences had taken place. In either scenario, however, horse is a resource with a complementary seasonality, i.e., it was exploited outside the period of reindeer migration, possibly during the monitoring of reindeer herd movements.

In the Gironde, seasonal information from the three sites surveyed can be interpreted similarly, as can data from the two Massif Central sites. In order to fully understand seasonal economic activity in the Gironde, where reindeer is less dominant (Delpech 1987), it would be necessary to expand the skeletochronological study to include saiga and perhaps even bovines. Similarly, ibex should be studied at Rond du Barry, because it is the second most important species at the site. Evidence from Duruthy points to a potential difference between local economies in the Aquitaine Basin and the northern border of the western Pyrénées.

## CONCLUSION

Thus, there is empirical evidence for the presence of seasonal growth layers in equid cementum. According to the present observations, determination of the season of death is possible based on observation of the final growth layer at, or just below, the gingival cuff.

The necessity of establishing a control sample for the study species is obvious. Like most physiological growth cycles, the appositional growth of cement is conditioned by both endogenous and exogenous factors

(Klevezal and Kleinenberg 1969; Grue and Jensen 1974; Castanet 1981, 1982). Once the presence of a seasonal depositional cycle is established for a given species, calendrical correspondences must be sought using animals of known date of death.

Finally, seasonal determinations can be obtained from fossil equid teeth when thin-sectioned and viewed under transmitted light. Results of the present study suggest that a certain degree of complementarity exists in the seasonal importance of reindeer and horse as human prey during the Pleniglacial (Dryas I) in southwestern France. Horse, as a resource exploited by humans, tends to "fill the gap" between putative reindeer migrations.

The implications for models of reindeer herd-following are serious and far-reaching, because humans were present in the Aquitaine during at least part of the proposed period of reindeer outmigration, i.e., summer (Gordon 1988). The alternative hypothesis proposed here and elsewhere is one of a more restricted pattern of seasonal mobility, accompanied by shifts in resource use (e.g., David 1973; Spiess 1979; Straus 1983, 1987; White 1985, 1987; Burke 1992).

## ACKNOWLEDGEMENTS

The author would like to acknowledge the members of her Ph.D. committee, without whom this research would not have been possible: Dr. White, Dr. Wright, and Dr. Crabtree, all from the Department of Anthropology at New York University; Dr. Meadow, Harvard University; Dr. Castanet, Université de Paris VII; and Dr. Pike-Tay, Vassar College. In addition, this research could not have been undertaken without the aid of numerous French archaeologists, who donated samples and assisted the author in various ways. Special thanks are due to Dr. Rigaud and colleagues at the Institut du Quaternaire, Université de Bordeaux.

### REFERENCES

Baglinière, J. L., J. Castanet, F. Conand, and F. J. Meunier
1992 Terminologie en sclérochronologie chez les vertébrés. In *Tissus durs et age individuel chez les vertébrés.*

Burke, A. M.
1992 *Prey Movements and Settlement Patterns during the Upper Palaeolithic in Southwestern France.* Ph.D. dissertation, Department of Anthropology, New York University.

Castanet, J.
1981 Nouvelles données sur les lignes cimentantes de l'os. *Archives Biologiques* (Bruxelles) 92:1-24.
1982 *Recherches sur la croissance du tissu osseux des reptiles. Application: La méthode squelettochronologique.* Thèse de Doctorat d'Etat, Université de Paris VII.

David, N.
1973 On Upper Palaeolithic society, ecology, and technologi-
cal change: The Noaillian Case. In *The Explanation of Culture Change.* C. Renfrew, ed. Pp. 277-383. Cambridge: Cambridge University Press.

Delpech, F.
n.d. L'environment animal des Magdaleniens. Actes du Colloque sur le Magdalenien, Mayence, 1987. (in press).

Gordon, B.
1988 *Of Men and Reindeer Herds in French Magdalenian Prehistory.* BAR International Series 390. Oxford: British Archaeological Reports.

Grue, H.
1976 Non-seasonal incremental lines in tooth cementum of domestic dogs (*Canis familiaris* L.). *Danish Revue of Game Biology* 10(2):1-8.

Grue, H., and B. Jensen
1979 Review of the formation of incremental lines in tooth cementum of terrestrial animals. *Danish Review of Game Biology* 11:1-48.

Jones, S. J., and A. Boyde
1974 Coronal cementogenesis in the horse. *Archives of Oral Biology* 19:605-614.

Klevezal, G. A.
1988 *Recording Structures of Mammals in Zoological Investigations.* Moscow: Nauta.

Klevezal, G. A., and S. E. Kleinenberg
1969 *Age Determination of Mammals From Annual Layers in Teeth and Bones.* Translation of U. S. S. R. Academy of Sciences publication by Israel Program for Scientific Translations, Jerusalem.

Levine, M.
1979 *Archaeo-Zoological Analysis of Some Upper Pleistocene Horse Bone Assemblages in Western Europe.* Ph.D. dissertation, Cambridge University.
1982 The use of crown height measurements and eruption-wear sequences to age horse teeth. In *Ageing and Sexing Animal Bones.* B. Wilson, C. Grigson, and S. Payne, eds. BAR British Series 109. Oxford: British Archaeological Reports.

Lieberman, D. E., T. W. Deacon, and R. Meadow
1990 Computer image enhancement and analysis of cementum increments as applied to teeth of *Gazella gazella. Journal of Archaeological Science* 17:519-533.

Miller, F.
1974 *Biology of the Kaminuriak Population of Barren Ground Caribou.* Canadian Wildlife Service Reports 31 (Part II). Ottawa: Canadian Wildlife Service.

Monks, G.
1981 Seasonality studies. In *Advances in Archaeological Method and Theory. Volume 4.* M. B. Schiffer, ed. Pp. 177-240. New York: Academic Press.

Peabody, F. E.
1961 Annual growth zones in living and fossil vertebrates. *Journal of Morphology* 108:11-62.

Perrin, W. F., and A. C. Myrrick, Jr.
1980 *Proceedings of the International Conference on Determining Age of Odontocete Cetaceans (and Sirenians).* Report of the International Whaling Commision Special Issue 3. La Jolla: National Marine Fisheries Service, SW Fisheries Center.

Pike-Tay, A.
1991 *Red Deer Hunting in the Upper Palaeolithic of Southwest France: A Study in Seasonality.* BAR International Series 596. Oxford: British Archaeological Reports.

Quéré, J. P., and M. Pascal
1983 Comparaison de plusieurs méthodes de la détermination de l'age individuel chez le cerf elaphe (*Cervus elaphus* L.). *Annales des Sciences Naturelles, Zoologie et Biologie Animale* 5:235-252.

Reimer, E., and O. Nordby
  1968   Relationship between age and tooth cementum layers in Norwegian reindeer. *Journal of Wildlife Management* 32:957-961.

Rigaud, J.-Ph., and J. Simek
  1987   Arms too Short to Box with God. In *The Pleistocene Old World*. O. Soffer, ed. Pp.47-60. New York: Plenum Press.

Saxon, A., and C. F. W. Higham
  1968   Identification of growth rings in the secondary dental cementum of *Ovis aries L. Nature* 219:634-635.

Spiess, A. E.
  1990   Deer tooth sectioning, eruption and seasonality of deer hunting in prehistoric Maine. *Man in the Northeast* 39:29-44.

Straus, L.
  1983   Terminal Pleistocene faunal exploitation in Cantabria and Gascony. In *Animals and Archaeology. Volume 1. Hunters and their Prey*. J. Clutton-Brock and C. Grigson, eds. Pp. 209-224. BAR International Series 163. Oxford: British Archaeological Reports.
  1987   Hunting in late Upper Palaeolithic Western Europe. In *The Evolution of Human Hunting*. M. H. Nitecki and D. V. Nitecki, eds. Pp. 147-175. New York: Plenum Press.

Welsh, D. A.
  1975   *Population, Behavioural and Grazing Ecology of the Horses of Sable Island, Nova Scotia*. Ph.D. dissertation, Dalhousie University.

White, R.
  1985   *Upper Palaeolithic Land-Use in the Perigord: A Topographic Approach to Subsistence*. BAR International Series 253. Oxford: British Archaeological Reports.
  1987   Glimpses of long-term shifts in late Palaeolithic land use in the Perigord. In *The Pleistocene Old World*. O. Soffer, ed. Pp. 263-277. New York: Plenum Press.

# 11

# Upper Palaeolithic Procurement and Processing Strategies In Southwest France

Katherine V. Boyle
Fenstanton, Huntingdon, U. K.

## ABSTRACT

Detailed consideration of faunal assemblage structure shows that regularities occur in the way resources were obtained during the Upper Palaeolithic of Western Europe; research into anatomical element representation and butchery marks sheds light on the probable function of individual sites and their role in the regional subsistence system. Both published and unpublished data from three Magdalenian deposits from southwest France (St.-Germain-la-Rivière, Limeuil, and Reignac) are considered. The predominance of species such as reindeer at Limeuil and Reignac reflects prevailing hunting and butchery strategies in addition to environmental conditions prevailing at the time of assemblage formation.

## INTRODUCTION

When Lartet and Christy published *Reliquiae Aquitanicae* in 1877, archaeological literature was largely characterized by description. This seminal volume, however, featured some interpretation of data and even introduced some issues which have only recently--within the last 25 years--been considered in a systematic manner. For example, the authors drew climatic inferences and discussed seasonality issues. Site- and assemblage-formation processes were briefly considered, with Buckland's (1823) influence apparent in the discussion of hyena and other carnivores as agents of accumulation. Of more interest here, however, human behavior was often inferred from the state of recovered bones. At Les Eyzies, reindeer vertebrae were found in articulation and considered in terms of kill and butchery strategies. Furthermore, with the addition of ethnographic data, conclusions were reached concerning the consumption of the brain and tongue as delicacies. The research reported here may, to some extent, be regarded as a continuation of this last approach.

In the course of research into Upper Palaeolithic large herbivore faunas from southwest France--more particularly the Périgord, Gironde, and Charente--I began the systematic compilation of anatomical element counts. Although a few quantitative lists are available in published form, they are usually only presented for major taxa such as reindeer. The current research represents an attempt to rectify the situation. However, when more than 90% of an assemblage is made up of one species and up to 25% of that is composed of loose teeth, the remaining material is often insufficient to warrant detailed quantitative consideration. Such analysis can be undertaken only when assemblage size is very large and/or the total number of species relatively small. Thus, great care must be taken when considering material attributable to species which make up only a very small proportion of the total assemblage, often less than 1%. As a result, I shall consider three sites, two from the Périgord and one from the Gironde. At Reignac six taxa are considered, with reindeer the dominant taxon. At Limeuil, where reindeer also dominates, horse is a distant second, while four other taxa total less than 1%. The Gironde site of St.-Germain-la-Rivière is dominated by saiga, although five other large herbivore species are present--reindeer, red deer, horse, ass, and bison (Table 11.1).

Reignac is located on the left bank of the Vézère river, at an altitude 15 m above river level (White 1985:189); the site extends over an area of 2,000 m². Discovered by Peyrony in 1949, the site was excavated between 1952 and 1962 by Dr. Chalcas Hulin, who owned the site at the time. Further excavation was undertaken by Alain Roussot of the Musée d'Aquitaine in Bordeaux in 1962 and 1963 and between 1967 and 1977 (Alain Roussot, personal communication, 1987). The material from Dr. Hulin's excavations is considered here.

The south-facing, open-air site of Limeuil, best known for its large quantity of engraved limestone plaques, is situated on the right bank of the confluence

**Table 11.1.** Frequencies of elements from selected ungulate species from Reignac, Limeuil, and St.-Germain-la-Rivière.

| | | Reignac reindeer | Reignac reddeer | Reignac bovids | Reignac horse | Reignac saiga | Reignac boar | Limeuil reindeer | Germain saiga |
|---|---|---|---|---|---|---|---|---|---|
| sk | skull | 104 | 4 | 0 | 0 | 2 | 1 | 20 | 11 |
| man | mandible | 353 | 6 | 0 | 5 | 24 | 20 | 88 | 32 |
| at | atlas | 14 | 1 | 0 | 0 | 0 | 3 | 9 | 0 |
| ax | axis | 0 | 0 | 0 | 0 | 0 | 0 | 9 | 0 |
| cer | cervical vertebrae | 70 | 0 | 0 | 0 | 3 | 0 | 15 | 0 |
| tho | thoracic vertebrae | 133 | 1 | 2 | 0 | 0 | 2 | 12 | 3 |
| lum | lumbar vertebrae | 62 | 0 | 0 | 0 | 2 | 0 | 16 | 1 |
| pel | pelvis | 175 | 3 | 0 | 2 | 0 | 0 | 14 | 0 |
| r | ribs | 108 | 1 | 12 | 1 | 0 | 0 | 3 | 0 |
| st | sternum | 0 | 0 | 0 | 0 | 0 | 0 | 0 | 0 |
| sc | scapula | 382 | 5 | 0 | 1 | 13 | 6 | 95 | 7 |
| ph | proximal humerus | 8 | 1 | 0 | 1 | 0 | 1 | 17 | 0 |
| dh | distal humerus | 316 | 8 | 2 | 2 | 16 | 6 | 148 | 32 |
| prc | proximal radio-cubitus | 169 | 1 | 2 | 2 | 9 | 8 | 95 | 11 |
| drc | distal radio-cubitus | 241 | 7 | 7 | 4 | 3 | 0 | 70 | 7 |
| car | carpals | 82 | 5 | 0 | 0 | 1 | 0 | 33 | 12 |
| pmc | proximal metacarpal | 192 | 4 | 2 | 6 | 3 | 0 | 4 | 2 |
| dmc | distal metacarpal | 353 | 6 | 4 | 11 | 17 | 0 | 129 | 41 |
| pf | proximal femur | 173 | 3 | 1 | 2 | 1 | 0 | 37 | 0 |
| df | distal femur | 68 | 0 | 0 | 0 | 0 | 0 | 39 | 1 |
| pt | proximal tibia | 366 | 0 | 4 | 1 | 1 | 2 | 22 | 1 |
| dt | distal tibia | 123 | 6 | 1 | 2 | 17 | 4 | 132 | 23 |
| tar | tarsals | 82 | 3 | 0 | 5 | 3 | 1 | 106 | 11 |
| ast | astragalus | 135 | 8 | 4 | 2 | 12 | 1 | 315 | 21 |
| cal | calcaneum | 183 | 4 | 2 | 2 | 4 | 4 | 34 | 9 |
| pmt | proximal metatarsal | 385 | 8 | 4 | 0 | 8 | 1 | 9 | 2 |
| dmt | distal metatarsal | 613 | 9 | 1 | 0 | 7 | 1 | 88 | 28 |
| phI | phalanx I | 427 | 5 | 3 | 3 | 20 | 1 | 37 | 47 |
| phII | phalanx II | 264 | 5 | 3 | 7 | 6 | 1 | 30 | 25 |
| phIII | phalanx III | 126 | 4 | 2 | 2 | 2 | 0 | 20 | 2 |

of the Vézère and Dordogne rivers in what is probably the most strategically impressive position in the area. Located approximately 10 m above present-day river level, the site was discovered in 1908. It was subsequently excavated by Capitan and published in conjunction with Bouyssonie (Capitan and Bouyssonie 1924).

St.-Germain-la-Rivière is a rock shelter located 10 km downstream from the modern town of Libourne (Gironde) on the right bank of the Dordogne river, a few kilometers below the Isle/Dordogne confluence. It is a large site; the infill deposit, which extends over a wide area, slopes down to the alluvial plain. Discovered in June 1929 by Lepront and Mirande, the site was excavated by Mirande and subsequently, during the 1960s, by Trecolle (Gambier 1991; Lenoir 1991). Assemblages from the two terraces were considered in this study, but sample size restrictions mean that only material from the upper terrace can, at this stage, be presented here in terms of quantified patterning.

All the material considered here is of Magdalenian age. Recent dates from St.-Germain-la-Rivière place this Middle Magdalenian site within the Older

Dryas: 15,300 ± 410 BP (Gif 5478); 16,200 ± 600 BP (Gif 5479); and 14,100 ± 160 BP (Gif 6037) (Ouzrit 1986). The site of Limeuil is dated to the Final Magdalenian (Magdalenian VI), largely on the basis of the burins and bone harpoons recovered. The dating of Reignac is less precise, but, in the absence of absolute dates, can be reasonably assigned to the Upper Magdalenian.

Only early collections are considered here, meaning that results and conclusions are somewhat restricted. The quality of excavation and data recovery during the nineteenth and early twentieth centuries was variable, which presents problems for modern scholars. These problems, however, are not insurmountable, and we are able to gain some idea as to the function of those sites which have yielded a sufficient quantity of material. In each case the assemblage is large, with sample sizes exceeding 1,700 identifiable bones.

Only large herbivores have been considered; the assumption is that the rare carnivores and microfauna present in the assemblages did not play an important part in the subsistence strategies. Such taxa total less

**Table 11.2**. Survival of proximal vs. distal humerus and tibia at Limeuil, St.-Germain-la-Rivière, and Reignac (data for Figures 11.1 and 11.2).

| | a | b | c | d |
|---|---|---|---|---|
| | humerus | | tibia | |
| | dist. | prox. | dist. | prox. |
| Limeuil | | | | |
| reindeer | 46.98 | 5.40 | 41.90 | 6.98 |
| horse | 33.33 | 16.67 | 66.67 | 16.67 |
| St.-Germain-la-Rivière | | | | |
| saiga (Up. Terr.) | 78.05 | 0.00 | 56.09 | 2.44 |
| saiga (Lw. Terr.) | 16.67 | 0.00 | 0.00 | 0.00 |
| Reignac | | | | |
| reindeer | 51.55 | 1.31 | 20.06 | 59.71 |
| red deer | 88.89 | 11.11 | 66.67 | 0.00 |
| bovids | 28.57 | 0.00 | 14.29 | 57.14 |
| horse | 18.18 | 9.09 | 18.18 | 9.09 |
| boar | 30.00 | 5.00 | 20.00 | 10.00 |
| saiga | 66.67 | 0.00 | 70.83 | 4.17 |

than 0.1% of the material from Limeuil, 0.4% at Reignac, and 0.25% in the Upper Terrace at St.-Germain-la-Rivière, but more than 10% in the much smaller sample from the Lower Terrace. At each site the material considered was found in close association with artifacts and bears direct evidence of human activity in the form of distinct cut marks, many of which can be "matched" with those described by Binford in *Nunamiut Ethnoarchaeology* (1978) and *Bones: Ancient Men and Modern Myths* (1981). The almost complete lack of evidence of carnivore activity (i.e., tooth marks) mirrors the rarity of these species. Only two horse bones at Limeuil show any form of

gnawing. At the other sites carnivore activity appears to have been completely absent--even at times during which the sites were unoccupied by man.

In the present study the assemblages considered were quantified using the approach advocated by Binford (1978) and employed subsequently by other researchers (Speth 1983; Thomas and Mayer 1983; Legge and Rowley-Conwy 1988; Landals 1990). After identifying element types, MAU (Minimal Animal Units, as defined by Binford 1984:51) values were calculated by dividing the observed number by the number of that bone in a complete animal carcass. No account is taken of the side of the animal from which the bone derives nor the apparent age of the individual, for reasons discussed by Binford (1978:69-72). Taking the highest MAU value to represent 100% of the MAU total observed, the proportion represented by each element was calculated by dividing the MAU value of one element by the highest MAU. Ratio values were then converted to percentage figures.

The figures obtained are used below in order to examine inter- and intra-site and -species variation in element representation at Limeuil, Reignac, and St.-Germain-la-Rivière. They are considered in relation to various index values, obtained by Binford (1978) as measurements of potential meat, marrow, and bone grease utility. General utility (modified) is also measured; this index represents a compound indication of potential value. For detailed discussion of index formulation and usage, the reader is referred to Binford's *Nunamiut Ethnoarchaeology* (1978), where the indices were first set out for caribou and sheep. In view of the fact that the indices were constructed for

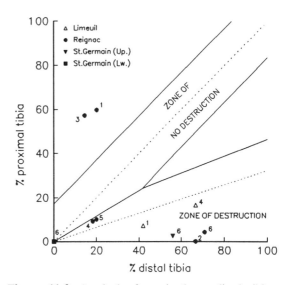

**Figure 11.1.** Survival of proximal vs. distal humerus at Reignac, Limeuil, and St.-Germain-la-Rivière (data from Table 11.2, cols. *a* and *b*). **Key:** 1 = reindeer; 2 = red deer; 3 = bovids; 4 = horse; 5 = boar; 6 = saiga.

**Figure 11.2.** Survival of proximal vs. distal tibia at Reignac, Limeuil, and St.-Germain-la-Rivière (data from Table 11.2, cols. *c* and *d*). **Key:** 1 = reindeer; 2 = red deer; 3 = bovids; 4 = horse; 5 = boar; 6 = saiga.

**Table 11.3.** Element representation frequencies, expressed as %MAU, of saiga, horse, boar, reindeer, red deer, and bovids for Reignac and the Modified General Utility Index, MGUI (Binford 1978:74, Tab. 2.7, col. 1) (data for Figures 11.3 to 11.8 and 11.14).

| | | a<br>saiga | b<br>horse | c<br>boar | d<br>reindeer | e<br>reddeer | f<br>bovids | g<br>MGUI |
|---|---|---|---|---|---|---|---|---|
| sk | skull | 16.67 | 0.00 | 5.00 | 16.97 | 44.44 | 0.00 | 8.74 |
| man | mandible | 100.00 | 45.45 | 100.00 | 57.78 | 66.67 | 0.00 | 13.89 |
| at | atlas | 0.00 | 0.00 | 30.00 | 4.56 | 22.22 | 0.00 | 9.79 |
| ax | axis | 0.00 | 0.00 | 0.00 | 0.00 | 0.00 | 0.00 | 9.79 |
| cer | cervical vertebrae | 1.67 | 0.00 | 0.00 | 4.57 | 0.00 | 0.00 | 35.71 |
| tho | thoracic vertebrae | 0.00 | 0.00 | 1.50 | 2.89 | 1.56 | 3.09 | 45.53 |
| lum | lumbar vertebrae | 2.38 | 0.00 | 0.00 | 3.37 | 0.00 | 0.00 | 32.05 |
| pel | pelvis | 0.00 | 18.18 | 0.00 | 28.55 | 33.33 | 0.00 | 47.89 |
| r | ribs | 0.00 | 0.51 | 0.00 | 1.26 | 0.80 | 12.24 | 49.77 |
| sc | scapula | 54.17 | 9.09 | 30.00 | 62.32 | 55.56 | 0.00 | 43.47 |
| ph | proximal humerus | 0.00 | 9.09 | 5.00 | 1.31 | 11.11 | 0.00 | 43.47 |
| dh | distal humerus | 66.67 | 18.18 | 30.00 | 51.55 | 88.89 | 28.57 | 36.52 |
| prc | proximal radio-cubitus | 37.50 | 18.18 | 40.00 | 29.73 | 11.11 | 28.57 | 26.64 |
| drc | distal radio-cubitus | 12.50 | 36.36 | 0.00 | 39.48 | 77.78 | 100.00 | 22.23 |
| car | carpals | 0.53 | 0.00 | 0.00 | 3.15 | 7.90 | 0.00 | 15.53 |
| pmc | proximal metacarpal | 12.50 | 54.54 | 0.00 | 31.89 | 44.44 | 28.57 | 12.18 |
| dmc | distal metacarpal | 70.83 | 100.00 | 0.00 | 57.75 | 66.67 | 57.14 | 10.50 |
| pf | proximal femur | 4.17 | 18.18 | 0.00 | 28.22 | 33.33 | 14.29 | 100.00 |
| df | distal femur | 0.00 | 0.00 | 0.00 | 11.09 | 0.00 | 0.00 | 100.00 |
| pt | proximal tibia | 4.17 | 9.09 | 10.00 | 59.71 | 0.00 | 57.14 | 64.73 |
| dt | distal tibia | 70.83 | 18.18 | 20.00 | 20.06 | 66.67 | 14.29 | 47.09 |
| tar | tarsals | 2.61 | 9.09 | 1.67 | 1.91 | 6.36 | 0.00 | 31.66 |
| ast | astragalus | 50.00 | 18.18 | 5.00 | 22.02 | 88.89 | 57.14 | 31.66 |
| cal | calcaneum | 16.67 | 18.18 | 20.00 | 29.85 | 44.44 | 28.57 | 31.66 |
| pmt | proximal metatarsal | 33.33 | 0.00 | 5.00 | 62.81 | 88.89 | 57.14 | 29.93 |
| dmt | distal metatarsal | 29.17 | 0.00 | 5.00 | 100.00 | 100.00 | 14.29 | 23.93 |
| phI | phalanx I | 20.83 | 13.64 | 1.25 | 17.45 | 13.90 | 10.71 | 13.72 |
| phII | phalanx II | 6.25 | 31.82 | 1.25 | 10.77 | 13.90 | 10.71 | 13.72 |
| phIII | phalanx III | 2.08 | 9.09 | 0.00 | 5.18 | 11.11 | 7.14 | 13.72 |

caribou (*Rangifer tarandus L.*), they should be of particular relevance to the reindeer-dominated assemblages of Upper Palaeolithic southwest France.

One point must be noted here regarding quantification. In the case of Limeuil and Reignac, antlers, although recovered in large quantities, were omitted. The decision was made to omit this material for three reasons: (1) the antler material from Limeuil has been removed from Les Eyzies, and thus, in order to be able to compare the assemblages, antler was omitted from Reignac; (2) the extreme degree of fragmentation of available antler prevented any serious attempt to estimate the number represented; and (3) antlers formed an important source of raw material for the Palaeolithic hunter, as cultural assemblages show. Unfortunately, raw material potential is not considered in the calculation of the Modified General Utility Index (MGUI), so that the importance of antler in tool manufacture is likely to be substantially underestimated by the utility indices. A potential raw-material index for antler would be of considerable value to the archaeozoologist working with Palaeolithic materials, as it would also be for bone.

## TAPHONOMIC CONSIDERATIONS

Preservation of identifiable bones and smaller fragments at Reignac, Limeuil, and St.-Germain-la-Rivière appears to be good. Root etching is virtually nonexistent; the surfaces of both complete and almost complete bones, as well as smaller fragments, show little evidence of the weathering that one might expect to find if the bones had spent a long time on the surface before burial. In general, elements of lowest density value are often less well represented--especially at St.-Germain-la-Rivière, where those elements of high density and high survival percentage value, as measured by Binford (1981:218), are relatively well represented (78.08% in the case of the mandible and distal humerus). Those of low to medium density value are rare--e.g., phalanges (I = 28.66%, II = 15.24%, III = 1.22%), tarsals (5.37%), carpals (4.88%), proximal tibia (2.44%), and humerus (0%). The relatively high frequencies of some medium density parts indicates that, although very low value elements may not be present, destruction was far from total.

If, as Binford (1981:219) recommends, we consider the ratio of distal to proximal humerus and tibia as a means of assessing the extent of destruction of anatomical elements, we can see that the distal humerus outnumbers the proximal epiphysis in all species at Reignac, both reindeer and horse at Limeuil, and saiga at St. Germain-la-Rivière (Figure 11.1, Table 11.2), placing the sites within Binford's **zone of destruction**. For the reindeer and bovid tibia at Reignac, however, the reverse is the case; the ratio places the site very firmly in the **zone of no destruction** (Figure 11.2, Table 11.2). These terms were primarily employed by Binford to distinguish between carnivore-ravaged assemblages (dog-yard sites) and those resulting from human activity. However, the distinction is not as clear-cut as this would imply, and, in the case of the three sites considered here, destruction is unlikely to be due to intense carnivore ravaging. Very few bones show recognizable signs of carnivore activity, while direct evidence of butchery is much more abundant. In view of the paucity of carnivore material at all three sites, it is more probable that destruction was due to postkill processing or removal from the site by man.

## BUTCHERY PRACTICES

### Morphological Observations

Several of the elements examined from each site bear indisputable evidence of human activity--namely cut marks of recognizable origin, many of which are

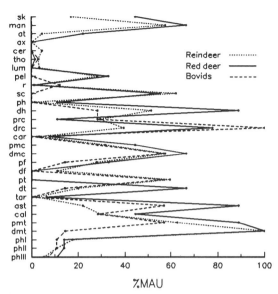

**Figure 11.4.** Element representation profiles for reindeer, red deer, and bovids at Reignac (data from Table 11.3, cols. *d*, *e*, and *f*).

similar to those recorded and named by Binford (1981:136-142). Secondary species, by definition, are less abundant than the major taxa. Nevertheless, those bones recovered which are attributable to these taxa often show greater evidence of intensive processing-- i.e., bear more cut marks and are more fragmentary. For example, if we omit teeth from our analysis, at St.-Germain-la-Rivière only 5.43% of the saiga material from the Lower Terrace bears direct evidence of butchery (stone-tool-inflicted incisions, etc.), in contrast to 24.6% of the material derived from other taxa. In the Upper Terrace the same trend is seen, namely 5.6% in contrast to 18.4%. At Limeuil the equivalent figures for reindeer and non-reindeer taxa are 5.63% and 34.71%, respectively; 30.61% of the horse bones alone show clear signs of butchery. Despite this, the overwhelming abundance of reindeer at Reignac and Limeuil and saiga at St.-Germain-la-Rivière means that most examples derive from these prevalent species.

Evidence of dismemberment on mandibles is rare. On the reindeer at Limeuil, marks are seen along the outside with some extending to the mandibular condyle and ascending ramus. They are also evident at Reignac, although they are markedly less common. At Limeuil they are more often parallel to the tooth row. In general, the rarity of dismemberment marks would seem to imply that carcasses were cut up and processed soon after the kill. This might suggest that the kill was close, if not immediately adjacent, to each site, with evidence of lower jaw removal in both cases. Marks which are found on saiga bones at St.-

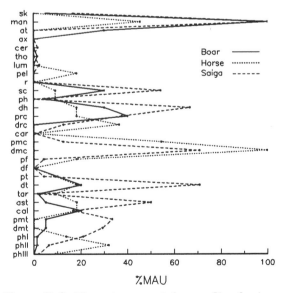

**Figure 11.3.** Element representation profiles for boar, horse, and saiga at Reignac (data from Table 11.3, cols. *a*, *b*, and *c*).

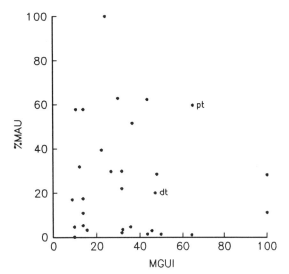

**Figure 11.5.** The relationship between %MAU frequencies for reindeer and MGUI values at Reignac (data from Table 11.3, cols. *d* and *g*).

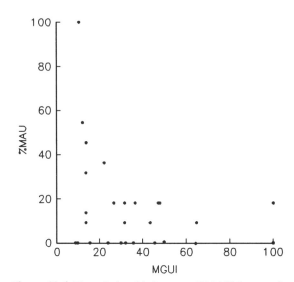

**Figure 11.6.** The relationship between %MAU frequencies for horse and MGUI values at Reignac (data from Table 11.3, cols. *b* and *g*).

Germain-la-Rivière may be attributed to tongue removal. They are rare, however, once again indicating that perhaps carcasses were dismembered soon after death.

At Reignac the distal humerus bears butchery marks similar to those recorded by Binford (Hd-1, Hd-2, and Hd-4 [Binford 1981:123, Fig. 4.30d-g]); the proximal end and its associated cut marks are rare. But, as Binford (1981:122-124) points out: "If the proximal humerus exhibits relatively few cut marks, probably because of the ease with which the joint may be disarticulated, the distal humerus generally sports a consistent and numerous collection of cut marks." This observation may be made for both reindeer at Reignac and saiga at St.-Germain. At the latter all butchery traces on the distal ends of the humerus may be attributed to dismemberment.

Evidence of skinning is present on both metatarsals and metacarpals. At both Reignac and St.-Germain-la-Rivière, reindeer and saiga metatarsals bear evidence of dismemberment (proximal end) and filleting (MTd-4 [Binford 1981:132, Fig. 4.38]). Marks resulting from filleting and skinning occur primarily on bones from the major species at all three sites. However, red deer and horse do show some evidence of such activity at Limeuil, as do both bison and horse at St.-Germain-la-Rivière. Transverse cuts occur on the anterior face (MCd-3), circular cuts around the distal shaft (MCd-1) (Binford 1981:142). It is possible that meat and skin were removed, leaving behind the distal metapodia which often form the maximum value at sites in southwest France. It should be noted that the unfused metapodia show little

or no evidence of dismemberment, filleting or skinning--especially in the case of the dominant saiga.

A few marks are found close to the head of the reindeer scapula at Reignac and Limeuil, marks which Binford (1981:104) notes are abundant at Combe-Grenal but are rare or absent in his Nunamiut collection. Saiga at St.-Germain-la-Rivière displays marks along the neck (S-2 [Binford 1981:122, Fig. 4.29]) and spine (S-3 [Binford 1981:98, Fig. 4.06]), although

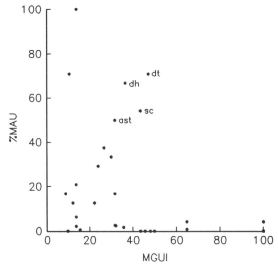

**Figure 11.7.** The relationship between %MAU frequencies for saiga and MGUI values at Reignac (data from Table 11.3, cols. *a* and *g*).

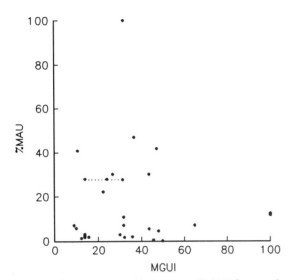

**Figure 11.8.** The relationship between %MAU frequencies for reindeer and MGUI values at Limeuil (data from Table 11.4, col. *d* and Table 11.3, col. *g*).

they, too, are not abundant and occur only on material from the Upper Terrace.

Dismemberment marks occur on reindeer, red deer, and horse distal tibiae at Reignac and Limeuil, where cut marks run across the anterior face from the dorsal projection to the medial malleolus (Td-3 [Binford 1981:118, Fig. 4.26e-f]). At St.-Germain-la-Rivière, such marks occur only on horse tibia.

At Reignac marks similar to Binford's (1981:113, Fig. 4.22) PS-7, PS-8, and PS-9 are noted above, below, and around the acetabulum, although only rarely. They are also seen on the inside surface, possibly inflicted during the severing of the upper hindlimb. At Limeuil we see PS-6 (Binford 1981:130, Fig. 4.36a) on one reindeer pelvis and PS-2, not illustrated by Binford, on one horse pelvis. The pelvis is absent from St.-Germain-la-Rivière.

Cut marks seen on reindeer astragali (TA-1, TA-2 [Binford 1981:120, Fig. 4.27e-f]) from Reignac and Limeuil, horse astragali from Limeuil, and saiga astragali from St.-Germain-la-Rivière result from dismemberment. Marks on the calcaneum are attributable to filleting in addition to dismemberment, especially in the case of the major species. At Reignac and Limeuil, for example, they are found on the proximal margins of the lateral face and across the distal end (TC-1, TC-2). Diagnostic marks are also seen at Limeuil on the few horse calcanea observed.

## ELEMENT REPRESENTATION

Having considered the direct evidence of butchery which is available, we can now turn our attention to

the question of element representation and begin to gain some idea as to the relative importance of each species in subsistence strategies practiced during the Magdalenian. Limb bones dominate in all but two element representation profiles at Reignac (Figure 11.3, Table 11.3). In these, the saiga and boar, the mandible accounts for 100% of the MAU total. The ribs and vertebrae are the parts of the carcass which are usually rare or absent, although the atlas is relatively abundant in the red deer and boar.

Although no profile closely resembles those presented by Binford (1978), the one for reindeer at Reignac is broadly similar to a fall hunting stand. Element representation is variable at such sites, but the relative abundance of mid- and lower-rear-leg, as seen at Reignac (Figure 11.4, Table 11.3), as well as the very low frequencies of vertebrae and pelvis, are typical at such sites (Binford 1978:358).

The much rarer red deer presents a somewhat similar profile, although it may be argued that a greater proportion of the carcass is represented. Nine elements account for more than 50% of the MAU, 14 for more than 25%. Meanwhile, bovids, horse, boar, and saiga yield profiles which indicate that more intensive processing of subsidiary species was carried out at Reignac.

Figures 11.5 to 11.7 (see also Table 11.3) show the relationship between Binford's MGUI and the frequency of skeletal elements from a selection of species at Reignac. Reindeer is represented by a "gourmet curve." This is defined by Binford (1978: 81) as one which selects "for high frequencies of parts of the

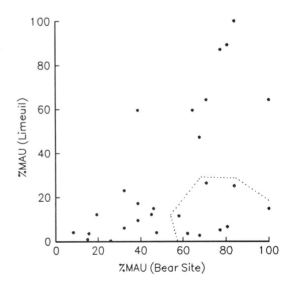

**Figure 11.9.** The relationship between %MAU frequencies for reindeer at Limeuil and modeled values from Binford's data on the Bear Site (data from Table 11.4, cols. *a* and *e*).

**Table 11.4**. Modeled %MAU frequencies for the Bear Site (Binford 1978:430, Tab. 8.1, col. 11), Site 64 (Binford 1978:234, Tab. 5.15, col. 2), and Kongumuvuk (Binford 1978:270, Tab. 6.6, col. 2), calculated %MAU frequencies of reindeer for Limeuil and saiga for St.-Germain-la-Rivière, and meat index values for reindeer (Binford 1978:23, Tab. 1.5) (data for Figures 11.8 to 11.14).

|  |  | a | b | c | d | e | f | g |
|---|---|---|---|---|---|---|---|---|
|  |  |  |  |  | Limeuil | Limeuil |  |  |
|  |  | Bear | Site | Kongu- | rein- | reindeer | Germain | meat |
|  |  | Site | 64 | muvuk | deer | excl. ast | saiga | index |
| sk | skull | 38.70 | 60.00 | 44.00 | 6.98 | 17.19 | 53.66 | 9.05 |
| man | mandible | 38.70 | 75.50 | 100.00 | 27.94 | 59.46 | 78.05 | 31.10 |
| at | atlas | 45.20 | 42.20 | 44.00 | 5.71 | 12.16 | 0.00 | 10.10 |
| ax | axis | 19.40 | 40.00 | 44.00 | 5.71 | 12.16 | 0.00 | 10.10 |
| cer | cervical vertebrae | 8.10 | 37.70 | 22.00 | 1.90 | 4.05 | 0.00 | 37.00 |
| tho | thoracic vertebrae | 14.90 | 12.00 | 4.40 | 0.43 | 0.91 | 1.13 | 47.20 |
| lum | lumbar vertebrae | 15.53 | 20.00 | 55.50 | 1.69 | 3.59 | 0.70 | 33.20 |
| pel | pelvis | 38.70 | 4.40 | 22.00 | 4.44 | 9.46 | 0.00 | 49.30 |
| r | ribs | 26.10 | 0.00 | 4.40 | 0.07 | 0.23 | 0.00 | 51.60 |
| st | sternum | 14.50 | 2.20 | 0.00 | - | - | 0.00 | 66.50 |
| sc | scapula | 100.00 | 2.20 | 77.70 | 30.16 | 64.19 | 17.07 | 44.70 |
| ph | proximal humerus | 58.10 | 25.50 | 0.00 | 5.40 | 11.49 | 0.00 | 28.90 |
| dh | distal humerus | 83.90 | 38.80 | 77.77 | 46.98 | 100.00 | 78.05 | 28.90 |
| prc | proximal radio-cubitus | 70.90 | 44.40 | 11.10 | 30.16 | 64.20 | 26.83 | 14.70 |
| drc | distal radio-cubitus | 67.70 | 44.40 | 11.10 | 22.22 | 47.29 | 17.07 | 14.70 |
| car | carpals | 47.70 | 95.50 | 11.10 | 1.84 | 3.92 | 4.88 | 5.20 |
| pmc | proximal metacarpal | 67.70 | 97.70 | 22.00 | 1.27 | 2.70 | 4.88 | 5.20 |
| dmc | distal metacarpal | 77.40 | 100.00 | 11.10 | 40.95 | 87.16 | 100.00 | 5.20 |
| pf | proximal femur | 83.90 | 95.50 | 11.10 | 11.74 | 25.00 | 0.00 | 100.00 |
| df | distal femur | 70.90 | 86.60 | 22.00 | 12.38 | 26.35 | 2.44 | 100.00 |
| pt | proximal tibia | 100.00 | 86.60 | 11.10 | 6.98 | 14.86 | 2.44 | 25.50 |
| dt | distal tibia | 80.60 | 86.60 | 77.70 | 41.90 | 89.19 | 56.09 | 25.50 |
| tar | tarsals | 46.20 | 91.10 | 44.00 | 6.98 | 14.86 | 5.37 | 11.20 |
| ast | astragalus | - | 91.10 | 44.00 | 100.00 | - | 51.22 | 11.20 |
| cal | calcaneum | 32.30 | 91.10 | 44.00 | 10.79 | 22.97 | 21.95 | 11.20 |
| pmt | proximal metatarsal | 32.30 | 97.70 | 66.00 | 2.86 | 6.08 | 4.88 | 11.20 |
| dmt | distal metatarsal | 64.50 | 86.60 | 11.10 | 27.94 | 59.46 | 68.29 | 11.20 |
| phI | phalanx I | 80.60 | 91.10 | 8.80 | 3.09 | 6.59 | 28.66 | 1.70 |
| phII | phalanx II | 77.20 | 91.10 | 5.50 | 2.38 | 5.06 | 15.24 | 1.70 |
| phIII | phalanx III | 62.10 | 91.10 | 2.60 | 1.70 | 3.55 | 1.22 | 1.70 |

very highest value" (MGUI greater than 60.00), while abandoning those of medium or low value. Thus, we see assemblages in which high value parts are either absent or relatively rare, and both low and medium value parts are more abundant. It is a pattern which may also be observed for red deer. Selection of primarily high utility value parts is usually associated with the major species at Upper Palaeolithic sites in southwest France. Where several species (at least three) were taken and one clearly dominated the assemblage (i.e., making up at least 75% of the large herbivore material), gourmet curves are almost invariably seen for the major species. Of the more than a dozen Magdalenian sites from southwest France that I have recently studied (Boyle 1990), only La Mège has a major taxon (reindeer) characterized by a "bulk curve." This represents processing strategies which "select for large quantities of parts of both high and

moderate value and abandon parts of the lowest utility at rapidly accelerating rates" (Binford 1978:81).

Only the proximal tibia is overrepresented for the reindeer at Reignac. This may be of significance, for, as Speth (1983) has demonstrated, the quality of the tibia (meat and marrow) varies markedly according to season and associated nutritional status of the animal concerned. Overrepresentation may therefore reflect discard by hunters selecting nutritionally rich elements and rejecting those of poor nutritional return. In spring, a time at which Gordon (1988:214) cites occupation at Reignac, the marrow quality of the proximal tibia declines, while fat content is low throughout the year. However, the distal tibia has a much higher marrow value (92.60) and is less prone to deterioration than is the proximal epiphysis. Its lower frequency at Reignac is therefore not very surprising; it may reflect either intensive processing, which renders the element unrecognizable, or removal from the site for use elsewhere. Both options indicate preferential selection of this body part.

Those species which show the most distinct bulk curves are horse and boar; the former is shown in Figure 11.6 (see also Table 11.3). The rarity or absence of high and medium value parts (MGUI > 30.00) may be explained in one of two ways. We have either a site from which butchery units were removed for consumption elsewhere or one at which processing was so intensive as to render units largely unrecognizable. The large quantity of unrecorded fragments and splinters of bone and antler at Reignac may lend support to this second interpretation. Thus, the concept of Reignac as some form of residential site cannot be ruled out (see below).

Finally, the picture for saiga (Figure 11.7, Table 11.3) is more complex than those observed for the other species. Four observed outliers include the distal humerus, scapula, distal tibia, and astragalus. This group of relatively abundant elements may represent two definable butchery units, namely the upper forelimb and lower hindlimb. The former is not complete because the proximal humerus is absent from the assemblage. Binford (1978:272) describes summer encounter-hunting camps where the distal tibia and tarsals are overrepresented. After the tibia and tarsals have been removed from the hindlimbs, the meat is retained along with the femur and taken elsewhere. In this way the meat is saved but the bone discarded. The overrepresentation of the humerus and scapula cannot be similarly explained because both parts have meat

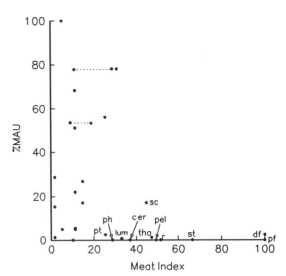

**Figure 11.11.** The relationship between %MAU frequencies for saiga at St.-Germain-la-Rivière and meat index values (data from Table 11.4, cols. _f_ and _g_).

and marrow values in the medium to high range. Despite these overabundances, the curve observed here is a bulk one; only two elements with MGUI values exceeding 50.00 (proximal tibia and proximal femur) were observed.

The picture at Limeuil is much the same as the one observed for reindeer at Reignac. Assemblage size is relatively large (N = 2,655), and reindeer predominates, far outnumbering four other large herbivore prey species (2,458 or 92%). All broadly defined age groups are present, with adults outnumbering juveniles and sub-adults by at least 4 : 1. The simplest measures of age at death (e.g., epiphyseal fusion and the distinction between deciduous and permanent teeth still adhering to bone) reveal that up to a quarter of the assemblage may derive from young adults. Distal femora remain unfused in 29.73% of cases. Similarly, 17.14% of distal radii are unfused. The former figure, and to some extent the latter, compare favorably with those of natural herd population structure in Canada, Alaska, and Scandinavia (Calef and Heard 1980; Davis et al. 1980), where up to 30% of fall herds may consist of calves and yearlings. However, little juvenile dental material survives; the equivalent figure is only approximately 7%. All stages of adult tooth wear are seen, with mature individuals more numerous than the very old. Further details concerning population structure are not available without more detailed age/sex data from incremental analysis and crown height measurements, neither of which have yet been undertaken.

Reindeer is represented by a gourmet curve at Limeuil (Figure 11.8, Tables 11.3 and 11.4), although no element, other than the maximum unit by definition

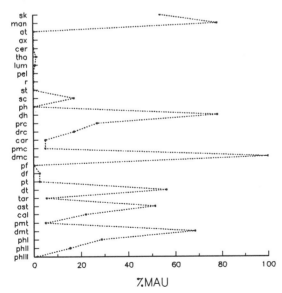

**Figure 11.10.** Element representation profile for saiga at St.-Germain-la-Rivière and meat index values (data from Table 11.4, col. _f_).

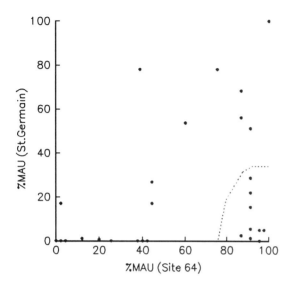

**Figure 11.12.** The relationship between %MAU frequencies for saiga at St.-Germain-la-Rivière and modeled values from Binford's data on Site 64 (data from Table 11.4, cols. *b* and *f*).

(in this case the astragalus, N = 315), represents more than 50% of the total MAU (see below). Several elements of medium MGUI value are, however, quite well represented, with the exception of those that make up the axial skeleton (vertebrae, ribs, and pelvis). If we ignore the astragalus and recalculate relative MAU frequencies employing the distal humerus as the dominant unit, additional meaning can be assigned to the pattern of element representation observed.

Limeuil can be likened to the Bear Site described by Binford (1978:429); this similarity is reflected if reindeer frequencies (excluding the astragalus) are plotted against modeled values from this winter camp (Figure 11.9, Table 11.4). The apparent underrepresentation of articular ends at the site may be explained in terms of potential grease-rendering strategies similar to those planned at the Bear Site. Articular ends were retained by the women at this winter camp in order to make bone grease towards the end of the occupation. The activity never occurred, however, and the bones, which would normally have been destroyed at a winter location, are overrepresented at the Bear Site in comparison with Limeuil. High percentage values of scapula, metacarpals, and phalanges at the Bear Site are explained "in terms of the sequence of consumption from stores. ... The pattern that emerges is one of consumption from the population of parts remaining after initial stages of consumption" (Binford 1978:429-431). These elements are underrepresented at Limeuil, suggesting that consumption was more

immediate. Similarity with the radical culling model based on the unmodified general utility index, such as that described for Site 17 (Binford 1978:Tab. 6.18, col.11), is also apparent when the astragalus is excluded. The combination of the two models suggests that processing and consumption occurred soon after the kill. Although a relatively large number of animals may have been dispatched, mass killing is not proposed.

At St.-Germain-la-Rivière (Figure 11.10, Table 11.4), saiga, the major species found in association with reindeer, bison, red deer, horse, and ass, is better represented in terms of element representation-- i.e., a larger number of element types are represented by a higher percentage MAU value. Seven elements represent more than 50% of the MAU total. Of these, five are limb bones, primarily lower limb bones. Once again the axial skeleton is largely absent, as are meat-rich units such as the femur.

Comparison of element representation with potential meat yield indicates that only parts of meat index value less than 30.00 are well represented, while those parts of value less than 15.00 exhibit an increase in frequency (Figure 11.11, Table 11.4). However, some of the parts with poor meat yields have high marrow index values. This pattern is evident at Binford's (1978:233) Site 64, where both migration hunting (spring) and processing occurred. Relatively high frequencies of head (cranium and mandible) and distal limb bones (humerus, metacarpals, tibia, and metatarsals) occur at both sites. Ribs, pelvis, and vertebrae are rare or absent. This compound or mixed

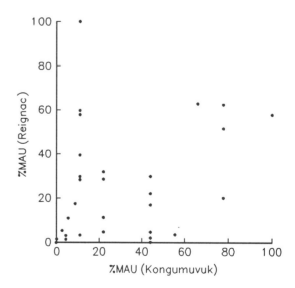

**Figure 11.13.** The relationship between %MAU frequencies for reindeer at Reignac and modeled values from Binford's data on Kongumuvuk (data from Table 11.3 col. *d* and Table 11.4 col. *c*).

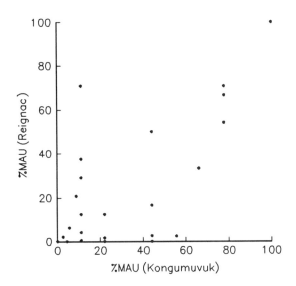

**Figure 11.14.** The relationship between %MAU frequencies for saiga at Reignac and modeled values from Binford's data on Kongumuvuk (data from Table 11.3 col. *a* and Table 11.4 col. *c*).

assemblage appears to result from a combination of kill, butchery, processing, drying, and consumption activities. The similarity between St.-Germain-la-Rivière and Site 64 is emphasized by comparing MAU values at St.-Germain with the modeled values suggested by Binford (1978:235) (Figure 11.12, Table 11.4).

## CONCLUSION

Reindeer hunting is commonly viewed as the major subsistence activity during at least part of the year during the Upper Palaeolithic in much of southwest France (Mellars 1985). Indeed, data from two of the three Magdalenian sites considered here (Limeuil and Reignac) do little to contradict this view. Only towards the west of the Périgord do other taxa take on a primary role. At St.-Germain-la-Rivière that role is played by saiga. Elsewhere, bovids and horse are of primary importance (Boyle 1990). In terms of element representation, the dominant species is characterized by a gourmet curve, suggesting that post-kill processing was not exhaustive and that it was not necessary to process low and some medium value parts. Instead, these parts remain, along with a smaller number of high value units, which ties in with Binford's (1978: 62) observation that increased meat availability is associated with increased discrimination in selecting parts of carcasses.

Secondary species more commonly display bulk curves and evidence of greater carcass processing--a greater proportion of elements display butchery marks and the bones themselves are more fragmentary. It is probable that carcasses of secondary species were processed more intensively than were those of the major taxon, probably in order to obtain greater yield. Perhaps a form of polyculture[1] can be discerned. Dependence on a single resource is risky because survival depends on diversification. By exploiting alternative resources in addition to reindeer (or saiga in the Gironde), elements of variety and security are maintained in the diet. During the Upper Palaeolithic, a triad of resources may have been exploited--reindeer; non-reindeer species, including fish and birds; and plant material, a variable of which we currently know relatively little. Perhaps secondary species (red deer, bovids, horse, boar, and saiga in the Périgord; reindeer, red deer, bovids, chamois, roe deer, and boar in the Gironde) were taken largely on an encounter basis, similar to the short-term encounter hunting which Binford (1978:265) attributes to the Nunamiut. An encounter hunting strategy is practiced when prey is not overly abundant and transport possibilities were limited, as they probably were during the Palaeolithic. Comparison of element frequencies with Nunamiut summer kill sites, such as Kongumuvuk Pass and the high mountain hunting camps, shows that, although reindeer displays little or no correlation at Reignac (Figure 11.13, Table 11.4), other species fit the predicted model reasonably well--particularly saiga (Figure 11.14, Tables 11.3 and 11.4). This patterning endorses the picture of a strategy which is based on encounter hunting for non-reindeer taxa and which intentionally exploits carcasses in such a way as to gain greater or maximum relative value (i.e., yield) for effort expended in processing rarer species. Such "complete" processing of reindeer was simply unnecessary, given the quantity available and the number taken.

## ACKNOWLEDGMENTS

Some of the data used here were collected with the support of a C. N. R. S. research fellowship in Bordeaux in 1987. I should like to thank A. Roussot of the Musée d'Aquitaine for granting me access to the material from Reignac and J.-J. Cleyet-Merle of the Musée National de Préhistoire in Les Eyzies for allowing me to examine the faunal material from Limeuil and St.-Germain-la-Rivière. Paul Mellars and Clive Gamble commented on earlier drafts and research. Finally, I should like to thank the organizers for inviting me to take part in the symposium. In addition, grants from the British Academy and Royal Society enabling me to travel to the U. S. A. are gratefully acknowledged.

## NOTES

[1]Polyculture is a term applied by Renfrew (1972) to the cultivation of and dependence on more than one staple during the third millennium BC in the Aegean.

## REFERENCES

Binford, L. R.
1978     *Nunamiut Ethnoarchaeology*. New York: Academic Press.
1981     *Bones: Ancient Men and Modern Myths*. New York: Academic Press.
1984     *Faunal Remains from Klasies River Mouth*. New York: Academic Press.

Boyle, K. V.
1990     *Upper Palaeolithic Faunas from South West France: A Zoogeographic Perspective*. BAR International Series 557. Oxford: British Archaeological Reports.

Buckland, W.
1823     *Reliquiae Diluvianae, or Observations on the Organic Remains Contained in Caves, Fissures and Diluvial Gravel, and on Other Geological Phenomena Attesting the Actions of a Universal Deluge*. London: John Murray.

Calef, G., and D. C. Heard
1980     The status of three tundra wintering caribou herds in northeastern mainland Northwest territories. In *Reindeer/Caribou Symposium II Norway 1979: Proceedings of the Second International Reindeer/Caribou Symposium, 17-21 September 1979, Røros, Norway*. E. Reimers, E. Gaare, and S. Skjenneberg, eds. Pp. 582-594. Trondheim: Direktoratet for vilt og Ferskvannsfisk.

Capitan, L., and J. Bouyssonie
1924     *Limeuil: Son gisement à gravures sur pierres de l'Age du Renne*. Paris: Nourry.

Davis, J. L., P. Valkenburg, and H. V. Reynolds
1980     Population dynamics of Alaska's western arctic caribou herd. In *Reindeer/Caribou Symposium II Norway 1979: Proceedings of the Second International Reindeer/Caribou Symposium, 17-21 September 1979, Røros, Norway*. E. Reimers, E. Gaare, and S. Skjenneberg, eds. Pp. 595-604. Trondheim: Direktoratet for vilt og Ferskvannsfisk.

Gambier, D.
1991     La sépulture de Saint-Germain-la-Rivière. In *Gironde. Préhistoire. Paysages, hommes et industries des origines à l'Age du Bronze*. I. Seguy, ed. Pp. 75-78. Canéjan: Imprimerie Balauze et Marcombe.

Gordon, B. C.
1988     *Of Men and Reindeer Herds in French Magdalenian Prehistory*. BAR International Series 390. Oxford: British Archaeological Reports.

Landals, A.
1990     The Maple Leaf site: Implications of the analysis of small-scale bison drives. In *Hunters of the Recent Past*. L. B. Davis and B. O. K. Reeves, eds. Pp. 122-151. London: Unwin Hyman Inc.

Lartet, E., and H. Christy
1877     *Reliquiae Aquitanicae, Being Contributions to the Archaeology and Palaeontology of Périgord and the Adjoining Provinces of Southern France*. London: H. Baillière.

Legge, A. J., and P. A. Rowley-Conwy
1988     *Star Carr Revisited: A Re-Analysis of the Large Mammals*. London: Centre for Extra-Mural Studies, University of London.

Lenoir, M.
1991     Saint Germain-la-Rivière. In *Gironde. Préhistoire. Paysages, hommes et industries des origines à l'Age du Bronze*. I. Seguy, ed. P. 75. Canéjan: Imprimerie Balauze et Marcombe.

Mellars, P. A.
1985     The ecological basis of social complexity in the Upper Palaeolithic of Southwestern France. In *Prehistoric Hunter-Gatherers: The Emergence of Cultural Complexity*. T. D. Price and J. A. Brown, eds. Pp. 271-297. London: Academic Press.

Ouzrit, L.
1986     *Recherches sur les faunes du Dryas ancien en Gironde. Le gisement de Saint-Germain-la-Rivière*. Thèse de Troisième Cycle, Université de Bordeaux I.

Renfrew, A. C.
1972     *The Emergence of Civilization: The Cyclades and the Aegean in the Third Millennium B.C.* London: Methuen and Co.

Speth, J. D.
1983     *Bison Kills and Bone Counts: Decision Making by Ancient Hunters*. Chicago: University of Chicago Press.

Thomas, D. H., and D. Mayer
1983     Behavioral faunal analysis of selected horizons. In *The Archaeology of Monitor Valley 2. Gatecliff Shelter*. D. H. Thomas, ed. Pp. 353-391. Anthropological Papers of the American Museum of Natural History 59 Part 1. New York: American Museum of Natural History.

White, R.
1985     *Upper Paleolithic Land Use in the Perigord: A Topographic Approach to Subsistence and Settlement*. BAR International Series 253. Oxford: British Archaeological Reports.

# 12

# Simulating Mammoth Hunting and Extinction: Implications for the Late Pleistocene of the Central Russian Plain

**Steven Mithen**
**University of Reading**

## ABSTRACT

Mammoths were an important resource for Upper Palaeolithic hunter-gatherers. Their remains are frequently found in faunal assemblages, their bones were used for the construction of dwellings, and they figure significantly in Palaeolithic art. Mammoths became extinct in North America at ca. 11,000 BP, in Eurasia at ca. 12,000 BP, and in Siberia at ca. 10,000 BP[1], and there has been considerable debate as to whether human predation was a causal factor. The computer simulation model described in this paper explores the effect of different types of hunting strategies on mammoth populations in a range of different environmental situations. It demonstrates that mammoth populations are extremely sensitive to predation. The simulation results are discussed with reference to the settlements on the Central Russian Plain. The results agree with Soffer's suggestion that the majority of mammoth remains probably derive from collecting, rather than hunting.

## INTRODUCTION

Debate continues to surround the nature of mammoth exploitation and the reason for their extinction at the end of the Pleistocene. Recent progress on this issue has come from further analyses of mammoth-bone assemblages (e.g., Haynes 1985, 1986, 1989, 1991; Saunders 1980), improved understanding of mammoth paleoecology (e.g., Guthrie 1984; Vereshchagin and Baryshnikov 1984), an increase in the number and quality of absolute dates on mammoth remains (Lister 1991; Stuart 1991), ethnoarchaeological studies (O'Connell et al. n.d.), and discovery of new sites (e.g., Yesner n.d.). I wish to add a further set of data to this debate--data from computer simulations of mammoth population dynamics and exploitation in constant, fluctuating, and deteriorating environments. My simulation of mammoths is based on a model of the population dynamics of modern elephants. The African elephant is generally regarded as an appropriate analogy for the mammoth (Haynes 1986:661).

In this simulation I will examine the relationship between the character and intensity of human predation on mammoth population decline and extinction. As such, it inevitably requires certain assumptions

about mammoth population dynamics and prehistoric hunting strategies. The aim is to derive a general understanding of the sensitivity of mammoth populations and then to reflect upon the archaeological data with this knowledge, notably that from the Central Russian Plain (Soffer 1985). The model described here represents a preliminary study for a more complex simulation of mammoth hunting presently underway at the University of Reading.

## MAMMOTH EXPLOITATION AND EXTINCTION IN THE OLD WORLD

The recovery of frozen mammoth carcasses, complete with gut contents, have provided us with considerable information about mammoth paleoecology. Certain critical gaps in our knowledge remain, such as mammoth migratory behavior and population densities. The dates we are acquiring from mammoth bones and ivory will allow us to monitor the variation in the timing of extinction throughout the world and to search for correlations with hunting pressure and climatic change. At present, it appears that mammoths became extinct throughout Europe by 12,000 BP, in North America slightly later at ca. 11,000 BP, and in Siberia as late as 10,000 BP (Stuart

1991).[1] Soffer (1991) describes the pattern of mammoth extinction as time transgressive from the southwest to the northeast of the Old World. As a large terrestrial mammal, mammoths exemplify the type of species that became extinct at the end of the Pleistocene.

Mammoth populations would certainly have suffered from the environmental changes at the end of the Pleistocene. Guthrie (1984) argues that the increase in seasonality and consequent zonation of vegetation was critical in having a detrimental effect on the viability of large mammal populations. In regions such as Siberia, the small size of mammoths and the evidence for naturally induced mass deaths suggest that the populations were suffering from environmental stress (Soffer 1991). It is likely that mammoths were pushed into refugia (Lister 1991), making the populations more vulnerable to local extinction due to short-term environmental fluctuations. Yet mammoths had survived previous glacial/interglacial cycles, and human hunting may have played a critical role in their extinction.

Various types of archaeological evidence indicate that Upper Palaeolithic hunters exploited mammoths and had a keen interest in their distribution and behavior. Most notable are the settlements on the Russian Plain with mammoth-bone dwellings (Soffer 1985). As many as 149 and 116 individual mammoths are represented in the faunal remains from Mezhirich and Mezin, respectively. Mammoths feature significantly in Palaeolithic art (Bahn and Vertut 1989:128-129), particularly on the engraved plaquettes from Gönnersdorf (Bosinski 1984), and indicate that the artists were knowledgeable about mammoth anatomy and keen to produce naturalistic images. We also have many carved objects made of mammoth ivory, including utilitarian items and those for decorative purposes. These include spear throwers, figurines, and bracelets. Some sites, such as Paviland cave in south Wales, appear to be specialist ivory procurement and processing locations (Jacobi 1980). Mammoth bones are frequently recorded within Lower/Middle and Upper Palaeolithic assemblages, and mammoths may have constituted an important source of food (see Haynes 1991 for a comprehensive review). As Soffer (1991) describes, the presence of large number of mammoths is a ubiquitous feature of Upper Palaeolithic sites in central and eastern Europe.

The extent to which this evidence indicates that mammoths were actively hunted is controversial. Many of the proboscidean bone assemblages which have been used to infer active hunting, such as those at Torralba (Howell 1965; Binford 1987) and La Cotte (Scott 1980), may have been acquired by scavenging from mammoth carcasses derived from natural processes and possibly accumulated over very long periods of time (Haynes 1991). Soffer (1985, 1991) and Haynes (1991) have argued that the large numbers of mammoth bones used to construct dwellings on the Central Russian Plain may have been taken from carcasses of animals dying of natural processes, rather than the victims of human hunting. Settlements may have been specifically located adjacent to large, naturally occurring accumulations of mammoth bones. Soffer provides some intriguing evidence for this, notably the wide range of bone weathering states within the same assemblage, suggesting that bones may have been acquired from animals long dead, and the rarity of cut marks that would be expected from defleshing--although Haynes suggests that a skillful butcher may have left few, if any, marks on the bones. Even if mammoths were not actively hunted, however, the human presence in their landscapes may still have had a serious affect on their populations by processes such as habitat destruction (cf. Diamond 1984:840-846). This would be extinction by "Sitzkrieg" rather than "Blitzkrieg" (Diamond 1989).

Even if Upper Palaeolithic hunters regularly hunted mammoths, there remain important arguments against the view that humans pushed mammoths into extinction. On cost-benefit grounds, it is questionable if mammoths were ever a preferred prey of Upper Palaeolithic hunters, particularly in light of the wide range of resources in the late Pleistocene environments. Webster and Webster (1984) argue that, once mammoth populations had been depleted, human hunters are likely to have switched to more profitable game, which may have allowed mammoth populations time to replenish. In addition, there may have been constraints on the intensity of mammoth hunting due to technical and organizational factors: mammoth hunting is likely to have been an activity requiring the cooperation of a large group, which may have only been feasible at certain times of the year, or, indeed, in certain years.

Before proceeding, we need to distinguish between the local extinction of a population and the total extinction of the species. The local disappearance of a mammoth/elephant population may have been a not uncommon occurrence throughout the Pleistocene because of short-term environmental events. As Haynes (1986) describes, a series of "die-offs" could lead to the local disappearance of a population, a situation he refers to as a "die-out." Such die-outs may have occurred as the climate moved into either a full glacial or a full interglacial state, and mammoths may have survived in a series of dispersed refugia across the world from which they expanded at more favorable times. For instance, mammoths appear to be absent from north and central Europe between 20,000-15,000 BP, the period of the last glacial maximum, although they survived in the Russian Plain. If a mammoth pop-

Table 12.1. Twenty-seven runs of the mammoth simulation model in a constant environment with varying population parameters and summary statistics on resulting population dynamics. Parameters $b$ and $e$ relate to the degree of density dependence on juvenile survival and age of female sexual maturity, respectively; parameter $f$ is percentage of sexually mature females reproducing in any one year.

| RUN | Parameter Values | | | Age at Reproduction | | | Juvenile Survival | | | Growth Rate | | Time to equilibrium | Equilibrium pop. size |
|---|---|---|---|---|---|---|---|---|---|---|---|---|---|
| | $b$ | $e$ | $f$ | Max | Min | Mean | Max | Min | Mean | Max | Mean | | |
| 1 | 0.05 | 0.05 | 0.15 | 10 | 10 | 10 | 0.93 | 0.89 | 0.91 | 1.02 | 0.22 | 510 | 1111.91 |
| 2 | 0.20 | 0.05 | 0.15 | 10 | 10 | 10 | 0.90 | 0.88 | 0.90 | 0.34 | -0.09 | 278 | 277.97 |
| 3 | 0.35 | 0.05 | 0.15 | 10 | 10 | 10 | 0.89 | 0.82 | 0.89 | -0.01 | -0.27 | 292 | 161.05 |
| 4 | 0.05 | 4.00 | 0.15 | 12 | 11 | 12 | 0.94 | 0.91 | 0.92 | 0.88 | 0.10 | ~ | 749.70 |
| 5 | 0.20 | 4.00 | 0.15 | 11 | 10 | 11 | 0.98 | 0.88 | 0.90 | 0.34 | -0.36 | 99 | 250.55 |
| 6 | 0.35 | 4.00 | 0.15 | 11 | 10 | 10 | 0.89 | 0.82 | 0.89 | -0.00 | -0.28 | 288 | 161.04 |
| 7 | 0.05 | 7.50 | 0.15 | 14 | 12 | 13 | 0.94 | 0.92 | 0.93 | 0.74 | 0.14 | 279 | 536.62 |
| 8 | 0.20 | 7.50 | 0.15 | 12 | 11 | 11 | 0.90 | 0.88 | 0.90 | 0.24 | -0.18 | 219 | 242.41 |
| 9 | 0.35 | 7.50 | 0.15 | 12 | 11 | 11 | 0.90 | 0.82 | 0.89 | -0.01 | -0.26 | 357 | 148.88 |
| 10 | 0.05 | 0.05 | 0.25 | 10 | 10 | 10 | 0.93 | 0.81 | 0.85 | 2.93 | 0.90 | 231 | 2852.39 |
| 11 | 0.20 | 0.05 | 0.25 | 10 | 10 | 10 | 0.88 | 0.81 | 0.83 | 2.48 | 0.38 | 183 | 713.00 |
| 12 | 0.35 | 0.05 | 0.25 | 10 | 10 | 10 | 0.84 | 0.81 | 0.82 | 2.03 | 0.08 | 160 | 407.47 |
| 13 | 0.05 | 4.00 | 0.25 | 17 | 11 | 15 | 0.93 | 0.86 | 0.88 | 2.72 | 0.58 | 286 | 1885.70 |
| 14 | 0.20 | 4.00 | 0.25 | 12 | 11 | 12 | 0.88 | 0.82 | 0.84 | 2.27 | 0.30 | 200 | 648.18 |
| 15 | 0.35 | 4.00 | 0.25 | 11 | 11 | 11 | 0.84 | 0.81 | 0.82 | 1.82 | 0.05 | 170 | 389.14 |
| 16 | 0.05 | 7.50 | 0.25 | 20 | 12 | 18 | 0.93 | 0.88 | 0.89 | 2.52 | 0.44 | 315 | 1413.85 |
| 17 | 0.20 | 7.50 | 0.25 | 14 | 12 | 13 | 0.88 | 0.83 | 0.85 | 2.07 | 0.23 | 204 | 588.07 |
| 18 | 0.35 | 7.50 | 0.25 | 12 | 12 | 12 | 0.85 | 0.82 | 0.83 | 1.62 | 0.02 | 179 | 370.36 |
| 19 | 0.05 | 0.05 | 0.35 | 10 | 10 | 10 | 0.93 | 0.75 | 0.82 | 6.35 | 1.53 | 158 | 3907.77 |
| 20 | 0.20 | 0.05 | 0.35 | 10 | 10 | 10 | 0.88 | 0.75 | 0.79 | 5.90 | 0.78 | 129 | 976.97 |
| 21 | 0.35 | 0.05 | 0.35 | 10 | 10 | 10 | 0.82 | 0.75 | 0.78 | 5.45 | 0.39 | 113 | 558.16 |
| 22 | 0.05 | 4.00 | 0.35 | 20 | 11 | 17 | 0.93 | 0.82 | 0.86 | 6.06 | 1.13 | 175 | 2555.55 |
| 23 | 0.20 | 4.00 | 0.35 | 13 | 11 | 12 | 0.88 | 0.77 | 0.80 | 5.61 | 0.62 | 146 | 884.23 |
| 24 | 0.35 | 4.00 | 0.35 | 12 | 11 | 11 | 0.82 | 0.77 | 0.79 | 5.16 | 0.31 | 120 | 523.55 |
| 25 | 0.05 | 7.50 | 0.35 | 24 | 12 | 20 | 0.93 | 0.86 | 0.88 | 5.77 | 0.95 | 177 | 1897.81 |
| 26 | 0.20 | 7.50 | 0.35 | 16 | 12 | 15 | 0.88 | 0.79 | 0.80 | 5.32 | 0.16 | 500 | 799.68 |
| 27 | 0.35 | 7.50 | 0.35 | 13 | 12 | 13 | 0.82 | 0.77 | 0.79 | 4.87 | 0.25 | 136 | 505.31 |

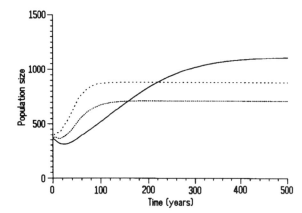

**Figure 12.1.** Simulated growth of mammoth populations in stable environment and with density dependence on juvenile survival and age of female sexual maturity. Run 1 (solid), run 11 (closed dash), and run 23 (open dash); see Table 12.1 for parameter values.

To develop our hypotheses concerning the role of human hunting in mammoth extinction, we need to acquire further information concerning the effect of predation on mammoth populations for both small-scale local populations and those covering continental areas. How many animals can be taken on an annual basis before populations begin to decline? How many can be taken before the population is pushed into extinction? Are these numbers feasible levels for humans to take with a Palaeolithic technology? How might climatic variables affect the level of hunting intensity required to push a mammoth population into extinction? While simulation cannot provide answers to these for a Pleistocene mammoth population, it can certainly provide some reasonable bounds for these values to considerably improve our discussion of the role of human predation as a factor in mammoth extinction.

ulation was hunted while it was also suffering from die-offs, the chance of a die-out may have increased. In other circumstances, local extinction may occur from hunting pressure alone, either by the increase in mortality or by the movement of a mammoth population away from the area of human exploitation, as has been observed among modern elephants (Dublin and Douglas-Hamilton 1987). Mammoth populations in refugia may be particularly susceptible to local extinction by hunting pressure because there is no possibility of immigration to replenish the population. Species extinction will simply occur when all local populations have become extinct. Between the two extremes of local and species extinction, it is also useful to think of regional extinction as the loss of mammoths from a large land mass, such as North America, although they may have remained present elsewhere in the world. Soffer (1991) has characterized the species extinction of mammoths as a mosaic of successive local and regional extinctions.

Our archaeological questions can be addressed at the level of either local, regional, or species extinction. With local extinction, we are more concerned with the detailed interactions between hunters and mammoths and must be concerned with issues such as hunting strategies and prey switching, as Webster and Webster (1984) suggest. Our appropriate timescales are in single, tens, or hundreds of years. When we are concerned with regional or species extinction and believe that human predation may have been significant, a major interest is the growth rate of the human population and the character of climatic deterioration over thousands of years. Ultimately, however, we will need to explain species extinction in terms of multiple local and regional extinctions.

## A SIMULATION MODEL

This section focuses on building a simulation model for mammoth populations. The following section will explore the exploitation of this simulated population. All computer programs were written by the author in Pascal and run on the University of Cambridge IBM 3084 mainframe.

The mammoth population is modeled using a Leslie matrix (Leslie 1945). This is a technique to model the population dynamics of a species with respect to the age/sex structure of the population. By using Leslie matrices, we can explore the effect of different types of hunting strategies and environmental events, which are age/sex specific in their effects, on the short- and long-term viability of the total population. I have discussed the use of Leslie matrices elsewhere, with examples concerning red deer and reindeer (Mithen 1990). For this simulation of mammoths, both female and male portions of the population are modeled and 60 age classes are used. Birth

**Table 12.2.** The effect of good (wet), bad (dry), and consecutive bad years on the fecundity and juvenile survival of elephants in Amboseli Park. The figures in parentheses denote the percentage change from the "average" figures in the first row (from Lee and Moss 1986; Phyllis Lee, personal communication, 1991).

| Year Type | % Fecundity | Juvenile Survival % Female | % Male |
|---|---|---|---|
| Average | 25 | 80 | 80 |
| Good | 30 (+20) | 90 (+12.5) | 90 (-12.5) |
| Bad | 15 (-40) | 65 (-18.75) | 55 (-31.25) |
| Consecutive bad | 5 (-80) | 65 (-18.75) | 40 (-50.0) |

and death parameter values are based on those of African elephants. There have been several recent models for elephant population dynamics, some using Leslie matrices (e.g., Hanks and McIntosh 1973; Croze et al. 1981; Pilgrim and Western 1986). I draw on parameter values used in these models and on more general discussion of elephant population dynamics (e.g., Laws et al. 1975). Elephants have been frequently used as an analogue for mammoths (e.g., Haynes 1991; Soffer 1991). My principal rationale is their equivalence in body size to mammoths, since body size is one of the main determinants of life-history characteristics.

In this section I move towards building an appropriate model in two steps. First, I describe a model in which population size is constrained by density dependence operating on juvenile survival and age of female sexual maturity. Since the role of density dependent factors on elephant populations is controversial, my second step is to introduce density independent constraints on population size in a model with only very weak density dependence.

## DENSITY DEPENDENT MODEL IN CONSTANT ENVIRONMENT

### Survival

The annual natural survival of non-juvenile elephants (> 5 yrs) is on the order of 97-98%, which decreases rapidly after the age of 50. Males appear to suffer higher non-juvenile mortality than females (Laws et al. 1975). In this model, I will use the following values: for females, I will use a value of 97.5% for animals aged 5-49 years, 95% for 50-59 years, and 50% for those 60 years or greater; for males, the values 95%, 90%, and 25% will be used for the same age classes. If density dependence is a factor controlling population size, then this is likely to operate on the survival of juvenile animals, i.e., those less than five years old, as these are most vulnerable from lack of nutrition. Here I will use a linear function of the form $S_t = a - bP_t/P_k$ where $S_t$ is the probability of survival at time $t$, $a$ and $b$ are constants ($b$ defining the rate fall in survival rate with population size), $P_t$ the population at time $t$, and $P_k$ the population level at carrying capacity. This is initially set at the arbitrary value of 1,000 to model relatively small populations and to explore the process of local extinction. The value of $a$ is kept constant at 0.95,

**Figure 12.2.** Age/sex structures for simulated mammoth populations at equilibrium: (a) = run 1; (b) = run 11; (c) = run 23. See Table 12.1 for parameter values.

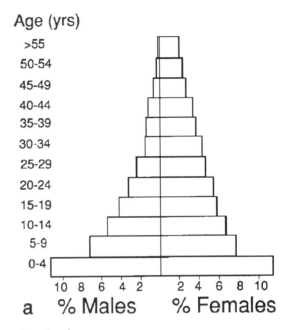

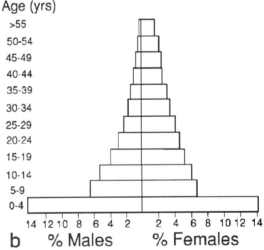

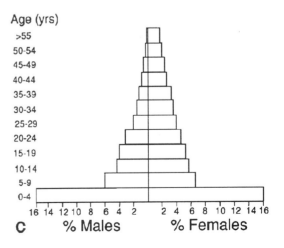

**Table 12.3.** The effect of random environmental fluctuations on the population dynamics from three runs (1, 11, 23) of the mammoth simulation model. Parameter $g$ defines the sensitivity of the population parameters to either good or bad years.

| Run/ Parameter Values | | $g$ | Age at First Reproduction | | | Juvenile Survival | | | Growth Rate | |
|---|---|---|---|---|---|---|---|---|---|---|
| | | | Max | Min | Mean | Max | Min | Mean | Max | Mean |
| 1 | $b = 0.05$ | 5.00 | 10 | 10 | 10 | 0.94 | 0.90 | 0.92 | 2.27 | 0.20 |
| | $e = 0.05$ | 15.00 | 10 | 10 | 10 | 0.94 | 0.93 | 0.94 | 5.00 | 0.08 |
| | $f = 0.15$ | 25.00 | 10 | 10 | 10 | 0.95 | 0.93 | 0.95 | 6.93 | -0.50 |
| 11 | $b = 0.20$ | 5.00 | 10 | 10 | 10 | 0.88 | 0.81 | 0.83 | 3.63 | 0.15 |
| | $e = 0.05$ | 15.00 | 10 | 10 | 10 | 0.91 | 0.81 | 0.85 | 9.28 | 0.25 |
| | $f = 0.25$ | 25.00 | 10 | 10 | 10 | 0.92 | 0.81 | 0.87 | 14.31 | 0.45 |
| 23 | $b = 0.20$ | 5.00 | 13 | 11 | 13 | 0.88 | 0.77 | 0.79 | 4.92 | 0.20 |
| | $e = 4.00$ | 15.00 | 13 | 11 | 12 | 0.89 | 0.76 | 0.81 | 12.64 | 0.35 |
| | $f = 0.35$ | 25.00 | 13 | 10 | 12 | 0.91 | 0.76 | 0.83 | 21.34 | 0.67 |

while three different values for $b$ are explored--0.05, 0.2, and 0.35. These give progressively stronger density dependence on juvenile survival.

### Fecundity

Following Pilgrim and Western (1986), the fecundity of animals aged 50 or over is set at zero. Annual fecundity itself is a function of interbirth interval and age at sexual maturity, both of which are variable in living populations and may be density dependent (Pilgram and Western 1986). In this model, I will treat age at sexual maturity as density dependent by using the linear function $F_t = d + eP_t/P_k$ where $d$ and $e$ are constants, the latter defining the rate of increase in age of sexual maturity with population size. An animal of age class $i$ at time $t$ is defined as sexually mature if $i > F_t$. The value of $d$ is kept constant at 9.0 (the age at which pregnancy becomes physiologically possible), and three different values for $e$ are explored--0.05, 4.0, and 7.5--giving a progressively stronger density dependent relationship. For animals between the age of sexual maturity and 50, three different values for fecundity, $f$, are used--0.15, 0.25, and 0.35.

### The Simulation

With three values for each of the parameters $b$, $e$, and $f$, 27 different models are possible. Some of these may be unrealistic for elephants and/or mammoths. To examine the pattern of population growth and the demographic characteristics of the equilibrium population, the growth of the population under each combination of parameter values was simulated. The population began with an arbitrary age/sex structure and size

--three in each age/sex class, making a starting population of 360 individuals. Growth was simulated until equilibrium was reached, defined as an absolute rate of growth of less than 0.0001% for ten successive years. On each of the 27 runs, the following data was recorded: time taken to reach equilibrium; maximum, minimum, and average survival rates for juveniles; maximum, minimum, and average ages of sexual maturity; maximum rate of growth and average rate of growth; total population at equilibrium; and age/sex structure of the equilibrium population.

The results for these 27 runs are given in Table 12.1. Figure 12.1 shows the growth of the population to equilibrium in three of these runs (nos. 1, 11, and 23), and Figure 12.2a-c shows their equilibrium age/sex structure. I will use these three runs throughout the paper to cover the range of feasible mammoth population models. Run 23 models a vigorous population--one that can grow rapidly, but is also sensitive to density dependent controls on population size; run 1 is a much less vigorous population with a slow growth rate; and run 11 falls between these extremes.

### DENSITY INDEPENDENT MODEL IN A FLUCTUATING ENVIRONMENT

In many, if not all, contemporary elephant populations, density independent factors may play a more significant role in both constraining population size and allowing periods of rapid growth than does the density of the population. For African elephants, rainfall is the main density independent factor; dry years reduce juvenile survival and fecundity rates from their average, while wet years increase them (Barnes 1982; Lee and Moss 1986). A sequence of dry years can have substantial cumulative effects on a population, particularly on the male portion, since juvenile males are particularly sensitive to drought (Lee and Moss 1986). In Amboseli the approximate effects of good (wet) and bad (dry) years on survival and fecundity is given in Table 12.2. There is no a priori reason to suppose that Pleistocene mammoth populations did not also suffer from such environmental events, causing density independent factors to be the main control on population size. While in low latitudes a good year may be one with high precipitation, in higher latitudes a good year may be one that is dry because high precipitation would have been in the form of snow, which would have made foraging more difficult. Extremely dry years, causing drought, would also have been detrimental to mammoth populations.

To explore the effect of such density independent (DI) effects, I define each year of the simulation as either good, average, or bad on a random basis. Initially these are defined so that any type of year may follow any other type with equal probability; this is done by using a Markov chain with transition matrix in which all elements are equal (Figure 12.3a). To model the density independent effects, I introduce a further parameter, $g$, and use this to define the effect of a good year on female fecundity in terms of the percentage increase of the average rate; in Table 12.2 this would have the value of 20.0. All other DI effects are defined as multiples of $g$. For instance, fecundity in the second of two consecutive bad years will be modified by $-4g$, while male survival in a good year will have the value of $0.625g$. By this means, I can introduce just one single new parameter and maintain the variation of DI effects across different population parameters.

To demonstrate the effects of the value of $g$, Table 12.3 shows three runs of the simulation (nos. 1, 11, and 23; Table 12.1), each made with three different values of $g$--5, 15, and 25. As equilibrium is no longer reached in such a fluctuating environment, the values in Table 12.3 are for the final year of the simulation. Simulation runs with $g$ values of 5 and 15 applied to run 11 are illustrated in Figure 12.4.

Using a Markov matrix to produce a pseudo-random sequence of good/average/bad years allows us to model climatic deterioration, as occurred for mammoth at the end of the last glacial. We can do this by beginning the simulation with a matrix as in Figure 12.3a, with an equal occurrence of good, average, and poor years. We can then gradually increase the probabilities for transitions to poor years (elements of the third row) and, accordingly, decrease those for transition to good or average years. For instance, Figure 12.3b shows a matrix that models an environment with a high frequency of poor years. To do this, we make the elements of the matrix linear functions of time. If the final probability for a transition to a poor year is denoted by $h$ and the initial value at $t = 1$ is 0.33, then the probability for a bad year at time $t$, $P_{bt}$, will equal $0.33 + ((h - 0.33)/tmax)t)$, in which $tmax$ denotes the period over which climatic deterioration is occurring (i.e., the time taken to move from the matrix in Figure 12.3a to that in 12.3b). The values for the transition to good or average years--$P_{g/at}$--are set equal at $(1-P_{bt})/2$. Such a model will simulate an increasing frequency of die-offs, which may create a die-out irrespective of hunting pressure. Figure 12.5 illustrates run 11 for $tmax = 750$, $g = 15$, and $h = 0.8$. In this example the population approaches extinction due to climatic deterioration alone.

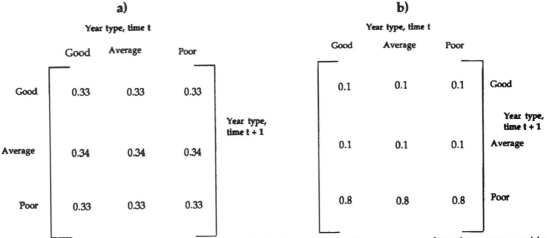

**Figure 12.3.** Markov chain transition matrices for simulating pseudo-random sequences of good, average, and bad years; (a) = matrix with equal-year-type probabilities; (b) = matrix for simulating an environment with higher frequency of poor years. When climatic deterioration is modeled, the elements of the matrices are treated as functions of time.

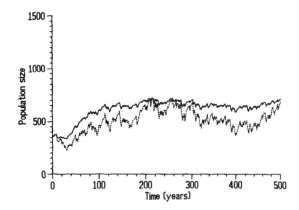

**Figure 12.4.** Simulated mammoth populations in fluctuating environments. Run 11 with $g = 5.0$ (solid) and $g = 15$ (dash); see Table 12.1 for parameter values for run 11.

## HOW APPROPRIATE ARE THESE MODELS FOR MODERN ELEPHANTS AND PLEISTOCENE MAMMOTHS?

Before exploring the effect of hunting on these simulated populations, we must briefly consider whether these simulated populations are viable models for modern elephants and Pleistocene mammoths. To do this, we need to compare aspects of the simulated populations with those of the real world using data independent from that employed in constructing the models. We have two points of contact: maximum rates of population growth and age structure.

Observed rates of population growth among elephants in Uganda have been between 3-4% (Hanks and McIntosh 1973). In Hwange National Park, Zimbabwe, they have been 5% since the 1930s (Haynes 1985). A population in the Addo National Park, South Africa, has maintained a growth rate of ca. 7% for 27 years between 1953-1979 (Calef 1988). Calef suggests that a growth rate of 7% is likely to be the maximum possible rate of growth for elephants. In light of these data, the maximum growth rates of the simulated populations in constant environments with density dependence the only control on population size appear to be rather low (Table 12.1). Only when fecundity reaches the relatively high value of 0.35% do maximum growth rates rise above 3%, and the maximum recorded is only 6.35%. Once the environmental fluctuations are added, however, and density independent factors play a significant role in controlling the population, we find a much wider, and generally higher, range of maximum growth rates (Table 12.3). When $g = 15$, maximum growth rates

of 5.0, 9.28, and 12.64 are recorded for runs 1, 11, and 23, respectively. The character of the population fluctuations represented in Figure 12.4, when $g = 15$, appears to be a good model for those of real elephant populations in historic times, although long-term sequences of elephant numbers are very difficult to reconstruct.

A comparison between observed and simulated age structures also indicates that the simulation model is realistic, particularly when environmental fluctuations are added. Figure 12.6 compares the frequency of animals aged between 0 and 10 years (inclusive) in a set of 10 real populations and 23 simulated populations. The real data is from Ottichilo's (1986) study of age structure of elephants in the Tsavo National Park between 1966 and 1980, a period during which drought and poaching led to fluctuations in the population size and structure. The proportion of 0-10 year olds vary between 29.9% and 63.82%, with most in the range 38-50%. The simulated age structures also fall in this range, both for the three equilibrium populations (runs 1, 11, and 23) and for a sample of 20 annual populations taken from a simulation run in a fluctuating environment (run 11, $g = 15$). These data suggest that the simulated mammoth population dynamics are similar to those of real elephant populations. The small sample size and variability within the data detracts from the value of this comparison. Nevertheless, if elephants are accepted as an analogy for mammoths, then the current model will be an effective tool for exploring the effect of human predation and climatic change on the decline and extinction of mammoths at the end of the Pleistocene.

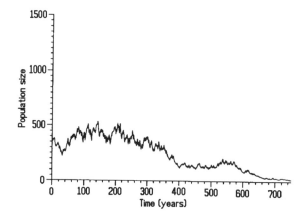

**Figure 12.5.** Simulated mammoth population in a deteriorating environment. Run 11 with $g = 15$, $h = 0.8$, *tmax* = 750. In this example, the mammoth population becomes extinct after ca. 750 years; see Table 12.1 for parameter values for run 11.

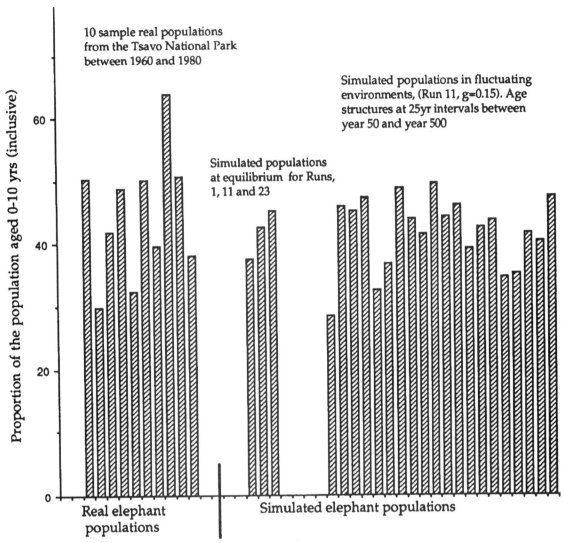

**Figure 12.6.** Age structure (proportion of population between 0-10 years) in real and simulated populations. Real samples from Tsavo National Park between 1960 and 1980 (after Ottichilo 1986). Simulated populations from runs 1, 11, and 23 in constant environment and run 11 in fluctuating environment with $g = 15$; see Table 12.1 for parameter values for runs 1, 11, and 23.

## SIMULATING PALAEOLITHIC HUNTING

All the simulations I describe will involve a random/catastrophic killing pattern rather than the selection of specific age/sex classes (this will be addressed in future work). Human hunting can be modeled in two ways, relating to different types of exploitation patterns. First, hunting can be modeled in terms of a "fixed percentage." In this a fixed percentage of each age/sex class of the population is killed each year. This creates a catastrophic mortality profile in the archaeological record (varying the percentage across age/sex classes would create an attritional

age/sex profile). If the percentage killed is large enough to cause the population to fall, the number of animals taken each year, as a fixed percentage, will also fall. In this scenario, human hunters are being modeled as responsive to the size/density of the mammoth populations--a constant effort is being modeled. If we assume that the human population size remains constant, then hunters are assumed to be switching to other prey as the size of the mammoth population/number killed declines (or switching from other prey as the size increases, should environmental factors cause population growth that outweighs the decline due to hunting). There is a related hunting pattern--"reduced percentage"--in which declining

**Table 12.4.** Fixed percentage hunting on three runs (1, 11, 23) of the mammoth simulation model. Parameter $K$ denotes the percentage of each age/sex class that is killed each year.

| Run/Parameter Values | | $K\%$ | Size of Kill Year 1 | Size of Kill At Equilibrium | Equilibrium/ Extinction Time | Population Size at Equilibrium |
|---|---|---|---|---|---|---|
| 1 | $b = 0.05$ | 1.0 | 11.16 | 1.79 | ~ | 177.53 |
| | $e = 0.05$ | 2.0 | 22.31 | 0.00 | 466 | 0.00 |
| | $f = 0.15$ | 3.0 | 33.47 | 0.00 | 236 | 0.00 |
| 11 | $b = 0.20$ | 1.0 | 7.14 | 5.05 | 175 | 500.13 |
| | $e = 0.05$ | 2.0 | 14.28 | 5.77 | 329 | 282.87 |
| | $f = 0.25$ | 3.0 | 21.42 | 1.97 | 1146 | 63.65 |
| | | 4.0 | 28.56 | 0.00 | 358 | 0.00 |
| 23 | $b = 0.20$ | 1.0 | 8.85 | 7.09 | 106 | 701.50 |
| | $e = 4.00$ | 2.0 | 17.70 | 10.21 | ~ | 500.14 |
| | $f = 0.35$ | 3.0 | 26.55 | 9.70 | 300 | 313.47 |
| | | 4.0 | 35.40 | 6.74 | 501 | 161.70 |
| | | 5.0 | 44.24 | 0.00 | 703 | 0.00 |

animal populations lead to a reduced level of exploitation in the percentage of the population take. This is used by game managers and may also be inferred from ethnographic accounts of North American hunters (John Rick, personal communication, 1991).

The second strategy is a "fixed number" kill of mammoths. This takes the same number of animals each year, irrespective of the size of the mammoth population. This number is distributed across age/sex categories in proportion to their frequencies; it also creates catastrophic mortality profiles and cannot easily be distinguished from a fixed percentage kill. For instance, if the fixed number kill was set at ten animals, and male animals aged 0-1 year represented 5% of the population, then their numbers would be reduced by 0.5 animals. Hence, this models the killing of a male calf every other year. With a fixed number kill, the percentage of the population which is taken annually increases as the population declines. Consequently, hunting effort is increased as the population declines (or decreased as the population increases) to maintain the same size kill.

Which of these two strategies is more appropriate for Palaeolithic hunters is debatable. It is likely to depend upon the role of mammoth in the economies. If mammoths were exploited as just another large mammal resource, along with reindeer, horse, and bison, then a fixed percentage cull is probably the most appropriate. If, however, it had a slightly different role due to its size, perhaps a specialized exploitation for ivory or a single organized mass hunt once a year, then a fixed number kill might be more appropriate.

The simulations I will initially describe are concerned with the exploitation and extinction of a local population--I use $P_k = 1000$. However, the qualitative results (i.e., the sensitivity of the populations to extinction) are directly applicable to much larger populations and to total extinction. It should be noted here that, by these simulations, I am exploring the consequences of the killing of animals which would have otherwise survived until the following year. Hunters may have been killing animals which were dying, or about to die, of natural causes, as Haynes (1991) has proposed for the Clovis hunters of North America.

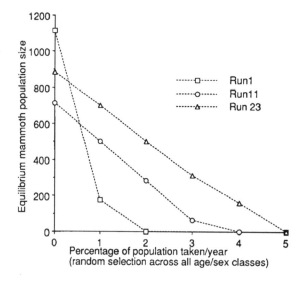

**Figure 12.7.** Equilibrium mammoth population sizes in constant environments and under varying intensities of fixed percentage culling. None of the three models for mammoth population dynamics (runs 1, 11, and 23) can sustain more than a 4% annual cull.

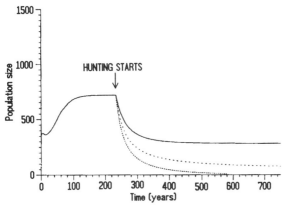

**Figure 12.8.** Fixed percentage culling of mammoth population (run 11) under three hunting intensities: 2% (solid), 3% (spaced dash), and 4% (closed dash). The population is allowed to reach equilibrium in a constant environment, free from predation, before hunting starts.

## RESULTS

Table 12.4 and Figure 12.7 present the results from exploring fixed percentage hunting of mammoths for three runs, numbers 1, 11, and 23, showing that hunting intensities of 2, 4, and 5% are sufficient to

push each of these into extinction, i.e., the equilibrium population size is zero. Figure 12.8 illustrates the exploitation of population number 11 at three hunting intensities. Table 12.5 and Figures 12.9 and 12.10 present similar results from fixed number hunting. Both of these show mammoth populations to be very sensitive to increased mortality through hunting pressure. They are only able to sustain low fixed percentage and number killing. Comparison with large (rather than mega-) herbivores is striking. In Figure 12.11 I compare fixed percentage hunting of mammoth (run 11) and reindeer; both populations have an equilibrium, unexploited level of ca. 4,000 individuals --in the present model this is achieved by manipulating the value of $P_k$. (The reindeer population is also simulated by a Leslie matrix and is described in Mithen 1990). Red deer are able to sustain an annual fixed percentage random kill of 21% (Mithen 1990). Fixed number hunting also shows mammoths to be very sensitive to predation. For run number 1, the kill size of four, which is sufficient to extinguish the population, is only 0.35% of an unexploited population size at equilibrium. Similarly, for run 11, the critical figure of seven animals represents 0.84%; and, for run 23, 11 animals represent 2.7%. It must be emphasized, however, that these fixed number kills are distributed across the population according to the

**Table 12.5.** Fixed number hunting on three runs (1, 11, 23) of the mammoth simulation model. Parameter $K$ denotes the total number of animals that are taken each year from the population; this figure is equally divided between all age/sex classes according to their frequency in the population.

| Run/Parameter Values | | $K$ | Size of Kill Year 1 | Size of Kill At Equilibrium | Equilibrium/ Extinction Time | Population Size at Equilibrium |
|---|---|---|---|---|---|---|
| 1 | $b = 0.05$ | 1 | 1 | 1 | 214 | 1036.07 |
| | $e = 0.05$ | 2 | 2 | 2 | 346 | 922.53 |
| | $f = 0.15$ | 3 | 3 | 3 | 624 | 749.25 |
| | | 4 | 4 | 0 | 838 | 0.00 |
| | | 5 | 5 | 0 | 449 | 0.00 |
| | | 10 | 10 | 0 | 153 | 0.00 |
| | | 20 | 20 | 0 | 73 | 0.00 |
| 11 | $b = 0.20$ | 1 | 1 | 1 | 87 | 683.78 |
| | $e = 0.05$ | 3 | 3 | 3 | 142 | 610.34 |
| | $f = 0.25$ | 5 | 5 | 5 | 247 | 504.26 |
| | | 6 | 6 | 6 | 678 | 382.09 |
| | | 7 | 7 | 7 | 338 | 0.00 |
| | | 9 | 9 | 9 | 164 | 0.00 |
| | | 20 | 20 | 20 | 55 | 0.00 |
| 23 | $b = 0.20$ | 5 | 5 | 5 | ~ | 749.14 |
| | $e = 4.00$ | 8 | 8 | 8 | 179 | 657.83 |
| | $f = 0.35$ | 9 | 9 | 9 | 254 | 594.28 |
| | | 10 | 10 | 10 | ~ | 500.53 |
| | | 11 | 11 | 0 | 946 | 0.00 |
| | | 12 | 12 | 0 | 286 | 0.00 |
| | | 15 | 15 | 0 | 134 | 0.00 |
| | | 20 | 20 | 0 | 81 | 0.00 |

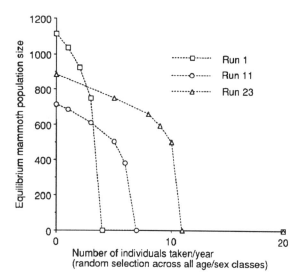

**Figure 12.9.** Equilibrium mammoth population sizes in constant environments and under varying intensities of fixed number culling. None of the three models for mammoth population dynamics (runs 1, 11, and 23) can sustain an annual cull of more than 11 animals distributed across all age/sex classes according to their frequency in the population.

frequency of each age/sex class within the population. If the fixed number kill targeted specific age/sex classes, then either higher, or lower, annual culls may be possible. Such selective culling awaits further modeling.

If we introduce random environmental fluctuations to let DI factors play the most significant role in controlling population growth and decline, we find that the sensitivity of the mammoth populations to hunting is increased (Table 12.6). This is in terms of both the size of the annual kill to cause extinction and the rate at which populations become extinct. Run 1 is unable to sustain any exploitation; run 11 becomes extinct with a fixed percentage of 3% or a fixed number of three; and run 23 with a fixed cull of 3% or a fixed number of eight.

The introduction of climatic deterioration will further increase the sensitivity of the mammoth populations to extinction. Table 12.7 shows three simulated populations suffering either a fixed percentage or fixed number cull in deteriorating environments (*tmax* = 500, *h* = 0.5, 0.6, and 0.7). Not surprisingly, there is a substantial reduction in extinction time from the non-deteriorating, fluctuating environment. Figure 12.12 illustrates the effect of a fixed 2% cull on a population modeled by run 11 in fluctuating (*g* = 15) and deteriorating (*g* = 15, *h* = 0.8, *tmax* = 500) environments.

## DISCUSSION

The simulations demonstrate that local mammoth populations are very sensitive to predation, which confirms previous suggestions made without quantitative support (e.g., Haynes 1991). The dramatic population collapses that we have seen following a slight increase in hunting intensity agree with the patterns observed among modern elephants--although, in the very recent past, the intensity of elephant hunting may have increased dramatically. For instance, in the Kabalega Falls National Park, Uganda, poaching led to a fall in elephant numbers from 14,337 in 1973 to 2,448 in 1976 (Eltringham and Malpas 1980). In Kenya, numbers of elephants are thought to have fallen from 75,300 in 1977 to 51,200 in 1980-1981 (Ottichilo 1986). This simulation indicates that such population falls are not only due to the specific ecological/economic/political conditions of the elephant populations and poaching in Africa today, but are also partly due to the inherent sensitivity of elephants (and mammoths) to predation. We can now

**Table 12.6.** The effect of random environmental fluctuations (*g* = 15) on the time to extinction in three runs (1, 11, 23) of the mammoth simulation model, for both fixed percentage and fixed number hunting with varying degrees of hunting intensities.

| Run/Parameter Values | Kill | Time to Extinction |
|---|---|---|
| 1   *b* = 0.05 | 1 | 330 |
|    *e* = 0.05 | 2 | 129 |
|    *f* = 0.15 | 3 | 82 |
| | 4 | 65 |
| | 1% | 462 |
| | 2% | 214 |
| | 3% | 129 |
| 11   *b* = 0.20 | 2 | Sustainable |
|    *e* = 0.05 | 3 | 932 |
|    *f* = 0.25 | 2% | Sustainable |
| | 3% | 323 |
| | 4% | 218 |
| 23   *b* = 0.20 | 7 | Sustainable |
|    *e* = 4.00 | 8 | 356 |
|    *f* = 0.35 | 9 | 302 |
| | 10 | 212 |
| | 11 | 149 |
| | 12 | 114 |
| | 3% | Sustainable |
| | 4% | 650 |
| | 5% | 269 |

**Table 12.7.** The effect of climatic deterioration in a randomly fluctuating environment on the time to extinction for three runs (1, 11, 23) of the mammoth simulation model (*tmax* = 500).

| Run/ Parameter Values | *h* | Kill | Time to Extinction |
|---|---|---|---|
| 1 *b* = 0.05 | 0.7 | 1 | 170 |
| *e* = 0.05 | 0.6 | | 219 |
| *f* = 0.15 | 0.5 | | 253 |
| 11 *b* = 0.20 | 0.7 | 3% | 227 |
| *e* = 0.05 | 0.6 | | 270 |
| *f* = 0.25 | 0.5 | | 295 |
| 23 *b* = 0.20 | 0.7 | 9 | 150 |
| *e* = 4.00 | 0.6 | | 196 |
| *f* = 0.35 | 0.5 | | 221 |

use these results to reflect upon the archaeology of the Central Russian Plain.

### Mammoth Hunting on the Central Russian Plain

As noted above, mammoth bones constitute a significant element of the faunal assemblages from many sites on the Central Russian Plain. They provided the basic construction material for dwellings, and mammoth ivory was an important raw material for utilitarian, decorative, and symbolic items. The Palaeolithic hunters of the Russian Plain, as well as those in many other regions of central and eastern Europe, have frequently been characterized as specialist mammoth hunters (see Soffer 1985, 1991). If the mammoth bones derived from fresh carcasses, and the

meat from these contributed to the sustenance of the human population, then much higher population levels may have existed than would have otherwise been the case. Even without the contribution of mammoth meat, human population levels in the Central Russian Plain are likely to have been relatively high for a hunter-gatherer population (Soffer 1985). In the absence of data concerning the age/sex structure of mammoth bone assemblages and relevant taphonomic studies, we have little guide as to whether bones derive from active hunting or from the collection of mammoth carcasses, perhaps of a considerable age (Soffer 1985, 1991). This is an important issue, with implications not only for the estimation of past human population densities (with their ramifications for social organization, etc.), but also for the organization of the subsistence-settlement system.

The results from this simulation support the ideas of Haynes (1991) and Soffer (1991) that bone collecting, rather than active hunting, is more likely as the source of the mammoth bone assemblages. The dates for settlements on the Central Russian Plain which have substantial mammoth bone assemblages range over a period of ca. 7,000 years, from ca. 20,000 to ca. 12,000 years BP. (Soffer 1986). If there was a significant level of active mammoth hunting, it becomes very difficult to understand how the mammoth population could have survived for such a long period, given their sensitivity to predation. An implication of these simulation results is that the relative longevity of the mammoth population on the Central Russian Plain during a period with relatively high human population densities would only have been possible if a substantial component of the mammoth bones in settlements came

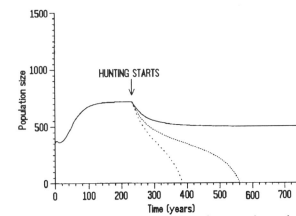

**Figure 12.10.** Fixed number culling of mammoth population (run 11) under three hunting intensities: five (solid), seven (closed dash), and nine (open dash). The population is allowed to reach equilibrium in a constant environment, free from predation, before hunting starts.

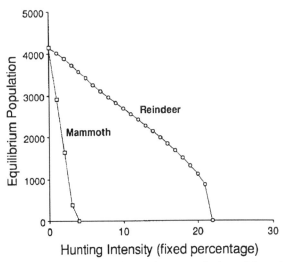

**Figure 12.11.** Comparison of mammoth (run 11) and reindeer equilibrium population sizes in constant environments under increasing intensities of fixed percentage hunting. Reindeer model from Mithen (1990).

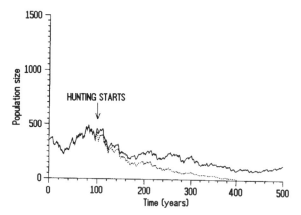

**Figure 12.12.** Two percent fixed percentage culling of mammoth population (run 11) in a fluctuating environment ($g = 15$) (solid) and in a deteriorating ($g = 15$, $h = 0.8$, *tmax* = 500) (dashed). In both cases, hunting begins at year 100. When the environment is deteriorating, extinction occurs.

from collecting. Active mammoth hunting must have been very light.

We can explore this proposition by making some speculations concerning mammoth and human population densities in the Central Russian Plain. Soffer (1985) used estimates of Pleistocene biomass to propose that the number of mammoths in her study area of 180,000 km² is likely to have been between 14,000-42,000 if the distribution was linearized along river valleys, or 7,000-21,000 if linearized and seasonal migration occurred. Let us slightly widen these bounds to between 5,000-50,000 or densities between 0.028 and 0.28 mammoths/km². These are densities which are at the lower end of the range recorded among modern African elephants by Croze et al. (1981) of 0.4-8.0 km² (with an outlier of 24). The simulations with the fixed cull models indicated that, for a vigorous population (run 23), extinction will occur if the cull is greater than 2.7% of the equilibrium population. For a less vigorous population (run 1), this proportion is as low as 0.35%. These imply that fixed number cull levels of 135-1,350 for a vigorous population and 1.4-140 for a less vigorous would have caused extinction. As we have seen in the models, such extinction would have been rapid.

Ethnographic estimates of human population levels in high latitude areas vary from between 0.01 and 0.178 people/km² (Burch 1972; David 1973). Soffer (1985) argues that human population densities would have been at the higher end of this range, if not beyond it. On the basis of these figures, the required hunting intensity to push mammoths into extinction in all possible combinations of mammoth/human population densities and population characteristics is only

0.75 mammoths/person/year. If we use the lower estimates for the number of mammoths, or the higher estimates for the human population density, this figure becomes markedly lower. There are two points that we must note. First, this estimate is based on simulations involving constant environments. As I have described, when we move to more realistic models involving environmental fluctuations, mammoths become even more sensitive to predation. Second, these hunting intensities relate to the killing of animals that would have otherwise survived until the following year. Hunters may have been killing mammoths which may have been fated to die from natural causes--hence not affecting the population dynamics of the mammoth population. Even if such hunting was occurring, the figure 0.75 mammoths/person/year as the maximum required hunting intensity for mammoth extinction certainly does not support the contention that we are dealing with specialized mammoth economies. For mammoths to have survived in this region for over 7,000 years, hunting intensities must have been very low.

Of course, the simulation may be inappropriate for the Central Russian Plain at the height and end of the last glacial. We may have been dealing with mammoth populations which were open and continuous over large geographic areas, so that predation was always compensated by immigration of animals. Such open populations, however, may have been unlikely because of the spatial patchiness of the landscapes in the Russian Plain and, by analogy, the social organization of elephants, which have relatively closed populations (Laws et al. 1975). Nevertheless, it remains an important possibility for evaluating the significance of the simulation results.

## SUMMARY

The models described in this paper face the problems of any simulation models in archaeology and in many other disciplines--limited and fuzzy data, a necessary set of assumptions, and the balances that must be found between generality/realism and simplicity/complexity. It is precisely because, not in spite, of the limited and fuzzy archaeological data that we need simulation models to improve our interpretations. The most uncontroversial and important result of this study has simply been to demonstrate that mammoth populations are extremely sensitive to predation. This increases the probability that human hunters played a significant role in the timing of mammoth extinction in the Old and New Worlds.

While deterministic models have remained at the core of this paper, I have tried to attain greater realism by exploring those which include stochastic environmental variability. By simulating pseudo-random sequences of good, average, and bad years, I have attempted to develop models which can combine the effects of human hunting and climatic deterioration in mammoth extinction. One of the main problems facing this work is that it may not have been the simple fact that environments were fluctuating or deteriorating that was critical to mammoths, but the specific sequence of bad years in relation to human hunting activity. Unfortunately, we cannot reconstruct paleoenvironments in sufficient detail to identify climatic fluctuations at the scale of resolution that our theoretical models require. However, it is hoped that this model, and more particularly the advanced model currently being developed (which includes spatial variability in population distributions and alternative hunting patterns), will improve our understanding of how human predation and climatic deterioration may interact to create the variability in the timing and cause of mammoth extinction at the end of the Pleistocene.

In this paper, I have used the simulation results to reflect upon the archaeological record of the Central Russian Plain. Since the archaeological record of this region documents a substantial use of mammoth bones and ivory over ca. 7,000 years, it is more probable, in light of these simulation results, that the majority of this material derived from carcass scavenging, as Soffer (1985, 1991) has argued, rather than from direct hunting.

## ACKNOWLEDGEMENTS

I would like to thank Harvey Bricker, Gail Larsen Peterkin, and Paul Mellars for inviting me to participate in their symposium at the 1991 SAA conference and The British Academy and University of Cambridge for travel funds. For valuable discussion about mammoths, advice on modeling, access to unpublished manuscripts, and comments on a previous version of this manuscript, I would like to thank Olga Soffer, Adrian Lister, Gary Haynes, Phyllis Lee, and John Rick.

## NOTES

[1]Note added in proof. This article was written before the sensational discovery of the mammoths on Wrangel Island in the Arctic Ocean, 200 km northeast of the Siberian coast, which date to between 7,000-4,000 years ago (Vartanyan et al. 1993).

## REFERENCES

Bahn, P., and J. Vertut
1989  *Images of the Ice Age*. London: Windward.
Barnes, R.
1982  A note on elephant mortality in Ruaka National Park, Tanzania. *African Journal of Ecology* 20:137-140.

Binford, L. R.
1987  Were there elephant hunters at Torralba? In *The Evolution of Human Hunting*. M. H. Nitecki and D. V. Nitecki, eds. Pp. 47-105. New York: Plenum Press.
Bosinski, G.
1984  The mammoth engravings of the Magdalenian site Gönnersdorf, Rhineland, Germany. In *La contribution de la zoologie et de l'ethologie à l'interpretation de l'art des peuples chasseurs préhistoriques*. H.-G. Bandi, W. Huber, M.-R. Sauter, and B. Sitter, eds. Pp. 295-322. Fribourg: Editions Universitaires.
Burch, E.
1972  The caribou/wild reindeer as a human resource. *American Antiquity* 37:339-368.
Calef, G. W.
1988  Maximum rate of increase in the African elephant. *African Journal of Ecology* 26:323-327.
Croze, H., A. K. K. Hillman, and E. M. Lang
1981  Elephants and their habitats: How do they tolerate each other. In *Dynamics of Large Mammal Populations*. C. W. Fowler and R. D. Smith, eds. Pp. 297-316. New York: John Wiley and Sons.
David, N. C.
1973  On Upper Palaeolithic society, ecology and technological change: The Noaillian case. In *The Explanation of Culture Change*. A. C. Renfrew, ed. Pp. 277-303. London: Duckworth.
Diamond, J. M.
1984  Historic extinction: A Rosetta Stone for understanding Pleistocene extinctions. In *Quaternary Extinctions: A Prehistoric Revolution*. P. S. Martin and R. G. Klein, eds. Pp. 824-862. Tucson: University of Arizona Press.
1989  Quaternary megafaunal extinctions: Variations on a theme by Paganini. *Journal of Archaeological Science* 16:167175.
Dublin, H. T., and I. Douglas-Hamilton
1987  Status and trends of elephants in the Serengeti-Mara ecosystem. *African Journal of Ecology* 25:19-33.
Eltingham, S. K., and R. C. Malpas
1980  The decline in elephant numbers in Rwenzori and Kabalega Falls National Park, Uganda. *African Journal of Archaeology* 18:73-86.
Guthrie, R. D.
1984  Mosaics, allelochemicals and nutrients: An ecological theory of late Pleistocene extinctions. In *Quaternary Extinctions: A Prehistoric Revolution*. P. S. Martin and R. G. Klein, eds. Pp. 259-298. Tucson: University of Arizona Press.
Hanks, J., and J. E. A. McIntosh
1973  Population dynamics of the African elephant (*Loxodonta africana*). *Journal Zoological Society of London* 169:29-38.
Haynes, G.
1985  Age profiles in elephant and mammoth bone assemblages. *Quaternary Research* 24:333-345.
1986  Proboscidean die-offs and die-outs: Age profiles in fossil collections. *Journal of Archaeological Science* 14:659-688.
1989  Late Pleistocene mammoth utilization in northern Eurasia and North America. *Archaeozoologia* 3:81-108.
1991  *Mammoths, Mastodons and Elephants: Biology, Behaviour and the Fossil Record*. Cambridge: Cambridge University Press.
Howell, F. C.
1965  *Early Man*. New York: Time-Life Books.
Jacobi, R. M.
1980  The Upper Palaeolithic in Britain, with special reference to Wales. In *Culture and Environment in Prehistoric Wales*. J. A. Taylor, ed. Pp. 15-99. BAR British Series

76. Oxford: British Archaeological Reports.

Laws, R. M., I. S. C. Parker, and R. C. B. Johnstone
1975    *Elephants and Their Habitats*. Oxford: Clarendon Press.

Lee, P. C., and C. J. Moss
1986    Early maternal investment in male and female African elephant calves. *Behavioural Ecology and Sociobiology* 18:353-361.

Leslie, P. H.
1945    On the use of matrices in certain population mathematics. *Biometrika* 33:183-212.

Lister, A.
1991    Late glacial mammoths in Britain. In *The Late Glacial in Europe*. R. N. E. Barton, A. J. Roberts, and D. A. Roe, eds. Pp. 51-59. CBA Research Report 77. London: Council for British Archaeology.

Mithen, S.
1990    *Thoughtful Foragers: A Study of Prehistoric Decision Making*. Cambridge: Cambridge University Press.

O'Connell, J. F., K. Hawkes, and N. B. Jones
n.d.    What do Clovis kill sites really represent? Skeptical comments from the Hadza perspective. Paper presented at the 56th annual meeting of the Society for American Archaeology, April 14-28, 1991, New Orleans.

Ottichilo, W. K.
1986    Age structure of elephants in Tsavo National Park, Kenya. *African Journal of Ecology* 26:323-337.

Pilgram, I., and D. Western
1986    Inferring hunting patterns on African elephants from tusks in the international ivory trade. *Journal of Applied Ecology* 23:503-514.

Saunders, J. J.
1980    A model for man-mammoth relationships in late Pleistocene North America. *Canadian Journal of Anthropology* 1:87-98.

Scott, K.
1980    Two hunting episodes of Middle Palaeolithic age at La Cotte de Saint-Brelade, Jersey (Channel Islands). *World Archaeology* 12:137-152.

Soffer, O.
1985    *The Upper Palaeolithic Settlement of the Russian Plain*. London: Academic Press.
1986    Radiocarbon accelerator dates for Upper Palaeolithic sites in European U. S. S. R. In *Archaeological Results from Accelerator Dating*. J. A. J. Gowlett and R. E. M. Hedges, eds. Pp. 109-115. Oxford University Committee for Archaeology Monograph 11. Oxford: Oxford University.
1991    Upper Paleolithic adaptations in central and eastern Europe and man/mammoth interactions. In *From Kostenki to Clovis: Upper Paleolithic-Paleoindian adaptations*. O. Soffer and N. D. Praslov, eds. Pp. 31-49. New York: Plenum Press.

Stuart, A. J.
1991    Mammalian extinctions in the late Pleistocene of northern Eurasia and North America. *Biological Reviews* 66:453-562.

Vartanyan, S. L., V. E. Garutt, and A. V. Sher
1993    Holocene dwarf mammoths from Wrangel Island in the Siberian Arctic. *Nature* 362:337-340.

Vereshchagin, N. K., and G. F. Baryshnikov
1984    Quaternary mammalian extinctions in Northern Eurasia. In *Quaternary Extinctions: A Prehistoric Revolution*. P. S. Martin and R. G. Klein, eds. Pp. 483-516. Tucson: University of Arizona Press.

Webster, D., and G. Webster
1984    Optimal hunting and Pleistocene extinction. *Human Ecology* 12:275-289.

Yesner, D.
n.d.    Late Pleistocene subsistence and paleoenvironments at the Broken Mammoth Site, Tanana Valley, Alaska. Paper presented at the 56th annual meeting of the Society for American Archaeology, April 14-28, 1991, New Orleans.

*13*

# Season and Reason: The Case for a Regional Interpretation of Mesolithic Settlement Patterns

**Peter Rowley-Conwy**
**University of Durham**

## ABSTRACT

Danish early and late Mesolithic lakeside settlements are examined. Season of occupation is examined through tooth eruption and bone growth of wild boar (*Sus scrofa*); the early Mesolithic sites were all occupied in summer (including Holmegaard V, previously believed to be a winter settlement), whereas late Mesolithic Ringkloster was occupied in winter and spring. Skeletal element frequency indicates that Ringkloster was a hunting camp and the early Mesolithic sites were not. There were considerable differences between sites of the two periods, despite their very similar locations, because of their different settlement systems. It is therefore argued that Mesolithic settlements cannot be understood by studying individual site location; the settlement system of which each site was a part exerts a crucial influence.

## INTRODUCTION

This contribution will argue that the location of a Mesolithic settlement is not sufficient in itself to enable archaeologists to understand what sort of site it is. Any attempt to reconstruct the economy of a site is likely to be at best partially successful, unless the settlement system in which the site was embedded is taken into account. Faunal remains are currently the best available means to examine the settlement system (Rowley-Conwy 1987a).

The examples to be used to support this statement are taken from the Mesolithic of Denmark. Comparisons will be made between the site of Ringkloster in Jutland (S. Andersen 1973-1974), dating from the late Mesolithic Ertebølle period (4th millennium bc[1]), and a number of sites from Zealand dating from the early Mesolithic Maglemose period (7th millennium bc). All these sites were in similar lakeside locations; all have similarly excellent conditions of faunal preservation; all appear to have been seasonal camp sites; and the same large mammals were hunted at them all. Despite these similarities, Ringkloster differs from the Maglemosian sites in a series of ways which cannot be accounted for, except by reference to the differing settlement systems in the two periods.

The large mammal bones from all the sites considered have been examined by the author. The hunting of five major species of land game was probably the most important activity; aurochs (*Bos primigenius*), moose (Br. elk) (*Alces alces*), red deer (*Cervus elaphus*), wild pig (*Sus scrofa*), and roe deer (*Capreolus capreolus*) are found in varying proportions. Several methods of faunal analysis are employed below to place the sites in their context by identifying (1) the approximate **season** of the year in which they were occupied and (2) the **reason** for their occupation, i.e., the general category of settlement to which they belong. It must be stressed at the outset that this work is at a relatively preliminary stage; however, because some other lines of evidence support the tentative conclusions presented here, the main conclusions are unlikely to suffer serious modification.

## SITE SEASONALITY

### Tooth Eruption

Examination of the teeth of wild pigs permits us to diagnose the season of occupation of the sites considered. Wild pigs in Denmark today give birth in March and April (Møhl 1978). If the assumption is made that their prehistoric counterparts were similar, then this restricted birth season may be used to determine the season of death of the animals whose jaws have been recovered archaeologically--if the various dental events can be aged fairly accurately.

**Table 13.1.** Stages of pig dental development and their ages (after Higham 1967:Appendix B).

| Stage | Dental Development | Est. Age in Months |
|---|---|---|
| 1 | Deciduous premolars unerupted | fetal |
| 2 | Deciduous PM2-3-4 in primary eruption | birth-one week |
| 3 | Deciduous PM2-3-4 in secondary eruption | 1-4 weeks |
| 4 | Deciduous PM2-3-4 in tertiary eruption | 4-7 weeks |
| 5 | Deciduous PM2-3-4 in primary wear, M1 unerupted | 2-4 |
| 6 | M1 in primary eruption | 4-5 |
| 7 | M1 in secondary eruption | 5-6 |
| 8 | M1 in tertiary eruption | 6-7 |
| 9 | M1 in primary wear, M2 unerupted | 7-8 |
| 10 | M1 in secondary wear, M2 unerupted | 8-9 |
| 11 | M2 in primary eruption | 9-10 |
| 12 | M2 in secondary eruption | 10-11 |
| 13 | M2 in tertiary eruption | 11-12 |
| 14 | PM2-4 in primary eruption | 12-14 |
| 15 | PM2-4 in secondary eruption | 14-15 |
| 16 | PM2-4 in tertiary eruption | 15-16 |
| 17 | PM2-4 in primary wear, M3 unerupted | 16-17 |
| 18 | M3 in primary eruption | 17-19 |
| 19 | M3 in secondary eruption | 19-21 |
| 20 | M3 in tertiary eruption, cusp one in primary wear | 21-23 |
| 21 | M3 cusp one in secondary wear | 23-25 |
| 22 | M3 cusp two in secondary wear | 25-27 |
| 23 | M3 cusp three in secondary wear | 27-29 |
| 24 | M3 all cusps in late secondary wear | 30+ |
| 25 | M3 all cusps in early tertiary wear | adult |
| 26 | M3 all cusps in late tertiary wear | late maturity |
| 27 | M3 all cusps in quaternary wear | old |

The work most usually quoted in connection with dental aging is the article by Silver (1969). For several domestic species, including pigs, this work presents two ages for the eruption of a particular tooth, one referring to modern animals and the other to eighteenth- and nineteenth-century animals assumed to have had poor nutrition. In each case, the modern animals are said to erupt their teeth at a younger age than the earlier animals. If nutrition has a major effect on the eruption ages of teeth, then the use of tooth eruption as a means of examining seasonal killing will be very problematic, although recent work gives grounds for greater confidence. For cattle, the reliability of the 18th- and 19th-century claims for later tooth eruption ages has been seriously questioned by Payne (1985) and Legge (Legge and Rowley-Conwy 1991). It is likely that the early data on sheep are similarly unreliable: the two very restricted killing peaks among the animals at the Romano-British temple

at Harlow (where seasonal sacrifice is likely) fall in the same month of the year only when the modern ages are used (Legge and Dorrington 1985). The situation pertaining to domestic pigs needs further research, but figures are available for three populations of wild pigs: animals in the former East Germany (Briedermann 1967), animals from Poland reared in the United States (Matschke 1967), and animals from Anatolia (Bull and Payne 1982). Despite the differences in environment and nutrition of these three populations, the quoted eruption ages are all closely similar to each other and to the modern domestic figures quoted by Silver (1969). This must cast some doubt on the notion that nutrition has a significant effect on eruption ages and lends confidence to the use of the recent figures for the Mesolithic wild specimens considered here.

The criteria used here for the aging of wild pig jaws are those of Higham (1967), based on an earlier edition of Silver's (1969) figures for modern domestic pigs (Table 13.1); Figure 13.1 shows the results for various sites. Each line represents one ageable jaw or fragment. Due to the fragmentary nature of some jaws, it was not always possible to allocate each piece to a single stage in the Higham scheme, so some lines are longer than just one stage. April 1 is taken as the average date of birth.

The Maglemosian sites of Holmegaard I and Lundby I are closely similar to each other (Figure 13.1) and to the other Maglemosian sites examined. No completely newborn specimens were observed, but a concentration appears at the ages of about two to five months. If the assumptions described above are correct, these certainly come from animals killed in the summer. There is then a gap, with little evidence for the killing of pigs in their first winter. Evidence for killing resumes in the second summer. There is also a concentration in the third summer, but allocation of a jaw or fragment to a particular stage here depends on how many cusps of the third molar are in wear (see Table 13.1), and these specimens may be more problematic. A few specimens appear to indicate dates of death in the second winter. Three possible explanations may be advanced: (1) the animals were killed during visits to the site outside the normal season of occupation; (2) these animals erupted their teeth at atypical ages; or (3) they were born outside the normal March-April period. It is not currently possible to choose which explanation is the most likely.

The evidence throughout, however, is consistent with markedly seasonal summer killing, and the jaws of the other large mammals are in agreement. This is reassuring in two ways. Firstly, the regular summer killing peaks suggest that the ages ascribed to particular tooth eruption events are more or less correct,

# WILD PIG DENTAL EVIDENCE

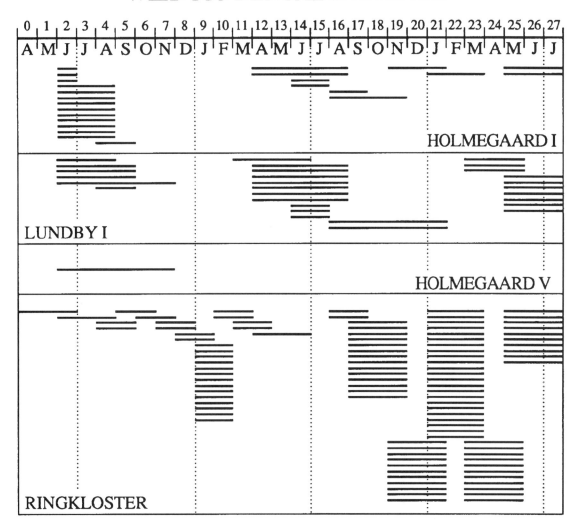

**Figure 13.1.** Seasonal information from wild pig jaws from Holmegaard I, Lundby I, Holmegaard V (all Maglemosian), and Ringkloster (Ertebølle), using the method of Higham (1967) and assuming a date of birth in April. Each line represents a single ageable pig jaw or jaw fragment. Only specimens not yet dentally mature are used (see Table 13.1).

because a single season of killing would not otherwise emerge from Figure 13.1 (cf. the Harlow sheep, above). Secondly, the new methods used here agree with earlier work carried out in Denmark. Most Maglemosian sites have long been believed to represent summer occupations, usually by virtue of their locations (e.g., K. Andersen 1973) and occasionally also because of their faunal evidence (Rosenlund 1980; Richter 1982).

One Maglemosian site that has hitherto been considered to be a winter site is Holmegaard V (Beck-er 1953; Petersen 1973; Grøn 1987). Unfortunately, the pig jaw data cannot resolve this because only a single doubtful specimen is available (Figure 13.1). This site will be discussed further below.

The Ertebølle site of Ringkloster stands in total contrast to Holmegaard I and Lundby I. A clear concentration is visible in the first winter. There is also a major group consistent with a kill in the second winter; the spread is wider, but the minimum period of occupation required to encompass all these jaws is November to May, suggesting a winter/spring occupa-

# WILD PIG HUMERUS SHAFT WIDTH

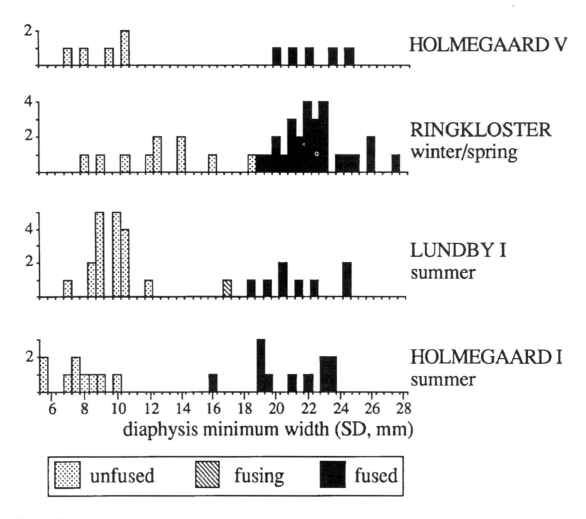

**Figure 13.2.** Histograms of humerus shaft width (measurement SD as defined by von den Driesch 1976) of wild pig from the same four sites used in Figure 13.1. The seasonal attributions are derived from Figure 13.1 (see text).

tion. A few specimens indicate killing outside the main season, and, as at the Maglemosian sites, the reason for this is unclear.

The results presented here are preliminary, and the ages ascribed to particular jaws and stages need not be as precise as Figure 13.1 implies. However, the conclusions are clear: the seasonality of Mesolithic sites can be determined by study of the wild pig jaws, and, equally clearly, the season of occupation of Ringkloster is fundamentally different from those of the determinable Maglemosian sites, despite the similar lakeside location.

## Bone Growth

Bone growth is a useful method of determining site seasonality. It was pioneered by Krause (1937) and Kollau (1943) for reindeer bones in northern Germany, and it has subsequently been applied to other ungulates, such as gazelle (Legge and Rowley-Conwy 1987), but not, apparently, to pigs. Pigs are eminently suited to this method because of the small size of piglets relative to adults.

Measurements of humerus shaft width (measurement SD as defined by von den Driesch 1976) are presented in Figure 13.2. The Maglemosian sites of

Lundby I and Holmegaard I, diagnosed as summer sites on the basis of their pig jaws, show a uniform pattern, with a group of very small unfused specimens clearly separated from the much larger adults. These very small specimens must correspond to the group of jaws aged about two to five months. The bone growth pattern on summer sites is therefore rather clear: animals in their first summer are visible as a separate size class. The gap between these and the older animals corresponds to the first winter; by the second summer, humerus shaft width has increased and merged with the adult range, even though second summer specimens have some way to go in terms of tooth eruption.

Other elements of the skeleton present the same pattern at these sites, and a similar picture emerges from the other Maglemosian summer sites studied. The winter/spring site of Ringkloster presents a major contrast (Figure 13.2); the first winter gap is filled in, corresponding to the jaw evidence for winter occupation put forward above. It is not clear why some individuals at Ringkloster apparently correspond to the summer kills at the Maglemosian sites; however, it must be remembered that the site was (on jaw evidence) occupied until May, after the March/April season of birth, so some very young individuals would be expected. The jaws from a few specimens also indicate killing in the first summer (Figure 13.1).

Despite some problems, the two patterns in Figure 13.2 are clearly different. It is further apparent that bone growth at Holmegaard V, the claimed winter site, in fact matches that at the summer sites. The conclusion from the bones is that Holmegaard V is a summer settlement, like the other Maglemosian sites considered here.

## THE MAGLEMOSIANS IN WINTER

The osteological conclusion that Holmegaard V is a summer settlement conflicts with earlier views of Maglemose seasonality. These earlier views must therefore be re-examined.

Becker (1953:182) regarded it as "quite certain" (my translation) that Holmegaard V was a winter site because (1) it lay on firm ground, not on peat, and (2) it had neither fish bones nor any of the barbed bone points with which the fish were believed to be caught. Regarding the first point, although it may be justified to use a location on peat as evidence for summer occupation if the area was flooded in winter, the converse--that a location on firm ground necessarily indicates a winter occupation--does not follow from this point. A summer settlement could surely occupy any suitable site, whether or not this happened to be on peat. Becker (1953:181) stresses that Holmegaard

V lay right at the lake edge, so location is otherwise similar to that of the other sites. This argument therefore seems less than conclusive.

The second point, the absence of fish, was also used to suggest that the British site of Star Carr was a winter site (Clark 1954:16). Subsequently, Star Carr has been demonstrated to be a summer site (Legge and Rowley-Conwy 1988). Reasons why fish were absent from Star Carr put forward by Wheeler (1978) may not be applicable to Holmegaard V, but Wheeler also makes the point that pike can be speared from February to late autumn. The absence of fish from a particular site does not therefore prove winter occupation, unless that occupation was very short-lived and restricted to midwinter. Other reasons for the absence of fish may thus have to be sought.

More recently, another argument for winter occupation of Holmegaard V has been put forward by Grøn (1987:311-312). He quotes observations made by Dr. Anders Fischer during the excavations of 1970-1971:

Fischer observed during the digging of a drainage ditch oriented north-south close to the excavation area that hazelnut shells, which are very often found at summer sites with good conditions for preservation, were found only in the northernmost part of the area. Cloven sticks of wood, more rarely preserved, were found in the excavated area farther to the south (Fischer, personal communication). Together these indications may reflect a situation in which the southwestern parts of the large settlement area were once-- or more likely several times--used for winter habitation withdrawn at least 15 m from the water, placed on solid ground, and oriented to the north (like the Flådet site), whereas the northern parts of the site were repeatedly used for "summer habitations" with dwellings situated only a few metres from the water on the peat deposits.

This seems to be a rather elaborate conclusion to base on a claimed spatial separation between hazel nuts and pieces of wood in a nonarchaeological drainage ditch. There is no stated indication that either the nuts or the wood derive from human activity. Even if they could be shown to do so, nuts become available for collection in autumn and may be stored for winter use, so their evidence would be inconclusive; it is harder to see why cloven sticks indicate winter.

The Maglemosian site of Flådet, mentioned in the quotation above, has also been claimed as a winter site by Grøn (1987), on purely locational grounds; the site lies some 20 m from the prehistoric lake shore, between ca. 1.20 and 1.40 m above its level (Grøn 1987:311, Fig. 5). This is minimally different from other Maglemosian sites and is hardly sufficient reason

ELEMENT FREQUENCY

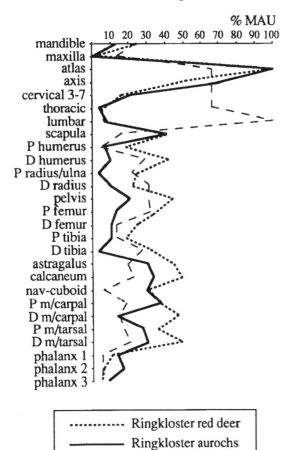

% MAU

Figure 13.3. Skeletal element frequency of the Ringkloster aurochs and red deer, quantified using Binford's %MAU method (see text) and compared to element frequency of the caribou from Aasivissuit (West Greenland) (Grønnow et al. 1983:Fig.83).

to postulate a winter occupation. The excavator of the site, in fact, considered that its location was typical of Maglemosian sites and that Flådet was probably occupied in summer (Skaarup 1979). Unfortunately, hardly any faunal material was preserved.

There is thus rather little evidence in favor of any of the known Maglemosian sites being occupied in winter. Certainly the claims advanced for Holmegaard V are most dubious, and the evidence from bone growth, pointing to a summer occupation, is to be preferred.

Maglemosian sites have been excavated for nearly a century, and the animal bones from about eight show that they were occupied in summer (Rowley-Conwy, work in progress). Had extensive winter

settlement taken place on the lake shores, it would seem reasonable to expect that some evidence of this would have been found by now. In the continuing absence of such evidence, it seems increasingly likely that Maglemosian winter settlements were not usually located on lakeshores. Where they were is open to question; numerous flint scatters are known at which no bones are preserved, and the winter settlements could certainly be among these. Another factor of importance is the rising sea level, which has inundated substantial areas that would have been available for Maglemosian settlement--a point stressed over half a century ago by Clark (1936). During Maglemosian times, the Baltic was a freshwater lake, drained by large rivers flowing out through the now-submerged lowlands into the North Sea. One possibility is that these rivers were the main focus of winter settlement at the time. Maglemosian flints have been recovered from sites on the bed of the Øresund (the strait between Denmark and Sweden) at depths of between 5 and 23 m (Larsson 1983). Whether these were winter sites cannot, of course, be determined, but they do lie on the banks of a submerged river (Larsson 1983), a completely different location from the lakeside settlements we have.

## SITE FUNCTION:
## SKELETAL ELEMENT FREQUENCY

The study of skeletal element frequency is at present fraught with problems, although there are grounds for hoping that the technique will become more useful as the problems become better understood (for applications to the Mesolithic, see Rowley-Conwy 1987a; Legge and Rowley-Conwy 1988, 1991). The intention in this section is to demonstrate that there is a major difference between Ringkloster, on the one hand, and the Maglemosian sites on the other.

For present purposes, it is important to note that preservation at all the sites considered was excellent. The bog peats preserve bones in superb condition, and it is believed that little or no post-depositional destruction has occurred. Because this is true of all the sites, inter-site comparisons should be valid in this respect. Excavation methods were also uniform, inasmuch as none of the sites was sieved. This is true also of Ringkloster, despite the recent date of the excavation, due to the impracticality of sieving peat. Recovery at all sites is believed to have been as good as could be achieved under these circumstances. Major distortions due to poor or differential recovery are thought to be unlikely. Traces of carnivore gnawing are relatively uncommon at all sites.

The method of quantification used here is that put forward by Binford (1984:50-51), most recently

Season and Reason                                                                                                                                                                                    185

referred to as "percent minimum animal unit" or
%MAU; for a fuller discussion under the name
%MNI, see Binford (1978:69-72). Despite the varying
nomenclature, this was the method employed at Star
Carr by Legge and Rowley-Conwy (1988). There are
two stages: first, the minimum number of each element (for example, distal humerus) must be estimated
from the fragments found; second, these numbers
must be adjusted because not all bones are equally
represented in a skeleton. For example, a ruminant
has one atlas vertebra, two distal humeri, and eight
proximal phalanges; the count for atlas vertebrae is
therefore doubled and that for proximal phalanges
divided by four, in order to bring them into line with
the long bone articulations. For the purposes of comparison, the figures for each assemblage are then
expressed as percentages of the most common element
in that assemblage; the most common element always
counts as 100%.

Three further points must be made about the
method as it is used here. First, all teeth and jaw
fragments have contributed to the minimum number of
elements. Although imprecise, this method was
considered preferable to counting just the complete
mandibles and maxillae and ignoring the large number
of loose teeth. The figures for these elements are
therefore more of an approximation than they are for
most other elements. The figure for maxilla is used
instead of the much less quantifiable fragments of
skull. Second, among the animals considered here,
pigs have more metapodials than do the ruminants.
For the purposes of comparability, the totals for
metapodials III and IV are therefore halved, and the
lateral metapodials and phalanges are ignored. Third,
newborn and very young animals are ignored. Even
on sites with excellent preservation, the bones of these
little creatures are prone to destruction, so the figures
would be distorted. Furthermore, because of their
much smaller size, such carcasses would be subject to
completely different decisions with regard to butchery
and transport than their sub-adult and adult counterparts. In practice this has meant that all the elements
deriving from first-summer animals have been omitted
from the Maglemosian totals; these are relatively easy
to distinguish, as Figure 13.2 shows. Bones of comparable size from Ringkloster are also omitted; numbers
in this category are small, and the decision is usually
easier to make than Figure 13.2 implies.

The %MAU of the Ringkloster red deer and
aurochs is plotted in Figure 13.3. Both the overwhelming importance of atlas and axis vertebrae and
the relative rarity of all other elements are immediately apparent for both species. This is not a pattern
known from other sites. It is difficult to envisage a
unique taphonomic action causing this (particularly
because pigs differ markedly--see below), so some
form of human activity is most probably responsible.

An activity that could account for the pattern seen
at Ringkloster emerges from a consideration of the
caribou bones from the Inuit site of Aasivissuit in
West Greenland (Grønnow et al. 1983). This site was
dominated by lumbar vertebrae, not the first two
cervical vertebrae (Grønnow et al. 1983:Table 6, Fig.
83), and in this way is substantially different from
Ringkloster. However, the relative rarity of all other
elements is similar (Figure 13.3).

The most recent occupations of Aasivissuit are
ethnographically recorded. People visited the site in
the months of July, August, and September in order to
hunt caribou, the only resource locally available in any
quantity. The majority of caribou were killed at the
end of a drive, very close to the site; after processing,
much meat was removed from the site by umiak to the
coastal settlement from which the people came. Many

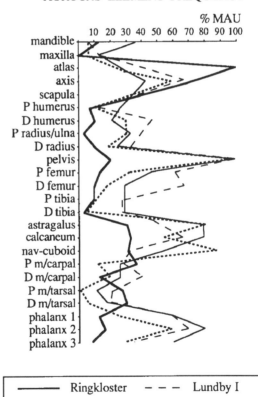

**Figure 13.4.** Skeletal element frequency of the Ringkloster
aurochs, quantified using Binford's %MAU method (see
text) and compared to element frequency of the aurochs
from the Maglemosian sites of Sværdborg I, Lundby I, and
Holmegaard V.

WILD PIG ELEMENT FREQUENCY

%MAU

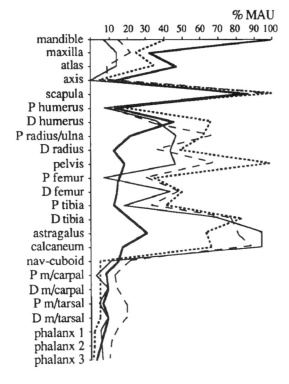

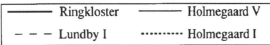

| ——— Ringkloster | ——— Holmegaard V |
| – – – Lundby I | ·········· Holmegaard I |

**Figure 13.5.** Skeletal element frequency of the Ringkloster wild pigs, quantified using Binford's %MAU method (see text) and compared to element frequency of the wild pigs from the Maglemosian sites of Holmegaard I, Lundby I, and Holmegaard V.

limbs, including the bones, are known to have been removed in this way, while the vertebrae were processed and abandoned at Aasivissuit. The possibility also exists that some limb bones were dumped in a part of the site not excavated.

Aasivissuit is thus a **hunting camp**. The high number of vertebrae is a result of the caribou having been killed close by; had they been killed individually and further away, as was probably the case with the Ringkloster aurochs and red deer, the vertebrae might have been abandoned at the kill site. This may account for the low number of vertebrae (except for atlas and axis) at Ringkloster.

Can Ringkloster be interpreted as a hunting camp by means of this comparison? The Aasivissuit and Ringkloster element frequencies are similarly peculiar, but this of course need not mean that the reasons for

this are similar. Nevertheless, it is difficult to envisage people introducing just the first two neck vertebrae to a site for any reason; it seems more likely that these elements are relatively common because some other elements were removed. The details of what was removed and what was never introduced remain unclear, but some meat removal was apparently taking place. The hunting camp explanation therefore seems likely.

At all events, some combination of activities was taking place at Ringkloster regularly enough over several centuries to cause a very unusual pattern of element frequency in the aurochs and red deer assemblages. It is worth stressing that this, at least, was similar at Aasivissuit; the ethnographic information derives mostly from this century, but the bones were excavated from Layer 3 of the site. This layer spans about a century, ca. AD 1650-1750. The bone assemblage is, like that from Ringkloster, a palimpsest representing the accumulated debris of a long period of activity consistent enough to produce a distinctive pattern, and the bones have gone through the taphonomic processes of discard, burial, and recovery. Evidence for carnivore gnawing is minimal (Grønnow et al. 1983).

The element frequency of the Ringkloster aurochs is compared to those from three Maglemosian lakeside sites in Figure 13.4 (Sværdborg I is used instead of Holmegaard I because of the small number of aurochs bones at the latter site). All three Maglemosian sites are similar to each other and different from Ringkloster: they have fewer atlas and axis vertebrae, more pelvis and upper rear limbs, more tarsals (astragalus, calcaneum, and naviculo-cuboid), and more phalanges. These sites are also palimpsests of many visits. It may be that the Maglemosian sites will in future be interpreted as base camps, as some current work assumes (e.g., Grøn 1987), but this remains to be seen. At all events, the activities that took place at them must have been regularly and consistently different from those that took place at Ringkloster--and this goes for Holmegaard V as much as for the others (Figure 13.4).

Finally, the pigs must be considered (Figure 13.5). Ringkloster differs very clearly from the Maglemosian sites in having relatively few elements from much of the skeleton. However, mandibles and scapulae are common, with maxilla, atlas, and distal humerus also fairly frequent. Once again, the Maglemosian sites (including Holmegaard V) are similar to each other and have a more "conventional" type of pattern. One is again tempted to invoke meat removal to account for the Ringkloster pig pattern--it is indeed hard to see what else could be involved. If this is correct, the frequency of the front end of the body could mean that this part of the carcass was consumed at Ringkloster by the hunters and not transported elsewhere. Pork contains more fat than beef or venison, and the importance of fat in the diet of active hunters in the winter, when Ringkloster was occupied, has been stressed (Speth and Spielmann 1983).

## CONCLUSIONS

Enough has now been done to demonstrate major differences between Ringkloster and the Maglemosian sites. Ringkloster was occupied in winter and spring, while work has so far failed to find a single definite Maglemosian winter site; Holmegaard V was most probably a summer site like all the rest. Ringkloster is argued to have been a hunting camp, probably used on rather brief visits by people who processed animals there and removed much of the meat. The Maglemosian sites were dissimilar; perhaps they were indeed base camps, as is often assumed.

Without detailed consideration of the animal bones, these conclusions could not be put forward. More specifically, because all the sites including Ringkloster are in identical locations on the edges of lakes in the low-lying Danish landscape, no consideration of the location or catchment of the individual sites would reveal the differences. The main works on site catchment analysis (e.g., Higgs and Vita-Finzi 1972; Jarman et al. 1972; Jarman et al. 1982:26-41) consider the isolated site in its catchment as the sole unit of study. The conclusion here, however, is that a single site cannot be treated in isolation from the settlement system of which it was a part. The archaeological study of Mesolithic settlement systems is complex (Rowley-Conwy 1987a), but this should not deter us.

In the present context, the differences between the Maglemosian and the Ertebølle settlement systems were enormous. During the Ertebølle the sea was close to its present level, and Ringkloster is only some 14 km from the present coast. It has been argued elsewhere (Rowley-Conwy 1983) that major sites on the coasts were permanently occupied by population units perhaps larger than the conventional hunter-gatherer band. A series of smaller sites functioned as temporary special-purpose extraction camps--and this is the role envisaged for Ringkloster. In the context of large population units in the coastal regions, winter and particularly spring would be times when fewer resources would be available (Rowley-Conwy 1984). The procurement of meat from the hinterland would thus be quite logical at this time of year.

The Maglemosian system was quite different. The sea was much further away, and Denmark was an extension of the North European Plain rather than the present collection of peninsulae and islands. It may be that the small summer communities gathered into

larger units in the winter, and, if so, then rivers in the now-submerged lowlands might have been where they gathered (Rowley-Conwy 1987b); this remains unknown. At all events, even that proportion of the Maglemosian settlement system that is currently known to us is sufficient to demonstrate that it was, not surprisingly, utterly unlike that of the Ertebølle.

Site location is thus likely to be difficult to interpret unless elements of the settlement system are understood. The conclusion is clear: although site catchment analysis is a very important source of hypotheses, it is no substitute for a detailed study of the faunal remains and other economic data. Such economic data are indeed the best, if not the only, means of testing site catchment hypotheses.

### NOTES

[1]Lowercase "bc" is used to indicate uncorrected radiocarbon years.

### REFERENCES

Andersen, K.
1983 *Stenalderbebyggelsen i den Vestsjællandske Åmose.* Copenhagen: Fredningsstyrelsen.
Andersen, S. H.
1973- Ringkloster: En jysk inlandsboplands med Ertebøllekultur
1974 (English summary). *Kuml* 1973-1974:11-108.
Becker, C. J.
1953 Die Maglemosekultur in Dänemark. Neue Funde und Ergebnisse. In *Actes de la III^ème Session, Zurich, 1950.* E. Vogt, ed. Pp. 180-183. Zurich: Congrès International des Sciences Préhistoriques et Protohistoriques.
Binford, L. R.
1978 *Nunamiut Ethnoarchaeology.* New York: Academic Press.
1984 *Faunal Remains from Klasies River Mouth.* New York: Academic Press.
Briedermann, L.
1968 Schwarzwild. In *Die Alterbestimmung der Erlegten Wilden.* E. Wagenknecht, ed. Pp. 76-86. East Berlin: Deutsche Landwirtschaftsverlag.
Brinch Petersen, E.
1973 A survey of the late Palaeolithic and Mesolithik of Denmark. In *The Mesolithic in Europe.* S. K. Kozlowski, ed. Pp. 77-127. Warsaw: Warsaw University Press.
Bull, G., and Payne, S.
1982 Tooth eruption and epiphyseal fusion in pigs and wild boar. In *Ageing and Sexing Animal Bones from Archaeological Sites.* B. Wilson, C. Grigson, and S. Payne, eds. Pp. 55-71. BAR British Series 109. Oxford: British Archaeological Reports.
Clark, J. G. D.
1936 *The Mesolithic Settlement of Northern Europe.* Cambridge: Cambridge University Press.
1954 *Excavations at Star Carr.* Cambridge: Cambridge University Press.
von den Driesch, A. E.
1976 *A Guide to the Measurement of Animal Bones from Archaeological Sites.* Peabody Museum Bulletin 1. Cambridge: Peabody Museum, Harvard University.
Grøn, O.
1987 Seasonal variation in Maglemosian group size and

structure: A new model. *Current Anthropology* 28:303-327.

Grønnow, B., M. Meldgaard, and J. B. Nielsen
1983   *Aasivissuit--the Great Summer Camp. Archaeological, Ethnographical and Zoo-Archaeological Studies of a Caribou-Hunting site in West Greenland.* Meddelelser om Grønland/Man and Society 5. Copenhagen: Kommissionen for Videnskabelige Undersøgelser i Grønland.

Higgs, E. S., and C. Vita-Finzi
1972   Prehistoric economies: A territorial approach. In *Papers in Economic Prehistory.* E. S. Higgs, ed. Pp. 27-36. Cambridge: Cambridge University Press.

Higham, C. F. W.
1967   Stock rearing as a cultural factor in prehistoric Europe. *Proceedings of the Prehistoric Society* 33:84-106.

Jarman, M. R., G. N. Bailey, and H. N. Jarman
1982   *Early European Agriculture.* Cambridge: Cambridge University Press.

Jarman, M. R., C. Vita-Finzi, and E. S. Higgs
1972   Site catchment analysis in archaeology. In *Man, Settlement and Urbanism.* P. J. Ucko, R. Tringham, and G. W. Dimbleby, eds. Pp. 61-66. London: Duckworth.

Kollau, W.
1943   Zur osteologie des Rentiers (nach den Funde von Stellmoor in Holstein). In *Die Alt- und Mittelsteinzeitlichen Funde von Stellmoor.* A. Rust. Pp. 60-105. Neumünster: Karl Wachholz.

Krause, W.
1937   Die eiszeitlichen Knochenfunde von Meiendorf. In *Das Altsteinliche Rentierjägerlager Meiendorf.* A. Rust. Pp. 48-61. Neumünster: Karl Wachholz.

Larsson, L.
1983   Mesolithic settlement on the sea floor in the Strait of Öresund. In *Quaternary Coastlines and Marine Archaeology: Towards the Prehistory of Land Bridges and Continental Shelves.* P. M. Masters and N. C. Flemming, eds. Pp. 283-301. New York: Academic Press.

Legge, A. J., and E. Dorrington
1985   Harlow Temple: The animal bones. In *The Romano-British Temple at Harlow, Essex.* F. R. Clark and I. K. Jones, eds. Pp. 122-133. Gloucester: West Essex Archaeological Group.

Legge, A. J., and P. A. Rowley-Conwy
1987   Gazelle killing in Stone Age Syria. *Scientific American* 257 (2):88-95.

Legge, A. J., and P. A. Rowley-Conwy
1988   *Star Carr Revisited: A Re-Analysis of the Large Mammals.* London: Centre for Extra-Mural Studies, London University.

Legge, A. J., and P. Rowley-Conwy
1991   "... Art made strong with bones:" A review of some approaches to osteoarchaeology. *International Journal of Osteoarchaeology* 1:3-15.

Matschke, G. H.
1967   Ageing European wild hogs by dentition. *Journal of Wildlife Management* 31:109-113.

Møhl, U.
1978   Aggersund-bopladsen zoologisk belyst. Svanejagt som årsag til bosættelse? (English summary). *Kuml* 1978:57-76.

Payne, S.
1984   The use of early 19th century data in ageing cattle mandibles from archaeological sites, and the relationship between the eruption of M3 and P4. *Circaea* 2 (August) 1984: 77-82.

Richter, J.
1982   Faunal remains from Ulkestrup Lyng Øst. In *Maglemose Hytterne ved Ulkestrup Lyng.* K. Andersen, S. Jørgensen, and J. Richter. Pp. 141-177. Copenhagen: Det Kongelige Nordiske Oldskriftselskab.

Rosenlund, K.
1980   Knoglematerialet fra bopladsen Lundby II (English summary). In *Lundby-holmen. Pladser af Maglemosetype i Sydsjælland.* B. B. Henriksen. Pp. 120-142. Copenhagen: Det Kongelige Nordiske Oldskriftselskab.

Rowley-Conwy, P.
1983   Sedentary hunters: The Ertebølle example. In *Hunter-Gatherer Economy in Prehistory.* G. N. Bailey, ed. Pp. 111-126. Cambridge: Cambridge University Press.
1984   The laziness of the short-distance hunter: The origins of agriculture in Denmark. *Journal of Anthropological Archaeology* 3:300-324.
1987a   Animal bones in Mesolithic studies: Recent progress and hopes for the future. In *Mesolithic Northwest Europe: Recent Trends.* P. Rowley-Conwy, M. Zvelebil, and H. P. Blankholm, eds. Pp. 74-81. Sheffield: Department of Archaeology and Prehistory.
1987b   Comment on Grøn (1987). *Current Anthropology* 28:322-323.

Silver, I. A.
1969   The ageing of domestic animals. In *Science in Archaeology.* 2nd edition. D. Brothwell and E. S. Higgs, eds. Pp. 283-302. London: Thames and Hudson.

Skaarup, J.
1979   *Flaadet. En Tidlig Maglemoseboplads på Langeland* (English summary). Rudkøbing: Langelands Museum.

Speth, J. D., and K. A. Spielmann
1983   Energy source, protein metabolism, and hunter-gatherer subsistence strategies. *Journal of Anthropological Archaeology* 2:1-31.

Wheeler, A.
1978   Why were there no fish remains at Star Carr? *Journal of Archaeological Science* 5:85-89.

# 14

# Lithic Use-Wear Evidence for Hunting by Neandertals and Early Modern Humans from the Levantine Mousterian

**John J. Shea**
**State University of New York at Stony Brook**

## ABSTRACT

Microwear analysis of stone tools from Levantine Mousterian sites provides evidence for the use of hafted stone spear points by Neandertals and early modern humans. Differences in the frequency of technologically assisted hunting may account for significant aspects of Levantine Mousterian variability. The ability to make and use hafted stone spear points is probably behaviorally "primitive" and one of many areas in which Neandertals and early modern humans did not differ from each other.

## INTRODUCTION

An effective investigation of the lithic evidence for hunting in the Late Pleistocene requires three developments in Paleolithic archaeology and paleoanthropology. First, there need to be reliable criteria for recognizing hafted stone spear points, which are the one category of lithic archaeological residue uniquely referable to hunting and not to other modes of meat acquisition, such as early-access scavenging. Second, evidence for the use of such implements must be sought in contexts where they are associated with a variety of human fossil morphotypes, so that one can determine how broadly such strategies were shared among Upper Pleistocene hominids. Third, realistic models must be formulated that describe the behavioral factors that led hominids to adopt technologically assisted hunting as a subsistence strategy.

This paper addresses these problems by examining the evidence for technologically assisted hunting in the Middle Paleolithic of the Levant. Lithic microwear analysis provides a reliable framework for the identification of prehistoric hunting implements. Use-wear analysis of Levantine Mousterian assemblages indicates the presence of impact-damaged hafted stone spear points in assemblages separately associated with the fossil remains of early modern humans at Qafzeh Cave and Neandertals at Kebara Cave during the period between 45,000 and 110,000 years ago. This evidence suggests that these hominids faced similar subsistence pressures and responded to these pressures in similar ways for a significant part of the early Upper Pleistocene.

## IDENTIFYING HUNTING RESIDUES

If one is interested in identifying technologically assisted hunting in the lithic record, then clearly the most immediately relevant archaeological evidence is those wear traces referable to the impact of stone projectile armatures against their targets. Such "impact wear" (Odell and Cowan 1986) has not yet been revealed by microwear studies of European Mousterian collections (Anderson-Gerfaud 1990), although it has been observed in the Middle Paleolithic of the Levant (Shea 1988). The use of hafted projectile armatures in the African Middle Stone Age seems plausible because of the pedunculated bases of Aterian points, the thinned bases of Stillbay points, and the design of Howiesonspoort crescents, although microwear evidence is thus far lacking. When pointed artifacts like Levallois points and other triangular artifacts from Middle Paleolithic contexts are lashed to a wooden haft and either thrown or thrust into large- or medium-sized animal targets, such as horse, deer, goat, and gazelle, they perform rather well, achieving deep penetration and causing massive internal injuries. Characteristic breakage patterns occur on the distal tips of most such points, often during the first such use and almost always after several applications.

Some of these wear patterns appear to be referable solely to the use of stone-tipped projectiles. In general, there are four kinds of impact-related damage (Figure 14.1):

(1) **Macrofracture**--a large shear or bending fracture begins at the point of impact and propagates broadly across either the dorsal or the ventral face of the tool, generally ending in either a "step" or "hinge" termination.

(2) **Burination**--a large shear or bending fracture begins at the point of impact and propagates parallel to one of the lateral edges, leaving an elongate scar not unlike the *coup de burin*.

(3) **Lateral Snapping**--bending or torsion forces a fracture to propagate between the dorsal and ventral surfaces or between the lateral edges at a point that is relatively distant from the part of a tool bearing the major load during impact.

(4) **Comminution**--the leading part of the tool collapses under load, resulting in a cluster of step-terminated bending fractures and incompletely propagated shear fractures.

Of the four kinds of impact wear, comminution and lateral snapping are of the least analytical value for identifying prehistoric spear points because they result from many wear vectors other than projectile impact. These vectors include other modes of stone tool use, including use as a wedge for splitting bone or shaping wood, accidental damage during flint-knapping, and even non-use-related phenomena, such as trampling and soil compaction. Distal fractures and burination smaller than 2 mm occasionally result from vigorous use during butchery, but macrofractures and burinations that are longer than 2 mm from initiation to termination appear uniquely referable to projectile impact.

It does not appear possible to reliably differentiate between wear resulting from throwing spears (javelins) and wear resulting from thrusting spears (lances). Nor do microwear traces alone allow one to differentiate hits on animal targets from impact against trees, rocks, or the ground. Because of this, the microwear record does not duplicate more direct methods of assessing hominid diet, such as stable-isotope and archaeofaunal analysis, but is instead complementary, providing a record of hunting effort rather than one of hunting success.

## THE LEVANTINE MOUSTERIAN EVIDENCE

Few parts of the Middle Paleolithic world feature so diverse an array of associated hominid fossils as does the Levant. Robust anatomically modern humans have been recovered from Qafzeh and Skhul caves, while anatomically archaic hominids with some

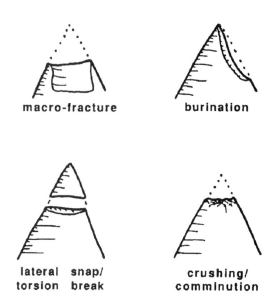

**Figure 14.1.** Four kinds of impact-related wear.

Neandertal autapomorphies have been recovered from Tabun, Amud, and Kebara Caves. While the relative chronological positions of these fossils and the nature of their biological relationships are hotly contested (Bar-Yosef 1989; Stringer 1989; Vandermeersch 1989; Wolpoff 1989), their archaeological associations are beyond dispute. All of these hominids are associated with a single lithic complex called the "Levantine Mousterian." Levantine Mousterian assemblages occur in both cave and open-air sites dating to between 45,000 to more than 120,000 years ago (Bar-Yosef 1989) (Figure 14.2).

Lithic microwear analysis was conducted on Levantine Mousterian stone tools from Kebara, Tabun, Hayonim, and Qafzeh caves and Tor Faraj rockshelter (Shea 1991). Once those sedimentary deposits were identified in which stone tool edges and surfaces were sufficiently well preserved for microwear analysis, every artifact larger than 2.5 cm in any dimension was examined for wear traces with a stereomicroscope (5-160X) and reflected light. Tools visibly worn from use were subsequently examined with a compound binocular microscope (70-300X) and incident lighting. In order to assure consistency in microwear interpretation, the values of nine variables were recorded for each concentration of wear identified in the archaeological record. The values of these variables indicate aspects of microfracture, striation, edge-dulling, and polish reflectivity, each of which has a close, experimentally verified relationship to specific aspects of stone tool use, including tool motion and worked materials (see Shea 1991). These microwear patterns were then interpreted by systematically comparing them to wear observed in an experimentally utilized reference collection of more than 1,200 stone artifacts worn from butchery, hide-working, bone-carving, soft plant processing, woodworking, flintknapping, and use as stone spear points. After this comparison, only those wear patterns replicating experimental stone tool uses were retained, so that the resulting archaeological sample contained the maximum number of reliably interpreted microwear traces.

Of the nearly 29,206 Levantine Mousterian artifacts examined, only 2,309 (7.9%) exhibited microwear traces referable to use. Of these, only 319 (13.8%) featured wear patterns replicating those produced by the experimental use of stone spear points. Such wear occurs in most of the assemblages examined, including assemblages associated with early modern humans from Qafzeh Units XV-XXIV and assemblages associated with archaic/Neandertal humans from Kebara Units IX-XII (Table 14.1). Microwear traces referable to impact are largely restricted to the distal tips of Levallois points, triangular flakes, and pointed blades (Figure 14.3).

Although wear referable to impact occurs on roughly one-third of all worn Levantine Mousterian points, impact damage is not the only kind of wear that occurs on these tools (Plate 14.1). Wear traces on the distal lateral edges generally consist of bifacial patterns of step- and feather-terminated microfractures propagating obliquely to the worn edge (Plate 14.1b). A matte-reflecting polish usually covers these microfractures, often extending far onto the tool surface before diminishing (Plate 14.1c). Edge-rounding and striations are both rare; when they are observed, striations are generally short, shallow, and aligned obliquely to the worn edge, and rounding is most pronounced near the distal tip. In replicative experiments, such wear results from cutting motions during the butchery of large animal carcasses, especially those in which there is contact between the cutting edge of the tool and animal bone and cartilage (see also Keeley 1980; Odell 1980).

Wear traces on the proximal lateral edges usually consist of a bilaterally symmetrical pair of either unifacial or alternatingly bifacial clusters of feather-terminated microfractures of variable size aligned perpendicularly to the edge (Plate 14.1d). Polish, striations, and edge-rounding almost never occur near such wear concentrations. When such abrasive wear occurs at all, it is usually on the dorsal scar ridges between the microfracturing clusters (Plate 14.1e). In replicative experiments, such wear results from the movement of a hafted stone tool against its handle and/or against the fibers that have been used to secure it (see also Odell and Cowan 1986).

Overall, such a patterned distribution of microwear traces is most consistent with use as a combination hafted spear point and butchery knife. Other kinds of wear traces, including some referable to woodwork-ing, also occur on some of these pointed artifacts, but there is no way of knowing how much time separated the various use-episodes represented on the edges of these tools. Damaged points may have been re-used for other tasks before finally being discarded, and tools worn from other activities may have been subsequently drafted into service as hafted stone spear points.

## BEHAVIORAL CONTEXT OF LEVANTINE MOUSTERIAN SPEAR POINT USE

Discussions of the role of hunting in hominid bio-behavioral evolution all too often adopt a stage-wise model in which hominids are shown moving in one direction through successively more complex subsistence strategies and leading inexorably to industrial agro-pastoralism. The subsistence adaptations of most living primates, including human foragers (Wilmsen 1989), however, are far more polyvalent than can comfortably be accommodated by such simple stage-wise models. A more scientific approach

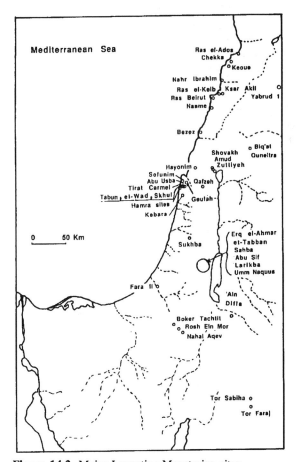

**Figure 14.2.** Major Levantine Mousterian sites.

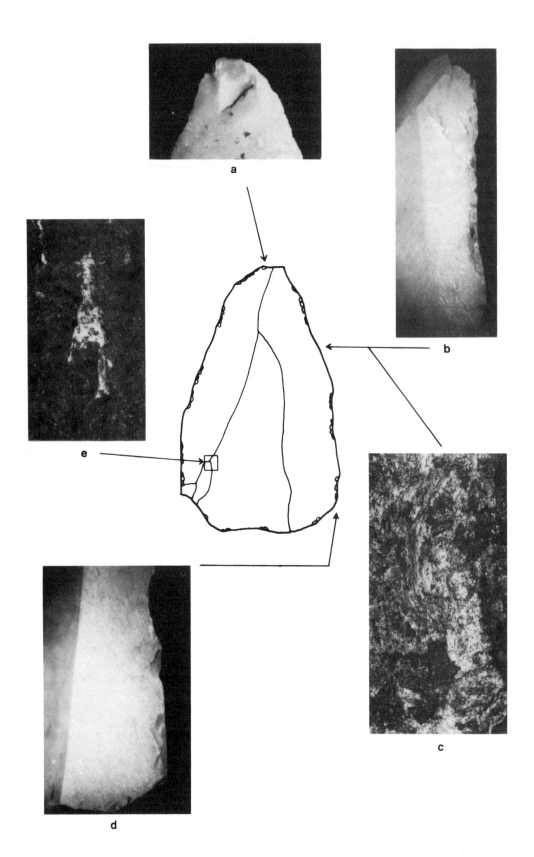

**Table 14.1.** Levantine Mousterian microwear sample parameters.

| Site and Assemblage | n Tools Examined | Tools Use-Worn | | Tools Worn from Impact | | |
| --- | --- | --- | --- | --- | --- | --- |
| | | n | % | n | % of Worn Tools | % of Tools Examined |
| Kebara IX | 2449 | 162 | 6.6 | 20 | 12.4 | 0.82 |
| KebaraX | 3258 | 433 | 13.3 | 68 | 15.7 | 2.09 |
| Kebara XI | 4169 | 363 | 8.7 | 49 | 13.5 | 1.18 |
| Kebara XII | 393 | 63 | 9.2 | 15 | 23.8 | 3.82 |
| Kebara XIII | 101 | 7 | 6.9 | 3 | 42.9 | 6.93 |
| Tabun I (Beds 1-17) | 431 | 19 | 4.4 | 4 | 21.1 | 0.93 |
| Tabun I (Beds 18-26) | 3985 | 139 | 3.4 | 4 | 2.9 | 0.10 |
| Tabun II | a1500 | 59 | 3.9 | 12 | 20.3 | 0.80 |
| Tabun IX | 1642 | 209 | 12.7 | 23 | 11.0 | 1.40 |
| Hayonim E | 2185 | 271 | 12.4 | 28 | 10.3 | 1.28 |
| Qafzeh XV | 5872 | 334 | 5.7 | 62 | 18.6 | 1.06 |
| Qafzeh XVII-XXIV | 2397 | 157 | 6.6 | 4 | 2.6 | 0.17 |
| Tor Faraj C | 824 | 93 | 11.2 | 27 | 29.0 | 3.28 |
| TOTAL | 29,206 | 2,309 | 7.9 | 319 | 13.8 | 1.09 |

aestimate, actual total not yet published.

to this problem is to view technologically assisted hunting as a behavioral strategy subject to a variety of ecological factors (Tooby and DeVore 1987), including the costs and risks of hunting large game with relatively simple tools.

It was probably not necessary for early Upper Pleistocene hominids to make and use spears in order to hunt small game. The predatory activities of our nearest primate relative, *Pan trogloydytes* (chimpanzee), provides an illustrative example. Chimpanzees regularly and successfully hunt a number of species (bushpig, bushbuck, colobus monkeys, and baboons) without using tools at all (Goodall 1986). Possibly because numerous alternative plant foods are available, however, chimpanzee hunting is largely opportunistic and almost always involves prey that are much smaller than the hunters. These animals are generally too small to inflict serious wounds on the hunters, and the risk of injury is further reduced by chimpanzee "pack" or "mob" hunting. Under such circumstances, there is little energetic incentive for chimpanzees to produce tools to aid in the capture and handling of animal prey, even though chimpanzees are quite capable of manufacturing and transporting tools for other purposes, such as sticks for termite "fishing" and stones for nut cracking.

Risk of injury must also have been a major factor in early hominid hunting strategies. Even today, with modern antibiotic medicines, field treatment of puncture wounds under subtropical conditions involves a high risk of infection. Hunting spears probably first appeared whenever and wherever hominids began to regularly hunt game that was large enough to inflict crippling wounds on the hunter, making it desirable for the hunters to inflict lethal wounds from a distance.

While sharpened wooden spears like those recovered from European Middle Pleistocene contexts at Clacton (England) and Lehringen (Germany) will penetrate the abdominal wall of most large terrestrial animals, such spears have significant disadvantages: the tip may puncture, but will not lacerate, internal organs; and, unless it is barbed, sharpened wooden spears can be dislodged by the movement of the wounded animal. The advantage of attaching stone points to spears is that, once they penetrate the abdominal cavity of their target, the thrashing of the wounded animal causes lacerations and massive internal hemorrhage, killing the animal relatively swiftly. Even if death does not occur immediately, the large slashing wounds created by such points assist in the formation of a blood trail that can be followed to the eventual

**Plate 14.1.** Distribution of wear on a Levallois point from Kebara Unit X: (a) macrofracture; (b) dorsal view of bifacial microfracturing on lateral edge; (c) incident-light photomicrograph (approximately 160X) of matte-reflecting polish and striations on the edge shown in (b); (d) cluster of microfractures on lateral edge near the base of the point; (e) isolated flattening of eminences on the dorsal ridge (approximately 120X).

death site. The principal disadvantages of using hafted stone spear points are that they require some investment of effort before use and that they also tend to break rather easily if they miss their target and hit some other hard object, like a tree or a rock.

In this sense, then, the kinds of spear points identified in the Levantine Mousterian tend more towards the "reliability" end of Bleed's (1986) "reliability vs. maintainability" continuum of hunting weapon design. Levallois points and pointed blades are very simple to produce (Boëda 1982) and are deadly effective when used. The fact that they are likely to become irreparably damaged once they hit their target would probably have been of small consequence, as they could have been easily replaced with relatively little effort. Given these functional considerations, greater numbers of points similar to those used as projectile armatures in the Levantine Mousterian should occur when and where the hunting of large game could be anticipated by hominid flintknappers. It also seems reasonable to suppose that such points may have been made less often when alternative low-risk food sources became available.

How does this help us to understand the Levantine Mousterian? The relative frequency of pointed artifacts is either a major factor in, or a strong correlate of, most current techno-typological classifications of Levantine Mousterian industrial variability (Copeland 1975; Jelinek 1982; Meignen and Bar-Yosef 1989). As many points appear to have been worn from use in hunting, the frequency of hunting by early Upper Pleistocene hominids may play a major role in Levantine Mousterian industrial variability. Indeed, as shown in Table 14.2, there is a strong correlation ($+0.79556$, $p = .01035$) between the percentage of worn tools exhibiting impact wear and the proportion of points among the Levallois debitage in the Kebara, Tabun, Qafzeh, and Tor Faraj assemblages. (No typological data are yet available for the Hayonim E assemblage.)

One of the most prominent features of Levantine Mousterian variability is the predominance of assemblages with large percentages of points in the southern and interior Levant (Copeland 1981; Jelinek 1982:91-96; Marks 1990). If we accept the hypothetical link between the production of points and hominid predatory activity in the Levantine Mousterian, then it is possible to explain this techno-typological pattern in ecological terms.

In the coastal and northern Levant, the presence of Mediterranean oak-pistachio woodland throughout most of the Upper Pleistocene probably furnished hominids with a dense and diverse array of plant and small-animal food sources that were available year-round (White 1977). While foraging deficits undoubtedly occurred in this region (and the lithic microwear

**Table 14.2.** Relationship between the occurrence of impact wear among the worn tools and the abundance of points in Levantine Mousterian assemblages. (Source Shea 1991.)

| Site and Assemblage | Tools Worn from Impact | | Levallois | | Pt/Flk Ratio |
|---|---|---|---|---|---|
| | n | % | Pts. n | Flks. n | |
| Kebara IX | 20 | 12.4 | 40 | 277 | 0.14 |
| Kebara X | 68 | 15.7 | 80 | 442 | 0.18 |
| Kebara XI | 49 | 13.5 | 62 | 740 | 0.08 |
| Tabun I (Beds 1-17) | 4 | 21.1 | 30 | 127 | 0.24 |
| Tabun I (Beds 18-26) | 4 | 2.9 | 54 | 687 | 0.08 |
| Tabun IX | 23 | 11.0 | 225 | 655 | 0.34 |
| Qafzeh XV | 62 | 18.6 | 225 | 1003 | 0.22 |
| Qafzeh XVII-XXIV | 4 | 2.6 | 6 | 269 | 0.02 |
| Tor Faraj C | 27 | 29.0 | 65 | 132 | 0.49 |

evidence clearly suggests that technological hunting occurred as well), it seems logical to suppose that hominids living in this part of the Levant would have had more "backup" low-risk food sources than those hominids living in the more steppic southern and interior Levant. Accordingly, they probably hunted large game less regularly and produced fewer pointed lithic artifacts.

In the southern and interior Levant, less rainfall, poor water retention by sandy loessic soils, and highly seasonal plant florescence schedules would probably have made it difficult for hominids living there to subsist year-round on plant and small-animal foods alone. While the known distribution of Levantine Mousterian sites is almost exactly coterminous with the maximum extent of the Mediterranean woodland phytogeographic zone (Horowitz 1989:13), the presence of habitually steppe-dwelling micro- and macro-fauna in the archaeofaunal remains from some southern Levantine Mousterian sites (Tchernov 1989) indicates that at least some hominid groups were living at or near the steppe-woodland ecotone. Seasonal shortfalls of plant and less mobile animal food sources may have forced hominids living in the southern and interior Levant to hunt large game more often, resulting in assemblages with greater proportions of pointed artifacts.

It would be tempting to equate the suggestion of a more predatory adaptation for the Mousterian of the interior and southern Levant with some measure of adaptive success. However, it must be remembered that the lithic record by itself only registers hunting effort and not hunting success. The southern and interior Levant may have been relatively marginal zones into which some hominid groups were periodi-

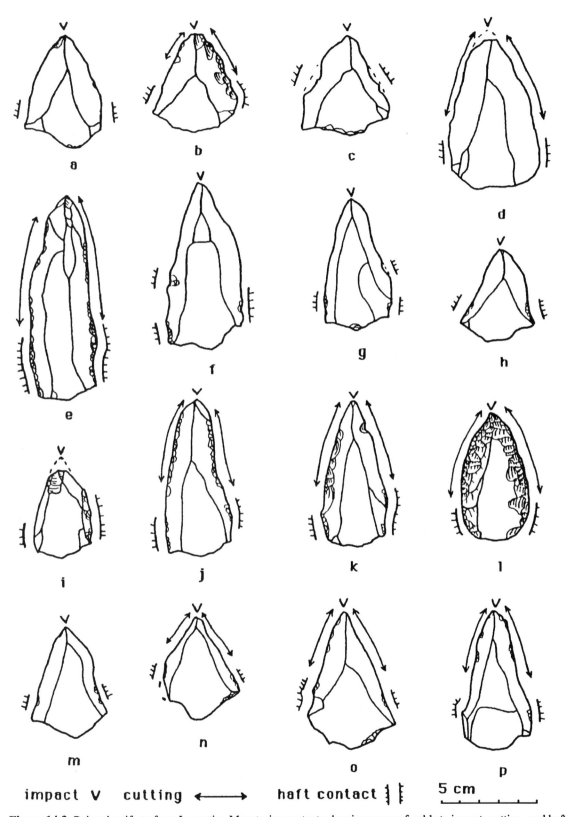

impact V    cutting ←——→    haft contact ⫫ ⫫    5 cm

**Figure 14.3.** Pointed artifacts from Levantine Mousterian contexts showing wear referable to impact, cutting, and haft contact: (a-d) Kebara Cave; (e-h) Tabun Cave; (i-l) Hayonim Cave; (m,n) Qafzeh Cave; (o,p) Tor Faraj.

cally displaced and within which they had to pursue more risky subsistence strategies in order to survive. If this was the case, then groups living in the southern and interior Levant would have experienced elevated risks of subsistence failure and extinction, but would also have stood to benefit far more profoundly than their counterparts in the northern and coastal Levant from even relatively minor improvements in behavioral strategies. In light of this consideration, it is interesting that the earliest evidence for a Middle/Upper Paleolithic transition comes from just this part of the Levant (Marks 1983).

## CONCLUSION

Much of the attention now being devoted to the Levantine Mousterian involves a search for the behavioral differences between the Neandertals and the early modern humans who are both associated with this lithic industry. Unfortunately, the cataloging of differences (e.g., Trinkaus 1986) all too often overlooks the many behavioral similarities that must have existed between these hominids. Such similarities are the logical point of departure for any investigation of their bio-behavioral differences.

Lithic microwear analysis suggests that both Neandertals and early modern humans living in the Levant between 45,000 and more than 110,000 years ago employed hafted stone spear points to hunt large terrestrial mammals. Inasmuch as there is no credible neurological evidence for major cognitive differences between these hominids (Deacon 1989:395-396), there is every reason to expect them to have produced approximately the same kinds of archaeological residues. While this expectation may seem counterintuitive from the point of view that sees early modern humans as the "new and improved" descendants of Neandertals (Trinkaus 1986; Wolpoff 1989), it is exactly what one should expect if the cognitive and manual skills needed to devise such weapons were behaviorally "primitive" characteristics shared by these hominids' last common ancestor.

Undoubtedly, there were important ways in which the activities of these hominids differed. However, there is simply no way of knowing a priori how, if at all, these differences are expressed in the lithic record. Further investigations of the behavioral similarities and differences between Neandertals and early modern humans in the Levantine Mousterian must move beyond simple characterization of the formal properties of the lithic and faunal evidence to examine the behavioral processes that create the archaeological record. When these are examined, most of the behavioral contrasts between anatomically archaic and anatomically modern humans will probably be not so much differences in the kinds of activities represented than variation in the relative frequencies of the same activities.

## REFERENCES

Anderson-Gerfaud, P.
1990   Aspects of behaviour in the Middle Palaeolithic: Functional analysis of stone tools from southwest France. In *The Emergence of Modern Humans: An Archaeological Perspective*. P. Mellars, ed. Pp. 389-418. Edinburgh: Edinburgh University Press.

Bar-Yosef, O.
1989   Upper Pleistocene cultural stratigraphy in southwest Asia. In *The Emergence of Modern Humans*. E. Trinkaus, ed. Pp. 154-180. Cambridge: Cambridge University Press.

Bleed, P.
1986   The optimal design of hunting weapons: Maintainability and reliability. *American Antiquity* 51:737-747.

Boëda, E.
1982   Etude experimentale de la technologie des pointes Levallois. *Studia Praehistorica Belgica* 2:23-56.

Copeland, L.
1975   The Middle and Upper Palaeolithic of Lebanon and Syria in the light of recent research. In *Problems in Prehistory: North Africa and the Levant*. F. Wendorf and A. Marks, eds. Pp. 239-263. Dallas: Southern Methodist University Press.
1981   Chronology and distribution of the Middle Paleolithic as known in 1980 in Lebanon and Syria. In *Préhistoire du Levant*. J. Cauvin and P. Sanlaville, eds. Pp. 239-263. Colloques Internationales du Centre National de Recherche Scientifique 598. Paris: Editions du Centre Nationale de Recherche Scientifique.

Deacon, T. D.
1989   The neural circuitry underlying primate calls and human language. *Human Evolution* 4:367-401.

Goodall, J.
1986   *The Chimpanzees of Gombe: Patterns of Behavior*. Cambridge: Harvard University Press.

Horowitz, A.
1989   The prehistoric cultures of Israel: Correlations with the oxygen-isotope scale. In *Investigations in South Levantine Prehistory/Préhistoire du Sud-Levant*. O. Bar-Yosef and B. Vandermeersch, eds. Pp. 5-18. BAR International Series 497. Oxford: British Archaeological Reports.

Jelinek, A. J.
1982   The Middle Paleolithic of the southern Levant, with comments on the appearance of modern *Homo sapiens*. In *The Transition from Lower to Middle Paleolithic and the Origin of Modern Man*. A. Ronen, ed. Pp. 57-104. BAR International Series 151. Oxford: British Archaeological Reports.

Keeley, L. H.
1980   *The Experimental Determination of Stone Tool Uses: A Microwear Analysis*. Chicago: University of Chicago Press.

Marks, A. E.
1983   The Middle to Upper Paleolithic transition in the Levant. In *Advances in World Archaeology. Volume 2*. F. Wendorf and A. Close, eds. Pp. 51-98. New York: Academic Press.
1992   Typological variability in the Levantine Middle Paleo-

ithic. In *The Middle Paleolithic: Adaptation, Behavior, and Variability*. H. Dibble and P. Mellars, eds. Pp. 127-142. University Museum Monograph 78. Philadelphia: The University Museum, University of Pennsylvania.

Meignen, L., and O. Bar-Yosef
1989    Nouvelles recherches sur le Paléolithique moyen d'Israël: La grotte de Kebara, unités VII à XII. In *Investigations in South Levantine Prehistory/Préhistoire du Sud-Levant*. O. Bar-Yosef and B. Vandermeersch, eds. Pp. 169-184. BAR International Series 497. Oxford: British Archaeological Reports.

Odell, G. H.
1980    Butchering with stone tools: Some experimental results. *Lithic Technology* 9:39-48.

Odell, G. H., and F. Cowan
1986    Experiments with spears and arrows on animal targets. *Journal of Field Archaeology* 13:195-212.

Shea, J. J.
1988    Spear points from the Middle Paleolithic of the Levant. *Journal of Field Archaeology* 15:441-450.
1991    *The Behavioral Significance of Levantine Mousterian Industrial Variability*. Ph.D. dissertation, Department of Anthropology, Harvard University. Ann Arbor: University Microfilms.

Stringer, C.
1989    Documenting the origin of modern humans. In *The Emergence of Modern Humans*. E. Trinkaus, ed. Pp. 67-96. Cambridge: Cambridge University Press.

Tchernov, E.
1989    The Middle Paleolithic mammalian sequence and its

bearing on the origin of *Homo sapiens* in the southern Levant. In *Investigations in South Levantine Prehistory/Préhistoire du Sud-Levant*. O. Bar-Yosef and B. Vandermeersch, eds. Pp. 25-42. BAR International Series 497. Oxford: British Archaeological Reports.

Tooby, J., and I. DeVore
1987    The reconstruction of hominid behavioral evolution through strategic modeling. In *Primate Models of Hominid Behavior*. W. Kinzey, ed. Pp. 183-237. New York: Plenum Press.

Trinkaus, E.
1986    The Neandertals and modern human origins. *Annual Review of Anthropology* 15:193-218.

Vandermeersch, B.
1989    The evolution of modern humans: Recent evidence from southwest Asia. In *The Human Revolution: Behavioural and Biological Perspectives on the Origins of Modern Humans*. P. Mellars and C. Stringer, eds. Pp. 155-164. Edinburgh: Edinburgh University Press.

White, J. C.
1977    *Stalking the Wild Legume: Pre-Agricultural Plant Exploitation Strategies in Palestine*. M.A. thesis, Department of Anthropology, University of Pennsylvania.

Wilmsen, E. N.
1989    *Land Filled with Flies: A Political Economy of the Kalahari*. Chicago: University of Chicago Press.

Wolpoff, M. H.
1989    The place of Neandertals in human evolution. In *The Emergence of Modern Humans*. E. Trinkaus, ed. Pp. 97-142. Cambridge: Cambridge University Press.

# 15

# *Zarzian Microliths from Warwasi Rockshelter, Iran: Scalene Triangles as Arrow Components*

## Deborah I. Olszewski
## University of Arizona

## ABSTRACT

The Zarzian Epipalaeolithic occupation at Warwasi yielded over 17,000 stone artifacts, with previous analyses resulting in a division of the Zarzian levels into four chronological units. Microliths comprise in excess of 35% of each of the unit assemblages, with geometric forms occurring in the top three units. The most common geometric is the scalene triangle (regular and elongated forms). A variety of metric and nonmetric attributes was recorded for various microlith forms. This paper discusses scalene triangles, elongated scalene triangles, and truncated bladelets. Truncated bladelets may represent unfinished or rejected attempts in the manufacture of the two scalene forms. Macroscopic examination failed to yield evidence of polish, suggesting that these microliths were not used to cut highly siliceous plants at Warwasi. Based on a comparison with attributes of Levantine lunate microliths, several preliminary hypotheses are offered regarding the manner in which scalene and elongated scalene triangles may have been hafted as arrow components.

## INTRODUCTION

Warwasi Rockshelter was tested in 1960 by Bruce Howe, as part of the Iranian Prehistoric Project (Braidwood et al. 1961) (Figure 15.1). The uppermost levels of the excavation yielded Zarzian Epipalaeolithic materials. These include Levels A through O, which were excavated in arbitrary levels of approximately 10 cm. The total depth of the Zarzian occupation was about 1.5 m, from modern ground surface to the uppermost of the Baradostian Upper Palaeolithic levels. The test unit was approximately 1 m x 8 m. About 12 m³ of sediments were removed.

The Zarzian lithic assemblage totaled 17,187 artifacts. Analyses by the author permitted the subdivision of the Zarzian levels into four chronological units. The distinctions between the units are based on changes in the relative frequencies of tool classes, the appearance of microburins, and changes within the microlith class. The most recent set of occupations is that of Levels A-D (Unit 4). Somewhat older are Levels E-G (Unit 3). Below these are the materials from Levels H-K (Unit 2). The oldest set of occupa-

tions is that of Levels L-O (Unit 1). Table 15.1 briefly summarizes the main lithic categories for each unit. Table 15.2 provides an overview of the tool classes by unit.

The Unit 1 Zarzian appears to have developed out of the Late Baradostian industry present at Warwasi (Olszewski 1993) and thus is probably later than 22,000 BP (Hole and Flannery 1967:153). The exact duration of the series of Zarzian occupations is difficult to ascertain in the absence of radiocarbon dates, although faunal evidence from the site and regional paleoclimatic studies suggest that repeated visits to Warwasi occurred sometime in the interval between 22,000 and 14,000 BP.

There are several chronological changes in the lithic assemblage. These include a shift in the microlith class from the dominance of inversely retouched bladelets (or "lamelles Dufour") in Unit 1 to the presence of scalene triangles in Units 2, 3, and 4--although various nongeometric forms are always the most common microliths. This change may parallel that observed by Garrod (1930:15) at Zarzi, where geometrics appeared in the upper levels. Other changes at Warwasi are the prevalence of curved microlith

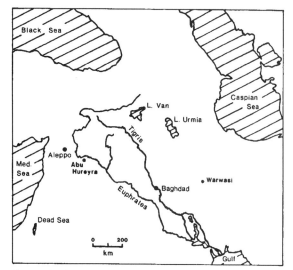

**Figure 15.1.** Location of sites mentioned in the text.

forms (microgravettes, curved backed bladelets, lunates) in Unit 3 and more varieties of geometric microliths in Unit 4.

## THE ZARZIAN AT WARWASI

The rockshelter at Warwasi is located above the Tang-i-knisht Valley and is a good location for observing game in the valley below. Paleoclimatic work (van Zeist and Bottema 1977, 1982) indicates a cool and dry regime during the Zarzian period--in fact, the harshest conditions of the late Pleistocene in the Zagros. Burrowing rodents, typical of cold, dry, and nonforested conditions, were identified in the Warwasi fauna (Turnbull 1975), lending further support to this climatic reconstruction.

The most parsimonious interpretation of the use of the rockshelter at Warwasi is that it functioned as a short-term campsite, where activities associated with locating game and initial processing of game occurred. This is suggested by several lines of evidence, including the rockshelter's ideal location as an overlook above the valley floor.

The fauna recovered can also be used to support an argument for a series of short-term occupations. Turnbull (1975) recorded *Equus hemionus* (onager), *Capra hircus aegagrus* (mountain goat), indeterminate *Capra/Ovis* (goat/sheep), *Sus scrofa* (wild boar), and *Hyaena* (hyena). Small rodents included *Meriones* cf. *persicus* (jird), *Ellobius* cf. *fuscocapillus* (mole vole), *Microtus* cf. *socialis* (social vole), *Ochotona* cf. *rufenscens* (pika), and *Lepus* cf. *capensis* (hare). The game animal sample from Warwasi is comprised mainly of teeth and a few leg and foot bones. Most of

these materials are extremely fragmentary. Based on the available fauna, Turnbull (1975:143-144) infers that the transport of most animal carcasses from the valley floor to the rockshelter was either impractical or that butchering and meat consumption occurred away from the rockshelter itself.

The presence of the teeth of game animals in the Zarzian sample may suggest that carcasses (or, at the very least, the heads) were transported to the rockshelter. There may have been further transport of various meat "packages" to other localities after initial butchering at Warwasi. The general absence of bone other than teeth could, however, simply reflect poor preservation conditions, so that it is possible that the inhabitants of Warwasi engaged in more extensive butchering activities than are apparent from the existing data.

Finally, the absence of hearths or other cultural features in the Zarzian levels may also indicate a somewhat limited or temporary use of the rockshelter.

## SCALENE TRIANGLES AND TRUNCATED BLADELETS

Although the Zarzian levels from Warwasi can be grouped into four different units, the oldest set of occupations from Unit 1 is not considered in this analysis because scalene triangles, except for probable intrusives, are not present in this unit. To obtain a numerically acceptable sample of the complete scalene triangles and truncated bladelets, it was necessary to collapse Units 2, 3, and 4 into one analytical unit. While this ignores overall changes in the lithic assemblages from the three units, the apparent lack of metric and nonmetric differences within each of the microlith types through time would seem to obviate this potential problem.

Within the geometric class of microliths, scalene and elongated scalene triangles are the most common type, comprising anywhere from 59.3% (Unit 4) to 95.9% (Unit 2) of this category. The majority of these are quite small and narrow (Figure 15.2).

**Table 15.1.** Zarzian lithics from Warwasi, summarized by units.

| Category | Units | | | | |
| | 1 | 2 | 3 | 4 | Sum |
|---|---|---|---|---|---|
| Tools | 574 | 878 | 784 | 1227 | 3463 |
| Hammerstones | - | - | 1 | - | 1 |
| Microburins | - | 22 | 38 | 36 | 96 |
| Cores | 265 | 212 | 91 | 113 | 681 |
| Debitage | 4032 | 5011 | 2381 | 1522 | 12946 |
| TOTAL | 4871 | 6123 | 3295 | 2898 | 17187 |

**Table 15.2.** Zarzian tools from Warwasi, by units.

| Class | Unit 1 | | Unit 2 | | Unit 3 | | Unit 4 | |
|---|---|---|---|---|---|---|---|---|
| | N | % | N | % | N | % | N | % |
| Scrapers | 70 | 12.2 | 119 | 13.6 | 46 | 5.8 | 33 | 27 |
| Burins | 17 | 2.9 | 27 | 3.1 | 19 | 2.4 | 3 | 02 |
| Borers | - | - | 11 | 1.2 | 20 | 2.5 | 68 | 55 |
| Backed Pieces | 16 | 2.8 | 35 | 3.9 | 8 | 1.0 | 11 | 09 |
| Truncations | 12 | 2.1 | 32 | 3.5 | 9 | 1.1 | 26 | 21 |
| Notches/Denticulates | 163 | 28.4 | 150 | 17.1 | 203 | 25.8 | 352 | 287 |
| Multiple Tools | 1 | 0.2 | 7 | 0.8 | 15 | 1.9 | 18 | 15 |
| Special Tools | 17 | 2.9 | 33 | 3.8 | 13 | 1.6 | 16 | 13 |
| Retouched Pieces | 60 | 10.4 | 116 | 13.2 | 89 | 11.5 | 155 | 126 |
| Truncated Bladelets | 8 | 1.3 | 32 | 3.6 | 37 | 4.7 | 73 | 59 |
| Other Nongeometrics | 202 | 35.2 | 216 | 24.6 | 266 | 33.9 | 377 | 307 |
| Scalenes | 1 | 0.2 | 23 | 2.6 | 21 | 2.7 | 18 | 15 |
| Elongated Scalenes | 6 | 1.0 | 70 | 7.9 | 31 | 3.9 | 36 | 29 |
| Other Geometrics | 1 | 0.2 | 4 | 0.5 | 7 | 0.9 | 37 | 30 |
| Varia | - | - | 3 | 0.3 | - | - | 4 | 03 |
| TOTAL | 574 | | 878 | | 784 | | 1227 | |

The probable manufacturing process for both types of scalene triangles suggests that truncated bladelets, a type of nongeometric microlith, may be related to the manufacture of scalenes within the Zarzian assemblages at Warwasi. Both types of scalenes are characterized by two converging truncated edges. Since a scalene triangle is defined by three edges of unequal length, one of these three edges is quite short. A truncated bladelet, which invariably has a short truncated edge, may then be seen as representing an early stage of modification of a bladelet into one of the types of scalene triangles. The retouched or truncated edge, since it is the shortest segment, may thus represent the least amount of effort expended in reshaping the bladelet by retouch. At this point, the prehistoric knapper decides whether the piece should be (1) modified further by truncating a second edge, therefore becoming a(n) (elongated) scalene triangle or (2) discarded, thereby remaining a truncated bladelet.

Table 15.3 lists the means and standard deviations for length, width, and thickness of scalenes, elongated scalenes, and truncated bladelets. A comparison of the means for each attribute for scalenes and elongated scalenes, and between each of these triangle types and the truncated bladelets, results in a significant difference at the $\alpha = .05$ level for all comparisons--with the exception of the thickness category for scalenes vs. elongated scalenes (t-Test; see Mendenhall and Ott 1972). The differences between the triangle and the truncated bladelet populations may reflect the termination of the manufacturing process after the production of one truncated edge, based on some combination of the features of width and thickness. Length is less likely to have been a critical variable, given that both scalene and elongated scalene triangles were produced.

Examination of the tips and the non-backed edge of the scalenes revealed the frequent presence of a finely abrupt retouch. This retouch can occur at either of the two tips, at both tips simultaneously, or along the entire non-backed edge. Table 15.3 shows the high percentage of complete scalenes with these modifications. Truncated bladelets also exhibit high frequencies of finely abrupt retouch in similar locations. It is technically possible that this "retouch" is related to bladelet segmentation prior to the production of truncated edges, perhaps in a manner analogous to the Krukowski microburin technique[1] (Brézillon 1968:129-130). If this is the case, it would help establish truncated bladelets as one stage in the manufacture of scalenes.

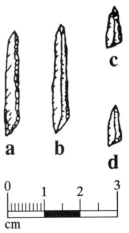

**Figure 15.2.** Zarzian triangles from Warwasi: elongated scalenes (a,b) and scalene triangles (c,d).

**Table 15.3.** Average metric measurements for selected Zarzian microliths. **Key:** L = length; W = width; T = thickness; RT = retouch of the nontruncated edge; N = sample of complete microliths measured; All N = total sample of complete and broken microliths; s.d. is standard deviation. All measurements in mm.

| Type | L | W | T | RT | N | All N |
|---|---|---|---|---|---|---|
| Scalene | 14.8 | 4.7 | 1.7 | 87% | 31 | 62 |
| (s.d.) | 3.1 | 1.1 | 0.4 | | | |
| Elongated | | | | | | |
| Scalene | 21.7 | 5.4 | 1.9 | 73% | 48 | 137 |
| (s.d.) | 3.5 | 1.0 | 0.5 | | | |
| Truncated | | | | | | |
| Bladelet | 19.5 | 7.4 | 2.4 | 71% | 49 | 151 |
| (s.d.) | 4.8 | 1.4 | 0.8 | | | |

Further support of this premise comes from an examination of the frequency of such truncations through time. In Unit 1, where scalenes and elongated scalenes are probably intrusive, truncations comprise a very low percentage of the nongeometric class (3.8%). They may also be intrusive. However, with the marked presence of scalene forms in Unit 2, and with their continuation into the later Units 3 and 4, truncations now comprise a moderate percentage of the nongeometric microlith class (14.5% in Unit 2, 12.5% in Unit 3, 17.1% in Unit 4). A parsimonious explanation would view truncations as a stage or stages in the reduction process associated with the two types of scalene triangles.

## SCALENE TRIANGLES AS ARROW ELEMENTS

The macroscopic analysis of the scalene triangles from Warwasi included a variety of nonmetric attribute observations. None of the scalenes examined, whether broken or complete, exhibited traces of polish. Although the formation of plant polish depends in part on the length of time a stone tool is utilized to cut plants containing silica and on the types of plants themselves (see Unger-Hamiliton 1983:245-247, 1989: 95), it is unlikely that the scalenes from Warwasi were used as elements of plant processing equipment. Existing paleoenvironmental data (van Zeist and Bottema 1977, 1982) suggest that the Zagros region was cool and dry prior to 14,000 BP. Potential plant foods such as the siliceous cereal grasses would not be abundant under these conditions, if indeed they were present at all.

Both types of scalene triangles were also examined for the presence of minute burin-like scars along the non-backed edge at both extremities. These types of scars are sometimes representative of breakage patterns that occur when an arrow tip impacts animal bone after penetrating the hide and soft tissues; this type of damage has been reported in the context of experimental archaeology (Bergman and Newcomer 1983; Shea, this volume). However, none of the complete scalenes produced evidence of this type of breakage. In addition, there are no traces of the mastic which may have been used to "set" these scalenes, possibly because of poor preservation conditions for the mastic, original cleaning procedures used on scalenes during field excavations in 1960, or hafting techniques that did not require the use of mastic.

Numerous archaeological and ethnographic sources describe the hafting of microliths (for example, Becker 1945:70; Clark et al. 1974; Deacon 1984:316; Larsson 1983:47-50; Leroi-Gourhan 1983: 155; Müller 1917:149; Odell 1978:46; Vayson de Pradenne 1936:219,221,226,229). The reconstructions shown in Figure 15.3 place an actual scalene and an elongated scalene triangle from Warwasi in tip and barb positions, as suggested by both archaeological and ethnographic evidence. I think it least likely that the Warwasi scalenes were hafted as transverse arrowheads or diagonal arrowtips (as in Figure 15.3 b,d,h,i) because both their form and their relative narrowness might be somewhat unsuitable for these techniques.

## COMPARISON WITH LEVANTINE LUNATES

Microliths were used in composite plant harvesting tools, as attested by the well-known sickle with microlithic bladelets still in place from the Natufian Epipalaeolithic level at el-Wad in Palestine (Garrod and Bate 1937:37). This example, however, does not have sickle polish nor do the bladelets appear to be backed. Much of the microwear research on various Levantine microliths seems to indicate their utilization as arrow elements; this is particularly true for the lunate form (Anderson-Gerfaud 1983; Büller 1983).

Microwear analyses of lunates have demonstrated meat polish (Büller 1983:110-111), as well as striations, microdamage, and polish location/features suggesting that they were hafted both as transverse arrowheads and as barbs (Anderson-Gerfaud 1983:81-84). My examination of the complete lunates (N = 319) from the late Epipalaeolithic (Natufian period) settlement at Abu Hureyra 1, northern Syria, revealed that 15.3% have burin-like scars at one of the tips (Olszewski n.d.). Based on experimental work by Bergman and Newcomer (1983), I think that some of the lunates at Abu Hureyra 1 were hafted so that one of the tips served as the arrowhead. The 50 lunates with this damage pattern, with one exception, have average lengths of at least 18 mm. In addition, Anderson-Gerfaud's (1983:84) work on lunates from Abu Hureyra 1 and from Mureybat (late Epipalaeolithic materials) indicates that longer lunates were hafted as transverse arrowheads, while shorter lunates functioned as barbs.

Some aspects of these data regarding lunate use may help clarify the use of scalene triangles as arrow components in the Zarzian assemblages from Warwasi. The average length of Warwasi scalene triangles falls near the average length for smaller lunates; the average width is also comparable. For example, lunates at el-Wad B1 have a length of 15.1 mm and a width of 4.9 mm, while those from Nahal Oren VI are 15.6 mm in average length and 4.5 mm in average width (Valla 1987:292). The overall similarity in these metric attributes might indicate that scalene triangles were more likely to serve as barbs than to function as arrowheads. Elongated scalene triangles from Warwasi, on the other hand, are similar in average length to collections of longer lunates from the Levant--for example, Kebara B with an average length of 23.4 mm, Mallaha IVa with an average length of 22.3 mm, and Oumm Qalaa with an average length of 21.7 mm (Valla 1987:292)--which suggests that the elongated scalenes may have been hafted transversely or with one tip of the triangle serving as the arrowtip.

While both of the above-mentioned styles of arrows may have been manufactured at Warwasi with elongated scalene triangles, I think it most likely that these geometrics were used with one tip of the triangle as the arrowtip (for example, Figure 15.3e,f). While the lack of burin-like scars at the tips of elongated scalene triangles might seem to argue against this style of placement, the formation of such impact fractures is not always a regular occurrence (see Shea, this volume).

Moreover, a comparison of the form of elongated scalene triangles with lunates suggests another potential argument against the transverse style arrowhead for the Warwasi elongated scalenes--width. Lunates which are comparable in average length to the Warwasi elongated scalene triangles generally have average width measurements of between 7 mm and 9 mm (Valla 1987:292). Thus, lunates are much wider for their length than the elongated scalene triangles from Warwasi, which average only 5.4 mm. The somewhat wider lunate, then, may be more amenable to hafting as a transverse arrowhead, since there is more surface to either fit into a slot or to be placed within mastic.

Finally, if truncated bladelets are an early stage in the manufacture of scalenes, then the average width of truncated bladelets also favors the arrowtip style of arrowhead for the Zarzian at Warwasi. Truncated bladelets are relatively wide for their length, averaging 7.4 mm. They are thus most similar to Levantine lunates in this respect. The fact that they may be

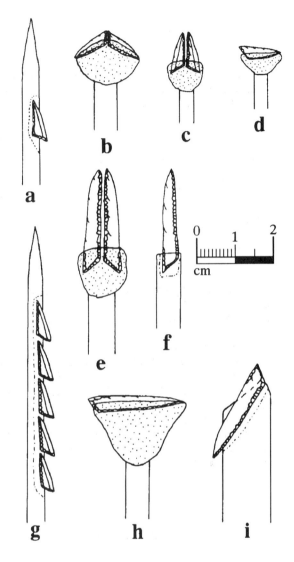

**Figure 15.3.** Warwasi scalene and elongated scalene triangles hypothetically hafted using techniques known from archaeological assemblages from Mesolithic Europe and from ethnographic contexts in Africa (Basarwa). Cf. Becker 1945:70 (a); Deacon 1984:316 (b); Vayson de Pradenne 1936:229 (c-f,h); Müller 1917:149 (d,h); Larsson 1983:47-50 (g); and hypothetical from Odell 1978:46 (i).

unfinished scalenes might suggest that "wide" scalenes were not the desired end product. If relative width is correlated with preferences in non-transverse arrowhead styles, then the fact that "wide" truncated bladelets are discarded before becoming scalenes indicates that elongated scalene triangles at Warwasi were infrequently hafted as transverse arrowheads.

## CONCLUSION

The Zarzian occupations at Warwasi Rockshelter, Iran, yielded tool assemblages in which microliths are the dominant component. Unit 1 is the oldest of the assemblages, and the existing geometrics are probably intrusive. Units 2, 3, and 4 are characterized by the presence of geometric microliths, primarily scalene and elongated scalene triangles. The manufacture of scalenes may have involved truncating selected bladelets to form the two "backed" edges of the triangle. Thus, the presence of truncated bladelets (a type in the nongeometric microlith class) may be representative of unfinished scalenes; that is, they are indicative of an early stage of the reduction process necessary to manufacture scalenes.

Based on several lines of evidence, I suggest that scalene and elongated scalene triangles functioned as components of arrows at Warwasi. The rockshelter is ideally situated to overlook game in the valley below and would have served as an ideal hunting, and possibly butchering, station. Environmental reconstructions indicate that the Zarzian occupation of the Zagros mountains occurred during a particularly harsh period, when conditions were quite cool and dry, between 22,000 and 14,000 BP. The microfauna recovered from Warwasi support this reconstruction of a nonforest cover during a cool and arid period. Edible plants requiring harvesting with stone tools, especially the cereal grasses, are unlikely to have been present in the region under these ecological conditions. Lack of macroscopic polish on scalenes also suggests that they were infrequently utilized for plant processing activities.

I propose that, at Warwasi, scalene triangles most likely functioned as arrow barbs (see Figure 15.3a,g), while elongated scalene triangles were more likely to be hafted with one of the triangle tips serving as an arrowtip (see Figure 15.3e,f). Although some of these conclusions are conjectural, they are based on metric attributes such as length, width, and thickness; comparisons of both types of scalenes from Warwasi with comparably sized lunate geometric microliths from the Levantine Epipalaeolithic; and information derived from microwear studies of lunates. Unfortunately, the moderate size of the Warwasi scalene sample, the absence of visible remaining mastic, and the fact that these scalenes have not been microscopically examined prevent more definitive conclusions at this time. The arguments presented above, however, do serve as a reasonable preliminary reconstruction for the use of scalenes and for the style of arrow employed at Warwasi rockshelter during the Zarzian Epipalaeolithic.

## ACKNOWLEDGEMENTS

The complete Warwasi Rockshelter lithics collection (Levels A through CCC) is on permanent loan to the University Museum, the University of Pennsylvania, Philadelphia, PA. Some of the research on the lithics collection from Abu Hureyra 1 was made possible by funding from the Fulbright Program, Sigma Xi Grants-in-Aid-of-Research, the Graduate Development Fund at the University of Arizona, and the Education Fund of the Department of Anthropology at the University of Arizona.

## NOTES

[1]The Krukowski microburin technique is characterized by retouching a bladelet along one lateral edge; this retouch replaces the notch technique used in true microburins. Pressure is applied to the retouched edge, resulting in a snap or segmentation of the bladelet. At least one, if not both, segment(s) can be modified into scalene triangles. In the case of Warwasi, the finely abrupt retouched edge might have been the original retouched and snapped lateral edge.

## REFERENCES

Anderson-Gerfaud, P.
   1983    A consideration of the uses of certain backed and 'lustred' stone tools from the late Mesolithic and Natufian levels of Abu Hureyra and Mureybat (Syria). In *Traces d'utilisation sur les outils néolithiques du Proche Orient*. M. C. Cauvin, ed. Pp. 77-105. Lyon: Maison de l'Orient.

Becker, C. F.
   1945    En 8000-Aarig Stenalderboplads i Holmegaards Mose. *Fra National-museets Arbejdsmark* 1945:61-72.

Bergman, C., and M. Newcomer
   1983    Flint arrowhead breakage: Examples from Ksar Akil, Lebanon. *Journal of Field Archaeology* 10:238-243.

Braidwood, R., B. Howe, and C. A. Reed
   1961    The Iranian prehistoric project. *Science* 133:2008-2010.

Brézillon, M. N.
   1968    *La dènomination des objects de pierre taillée: Matériaux pour un vocabulaire des préhistoriens de langue française.* Supplément à *Gallia Préhistoire* 4. Paris: Editions du Centre National de Recherche Scientifique.

Büller, H.
   1983    Methodological problems in the microwear analysis of tools selected from the Natufian sites of el-Wad and Ain Mallaha. In *Traces d'utilisation sur les outils néolithiques du Proche Orient*. M. C. Cauvin, ed. Pp. 107-125. Lyon: Maison de l'Orient.

Clark, J. D., J. L. Phillips, and P. S. Staley
   1974    Interpretations of prehistoric technology from ancient Egyptian and other sources. Part 1: Ancient Egyptian bows and arrows and their relevance for African prehistory. *Paléorient* 2:323-388.

Deacon, J.
   1984    Later stone age people and their descendants in Southern Africa. In *Southern African Prehistory and Paleoenvironments*. R. Klein, ed. Pp. 221-328. Boston: A.A. Balkema.

Garrod, D. A. E., and D. M. A. Bate
  1937   *The Stone Age of Mount Carmel. Volume 1.* Oxford: Clarendon Press.
Hole, F., and K. Flannery
  1967   The prehistory of southwestern Iran: A preliminary report. *Proceedings of the Prehistoric Society* 33:147-206.
Larsson, L.
  1983   *Ageröd V: An Atlantic Bog Site in Central Scania.* Acta Archaeological Lundensia Number 12. Lund: C. W. K. Gleerups.
Leroi-Gourhan, A.
  1983   Une tête de sagaie à armature de lamelles de silex à Pincevent (Seine-et-Marne). *Bulletin de la Société Préhistorique Française* 80:154-156.
Mendenhall, W., and L. Ott
  1972   *Understanding Statistics.* Belmont: Duxbury Press.
Müller, S.
  1917   Archaeologisk Udbytte af Mosearbeidet i Krigsaaret. *Aarböger* 1917:148-174.
Odell, G. H.
  1978   Préliminaires d'une analyse fonctionnelle des pointes microlithiques de Bergumermeer (Pays-Bas). *Bulletin de la Sociétié Préhistorique Française* 75:37-49.
Olszewski, D. I.
  1993   The Zarzian occupation at Warwasi rockshelter, Iran. In *The Paleolithic Prehistory of the Zagros-Taurus.* D. I. Olszewski and H. L. Dibble, eds. Pp. 206-236. Philadelphia: University Museum Press.
  n.d.    The chipped stone from Abu Hureyra 1. In *Abu Hureyra and the Advent of Agriculture.* A. M. T. Moore, A. Legge, and G. C. Hillman, eds. New Haven: Yale University Press. (in press).

Turnbull, P.
  1975   The mammalian fauna of Warwasi rockshelter, west-central Iran. *Fieldiana Geology* 33(8):141-155.
Unger-Hamilton, R.
  1983   An investigation into the variables affecting the development and the appearance of plant polish on flint blades. In *Traces d'utilisation sur les outils néolithiques du Proche Orient.* M. C. Cauvin, ed. Pp. 243-250. Lyon: Maison de l'Orient.
  1989   The Epi-Palaeolithic southern Levant and the origins of cultivation. *Current Anthropology* 30:88-103.
Valla, F.
  1987   Chronologie absolue et chronologie relative dans le Natoufien. In *Chronologies in the Near East.* O. Aurenche, J. Evin, and F. Hours, eds. Pp. 267-294. BAR International Series 379. Oxford: British Archaeological Reports.
van Zeist, W., and S. Bottema
  1977   Palynological investigations in western Iran. *Palaeohistoria* 19:19-85.
  1982   Vegetational history of the eastern Mediterranean and the Near East during the last 20,000 years. In *Paleoenvironments and Human Communities in the Eastern Mediterranean Region in Later Prehistory.* J. L. Bintliff and W. van Zeist, eds. Pp. 277-321. BAR International Series 133. Oxford: British Archaeological Reports.
Vayson de Pradenne, A.
  1936   Sur l'utilisation de certains microliths géometriques. *Bulletin de la Sociétié Préhistorique Française* 33:217-232.
Vignard, E.
  1935   Armatures de fléches en silex. *L'Anthropologie* 45:85-92.

# 16

# Variability in Hunter-Gatherer Seasonal Mobility in the Southern Levant: From the Mousterian to the Natufian

Daniel E. Lieberman
Harvard University

## ABSTRACT

Evidence for the season of occupation of several deeply stratified cave sites from the Levant demonstrate that there have been major changes in hunter-gatherer mobility patterns between the Middle Palaeolithic and the Natufian. Models of hunter-gatherer mobility and resource acquisition strategies based on the current distribution of plant, animal, and technological resources in the southern Levant are tested using seasonal data on gazelle exploitation derived from cementum increment analysis. The strategy of seasonal mobility from habitat to habitat appears to be a quintessential behavior for modern human hunter-gatherers throughout the Middle and Upper Palaeolithic and until the end of the Epipalaeolithic. This pattern contrasts with the less mobile strategy associated with archaic humans.

## INTRODUCTION

Ethnographic studies demonstrate that seasonal migration from habitat to habitat is an important strategy employed by almost all hunter-gatherers to cope with changes in the temporal and spatial distribution of critical resources (Kelly 1983). But when did the modern human pattern of high seasonal mobility become established, and how did it change? It is particularly interesting to examine the evolution of hunter-gatherer mobility strategies in the Levant. Because it forms a small, environmentally diverse corridor between Africa and Eurasia, the Levant has been occupied by hominids for roughly 1.5 million years. Until recently, however, there have been almost no data on the season of occupation of most Palaeolithic archaeological sites in this region. Archaeologists have been forced to rely on general models of mobility strategies, and there has been little success examining variability in hunter-gatherer mobility in the archaeological record of the Levant.

This study examines the season of occupation of five deeply stratified cave sites from northern Israel--Qafzeh, el-Wad, Tabun, Kebara, and Hayonim--to test whether ancient hunter-gatherers used the Levantine landscape differently over the course of the Late Pleistocene. These five caves are the focus of this study because they are among the few sites from the southern Levant with archaeological remains that span much of the Late Pleistocene and that contain enough

fauna for analysis of seasonality. There are two major reasons why determining their season of occupation is important. First, both anatomically modern and archaic *Homo sapiens* are associated with Levantine Mousterian industries in these sites: modern human fossils have been uncovered at Qafzeh and perhaps Tabun, and archaic human fossils have been uncovered at Tabun and Kebara. Despite their morphological differences, there has been little available evidence for any behavioral differences between these taxa in the archaeological record (Clark and Lindly 1989). Second, the high environmental diversity of the region suggests that a variety of resource acquisition strategies could have been used at any time. These sites provide a heuristic test of diachronic changes in the seasonal pattern of hunting and site occupation.

Evidence for the seasonal hunting of gazelle and other prey species is derived principally from the study of cementum bands in teeth, which is described below. The results of these analyses demonstrate considerable diversity in mobility patterns over time, so that no single model can explain the variability in the seasonal use of these sites during the Late Pleistocene. However, several patterns of seasonal site use do emerge. With the exception of the Natufian period just prior to the origins of agriculture, modern human hunter-gatherers used most environments on a highly seasonal basis. Almost every site was occupied for just a single season, and changes in the season of occupation of sites are best explained by local and regional

## Schematic Topographic Cross-Section of the Southern Levant

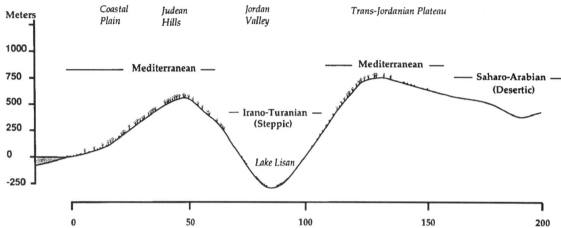

**Figure 16.1.** Idealized topographic transect across the southern Levant, showing relationships between geographical and environmental zones.

paleoenvironmental conditions. In contrast, archaic humans appear to have been less seasonally mobile than modern humans--a behavioral difference with interesting implications that are discussed in the conclusion. The only other period in which sites were occupied on a multiseasonal basis was during the Natufian, which dates to between 12,800 and 10,300 BP (Bar-Yosef and Belfer-Cohen 1989).

## BACKGROUND

### Assessing Variability in Ancient Mobility Patterns

Modeling mobility patterns in the southern Levant is complicated because the small size and varied topography of the region suggest that hunter gatherers could have adopted diverse strategies during any given period to acquire sufficient resources. The Levant has five major environmental zones (Horowitz 1979; Zohary 1962) that provide hunter-gatherers with a transect of habitats, all within a several-day walk (see Figure 16.1): (1) the Mediterranean coastal plain, which has varied in size with sea-level changes; (2) the forested Mediterranean hills; (3) the steppic Irano-Turanian zone in the Jordan valley; (4) the forested hills of the Transjordanian Plateau; and (5) the desertic Saharo-Arabian vegetational zone that surrounds the region to the south and east. How were these environmental zones used on a seasonal basis, and how did hunter-gatherer strategies change over time in the southern Levant?

Typically, hunter-gatherer mobility and resource acquisition models are proposed using assumptions of optimality and then "tested" by examining whether the

available archaeological data conform to the model. In the southern Levant, researchers have attempted to relate the known distribution of archaeological sites to the region's geography using either models of transhumance based on the movements of modern Bedouin (e.g., Vita-Finzi and Higgs 1970; Henry 1983, 1989; Bar-Yosef 1987) or using models of circulating versus residential mobility, based on Mortenson's (1972) distinction between villagers and hunter-gatherers and Binford's (1980) dichotomy between collectors and foragers (e.g., Marks and Friedel 1977; Coinman et al. 1986). Such a methodology can be problematic when there is a paucity of data, resulting in the likelihood of accepting a false null hypothesis because of insufficient evidence to reject it (Foley 1983). A different approach is preferable for estimating and testing ancient hunter-gatherer mobility strategies. First, we need to consider the full universe of possible strategies and then eliminate those that were either unlikely for environmental reasons or are refutable on the basis of archaeological data.

This study assumes that hunter-gatherers could have occupied a given site in **any** environmental zone during **any** season. Assuming that one can make some generalizations about mobility patterns within archaeologically discernible regions and time periods (Cross 1989), it is necessary to (1) determine the spatial distribution of sites within well-defined time periods; (2) assess the paleoenvironmental context of these sites from paleoclimatic, geological, and archaeological data; (3) determine the seasons during which sites were occupied; and (4) relate the seasonal use of environments with other archaeological data, such as the extractive and productive activities evident at particular sites. Before presenting data on site seasonality, I will discuss briefly the geographical, chronological, and paleoenvironmental context of the sites analyzed in this study.

## Temporal and Spatial Distribution

Tabun, el-Wad, Kebara, Hayonim, and Qafzeh caves (see Figure 16.2) provide the longest, well-studied sequence in the region from which to estimate site seasonality from the Middle Palaeolithic through the Epipalaeolithic. These sites are located in a limited area and from several contiguous environmental zones and thus yield data with considerable heuristic potential for examining how mobility is tested in the archaeological record. Moreover, several of these caves (Kebara, Tabun, and Qafzeh) contain the remains of either anatomically modern or archaic *Homo* in Mousterian levels.

Tabun and el-Wad, located four km from the present coast at the Wadi Mughara, were originally excavated by Dorothy Garrod in the 1930s (Garrod and Bate 1937); Tabun was recently re-excavated by Jelinek (1982). Located on the boundary between Mt. Carmel and the coastal plain, these caves were situated on the ecotone between the Mediterranean oak forest and the more open marsh and Mediterranean vegetation of the coastal plain (Vita-Finzi and Higgs 1970). These caves offered hunter-gatherers proximity to several environmental zones, as well as to the high concentration of game likely to have been found in the wadi.

The Tabun sequence extends from the final Acheulian (Levels G and F) through the Acheulo-Yabrudian (Level E) and the Mousterian (Levels D, C, and B). In this study, samples were analyzed from Tabun Ea (Amudian) through Tabun B. Levels D, C, and B are characterized by different industrial variants of the Levantine Mousterian (Jelinek 1982; Meignen and Bar-Yosef 1989). Recently published radiometric dates of these levels (Grün and Stringer 1991) indicate that they are older than originally supposed (see Table 16.1): Tabun B is now estimated to date to Oxygen Isotope Stage (OIS) 4 and/or late OIS 5; Tabun C is dated to between early OIS 5 and/or late OIS 6; and Tabun D is dated to OIS 6 or possibly OIS 7. The partial skeleton of an archaic *Homo sapiens* female was recovered from either Level B or C, and a mandible of questionable taxonomic affinity was found in Level C (Garrod and Bate 1937; McCown and Keith 1939).

The fauna from Tabun Cave is similar to that from other sites in the Mt. Carmel region. Levels Ea through B are dominated by *Gazella gazella* and *Dama mesopotamica*, with gazelle comprising between 50% and 80% of the fauna in Levels D and C (Garrod and Bate 1937; Davis 1982; Garrard 1982). A number of other medium- to large-sized mammals are present

in smaller quantities in most levels, including *Cervus elaphus*, *Capra* sp., *Bos primigenius*, *Equus* spp., *Sus* spp., *Capreolus capreolus*, *Hyaena* spp., *Vulpes* spp., and *Canis* spp.

El-Wad cave, 70 m north of Tabun, contains industries from the Mousterian (Levels G and F), the early and late Upper Palaeolithic (Levels E-C), and the Natufian (Level B). The Natufian at el-Wad is divided into late (B1) and early (B2) levels that are dated to ca. 9800 BP and 12,800 BP, respectively. The fauna from el-Wad were studied by Bate (1937) and Garrard (1980, 1982). *G. gazella* is the predominant species in Levels B-D. Also present at el-Wad are small numbers of *S. scrofa*, *Bos* sp., *C. elephus*, *C. capreolus*, *Equus* spp., and *Capra* sp. Only samples from Levels D through B₂ were selected from the few fauna that remain from Garrod's excavations.

Kebara Cave, three km from the present shore and 13 km south of the Wadi Mughara, is located on the ecotone between the Mt. Carmel uplands and the more open coastal plain. Excavations of the cave were first undertaken by Turville-Petre (1932) and then by Stekelis in the 1960's (Schick and Stekelis 1977). Recent excavations (1982-1990) at Kebara Cave have

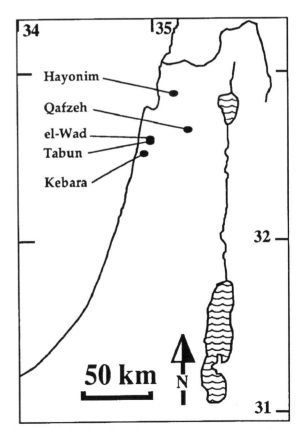

**Figure 16.2.** Map of southern Levant with locations of sites analyzed in this study.

**Table 16.1.** Results of cementum increment analysis with associated dates and climatic phases.

| Site/Level | Age (ka) | Cultural Period | Sample | Estimated Season | % F/W | % Sp/Sm | Climate |
|---|---|---|---|---|---|---|---|
| Hayonim B | 12 | E. Natufian | 15 | Year round | 55 | 45 | Warm & dry |
| Hayonim C | 17-14 | Kebaran | 8 | Winter | 100 | 0 | Cold & dry |
| Hayonim D | 27-29 | Aurignacian | 12 | Fall/Winter | 100 | 0 | Cold & wet |
| Hayonim E | ? | Mousterian | 8 | Fall | 20 | 80 | ? |
| Kebara B | 12-10 | Natufian | 12 | Year round | 42 | 58 | Warm & dry |
| Kebara C | 14-20 | Kebaran | 12 | Fall/Winter | 83 | 17 | Cold & dry |
| Kebara UP | 27-34 | Aurignacian | 21 | Spring | 0 | 100 | Cold & wet |
| Kebara MP | 48-65 | Mousterian (Tb) | 30 | Year round | 52 | 48 | Cold & dry |
| Tabun B | 60-80 | Mousterian (Tb) | 12 | Year round | 50 | 50 | Cold & dry |
| Tabun C | 80-130 | Mousterian (Tc) | 10 | Winter | 90 | 10 | Cold & wet |
| Tabun D | >130 | Mousterian (Td) | 10 | Winter | 100 | 0 | ? |
| Tabun Ea | ? | Amudian | 8 | Winter | 100 | 0 | ? |
| El Wad B | 9.8-12 | Natufian | 15 | Year round | 60 | 40 | Warm & dry |
| El Wad C | =20-25 | Late UP | 15 | Spring | 0 | 100 | Cold & wet |
| El Wad D | 30-27 | Aurignacian | 12 | Fall/Winter | 100 | 0 | Cold & wet |
| Qafzeh XVI-XXII[1] | 92-115 | Mousterian (Tc) | 14 | Spring/Summer | 8 | 92 | Cold & wet |

[1]Qafzeh sample includes *Capra* and *Dama* in addition to *Gazella*. **Key:** F/W = Fall/Winter; Sp/Sm = Spring/Summer.

been conducted by Bar-Yosef et al. (1992). Kebara contains approximately 5 m of a Tabun B-type Mousterian industry (Units XII-VII) overlain by mixed (Units VI-IV), Upper Palaeolithic (Units III-I), Kebaran (Level C), and Natufian (Level B) levels. Thermoluminescence (TL) and electron spin resonance (ESR) assays date the Kebaran Mousterian to ca. 48,000-65,000 BP and the Upper Palaeolithic (Unit VI) to between 44,000-54,000 BP (Valladas et al. 1987, 1988) A nearly complete burial of an adult archaic *Homo* from Unit XII is dated to approximately 62,000 BP (Valladas et al. 1988). The faunal remains from the site, which have been only partially studied, are dominated by *G. gazella*, although there are also large numbers of *D. mesopotamica* as well as smaller numbers of *C. capreolus*, *C. elaphus*, *S. scrofa*, *Alcephalus* sp., *Bos primigenius*, and *Equus* spp. (Saxon 1974; Davis 1977; Bar Yosef et al. 1992). Gazelle constitute at least 75% of the bones in all levels, with the exception of the Upper Palaeolithic, where they are about 63%. Speth's taphonomic analysis of the fauna from the Mousterian and Upper Palaeolithic levels indicates that most of the bones were introduced into the cave by humans, but that some were subsequently modified by hyenas (Bar Yosef et al. 1992). The paleoenvironment around Kebara was essentially the same as the Wadi Mughara.

Hayonim Cave, located 20 km north of the Wadi Mughara in the oak-forested hills 13 km from the present-day coast and 250 m above sea-level, was excavated by Bar-Yosef, Tchernov, and Arensburg

(Bar-Yosef and Tchernov 1966). Hayonim Cave contains deposits from the Mousterian (Level E); the Aurignacian (Level D); the Kebaran (Level C), which is generally dated to between ca. 17,000 and 14,000 BP; and the Natufian (Level B), dated to ca. 12,000 BP (Bar-Yosef 1991). Faunal and lithic correlations tentatively suggest that the Mousterian and Aurignacian levels probably date to OIS 5 and the end of OIS 3, respectively (Bar-Yosef 1992a). The fauna from Hayonim have not been studied completely for all the levels, but it is clear that gazelle is the most abundant mammal throughout the sequence, accounting for approximately 80% of the remains in Level B, at least 60% in Level C, 89% in Level D, and 86% in Level E; *D. mesopotamica* is present in small numbers in most levels (Davis 1982; Bar-Yosef 1983). The seasons of occupation of the Epipalaeolithic levels at Hayonim Cave have been independently estimated using various kinds of faunal data by Tchernov (1984), Davis (1983), Pichon (1987), and Lieberman (1991).

Qafzeh Cave, 35 km from the present-day coast and 220 m above sea level, was recently excavated by Vandermeersch (1981). Qafzeh is particularly important because of the remains of several early anatomically modern *Homo sapiens* that were excavated from Levels XVI-XXIII. Although the interior of Qafzeh contains numerous artifacts and faunal remains embedded in fine-grained sediments, the terrace levels from which all of the Mousterian hominid fossils were excavated have attracted more interest. The Mousterian levels on the Qafzeh terrace are dated by TL and ESR assays to between 92,000 and 115,000 BP

(Valladas et al. 1988; Schwarcz et al. 1988; Bar-Yosef 1992a). The lithic assemblage from Qafzeh resembles that from Tabun C, with a relatively high percentage of Levallois flakes and cores with radial/centripetal preparation (Boutié 1989). The faunal remains from Qafzeh have not been completely studied, but suggest a very diversified diet. According to a preliminary report by Bouchud (1974), *G. gazella* bones are the most common medium- to large-sized mammal from Levels XVI-XXIII, comprising 22% of the identified elements. Other large mammals are also present in similar proportions: *B. primigenius* accounts for 20%, *E. mauritanicus* accounts for 17%, and *C. elaphus* and *D. mesopotamica* constitute 16% and 13% of the fauna, respectively. Suids and caprids are present in small quantities in the lower levels of Qafzeh. In contrast to the lower levels, the upper levels of the terrace are dominated by *C. elaphus*, which constitutes about 40% of Levels XI-XV (Bouchud 1974).

## Paleoclimates

The paleoenvironmental context of the sites analyzed in this study is essential for interpreting data on season of occupation because seasonal site use by humans is most directly related to the temporal and spatial availability of plant and animal resources. Throughout the Late Pleistocene and up to the present, the southern Levant has been dominated by three major phytogeographic zones: the Mediterranean, the Irano-Turanian, and the Saharo-Arabian (Danin 1988; Zohary 1962). The Mediterranean zone presently extends from the Taurus foothills in the northern Levant to the coastal lowlands and Transjordanian plateau of the southern Levant. This zone, which receives annual precipitation of 400 mm to over 1,000 mm (Jaffe 1988), can be subdivided into highland and lowland coastal regions. Oak, pistachio, and pine forests predominate in the highlands, whereas the coastal/alluvial plain includes both open and shrub (maquis) woodlands (Zohary 1962). Until recently, the coastal plain also contained numerous marshes. The steppic Irano-Turanian zone, characterized by small tree, shrub, and herbaceous communities, occurs in regions that receive annually between 150 mm and 400 mm of rain and experience great annual and diurnal temperature variation. Irano-Turanian vegetation is highly seasonal and relatively open in comparison to that of the Mediterranean zone. The desertic Saharo-Arabian zone receives less than 150 mm of rainfall per year and is characterized by sparsely distributed vegetation, principally annuals with short-term growth in response to locally available moisture (Horowitz 1979).

While the major phytogeographic zones and faunal assemblage zones have varied in size with climatic fluctuations over the last 200,000 years, palynological and paleontological evidence suggest that climatic changes have affected the relative distribution of environmental zones more than their species composition (Horowitz 1979, 1988). The three major zones with corresponding fauna have persisted in a mosaic, with the Mediterranean zone retreating along rivers and lakes during dry periods (Tchernov 1988). Under warm interglacial conditions like the present, pulses and legumes are available from April through early July in the Mediterranean and Irano-Turanian zones; cereals are mostly available on the ecotone between the woodland and open environments during the same seasons; fruits and nuts ripen in the Mediterranean zones between late August and October-November; leafy foods are plentiful from December to April; and roots and tubers are widely distributed both temporally and spatially. *G. gazella* and *D. mesopotamica* comprise the majority of hunted game. These territorial species would have been available throughout the year in a variety of environments, although they would have been leanest during the winter, which is most likely the period of resource stress for humans as well as for their prey.

The distribution of major environmental zones in the southern Levant during the Quaternary can be estimated using palynological, faunal, isotopic, and geological data. It is convenient to distinguish between three recurring climatic patterns--cold and wet (interstadial), cold and dry (glacial), and warm and dry (interglacial)--that have recently been summarized by Bar-Yosef (1992b) and Horowitz (1988) (see Figure 16.3).

During interglacial conditions, such as the Holocene and early OIS 5, the Mediterranean phytogeographic belt covered much of the coastal plain, central hills, and Transjordanian plateau, although it diminished to the south, becoming desertic at the Negev. The Jordan Valley contained mostly Irano-Turanian vegetation. Precipitation was limited to the winter, when cyclonic rains from the Mediterranean were pushed southward by cold air masses from the north. Such conditions probably prevailed during the Natufian period, and perhaps during certain phases of the Levantine Mousterian.

Rainfall levels were higher and perhaps less seasonal during the relatively cool and wet phases of the latter part of OIS 5 and OIS 3, and at the end of OIS 2. These changes resulted in the growth of deciduous oak Mediterranean forests at the expense of the steppic and desertic zones. The Negev and parts of the Sinai were covered by Irano-Turanian vegetation at these times. Pluvial phases also resulted in larger lakes, extensive paleosol formation (Goldberg 1976), and an increase in the size of the coastal plain. Cool, wet climatic conditions correlate with the Aurignacian, the Geometric Kebaran, and most likely with the

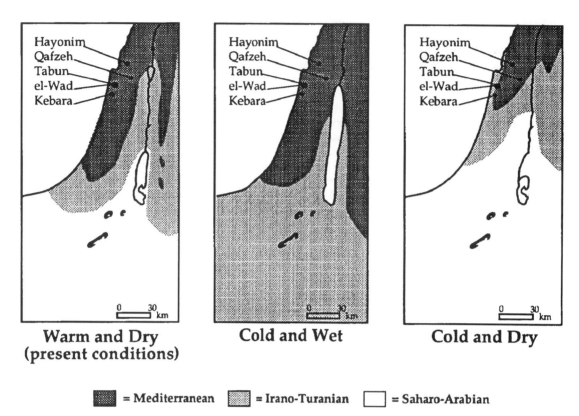

**Warm and Dry**      **Cold and Wet**      **Cold and Dry**
**(present conditions)**

▓ = Mediterranean    ▒ = Irano-Turanian    ☐ = Saharo-Arabian

**Figure 16.3.** Map of the estimated distributions of Mediterranean, Irano-Turanian, and Saharo-Arabian phytogeographic zones during warm and dry, cold and wet, and cold and dry climatic conditions.

Tabun C phase of the Mousterian, which includes the occupation of Qafzeh XVI-XXIII and Tabun C.

The climate in the Levant was cold and dry during much of OIS 4 and the latter part of OIS 2. The highly seasonal and low levels of rainfall during these periods resulted in the retreat of Mediterranean vegetation to the northern part of the southern Levant and to the central mountainous backbone of the region. The coastal plain and hills were covered with open forest and steppic vegetation, while the Negev and much of the Jordan valley were dominated by Saharo-Arabian vegetation. Dunes invaded the coastal plain, and the Jordan valley lakes were restricted to marshes in the Hula Basin and a less saline Dead Sea. Such phases were probably stressful times for hunter-gatherers in the southern Levant. Cold and dry climatic phases are correlated with the Mousterian occupation of Kebara, perhaps with the occupations of Tabun B and Tabun D, and with the Kebaran Culture.

Figure 16.3 shows the five caves analyzed in this study with respect to the inferred distribution of phytogeographic zones. It is important to note that, throughout the entire Late Pleistocene and Holocene, these sites were **within or on the margin of the Mediterranean phytogeographic zone**. During warm

and dry interglacial periods, like today or OIS 5e, they were all situated in a mixed maquis/forest Mediterranean zone; during cold and wet phases, they were situated in a more arboreal forest with the steppic zone much further away; and, during cold and dry phases, they were situated in the open woodland Mediterranean phytogeographic zone, but close to or on the margin of the steppic zone.

### Seasons of Site Occupation

There has been very little information available on the seasons of occupation of Levantine Palaeolithic sites. Reliable data on site seasonality, however, can be obtained from the analysis of incremental growth structures in mammalian teeth. This study uses seasonally deposited acellular cementum increments in the mountain gazelle (*Gazella gazella*) to estimate when these sites were occupied. Gazelle is the most appropriate species for this analysis for two reasons: gazelle is the dominant fauna in the Levantine Palaeolithic and Epipalaeolithic, comprising 60-90% of the fauna in most sites (Bar-Yosef 1981; Garrard 1980); and they are territorial, non-migratory, rapid breeders that are plentiful in most environmental zones (Baharav 1981,

1983). The absence of gazelle at a site from a particular season most likely indicates that the site was not then occupied, although this assumption should be confirmed by using other sources of data.

Between 8 and 30 gazelle mandibles were analyzed from each level of each site, according to availability (see Table 16.1). Gazelle is the dominant prey species, comprising between 50-80% of the fauna from all levels of these sites, with the possible exception of Tabun B with its very high percentage of deer (Garrod and Bate 1937; Bouchud 1974; Davis 1982; Garrard 1982). At Qafzeh, fallow deer (*Dama mesopotamica*) and mountain goat (*Capra ibex*) were also included because of the small sample sizes available. These species are expected to have a banding pattern similar to that of gazelle (Lieberman 1993). Only mandibles from anthropogenic contexts and without gnaw marks were studied; in addition, only teeth embedded in the alveolar bone of the mandible or maxilla were analyzed, in order to reduce possible false estimations of season of death resulting from the loss of the outermost level of cementum in loose teeth.

Cementum (see Figure 16.4) is a bone-like tissue that surrounds the roots of mammalian teeth, anchoring them to the periodontal ligament by means of collagen fiber bundles. Changes in the mineralization of these collagen bundles (Sharpey's fibers) under diets that vary seasonally produce bands that are well-correlated with seasonal growth (Lieberman and Meadow 1992). Previous study has demonstrated a precise relationship between cementum bands and their seasonal deposition in *Gazella* (for details, see Lieberman et al. 1990). Translucent bands in gazelle are laid down at a steady rate in the spring/summer (between April and October), while opaque bands are deposited at a slower rate during the fall/winter (between November and March). A sample of 20 teeth of modern gazelle from Israel with known date of death was analyzed in two blind tests: the season of death was correctly predicted for 18 out of 20 by the first blind test and for 17 out of 20 by the second blind test. Detailed explanations of the biology of cementum and the techniques of analysis used in this study are published elsewhere (Lieberman et al. 1990; Lieberman and Meadow 1992; see also Klevezal and Kleinenberg 1967; Grue and Jensen 1979; Pike-Tay 1990; Burke, this volume). All the teeth in this study were analyzed using computer-image analysis techniques to reduce error and subjectivity.

## RESULTS

The results of the analyses of the cementum increments of gazelle from major levels of Kebara, Qafzeh, Tabun, Hayonim, and el-Wad caves are summarized in Table 16.1. These data are part of a larger study of Levantine Palaeolithic and Epipalaeolithic sites (Lieberman 1992). It must be remembered that estimations of the season of death of gazelle, no matter how reliable, do not constitute definitive evidence for the season of occupation of these sites; rather, they should be considered minimal estimates of seasonal site use. Because of space limitations, the raw data are available elsewhere (Lieberman 1993).

Several interesting patterns are evident from these data. Most importantly, there is a more consistent pattern of seasonal gazelle hunting within levels than between levels of sites. In all the sites surveyed, gazelle killed during one season constitute either around 40-60%, 0-10%, or around 90-100% of the total sample, suggesting that the seasonal use of sites by hunter-gatherers within archaeological levels was relatively constant. This is particularly remarkable given the long period of deposition at some sites, such as the Upper Palaeolithic levels of Kebara. In addition, it is unlikely that the multiseasonal signature from Middle Palaeolithic sites results from the mixing of different seasonal occupations. Evidence for multiseasonal hunting of gazelle in the Kebara Mousterian is documented on samples from both the original Stekelis excavations and from a single level (Unit X) of the 1987 excavation of the *décapage* (a single horizontal exposure); these samples originate from a single layer and are unlikely to result from more than one occupation of the cave or from other non-anthropogenic processes (see Bar-Yosef et al. 1992). There is, however, variation both between sites from the same archaeological phase and between different levels of the same site. Site use during the Middle and Upper Palaeolithic seems to have been complex and variable.

## Middle Palaeolithic

Qafzeh Levels XXII-XVI were probably inhabited during the spring and/or summer; at both Tabun B and Kebara XII-VII, there is evidence for gazelle culling during both the fall/winter and the spring/summer, while at Tabun C, D, and Ea and at Hayonim E, gazelle only seem to have been killed during the fall/winter. These data suggest an interesting correlation between Tabun B-type industries at Tabun and Kebara caves and multiseasonal site use. These levels are the only occupations, except for some in the Natufian, that show any evidence for multiseasonal site use in the southern Levant (Lieberman 1993). So far, Tabun-B industries have only been associated with archaic *Homo*.

## Upper Palaeolithic

Upper Palaeolithic hunter-gatherers obviously had relatively complex and mobile subsistence strategies. At el-Wad D it appears that gazelle was killed only

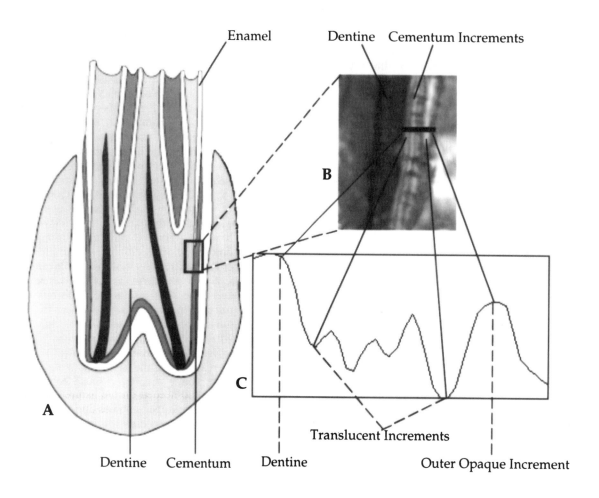

**Figure 16.4.** Schematic cross-section of a gazelle tooth (A) showing disposition of cementum and other dental tissues; (B) is a transmitted light polarized micrograph (100X) of a gazelle tooth thin-section showing translucent and opaque cementum increments; (C) is a graph of the relative luminance of pixels across the cementum, allowing a quantitative measure of the number of increments and the nature of the outermost increment.

during the fall/winter, but, at el-Wad C, gazelle killing seems to have been limited to the spring/summer. The Kebara Upper Palaeolithic levels were most likely occupied between spring and summer.

### Epipalaeolithic

All three three sites with Natufian remains, Kebara, el-Wad, and Hayonim, show a shift from single-season to multiseasonal hunting of gazelle. These changes in seasonal activity and mobility patterns are correlated with a variety of other novel occurrences: more permanent architecture, burials, an increase in lithic density, and, at Hayonim, the pres-

ence of human commensals. While none of these occurrences alone is sufficient to argue for permanent year-round occupation of sites, together they constitute reasonable evidence for reduced mobility and a significant shift in resource acquisition strategies (Lieberman 1991, 1993).

### DISCUSSION

The above results suggest that late Palaeolithic and Epipalaeolithic hunter-gatherer mobility patterns were complex and dynamic. No single model can account for the mobility patterns of southern Levantine hunter-gatherers during the Pleistocene. While there is evidence for a possible increase in the complexity of mobility strategies in the southern Levant at the end of the Epipalaeolithic, with multiseasonal and perhaps even permanent use of several Natufian sites, multi-seasonal site use is not a novel behavioral occurrence at these sites. Multiseasonal site use is documented in the Mousterian at Kebara, dated to approximately 60,000 years ago, and the slightly older Tabun B level. The presence of gazelle that were killed in both the growth and non-growth seasons means that the hunters who occupied these cave must have visited the site during **at least** two different seasons. Additionally, the season during which hunter-gatherers occupied certain sites changed over time, particularly at el-Wad and Kebara.

These seasonality data reinforce the importance of each site's unique context, as well as the fact that one could not reconstruct seasonal mobility patterns solely on the basis of resource acquisition models. The season of occupation of any given site may be the result of a variety of factors, including the contemporary distribution of environmental zones and the local conditions at the cave. As mentioned above, the later Upper Palaeolithic level at el-Wad (Level C) seems to have been occupied only during the dry season. In contrast, the earlier Aurignacian at el-Wad (Level D) was probably occupied during the wet season, while the roughly contemporaneous Kebara Upper Palaeolithic levels seem to have been occupied during the dry season. Since these sites are all located in similar environments during similar pluvial climatic conditions, explanations other than climate must be sought. Geological analyses indicate that Kebara Cave was very wet during the Upper Palaeolithic and contained a little pond in the back (Goldberg and Laville 1988), probably making it an unpleasant place to be in the winter.

Testing models of mobility strategies, however, is more complicated than the (already difficult) task of identifying which sites were occupied during which seasons. During the fluctuating but generally cool climatic conditions of Oxygen Isotope Stages 5d to 2, the Mediterranean forests and open woodlands that covered much of the northern part of Israel (in contrast to the south) were probably rich enough in resources to allow small hunter-gatherer bands to exploit relatively small territories in many different ways. Two profound limitations preclude more specificity about the exact nature of mobility strategies used during any given time period. First, not enough is known about the distribution and nature of open-air sites from this region during the Late Pleistocene. The caves analyzed in this study represent just a small sample of possible sites, many of which were submerged by recent sea level rises. The seasonality data provided above can help distinguish which environments were used during certain seasons, but do not

suggest which were or were **not** used during other seasons. Second, the lack of chronological control hampers our ability to make more precise inferences about the relationships between sites. There is little consensus on the dates of the Tabun levels, and the Middle Palaeolithic occupations from Hayonim and el-Wad have yet to be radiometrically dated.

Figure 16.5 illustrates the four Late Pleistocene mobility strategies which are substantiated by the most evidence. While it is likely that some hunter-gatherer groups--perhaps those associated with Tabun C-type industries--migrated along east-west transects, spending the spring and summer in the highlands (e.g., at Qafzeh) and the cooler and wetter winters near the coastal plain (e.g., at Tabun) (Model 1), some perhaps migrated along either north-south transects or entirely within the coastal plain (Model 2). Alternatively, the evidence for fall/winter occupation of Hayonim Cave suggests that some hunter-gatherers may have migrated from the lowlands in the spring/summer to the highlands in the fall/winter to take advantage of the patches of nuts and fruits in the oak forests (Model 3). Finally, it seems that some hunter-gatherers were less mobile (Model 4), living in relatively permanent base-camps as either sedentary hunter-gatherers, during the Natufian, or as part of a radiating mobility strategy, which characterizes the occupations of Tabun B sites. More data are needed on the nature and seasonality of contemporary open-air sites during the Late Pleistocene in central and northern Israel in order to be more precise about the nature of mobility strategies in this region.

In spite of the inability to identify which factors contribute to the observed variability in Late Pleistocene mobility patterns, the pattern of multiseasonal site use from Kebara XII-VII and Tabun B may represent a significant and radically different resource acquisition strategy. Such evidence for behavioral differences in the Middle Palaeolithic has implications for current debates on the origins of modern humans. In particular, much attention has been focused on the lack of correlation between the fossil and archaeological records in the southern Levant, where both archaic and anatomically modern human taxa appear to have made similar Mousterian tools, hunted the same animals, and inhabited the same geographical region for at least 60,000 years--although it is unclear whether they were sympatric at any particular time. While morphological differences between these taxa imply that they behaved in different ways (see, for example, Trinkaus 1983, 1986), archaeological traces of such differences have yet to be demonstrated. Some researchers (e.g., Wolpoff 1989; Clark and Lindly 1989) interpret these archaeological similarities as evidence for the presence of only one species that gradually evolved into a more modern morphology; others (e.g., Stringer and Andrews 1988) argue that these industries

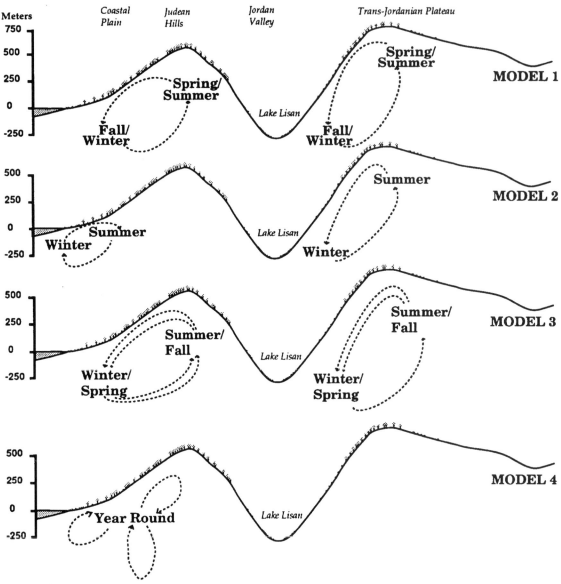

**Figure 16.5.** Alternative Late Pleistocene transhumance models (see text for explanation).

and sites were produced by at least two species with different behaviors that cannot be currently distinguished in the archaeological record.

Behavioral information from the late Pleistocene Levantine archaeological record has generally been limited to attempts to understand the formal, functional, and technological characteristics of stone tools (e.g., Meignen and Bar-Yosef 1989; Shea 1989) and to identify which mammalian species were utilized and whether they were hunted or scavenged (e.g., Davis 1977; Bar Yosef et al.). However, perhaps it should not be too surprising if two closely related and similar taxa made essentially the same tools, used them

similarly, and hunted the same medium- to large-sized mammals that lived around them (Stiner 1992). While it would be premature to draw too many conclusions from the limited data presented above (samples from Skhul and Amud are currently being analyzed), the correlation between these Tabun B-type industries, multiseasonal site use, and the presence of archaic *Homo sapiens* from the same levels suggests the possibility that Neanderthals may have used habitats in a different, less seasonally mobile manner than modern *Homo sapiens*. Trinkaus (1983, 1986) has outlined numerous Neanderthal morphologies--such as overall greater cortical robusticity, thicker lower-limb shaft diameters, larger femoral heads, lower femoral neck angles, etc.--which suggest that the limbs of archaic *Homo sapiens* were subjected to greater biomechanical stresses than modern *Homo sapiens*. It is possible that such stresses were incurred by the less mobile resource acquisition strategy evidenced at Kebara and Tabun, also suggested by Marks and Friedel (1976) in the Negev. In a small but environmentally diverse region like the southern Levant, high residential mobility may be an energetically more efficient means of acquiring sufficient resources than low residential mobility. Reduced mobility among contemporary hunter-gatherers has been shown to increase the energetic costs of foraging as the density of usable resources declines over time (e.g., Silberbauer 1981). Clearly, more data are needed to test this hypothesis.

It should not come as a surprise that ancient hunter-gatherer mobility and resource acquisition stategies were diverse and complex. New techniques that can estimate the season of death of fauna from archaeological contexts, such as cementun increment analysis, allow researchers to examine variability in the seasonal use of resources as a means of testing hypotheses relating to behavioral variability and the interpretation of past economies.

## ACKNOWLEDGMENTS

Thanks are due to Ofer Bar-Yosef, Richard Meadow, David Pilbeam, John Shea, John Speth, Eitan Tchernov, and Bernard Vandermeersch for their help in providing data and comments. I am grateful to the Natural History Museum (London) and the Israel Antiquities Authority for allowing me to study their collections. This research was funded by grants to the author from the National Science Foundation (BNS 9015973), the Wenner-Gren Foundation, the L. S. B. Leakey Foundation, and the CARE Foundation. I would also like to thank H. Bricker, P. Mellars, and G. Peterkin for their invitation to participate in this symposium and its publication.

## REFERENCES

Baharav, D.
  1981    Food habits of the mountain gazelle in semi-arid habitats of eastern Lower Galilee, Israel. *Journal of Arid Environments* 4:63-69.
  1983    Reproductive strategies in female mountain and dorcas gazelle. *Journal of the Zoological Society of London* 200:445-453.
Bar-Yosef, O.
  1981    The Epi-Palaeolithic complexes in the southern Levant. *Préhistoire du Levant*. J. Cauvin and P. Sanlaville, eds. Pp. 389-408. Colloques Internationales du Centre National de Recherche Scientifique 598. Paris: Editions du Centre National de Recherche Scientifique.
  1983    The Natufian in the southern Levant. In *The Hilly Flanks*

and *Beyond*. T. C. Young, P. E. L. Smith, and P. Mortensen, eds. Pp. 11-42. Oriental Institute Studies in Ancient Oriental Civilization 36. Chicago: University of Chicago.
  1987    Late Pleistocene Adaptations in the Levant. In *The Pleistocene Old World: Regional Perspectives*. O. Soffer, ed. Pp. 219-236. New York: Plenum Press.
  1991    The Archaeology of the Natufian layer at Hayonim Cave. In *The Natufian Culture in the Levant*. O. Bar-Yosef and F. Valla, eds. Pp. 81-92. Ann Arbor: International Monographs in Prehistory.
  1992a   The role of western Asia in modern human origins. *Philosophical Transactions of the Royal Society* 337:193-200.
  1992b   Middle Palaeolithic human adaptations in the Mediterranean Levant. In *The evolution and Dispersal of Modern Humans in Asia*. T. Akazawa, ed. Pp. 189-216. Tokyo: Hokusen-sha.
Bar-Yosef, O., and E. Tchernov
  1966    Archaeological finds and fossil faunas of the Natufian and microlithic industries at Hayonim cave, Western Galilee (Israel). *Israel Exploration Journal* 15:104-140.
Bar-Yosef, O., and A. Belfer-Cohen
  1989    The origins of sedentism and farming communities in the Levant. *Journal of World Prehistory* 4:447-498.
Bar-Yosef, O., B. Vandermeersch, B. Arensburg, P. Goldberg, H. Laville, L. Meignen, Y. Rak, E. Tchernov, and A.-M. Tillier
  1986    New data on the origin of modern man in the Levant. *Current Anthropology* 27:63-64.
Bar-Yosef, O., B. Vandermeersch, B. Arensburg, A. Belfer-Cohen, P. Goldberg, H. Laville, L. Meignen, Y. Rak, J. D. Speth, E. Tchernov, A.-M. Tillier, and S. Weiner
  1992    The excavations in Kebara Cave, Mt. Carmel. *Current Anthropology* 33:497-550.
Binford, L. R.
  1980    Willow smoke and dogs' tails: Hunter-gatherer settlement systems and site formation processes. *American Antiquity* 45:4-20.
Bouchud, J.
  1974    Etude préliminaire de la faune provenant de la Grotte du Djebel Qafzeh près de Nazareth (Israël). *Paléorient* 2:87-102.
Boutié, P.
  1989    Etude technologique de l'industrie mousterienne de la grotte de Qafzeh (près de Nazareth, Israël). In *Investigations in Southern Levantine Prehistory/Préhistoire du Sud Levant*. O. Bar-Yosef and B. Vandermeesrch, eds. Pp. 213-230. BAR International Series 497. Oxford: British Archaeological Reports.
Clark, G. A., and J. M. Lindly
  1989    Modern human origins in the Levant and western Asia: The fossil and archaeological evidence. *American Anthropologist* 91:962-985.
Coinman, N., G. Clark, and J. Lindly
  1986    Prehistoric hunter-gatherer settlement in the Wadi el'Hasa, west-central Jordan. In *The Prehistory of Jordan*. A. Garrard and H. G. Gebel, eds. Pp. 209-285. BAR International Series 284. Oxford: British Archaeological Reports.
Cross, J. R.
  1989    Expanding the scope of seasonality reasearch in archaeology. In *Coping with Seasonal Constraints*. R. Huss-Ashmore, J. Curry, and R. K. Hitchcock, eds. Pp. 55-63. MASCA Research Papers in Science and Archaeology 5. Philadelphia: The University Museum, University of Pennsylvania.
Danin, A.
  1988    Flora and vegetation of Israel and adjacent areas. In *The Zoogeography of Israel*. Y. Yom-Tov and E. Tchernov,

eds. Pp. 129-157. Dordrecht: W. Junk.

Davis, S. J. M.
1977 The ungulate remains from Kebara Cave. *Eretz Israel* 13:150-163.
1982 Climatic change and the advent of domestication: The successions of ruminant artiodactyls in the late Pleistocene-Holocene in the Israeli region. *Paléorient* 8:5-15.
1983 The age profiles of gazelle predated by ancient man in Israel: Possible evidence for a shift from seasonality to sedentism in the Natufian. *Paléorient* 9:55-62.

Foley, R.
1983 Optimality theory in anthropology. *Man* (n.s.) 20:222-242.

Garrard, A.
1980 *Man-Animal-Plant Relationships During the Upper Pleistocene and Early Holocene of the Levant.* Ph.D. dissertation, University of Cambridge.
1982 The environmental implications of the re-analysis of the large mammal fauna from the Wadi-el-Mughara caves, Palestine. In *Paleoclimates, Paleoenvironments and Human Communities in the Eastern Mediterranean Region in Later Prehistory.* J. L. Bintliff and W. Van Zeist, eds. Pp. 165-198. BAR International Series 133. Oxford: British Archaeological Reports.

Garrod, D. A. E., and D. M. A. Bate
1937 *The Stone Age of Mount Carmel. Volume 1.* Oxford: Clarendon.

Goldberg, P.
1976 Upper Pleistocene geology of the Avdat/Aqev Area. In *Prehistory and Paleoenvironments in the Central Negev, Israel. Volume 1.* A. Marks, ed. Pp. 25-55. Dallas: Southern Methodist University Press.

Goldberg, P., and H. Laville
1988 Le contexte stratigraphique des occupations paléolithiques de Kebara (Israël). *Paléorient* 14:123-130.

Grue, H., and B. Jensen
1979 Review of the formation of incremental lines in tooth cementum of terrestrial mammals. *Danish Review of Game Biology* 11:1-48.

Grün, R., and C. B. Stringer
1991 Electron spin resonance dating and the evolution of modern humans. *Archaeometry* 33:153-199.

Henry, D. O.
1983 Adaptive evolution within the Epipalaeolithic of the Near East. *Advances in World Archaeology* 2:99-160.
1989 *From Foraging to Agriculture: The Levant at the End of the Ice Age.* Philadelphia: University of Pennsylvania Press.

Horowitz, A.
1979 *The Quaternary of Israel.* New York: Academic Press.
1988 The Quaternary environments and paleogeography in Israel. In *The Zoogeography of Israel.* Y. Yom-Tov and E. Tchernov, eds. Pp. 35-58. Dordrecht: W. Junk.

Jaffe, S.
1988 Climate of Israel. In *The Zoogeography of Israel.* Y. Yom-Tov.and E. Tchernov, eds. Pp. 79-94. Dordrecht: W. Junk.

Jelinek, A.
1982 The Tabun Cave and Palaeolithic man in the Levant. *Science* 216:1369-1375.

Kelly, R. L.
1983 Hunter-gatherer mobility strategies. *Journal of Anthropological Research* 39:277-306.

Klevezal, G. A., and S. E. Kleinenberg
1967 *Age Determination of Mammals by Layered Structure in Teeth and Bone.* Academy of Sciences, U. S. S. R. Trans. 1969 Foreign Lang. Div., Dept. Sec. State, Canada. Quebec: Fisheries Research Board.

Lieberman, D. E.
1991 Seasonality and gazelle hunting at Hayonim Cave: New evidence for "sedentism" during the Natufian. *Paléorient* 17:47-57.
1993 *Mobility and Strain: The Biology of Cementum and the Evolution of Hunter-Gatherer Mobility Strategies in the Southern Levant.* Ph.D. dissertation, Department of Anthropology, Harvard University.

Lieberman, D. E., T. W. Deacon, and R. H. Meadow
1990 Computer image enhancement and analysis of cementum increments as applied to teeth of *Gazella gazella. Journal of Archaeological Science* 17:519-533.

Lieberman, D., and R. H. Meadow
1992 The biology of cementum increments (with an archaeological perspective). *Mammal Review* 22:57-77.

Marks, A. E., and D. Friedel
1977 Prehistoric settlement patterns in the Avdat/Aqev area. In *Prehistory and Palaeoenvironments in the Central Negev, Israel. Volume 2.* A. Marks, ed. Pp. 131-159. Dallas: Southern Methodist University Press.

McCown, T., and A. Keith
1939 *The Stone Age of Mt. Carmel. Volume 2.* Oxford: Clarendon.

Meignen, L., and O. Bar-Yosef
1989 Nouvelles recherches sur le Palaeolithique Moyen d'Israel: La grotte de Kebara, unités VII-XII. In *Investigations in Southern Levantine Prehistory.* O. Bar-Yosef and B. Vandermeersch, eds. Pp. 169-184. BAR International Series 497. Oxford: British Archaeological Reports.

Mortensen, P.
1972 Seasonal camps and early villages in the Zagros. In *Man, Settlement and Urbanism.* P. Ucko, R. Tringham, and G. W. Dimbleby, eds. Pp. 293-297. London: Duckworth.

Pichon, J.
1987 L'avifaune. In *La faune du gisement de Mallaha (Eynan), Israël.* J. Bouchud, ed. Pp. 115-150. Mémoires et Travaux du Centre de Recherche de Jérusalem 4. Paris: Paléorient.

Pike-Tay, A.
1990 *Red Deer Hunting in the Upper Palaeolithic of Southwest France: A Case Study in Seasonality.* BAR International Series 569. Oxford: British Archaeological Reports.

Saxon, E. C.
1974 The mobile herding economy of Kebarah Cave, Mt. Carmel: An economic analysis of the faunal remains. *Journal of Archaeological Science* 1:27-45.

Schick, T., and M. Stekelis
1977 Mousterian assemblages from Kebara Cave, Mount Carmel. *Eretz Israel* 13:97-149.

Schwarcz, H. P., R. Grün, B. Vandermeersch, O. Bar-Yosef, H. Valladas, and E. Tchernov
1988 ESR Dates for the Hominid Burial Site of Qafzeh in Israel. *Journal of Human Evolution* 17:733-737.

Shea, J. J.
1989 Tool use in the Levantine Mousterian of Kebara Cave, Mt. Carmel. *Mitekufat Haeven* 22:15-30.

Silberbauer, G.
1981 *Hunter and Habitat in the Central Kalahari Desert.* Cambridge: Cambridge University Press

Stiner, M.
1992 Species "choice" by Italian Upper Pleistocene predators. *Current Anthropology* 33:433-451.

Stringer, C., and P. Andrews
1988 Genetic and fossil evidence for the origin of modern humans. *Science* 239:1263-1268.

Tchernov, E.
1984 Commensal animals and human sedentism in the Middle

East. In *Animals and Archaeology. Volume 3. Early Herders and Their Flocks*. J. Clutton-Brock and C. Grigson, eds. Pp. 91-115. BAR International Series 202. Oxford: British Archaeological Reports.

1988    The biogeographical history of the southern Levant. In *The Zoogeography of Israel*. Y. Yom-Tov and E. Tchernov, eds. Pp. 159-250. Dordrecht: W. Junk.

Trinkaus, E.

1983    Neanderthal postcrania and the adaptive shift to modern humans. In *The Mousterian Legacy: Human Biocultural Change in the Upper Pleistocene*. E. Trinkaus, ed. Pp. 165-200. BAR International Series 164. Oxford: British Archaeological Reports.

1986    The Neanderthals and modern humans. *Annual Review of Anthropology* 15:193-218.

Turville-Petre, F.

1932    Excavations in the Mugharet el-Kebarah. *Journal of the Royal Anthropological Insitute of Great Britain and Ireland* 62:271-276.

Valladas, H., J. L.. Joron, G. Valladas, B. Arensburg, O. Bar-Yosef, A. Belfer-Cohen, P. Goldberg, H. Laville, L. Meignen, Y.

Rak, E. Tchernov, A.-M. Tillier, and B. Vandermeersch

1987    Thermoluminescence dates for the Neanderthal burial site at Kebara in Israel. *Nature* 330:159-160.

Valladas, H., J. L. Reyss, J. L. Joron, G. Valladas, O. Bar-Yosef, and B. Vandermeersch

1988    Thermoluminescence dating of Mousterian 'Proto-Cro-Magnon' remains from Israel and the Origin of Man. *Nature* 331:614-615.

Vandermeersch, B.

1981    *Les hommes fossiles de Qafzeh (Israël)*. Paris: Editions du Centre National de Recherche Scientifique.

Vita-Finzi, C., and E. S. Higgs

1970    Prehistoric economy in the Mount Carmel area of Palestine: Site catchment analysis. *Journal of the Prehistoric Society* 36:1-37.

Wolpoff, M.

1989    Multiregional evolution: The fossil alternative to Eden. In *The Human Revolution*. P. Mellars and C. B. Stringer, eds. Pp. 62-108. Edinburgh: Edinburgh University Press.

Zohary, M.

1962    *Plant Life of Palestine*. New York: Ronald Press.

# 17

# The Human Food Niche in the Levant Over the Past 150,000 Years

**Michael P. Neeley**
**Arizona State University**

**Geoffrey A. Clark**
**Arizona State University**

## ABSTRACT

Archaeologists have tended to accept Flannery's (1969) broad spectrum revolution (BSR) as a general phase in an evolutionary sequence of subsistence changes leading to the appearance of domestication economies. Previous partial tests of the Flannery model in both hemispheres have tended to support it, especially those aspects of it that predict increasing subsistence diversity over time and increases in the relative intensity of food procurement. Phillip Edwards has recently claimed, however, that the BSR is not documented in Levantine archaeofaunal data and that its generality as a phase in the domestication process in that region can therefore be called into question. We re-analyzed Edwards's data using a simulation approach and came to the conclusion that there was, in fact, considerable support for the BSR. We attribute the disparity between our results and those of Edwards to the way in which diversity is measured.

## INTRODUCTION

Archaeologists have tended to accept Flannery's (1969) broad spectrum revolution (BSR) as a general phase in an evolutionary sequence of subsistence changes leading to the appearance of domestication economies. Previous partial tests of the Flannery model in both hemispheres have tended to support it, especially those aspects that predict increasing subsistence diversity over time and increases in the relative intensity of food procurement (e.g., Earle 1980; Christenson 1980; Clark and Yi 1983; Clark 1987). Phillip Edwards has recently claimed, however, that the BSR is not documented in Levantine archaeofaunal data and that its generality as a phase in the domestication process in that key region can, therefore, be called into question (Edwards 1989; cf. Binford 1968, 1983). He contends that diversified archaeofaunas have been present in the Levant since the Middle Palaeolithic and that no changes in the direction of increasing diversity are discernible in the period immediately preceding the appearance of domestication economies there. Edwards's construal of pattern is juxtaposed here with the expectations of long-term, diachronic niche-width models developed by Cohen (1977), Earle (1980), and Redding (1988). Although

his conclusions partly mirror our own, we think there are problems with how Edwards measures diversity, with his construal of what constitutes the BSR, and what it means.

This essay addresses three major, related issues that bear on attempts to explain long-term subsistence change. First, test implications of the BSR, and of other general models of subsistence change that incorporate it, are reviewed, and a summary of Edwards's results is provided. Second, the concept of diversity itself, and how to measure it, is examined. It can be argued that the diversity index used by Edwards (Shannon's *J*) is probably inappropriate for the study he undertook. Finally, the same corpus of Levantine archaeofaunal data analyzed by Edwards is reanalyzed using Kintigh's (1984, 1989) simulation approach. Problems affecting our capacity to monitor changes in subsistence organization in Levantine Pleistocene contexts are also addressed.

## THE BROAD SPECTRUM REVOLUTION

In the classic formulation, Flannery's (1969) broad spectrum revolution is characterized by a series of changes in the subsistence economy beginning ca.

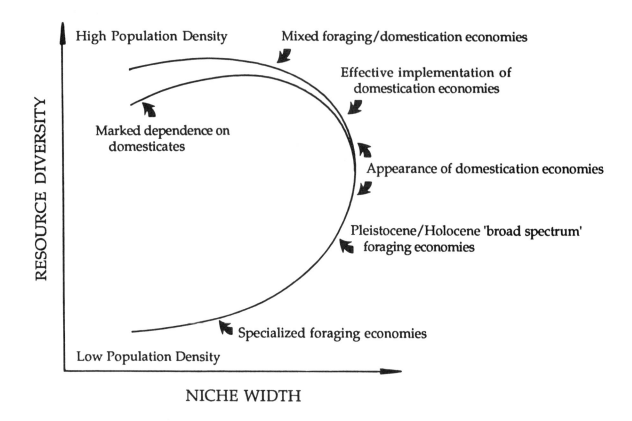

**Figure 17.1.** Theoretical relationship between niche width and resource diversity under conditions of population growth and with the least-cost selection assumption in effect (from Clark 1987:296; modified from Christenson 1980:37).

20,000 BP (the Upper/Epipalaeolithic boundary in the Middle East) that are manifest in a broadening of the human food niche. This increase in resource diversity was thought to continue until ca. 8000 BP (the Neolithic), when reliance upon domestication economies is achieved in some areas. In the Levantine context, the broadening of the diet is thought to have included a greater emphasis on smaller, more labor intensive, lower yield, but more reliable food packages (e.g., deer, gazelle, equids, ovicaprines) than those that are the basis for Middle and Upper Palaeolithic subsistence. While a substantial part of the diet continued to be provided by large- and medium-sized game (i.e., the change did not result in the replacement of traditional resources, but in the addition of new ones), the most notable difference is thought to lie in the greater diversity of resources utilized over time, with consequent increases in labor expended in food procurement and processing as more "high cost, low yield" resources are added to the diet. It is this pattern of increased diversity, attributed to a causal nexus involving population increase, environmental change, technological change, and to changes in the organiza-

tion of the subsistence subsystem, that is believed to lead to the appearance of domestication economies (Flannery 1969:79).

Flannery (1969:75) originally suggested that, of the variables just noted, population pressure, as it relates to differentials in carrying capacity, might be a possible "prime mover" of changes in the subsistence economy. This idea, since adopted by many workers, has been jettisoned by Flannery himself (cf. 1969, 1986). Flannery relied heavily on the population equilibrium model proposed by Binford (1968), in which population growth exceeded the resource base in some areas, internal population control mechanisms eventually failed, and emigration into adjacent areas of lower population density/carrying capacity became the only option. These conditions in "adaptive tension zones," as Binford called them (i.e., ecotones between areas of relatively high and relatively low population density/carrying capacity), would have tended to stress both donor and recipient groups and would have selected for means to increase the width of the human food niche for both of them. Over the long run, this process would have tended to restore population/resource imbalances at higher and higher carrying capacities, but at the cost of increased labor investment in food procurement. From this perspective, domestication, perhaps the ultimate form of intensification, was only the last in a long series of subsistence shifts that were fairly predictable given adequate, and independent, controls over resource diversity and population density. Nevertheless, these early models tended to focus on subsistence changes in relatively close temporal proximity to agricultural origins.

Since the late 1970s, it has been widely recognized that evidence for the BSR predates the appearance of domestication economies by as much as 10,000-15,000 years. All subsequent workers have, therefore, sought to generalize the Flannery/Binford model to include all long-term subsistence change, invoking population/resource imbalances as the primary causal mechanism involved (e.g., Cohen 1977; Christenson 1980; Earle 1980; Clark and Yi 1983; Clark 1987; Redding 1988). Given a mosaic of different population densities, resource mixes, and subsistence strategies, a major assumption of these models is that, as population density increases, there is a concomitant need to broaden or diversify the resource base. As food resources are stretched to their limits by population growth (other factors being held constant), the trajectory of increasing resource diversity results in the appearance of the earliest domestication economies as a point on a continuing spiral of intensification. Following the achievement of reliance upon domesticated plants and animals, diversity is generally thought to decline as agricultural economies become established and intensified, and as the proportion of resources obtained through hunting and collecting declines (Christenson 1980).

If simple diversity (number of economic species) is plotted against niche width (proportional contribution of economic species measured by some "currency," such as calories, over time, the resulting curve is believed to have some generality and to allow for the prediction of one variable, given a known value for the other (Figure 17.1). The curve resembles a "backward C," with (1) specialized foraging economies characterized by relatively low resource diversity occurring under conditions of low population density; followed by (2) the BSR, where, driven by population increases, both resource diversity and niche width tend to increase and to reach maximum values; (3) the appearance of domestication economies; and (4) their effective implementation, marked by decreases in diversity and niche width and by increases in the rate of population growth. In extreme cases of agricultural intensification, both resource diversity and niche width would theoretically approach unity, although in practice this never actually happens. It is this sort of diversification and intensification trajectory (the

"backward C"), ultimately powered by increases in population density and by regional population/resource imbalances, that has been presented in support of the BSR as a general evolutionary phase for regions outside the Middle East. These studies either assume or independently control for increases in regional population density over time (e.g., Christenson 1980; Clark and Yi 1983; Clark 1987).

In order for a model based on population growth and resource diversity to be used with some degree of confidence, both variables must be measured independently. Although it is admittedly quite difficult to document population growth archaeologically, a crude measure of growth is one based on the scaled or standardized number of sites or levels known per unit time. Such data are usually accessible from areas where archaeological inquiry has some historical depth and where surveys are a standard and accepted part of the research protocol. Fortunately, both conditions obtain in the Levant. By using site numbers standardized per unit time as a surrogate for regional population densities, general trends indicating increase, decrease, and/or stability can usually be ascertained. The definition and measurement of diversity in archaeological contexts is a much-debated subject; various ways that have been proposed to measure different aspects of diversity are discussed below.

In a recent paper, Richard Redding (1988) has developed a universal generalization of the Flannery model, couched in terms of four evolutionary stages characterized by a prioritized hierarchy of tactics. It is assumed that local hunter-gatherer populations grew and stressed the resource base, thus forcing groups to adopt these tactics in order to cope with stress. Redding argues that the tactics (emigration, diversification, storage, and domestication) are adopted in a predictable general order or sequence. Of interest to us is the role of diversification and the options associated with this subsistence tactic. In the Redding model, decisions must be made at various population and carrying capacity thresholds. These decisions are viewed in evolutionary terms and are expected to increase the overall fitness of the groups involved in the decision making process. At the first threshold level (Stage I), the mechanisms available for alleviating stress are population regulation and emigration/mobility. At subsequent thresholds, diversification (Stage II), storage (Stage III), and plant/animal manipulation (Stage IV) are successively added to those characteristic of earlier stages (Figure 17.2). Although the model is not intended to portray the change as unilineal, the ordering presented is believed to be the most likely general sequence of events or processes (Redding 1988:75). Several aspects of his model are interesting for our purposes. One is the notion that the threshold of stress due to carrying capacity and population/resource imbalances does not have to be

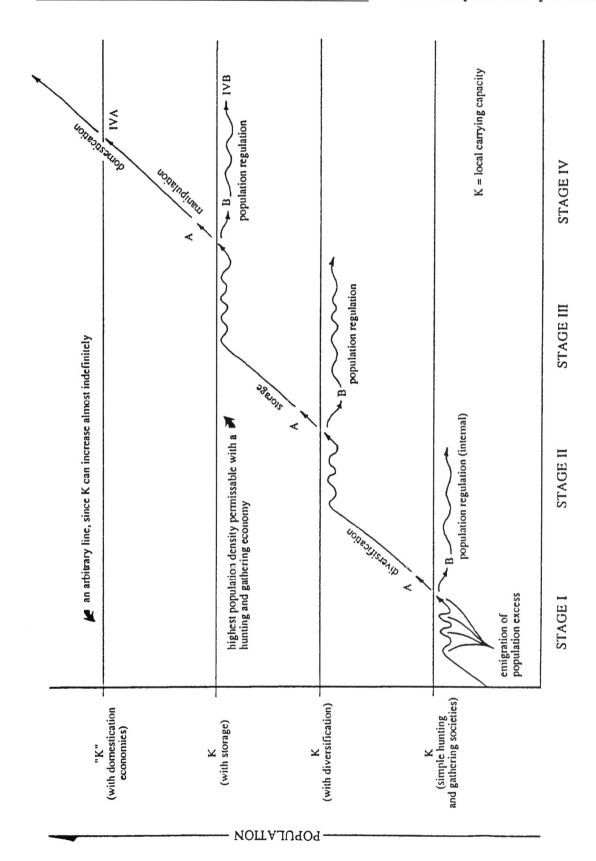

reached by all groups simultaneously. This implies that groups in relative proximity to each other might be operating on different levels in terms of the tactics or strategies employed. For our purposes it would not be unusual to see some variability in the regional data set that might be attributable to variable subsistence practices and not just the result of "noisy data." Redding (1988:85) also indicates that diversity should be greatest prior to the advent of storage technology. This suggests that we might observe a **decrease** in the overall diversity of site assemblages prior to the appearance of domestication economies as a result of the implementation of storage technologies.

Several trends can be predicted from the concept of the BSR and from the other models of subsistence change to which we have just alluded. First, in terms of the placement of the BSR in time, there should be discernible, albeit gradual, change beginning in the late Upper Palaeolithic and continuing throughout the succeeding Kebaran, Natufian, Neolithic, Chalcolithic, and Metal Ages, as domestication economies become established and as both resource diversity and niche width decline. Second, changes in subsistence should be additive and should not result in the replacement or substitution of one resource or group of resources with another (Earle 1980). As a result, change in diversity might best be monitored by the number of different species utilized over time--here and subsequently referred to as **richness**, rather than by **evenness**, the proportional contribution of a given species to the overall diet. This distinction is anticipated by the BSR model in which the proportional contribution of a species to the diet might not change appreciably over time, even though more species are being added to the diet (Flannery 1969:77). Third, these models rely heavily on the notion that there is an increase in regional population density over time, which, other things being equal, causes the diversification of the resource base to take place (Cohen 1977; Christenson 1980; Earle 1980; Clark 1987). Therefore, estimates of population density should indicate an increase in site numbers and levels through time.

### EDWARDS'S RESULTS SUMMARIZED

The recent work of Phillip Edwards (1989) contrasts with the expectations of the BSR model and studies derived from its basic premises. After examining 72 Levantine archaeofaunal assemblages (although only 29 are used for the "diversity" test) distributed across eight analytical units ranging in time from the Mugharan (ca. 120,000 BP) to the Pre-Pottery Neo-

**Table 17.1.** Estimate of population growth over time[a].

| Culture-Stratigraphic Unit | # of Sites | Temporal Duration | # of sites per millen. |
|---|---|---|---|
| Middle Palaeolithic | 347 | 65,000 | 5.33 |
| Upper Palaeolithic | 151 | 17,000 | 8.88 |
| Epipalaeolithic | 79 | 10,000 | 7.90 |
| Neolithic | 88 | 4,000 | 22.00 |
| Chalcolithic | 37 | 1,000 | 37.00 |
| Bronze Age | 102 | 1,800 | 56.66 |
| Iron Age | 114 | 700 | 162.85 |

[a] The data for this table represents results from five surveys in the Levant: (1) the Wadi el-Hasa (Clark et al. 1988a; MacDonald 1988a, 1988b); (2) the Southern Ghors and Northeast Araba (MacDonald et al. 1988; Neeley 1989); (3) the Negev and Sinai (Marks 1977); (4) the Hisma region (Henry et al. 1983); and (5) the Azraq Basin (Garrard et al. 1988a).

lithic (ca. 8000 BP), Edwards suggested that, by the Middle Palaeolithic (82,000-37,000 BP), a wide range of animals were being exploited for dietary purposes throughout western Asia and that there was no evidence to support a broadening of the diet immediately prior to the appearance of domestication economies. He concluded from this pattern search that the BSR, which predicts an increase in diversity beginning around 20,000 BP, is inappropriate as a general evolutionary phase in the Levant. Leaving aside the issue of plant foods and the contribution of plants such as cereal grasses to the overall subsistence base, the issues that concern us here are (1) Edwards's use of a diversity index that measures only one of several components of diversity and (2) his decision to terminate his study with the 6th millennium BC, when mixed predation/domestication economies were becoming fairly widespread in the region, but before reliance upon domesticates is well documented.[1]

### ESTIMATING POPULATION GROWTH

One of the basic tenets of the model used here is that increases in population density over time are believed to drive the need to diversify the diet. Rather than simply reporting the number of sites or levels per culture-stratigraphic unit, it is clearly more appropriate to relate these numbers to a standardized measure of time. Scaling site numbers to unit time allows for comparability across culture-stratigraphic units of vastly different durations. This scaling method, first

**Figure 17.2.** Redding's model: changes in local carrying capacity under conditions of population growth and with the adoption of emigration (Stage I), diversification (Stage II), storage (Stage III), and manipulation-domestication (Stage IV) strategies (after Redding 1988:76,79).

advocated by Clark and Yi (1983), is also used here. The seven culture-stratigraphic units most commonly employed in these analyses are given in Table 17.1. The data used for these population estimates are derived from five areas of more-or-less systematic survey in the Levant. While the individual data sets are broadly comparable, there are, of course, inevitable biases; different research questions, of course, tend to dictate what types of sites are recorded. As a result, most of the post-Neolithic periods are apt to be underrepresented because of the site-centered orientation of much Metal Age research. Similarly, when dealing exclusively with surface collections, assignment of assemblages to particular culture-stratigraphic units is often difficult in the absence of test excavations. This results in many sites being placed in indeterminate, bracketing categories (e.g., Epipalaeolithic/Pre-Pottery Neolithic), which, of course, precludes the kind of temporal resolution that would be desirable for the present purposes.

Table 17.1 also gives the incidence of Levantine sites per millennium. It is apparent from inspection of the table that the general expectation of population growth over time is well supported. After millennia of low values for the Middle, Upper, and Epipalaeolithic (5.33, 8.88, and 7.90, respectively), there is almost a three-fold increase when the Epipalaeolithic (7.90) is compared with the Neolithic (22.00). Chalcolithic values nearly double again (to 37.00), and there is a substantial, although incremental, increase during the Bronze Age (to 56.66). Finally, in the Iron Age (sensu stricto), scaled site numbers almost triple (to 162.85). While these trends are robust and are generally replicated within individual surveys, they are also clearly influenced by the variable quality of the survey data upon which they are based. Different survey teams also used somewhat different analytical units, and there are differences in resolution dependent upon the units employed in the field and the sophistication of the collection strategies and of subsequent laboratory analysis. Some surveys are supported by extensive test excavations (this is particularly true of the Azraq Basin data set), although most are not. The Wadi Hasa Survey, for example, recorded only 10 single-component Epipalaeolithic sites, although no less than 58 were assigned to an undifferentiated "Epipalaeolithic/ Pre-Pottery Neolithic" category and were not used here (MacDonald 1988c; Clark et al. 1988a; Coinman et al. 1988). The Negev and Sinai Desert surveys, the Azraq Basin survey, and that in the Wadi Hisma region all indicate higher Epipalaeolithic site densities than Upper Palaeolithic ones, whereas the reverse is true in the Hasa. If it were possible to better differentiate Epipalaeolithic sites in the Wadi Hasa "Epi/PPN" category, that pattern would almost certainly be replicated there as well.

## THE COMPONENTS OF DIVERSITY

The concept of diversity, as developed and employed in ecology, has often been misunderstood and, consequently, misapplied in archaeological research. As a general notion, diversity connotes the amount of variability present in a sample or population. However, such a definition is inappropriately vague when trying to measure diversity quantitatively. The diversity concept encompasses a number of distinct components, and part of the problem in using it analytically is that archaeologists rarely have a clear idea about what component of diversity is being measured by a particular diversity index. In a recent volume devoted to archaeological diversity questions (Leonard and Jones 1989), the component parts of diversity are identified as richness, evenness, and heterogeneity (Bobrowsky and Ball 1989:5).

**Richness** is the number of species/types in a given sample or collection. Since it can be shown statistically that richness is a function of sample size, the unqualified use of the simple number of species/types present in a collection might be an inaccurate measure of richness. To assess richness with some degree of reliability, the effects of sample size must be taken into account. **Evenness** refers to the proportional distribution of the species/types in the sample. This measure helps us determine whether or not all of the species/types are represented more or less equally in a sample, or whether the sample is dominated by a few very abundant species/types. As might be expected, the most commonly used evenness measures are also affected by sample size, as well as by richness (Bobrowsky and Ball 1989:7).

**Heterogeneity** measures the relationship between richness and evenness and expresses this relationship as a single index. It is this aspect of diversity that is most often taken to signify overall diversity (i.e., diversity in the colloquial usage of the term). Heterogeneity measures are very popular with archaeologists, but they suffer from the drawback that we typically do not know which aspect of diversity (richness or evenness) is most heavily influencing the index. In fact, identical heterogeneity statistics can result from analyses of two assemblages of very different composition, with the value determined in the first case by evenness and in the second by richness.

Because of the interest in diversity measures in the life sciences, a number of equations have been published over the years (mostly by ecologists) that attempt to measure accurately the two generally recognized components of diversity. In their review of these measures, Bobrowsky and Ball (1989:7-8) suggest that only a few of them are actually applicable to the kinds of data usually available to answer archaeological research questions. Heterogeneity measures

**Table 17.2.** Faunal assemblages used for this study.

Middle Palaeolithic

| | |
|---|---|
| Douara Cave | Payne 1983 |
| Far'ah II | Gilead and Grigson 1984 |
| Qafzeh 11 | Bouchud 1974 |
| Qafzeh 15 | Bouchud 1974 |
| Qafzeh 22 | Bouchud 1974 |
| Wadi Hasa 621 | Clark et al. 1988b |
| Tabun D | Bar-Yosef 1989 |
| Bezez B | Garrard 1983 |
| C-Spring | Clutton-Brock 1970 |

Upper Palaeolithic

| | |
|---|---|
| Kebara D | Saxon 1974 |
| Kebara E | Saxon 1974 |
| Wadi Hasa 618 | Clark et al. 1988b |
| Qafzeh 9 | Bouchud 1974 |
| Jilat 9 | Garrard et al. 1988b |
| Azraq 17 | Garrard et al. 1988b |
| El Wad D | Bar-Yosef 1989 |

Kebaran

| | |
|---|---|
| Ein Gev I | Davis 1974 |
| Wadi Hammeh 26 | Edwards et al. 1988 |
| Uweinid 18 | Garrard et al. 1988b |
| Wadi Hasa 784x | Clark et al. 1988b |
| Jilat 6 | Garrard et al. 1988b |
| Kebara C | Saxon 1974 |
| Nahal Hadera V | Saxon et al. 1978 |
| Hefsibah | Saxon et al. 1978 |
| Tor Hamar | Henry and Garrard 1988 |
| Iraq e Zigan | Heller 1978 |

Natufian

| | |
|---|---|
| Beidha | Hecker 1989 |
| Wadi Hammeh 27 | Edwards et al. 1988 |
| Hayonim Terrace | Henry et al. 1981 |
| Wadi Hasa 1065 | Clark et al. 1988b |
| Kebara B | Saxon 1974 |
| Wadi Judayid | Henry and Turnbull 1985 |
| Rosh Horesha | Butler et al. 1977 |
| Jilat 8 | Garrard et al. 1988b |
| Jilat 10 | Garrard et al. 1988b |
| Azraq 18 | Garrard et al. 1988b |
| Jilat 6 | Garrard et al. 1988b |

Neolithic

| | |
|---|---|
| Jericho PPNA | Clutton-Brock 1979 |
| Gilgal | Noy et al. 1980 |
| Abu Salem | Butler et al. 1977 |
| Jericho PPNB | Clutton-Brock 1979 |
| Beidha | Hecker 1982 |
| Ain Ghazal PPNB | Köhler-Rollefson et al. 1988 |
| Wadi Tbeik | Tchernov and Bar-Yosef 1982 |
| Ain Ghazal PPNC | Köhler-Rollefson et al. 1988 |
| Ain Ghazal Yarmoukian | Köhler-Rollefson et al. 1988 |
| Ujrat | Dayan et al. 1986 |

(Table 17.2--continued)

Neolithic, cont.

| | |
|---|---|
| Jilat 7 | Garrard et al. 1988b |
| Azraq 31 | Garrard et al. 1988b |
| Jericho PN | Clutton-Brock 1979 |

Chalcolithic

| | |
|---|---|
| Jebel Jill | Henry and Turnbull 1985 |
| Shiqmim | Grigson 1987 |
| Sabi Abyad | Akkermans 1987 |

Bronze Age

| | |
|---|---|
| Jericho EB | Clutton-Brock 1979 |
| En Shadud | Horowitz 1985 |
| Arad EB I | Lernau 1978 |
| Arad EB II | Lernau 1978 |
| Jericho MB | Clutton-Brock 1979 |
| Tel Michel MB | Hellwing and Feig 1989 |
| Tel Michel LB | Hellwing and Feig 1989 |

Iron Age

| | |
|---|---|
| Jericho Iron | Clutton-Brock 1979 |
| Tel Michel Iron | Hellwing and Feig 1989 |
| Tel Michel Persian | Hellwing and Feig 1989 |

are deemed too problematic to be useful when applied to the common kinds of archaeological data bases, and they should probably be avoided.

Given the problems with diversity indices expressed as heterogeneity measures, any assessment of the Levantine archaeofaunal record should utilize separate measures of richness and evenness. Edwards (1989:236-237) does not use an undifferentiated heterogeneity index; he measures only assemblage evenness. Ignoring richness, however, could result in an inadequate assessment of subsistence change in light of expectations derived from models in which the BSR plays a prominent role. These models predict that more resources will be added to the diet until the point at which domestication economies take hold, resulting in greater richness; the evenness component of diversity, the proportional contribution of staples, would not necessarily change. In fact, Flannery (1969:77-78) more or less anticipated Edwards findings when he pointed out that the BSR itself is not usually characterized by changes in the major food procurement subsystems; the proportional contribution of staple foods might not change at all, so long as those staples remained the dominant components of the diet. The real significance of the diversity characteristic of the BSR lies in the potential for amplification of novel and initially rather minor food procurement subsystems as selective pressure makes such amplification adaptive over the long run. This suggests that, of the two components of diversity, the richness index might be a more meaningful indicator of BSR trends than the evenness index favored by Edwards.

## KINTIGH'S SIMULATION APPROACH

Having noted some of the problems associated with diversity indices, we examine here the richness component of Levantine archaeofaunas using a simulation approach developed by Keith Kintigh (1984, 1989). Kintigh (1989) has published simulation algorithms for both richness and evenness; however, McCartney and Glass (1990) have recently argued that the evenness measure he employs is, in fact, a heterogeneity statistic. While their point might be valid, Kintigh's evenness statistic is a standardized statistic which allows general comparability between cases along with the construction of a confidence interval of expected values. For a true evenness statistic, the construction of an expected curve is somewhat problematic. We will use this evenness measure in conjunction with the richness statistic to identify cases of interest, given the potential interpretive problems just summarized.[2] A strength of the simulation approach is that values for expected richness and evenness are generated for given sample sizes and are accompanied by confidence intervals. Thus, the sample-size problem is avoided at the individual assemblage level. Observed richness and evenness values for each assemblage are computed and then compared with the corresponding expected values and their confidence intervals generated by the simulation. On an intuitive level, the confidence intervals generated by the simulation program would be expected to contain most of the cases. However, because the expected values are based on the combined richness and evenness of all cases rather than on each individual case, many samples fall below the expected values--an adjustment of the algorithm that might provide a better fit for each individual case is suggested by McCartney and Glass (1990). Rather than using the confidence interval as an absolute expectation, these results suggest the expected form of the relationship due to richness and sample size. Samples that deviate from the expected range of variation are easily identified. Since richness and evenness are analyzed separately, the problem of isolating their effects from other components of diversity is circumvented. While simulation approaches are the favored means of assessing diversity in this study, another method utilizing regression techniques might also prove useful (Jones et al. 1983; Grayson 1984; see Rhode [1988] for a comparison of these techniques).

## LEVANTINE ARCHAEOFAUNAL DATA

Edwards's (1989) analysis of Levantine archaeofaunas relies on data from published site reports. In an attempt to maintain comparability with Edwards's study, we have tried to obtain as many of the same site reports as we could, while supplementing them with a few additional, more current references. In some instances, we both resort to faunal data derived from synthetic reports (e.g., Bar-Yosef 1989). It comes as no surprise that exact comparability was not attained. However, if there is robust pattern in Levantine subsistence trends, relatively minor differences in the two data bases should tend to cancel out and have relatively little effect on the overall results.

The temporal span of this study covers approximately 100,000 years, divided into eight culture-stratigraphic analytical units: (1) the Middle Palaeolithic (100,000-37,000 BP); (2) the Upper Palaeolithic (37,000-20,000 BP); (3) the Kebaran (20,000-12,000 BP); (4) the Natufian (12,500-10,000 BP); (5) the (undifferentiated) Neolithic (10,000-6000 BP); (6) the Chalcolithic (6000-5000 BP); (7) the Bronze Age (5000-3200 BP); and (8) the Iron Age (3200-2500 BP). The choice of these analytical units is partly a matter of convention--they are the ones most commonly used in the Levant and largely replicate Edwards's categories--but they are also predicated on the assumption that, in order to detect possible changes in diversity associated with the BSR, bracketing periods of sufficient duration must be examined. If it is assumed that the BSR begins in the late Upper Palaeolithic and continues well into the Neolithic, Middle Palaeolithic and Metal Age archaeofaunas should also be included in the analysis. If the BSR-based models are accurate predictors of vectored change, then there should be a decrease in diversity in the domestication economies of the post-Neolithic era. A time frame of insufficient duration is believed to be a defect of the Edwards study, since he stops at a relatively early point in the Neolithic (8000 BP) and thus would have been unable to detect probable decreases in diversity associated with the effective implementation of intensive agro-pastoral economies of the late Neolithic and Metal Ages.

Although it would have been desirable for statistical purposes, each analytical unit is not represented by an equal number of sites or levels because of problems of preservation, selective excavation, and/or consistency in reporting. Faunal data often consisted only of species lists, without even minimal quantification (e.g., abundance ranking, number of identified specimens [NISP], minimum number of individuals [MNI], etc.). In order to take advantage of a large number of data sets, bone counts (NISPs) were utilized over MNIs to measure elements of diversity (cf. Cruz-Uribe 1988). Periods best represented in terms of the frequency of usable data are the Natufian and the Neolithic, probably reflecting the traditional emphasis on research questions aimed at various aspects of the

**Table 17.3.** Levantine archaeofaunal genera and species.

1. *Equus equus, asinus* (horse, hemione, zebra, ass)
2. *Sus scrofa* (boar, domestic pig)
3. *Dama mesopotamica* (fallow deer)
4. *Capreolus capreolus* (roe deer)
5. *Cervus elaphus* (red deer)
6. *Bos primigenius* (auroch)
7. *Bos taurus* (domestic cattle)
8. *Alcelaphus bucelaphus* (hartebeest)
9. *Gazella gazella* (gazelle)
10. *Capra ibex* (ibex)
11. *Ovis* cf. *aries* (sheep)
12. *Capra/Ovis*
13. *Camelus* cf. *dromedarius* (camel)
14. *Dicerorhinus merki, hemitoechus* (rhino)
15. *Hippopotamus amphibius* (hippo)
16. Large ungulate
17. Small ungulate
18. *Lepus europaeus* (hare)
19. *Vulpes vulpes* (fox)
20. *Erinaceus europaeus* (hedgehog)
21. *Hemiechinus* (long eared hedgehog)
22. *Felis* sp. (cat)
23. *Canis lupus* (wolf)
24. *Panthera pardus, leo* (leopard, lion)
25. *Lynx lynx* (lynx)
26. *Martes martes* (marten)
27. *Meles taxus* (badger)
28. *Hyrax hyrax* (hyrax)
29. *Hystrix* (porcupine)
30. *Testudo* (tortoise)
31. *Clemmys* (tortoise)
32. *Teleostomi* (boney fish)
33. *Sciurus* (squirrel)
34. *Struthio* (ostrich shell)
35. *Otididae* (shell)
36. *Potamon* (crab)
37. *Aves*
38. *Anas* (duck)
39. *Anser* (goose)
40. *Alectoris* (partridge)
41. *Rallus* (water bird)
42. *Phasianidae* (pheasant)
43. *Pteroclidae* (sand grouse)
44. *Fulica* (coot)
45. *Ciconia* (stork)
46. *Columba* (pigeon)
47. *Syrrhaptes* (sand grouse)
48. *Gallus* (wild chicken)
49. *Cygnus* (swan)
50. *Larus* (gull)
51. *Streptopelia* (dove)
52. *Tadorna* (shellduck)
53. *Vanellus* (harpwing)

(Table 17.3--continued)

54. *Bucephala* (duck)
55. *Ammoperdix* (partridge)
56. *Porphyrio* (gallinule)
57. *Chlamytodis* (bustard)
58. *Coturnix* (quail)
59. *Clarias* (fish)

Dropped

1. *Hyaena* (striped hyena)
2. *Crocuta* (spotted hyena)
3. *Mustela nivalis* (polecat)
4. *Buteo* (buzzard)
5. *Bubo* (owl)
6. *Vormella* (polecat)
7. *Aquila* (eagle)
8. *Passeriformes* (sm. birds)
9. *Galerida* (lark)
10. *Corvus* (crow)
11. *Falconiformes* (falcons)
12. *Neophron* (vulture)
13. *Ketupa* (brown fish owl)
14. *Circus* (harrier)

transition in what is usually regarded as a "nuclear area."

We recognize that environmental conditions in the Levant have fluctuated over the past 100,000 years and that these fluctuations likely affected both species ranges and densities. We are also aware of the potential effects of changing environment on species diversity and how such changes might have altered human behavior in relation to species procurement. However, modeling and testing the effects of environmental change in the Levant, an area in which there is no single agreed-upon paleoenvironmental model, and its impact on species diversity and availability lies beyond the scope of this paper (see Schuldenrein [1983] for a discussion of competing paleoenvironmental models). Although certain species were not available at all loci throughout the temporal and spatial range of this study, we think that the inability to control for environmental variability, given the lack of consensus just mentioned, does not invalidate our results, which focus on general evolutionary trends. Moreover, the data are region-wide, so that any sub-regional differences would presumably average out.

The publications that have contributed data to this study are listed in Table 17.2. Sixty-three assemblages are analyzed, compared with the 72 studied by Edwards (1989:228-229), although it appears he only used 29 in his diversity test. Since some reports present information on all species recovered, regardless of their economic potential, a screening process was initiated in order to isolate probable economic species.[3] Only three publications separated economic species from those thought to be non-economic and

**Table 17.4.** Mean values and frequencies of species richness for Levantine archaeofaunas.

| Period | N | # of species | Max # of species | Mean Richness |
|---|---|---|---|---|
| Middle Palaeo. | 9 | 26 | 14 | 8.55 |
| Upper Palaeo. | 7 | 22 | 17 | 8.28 |
| Kebaran | 10 | 27 | 14 | 8.40 |
| Natufian | 11 | 35 | 20 | 10.72 |
| Neolithic | 13 | 43 | 17 | 11.15 |
| Chalcolithic | 3 | 15 | 12 | 8.66 |
| Bronze Age | 7 | 23 | 13 | 9.14 |
| Iron Age | 3 | 17 | 12 | 9.00 |

**Key:** N = number of assemblages; # of species = number of species represented in the archaeofaunas of this time period; max # of species = greatest number of species represented in any one assemblage for this period; mean richness = average number of species in each assemblage for this period.

likely intrusive in cultural deposits (Noy et al. 1980; Payne 1983; Saxon 1974). Building on these and other assessments of economic status, we decided to eliminate all rodents, insectivores, raptors, and reptiles except for tortoises. All Mollusca were eliminated because of inconsistent reporting (i.e., lack of counts) and because the common ornamental use of shell and absence of shell middens suggested that they were not major dietary components (Edwards 1989:231). This screening left the rest of the mammals, birds, and fish as potential food items. Of the 59 species that remained, 22 were birds.

In addition to preliminary screening of the kind just described, a second procedural issue in a diversity study centers on how to classify the remaining "economic" species. Should every species be represented by a single unique category, or should some species be combined in a more inclusive taxon (e.g., *Lepus* spp.)? The former tends to inflate richness levels, while the latter tends to depress them. Although the avifaunal classification used here might be somewhat overfine, it replicates the approach taken by Edwards. Unlike Edwards, we aggregate mammalian species into genera (e.g., *Equus* spp.). The faunal categories used in this study are given in Table 17.3 (cf. Edwards 1989:229-230).

## SPECIES RICHNESS AND EVENNESS SIMULATIONS

Two measures of species richness and evenness were undertaken using mean values and Kintigh's program (1989). This allowed us to compare assem-

blages aggregated by analytical units and to look at time trends. The richness/evenness program analysis comprised eight runs which treated each individual culture-stratigraphic unit as the analytical universe. The intent here was to examine within-period diversity to isolate any apparent internal trends. A combined-group run would have swamped any trends and is considered irrelevant to this study. Simple comparisons of the number of different species utilized by time period are also provided to assess very general trends that ignore the effects of sample-size differences. We first discuss the least complex measure, means and frequencies, and then the within-period simulations.

### Species Diversity: Means and Frequencies

An examination of the richness and evenness statistics that ignores sample-size differences indicates some interesting trends (Table 17.4). The total number of economic species per culture-stratigraphic unit fluctuates from the Middle Palaeolithic through the Kebaran and then rises sharply and attains a maximum during the Natufian and the Neolithic. This peak is followed by an even sharper decline during the Chalcolithic and by subsequent partial recovery and fluctuation in the post-Neolithic periods. Taken at face value, such a crude measure tends to support the BSR concept, but maximum diversity appears to occur in the late, rather than in the early, Epipalaeolithic. The decline in richness associated with the effective implementation of domestication economies during the post-Neolithic eras also agrees well with vectored subsistence change under conditions of increased population density predicted by BSR-based models (e.g., Christenson 1980; Clark 1987; cf. Figure 17.1).

Maximum single-site species richness values and mean species richness statistics are also given in Table 17.4. Inspection of maximum richness values indicates a trend toward increasing richness through time, with a peak during the Natufian and the Neolithic, followed by a rather sharp decline. While again supportive of the BSR concept, this measure represents only the single most diverse faunal assemblage from each time period. A better indicator of general time trends is the mean species richness statistic, which peaks in the Natufian/Neolithic and is, once again, followed by a sharp decline. The mean richness values are probably affected to some extent by sample-size differences.

The summary statistics for evenness (Table 17.5) tend to support Edwards's (1989:237) conclusion that the highest mean evenness values coincide with the Middle Palaeolithic and then decline steadily through the Neolithic. In the post-Neolithic periods, mean evenness increases slightly, but never to the level reached in the Middle Palaeolithic. It was this sort of

**Table 17.5.** Summary statistics of species evenness[a] for Levantine archaeofaunas.

| Period | N | Max. | Min. | Mean | Median |
|---|---|---|---|---|---|
| Middle Palaeolithic | 9 | .6305 | .2391 | .4736 | .5000 |
| Upper Palaeolithic | 7 | .6159 | .0854 | .3438 | .4194 |
| Kebaran | 10 | .5732 | .2374 | .3781 | .3501 |
| Natufian | 11 | .5884 | .1859 | .3312 | .2586 |
| Neolithic | 13 | .5216 | .1262 | .3167 | .3074 |
| Chalcolithic | 3 | .5951 | .2191 | .4337 | .4871 |
| Bronze Age | 7 | .5518 | .2186 | .3878 | .3550 |
| Iron Age | 3 | .5283 | .1436 | .2857 | .1853 |

[a]An evenness value of 1.0 indicates that each class of species in the assemblage is represented by a uniform number of parts--e.g., an assemblage with three species each containing two bones would have a value of 1.0. Low evenness values suggest specialization or an increase in the number of species represented. For example, an assemblage comprised of one species would have an evenness value of 0.0, while another dominated by high frequencies of one species and lower frequencies of several other species would also tend to have a low evenness value.

trend and statistic--mean values regardless of sample size--that Edwards (1989) used to support his claim that diversity was highest early on, in the Middle Palaeolithic, and not in the Epipalaeolithic, as the BSR model would suggest. Aside from the sample-size problem, other factors need to be considered in his interpretation. Foremost is the assumption that higher evenness is equal to greater diversity. Since evenness is a monitor of the proportional distribution of species, a high evenness value might indicate a relatively equal proportion of species utilization, while a lower evenness statistic might correspond to more selective species utilization or to an increase in the number of species utilized. In the latter instance, the traditional resources might be utilized in the same frequencies, but, because of added species, their proportional representation declines. It is possible that the decline in mean evenness over time is in response to the increase in number of species utilized, a trend which is apparent from the mean richness values.

In summary, at this low level of resolution, some of the trends predicted by BSR-based models appear to be verified. However, we wish to emphasize that these basic statistics, while they produce results supportive of the model, are fraught with sampling problems of various kinds and should be utilized only as a first approximation before proceeding to analytical approaches that scale diversity indices to sample-size differences.

## Species Diversity:
## Simulations Within Time Periods

Here simulations are confined to each of the eight analytical units. The results of these simulations are summarized in Figures 17.3-17.4. The range of expected values generated from the different site-specific sample sizes are represented by the three lines, and the placement of individual assemblage scores in relation to them by squares. The solid center line is the mean expected value, and the dashed lines that bracket it are the upper and lower confidence intervals. A 90% confidence interval is used throughout. In all the figures, sample size, richness, and evenness represent the actual values for each of the assemblages.

### Middle Palaeolithic

As might be expected, interpretation of the within-period patterns is not as straightforward as was the case with the mean and frequency data. This is due in part to the general tendency for all periods to exhibit levels of richness beneath the confidence interval. These lower-than-expected levels are a function of how the program calculated the expected values (see McCartney and Glass [1990] for a discussion of this phenomenon). All Middle Palaeolithic sites fall well below the lower confidence interval, which initially suggested lower-than-expected diversity in these faunal assemblages (Figure 17.3a,b). However, given the nature of the program and the fact that all assemblages tend to fall below the expected interval, our interpretation utilizes the confidence interval as a general model of the sample-size effect to which the data are expected to conform. Exact fit within the bounds of the confidence interval is not expected. Deviations from the general relationship expressed by the model (e.g., assemblages within or above the confidence interval, those outside the expected sample-size trend) are apt to be the most interesting aspects of these data in terms of diversity questions. Working with these assumptions, the Middle Palaeolithic pattern indicates that richness (Figure 17.3a) and evenness (Figure 17.3b) tend to be a result of the sample-size effect. No assemblage deviates substantially from its expected values--i.e., there are no large samples with either very low or very high richness/evenness statistics. This suggests that observed richness and evenness values can be explained in terms of the sample-size effect. On an interpretative level, these assemblages appear to represent essentially the same range of economic activities; there are no indications of specialization or intensification in food procurement at any one site. This apparently generalized economic behavior might reflect a random sample of species from the local environment. These results are somewhat surprising, given the general expectation that rockshelter contexts are thought to have, on average, more diverse faunas than open sites. It might be the case, since the human component in the accumulation of these faunas was overall probably very low, that similar background faunas are primarily being sampled, regardless of whether they come from rockshelters or open sites. Other studies indicate that the overall intensity of human use of caves and rockshelters during the Middle Palaeolithic was, in general, minimal, with the result that the human contribution to the accumulation of faunas in such sites was also probably minimal (see Straus 1982; Jelinek 1988; Stiner 1990).

## Upper Palaeolithic

The Upper Palaeolithic simulations indicate that most of the sites follow the linear sample-size trend predicted by the simulation model. However, one assemblage (Kebara E) is richer than expected, and another (Kebara D) falls just below the lower confidence interval (Figure 17.3c). The remainder adhere to a pattern consistent with the sample-size effect. It is interesting to note that, overall, Upper Palaeolithic mean richness is slightly lower than that of the Middle Palaeolithic (8.28 vs. 8.55; see Table 17.4), thus underscoring how the use of grand means to ascertain changes in resource diversity can sometimes be misleading when sample size is not taken into account. While the richest Upper Palaeolithic assemblages are from Kebara Cave, other rockshelter assemblages (e.g., Qafzeh 9, el-Wad D) conform to expected trends, as do all the Upper Palaeolithic open sites (e.g., Azraq 17, Hasa 618). The Upper Palaeolithic graph indicates more differentiation in richness values than that of the Middle Palaeolithic, with at least some sites substantially richer than any Levantine Middle Palaeolithic site. There is no correlation with site context. The evenness simulation tends to reinforce

our interpretation of richness, in that the same Kebara samples also deviate from the expected values (Figure 17.3d). This suggests that greater richness was associated with a more equitable resource usage than would be expected if the local environments were sampled at random.

## Kebaran

The early and late Epipalaeolithic plots are given in Figure 17.3e,f (Kebaran) and 17.3g,h (Natufian). As we approach the BSR interval, analytical units are of shorter duration. The Kebaran simulation is comprised of both Kebaran and Geometric Kebaran assemblages (Figure 17.3e,f). In examining the richness simulation, the tight, linear sample-size effect noted for the Middle and Upper Palaeolithic is less apparent when the individual assemblage distribution is compared to the the confidence interval. Three assemblages fall in or above the expected range (Iraq e'Zigan, Kebara C, Hammeh 26). Even if the Hammeh 26 and Kebara C assemblages are ignored, a considerable amount of variability in the distribution of the remaining assemblages suggests a difference in animal exploitation which is not apparent in the earlier periods.

Evenness plots for the Kebaran assemblages also suggest exploitation patterns distinct from those of the earlier periods (Figure 17.3f). Five assemblages (Iraq e'Zigan, Ein Gev I, Hammeh 26, Kebara C, Hefsibah) fall within or above the confidence interval. The remainder only very roughly conform to the sample-size trend expected if these were random selections from the environment. The expected sample-size trend does not adequately describe the distribution of these Kebaran assemblages (cf. the Middle Palaeolithic pattern), and the variability in evenness could correspond to a different pattern of species utilization. Kebaran samples appear to be more diverse in a relative sense, since the number of species present in the Middle and Upper Palaeolithic, and in the Kebaran, is rather similar (26, 22, 27, respectively; see Table 17.4).

## Natufian

In some contrast to the Kebaran plots, the Natufian assemblages tend to conform to the expected sample-size trend generated by the simulation. Only 3 of the 11 assemblages (Hammeh 27, Kebara B, Hasa 1065) fall within or above the confidence intervals (Figure 17.3g), suggesting that, in the latter part of the Epipalaeolithic, significantly richer faunal assemblages

**Figure 17.3.** Richness (a,c,e,g) and evenness (b,d,f,h) simulations for four of the eight analytical units used by convention to structure Levantine archaeological research. The bracketing lines represent a 90% confidence interval, which provides a general model of the sample-size effect. Exact fit within the bounds is not expected. See Figure 17.4 for the four remaining analytical units.

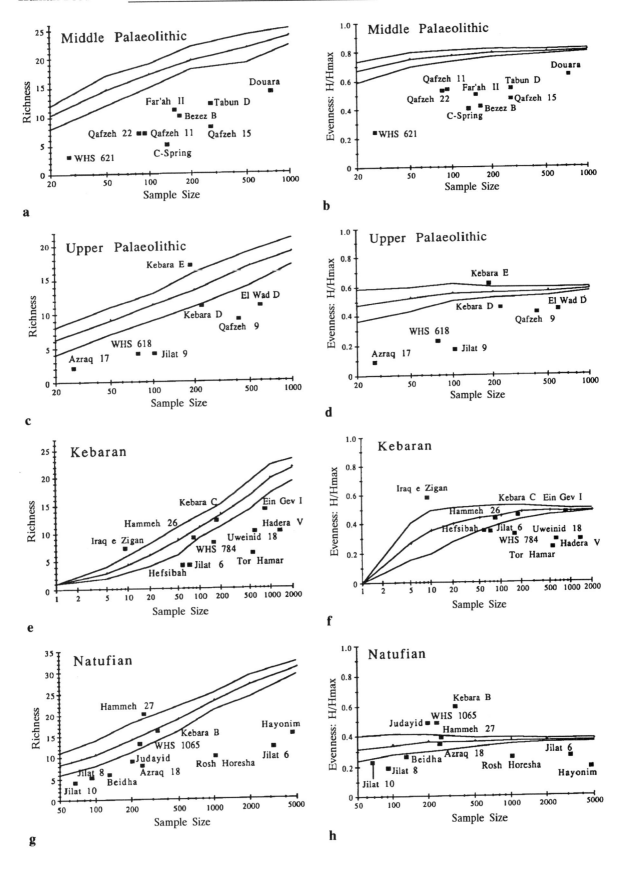

a

b

c

d

e

f

g

h

were being created by human behavior, thus conforming to the expectations of BSR-based models. Although all assemblages do not deviate from the sample-size effect, the fact that some do indicates a continuation of behavioral activities that were largely absent prior to the early Epipalaeolithic.

The evenness simulation shows that slightly more than half of the assemblages follow sample-size trend expectations, while five (Kebara B, Hasa 1065, Hammeh 27, Azraq 18, Judayid) deviate from this pattern (Figure 17.3h). These departures from expected evenness indicate assemblages utilizing species in a proportion greater than would be expected from a more random pattern. It is not a coincidence that the three assemblages with high richness values also deviate from the expected evenness pattern.

It is of some interest to note that the sustained, episodic, but relatively intensive use of the Levantine rockshelters appears to have come to an end sometime in the late Epipalaeolithic/early Neolithic, possibly because they were becoming filled with accumulated natural and cultural debris. After about 8,000 years ago, tangible evidence of human use of rockshelters is largely confined to layers of goat and sheep droppings and to the casual hearths produced by generations of shepherds who used, and continue to use, these natural shelters as temporary corrals. This region-wide change in site context may have had a general effect on the composition of archaeofaunas, since it effectively eliminated the better preservation characteristic of protected, sediment-trap localities.

## Neolithic

The higher richness values continue into the Neolithic, where three collections fall within or above the confidence intervals (Azraq 31, Jericho PN, Gilgal). In general, a roughly linear trend due to the sample-size effect can be detected for most of the other samples, though many are of a similar size and tend to cluster in the center of the diagram (Figure 17.4a). Perhaps most interesting is the appearance of a very large collection with a low richness value (Beidha). This is the first indication of some sort of fairly clear-cut economic specialization--i.e., the intensive utilization of a few species. It is not surprising that this signature appears for the first time in the Neolithic, when the earliest undisputed domestication economies occur. Two other collections (Ujrat, Ain Ghazal PPNB) are more ambiguous in this respect, but

may also represent this tendency toward specialization. The evenness simulation for the Neolithic tends to confirm these conclusions (Figure 17.4b). Both Beidha and Ujrat are lower in evenness than would be expected (i.e., they cannot be explained by the sample-size effect), suggesting that some sort of specialization in animal procurement and use was occurring. In fact, both these assemblages are dominated by high frequencies of *Capra*. Most of the collections can be explained in terms of the sample-size effect (interpreted here as a sort of random selection from the environment), while a few represent greater evenness than expected (Gilgal, Jericho PN, Jericho PPNB, Azraq 31, Ain Ghazal PPNB).

In sum, the Neolithic collections appear to signal the beginnings of a shift in animal resource utilization when compared with earlier periods. Some assemblages indicate a continuation of the trend towards greater richness and evenness noted for much of the Epipalaeolithic and believed to correspond to the beginning of the BSR. Others, however, indicate a **decrease** in diversity (richness and evenness) that can be argued to mark the onset of intensified selection of a few economically important species, such as sheep or goats, at the expense of others less amenable to manipulation. Since the Neolithic sample aggregates all periods, we might be detecting the beginning of intensified agro-pastoral economies characterized by a progressive narrowing of the human food niche.

There is another aspect to these data that has nothing directly to do with economic changes, but which effects our capacity to detect and make sense of economic patterns. The Neolithic sample is heavily dominated by open-air sites, whereas many of the pre-Neolithic samples were recovered from cave and rockshelter contexts. The latter tend to have better-preserved faunas and to serve as carnivore lairs and dens; they are also frequented by raptors (e.g., Kebara). In general, it seems likely that there would be a larger non-human component in the bone assemblages from caves and rockshelters than from open air sites, at least from the Upper Palaeolithic on. This probably holds true regardless of culture-stratigraphic unit affiliation and would only be questionable for pre-Upper Palaeolithic units, where recent taphonomic studies have cast doubt on the predatory abilities of pre-modern hominids (see, e.g., Binford 1981, 1985). This means that, from the Neolithic "on up," we can probably have more confidence that archaeofaunal patterns are, indeed, monitoring economic, or at least

**Figure 17.4.** Richness (a,c,e,g) and evenness (b,d,f,h) simulations for four of the eight analytical units used by convention to structure Levantine archaeological research. The bracketing lines represent a 90% confidence interval, which provides a general model of the sample-size effect. Exact fit within bounds is not expected. See Figure 17.3 for the other four analytical units.

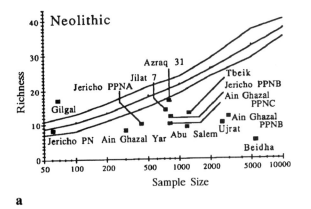

a

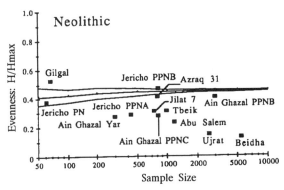

b

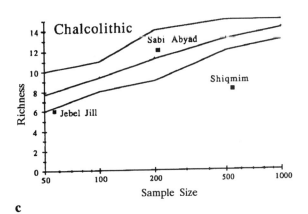

c

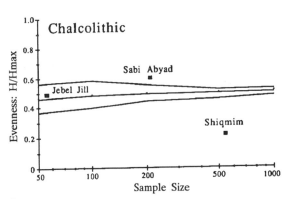

d

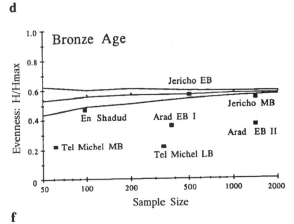

e

f

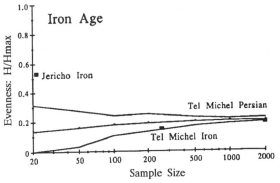

g

h

human behavioral, change, since the confounding effects of non-human agencies are minimized.

## Chalcolithic

Two of the three Chalcolithic assemblages (Jebel Jill, Sabi Abyad) fall within the expected range of richness (Figure 17.4c,d). While, on the face of it, this might suggest that Chalcolithic sites are comparable in terms of richness to those of the preceding Neolithic, the sharp drop in the number of species exploited (53 in the Neolithic vs. 15 in the Chalcolithic) in fact indicates a significant difference in resource exploitation. This pattern is also replicated in a decline in the maximum number of species recorded at a single site (20 vs. 12) and in a drop in the mean richness statistic from 11.15 (Neolithic) to 8.66 (Chalcolithic) (Table 17.4). However, because the sample size is so small (n = 3), there is a high likelihood that the richness and evenness simulations are compromised, since one collection usually falls above the confidence interval, one below it, and one within it (Kintigh, personal communication, 1992). Thus, the results from very small samples, such as those of the Chalcolithic and Iron Age, should be set aside until a more robust data set can be compiled for testing.

## Bronze and Iron Ages

No Bronze Age sample falls within the range of expected richness values, and they generally conform to the sample-size trend (Figure 17.4e). This suggests that the increased diversity characteristic of the Kebaran, Natufian, and Neolithic has begun to decline in subsequent periods, probably because of the combined effects of intensive agro-pastoral economies, on the one hand, and increasingly widespread habitat destruction, on the other (for a well-documented example of these processes at the Jordanian Neolithic site of Ain Ghazal, see Köhler-Rollefson et al. 1988; Rollefson and Simmons 1988).

The evenness plot also generally follows the sample-size effect, but two modes are apparent: one well below the expected confidence interval, interpreted here as essentially a random choice of species, and a second one higher up on the graph indicating sites with greater evenness (En Shadud, Jericho EB, Jericho MB) (Figure 17.4f). Although the latter three assemblages do not appear to be significantly richer than the others, they do seem to indicate a more even use of economic species than might be expected (cf. Figures 17.4e,f). Such a trend could indicate sedentary or semi-sedentary community use of several domesticated species in a roughly equivalent manner, rather than the highly focused specialization on one or two species that occurs in some pastoral adaptations. Finally, the three Iron Age assemblages suffer from the same

small sample-size effect as the Chalcolithic assemblages (Figure 17.4g,h). Any attempt to identify and interpret pattern in the Iron Age sample would be fruitless.

In summary, the patterns noted in the within-period simulations are by no means conclusive by themselves, although the overall trend is at least suggestive of support for the BSR model. Because richness and evenness generally follow a sample-size trend in all analytical units, exact replication of patterns expected under BSR-based models is not achieved (cf. Figure 17.2). While the patterns detected here might be affected by the variables selected (unlikely, in our view) or by the fact that some units are only represented by a few collections (the effects of which have been noted for the Chalcolithic and Iron Age samples) or by some defect in the simulation algorithm itself (see above), we can only partition potential sources of error impressionistically. Once sample-size effects are taken into account, however, these Levantine archaeofaunas do, in fact, appear to become more, rather than less, diverse through time. This directly contradicts Edwards's (1989:240-242) conclusions that they are relatively diverse throughout the entire sequence and that no marked increases in diversity can be detected that might correspond to the BSR.

Assuming the foregoing to be an accurate account of prehistoric subsistence change in the Levant, within the limitations of the evidence, some general conclusions can be made on the basis of the within-period simulations of richness and evenness. Contra Edwards's (1989:237) contention that diversity was already high at the beginning of the sequence (1989: 237), the richness/evenness simulations for the Middle Palaeolithic conform to an expected relationship determined by sample-size effects (the reader is reminded that Edwards was measuring only evenness). This is the only period in which the richness and evenness values for all assemblages fall below the confidence bands and exhibit a single linear relationship based on sample size. The Upper and early Epipalaeolithic periods show some increases in diversity, as a few of the assemblages deviate from the expected sample-size trend. Those analytical units with the largest numbers of divergent assemblages are, once again, the Kebaran, the Natufian, and the Neolithic--the periods just prior to and including the "domestication" interval. Subsequent periods tend to be less diverse, although this is not always apparent from the graphs alone (see Table 17.4).

We believe that these trends offer some support for BSR-based models, but acknowledge that they also fail to account for a substantial part of the variability present in the data. As Edwards (1989:232) notes, one problem with coarse-grained analyses like these is that they must assume site function and site duration to be relatively equal and constant across time, or at least across the analytical units being compared. In actuality, this is not likely to be the case. Much of the assemblage discordance might be due to such functional and temporal variation--factors not usually addressed or even discernible in individual site reports. This tends to make the data noisy and renders the quest for pattern somewhat problematic (see, e.g., the questions raised by Stiner [1992]). However, we can discern no ready solution to this dilemma, which is universal in all regional archaeological research. Presumably, as more sites are excavated and published, the regional archaeofaunal data base will improve.

## CONCLUSIONS

At the beginning of this essay, we suggested that the BSR model should be re-examined in the Levant using a diversity index, richness, that might be more sensitive to subsistence changes caused by population/resource imbalances than those monitored by another component of diversity, evenness. We also indicated that conclusions drawn from a previous study of Levantine archaeofaunas by Phillip Edwards (1989) were problematic because of (1) his use of an evenness measure, Shannon's *J*, and the fact that he ignored richness; (2) his failure to consider subsistence changes more recent than a relatively early phase of the Neolithic; (3) his failure to distinguish between economic and non-economic faunas; and (4) his failure to take sample-size effects into account. His contention that Levantine archaeofaunas were diverse from start to finish and that no vectored change in the direction of increasing diversity was apparent during the most likely BSR interval, the Epipalaeolithic, appears to us to be unfounded. These considerations led him to conclude that there was no evidence to support the BSR in the Levant and that taxonomic diversity was unrelated to trends towards food production at the end of the Pleistocene. We were inclined to be skeptical, since there is considerable support for BSR-based models in other parts of the world, and we could see no reason why the Levant should be exceptional in this regard. We tried to make our evaluation comparable to his by examining essentially the same data base (63 collections analyzed vs. 72[29] for Edwards). Unlike Edwards, however, we made a distinction beforehand between economic and non-economic faunas, since we thought that economic patterns might be swamped by the general characteristics of similar and numerically predominant background faunas.

Of our original expectations, we were able to tentatively document population growth over time, using a procedure that scaled site numbers to time

within culture-stratigraphic analytical units. After millennia of near stasis, episodes of accelerated population growth apparently occurred during the Neolithic and again in the Metal Ages. We also computed a number of species richness statistics on the faunal data by culture-stratigraphic unit. These means and frequencies provided the clearest indications of support for BSR-based models, since, as expected, they attained maximum values in the Epipalaeolithic and Neolithic. Since these are the analytical units best represented by archaeofaunal data and since there is a generally acknowledged correlation between diversity and the size of an archaeofaunal assemblage, the mean and frequency data can only be used as a first approximation (Grayson 1984; Meltzer et al. 1992).

The simulations corrected for these sample-size problems by imposing confidence intervals around individual sample means and providing a display of the expected relationship between richness/evenness and sample size. This allows comparison between the heuristic model and the data. However, pursuing diversity questions with simulation approaches proved to be a complex endeavor. The within-period simulations provided tentative support for the BSR, since patterns indicating greater richness and evenness occurred in the Kebaran, Natufian, and Neolithic, followed by predicted declines during the Metal Ages. A problem with the within-period simulations is that the scales used to derive these trends are not directly comparable. We were thus forced to monitor the relative frequency of sites that deviated from the expected relationship by using data with some analytical units poorly represented.

Despite some doubts about their utility, but because Edwards (1989) used them, within-period simulations of evenness were also run on the data. Surprisingly, these tended to confirm the results of the within-period simulations of richness, again indicating tentative support for an Epipalaeolithic/Neolithic BSR in the Levant. Given Edwards's (1989) results, we expected that the evenness simulations would provide indications of high diversity throughout the sequence. Our efforts to employ the latter on the same data set should have produced results comparable to those of Edwards. It did not. Instead, Levantine archaeofaunas tended to exhibit variability around the sample-size trend for evenness which increased through time, essentially corresponding to the expectations of the BSR. This pattern obtained regardless of the diversity measure (richness or evenness) used.

There are several reasons why we think our results are at such variance with those of Edwards (1989). First, he ignores richness as a component of diversity. We think that a richness index is easier to interpret than an evenness index. Second, he equates higher evenness with greater diversity. This assumes that a decrease in evenness is also a decrease in diversity, but this is not necessarily so. Third, his analysis provides no control for sample size, which is known to correlate with diversity, in general, and, in specific, with evenness and richness (Grayson 1984). Because of this, his explanation of the variability in his data is suspect, since we cannot determine the relationship between his values and the samples from which they were derived. Kintigh's (1984, 1989) simulation program has the advantage that expected relationships between the two are graphically displayed. Finally, the number of assemblages analyzed for each period (generally three to four) is often very small and is, therefore, apt to be misleading (e.g., the problems noted for the Chalcolithic and Iron Age samples).

Defects in both studies are mainly related to the poor and variable resolution of the Levantine archaeofaunal record itself. They are aggravated by variable field procedures, such as differences in recovery techniques, and inconsistencies in the ways in which basic data are reported. Future efforts should, of course, attempt to incorporate economic plant data; this would obviously provide a more complete picture of prehistoric adaptations than the consideration of faunal data alone. For a variety of reasons, however, efforts to include plant data in diversity studies have not met with much success (Clark 1987:299-301). Everyone acknowledges that, except perhaps in arctic "photosynthetic deserts," plants have been important in the human diet from time immemorial, but they are notoriously resistant to quantification. A more subtle deficiency has to do with a failure to control for the geographical distribution of site locations over time. It would be important to know, for example, whether or not similar habitats were equally accessible during each period, so that similarities in access to faunal resources could be assumed.

Unravelling the relationships among diversification, intensification, population growth, and the appearance of domestication economies is a complex and frustrating process. However, a positive aspect of this research is that model building has proceeded to the point where fairly explicit test implications can be generated about pattern and subsequently compared with regional data sets. BSR-based models are in the vanguard of this research and have, in our opinion, considerable explanatory potential. We would be loath to abandon them simply because of instances where construals of pattern do not neatly coincide with expectations, especially in the absence of viable alternatives.

## ACKNOWLEDGMENTS

This is Wadi Hasa Palaeolithic Project Contribution Number 12, supported by the National Science Foundation (Grant Nos. BNS-8405601, BNS-8921863, BNS-9013972), the National Geographic Society (Grant No. 2914-84), the Chase Bank of Arizona, and the Research Vice-President's Office, Arizona State University (Grant No. 90-0729). The support of the Department of Antiquities, Hashemite Kingdom of Jordan, and the American Center for Oriental Research (Amman) is gratefully acknowledged.

## NOTES

[1]Like most Levantine prehistorians, we are of the opinion that plant foods were important components in the human diet from the earliest colonization of the region by hominids ca. 1,400,000 years ago (Tchernov 1987) until the present. The problem, of course, is quantification. While we have more or less defensible monitors of the relative importance of animal species in archaeological sites, no corresponding quantitative measures of the dietary importance of plant resources have been devised. Consequently, it is hard to put empirical "teeth" into studies of the relative importance of plants, even when plant data are reasonably common in the archaeological records, as during the Bronze and Iron Ages.

[2]Because of inadequacies in the archaeological data matrices, many of the diversity indices for both richness and evenness are of little use for archaeological applications, according to Bobrowsky and Ball (1989). In fact, they favor only three for richness and two for evenness. They recommend that undifferentiated heterogeneity measures be avoided because they confound the effects of different components of diversity.

[3]In his statistical calculations, and in subsequent discussion, Edwards (1989) apparently did not attempt to separate the faunal remains into economic and non-economic (i.e., background) components. It is therefore possible that economic patterns are swamped, or at least obscured, by patterns in the sometimes numerically overwhelming non-economic faunas. In our opinion, his failure to make this distinction has led him to conclude, probably erroneously, that Levantine archaeofaunas are essentially the same and about equally diverse throughout the sequence.

## REFERENCES

Akkermans, P. M. M. G.
1987    A late Neolithic and Early Halaf village at Sabi Abyad, northern Syria. *Paléorient* 13:23-40.
Bar-Yosef, O.
1989    Upper Pleistocene cultural stratigraphy in southwest Asia. In *The Emergence of Modern Humans*. E. Trinkaus, ed. Pp. 154-180. Cambridge: Cambridge University Press.
Binford, L. R.
1968    Post-Pleistocene adaptations. In *New Perspectives in Archaeology*. S. R. Binford and L. R. Binford, eds. Pp. 313-341. Chicago: Aldine.
1981    *Bones: Ancient Men and Modern Myths*. Orlando: Academic Press.
1983    *In Pursuit of the Past*. New York: Thames and Hudson.
1985    Human ancestors: Changing views of their behavior. *Journal of Anthropological Archaeology* 4:292-327.
Bobrowsky, P. T., and B. F. Ball
1989    The theory and mechanics of ecological diversity in archaeology. In *Quantifying Diversity in Archaeology*. R. D. Leonard and G. T. Jones, eds. Pp. 4-12. Cambridge:

Cambridge University Press.

Bouchud, J.
1974   Etude préliminaire de la faune provenant de la grotte du Djebel Qafzeh, près de Nazareth, Israël. *Paléorient* 2:87-102.

Butler, B. H., E. Tchernov, H. Hietala, and S. Davis
1977   Faunal exploitation during the Late Epipaleolithic in the Har Harif. In *Prehistory and Paleoenvironments in the Central Negev, Israel. Volume 2.* A. E. Marks, ed. Pp. 327-345. Dallas: Southern Methodist University Press.

Christenson, A. L.
1980   Change in the human food niche in response to population growth. In *Modeling Change in Prehistoric Subsistence Economies.* T. K. Earle and A. L. Christenson, eds. Pp. 31-72. New York: Academic Press.

Clark, G. A.
1987   From the Mousterian to the Metal Ages: Long-term change in the human diet of northern Spain. In *The Pleistocene Old World: Regional Perspectives.* O. Soffer, ed. Pp. 293-316. New York: Plenum Publishing.

Clark, G. A., and S. Yi
1983   Niche-width variation in Cantabrian archaeofaunas: A diachronic study. In *Animals and Archaeology. Volume 1. Hunters and their Prey.* J. Clutton-Brock and C. Grigson, eds. Pp. 183-208. BAR International Series 163. Oxford: British Archaeological Reports.

Clark, G. A., D. Majchrowicz, and N. R. Coinman
1988a  A typological and technological study of Upper Paleolithic collections from the WHS with observations on adjacent time-stratigraphic units. In *The Wadi Hasa Archaeological Survey 1979-1983, West-Central Jordan.* B. MacDonald, ed. Pp. 87-127. Waterloo: Wilfrid Laurier University Press.

Clark, G. A., J. Lindly, M. Donaldson, A. Garrard, N. Coinman, J. Schuldenrein, S. Fish, and D. Olszewski
1988b  Excavations at Middle, Upper and Epipaleolithic sites in the Wadi Hasa, west-central Jordan. In *The Prehistory of Jordan.* A. N. Garrard and H. G. Gebel, eds. Pp. 209-285. BAR International Series 396. Oxford: British Archaeological Reports.

Clutton-Brock, J.
1970   The fossil fauna from an Upper Pleistocene site in Jordan. *Journal of Zoology* 162:19-29.
1979   The mammalian remains from the Jericho tell. *Proceedings of the Prehistoric Society* 45:135-157.

Cohen, M. N.
1977   *The Food Crisis in Prehistory: Overpopulation and the Origins of Agriculture.* New Haven: Yale University Press.

Coinman, N. R., G. A. Clark, and J. Lindly
1988   A diachronic study of Palaeolithic and Early Neolithic site placement patterns in the southern tributaries of the Wadi el Hasa. In *The Wadi el Hasa Archaeological Survey 1979-1983, West-Central Jordan.* B. MacDonald, ed. Pp. 48-86. Waterloo: Wilfrid Laurier University Press.

Cruz-Uribe, K.
1988   The use and meaning of species diversity and richness in archaeological faunas. *Journal of Archaeological Science* 15:179-196.

Davis, S.
1974   Animal remains from the Kebaran site of Ein Gev I, Jordan Valley, Israel. *Paléorient* 2:453-462.

Dayan, T., E. Tchernov, and O. Bar-Yosef
1986   Animal exploitation in Ujrat el-Meked, a Neolithic site in southern Sinai. *Paléorient* 12:105-116.

Earle, T. K.
1980   A model of subsistence change. In *Modeling Change in Prehistoric Subsistence Economies.* T. K. Earle and A.

L. Christenson, eds. Pp. 1-29. New York: Academic Press.

Edwards, P. C.
1989   Revising the Broad Spectrum Revolution: Its role in the origins of southwest Asian food production. *Antiquity* 63:225-246.

Edwards, P. C., S. J. Bourke, S. M. Colledge, J. Head, and P. G. Macumber
1988   Late Pleistocene prehistory in Wadi al-Hammeh, Jordan Valley. In *The Prehistory of Jordan.* A. N. Garrard and H. G. Gebel, eds. Pp. 525-565. BAR International Series 396. Oxford: British Archaeological Reports.

Flannery, K. V.
1969   Origins and ecological effects of early domestication in Iran and the Near East. In *The Domestication and Exploitation of Plants and Animals.* P. J. Ucko and G. W. Dimbleby, eds. Pp. 73-100. Chicago: Aldine.
1986   *Guila Naquitz.* New York: Academic Press.

Garrard, A. N.
1983   The Palaeolithic faunal remains from Adlun and their ecological context. In *Adlun in the Stone Age: The Excavations of D.A.E. Garrod in the Lebanon, 1958-1963.* D. Roe, ed. Pp. 397-409. BAR International Series 159. Oxford: British Archaeological Reports.

Garrard, A. N., A. Betts, B. Byrd, S. Colledge, and C. Hunt
1988a  Summary of paleoenvironmental and prehistoric investigations in the Azraq Basin. In *The Prehistory of Jordan.* A. N. Garrard and H. G. Gebel, eds. Pp. 311-337. BAR International Series 396. Oxford: British Archaeological Reports.

Garrard, A. N., S. Colledge, C. Hunt, and R. Montague
1988b  Environment and subsistence during the Late Pleistocene and Early Holocene in the Azraq Basin. *Paléorient* 14:40-49.

Gilead, I., and C. Grigson
1984   Far'ah II: A Middle Palaeolithic open-air site in the northern Negev, Israel. *Proceedings of the Prehistoric Society* 50:71-97.

Grayson, D. K.
1984   *Quantitative Zooarchaeology.* New York: Academic Press.

Grigson, C.
1987   Shiqmim: Pastoralism and other aspects of animal management in the Chalcolithic of the northern Negev. In *Shiqmim I.* T. E. Levy. Pp. 219-241. BAR International Series 356. Oxford: British Archaeological Reports.

Hecker, H. M.
1982   Domestication revisited: Its implications for faunal analysis. *Journal of Field Archaeology* 9:217-236.
1989   Beidha Natufian: Faunal report. In The *Natufian Encampment at Beidha.* B. F. Byrd. Pp. 97-101. Jutland Archaeological Society Publications XXIII. Aarhus: Aarhus University Press.

Heller, J.
1978   The faunal remains of Iraq e Zigan, a Late Pleistocene site on Mt. Carmel. *Israel Journal of Zoology* 27:11-19.

Hellwing, S., and N. Feig
1989   Animal bones. In *Excavations at Tel Michel, Israel.* Z. Herzog, G. Raap, Jr., and O. Negbi, eds. Pp. 236-247. Minneapolis and Tel Aviv: The University of Minnesota Press and The Sonia and Marco Nadler Institute of Archaeology.

Henry, D. O., and A. N. Garrard
1988   Tor Hamar: An Epipaleolithic rockshelter in southern Jordan. *Palestine Exploration Quarterly* 120:1-25.

Henry, D. O., A. Leroi-Gourhan, and S. Davis
1981   The excavation of Hayonim Terrace: An examination of terminal Pleistocene climatic and adaptive change.

*Journal of Archaeological Science* 8:33-58.

Henry, D. O., F. A. Hassan, K. Cooper Henry, and M. Jones
1983    An investigation of the prehistory of southern Jordan. *Palestine Exploration Quarterly* 83:1-24.

Henry, D. O., and P. F. Turnbull
1985    Archaeological and faunal evidence from Natufian and Timnian sites in southern Jordan. *Bulletin of the American Schools of Oriental Research* 257:45-64.

Horowitz, L. K.
1985    The En Shadud faunal remains. In *En Shadud: Salvage Excavations at a Farming Community in the Jezreel Valley, Israel*. E. Braun, ed. Pp. 168-177. BAR International Series 249. Oxford: British Archaeological Reports.

Jelinek, A. J.
1988    Technology, typology, and culture in the Middle Palaeolithic. In *Upper Pleistocene Prehistory of Western Eurasia*. H. L. Dibble and A. Montet-White, eds. Pp. 199-212. University Museum Monograph 54. Philadelphia: The University Museum, University of Pennsylvania.

Jones, G. T., D. K. Grayson, and C. Beck
1983    Artifact class richness and sample size in archaeological surface assemblages. In *Lulu Linear Punctated: Essays in Honor of George Irving Quimby*. R. C. Dunnell and D. K. Grayson, eds. Pp. 55-73. Anthropological Papers 72. Ann Arbor: Museum of Anthropology, University of Michigan.

Kintigh, K. W.
1984    Measuring archaeological diversity by comparison with simulated assemblages. *American Antiquity* 49:44-54.
1989    Sample size, significance, and measures of diversity. In *Quantifying Diversity in Archaeology*. R. D. Leonard and G. T. Jones, eds. Pp. 25-36. Cambridge: Cambridge University Press.

Köhler-Rollefson, I., W. Gillespie, and M. Metzger
1988    The fauna from Neolithic Ain Ghazal. In *The Prehistory of Jordan*. A. N. Garrard and H. G. Gebel, eds. Pp. 423-430. BAR International Series 396. Oxford: British Archaeological Reports.

Leonard, R. D., and G. T. Jones, eds.
1989    *Quantifying Diversity in Archaeology*. Cambridge: Cambridge University Press.

Lernau, H.
1978    Faunal remains, Strata III-I. In *Early Arad*. R. Amiran, ed. Pp. 83-113. Jerusalem: Israel Exploration Society.

MacDonald, B.
1988a   The Early to Late Bronze periods. In *The Wadi el Hasa Archaeological Survey 1979-1983, West-Central Jordan*. B. MacDonald, ed. Pp. 155-170. Waterloo: Wilfrid Laurier University Press.
1988b   The Iron Age periods. In *The Wadi el Hasa Archaeological Survey 1979-1983, West-Central Jordan*. B. MacDonald, ed. Pp. 171-189. Waterloo: Wilfrid Laurier University Press.

MacDonald, B., ed.
1988c   *The Wadi el Hasa Archaeological Survey 1979-1983, West-Central Jordan*. Waterloo: Wilfrid Laurier University Press.

MacDonald, B., G. A. Clark, and M. Neeley
1988    Southern Ghors and northeast Araba archaeological survey 1985 and 1986, Jordan: A preliminary report. *Bulletin of the American Schools of Oriental Research* 72:23-45.

Marks, A. E.
1977    Introduction: A preliminary overview of central Negev prehistory. In *Prehistory and Paleoenvironments in the Central Negev, Israel. Volume 2*. A. E. Marks, ed. Pp. 3-34. Dallas: Southern Methodist University Press.

McCartney, P. H., and M. F. Glass
1990    Simulation models and the interpretation of archaeological diversity. *American Antiquity* 55:521-536.

Meltzer, D. J., R. D. Leonard, and S. K. Stratton
1992    The relationship between sample size and diversity in archaeological assemblages. *Journal of Archaeological Science* 19:375-387.

Neeley, M. P.
1989    *The Late Pleistocene and Early Holocene Prehistory in the Southern Ghor and Northeast Araba, Jordan*. Master's Thesis, Department of Anthropology, Arizona State University.

Noy, T., J. Schuldenrein, and E. Tchernov
1980    Gilgal, a Pre-Pottery Neolithic A site in the Lower Jordan Valley. *Israel Exploration Journal* 30:63-82.

Payne, S.
1983    The animal bones from the 1974 excavations at Douara Cave. In *Palaeolithic Site of the Douara Cave and Paleogeography of Palmyra Basin in Syria. Part III*. K. Hanihara and T. Akazawa, eds. Pp. 1-108. The University Museum Bulletin 21. Tokyo: University of Tokyo.

Redding, R.
1988    A general explanation of subsistence change: From hunting and gathering to food production. *Journal of Anthropological Archaeology* 7:56-97.

Rhode, D.
1988    Measurement of archaeological diversity and the sample-size effect. *American Antiquity* 53:708-716.

Rollefson, G. O., and A. H. Simmons
1988    The Neolithic settlement at Ain Ghazal. In *The Prehistory of Jordan*. A. N. Garrard and H. G. Gebel. Pp. 393-421. BAR International Series 396. Oxford: British Archaeological Reports.

Saxon, E. C.
1974    The mobile herding economy of Mt. Carmel: An economic analysis of the faunal remains. *Journal of Archaeological Science* 1:27-45.

Saxon, E. C., G. Martin, and O. Bar-Yosef
1978    Nahal Hadera V: An open-air site on the Israeli coast. *Paléorient* 4:253-266.

Schuldenrein, J.
1983    *Late Quaternary Paleo-environments and Prehistoric Site Distributions in the Lower Jordan Valley*. Ph.D. dissertation, Department of Anthropology, University of Chicago.

Stiner, M. C.
1990    *The Ecology of Choice: Procurement and Transport of Animal Resources by Upper Pleistocene Hominids in West-Central Italy*. Ph.D. dissertation, Department of Anthropology, University of New Mexico.
1992    Overlapping species "choice" by Italian Upper Pleistocene predators. *Current Anthropology* 33:433-451.

Straus, L. G.
1982    Carnivores and cave sites in Cantabrian Spain. *Journal of Anthropological Research* 38:75-96.

Tchernov, E.
1987    The age of the Ubeidiya formation, an Early Pleistocene hominid site in the Jordan Valley, Israel. *Israel Journal of Earth Sciences* 36:3-30.

Tchernov, E., and O. Bar-Yosef
1982    Animal exploitation in the Pre-Pottery Neolithic B period at Wadi Tbeik. *Paléorient* 8:17-37.

# 18

# Issues in Palaeolithic and Mesolithic Research

T. Douglas Price
University of Wisconsin--Madison

The papers in this volume offer a set of detailed, analytical studies examining the relationship between humans and animals; between bones, weapons, and people; and between technology and subsistence in the Upper Pleistocene and early Holocene. I have been asked to consider these studies and to comment on some of the major issues and themes. Why do we want to know about hunting technologies? What are the broader implications of such detailed technological and subsistence information? Is there an underlying approach or paradigm that unites the essays? What kinds of questions drive such research? Below, I review the contributions of some of the papers in this volume in light of these questions. I have grouped my comments on the papers under the specialized topics of weapons technology, hunting tactics, faunal analysis, and miscellaneous. I conclude with some remarks on more general issues in the archaeology of hunter-gatherers.

## WEAPONS TECHNOLOGY

Several of the initial papers in this volume consider aspects of hunting technology. Steven Churchill examines the relationship between weaponry, prey size, and hunting locales as reported in the ethnographic record. Churchill concludes from his comparative study that hominids armed only with hand spears would have been limited to hunting larger animals in areas where they could have been trapped or constrained in some fashion. The atlatl, and subsequently the bow, increased the range of animals that could be hunted and reduced the need for particular kinds of terrain. Such evidence may help to explain why we refer to "large-game hunters" in the Palaeolithic. Rapid changes in hunting weaponry toward the end of the Pleistocene may perhaps best be seen in terms of efforts toward the expansion of the subsistence base.

Steven Kuhn examines core reduction patterns and stone tool transport in the Mousterian of west-central Italy in light of a reported shift in hunting strategies after 55,000 BP. A change from scavenging to ambush hunting is associated with a shift from sedentism to mobility at that time. Kuhn notes that, although

hunting equipment showed no change with this shift, there were significant differences in the lithic assemblages. Comparison of the assemblages indicates that core reduction is less expedient, that resharpening is more common, and that exotic raw material is less abundant in the levels associated with hunting.

John Shea reports that impact wear on Levallois and Mousterian points reveals their use as projectile points. Such evidence is lacking in the European Mousterian and points to another aspect of the isolation of Europe from the remainder of the Old World during the Middle Paleolithic. Deborah Olszewski looks at the function of Zarzian microliths, which often comprise 35% of these Epipalaeolithic assemblages. Scalene triangles appear to have been arrow components, and truncated bladelets may have been a by-product from the production of microliths.

Heidi Knecht recreates and examines the bone and antler weapons of the early Upper Palaeolithic. She reports in great detail on their evolution in efficiency. Gail Larsen Peterkin undertakes a statistical study of both lithic and organic armatures from the Upper Palaeolithic. She demonstrates that morpho-functional classes cross-cut traditional typological categories and can be readily distinguished by several metric variables. Francis Harrold's study of Gravette points suggests that these artifacts function along a continuum of use, from knives to points. Detailed technical studies such as these refine our understanding of the meaning and function of lithic artifacts.

## HUNTING TACTICS

Lawrence Straus points out that Upper Palaeolithic sites in western Europe are more common in areas of moderate relief; he argues that land forms must have been important in animal kills where drives and trapping were needed. Such strategic use of the landscape may have been important, but other factors are also involved in the known distribution of sites. It is more likely that the concentration of sites in areas of moderate relief is a consequence of deposition and erosion during the Pleistocene. Sites in the valleys and plains of western Europe were often very deeply buried or destroyed by erosion. On the other hand, the caves and rock shelters of southern Europe protected prehistoric remains and bias our perspective on the distribution of populations and archaeological materials.

## FAUNAL ANALYSIS

Mary Stiner presents data on food gathering during the Middle Palaeolithic of Italy, documenting the presence of mussels and clams as evidence for collecting activities by *Homo sapiens neanderthalensis*. Other small animals, such as hare and rabbit, were apparently introduced by other predators and are not associated with human subsistence. This European evidence directly contrasts with Middle Stone Age data from Africa and the Near East, where a variety of species of different sizes were exploited. The faunal evidence also contrasts with the ideas of those who would have us think that hunting was not a common practice in the Middle Palaeolithic. As Stiner notes, "passive scavenging of large mammals did not provide the mainstay of diet" in this period--rather, the hunting of large game was the basis of subsistence. Her discussion of the consumption of shellfish in combination with animal brains fits well with the work of Speth and Spielmann (1983) on the need for both fat and protein in the human diet.

Stiner's consideration of evidence from Palaeolithic coastal Europe also serves as a very important reminder. Although most of the Pleistocene coasts of Europe are today deeply submerged and generally inaccessible to the archaeologist, these areas, particularly the Atlantic and Mediterranean shorelines, must have been very propitious localities for groups of hunter-gatherers. The general concern with large-game hunting in Palaeolithic archaeology may reflect only archaeologically visible inland facies of a wider human presence.

For example, recent investigations of Mesolithic diet in southern Scandinavia have eradicated a previous bias toward large-game hunting and terrestrial foods that dominated earlier views. Tauber (1981) used carbon isotopes in human bone to examine the importance of marine resources in the diet of the inhabitants of Mesolithic and early Neolithic Denmark. Mesolithic hunter-gatherers in southern Scandinavia had been assumed to have been largely dependent on terrestrial resources. Although a variety of marine foods, including fish, seal, and whale bones, were known from sites of this period, their contribution to the diet was thought to be relatively small. However, carbon isotope ratios in Mesolithic hunter-gatherers were shown to be comparable with those of the Eskimo of Greenland, where marine foods contrib-

ute more than 75% of the diet. Thus, it appears that coastal hunter-gatherers in Mesolithic Denmark only supplemented their diet with terrestrial foods.

Anne Pike-Tay and Harvey Bricker examine both weaponry and fauna, using age and season of death in animals from Gravettian sites to investigate hunting practices. The ages of individual animals from faunal assemblages at sites in southwestern France reflect catastrophic hunting patterns, thus indicating that hunters were very effective. Seasonal data from these animals emphasize a common pattern of individual kills rather than mass slaughter. Such information explains sites with large numbers of animal kills as the result of many repeated hunting episodes rather than mass slaughter. The almost total focus on reindeer in Upper Palaeolithic Dordogne, in contrast to other areas of western Europe, is noted in this paper and elsewhere; this pattern is very intriguing and requires further investigation. Katherine Boyle's study of element representation and butchery marks on reindeer bone from Magdalenian sites indicates an abundance of choice cuts. Reindeer appear to have been readily available in large number. Ariane Burke's study of cementum annuli in horse teeth from the Upper Palaeolithic of southwestern France reveals an emphasis on horse hunting during the summer when reindeer was of limited importance.

Daniel Lieberman uses cementum annuli in gazelle to examine changes in duration of occupation during the late Pleistocene and early Holocene of the Near East. Several trends are noted. The mobility of archaic humans appears to have been less than that of modern, a fact that corroborates the argument that Middle Palaeolithic sites in western Europe may have been permanently occupied. The evidence also indicates that the first true sedentary settlements appeared in the Natufian.

Peter Rowley-Conwy examines tooth eruption and bone growth in faunal assemblages from inland Mesolithic sites of southern Scandinavia for changes in subsistence and settlement. Early Mesolithic sites appear to have been summer base camps, but later sites were winter/spring hunting stations. It is the case, however, that virtually all known early Mesolithic sites are inland summer settlements. The likely locations for winter settlement--what were, at the time, the coasts--are today under the sea. In the later Mesolithic, both inland and coastal sites are recorded; the question of residential sedentism vs. mobility and relationships between the coastal and inland sites is important for understanding the transition to the Neolithic in this area. New information from bone chemistry has helped to resolve this question. Noe-Nygaard (1988) used the $\delta^{13}C$ levels in dog bones at inland and coastal Mesolithic sites as a proxy for humans. Dogs at coastal sites consumed a diet dominated by marine foods, while dogs at inland sites ate an almost exclusively terrestrial diet. Such evidence indicates that the dogs, and most likely their human owners, spent most of the year inland. This study provides strong evidence for a sedentary pattern in both areas, as well as a distinction between coastal and inland settlements.

## MISCELLANEOUS

Computer simulations of mammoth populations by Steven Mithen indicate the susceptibility of these animals to human hunting. According to his model, a cull rate of only 2% may have be sufficient to extirpate a local population of 1,000 animals. Mithen suggests that the hunters of Upper Pleistocene Europe did not eat mammoth, but may have scavenged their carcasses for bones and skins for construction (per Soffer 1985). However, until the question of what those folks on the cold steppes of eastern Europe **did** eat can be answered satisfactorily, the utility of the model remains in question.

Michael Neeley and Geof Clark re-examine the faunal evidence for Flannery's Broad Spectrum Revolution in light of recent questions regarding the concept in the prehistoric Near East (Edwards 1989). They model the human food niche for the last 150,000 years, using an index of diversity based on the presence of various animal species per unit of time. This index indicates relatively little change in faunal utilization until the Natufian and then shows a decrease in diversity through the Neolithic. The absence from this study of plants and other collected foods, however, makes it difficult to assess fully the significance of the Broad Spectrum Revolution. Given the recent discovery in the Near East of large quantities of plant foods in the human diet by 18,000 BP (Kislev et al. 1992; Nadel and Hershkovitz 1991), it seems essential that both animal and plant foods be incorporated in any investigation of changes in diet over time in this area.

## CONCLUSIONS

Detailed studies of stone, bone, and teeth, such as those represented in this volume, are indeed informative. These types of studies inform on the nature of past human behavior and, in particular, on larger questions about differences between archaic and modern humans and between early modern humans and ourselves. Some of the most critical questions about the past are involved in these studies. The chronological span of the volume incorporates two of the most important transitions in prehistory, that from archaic to fully modern humans and from food collec-

tion to food production. Both of these changes are fundamental in the evolution of human society and essential for an understanding of the past. With regard to the transition from _Homo sapiens neanderthalensis_ to _Homo sapiens sapiens,_ studies directed toward hunting skills, abilities, and strategies have a great deal to tell us about the similarities and/or differences between these subspecies, so that we may better understand the evolution of genus _Homo_. Questions such as the importance of hunting vs. scavenging in the Palaeolithic can best be approached by the kinds of studies represented in this volume. Information on behavioral differences between the archaic hominids of Europe and the Near East is particularly intriguing.

It seems clear that subsistence determines most aspects of human adaptation among hunter-gatherers. In contrast to the more hierarchical societies of food producers, the organization of life in hunter-gatherer groups generally revolves around the economics of the food quest. The settlements of hunter-gatherers largely reflect this food quest. The major dimensions of variability in the hunter-gatherer sites are, in large part, a result of subsistence strategies. Site size and population, as well as the season and duration of occupation, are primarily determined by the accessibility and reliability of food sources. Definition of these variables is the immediate goal of studies such as those included in this volume, in an attempt to better understand prehistoric settlement and subsistence activities.

Other important concerns in the volume include the nature and composition of human diet in the Upper Pleistocene and early Holocene. With regard to the transition to agriculture, shifts in subsistence and the nature of food gathering are critical to an understanding of this major change in human adaptation. Information on the nature of subsistence and settlement is fundamental; specifically, the diversity of diet and the permanence of settlement are crucial aspects of early farming communities. Documenting the presence of both is an essential task of the archaeology of the late Pleistocene and early Holocene.

The studies in this volume also point out certain lacunae. For example, we need to know much more about the formation of sites in the Palaeolithic. We need to remember that prehistoric peoples removed things from sites in addition to importing them. Sweeping and cleaning activities at longer-term residential sites must greatly affect the composition of assemblages. We also need to know more about the behavior of prey animals in relation to hunting technologies. Reindeer, for example, are remarkably stupid animals, and they can be taken very easily with pits and deadfalls. Other simple hunting techniques were likely employed as well in the later Pleistocene and are important in the repertoire of food-getting activities.

These studies also point out the power, and the limitations, of the concepts that direct research. The concepts used to characterize hunter-gatherers are a major factor in how we view the past: scavenging vs. hunting, maintainable vs. reliable technologies (Bleed 1986), logistical collecting vs. foraging (Binford 1980), sedentary vs. mobile, simple vs. complex. Such dichotomous perspectives make the colorful prehistoric tapestry merely black and white.

One of the reasons that archaeology often seems to be so complex is that we are just beginning to define the range of variability present in the prehistoric world. An emphasis on dichotomization reinforces a simplistic and limited view of the past. It is more useful to emphasize the range between the two extremes and to seek variability rather than deny it. O'Connell et al. (1988), for example, have noted that modern foragers incorporate a range of meat-getting techniques from scavenging to hunting. Such behaviors undoubtedly characterized our late Pleistocene and early Holocene ancestors as well.

Most models for prehistoric hunter-gatherer societies are based on evidence from the recent foragers of the ethnographic record who inhabited the most marginal environments on the planet--people who lived in small groups and moved around a lot. Over the last 30 years, this limited perspective has essentially become doctrine and has practically dominated archaeological interpretations of past hunter-gatherer adaptations. Archaeologists tend to see hunter-gatherer groups as small, mobile, and simple rather than large, sedentary, and complex.

We have very little evidence in most areas for the coastal aspect of these adaptations. It is critical to remember that the rising sea levels of the Holocene have submerged the early postglacial coastlines of much of the globe. It is now clear that sea levels in the Atlantic and Mediterranean did not stabilize at modern shorelines until late in the postglacial, perhaps around 2500 BP (Ters 1976). The late Pleistocene and early Holocene coastlines of most of Europe are missing from the archaeological record.

Evidence from the many times and places in the prehistoric record demonstrates that foraging groups do not often fit the simple, dichotomous labels that we attach to them. If the dominant theme of this volume is the wide range of variability of the archaeological record from the late Pleistocene and the early Holocene, it would appear that we are moving closer to an understanding of this past.

## REFERENCES

Binford, L. R.
  1980    Willow smoke and dogs' tails: Hunter-gatherer settlement systems and archaeological site formation. *American Antiquity* 45:4-20.
Bleed, P.
  1986    The optimal design of hunting weapons: Maintainability or reliability. *American Antiquity* 51:737-747.
Edwards, P. C.
  1989    Revising the Broad Spectrum Revolution: Its role in the origins of southwestern Asian food production. *Antiquity* 63:225-246.
Kislev, M. E., D. Nadel, and I. Carmi
  1992    Epi-Palaeolithic (19,000 BP) ceral and fruit diet at Ohalo II, Sea of Galilee, Israel. *Review of Palaeobotany and Palynology* 71:161-166.
Nadel, D., and I. Hershkovitz
  1991    New subsistence data and human remains from the earliest Levantine Epipalaeolthic. *Current Anthropology* 32:631-635.
Noe-Nygaard, N.
  1988    $\delta^{13}C$ values of dog bones reveal the nature of changes in man's food resources at the Mesolithic-Neolithic transition, Denmark. *Isotope Geoscience* 73:87-96.
O'Connell, J. F., K. Hawkes, and N. B. Jones
  1988    Hadza hunting, butchering, and bone transport and their archaeological implications. *Journal of Anthropological Research* 44:113-161.
Soffer, O.
  1985    *The Upper Paleolithic of the Central Russian Plain.* New York: Academic Press.
Speth, J. D., and K. A. Speilman
  1983    Energy source, protein metabolism, and hunter-gatherer subsistence strategies. *Journal of Anthropological Archaeology* 2:1-31.
Tauber, H.
  1981    $\delta^{13}C$ evidence for dietary habits of prehistoric man in Denmark. *Nature* 292:332-333.
Ters, M.
  1976    Les lignes de rivage holocéne, le long de côte atlantique français. In *La préhistoire français. Tome II. Les civilisations néolithiques et protohistoriques de la France.* J. Guilaine, ed. Pp. 27-30. Paris: Editions du Centre National de la Recherche Scientifique.

# 19

# *Comments on This Volume and Recent Research by Scholars in Non-Anglophone Europe*

Marcel Otte
Université de Liège

## METHODOLOGY, THEORY, AND DOCUMENTATION

The New Orleans meetings on prehistoric hunting and the thick volume that has resulted from them are impressive with respect to both quality and innovation. The following general remarks are made from the European point of view and with specific comparative reference to a similar meeting held recently in Belgium.

The methodological aspects of the contributions are probably those that are the most developed and the best adapted to the body of questions under consideration. It is certainly in this area that members of "the American school" show themselves to be the most innovative and the most effective. They develop a research strategy that is well constructed, logical, and bounded--a strategy that proceeds from a clear question to a precise answer.

The theoretical aspects, which are also very different from those of Europe, are very distinctive in that they represent a traditionally American orientation while covering only one part of general archaeological thought. This orientation, which is traditionally called "anthropological" (to the francophone world, "ethnographic" would seem more comfortable), constitutes what is, in my view, an excess that merits reconsideration in various ways, including in institutional terms--what should be the place of the discipline of archaeology within the university?

Finally, the documentary aspects are quite clearly those with which most of the problems arise. It is often the case that analytic efforts are applied to only one region of the Old World. Such work tends to be too limited in both geographic scope--generally centered on western Europe--and in the "classical" sources of documentation which were utilized--defined by the historical accidents of site discovery and, probably, by the fact of their translation into English. This deficiency in the documentary aspects of research blunts the cutting edge of the methodology that has been so carefully constructed and, of necessity, diminishes the significance of the results. I would, therefore, argue for extending the scope of research questions to the central and eastern parts of the continent while surmounting the barriers of linguistic compartmentalization.

## EXAMPLES FROM THIS VOLUME

The work of Steven Churchill is certainly the most productive in terms of its methodology and its long-term significance. He has provided an excellent summary of numerous ethnographic data on weapons and their relationships to prey animals. The interpretation within the context of the Palaeolithic remains weak, however, because of the poverty and lack of timeliness of the data used by the author. The very classic ideas he develops about Mousterian behavior have long been superceded by studies of raw material sources, lithic reduction sequences, and planning in settlement shifts. Mousterian hunting practices are now clearly documented by the use-wear damage on stone tools caused by woodworking, by the Lehringen spear discovered within the body of an elephant (Thieme and Veil 1985), and by the many specialized hunting sites that have been excavated, primarily in eastern and central Europe. This body of data, which is often poorly known and poorly understood, has given rise to the development outside Europe of some rather confused theories, whose influence seems to linger on among today's younger generation of researchers, about the limited abilities of the makers of Mousterian tools.

Among the specialized hunting sites of the Mousterian that are known, we could cite Zwollen in southern Poland, where horse dominates the faunal sample (Schild and Gautier 1988), and Neumark in eastern Germany (Saxony-Thuringia), where bovids predominate (Mania 1990). At the Belgian site of Sclayn, an interglacial occupation has a predominance of roe deer (Patou and Otte 1992). In France, horse dominates the fauna at the site of Genay (Patou 1987) and aurochs at La Borde (Jaubert et al. 1990). Finally, it should not be forgotten that Lioubin (Lioubin and Barychnikov 1984) presented evidence for the specialized hunting of mountain goat in the Caucasus some time ago.

The same influences can be detected in the contribution of John Shea, who continues his search for behavioral differences between what he calls "modern" and "archaic" humans. This search seems futile to the extent that differences in **ability** can not now be detected in Europe itself. It is, rather, simply a question of different **choices** that have been made-- options that are of a traditional or historic nature, not ones determined by evolutionary stage. Moreover, given the extreme variability within the Mousterian and its very long duration of at least 300,000 years in Europe, the variables considered here cannot be reduced simply to a superficial anatomical dichotomy with no further consequences.

The contributions of Mary Stiner and Steven Kuhn on the relationships between hunting practices and lithic industries in central Italy are particularly stimulating and intellectually rich. However, this kind of approach also should be supported by some external comparisons, in order to verify that the regularities at issue really do repeat under the same conditions. The various attempts to explain differences in lithic industries in terms of differences in fauna have shown the enormous complexity of this observed variability. There is obviously not a single variable, such as fauna, that can be set in counterpoint to the lithic industry; rather, multiple variables are involved. Relationships to the environmental context of settlement (Brugal and Jaubert 1991), to the acquisition of raw materials (Turq 1989), and to shifts in settlement (Otte n.d.) are certainly of importance here. The different variables, including the fauna, exhibit a structural coherence, linked one to the other, but they are not univocal in their effect upon the whole structure (Otte 1992). It seems that, once again, the application of a theory constructed outside the area studied suffers from the absence of intellectual competition in the region where it is used and from the urgent wish to produce the results expected from the application of the analysis in question. The New Orleans meetings, providing for the confrontation of different points of view and different experiences, offers the potential to change this state of affairs.

The contribution by Heidi Knecht is filled with good ideas and excellent experimental observations, although one rather regrets the overly narrow focus of the treatment, which could, I believe, lead to a more integrated approach if it were followed up and extended. In particular, she does not deal with the consequences of having particular kinds of organic weapons on other technological components--for example, the modalities of stone-working, the question of intermediate tools, and the general balance among objects made from different kinds of raw material within the same assemblage. Here we see an unfortunate side of specialization: the analysis, while producing new

information, does not proceed to the necessary next step of returning to the fundamental postulates from which it started.

Somewhat similar remarks may be made about the contribution of Gail Larsen Peterkin. The very legitimate wish to discover some connection between the properties of the armatures, on the one hand, and the prey animals, on the other, must, it seems to me, be tempered by the results of her own analysis. It seems quite obvious that there is no simple and univocal relationship between prey and technology, and this is a hard fact that should lead the author to consider other variables. It seems to me that there is, beyond some simple mechanical determinism, the firm and unyielding effect of cultural tradition, which has once again been underestimated.

It is always amusing to encounter very similar bibliographic items from the two sides of the Atlantic-- never mind that the motivations of the authors may have been very different! However, the areas of overlap are now such that some measure of exchange would certainly be profitable to both sides. A good example of this is provided by the contribution of Francis Harrold, which is rigorous and rich in data, although both the analysis and the results line up, point by point, with those recently published in Kraków by Kozlowski and Lenoir (1988). The recent opening of frontiers in eastern Europe should reduce the frequency of such duplication of effort.

One could cite even more examples of these situations that strike a jarring note for someone of the European school, although it is probably not necessary, given what was asked of me, to deal further with individual contributions. I will, instead, take refuge in the amicable professional relationships that link me with American researchers and hope that they will accept with good will the observations made here.

Problems of sample definition arise in almost every contribution. What does the sample represent with respect to the often very ambitious question originally raised? Should it not be extended to include wider cultural areas? Is it really representative of some Palaeolithic entity, rather than of the literature available in one modern language? The dominant impression is of a feverish search for some general covering law rather than the respectful consideration of the specifics of each case. Palaeolithic reality seems to me to have been every bit as complex as that of our own contemporary society.

## COMPARISONS WITH TREIGNES

The meetings that my colleagues, Claire Bellier and Pierre Cattelain, and I recently organized at Treignes (Belgium) dealt with topics that are very similar to those discussed in New Orleans. Perhaps by discussing how the European scientific community responded to some of the same sort of opportunities afforded to the New Orleans symposiasts, I will be able to shed some light on the differing approaches of the Europeans and Americans.

The papers at Treignes were concerned with technological approaches of an experimental nature--a bit like that given in New Orleans by Christopher Bergman, who is, after all, English. This approach is more optimistic than in the U. S. A., or, depending on one's point of view, more naive or less rigorous. A sort of quiet confidence leads from experiment to interpretation without the methodological maneuvering, referred to above, that seems indispensable to members of the American school.

A series of focused presentations of sites given at the Treignes meetings reveals another consideration which is rather close to the first point. The detailed statement of anatomical facts, such as species, age, and body parts represented, seems to be sufficient to the needs of European archaeologists, who are spared from obligatory theoretical wrangling. It is like putting back together so many "contexts"--situations that, once assembled in time and space, lead inevitably to the composition of a harmonious picture. Having been brought up professionally in this way of thinking, I know that it has its very comfortable aspects. It is to these matters that we now turn our attention.

Some of the important contributions at Treignes rest directly upon the definition of "traditions" in prehistory. This notion, which certainly comes from our side of the Atlantic, is so natural in this context that it does not need to be defended here. We then move straight away to the question of its provisioning through hunting--i.e., what are its methods and its practices? A population $X$ procures its meat to eat by using technique $Y$ in a given situation. Any errors in this determination cannot be methodological, because the "facts" are known; it must, rather, be an error of context, caused by the environment. A European history that implies migrations, contacts, and exchanges is thus constructed, and this history simply precedes that of the Greeks and Romans.

Other topics considered at Treignes include sociological matters, such as meat-sharing after the hunt; questions of seasonality (nomadism); and the influence of the environment (migrations). In addition, the role of hunting in relation to art and religion was the subject of some excellent contributions. It is, in fact, difficult to overstate the importance of this relationship in hunting societies, where fundamental mythological elements are closely tied to the connections between man and nature. These connections, sustained by the practice of hunting, determine religious practices to a considerable extent; at the same time, they have a retroflexive effect on predation

itself. Here, too, the European approach, which is close to the tradition of the philological sciences in Europe, is very different from the American approach.

Finally, the Treignes contributions on evolutionary process point to what is, without question, the greatest contrast between the two sides of the Atlantic. In Europe we are always trying to grapple with synchronous phenomena--to define them and to make some sense of them. It seems quite natural to us that the key factor in understanding the differences we observe in prehistory is, quite obviously, time itself. The frantic research on chronologies, stratigraphies, superposed columns, evolutionary diagrams, and dating all stem from this obsession.

This kind of research, employed most often without conscious thought, is essentially that of the historian, which stacks anecdotal slices one upon another and then backs off to analyze what is going on. This is our only metaphysical anxiety! And, indeed, I have some feelings of betraying my own community by denouncing it to you. This conception, which now approaches biology and the life sciences, insists upon origins and destinations. Our principal task is to trace the branches of this tree and thus to specify the **heritage** of ideas, including the idea of hunting.

## CONCLUSIONS AND REFLECTIONS

The European approach to hunting is probably determined primarily by the structures of the institutions in which our researchers are trained. These institutional structures determine, quite unconsciously, what things are accepted as certainties or laws and what things belong in the category of discoveries that it would be useful to make. These schools follow the disciplinary traditions of history in important ways, and they are closely related to university faculties in which literary traditions dominate. We thus find both the enthusiastic desire to establish a chronology leading to the evolution of hunting behavior and, at the same time, feelings of certainty concerning the appropriateness of the analysis. Archaeology gives us a mass of data which can be added to the omnipotent and immutable body of thought that comes from the history of the peoples of the West. Data on prehistoric hunting, provided by the so-called auxiliary sciences, are immediately subsumed and integrated into a more general field of research, the bases of which often lie beyond the competence of the archaeologists themselves. The newer goals seem to require that archaeologists become more truly "pre-historians" rather than the archivists of Pleistocene hunters.

The American approach, on the other hand, derives quite obviously from the discipline of anthropology, whose theoretical framework is no less constraining than that of history is for the Europeans. From an American point of view, this kind of analysis seems to require that each stage of prehistory is considered a "fixed moment" in time. In large measure, it permits, encourages, and even requires a functionalist approach to the same observations that are considered quite differently by Europeans. The never-ending search for the explanation of these observations reveals much about this way of thinking. Although explanation is necessary to provide balance and legitimacy to archaeological analysis, it is challenged by the very movement of life, including the movement of time, and thus remains inaccessible.

Europe, therefore, is dominated by the collection and dissemination of data. It refrains from using overly learned terms for this sort of research and hesitates between the "scientific" and the "cultural." Knowledge is embraced directly, in and for itself; facts have their own intrinsic value. The study of a site often stops with the presentation of the basic data. Here it is the fact that rules. In America, however, the theoretical construct is sovereign. The anthropological approach impels researchers to seek out scientific-sounding titles and to look to the exact sciences for recognition of the quality of their research. This approach produces very carefully constructed models, explicit in their structure and designed in advance for the collection of data.

Thanks to these two sets of meetings, those in Treignes and those in New Orleans, and thanks to the spirit of intellectual openness that both have fostered, these differences may become less pronounced. We hope that some integration of the two ways of doing research may provide new perspectives regarding our knowledge of the basic nature of mankind and the ways in which this nature has changed through time.

## REFERENCES

Auguste, P.
1991    Chasse ou charognage au Paléolithique moyen: l'Exemple du site de Biache-Saint-Vaast. *Bulletin de la Société Préhistorique Française* 88:68-69.

Brugal, J. P., and J. Jaubert
1991    Les gisements paléontologiques pléistocènes à indices de fréquentation humaine: Un nouveau type de comportement de prédation. *Paléo* 3:15-41.

Jaubert, J., M. Lorblanchet, H. Laville, R. Slott-Moller, A. Turq, and J.-Ph. Brugal
1990    *Les chasseurs d'aurochs de La Borde, un site du Paléolithique moyen (Livernon, Lot).* Documents d'Archéologie Française 27. Paris: Maison des Sciences de l'Homme.

Kozlowski, J. K., and M. Lenoir
1988    Analyse des pointes à dos des gisements périgordiens de l'Aquitaine. *Prace Archeologiczne - Zeszyt* 43:1-94.

Lioubin, V. P., and G. F. Barychnikov
1984    L'activité de chasse des plus anciens habitants du Caucase (Acheuléen, Moustérien). *L'Anthropologie* 88:221-229.

Mania, D.
1990    Das Mittelpaläolithikum von Neumark Nord--eine besondere ökologische Fazies. *Ethnographisch-Archäologische Zeitschrift* 31:16-23.

Otte, M.
n.d.    L'illusion charentienne. Colloque International de Brives 1990, "Les Moustériens charentiens." (in press).
1992    The significance of variability in the European Mousterian. In *The Middle Palaeolithic: Adaptation, Behavior, and Variability* H. Dibble and P. Mellars, eds. Pp. 45-52. University Museum Monograph 72. Philadelphia: The University Museum, University of Pennsylvania.

Patou, M.
1987    La grande faune de la brèche de Genay (Côte-d'Or): Fouilles de l'abbé Joly. *L'Anthropologie* 91:97-108.

Patou, M., and M. Otte
1992    Comportements de subsistence au Paléolithique moyen en Europe. *Paléo* 4:29-31.

Schild, R., and A. Gautier
1988    The Middle Paleolithic of the North European Plain at Zwollen: Preliminary results. In *L'homme de Neandertal. Tome 8. La mutation.* J. Kozlowski, ed. Pp. 149-167. ERAUL 35. Liège: Université de Liège.

Thieme, V. H., and St. Veil
1985    Neue Untersuchungen zum eemzeitlichen Elefanten-Jagtplatz Lehringen, Ldkr. Verden. *Die Kunde* N.F. 36:11-58.

Turq, A.
1989    Exploitation des matières premières lithiques et occupation du sol: l'Exemple du Moustérien entre Dordogne et Lot. In *Variations des paléomilieux et peuplement préhistorique.* Pp. 179-203. Cahiers du Quaternaire 13. Paris: Editions du Centre National de la Recherche Scientifique.